Frommer's®

Caribbean
Ports of Call

Here's what the critics say about Frommer's:

"Amazingly easy to use. Very portable, very complete."
—Booklist

◆

"The only mainstream guide to list specific prices. The Walter
Cronkite of guidebooks—with all that implies."
—Travel & Leisure

◆

"Complete, concise, and filled with useful information."
—New York Daily News

Other Great Guides for Your Trip:

Frommer's Bahamas

Frommer's Caribbean

Frommer's Caribbean Cruises & Ports of Call

Frommer's Caribbean Hideaways

Frommer's Jamaica & Barbados

Frommer's Puerto Rico

Frommer's Virgin Islands

Frommer's Caribbean from $60 a Day

Frommer's Born to Shop Caribbean

Frommer's Portable Bahamas

The Complete Idiot's Travel Guide to Cruise Vacations

The Complete Idiot's Travel Guide to the Caribbean

The Unofficial Guide to Cruises

Frommer's

2nd Edition

Caribbean Ports of Call

By Darwin Porter & Danforth Prince

MACMILLAN • USA

ABOUT THE AUTHORS

A native of North Carolina, **Darwin Porter** was a bureau chief for *The Miami Herald* when he was 21, and later worked in television advertising. A veteran travel writer, he is the author of numerous best-selling Frommer guides, notably to England, France, Italy, and Spain. He is assisted by **Danforth Prince,** formerly of the Paris Bureau of *The New York Times.* They have been frequent travelers to the Caribbean for years, and are intimately familiar with what's good there and what isn't. They have also written *Frommer's Caribbean Cruises,* the most candid and up-to-date guide to cruise vacations on the market. In this guide, they share their secrets and discoveries with you.

MACMILLAN TRAVEL

A Simon & Schuster Macmillan Company
1633 Broadway
New York, NY 10019

Find us online at **www.frommers.com**

ISBN 0-02-862269-3
ISSN 1090-2619

Editor: Jeff Soloway
Production Editor: Donna Wright
Photo Editor: Richard Fox
Design by Michele Laseau
Digital Cartography by Ortelius Design and Peter Bogaty
Page Creation by Jena Brandt, Eric Brinkman, Natalie Evans, Heather Pope, Karen Teo

SPECIAL SALES

Contents

List of Maps

AN INVITATION TO THE READER

In researching this book, we discovered many wonderful places—hotels, restaurants, shops, and more. We're sure you'll find others. Please tell us about them, so we can share the information with your fellow travelers in upcoming editions. If you were disappointed with a recommendation, we'd love to know that, too. Please write to:

Frommer's Caribbean Ports of Call, 2nd Edition
Macmillan Travel
1633 Broadway
New York, NY 10019

AN ADDITIONAL NOTE

Please be advised that travel information is subject to change at any time—and this is especially true of prices. We therefore suggest that you write or call ahead for confirmation when making your travel plans. The authors, editors, and publisher cannot be held responsible for the experiences of readers while traveling. Your safety is important to us, however, so we encourage you to stay alert and be aware of your surroundings. Keep a close eye on cameras, purses, and wallets, all favorite targets of thieves and pickpockets.

WHAT THE SYMBOLS MEAN

✪ Frommer's Favorites

Our favorite places and experiences—outstanding for quality, value, or both.

The following abbreviations are used for credit cards:

AE	American Express	EURO	Eurocard
CB	Carte Blanche	JCB	Japan Credit Bank
DC	Diners Club	MC	MasterCard
DISC	Discover	V	Visa
ER	EnRoute		

FIND FROMMER'S ONLINE

Arthur Frommer's Outspoken Encyclopedia of Travel (www.frommers.com) offers more than 6,000 pages of up-to-the-minute travel information—including the latest bargains and candid personal articles updated daily by Arthur Frommer himself. No other website offers such comprehensive and timely coverage of the world of travel.

What This Guide Will Do for You

You've picked your Caribbean cruise and are ready to sail. What you do on board will depend on what the ship offers, but when you anchor at a port of call, you need to know how to make the most of your time ashore. Should you take a shore excursion or arrange a tour yourself? Where are the best beaches? Are there outfitters that can arrange scuba diving or snorkeling? Where can you find the best duty-free bargains and island handcrafts? What's the best place to have lunch? We'll answer all those questions and more as we take you to 21 ports of call, mainly in the Caribbean, but also in The Bahamas, Mexico, and Key West.

First off, in chapter 2 we cover six major ports of embarkation: the four major Florida ports—Miami, Fort Lauderdale, Tampa, and Cape Canaveral—plus New Orleans and San Juan. We describe each port, telling you how to get there and how to take care of all the logistics. And since many passengers spend a few days in the port before the ship sails, we also discuss each city's highlights and best beaches, plus where to dine, where to stay, and what to do after dark.

Chapter 3 features complete A-to-Z coverage of each port of call. We give you all the options you need to know to structure your day, whether you want to shop, relax at the beach, see the sights, gamble, or find the best outdoor activities or water sports. We also highlight our favorite experiences, moments that can make exploration special, from submarine sightseeing to authentic island bars.

On some islands, it's best to take an arranged shore excursion rather than setting off on your own, because roads may be poor and driving difficult. But often there's no better way to experience an island than to do your own exploration, whether on foot, by taxi, or by rental car. We'll give you all the information you need to choose for yourself. It may also be cheaper to book an arranged excursion yourself, rather than through the cruise ship, and we'll share our insider advice on how to do that, too.

1 Going Ashore

As a general rule, most cruise ships arrive at a port of call in the morning, around 7am, but passengers don't start disembarking until around 9am. (This can vary considerably depending on an

The Caribbean Islands

FLORIDA

Miami

Straits of Florida

THE BAHAMAS

Havana

Cuba

Little Cayman

Cayman   Cayman Brac

CAYMAN ISLANDS

Montego Bay

JAMAICA   Kingston

Haiti

Port-au-Prince

GREATER

C a r i b b e a n   S e a

COLOMBIA

2-0140

Atlantic

Ocean

TURKS AND CAICOS ISLANDS

Dominican Republic

San Juan

Santo
Domingo

Puerto Rico

ANTILLES

VIRGIN   ISLANDS

Tortola   Anegada
          Virgin Gorda Anguilla
St. John   St. Maarten/
St. Thomas   Saba   St. Martin
                                Barbuda
St. Croix
          St. Barthélemy   St. Kitts
                  Nevis   Antigua
                  Montserrat
St. Eustatius

Guadeloupe

LEEWARD ISLANDS

Dominica

Martinique

St. Lucia

St. Vincent   BARBADOS

THE
GRENADINES

WINDWARD ISLANDS

DUTCH LEEWARD ISLANDS
Aruba   Curaçao
              Bonaire   LESSER ANTILLES   Grenada

Tobago

Port of Spain

Trinidad

Caracas

VENEZUELA

individual cruise.) You rarely have to clear Customs or immigration, because the ship's purser already has your passport and has done all the paperwork for you. So when local officials give the word, you go ashore. Sometimes you can walk right down the gangplank onto dry land. But if the port isn't big enough to accommodate large cruise ships, the custom is to anchor offshore and ferry passengers to land via a tender. You may have to wait in line.

Most passengers start heading back to the ship around 4pm, or not much later than 5pm. By 6pm, you're usually sailing off to your next destination.

PASSPORTS & VISAS

Even though the Caribbean islands are, for the most part, independent nations and thereby classified as international destinations, passports are not generally required. However, you must have identity documents, and a passport is often the best form of identification. Other acceptable documents include an ongoing or return ticket, plus a current voter registration card or a birth certificate (the original or a copy that has been certified by the U.S. Department of Health). If you use one of these other documents, you will also need some photo ID, such as a driver's license or an expired passport. A driver's license is not acceptable as a sole form of identification. Visas are usually not required, but some countries may require you to fill out a tourist card.

Technically, a "valid" passport is one that isn't scheduled to expire for 6 months. For more information, call the Department of State Office of Passport Services' information line at ☎ **202/647-0518.**

Aliens residing in the United States need to have valid passports and alien registration cards. All non-U.S. or Canadian citizens must have valid passports and the requisite visas when boarding any cruise ship or aircraft departing from or returning to American soil.

Canadians need an identity card for entry and re-entry into the United States. It's better, however, to travel with a passport, available at 28 regional offices in Canada, as well as at certain travel agencies or post offices. For further information call ☎ **800/567-6868** or 819/994-3500.

2 Money Matters

The safest way to carry large amounts of money is to use traveler's checks, although credit cards are accepted virtually everywhere on Caribbean waters or land. The U.S. dollar is also widely accepted on the islands. Specific currency information is included in chapter 3, "The Ports of Call."

Three major traveler's check issuers are **American Express** (☎ **800/221-7282** in the U.S. and Canada, with many regional representatives around the world); **Citicorp** (☎ **800/645-6556** in the U.S. and Canada, or 813/623-1709, collect, from other parts of the world); and **Thomas Cook** (☎ **800/223-7373** in the U.S. and Canada, or 609/987-7300, collect, from other parts of the world).

Cirrus, Plus, and other automated-teller machine networks operate in the Caribbean. For locations of **Cirrus** abroad, call ☎ **800/424-7787.** For **Plus** locations abroad, call ☎ **800/843-7587.** You can also access the Visa/PLUS International ATM Locator Guide Web site at **www.visa.com/visa.** Most large cruise lines, such as Carnival, now have ATMs aboard—but not the smaller lines. Check before embarking, and make appropriate arrangements.

You'll probably be able to charge the cost of shore excursions to your onboard ship account.

3 Duty-Free Shopping: Is It Such a Good Deal?

Duty-free means a traveler can make purchases free of duty, or tax, on the assumption that those goods will be used or consumed after departing the country. Tobacco, liquor, and perfumes once dominated duty-free purchases, but now virtually all premium luxury goods are sold duty-free, including jewelry and electronics. In a port of call in the Caribbean, the savings on duty-free merchandise can range from as little as 5% up to 50% on a particular item. Unless there's a special sale being offered, most products will carry comparable price tags from island to island. It pays, before you leave home, to check out your local discount retailer's prices on goods you may want to buy so you really know whether you're getting a bargain or not.

In chapter 3, we detail shopping in each port, providing tips on that island's best buys, as well as recommendations for specific stores.

4 Coming Home: Customs

Customs officers are most interested in expensive, big-ticket items like cameras, jewelry, china, or silverware. They don't really care much about your souvenir items unless you've bought so many that they couldn't possibly be intended for your personal use.

U.S. CUSTOMS

The U.S. rate of tax for those who exceed their duty-free exemptions in foreign countries is 10%; it's only 5% in the U.S. Virgin Islands. The U.S. duty-free exemption is $400 for the French islands of Guadeloupe and Martinique, $1,200 in the U.S. Virgin Islands, and $600 for most other islands in the Caribbean. If you visit only Puerto Rico, you don't have to go through Customs at all, since it's an American commonwealth. For more information and updates, contact the U.S. Customs offices in Washington D.C. at ☎ **202/927-6724,** or check their Web site at **www.customs.ustreas.gov.**

U.S. citizens, or returning residents 21 years of age, traveling directly or indirectly from the U.S. Virgin Islands, are allowed to bring in free of duty 1,000 cigarettes, 5 liters of alcohol, and 100 cigars (so long as they're not Cuban). Duty-free limitations on articles from other countries are generally 1 liter of alcohol, 200 cigarettes, and 200 cigars. Unsolicited gifts can be mailed to friends and relatives at the rate of $100 per day. Most meat or meat products, fruit, plants, vegetables, or plant-derived products will be seized by U.S. Customs agents unless they're accompanied by an import license from a U.S. government agency.

Joint Customs declarations are permitted for members of a family traveling together. For instance, a husband and wife with two children have a total duty-fee exemption in the U.S. Virgin Islands of $4,800.

Collect receipts for all purchases made abroad. Beware of friendly merchants offering a false receipt to undervalue your purchase (thereby stretching your duty-free allowance)—the merchant might be an informer to U.S. Customs. You must also declare on your Customs form all gifts received during your stay abroad. If you're carrying expensive cameras or jewelry, it's a good idea to bring proof that you purchased them on the U.S. mainland. Or if you purchased them during an earlier trip abroad, you should carry proof that you have previously paid the Customs duty.

If you use any medication containing controlled substances or requiring injection, carry an original prescription or note from your doctor.

For additional information contact the U.S. Customs Service, 1301 Constitution Ave., P.O. Box 7407, Washington, DC 20044 (☎ **202/927-6724**). The Web site is www.customs.ustreas.gov.

CANADIAN CUSTOMS

Exemptions for Canadian citizens depend on their time abroad. Canadians who have spent 24 hours or less outside their country are allowed a (CAN) $50 exemption from taxation on goods they've bought abroad, but any tobacco or liquor products are subject to the Canadian tax code. Canadians who have spent more than 48 hours abroad are allowed a (CAN) $300 exemption, and are permitted to bring back duty-free 200 cigarettes, 200 grams of tobacco, 40 imperial ounces of liquor, and 50 cigars. For Canadians who have spent 7 days or more abroad, the exemption is raised to (CAN) $500, and the same quantities of tobacco and liquor mentioned above can be brought in duty-free.

In addition to the exemptions noted above, and regardless of the amount of time they spend away from Canada, Canadians are allowed to mail gifts from abroad to friends, clients, and relatives in Canada (but not to themselves), at the rate of (CAN) $60 per day, provided the gifts are unsolicited and aren't alcohol or tobacco products. Be sure to write "Unsolicited gift, under $60 value" on the outside of the package.

All valuables such as expensive cameras and jewelry should be declared on the Y-38 Form before your departure from Canada, with the article's serial number, if possible. When serial numbers aren't available, as in the case of jewelry, it's wise to carry a photocopy of either the original bill of sale or a bona fide appraisal.

For more information, contact **Revenue Canada,** 2265 St. Laurent Blvd., Ottawa ON K1G 4K3 (☎ **613/993-0534**), and ask for the free booklet "I Declare." You can also check the agency's Web site at **www.rc.gc.ca.**

BRITISH CUSTOMS

On returning from the Caribbean, if you arrive either directly in the United Kingdom or via a port in another EC country where you did not pass through Customs with all your baggage, you must go through U.K. Customs and declare any goods in excess of the allowances. The allowances are 200 cigarettes, 100 cigarillos, 50 cigars, 250 grams of tobacco; 2 liters of still table wine; 1 liter of spirits or strong liqueurs over 22% volume, or 2 liters of fortified or sparkling wine or other liqueurs; and £145 worth of all other goods, including gifts and souvenirs. (No one under 17 years of age is entitled to a tobacco or drinks allowance). Only go through the green "nothing to declare" channel if you're sure you have no more than the Customs allowances and no prohibited or restricted goods. British Customs tends to be strict and complicated in its requirements. For details, get in touch with **Her Majesty's Customs and Excise Office,** Dorset House, Stamford St., London SE1 9PY (☎ **0171/202-4227;** fax 0171/202-4216. The government's Web site, located at **www.open.gov.uk/,** is also helpful.

5 Ship Itineraries

Listed below are the itineraries of ships plying the waters of the Caribbean. Of course, these itineraries are highly abbreviated, and subject to changes based on new ship acquisitions and last-minute tropical storms, so check with the cruise line or your travel agent. For in-depth profiles of these lines and their individual ships, see *Frommer's Caribbean Cruises.*

In general, the **best beaches** are found in the western Caribbean, including the Seven Mile Beach in Grand Cayman, and Palm Beach and Eagle Beach on Aruba. In the eastern Caribbean, you'll sometimes find beaches of beige, brown, or black volcanic sand that absorb the heat of the sun. Notable beaches here include Cane Garden Bay, Tortola, in the British Virgin Islands, and Trunk Bay on St. John. In the French West Indies, the best beach is Le Diamant on Martinique.

Aruba and San Juan are the most diverse, grand, and exciting **gambling centers** in the Caribbean, rivaling the razzle-dazzle of Las Vegas. For size, scope, and ambiance, the best casinos are the San Juan Grand Beach Hotel & Casino at Isla Verde, San Juan, or The Alhambra on Aruba. There's lots of gambling in St. Maarten as well, but the casinos are a bit dowdier.

To **shop** until you drop, head to the U.S. Virgin Islands, particularly St. Thomas, the leading shopping bazaar in the Caribbean. Here you'll find discounted jewelry, liquor, china, linens, perfume, and electronics. St. Maarten and St. Croix are also contenders in the shopping sweepstakes, with discounts of up to 25% to 50%.

American Canadian Caribbean Line. 461 Water St., Warren, RI 02885. ☎ **800/556-7450** or 401/247-0955. Fax 401/247-2350. www.accl-smallships.com.

Grande Mariner: Exact itineraries for this newest ship within ACCL's fleet were still being hammered out at the time of this writing. Look for forays to yachting paradises such as the less-frequently visited cays of the Virgin Islands, or to St. Lucia and Trinidad.

Cape Canaveral Cruise Line. 7099 N. Atlantic Ave., Cape Canaveral, FL 32920. ☎ **800/910-SHIP** or 407/783-4052. Fax 407/783-4120. www.cccruiseline.com.

Most cruises aboard this line are 2-day, 2-night experiences, with absolutely no variation in the oft-traveled route. *Dolphin IV* sails from Port Canaveral's Terminal 3 at 4pm, arriving in Freeport, on Grand Bahama Island, the following morning at 8am. Check for actual days of departure. Passengers spend the day at Freeport shopping, sunning, cycling, gambling, or whatever, then depart that evening for their return to Port Canaveral.

In 1997, the company inaugurated twice-per-month 4-day cruises. These incorporate a stopover at Key West in addition to Freeport. The length of the stop (16 hours) in Key West is longer than that offered by any other cruise line, allowing plenty of carousing time for partying passenger. As the morning light breaks over the rooftops of the town, expect at least a handful of tired, slightly inebriated celebrants to rush hysterically back to the ship just before its 6am departure from Mallory Docks.

Carnival Cruise Lines. 3655 NW 87th Ave., Miami, FL 33178-2428. ☎ **800/327-9501** or 305/599-2200. Fax 305/406-4740. www.carnival.com.

Carnival keeps costs low by scheduling fewer stops at port and more days at sea. Thus, the shipboard parties are allowed to continue unabated. When you do make landfalls, you can expect them to be at the larger and more obvious Caribbean destinations, where deep ports can accommodate Carnival ships' circus-sized girths and bulks. Cruise & Tour packages offered by the company usually include a stay at a hotel near (but not inside the perimeter of) Disney World.

Celebration: Year-round, 7-day cruises originate in New Orleans and meander through the western Caribbean to Grand Cayman and Playa del Carmen/Cozumel in Mexico, and Montego Bay in Jamaica. There are usually three "fun" days at sea. At press time, Celebration was the only Caribbean cruise ship based year-round in New Orleans.

Carnival Destiny: Carnival's newest and largest ship, launched late in 1996, departs from Miami and remains in the Caribbean throughout the year. It alternates 7-day cruises through the Eastern Caribbean (with stops at San Juan and ports in the U.S. Virgin Islands) with excursions to such western Caribbean resorts as Playa del Carmen/Cozumel, Grand Cayman, and Ocho Rios.

Ecstasy: The ship makes 3-day cruises from Miami to Nassau and back year-round, and 4-day cruises from Miami to Key West, Playa del Carmen/Cozumel, and Miami. Both itineraries include at least 1 day at sea.

Fantasy: Three-day cruises from Port Canaveral to Nassau and back leave year-round, as do 4-day cruises from Port Canaveral to Nassau to Freeport and back to Port Canaveral. Both itineraries include at least 1 day at sea. *Fantasy,* the first of Carnival's megaships, is one of the largest vessels employed year-round on short-term cruises.

Fascination: The ship makes 7-day cruises year-round, leaving from San Juan and calling at St. Thomas, St. Maarten, Dominica, Barbados, and Martinique, with one full day at sea.

Imagination: The ship makes 7-day cruises year-round from its home port of Miami. One route calls at Cozumel/Playa del Carmen, Grand Cayman, and Ocho Rios; the other stops at San Juan, St. Thomas, and St. Maarten.

Inspiration: The ship makes 7-day cruises departing from San Juan every Sunday, calling at St. Thomas, Guadeloupe, St. Lucia, Grenada, and Santo Domingo.

Jubilee: Between November and March, *Jubilee* makes 10- and 11-day cruises from Miami to points farther south in the Caribbean than any other Miami-based cruise ship. The most distant stop on the ship's 11-day cruises is Lake Gatun, the approximate midway point along the Panama Canal. Other stops include Aruba, Cartagena, the San Blas Islands, Puerto Limón (Costa Rica), and Key West.

Ten-day cruises aboard the same ship follow one of two different itineraries to the southern Caribbean. Stops include Tortola, Martinique, Barbados, St. Lucia, St. Thomas; or alternatively, St. Thomas, St. Kitts, Barbados, Trinidad, and Aruba. In summer, the Jubilee heads through the Panama Canal for cruises northwest to Alaska.

Paradise: From its home port in Miami, the newest of the Carnival ships has the same routes as the *Imagination,* but when the *Imagination* is in the western Caribbean, *Paradise* is in the eastern Caribbean, and vice versa. The only exception is that *Paradise* substitutes Tortola for St. Maarten during its treks through the eastern Caribbean.

Sensation: The ship makes 7-day cruises year-round through the Eastern Caribbean from its home base in Tampa. Stops include New Orleans, Playa del Carmen/Cozumel, and Grand Cayman.

Tropicale: Based year-round in Tampa, this smaller and older Carnival ship specializes in short-term treks through the Western Caribbean, managing to travel farther in less time than virtually any other cruise ship in the industry. Four-day cruises stop at Key West and Cozumel; 5-day cruises anchor at Grand Cayman and Cozumel.

Celebrity Cruises. 1050 Caribbean Way, Miami, FL 33132. ☎ **800/327-6700** or 305/539-6000. Fax 800/722-5329. www.celebrity-cruises.com.

Century: Celebrity aims to keep Century, the first and most widely publicized of the line's megaships, within the Caribbean throughout the year. Departing and arriving from Fort Lauderdale, it alternates visits to the western and eastern Caribbean at weekly intervals. Its eastern Caribbean route includes stopovers at San Juan, St. Thomas, St. Maarten, and Nassau; its western Caribbean route takes in Ocho Rios, Grand Cayman, Cozumel, and Key West.

Galaxy: Unlike its older sibling, described above, Galaxy spends winters in the Caribbean and summers along the Pacific Coast of North America and in Alaska, with interim cruises spent traversing the Panama Canal. Between October and April, San Juan is the beginning and end point for cruises that depart every Saturday for Catalina Island (a beach island off the southeast coast of the Dominican Republic), Barbados, Martinique, Antigua, and St. Thomas.

Horizon: Between late October and mid-April, Horizon makes 10- or 11-day jaunts that depart from Fort Lauderdale and include visits to St. Maarten or Curaçao, St. Lucia or Grenada, Antigua or LaGuaira, and Martinique or Antigua, depending on the week of your journey. Midwinter cruises usually stop at both Barbados and St. Thomas. More than any other vessel within the Celebrity fleet, *Horizon* makes itself available for one-of-a-kind charterings by special interest groups and travel-industry entrepreneurs.

Mercury: Celebrity's newest ship spends every week throughout the winter cruising from its home port of Fort Lauderdale to such western Caribbean ports as Key West, Calica, Cozumel, and Grand Cayman.

Zenith: With cruises that last between 7 and 18 nights, this ship specializes in long-term sailings. The longest of these travels from Acapulco, Mexico, through the canal to New York City, with stops en route at Cartagena, Grand Cayman, Cozumel, and at least two of the major ports of eastern Florida. In summer, the ship embarks on 1-week sailings between New York and Bermuda.

Clipper Cruise Line. 7711 Bonhomme Ave., St. Louis, MO 63105-1956. ☎ **800/325-0010** or 314/727-2929. Fax 314/727-6576. www.ecotravel.com/clipper.

Nantucket Clipper: Every winter, between December and February, this ship makes a 7-day transit through isolated, less-visited corners of the British and U.S. Virgin Islands from its home port in St. Thomas. Ports of call include St. John, Jost van Dyke, Sopers Hole, Tortola, Virgin Gorda, Salt Island, Norman's Island, and Christmas Cove.

Yorktown Clipper: Every winter, between November and March, this ship cruises through the Leeward and Grenadine islands of the southern Caribbean. From twin bases in St. Kitts and Grenada, it embarks on 7-day excursions through the central and southern Caribbean, focusing on such lesser-visited islands as Bequia, Dominica, Union Island, Nevis, and St. Kitts. Sometimes the line charters smaller sailing vessels from outside entrepreneurs to carry passengers to such smaller islands as Mustique, Mayreau, or Petit St. Vincent.

Club Med Cruises. 40 W. 57th St., New York, NY 10019. ☎ **800/CLUBMED** or 212/977-2100. Fax 800/727-5306. www.clubmed.com.

Club Med 2: Between early October and early May, the ship departs from Martinique for 7-day excursions that begin and end on Saturday. Ports of call include St. Martin, St. Barts, Marie-Galant, Dominica, and Mayreau, as well as Guadeloupe, Barbados, the Tobago Cays, St. Kitts, Nevis, Virgin Gorda, and scattered ports along the coast of Venezuela.

Commodore Cruise Line. 4000 Hollywood Blvd., South Tower 385, Hollywood, FL 33021. ☎ **800/237-5361** or 954/967-2100. Fax 954/967-2147. www.e-trade.com/commodore.htm.

Enchanted Isle: Battered but durable, and known for its reasonably priced accommodations, this ship departs on Saturday for 7-day cruises from New Orleans to the western Caribbean and along the Gulf coast of Mexico. Stopovers include Plaza del Carmen/Cozumel, Grand Cayman, and Montego Bay (Jamaica). In some cases, the

Honduran ports of Roatan Island and/or Puerto Cortes are substituted for Grand Cayman and/or Ocho Rios.

Costa Cruise Lines. World Trade Center, 80 SW 8th St., Miami, FL 33130-3097 (mailing address: P.O. Box 01964, Miami, FL 33101-9865). ☎ **800/462-6782** or 305/358-7325. Fax 305/375-0676. www.costacruises.com.

CostaRomantica: Every Sunday throughout the winter, the ship departs from Port Everglades in Fort Lauderdale on one of two routes that alternate weekly. The eastern Caribbean cruises call at San Juan, St. Thomas, Serena Cay (Costa's private island off the coast of the Dominican Republic), and Nassau. The western Caribbean cruises dock at Key West, Playa del Carmen/Cozumel, Ocho Rios, and Grand Cayman.

CostaVictoria: Its winter itinerary is almost exactly the same as that of the Romantica, but when *Romantica* does the eastern route, *Victoria* does the western route, and vice versa.

Cunard. 6100 Blue Lagoon Dr., Miami, FL 33126. ☎ **800/5-CUNARD** or 305/463-3000. Fax 305/269-6950. www.cunardline.com.

On December 31, 1999, both Sea Goddesses below will meet on the same isolated beachfront on Virgin Gorda, for a shared "changeover of the millennium" party that promises to be particularly spectacular.

Sea Goddess I: This ship spends November through February in the Caribbean, on 7-day circular itineraries from bases in both Barbados and St. Thomas. Stopovers include St. John, St. Maarten, St. Barts, Antigua, Virgin Gorda, Jost Van Dyke, Grenada, Nevis, Mayreau, Carriacou, and Grand Turk. There's also a 14-day odyssey that calls at each of the above-mentioned islands, but with slightly longer stopovers.

Sea Goddess II: During the winter months, this ship follows the same itinerary as the Sea Goddess I, embarking on 7-day tours through the Caribbean from bases in either Barbados or St. Thomas. It's rare that both ships are in the same port at the same time, however.

Holland America Line-Westours. 300 Elliott Ave. W., Seattle, WA 98119. ☎ **800/426-0327** or 206/281-3535. Fax 800/628-4855. www.hollandamerica.com.

Maasdam: Between November and April, the ship departs from Fort Lauderdale for 10-day cruises in the Caribbean, trekking through the Panama Canal to Acapulco.

Noordam: From mid-October to April, *Noordam* leaves from Tampa for 7-day cruises through the western Caribbean, with stops at Grand Cayman, Santo Tomás de Castilla, Guatemala (departure points for visits to the Mayan ruins of Tikal and Copán), and Cozumel/ Playa del Carmen.

Ryndam: From October to April, *Ryndam* sails from Fort Lauderdale for 10-day treks through central and southern Caribbean ports that include St. Lucia, Barbados, Guadeloupe, St. Maarten, St. Thomas, and Nassau.

Statendam: From October to March, *Statendam* makes 10-day treks from Fort Lauderdale to ports whose specifics change with every cruise. Stops may include St. John, St. Thomas, Dominica, Grenada, Trinidad, and Curaçao, with 3 days at sea.

Veendam: Between October and July, *Veendam* spends 90% of its time making 7-day cruises from Fort Lauderdale through the western and, to a slightly lesser degree, eastern Caribbean, with stopovers at Nassau, San Juan, St. John, and St. Thomas, and 3 days at sea. On rare intervals, there are 7-day cruises from Fort Lauderdale that stop at Key West, Playa del Carmen/Cozumel, Ocho Rios, and Grand Cayman, with 2 days at sea.

Westerdam: From October to April, the *Westerdam* specializes in 7-day cruises from Fort Lauderdale that stop at Nassau, San Juan, St. John, St. Thomas, and Half Moon Cay, which is the cruise line's private Bahamian island.

Mediterranean Shipping Cruises. 420 Fifth Ave., New York, NY 10018. ☎ **800/666-9333** or 212/764-8593. Fax 212/764-8593.

Melody: Between January and April, from a base in Fort Lauderdale, this ship embarks on 12-day cruises of either the western or eastern Caribbean. Eastern Caribbean ports of call include St. Thomas, Guadeloupe, Grenada, Barbados, Antigua, and Grand Turk. Western Caribbean stopovers include Playa del Carmen, Cozumel, Ocho Rios, Santo Domingo, Grand Turk, and Key West.

Norwegian Cruise Line. 7665 Corporate Center Dr., Miami, FL 33126. ☎ **800/327-7030** or 305/436-4000. Fax 305/436-4126. www.ncl.com.

Norwegian Dream: From January through April and from October through December, the ship departs every Sunday from Miami for 7-day cruises, stopping at such western Caribbean ports as Grand Cayman, Playa del Carmen/Cozumel, Cancún, and Great Stirrup Cay (NCL's private island in The Bahamas). During other months, trips leave from New York and include visits to Bermuda. At other, relatively infrequent, intervals, the ship makes 7-day circuits from San Juan to such southern Caribbean ports as Aruba and Curaçao.

Leeward: The *Leeward*, along with the company's recently acquired *Norwegian Majesty,* is NCL's foremost specialist in relatively inexpensive, short-haul, short-term, hard-partying cruises that never extend more than 4 days. Year-round, 3-day "extended weekend" cruises depart from the Port of Miami every Friday at 5pm, calling at Great Stirrup Cay and either Key West or Nassau. These alternate with 4-day weekday cruises that leave Miami every Monday and stop at Key West, Cancún, and Cozumel.

Norway: Except for the summer months (April to October), when it stays in Europe, this ship leaves on 7-day cruises from Miami every Saturday. Mostly they head for the eastern Caribbean, stopping at St. Maarten, St. John, St. Thomas, and Great Stirrup Cay, with 3 days at sea. On selected Saturdays, however, they depart for the western Caribbean, stopping at Ocho Rios, Grand Cayman, Cozumel, and Great Stirrup Cay, with 2 days at sea.

Norwegian Majesty: In winter, it specializes exclusively in short-term, short-haul itineraries. Three-day cruises from Miami visit The Bahamas and Key West. Four-day cruises pay brief calls at Cozumel, and sometimes at the nearby Mexican beach resort of Puerto Morelas. Some itineraries are themed. For example, one 3-day cruise is devoted to Elvis, with impersonators, Elvis costumes, Elvis dance contests, and Elvis trivia questions. Other themes include country-western music, Irish or Greek culture, and bobby-sock and bubble-gum rock 'n' roll.

Norwegian Sea: More than any other ship within NCL's armada, *Norwegian Sea* makes stops that are a bit off the beaten track. From its year-round home port in San Juan, it embarks on a half-dozen different routings that make stops at St. Thomas and St. Maarten, as well as such less-visited ports as Santo Domingo, Antigua, St. Kitts, and Dominica. Other stops might include St. Lucia, Barbados, and Antigua. Regardless of the specific routing, all cruises include a full day at sea.

Norwegian Wind: The *Wind* spends its summers in Alaska, and its winters in Miami, leaving for 7-day cruises through the Western Caribbean. Ports of call include Grand Cayman, Cancún, Cozumel, and Great Stirrup Key, with 2 full days at sea.

Premier Cruises. 400 Challenger Rd., Cape Canaveral, FL 32920. ☎ **800/990-7770** or 407/ 783-5061. Fax 407/784-0954. www.premiercruises.com.

Island Breeze: A dowager vessel built in the early 1960s, and most recently under the auspices of the now-defunct Dolphin Cruise Line, this ship offers 7-day cost-conscious cruises from its home port of Santo Domingo. Ports of call vary on alternate weeks, but visits on its southeastern run are likely to include Barbados, St. Lucia, Guadeloupe, St. Maarten, and St. Thomas. Tours through the Caribbean's southwestern tier include Curaçao, Caracas, Grenada, Martinique, and St. Croix.

Big Red Boat: This ship is based year-round in Port Canaveral, and devotes its time exclusively to 3- and 4-day cruises to Nassau and Port Lucaya. Cruises can be combined with a 3- or 4-night Disney Vacation.

Sea Breeze: From a wintertime base in Fort Lauderdale, this ship specializes in 7-night cruises to "The Mayan Americas," focusing on the Isthmus of Central America. Stopovers are at Playa del Carmen/Cozumel, Roatan (Honduras), Belize, and Key West.

Seawind Crown: Medium-sized and sturdy, although not particularly stylish, this is the only major cruise ship based in the southern Caribbean port of Aruba. Most of its cruises last for 7 nights, and focus on southern Caribbean islands too far from South Florida for most major cruise ships. Ports of call include Margarita Island, Caracas, Barbados, and St. Lucia.

Princess Cruises. 10100 Santa Monica Blvd., Los Angeles, CA 90067-4189. ☎ **800/ 421-0522** or 310/553-1770. Fax 310/284-2845. www.princesscruises.com.

Dawn Princess: From its home port of San Juan, this twin of the Sun Princess sails on a series of 7-day cruises, departing every Saturday. About half its trips visit Aruba, Caracas, Grenada, St. Thomas, and Dominica. The others stop at St. Thomas, St. Maarten, Barbados, Martinique, and St. Lucia.

Grand Princess: Launched with lots of fanfare in 1998, the newest and biggest of the company's megaships is too large to fit through the Panama Canal. Consequently, *Princess* plans to keep it plying the waters of the Eastern Caribbean every winter, and the seas of Europe every summer. Look for stopovers at St. Thomas, St. Maarten, and Princess Cays, the company's private island.

Regal Princess: During the winter months, this ship travels from Fort Lauderdale across the Caribbean to Cartagena and Colombia, then through the Panama Canal (it's so wide it can barely squeeze through) as far as the Gatun Lock, then into the Caribbean again to Costa Rica, Grand Cayman, and Cozumel. Most of its winter cruises last for 10 days, with the exception of a late spring "repositioning cruise" that lasts 15 days and ends in San Diego. Summer months are spent cruising along the coast of Alaska.

Sea Princess: The launch date for this ship was scheduled for several months after this writing. Expect a home port of Fort Lauderdale, and an itinerary that includes such western Caribbean ports as the Princess Cays, Ocho Rios, Grand Cayman, and Cozumel.

Sun Princess: In winter months, this ship travels in wide-ranging, 10- and 11-day sweeps between San Juan and Acapulco. Ports of call en route include Martinique, San Juan, Ocho Rios, Grenada, Costa Rica, and such Pacific coast Mexican resorts as Huatulco and Acapulco.

Radisson Seven Seas Cruises. 600 Corporate Dr., Suite 410, Fort Lauderdale, FL 33334. ☎ **800/477-7500** or 305/776-6123. Fax 305/772-3763. www.rssc.com.

Radisson Diamond: In winter, this vessel conducts cruises that last between 4 and 9 nights each. The shorter ones tend to begin and end in San Juan, and make circular routes that include visits to Tortola, St. Barts, St. Maarten, St. Thomas, Bonaire, and in some cases, Ponce, in Puerto Rico. The longer ones travel west from either Aruba or San Juan, to Puerto Caldera, Costa Rica.

Regal Cruises. 300 Regal Cruise Way, Palmetto, FL 34221. ☎ **800/270-7425** or 941/721-7300. Fax 941/723-0900. www.regalcruises.com.

Regal Empress: From late October through late May, the ship makes cruises of varying duration, each of which departs from the company's home base of Port Manatee, 3 miles south of St. Petersburg. Five-day cruises stop at Playa del Carmen/Cozumel and include 2 days at sea. Six-day cruises call on Key West and Playa del Carmen/Cozumel, and include 1 day at sea. Seven-day cruises visit Grand Cayman, Montego Bay, and Key West, with 2 days at sea. Eight-day cruises call at Ocho Rios, Grand Cayman, and Playa del Carmen/Cozumel, also with 2 days at sea.

Royal Caribbean Cruises, Ltd. 1050 Caribbean Way, Miami, FL 33132. ☎ **800/327-6700** or 305/539-6000. Fax 800/722-5329. www.royalcaribbean.com.

Enchantment of the Seas: This ship departs every Sunday year-round from Miami on alternating tours of the western and eastern Caribbean. Eastern Caribbean stops include St. Maarten, St. John, St. Thomas, and CocoCay; western Caribbean stops include Key West, Cozumel, Ocho Rios, and Grand Cayman.

Grandeur of the Seas: Based in Miami, and departing every Saturday throughout the year, this ship makes 7-day circuits of the Eastern Caribbean, with stops at Labadee, San Juan, St. Thomas, and CocoCay.

Legend of the Seas: Throughout the winter, from a base in San Juan, this ship departs on trips through the Panama Canal, as far as Acapulco, that usually last from 10 to 11 days, and in rare instances, as much as 14 days. Cruises heading west make stops in St. Thomas, Catalina Island (off the coast of the Dominican Republic), Curaçao, and Caldera (Costa Rica). Eastbound transits call at Aruba.

Majesty of the Seas: Every Sunday, year-round, it departs from Miami for tours of the Western Caribbean, making stops at Playa del Carmen/Cozumel, Grand Cayman, Ocho Rios, and Labadee.

Monarch of the Seas: Using San Juan as its home port, this ship departs every Sunday throughout the year on 7-day cruises that stop at St. Thomas, Martinique, Barbados, Antigua, and St. Maarten.

Nordic Empress: Between May and August it uses Port Canaveral as its base, departing for 3- and 4-night treks to Nassau and CocoCay. From September to May, it moves to San Juan, and makes an alternating series of 3- and 4-night cruises. Three-night cruises stop at St. Thomas and St. Maarten; 4-night cruises add an additional stop at St. Croix.

Rhapsody of the Seas: Between October and April, this ship departs every Saturday from San Juan for southern Caribbean ports, including Aruba, Curaçao, St. Maarten, and St. Thomas.

Sovereign of the Seas: Throughout the year, it embarks from Miami on 3- and 4-night circuits. Three-night cruises stop at Nassau and CocoCay; 4-night cruises add an additional stop in Key West.

Splendour of the Seas: Between November and March, from a base in Miami, it embarks on 10- and 11-night circuits through the Caribbean. Ten-night cruises stop at Cozumel/Playa del Carmen, Grand Cayman, Ocho Rios, St. Thomas, San Juan, and Labadee. Eleven-night itineraries include Key West, Curaçao, Aruba, Ocho Rios, Grand Cayman, and Cozumel.

Vision of the Seas: Between October and March, this glistening new ship (launched in May of 1998), will set sail on 10- and 11-night cruises through the Panama

Canal, between San Juan and Acapulco. Stops en route will include St. Thomas, Curaçao, and Aruba.

Seabourn Cruise Line. 55 Francisco St., Suite 710, San Francisco, CA 94133. ☎ **800/929-9595** or 415/391-7444. Fax 415/391-8518.

Seabourn Legend: Between November and April, it features Caribbean itineraries of between 7 and 16 days, some of which originate in Fort Lauderdale, others in San Juan. Ports of call vary according to the individual cruise, but are likely to include scattered ports in The Bahamas, as well as St. John, Virgin Gorda, St. Barts, Aruba, Cartagena, the San Blas islands of Panama, Panama City, and Caldera, Costa Rica.

Seabourn Pride: Between January and March, this vessel schedules a 10-week circumnavigation of South America, with Caribbean stops at the tour's beginning and end. The odyssey begins in Fort Lauderdale, and continues through the Canal, stopping at Valparaiso, Chile, before cruising around the tip of Cape Horn, and then to ports in Brazil, Venezuela, and such Caribbean ports as St. John and San Juan, just before the ship's return to Fort Lauderdale. The ship also makes 6-day cruises through the Eastern Caribbean.

Star Clippers. 4101 Salzedo Ave., Coral Gables, FL 33146. ☎ **800/442-0553** or 305/442-0550. Fax 305/442-1611. www.star-clippers.com.

Star Clipper: Between November and May, this modern-day replica of a 19th-century clipper ship operates from a base in Antigua. The *Star Clipper*'s "Treasure Islands" tour makes stops at St. Barts, Virgin Gorda, St. Maarten, and St. Kitts. This cruise alternates with 7-day excursions through the Grenadines, with stops at Dominica, St. Vincent, the Tobago Cays, St. Lucia, Martinique, and the isolated Ile des Saintes. Both routes defer to prevailing wind patterns.

Royal Olympic Cruises. 1 Rockefeller Plaza, Suite 315, New York, NY 10020. ☎ **800/872-6400** or 212/397-6400. Fax 212/765-9685. www.royalolympiccruises.com.

Stella Solaris: In winter, this Greek-owned ship offers several different trips. Cruises of between 12 and 16 days may offer stopovers at Key West, Cozumel, Trinidad, St. Vincent, Antigua, San Juan, Curaçao, St. Lucia, St. Thomas, Bequia, and Barbados. Some tours chug on toward the Mediterranean. Fort Lauderdale and Galveston, Texas, are the points of origin for many of these cruises, a fact that offers easy access to clients based in Texas.

Tall Ship Adventures. 1389 S. Havana St., Aurora, CO 80012. ☎ **800/662-0090** or 303/755-7983. Fax 303/755-9007. www.tallshipadventures.com.

Sir Francis Drake: Each winter, this line's only ship, the *Sir Francis Drake,* departs from a home port on Beef Island, near Tortola, and ventures to Peter Island, Cooper Island, Marina Cay, Norman Island, and sites on or off the coast of Virgin Gorda.

During the summer and autumn, the ship's home port will probably be St. Lucia, and it will offer cruises to French-oriented islands such as Dominica, Martinique, Guadeloupe, and the Ile des Saints. On alternate weeks, look for southbound excursions through St. Vincent and the scattered miniarchipelago of the Grenadines.

Windjammer Barefoot Cruises, Ltd. 1759 Bay Rd. (P.O. Box 120), Miami Beach, FL 33139. ☎ **800/327-2601** or 305/672-6453. Fax 305/674-1219. www.windjammer.com.

Captains on this cruise line often adjust their itineraries in mid-cruise to reflect changing wind and weather patterns, as well as any island event of particular interest.

Amazing Grace: A motorized, diesel-driven supply ship responsible for replenishing the stocks of its siblings, *Amazing Grace* has a more rigid timetable than any of the other ships in the fleet. Cruises last for 13 days and call at most of the ports between

Freeport, The Bahamas, and Port-of-Spain, Trinidad. This route encompasses greater distances and more ports of call (almost 20) than that of almost any other cruise line.

Fantôme: Based year-round in Nelson's Harbour, Antigua, *Fantôme* maintains an ongoing roster of 6-day cruises that stop at St. Lucia, Martinique, St. Barts, Statia, and Saba—with an occasional spontaneous change en route.

Flying Cloud: Six-day cruises depart every Monday from Tortola, British Virgin Islands, calling at a selected roster of some of the archipelago's least-visited, least-touristy sites, such as Jost van Dyke, Virgin Gorda, Peter Island, and Norman Island.

Legacy: Windjammer's newest vessel is based year-round in Fajardo, along Puerto Rico's eastern shore. From there, it embarks on 7-day excursions that include visits to offshore dependencies of Puerto Rico, such as Vieques and Culebra, and scattered ports of the Virgin Islands, such as St. Croix, Culebra, Norman Island, Jost van Dyke, Virgin Gorda, and St. John.

Mandalay: Between December and May, 13-day cruises depart on Mondays from either Grenada or Antigua and feature stops in St. Vincent and isolated harbors in the Grenadines, including Bequia, Palm Island, St. Lucia, Guadeloupe, Martinique, St. Kitts, and Carriacou. Between June and November, the ship conducts 7-day cruises between Grenada and Margarita Island, Venezuela, with lots of beach time.

Polynesia: Six-day cruises depart every Monday from St. Maarten, with stops at a selection of islands including St. Barts, St. Kitts, Saba, Statia, Prickly Pear, Anguilla, Nevis, and Tintamarre.

Yankee Clipper: Six-day cruises depart every Monday from Grenada, with stops at islands throughout the Grenadines.

Windstar Cruises. 300 Elliott Ave. W., Seattle, WA 98119. ☎ **800/258-7245** or 206/281-3535. Fax 206/281-0627. www.windstarcruises.com.

Wind Spirit: The ship uses Charlotte Amalie, St. Thomas, as a base for its 7-day cruises in winter, fall, and spring. Stops include St. John, St. Martin, St. Barts, Tortola, Virgin Gorda, and Jost van Dyke. In summer, it sails in the Mediterranean.

Wind Surf: In fall, winter, and spring, this newest member of the Windstar fleet sails from Bridgetown, Barbados, on either northbound or southbound itineraries. The southbound cruise includes stops at the Tobago Cays, Tobago, Grenada, Martinique, St. Lucia, and Barbados. Northbound stops include Nevis, St. Martin, St. Barts, Ile des Saintes, and Bequia. In summer, the ship sails in the Mediterranean.

2 Ports of Embarkation

The busiest of the ports of embarkation is Miami, followed by Port Everglades in Fort Lauderdale and Port Canaveral at Cape Canaveral. Tampa, on Florida's west coast, is also becoming a major port, especially for cruise ships visiting the eastern coast of Mexico. New Orleans is popular for ships sailing to Mexico. San Juan is both the major port of embarkation in the Caribbean Basin and a major port of call. (We've also covered San Juan in chapter 3, "The Ports of Call.")

All of these ports are tourist destinations themselves, so cruise lines now offer special deals to extend all Caribbean or Bahamian cruise vacations in the port either before or after the cruise, sometimes in a line-owned hotel. These packages, for 2, 3, or 4 days, often offer major hotel and car-rental discounts. Have your travel agent or cruise specialist check for the best deals.

In this chapter, we describe each port of embarkation, tell you how to get to it, and suggest things to see and do there, whether hitting the beach, sightseeing, or shopping. We also recommend restaurants and places to stay, as well as bars, clubs, and other evening entertainment. You'll find more detailed information about each destination in *Frommer's Florida; Frommer's Miami & the Keys; Frommer's New Orleans;* and *Frommer's Puerto Rico.*

1 Miami & the Port of Miami

Miami is the cruise capital of the world. More cruise ships, especially super-sized ones, berth here than anywhere else on earth, and more than 3 million cruise ship passengers pass through yearly. Not surprisingly, its facilities are extensive and state-of-the art. The port's success has come from a sophisticated blend of public and private investment, aggressive marketing, and a package of tax breaks and sales incentives during the early years. It also helps that the Port of Miami is well-connected to a major airport, Miami International, only 8 miles away.

Some very large cruise ships call Miami home. These include Carnival Cruise Line's 2,600-passenger super-triplets *Ecstasy, Imagination,* and *Paradise,* as well as the smaller and less impressive *Jubilee,* and the largest of all, *Carnival Destiny.* Royal Caribbean Cruises, whose corporate headquarters lie very near the port, assembles a fleet here larger than most national navies. It includes *Enchantment of the Seas, Grandeur of the Seas, Majesty of the Seas, Sovereign of the Seas,* and *Splendour of the Seas.* Norwegian Cruise Line's 2,044-passenger flagship, *Norway,* also pulls into the port, along with such smaller vessels as *Norwegian Dream, Leeward,* and *Norwegian Majesty.* Finally, Cunard's *QE2,* along with its *Sea Goddesses,* make occasional appearances in Miami.

Just across the bridge from the Port of Miami is Bayside Marketplace, downtown Miami's waterfront and restaurant shopping complex, which can be reached via regular shuttle service between each cruise terminal and Bayside's main entrance. In the coming years, the port plans to increase its cruise ship capacity 40% by adding four new passenger terminals as part of a 53-acre waterfront park. This combination cruise facility and entertainment village will come complete with shops, restaurants, museums, and theme parks. Also planned for the area is a world trade center and a performing-arts center.

The **Port of Miami** is at 1015 N. America Way, in central Miami. The port lies on Dodge Island, reached via a five-lane bridge from the downtown district. For information, call ☎ **305/371-PORT.**

Note: All 305 area codes in Miami will remain the same; however, because of an overload on that circuit, new businesses and residences will take a 786 area code.

GETTING TO MIAMI & THE PORT

BY AIR   **Miami International Airport** is about 8 miles west of downtown Miami and the port. The fare from the airport to the Port of Miami is about $18. The meter must read $1.10 at the start of your trip, and one fare pays for all passengers in the cab. Some leading taxi companies include **Central Taxicab Service** (☎ **305/532-5555**), **Diamond Cab Company** (☎ **305/545-5555**), and **Metro Taxicab Company** (☎ **305/888-8888**).

You can also take a **Metrobus** (☎ **305/638-6700**) from the airport to the port for only $1.25, but you'll have to carry your luggage.

You can go by van on **SuperShuttle** (☎ **305/871-2000**), which charges $7 to $14 per person, with two pieces of luggage, for a ride within Dade County, which includes the Port of Miami. Their vans operate 24 hours a day.

BY CAR   **The Florida Turnpike,** a toll road, and **Interstate 95** are the main arteries for those arriving from the north. Ongoing road construction on Interstate 95 virtually guarantees slow-moving traffic. Coming in from the northwest, take **Interstate 75** or **U.S. 27** to reach the center of Miami.

Avis (☎ **800/331-1212**), **Budget** (☎ **800/527-0700**), **Dollar** (☎ **800/800-4000**), **Hertz** (☎ **800/654-3131**), **National** (☎ **800/227-7368**), and **Value** (☎ **800/468-2583**) can all be found on Miami International Airport's lower level near the baggage-claim area.

Parking at the Port   Parking lots right at street level face the cruise terminals. Parking runs $8 per day. Porters can carry your luggage to the terminals.

BY TRAIN   **Amtrak** (☎ **800/872-7245**) offers 3 trains daily between New York and Miami, and daily service between Los Angeles and Miami. You'll pull into Amtrak's Miami terminal at 8303 NW 37th Ave. (☎ **305/835-1205**).

EXPLORING MIAMI

Miami is no longer just a beach vacation—you'll also find high-quality hotels, distinctive restaurants, unusual attractions, and top shopping. After a relaxing day on the water, take advantage of choice theater or opera, restaurants serving exotic and delicious food, the hopping club scene, or the lively cafe culture.

Miami at a Glance

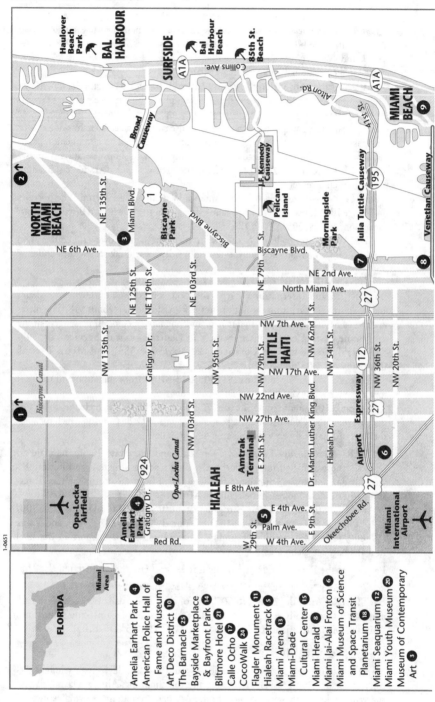

Amelia Earhart Park 4
American Police Hall of
Fame and Museum 10
Art Deco District 23
The Barnacle 25
Bayside Marketplace
& Bayfront Park 14
Biltmore Hotel 21
Calle Ocho 17
CocoWalk 24
Flagler Monument 11
Hialeah Racetrack 5
Miami Arena 13
Miami-Dade
Cultural Center 15
Miami Herald 8
Miami Jai-Alai Fronton 6
Miami Museum of Science
and Space Transit
Planetarium 18
Miami Seaquarium 12
Miami Youth Museum 20
Museum of Contemporary
Art 3

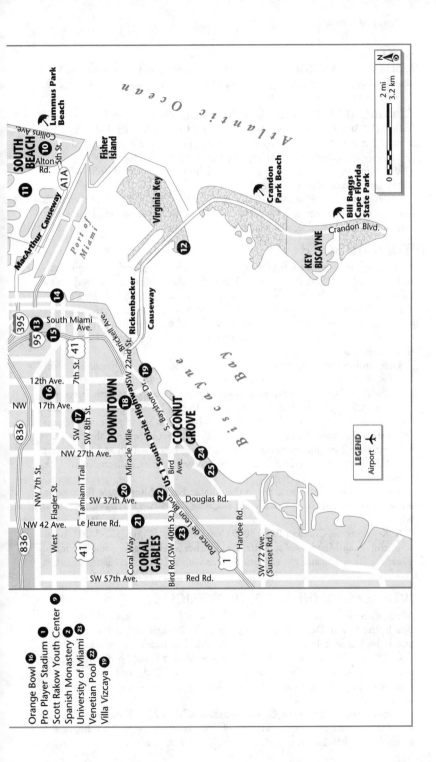

LEGEND
✈ Airport

N

2 mi
3.2 km
0

Atlantic Ocean

Lummus Park Beach
Collins Ave.
SOUTH BEACH
Alton Rd.
5th St.
A1A
MacArthur Causeway
Port of Miami
Fisher Island

Virginia Key

Crandon Park Beach
Bill Baggs Cape Florida State Park
Crandon Blvd.
KEY BISCAYNE

Rickenbacker Causeway

Biscayne Bay

395
95
41
South Miami Ave.
7th St.
12th Ave.
17th Ave.
NW
SW 8th St.
SW
DOWNTOWN
Brickell Ave.
SW 22nd St.
S. Bayshore Dr.
COCONUT GROVE
836
NW 7th St.
NW 27th Ave.
Miracle Mile
Tamiami Trail
Flagler St.
NW 42 Ave.
SW 37th Ave.
Le Jeune Rd.
West
Coral Way
CORAL GABLES
SW 57th Ave.
US 1 South Dixie Highway
Ponce de Leon Blvd.
Bird Rd.(SW 40th St.)
Bird Ave.
Douglas Rd.
Hardee Rd.
Red Rd.
SW 72 Ave. (Sunset Rd.)
41

Orange Bowl 16
Pro Player Stadium 1
Scott Rakow Youth Center 9
Spanish Monastery 2
University of Miami 23
Venetian Pool 22
Villa Vizcaya 19

ESSENTIALS

VISITOR INFORMATION   Contact the **Greater Miami Convention and Visitors Bureau,** 701 Brickell Ave., Miami, FL 33131 (☎ **800/283-2707** or 305/539-3000) for the most up-to-date information.

GETTING AROUND   For a taxi in Miami, call **Metro** (☎ **305/888-8888**) or **Yellow** (☎ **305/444-4444**); on Miami Beach, call **Central** (☎ **305/532-5555**). The meter starts at $1.50, and ticks up another $2 each mile and 25¢ for each additional minute, with standard flat-rate charges for frequently traveled routes.

Bus transportation in Miami is often a nightmare. Call ☎ **305/638-6700** for public transit information. Fare is $1.25.

Metromover (☎ **305/638-6700**), a 4.4-mile elevated line, circles downtown, stopping near important attractions and shopping and business districts. It runs daily from about 5am to midnight. The fare is 25¢.

HITTING THE BEACH

A 300-foot-wide sand beach runs for about 10 miles from the south of Miami Beach to Haulover Beach Park in the north. Although most of this stretch is lined with a solid wall of hotels, beach access is plentiful, and you are free to frolic along the entire strip. There are lots of public beaches here, wide and well-maintained, complete with lifeguards, toilet facilities, concession stands, and metered parking (bring lots of quarters). A wooden boardwalk runs along the hotel side of the beach from 21st to 46th streets—about 1¹/₂ miles.

Lifeguard-protected public beaches include **21st Street,** at the beginning of the boardwalk; **35th Street,** popular with an older crowd; **46th Street,** next to the Fontainebleau Hilton; **53rd Street,** a narrower, more sedate beach; **64th Street,** one of the quietest strips around; and **72nd Street,** a local old-timers spot. On the southern tip of the beach is family favorite **South Pointe Park,** where you can watch the cruise ships. **Lummus Park,** in the center of the Art Deco district, is the best place for people-watching and model-spotting. The beach between 11th and 13th streets is popular with the gay crowd. Senior citizens prefer the beach from 1st to 15th streets.

To escape the crowds, head up to the 40-acre **North Shore State Recreation Area,** 3400 NE 163 St. at Collins and Biscayne (☎ **305/919-1844**). Parking is $3.25.

In Key Biscayne, **Crandon Park,** 4000 Crandon Blvd. (☎ **305/361-5421**), is one of metropolitan Miami's finest white sand beaches, stretching for some 3¹/₂ miles. There are lifeguards, and you can rent cabanas with a shower and chairs. Saturdays and Sundays the beach can be especially crowded. Parking nearby is $3.50.

SOUTH BEACH & THE ART DECO DISTRICT

Miami's best sight is a part of the city itself. Located at the southern end of Miami Beach, the ✪ **Art Deco District** is filled with outrageous and fanciful 1920s and 1930s architecture that shouldn't be missed. This treasure trove features more than 900 buildings in the Art Deco, Streamline Moderne, and Spanish Mediterranean Revival style. The district stretches from 6th to 23rd streets, and from the Atlantic Ocean to Lennox Court. Ocean Drive boasts many of the premier Art Deco hotels.

Also in South Beach is the ✪ **Bass Museum of Art,** 2121 Park Ave. (☎ **305/673-7533**), with a permanent collection of Old Masters, along with textiles, period furnishings, objets d'art, ecclesiastical artifacts, and sculpture.

CORAL GABLES & COCONUT GROVE

These two Miami neighborhoods are fun to visit for their architecture and ambiance. In **Coral Gables,** the old world meets the new, as curving boulevards, sidewalks, plazas, fountains, and arched entrances evoke Seville. Today the area is home to the **University of Miami** and the **Miracle Mile** (it's actually half a mile), a 5-block retail mecca stretching from Douglas Road (37th Avenue) to Le Jeune Road (42nd Avenue). You can even visit the boyhood home of George Merrick, the man who originally developed Coral Gables. The **Coral Gables Merrick House & Gardens,** 907 Coral Way (☎ **305/460-5361**) has been restored to its 1920s look and is filled with Merrick memorabilia. The house and garden are open for tours on Wednesday and Saturday between 1 and 4pm.

Coconut Grove, South Florida's oldest settlement, remains a village surrounded by the urban sprawl of Miami. It dates back to the early 1800s when Bahamian seamen first sought to salvage treasure from the wrecked vessels stranded along the Great Florida Reef. Mostly people come here to shop, drink, dine, or simply walk around and explore. But don't miss the ✪ **Vizcaya Museum & Gardens,** 3251 S. Miami Ave. (☎ **305/250-9133**), a spectacular 70-room Italian Renaissance–style villa.

ANIMAL PARKS

Just minutes from the Port of Miami in Key Biscayne, the **Miami Seaquarium,** 4400 Rickenbacker Causeway (☎ **305/361-5705**) is a delight. Performing dolphins such as Flipper, TV's greatest sea mammal, perform along with "Lolita the Killer Whale." You can also see endangered manatees (often victims of speeding motorboats), sea lions, tropical theme aquariums, and the gruesome shark feeding. It's open daily from 9:30am to 6pm. Admission is $18.95 for adults, $13.95 for seniors over 55, and $16.95 for children 3 to 9.

At **Monkey Jungle,** 14805 SW 216th St., Homestead (☎ **305/235-1611**), the trick is that the visitors are caged, and nearly 500 monkeys frolic in freedom and make fun of them. The most talented of these free-roaming primates perform shows daily for the amusement of their guests. The site also contains one of the richest fossil deposits—some 5,000 specimens—in South Florida. It's open daily from 9:30am to 5pm. Admission is $11.50 adults, $6 children 4 to 12, under 3 free.

In South Miami, **Parrot Jungle and Gardens,** 11000 SW 57th Ave. (☎ **305/666-7834**), is actually a botanical garden, wildlife habitat, and bird sanctuary all rolled into one. Children can enjoy a petting zoo and a playground. It's open daily from 9:30am to 6pm. Admission is $12.95 adults, $9.95 children 3 to 10, free for children under 3.

ORGANIZED TOURS

BY BOAT   **Heritage Tours of Miami II** features jaunts aboard an 85-foot topsail two-masted schooner. Tours depart from the Bayside Marketplace at 401 Biscayne Blvd. (☎ **305/442-9697**) and are offered September through May only. The daily 2-hour cruises pass by Villa Vizcaya, Coconut Grove, and Key Biscayne and put you in sight of Miami's spectacular skyline. They leave at 1:30pm, 4pm, and 6pm. Tickets cost $12 for adults, $7 for children under 12. On Friday, Saturday, and Sunday evenings, there are 1-hour tours to see the lights of the city at 9pm, 10pm, and 11pm.

BY FOOT   An **Art Deco District Walking Tour,** sponsored by the Miami Design Preservation League (☎ **305/672-2014**), leaves every Saturday at 10:30am from the Art Deco Welcome Center at 1001 Ocean Dr., South Beach. The 90-minute tour costs $10.

SHOPPING

Most cruise ship passengers shop right near the Port of Miami at **Bayside Marketplace,** a mall with 150 specialty shops at 401 Biscayne Blvd. Some 20 eateries serve everything from Nicaraguan to Italian food; there's even a Hard Rock Café. You can also watch the street performers or take a boat tour from here.

A free shuttle from the Hotel Inter-Continental in downtown Miami takes you to the **Bal Harbour Shops** (9700 Collins Ave.), which houses big-name stores from Chanel to LaCoste. Stores at this lavishly landscaped mall include Neiman-Marcus and Florida's largest Saks Fifth Avenue.

In South Beach, **Lincoln Road,** an 8-block pedestrian mall, runs between Washington Avenue and Alton Road, near the northern tier of the Art Deco district. It's filled with antique shops, interior design stores, art galleries, and even vintage clothing outlets, as well as coffee houses, restaurants, and cafes.

Just a short drive south of Downtown, the **Dadeland Mall** (at the corner of U.S. Highway 1 and SW 88th Street (☎ **305/665-6226**), is the most popular shopping plaza in suburban Dade County. Its tenants include Burdines and Burdines Home Gallery, Lord & Taylor, and Saks Fifth Avenue. The food court offers many quick bite options from fast food to sweets.

Coconut Grove, centered around Main Highway and Grand Avenue, is the heart of the city's boutique district. **Coco Walk,** 3015 Grand Ave., between Main Highway and Virginia Street (☎ **305/444-0777**), is more for novelties, movies, a late-night rendezvous, or a bookstore browse. For swanky shopping, go to **Mayfair Shops in the Grove,** 2911 Grand Ave. (☎ **305/448-1700**), just east of Commodore Plaza.

In Coral Gables, **Miracle Mile,** actually a half-mile stretch of SW 22nd Street between Douglas and Le Jeune roads, features more than 150 shops.

Island Trading, 1400 Ocean Dr. (☎ **305/673-6300**), is the shop to ensure that you arrive at your Caribbean destination of choice looking less like a tourist. Here you can pick up Batik sarongs, bathing suits, and other tropical beachwear. Many of the unique styles are designed on the premises by a team of young and creative employees.

At **The International Jewelry Exchange,** in Fashion Island (18861 Biscayne Bay), North Miami Beach (☎ **305/931-7032**), more than 50 jewelry dealers hustle their wares from separate booths. Try haggling for great deals on pieces from Tiffany or Cartier, or you can create your own design for a custom-made bracelet or necklace.

For Caribbean art, stop by **Gallery Antigua,** in the Boulevard Plaza Building, (☎ **305/759-5355**). This gallery features a wide array of prints and originals, and also hires artists-in-residence (usually from the Caribbean), who display and sell their own work.

If a bottle of Jim Beam just won't do, try **Crown Liquors,** 6751 Red Rd., Coral Gables (☎ **305/669-0225**), the prince of liquor stores in Miami. The owners can afford to stock this store with rare spirits from around the world. Of course, you can also find that trusty bottle of sour mash whiskey here—usually at a better price than most other stores. Their selection of wines and champagnes is reason enough for stopping in.

For offbeat shopping, hop over to **Ba-balú,** 500 Española Way (☎ **305/ 538-0679**), a few blocks off South Beach's Ocean Drive. At this Havana-style haven, Herb Sosa capitalizes off the current nostalgia craze for Cuba. Try the Cuban coffee, the hand-rolled Ba-balú brand cigars, and the tropical-flavored ice cream that only needs Carmen Miranda to serve it. You'll also find such memorabilia as vintage magazine covers, Cuban flags, linen guayaberas, and Batista-era cigar-box labels.

For a change of pace from the fast-paced glitz of South Beach or the serene luxury of Coral Gables, head for Little Havana, just west of downtown Miami on SW 8th Street. **Do Re Mi Music Center,** 1829 SW 8th St. (☎ 305/541-3374) has a great collection of Cuban music, ranging from classic to contemporary. Traditional guayaberas (shirts) come in every style and size imaginable at **La Casa de las Guayaberas,** 5840 SW 8th St. (☎ 305/266-9683). Finally, **El Credito Cigars,** 1106 SW 8th St. (☎ 305/858-4162), sells hand-rolled cigars just like the ones made when the company was founded in 1807 in Havana.

WHERE TO STAY

Thanks to the network of highways that cut through Miami, you can stay virtually anywhere in Greater Miami and still be within 10 to 20 minutes of your cruise ship.

Carnival Cruise Lines owns the **Wyndham Hotel,** 1601 Biscayne Blvd. (☎ **800/ 996-3426** or 305/374-000), above the Omni International Shopping Mall. This multistory structure of chrome and glass overlooks the Venetian Causeway and Biscayne Bay. Its central location is also near one of Miami's high-crime districts. Radically renovated in 1994, the hotel now hosts more pre- and post-cruise bookings (about 35,000 room nights a year) than any other in Miami. Rooms are large, comfortable, and traditionally decorated.

Brickell Point Miami, 495 Brickell Ave. (☎ **800/235-3535** or 305/373-6000), is in a park-like area flanking the riverside, between Brickell Park and Biscayne Bay. All rooms offer both city and water views; the best units are on floors 17 and 18.

Set across the bay from the cruise ship piers, the ✪ **Miami Inter-Continental Hotel,** 100 Chopin Plaza (☎ **800/327-3005** or 305/577-1000), is a bold triangular tower soaring 34 stories. Bedrooms and bathrooms are big and comfortable.

In trendy South Beach, the Art Deco **Astor,** 956 Washington Ave. (☎ **800/ 270-4981** or 305/531-8081), originally built in 1936, reopened after a massive renovation in 1995. Standard bedrooms are small, but elegantly decorated, with French-milled cabinetry and large bathrooms. The hotel bar, next to a waterfall, is a chic rendezvous, as is the hot, hot restaurant, the Astor Place Bar & Grill.

The Astor is only 2 blocks from the beach, but if that's still too far for you, try the **Ocean Front Hotel,** 1230-38 Ocean Dr. (☎ **800/783-1725** or 305/672-2579). This upscale South Beach stopover has a French ambience, good-sized rooms, and comfortable bathrooms.

✪ **The Delano,** 1685 Collins Ave. (☎ **800/555-5001** or 305/672-2000), is a sleek, postmodern, and self-consciously hip celebrity hot spot. This "seductive space" was the creation of world renowned hotelier Ian Schrager and designer Philippe Starck. Madonna once owned the hotel restaurant, the Blue Door, but the Delano bought it back. The chic rendezvous still attracts "material girls and trophy boys," however.

Inland in Miami Beach is the ✪ **Indian Creek Hotel,** 2727 Indian Creek Dr. at 28th Street. (☎ **800/491-2772** or 305/531-2727). Each room here is a homage to the 1930s Art Deco age. The hotel won an award from the Miami Design Preservation League for its outstanding restoration of the whole structure, including the lobby and restaurant. The location is only 1 block from the beach, and boardwalk. Although little known, the hotel's Pan Coast Restaurant is a gem serving a Pan Asian/Caribbean cuisine.

If you've got the right pecs and abs, consider checking into the latest sensation, **The Tides,** 1300 Ocean Dr., (☎ **800/688-7678** or 305/604-5000). Right on the beach, a block and a half from the now-infamous Versace mansion, this hotel offers rooms with telescopes, for focusing on the beach and the beachgoers. A $10 million renovation brought life to this Art Deco monument (rooms were trimmed from 115 to 43). Bedrooms are a bit spare but comfortable.

The 50-room art-deco **Abbey Hotel,** 300 W. 21st St., (☎ **888/612-2239** or 305/ 531-0031) opened in 1997. It has decorated its generous-sized bedrooms in pink and green, with marble floors. After leaving the lobby, painted a whimsical blue, you're out the door and staring at the Bass Museum of Art across the street. The hotel is 2 blocks from the beach.

Right in the heart of the South Beach scene, **The Kent,** 1131 Collins Ave. (☎ **305/ 531-6771**), like The Tides, is part of Chris Blackwell's Island Outpost chain and also an Art Deco monument. It caters to movers and shakers in the fashion industry, among others. Rooms are modest in size but tasteful and comfortably furnished. Prices are reasonable.

Farther north in Miami Beach, you can stay at popular updated 1950s resorts: the **Eden Roc,** 4525 Collins Ave. (☎ **800/327-8337** or 305/531-0000), or the **Fontainebleau Hilton Resort & Towers,** next door at 4441 Collins Ave. (☎ **800/ 548-8886** or 305/538-2000). Both hotels have spas, health clubs, outdoor swimming pools, and beach access.

In Coconut Grove, near Miami's City Hall and the Coconut Grove Marina, the ✪ **Grand Bay Hotel,** 2669 S. Bayshore Dr. (☎ **800/327-2788** or 305/838-9600), overlooks Biscayne Bay. It's the most glamorously European-style hotel in the Greater Miami area.

In Coral Gables, the famous **Biltmore Hotel,** 1200 Anastasia Ave. (☎ **800/ 228-3000** or 305/445-1926) was recently restored. Everything here is monumental except the rooms. There's also the **Hotel Place St. Michel,** 162 Alcazar Ave. (☎ **800/848-HOTEL** or 305/444-1666), a three-story establishment that seems like an inn in provincial France.

In Key Biscayne, the **Sonesta Beach Resort Key Biscayne,** 350 Ocean Dr. (☎ **800/ SONESTA** or 305/361-2021) offers relative isolation from the rest of congested Miami. This eight-story structure is set on 10 landscaped acres with a white sandy beach.

WHERE TO DINE

Lombardi's, in Bayside Marketplace (☎ **305/381-9580**), is a moderately priced Italian restaurant. One of the best menu items is lobster *fra diavolo*. Also available are a dozen zesty risottos and pastas; veal, fish, beef, and chicken dishes; and freshly prepared salads.

East Coast Fisheries & Restaurant, 360 W. Flagler at South River Drive (☎ **305/ 373-5516**), is a no-nonsense retail market and restaurant, offering a terrific variety of the freshest fish available. The absolutely huge menu features every fish you could think of, cooked the way you want it.

Only a 5-minute taxi ride from the cruise docks, ✪ **The Fish Market,** on the fourth floor of the Wyndham Hotel, 1601 Biscayne Blvd. (☎ **305/374-0000**), is one of Miami's finest and most elegant restaurants, and the prix-fixe lunch is one of the best bargains in town. Try the herb-seared salmon burgers with boursin cheese or sesame-flavored snapper with oriental vinaigrette. Better seafood than this is hard to find.

In the lobby of the elegant Hotel Inter-Continental Miami, ✪ **Le Pavilion,** 100 Chopin Plaza (☎ **305/577-1000**), is one of the most artful and European restaurants in town. The menu blends continental and Floridian cuisine in dishes like a mélange of Florida seafood simmered in a light saffron broth; pan-fried, corn-fed squab; and roast filet of milk-fed veal with wild mushrooms and an herb compote.

If you're heading for South Beach, join the celebs and models at **Nemo,** 100 Collins Ave. (☎ **305/532-4550**). Self-taught chef Michael Schwartz dazzles the palate by borrowing liberally from Japan and Southeast Asia and the Caribbean. Nemo features a constantly changing array of daily specials and beautifully prepared featured dishes. Try the wok-charred salmon flecked with toasted pumpkin seeds sitting atop a salad with four kinds of sprouts. Save room for Hedy Goldsmith's succulent desserts—none better on South Beach.

Take time to stroll down the pedestrian mall on Lincoln Road, which offers art galleries, specialty shops, and one of the area's best dining establishments, **South Beach Brasserie,** 910 Lincoln Rd. (☎ **305/534-5511**), the creation of actor-cum-restaurateur Michael Caine. Housed in a beautifully renovated 1929 Mediterranean-style building, once a Jehovah's Witnesses meeting house, this restaurant redefines urban cool, with a relaxing, tropical atmosphere and a menu that features such delectable choices as pan-seared lemongrass red snapper and quail stuffed with wild rice and apple.

At the legendary **Joe's Stone Crab,** 227 Biscayne St., between Washington and Collins avenues (☎ **305/673-0365**), about a ton of stone-crab claws are served daily when in season. Unless you go very early, you'll have to wait.

Even if Gloria Estefan weren't part-owner of **Larios on the Beach,** 820 Ocean Dr. (☎ **305/532-9577**), the crowds would still flock to this bistro serving old-fashioned Cuban dishes, such as *masitas de puerco* (fried pork chunks). Live Cuban jazz is performed Friday and Saturday nights.

Joining other New York restaurants that have migrated to Florida, **Smith & Wollensky,** the fabled steak house of Manhattan, has opened a branch here at 1 Washington Ave. (☎ **305/673-1708**). It's almost twice the size of its Manhattan mama, seating 600. Go here for amazing steaks.

If you're strolling along Ocean Drive, stop by **The News Café,** 800 Ocean Dr. (☎ **305/538-6397**), at any time of the day or night for drinks, ice cream, sandwiches, and more. This is one hip joint.

In Coconut Grove, **The Chart House,** 51 Chart House Dr. (off South Bayshore Drive, ☎ **305/856-9741**), overlooks an upscale marina. Steaks, chicken, pork, and fish are thick and appropriately juicy; lobsters are fresh from the tank, and never overcooked. There can be a long wait.

In the Grand Bay Hotel, ✪ **Grand Café,** 2669 S. Bayshore Dr. (☎ **305/ 858-9500**), lives up to its name. Culinary-star-of-the-minute Pascal Oudin serves "fussed over" dishes such as a coronet of home-smoked ginger salmon with a lime-tarragon mousseline sauce. There's also a wonderful luncheon buffet.

If you'd like to people-watch while you eat, head for **Café Tu Tu Tango,** 3015 Grand Ave. on the second floor of Coco Walk. This second floor restaurant is designed to look like a disheveled artist's loft, complete with original paintings (some half-finished) on easels or hanging from the walls. The artists themselves often work in the restaurant. Here the best offerings are pastas, ribs, and fish. You can order dishes to be shared in small portions (tapas style), including the likes of seared tuna sashimi.

One of the hottest new dining spots in Greater Miami is in Coral Gables. **Norman's,** 21 Almeria Ave. (☎ **305/446-6767**), is run by its namesake, Norman Van Aken, a specialist in American and West Indian cuisine, although he borrows liberally from Asia and Mexico as well. He's even improved on conch chowder by adding a saffron-tinged cream with hints of star anise, coconut, and fresh orange. The soft-shell crabs are as good here as at the legendary Joe's Stone Crab (see above) on Miami Beach.

The surf and turf is routine at the **Rusty Pelican,** 3201 Rickenbacker Causeway (☎ **305/361-3818**) in Key Biscayne, but it's worth coming for a drink and the spectacular sunset view.

One reason to visit Little Havana is to enjoy its excellent Hispanic cuisine. There's none better than at **Victor's Café,** 2340 SW 32nd Ave., in Miami (☎ **305/445-1313**), where the elite meet to eat black beans. Victor's tantalizes with updated versions of Cuban classic dishes, such as oak-grilled top sirloin with a Cuban-style polenta.

MIAMI AFTER DARK

Miami night life is as varied as its population. On any night, you'll find world-class opera or dance, as well as grinding rock and salsa. Restaurants and bars are open late, and many clubs, especially on South Beach, are still going past dawn.

The Miami Herald lists major cultural events. You can buy tickets to many of them through **TicketMaster** (☎ 305/358-5885).

The 2,500-seat **Dade County Auditorium** at 2901 W. Flagler St., in downtown Miami (☎ **305/547-5414**), is home to the city's Greater Miami Opera and also productions of the Concert Association of Florida and the Miami Ballet Company.

Broadway shows, opera, and dance performances are often held at the **Jackie Gleason Theater of the Performing Arts,** 1700 Washington Ave., South Beach (☎ **305/673-7300**).

You can watch the **Miami City Ballet** (☎ **305/532-4880**), directed by Edward Villella, practice at its Lincoln Road studio (no. 905) or perform from September through April at the Dade County Auditorium.

Greater Miami Opera, 1200 Coral Way, Coral Gables (☎ **305/854-1643**), performs all year at the Dade County Auditorium.

THE CLUB & MUSIC SCENE

It's hopping in South Beach, with beachfront bars, clubs, and more. **Amnesia,** 136 Collins Ave. (☎ **305/531-5535**), has been compared to a semitropical amphitheater. It's one of the leading straight discos at the beach.

Opened by the-artist-formerly-known-as-Prince, **Glam Slam,** 1235 Washington Ave. (☎ **305/672-2770**), is ever so fashionable once again. It often hosts special nights with themes like "Let's All Go Gay" and "Glamour Gals."

MoJazz Club, 928 71st St. (☎ **305/867-0950**), in the upper Normandy Isle section of the beach, offers the best jazz around, and has since 1993. It's nonfusion jazz—that is, the pure thing—in a neighborhood cafe. Some of the country's best jazz artists have been known to show up here. You can even order Vietnamese and Chinese food.

Many of the best bands in Miami perform at **Rosa's Bar & Lounge,** 754 Washington Ave. (☎ **305/532-0228**). The beat is often African, but also Latin (especially Cuban), jazz, and funk/rap.

You can dance to a 10-piece orchestra and enjoy a Las Vegas–style floor show at the **Tropicana,** in the Fontainebleau Hilton Resort & Towers, 4441 Collins Ave. (☎ **305/672-7469**).

Opened in 1912, landmark ✪ **Tobacco Road,** 626 S. Miami Ave. (☎ **305/374-1198**), has hosted practically all the big names who ever visited Miami. Local and national blues bands perform at night, and you can also hear funk, R&B, and jazz.

Coco Loco's, in the Sheraton Biscayne Bay Hotel, 495 Brickell Ave. (☎ **305/373-6000**), has the area's best happy hour buffet. You might not need dinner! Happy hour is Monday through Friday from 5 to 8pm.

The lavish and glitzy ○ **Les Violins Supper Club,** 1751 Biscayne Blvd. (☎ **305/ 371-8668**), re-creates nightlife in the pre-Castro era. Its floor shows are among the best in Miami, and who can resist tipping those strolling violinists? The crowd dances on a wooden floor to the tunes of a live dance band.

In Coconut Grove, **The Hungry Sailor,** 3426 Main Hwy. (☎ **305/444-9359**), is a British-inspired pub, with live entertainment or a DJ Tuesday through Saturday. For a lively happy hour, stop by **Monty's Raw Bar,** 2560 S. Bayshore Dr. (☎ **305/ 858-1431**), atop a pier with great views and live music. Fresh oysters and chowders are available. The **Taurus Steak House,** 3540 Main Hwy. (☎ **305/448-0633**), in spite of its name, is one of the most frequented nighttime rendezvous spots in the Grove, drawing a crowd mainly 35 and older with its live music, Tuesday through Saturday nights.

In Coral Gables, head for happy hour at **Alcazaba,** in the Hyatt Regency Hotel, 50 Alhambra Plaza (☎ **305/441-1234**), which has the best tapas and tropical drinks around.

2 Fort Lauderdale & Port Everglades

Home to more four- and five-star ships than even Miami, Port Everglades, in Broward Country, is the second-busiest cruise port in the world. It boasts the deepest harbor along the eastern seaboard south of Norfolk, an ultra-modern cruise-ship terminal, and an easy access route to the Fort Lauderdale airport, less than a 5-minute drive away. The port lies some 40 miles north of Miami's center.

The port itself is fairly free of congestion. Ten modern cruise terminals offer covered loading zones, dropoff and pickup staging, and curbside baggage handlers. Terminals are comfortable and safe. If you're waiting between ships, you'll find comfortable seating areas, snack bars, lots of taxis, clean restrooms, and plenty of pay phones. Two separate parking lots provide a total of 4,500 parking places, priced at $8 per day.

Ships that make Port Everglades their home tend to be upscale, and include *Century, Horizon, Mercury,* and on a less regular basis, *Zenith,* all from the Celebrity line; *CostaVictoria* and *CostaRomantica* from Costa Cruises; *Westerdam, Statendam, Maasdam, Ryndam,* and *Veendam* from Holland America; *Melody* from Mediterranean Shipping Cruises; *Regal Princess* and *Grand Princess* from Princess; the *Pride* and the *Legend* from Seabourn; and the *Sea Breeze* from Premier Cruises.

For information about the port, call **Port Everglades Authority** at ☎ **954/ 523-3404**.

GETTING TO FORT LAUDERDALE & THE PORT

BY AIR   The **Fort Lauderdale/Hollywood International Airport** (☎ **954/ 359-6100**) is small, extremely user-friendly, and less than 2 miles from Port Everglades. **Carnival** (☎ **305/599-2200**) flies into Fort Lauderdale.

Cruise ship buses meet incoming flights when they know transfer passengers are on board, so make arrangements for pickup when you book your cruise. Taking a taxi to the port costs $9 to $12.

BY CAR   The port has a trio of passenger entrances: **Spangler Boulevard,** an extension of State Road 84 East; **Eisenhower Boulevard,** running south from the 17th Street Causeway (A1A); and **Eller Drive,** connecting directly with Interstate 595. Interstate 595 runs east/west, with connections to the Fort Lauderdale/Hollywood Airport, Interstate 95, State Road 7 (441), Florida's Turnpike, Sawgrass Expressway, and Interstate 75.

The following car rentals provide shuttle service from the port to their rental terminal sites: **Avis** (☎ **800/331-1212** or 954/359-3255); **Budget/Sears Rent-a-Car** (☎ **800/527-0700** or 954/359-4747); **National** (☎ **800/227-7368** or 954/359-8303); and **Dollar** (☎ **800/800-4000** or 954/359-7800).

Parking at the Port   Convenient parking is available at two large garages. The 2,500-space Northport Parking Garage, next to the Greater Fort Lauderdale/Broward County Convention Center, serves terminals 1, 2, and 4. The 1,000-space Midport Parking Garage serves terminals 18, 19, 21, 22, 24, 25, and 26. Garages are well-lit, security-patrolled, and designed to accommodate RVs and buses. The 24-hour parking fee is $7.

BY TRAIN   Amtrak (☎ **800/USA-RAIL**) trains from New York to Miami make various stops along the way, including Fort Lauderdale. The local station is at 200 SW 21st Terrace (☎ **954/587-6692** or 305/835-1123). Taxis are lined up to deliver you to Port Everglades for a $10 to $15 fare.

EXPLORING FORT LAUDERDALE

Fort Lauderdale Beach, a 2-mile strip along Florida A1A, gained fame in the 1950s as a spring-break playground, popularized by the movie *Where the Boys Are.* But in the 1980s, partying college kids, who brought the city more mayhem than money, began to be less welcome. Fort Lauderdale tried to attract a more mainstream, affluent crowd in an effort to transform itself into the "Venice of the Americas." The city has largely been successful.

In addition to miles of beautiful wide beaches, Fort Lauderdale has more than 300 miles of navigable natural waterways, in addition to innumerable artificial canals that permit thousands of residents to anchor boats in their backyards. You too can easily get on the water, by renting a boat or hailing a private, moderately priced water taxi.

ESSENTIALS

VISITOR INFORMATION   The **Greater Fort Lauderdale Convention & Visitors Bureau,** 1850 Eller Dr., Suite 303, Fort Lauderdale, FL 33316 (☎ **954/765-4466**), is an excellent resource, distributing a comprehensive guide on events and sightseeing in Broward County.

GETTING AROUND   For a taxi, call **Yellow Cab** (☎ **954/565-5400**). Rates start at $2.45 for the first mile and $1.75 for each additional mile.

Broward County Mass Transit (☎ **954/357-8400**) runs bus service throughout the county. Each ride costs $1.15 for the first transfer and 15¢ for each additional same-day transfer.

HITTING THE BEACH

The Fort Lauderdale Beach Promenade underwent a $20 million renovation—and it looks marvelous. This beach is still backed by an endless row of hotels and is popular with visitors and locals alike. On weekends, parking at the oceanside meters is difficult to find. Try biking or blading to the beach instead. It's located along Atlantic Boulevard (Fla. A1A), between SE 17th Street and Sunrise Boulevard. The fabled strip from *Where the Boys Are* is Ocean Boulevard, between Las Olas Boulevard and Sunrise Boulevard.

Ft. Lauderdale Beach at the Howard Johnson is a perennial local favorite. A jetty bounds the beach on the south side, making it rather private, though the water gets a little choppy. High school and college students share this area with an older crowd. The beach is located at 4660 N. Ocean Dr. in Lauderdale by the Sea.

Fort Lauderdale at a Glance

To Orlando & West Palm Beach ↑

DEERFIELD BEACH

To Palm Beach ↑ A1A

0 ___ 3 mi / 4.8 km N

Sample Rd.

441

Coconut Creek

Margate

845

Old Dixie Hwy.

✈ **POMPANO BEACH**

1

Atlantic Blvd.

Fort Lauderdale Executive Airport

N. Lauderdale

N. Ocean Blvd.

95

University Dr.

N.W. 56th St.

Tamarac ✈

Florida Turnpike

Power Line Rd.

Commercial Blvd.

N. Andrews Ave.

Federal Hwy.

870

Sea Ranch Lakes

Lauderdale-by-the-Sea

817

Inverrary Blvd.

Midriver Canal

N.W. 31st St.

816

Lauderhill

Oakland Park Blvd.

Oakland Park

Wilton Manors

Intracoastal Waterway

A1A

N.W. Sunset Strip

N.W. 68th Ave.

N.W. 61st A.

Sunrise

838

N.W. 19th St.

N.W. 9th Ave.

N.E. 4th

Sunrise Blvd.

1

2

To Everglades Pkwy (Alligator Alley) and Naples ←

Plantation

842

Broward Blvd.

Riverland Rd.

3

4

S. Andrews Ave.

Las Olas Blvd.

S. Fed. Hwy.

Atlantic Ocean

N. New River Canal

595

Peters Rd.

S.W. 12th

Davie Blvd.

82

Fort Lauderdale

S. New River Canal

Fern Crest Village

Nova Dr.

Davie Rd.

84

Hacienda Village

595

S.W. 24th

S.W. 17th St.

Port Rd.

Stranahan River

College Ave.

Orange Dr.

Griffin Rd.

818

Davie

✈ Fort Lauderdale Hollywood International Airport

Ravenswood

Ocean Dr.

Stirling Rd.

848

S.W.48th St.

1

S.W. 60th St.

Dania

Dania Beach Bl.

A1A

Davie Rd. Ext.

822

Sheridan St.

N. 18th Ave.

West Lake

Pembroke Pines

Taft St.

Pines Blvd.

820

HOLLYWOOD

Hollywood Blvd.

Ocean Blvd.

✈ Hollywood North Perry Airport

441

95

Miramar

Pembroke Rd.

Moffet St.

N.E. 6th Ave.

Miramar Pwky.

858

Hallandale Beach Blvd.

N.E. 215th St.

S.W. 40th A

Pembroke Park

Hallandale

To Homestead and Key West ←↓

To Miami & Coral Gables ↓

872

To Miami Beach ↓

1-1070

Bonnet House **2**   Museum of Art **3**

Butterfly World **1**   Museum of Discovery and Science **4**

Airport ✈   Beach ⦓   Cruise Ship Terminal ⛴

SEEING THE SIGHTS

The **Museum of Discovery & Science,** 401 SW Second St. (☎ **954/467-6637**), is an excellent interactive science museum, with an IMAX theater. Check out the 52-foot-tall "Great Gravity Clock," located in the museum's atrium.

The **Museum of Art,** 1 Las Olas Blvd. (☎ **954/763-6464**), is a truly terrific small museum of modern and contemporary art.

A guided tour of the **Bonnet House,** 900 N. Birch Rd. (☎ **954/563-5393**), offers a glimpse into the lives of the pioneers of the Fort Lauderdale area. This unique 35-acre plantation home and estate survives in the middle of an otherwise highly developed beachfront condominium area. Tours are offered Wednesday through Friday at 10am or 1pm, Saturday and Sunday at 1 or 2pm; arrive 15 minutes before the tour.

Butterfly World, Tradewinds Park South, 3600 W. Sample Rd., Coconut Creek (west of the Florida Turnpike; ☎ **954/977-4400**), cultivates more than 150 species of these colorful and delicate insects. In the park's walk-through, screened-in aviary visitors can watch newborn butterflies emerge from their cocoons and flutter around as they learn to fly.

ORGANIZED TOURS

BY BOAT   The Mississippi River–style steamer *Jungle Queen,* Bahia Mar Yacht Center, Florida A1A (☎ **954/462-5596**), is one of Fort Lauderdale's best-known attractions. Dinner cruises and 3-hour sightseeing tours take visitors up the New River past Millionaires' Row, Old Fort Lauderdale, the new downtown, and the Port Everglades cruise-ship port. Call for prices and departure times.

✪ **Water Taxi of Fort Lauderdale,** 651 Seabreeze Blvd. (☎ **954/467-6677**), is a fleet of old-port boats that navigate this city of canals. The boats operate taxi service on demand and carry up to 48 passengers each. You can be picked up at your hotel and shuttled to the dozens of restaurants and bars on the route for the rest of the night. The service operates daily from 10am to midnight or 2am. The cost is $7 per person per trip, $13 round-trip, $15 for a full day. Opt for the all-day pass—it's worth it.

BY TROLLEY BUS   South Florida Trolley Tours (☎ **954/946-7320**) covers Fort Lauderdale's entire history during a 90-minute open-air trolley tour. Tours cost $12 for adults; children under 12 are free. The trolleys pick up passengers from most major hotels for three tours daily, at 9:30am, 12:05pm, and 2:10pm.

BY FOOT   The **Historical Society Museum,** 219 SW Second Ave. (☎ **954/ 463-4431**), offers walking tours of the city's historic center. Tours must be requested and are conducted Tuesday through Friday from 10am to 4pm. They cost $10 to $15 per person.

You can also walk along **Riverwalk,** a 10-mile linear park along the New River that connects the cultural heart of Fort Lauderdale to its historic district.

SHOPPING

Not counting the discount "fashion" stores on Hallandale Beach Boulevard's "Schmatta Row," there are three places every visitor to Broward County should know about.

The first is **Antique Row,** a strip of U.S. 1 around North Dania Beach Boulevard (in Dania, about 1 mile south of Fort Lauderdale/Hollywood International Airport) that holds about 200 antique shops. Some are a bit overpriced, but if you're persistent you'll find some good buys in furniture, silver, china, glass, linens, and more. Most shops are closed Sundays.

The **Fort Lauderdale Swap Shop,** 3291 W. Sunrise Blvd. (☎ **954/791-SWAP**), is one of the world's largest flea markets. In addition to endless acres of vendors, there's a mini–amusement park, a 12-screen drive-in movie theater, weekend concerts, and even a free circus complete with elephants, horse shows, high-wire acts, and clowns. It's open daily.

Sawgrass Mills, 12801 W. Sunrise Blvd., Sunrise (☎ **954/846-2300**), a behemoth mall shaped like a Florida alligator, is nearly 2.5 million square feet. Wear your Nikes to trek around the more than 300 shops and kiosks, which include Donna Karan, Saks Fifth Avenue, Levi's, Ann Taylor, Barney's New York, Cache, Waterford Crystal, and hundreds more, all claiming to sell at 30% to 80% below retail. A spot check revealed that many stores offered prices 20% to 60% lower than in the Caribbean. Take Interstate 95 North to 595 West until Flamingo Road, where you'll exit and turn right. Drive 2 miles to Sunrise Boulevard. You can't miss this monster on the left. Parking is free.

Not for bargain hunters, swanky **Las Olas Boulevard** hosts literally hundreds of unusual boutiques. Close to Fort Lauderdale Beach, the **Galleria** mall, 2414 E. Sunrise Blvd., between NE 26th Avenue and Middle River Drive (☎ **954/564-1015**), has Neiman-Marcus, Saks, Macy's, Cartier, Brooks Brothers, Lord & Taylor, and many other stores.

WHERE TO STAY

Fort Lauderdale Beach has a hotel or motel on nearly every block, and the selection ranges from run-down to luxurious. A number of chains operate here, including **Best Western** (☎ **800 528-1234**), **Days Inn** (☎ **800/325-2525**), **Doubletree Hotels** (☎ **800/222-8733**), and **Holiday Inn** (☎ **800/465-4329**). Call the **Fort Lauderdale Convention and Visitors Bureau** (☎ **954/765-4466**) for its *Superior Small Lodgings* guide to the area.

There are also two Marriotts: **The Fort Lauderdale Marina Marriott,** 1881 SE 17th St. (☎ **800/433-2254** or 954/463-4000) and the far superior **Marriott in Harbor Beach** at 3030 Holiday Dr.

✪ **Hyatt Regency Fort Lauderdale** at Pier 66 Marina, 2301 17th St. Causeway (☎ **800/233-1234** or 954/525-6666), is a circular landmark that recently received a much-needed facelift. Its famous Piertop Lounge, a revolving bar on its roof, is often filled with cruise-ship patrons. Bedrooms are larger than those of some equivalently priced hotels in town.

La Casa del Mar Bed & Breakfast, 3003 Grand Granada St. (☎ **800/739-0009** or 954/467-2037) appeals to the bed-and-breakfast fancier. The 10 generally spacious bedrooms in this Spanish-inspired inn are comfortable and reasonably priced. It lies only a block away from Fort Lauderdale Beach. The price includes breakfast and also wine and cheese beside the pool in the afternoon.

Marriott's Harbor Beach Resort, 3030 Holiday Dr. (☎ **800/222-6543** or 954/525-4000), is the only resort set directly on the beach. Its modest-sized bedrooms have water views.

The Pillars Waterfront Inn, 111 N. Birch Rd. (☎ **954/467-9639**), is a small, 22-room inn, the best of its size in the region. The clean and simple accommodations have very comfortable beds.

Radisson Bahia Mar Beach Resort, 801 Seabreeze Blvd. (☎ **800/327-8154** or 954/764-2233), is scattered over 42 acres of seacoast. A four-story row of units is adjacent to Florida's largest marina.

The Riverside Hotel, 620 E. Las Olas Blvd. (☎ **800/325-3280** or 954/ 467-0671), which opened in 1936, is a local favorite. Try for a ground-floor room, which has higher ceilings and more space.

WHERE TO DINE

The only restaurant at Port Everglades, ✪ **Burt & Jacks,** at Berth 23 (☎ **954/ 522-2878**), is a collaboration between actor/director Burt Reynolds and restaurateur Jack Jackson. As you sit at this elegant restaurant, you can watch the cruise ships and other boats pass by. A waiter will arrive with raw steaks, lobster, veal, or pork chops, etc.; you choose and your dish will arrive perfectly cooked.

Bahia Cabana Beach Resort, 3001 Harbor Dr. (☎ **954/524-1555**), offers American-style meals three times a day in hearty portions. And the hotel's bar, known for its Frozen Rumrunner, is the most charming and laid-back in town.

In the Quarry Shopping Center, **Bimini Boat Yard,** 1555 SE 17th St. Causeway (☎ **954/525-7400**), serves sandwiches (grilled grouper or roast beef foccacia), the best burgers in town, salads, and pizzas at any hour you want.

In the shadow of the Hyatt Pier 66 Hotel, **California Café,** Pier 66, 2301 SE 17th St. Causeway (☎ **954/728-8255**), serves avant-garde modern cuisine at affordable prices. Dishes are flavorful and zesty. Try the pepper-grilled tuna with jasmine-flavored rice, or the potato-crusted salmon with lemongrass butter.

Cap's Place, 2765 NE 28th Ct., in Lighthouse Point (☎ **954/941-0418**), is a famous old-time seafood joint, offering good food at reasonable prices. The restaurant floats on a barge; you get a ferry ride over. Dolphin (a local saltwater fish, not the mammal) and grouper are popular, and like the other meat and pasta dishes here, can be prepared any way you want.

Evangeline, 211 Hwy. A1A at Las Olas Boulevard (☎ **954/522-7001**), is like a restaurant in Arcadian Louisiana. At lunch, enjoy an oyster or catfish po' boy, or rabbit gumbo for dinner. You can also try the alligator.

Il Tartufo, 2400 E. Las Olas Blvd. (☎ **954/767-9190**), is the most charming and fun Italian restaurant in Fort Lauderdale. It serves pizzas, oven-roasted specialties, and other Italian standards, plus a selection of fish baked in rock salt.

Mark's Las Olas, 1032 E. Las Olas Blvd. (☎ **954/463-1000**), is the showcase of Miami restaurant mogul Mark Militello. The food is as carefully prepared as you'd expect, but the place is a lot less fun than it should be. The daily changing menu might include Jamaican jerk chicken with fresh coconut salad or a superb sushi-quality tuna, crusted in peppercorns, with root vegetable mash, foie gras, and veal drippings.

Zan Z Bar, 602 E. Las Olas Blvd. (☎ **954/767-3377**), serves the food and the wine of South Africa, and not many places can boast that. For a "taste" of the country, order a sample platter for two that includes ostrich tips, cured beef strips, and savory sausages. Some dishes are topped with a thick cornmeal called "pap" and served with a tomato and onion flavored gravy. It's not for everybody, but it's certainly different.

Set across the highway from the beach on "the strip" is hip **Mistral,** 201 Hwy. A1A near Las Olas Boulevard (☎ **954/463-4900**). Portions here are generous, dishes flavorful, and prices moderate. The varied menu includes pan-seared dolphin, lasagna of baby artichokes, and designer pizzas that are larger than you'd expect. The pizza with seafood and herbs is great.

Paesano, 1301 E. Las Olas Blvd. (☎ **954/467-3266**), is chic and elegant, with good, albeit old-fashioned, food. The 16-ounce T-bone steak is usually grilled to perfection, or you may prefer one of the numerous pasta dishes.

Garlic crabs are the specialty at the **Rustic Inn Crabhouse,** 4331 Ravenswood Rd. (☎ **954/584-1637**), located west of the airport. This riverside dining choice has an open deck over the water.

One of the city's two four-star restaurants is ✪ **Sheffield's,** in the Marriott's Harbor Beach Resort, 3030 Holiday Dr. (☎ **954/525-4000**). The menu appears simpler than it actually is; dishes are original and, if slow to arrive, at least worth the wait.

FORT LAUDERDALE AFTER DARK

With the 1991 completion of the **Broward Center for the Performing Arts,** 201 SW Fifth Ave. (☎ **954/462-0222**), Fort Lauderdale finally got itself the venue it craved. This stunning $55 million complex contains both a 2,700-seat auditorium and a smaller 590-seat theater. The center attracts top opera, symphony, dance, and Broadway productions, as well as more modest-sized shows.

The region has some superb theater groups, whose seasons run roughly from October through May. **Hollywood Boulevard Theatre,** 1938 Hollywood Blvd., Hollywood (☎ **954/929-5400**), is the newest addition. **Off Broadway,** 1444 NE 26th St. (between Federal Highway and Dixie Highway), Fort Lauderdale (☎ **954/ 566-0554**), specializes in smaller, independent, and sometimes offbeat productions of contemporary plays. A landmark in the Fort Lauderdale theater community is the **Parker Playhouse,** 707 NE Eighth St. (☎ **954/763-2444**), which offers a popular series of touring Broadway shows. There's also the **Vinnette Carroll Repertory Company,** 503 SE 6th St., Fort Lauderdale (☎ **954/462-2424**).

Another long-time local tradition is the **Opera Guild** (☎ **954/462-0222**), a society of music lovers that stages a wide-ranging series of shows. Other good classical music is performed in season by the **Florida Philharmonic** (☎ **954/561-2997**) and the **Symphony of the Americas** (☎ **954/561-5882**). Look for listings in the *Sun-Sentinel* or *The Miami Herald* for schedules and performers or call the 24-hour **Arts & Entertainment Hotline** (☎ **954/357-5700**).

THE BAR & CLUB SCENE

From the area's most famous bar, the ✪ **Piertop Lounge,** in the Hyatt Regency at Pier 66 (☎ **954/525-6666**), you'll get a 360° panoramic view of Fort Lauderdale. The bar turns every 66 minutes. There's a dance floor and floor shows Tuesday through Saturday, but no cover or drink minimum.

Inspired by the TV series, **Cheers,** 941 E. Cypress Creek Rd. (☎ **954/771-6337**), has two bars and a dance floor. Its specialty is "Acoustic Blues" Sunday through Tuesday, with rock and roll the rest of the week.

On weekends it's hard to get in **Club M,** 2037 Hollywood Blvd. (☎ **954/ 925-8396**), one of the area's busiest music bars. Although the small club is primarily a local blues showcase, electric and traditional jazz bands also perform.

O'Hara Pub & Sidewalk Café, 722 E. Las Olas Blvd. (☎ **954/524-2801**), is often packed with a trendy crowd, who come here to listen to live blues and jazz. Call their jazz hotline (☎ **954/524-2801**) to hear the lineup.

If you want to dance, try the **Baja Beach Club,** 3200 N. Federal Hwy. (☎ **954/ 561-2431**), perhaps the world's only dance club that anchors an entire shopping mall. Kids just want to have fun, and the club delivers with a great sound system and crowd-pleasing promotions.

Desperado, 2520 S. Miami Rd. (☎ **954/463-2855**), is the area's best Country and Western club, offering free line-dance lessons. Live entertainment starts nightly at 9:30pm.

3 Cape Canaveral & Port Canaveral

Port Canaveral is Florida's most unusual and multifaceted port—and also its most underrated. Its facilities are the most up-to-date, stylish, and least congested of any port in Florida. And the cruise ship world is starting to take notice. In 1997, 1.4 million cruise ship passengers embarked or disembarked here—an increase of 50% from only 3 years before. Cruise lines also appreciate the port's proximity to Cape Canaveral's Kennedy Space Center and Walt Disney World at Orlando. Many lines offer pre- or post-cruise packages.

Port Canaveral has an abundance of bars and restaurants, facilities noticeably absent at many other Florida harbors. The best ones are positioned adjacent to the frequently dredged deepwater access channels used by most ships. Sitting at one of these restaurants' sundecks during happy hour, you'll feel as if you could shake the hand of a cruise ship passenger gliding in or out of the port.

The 3,300-acre port covers an area larger than the Port of Miami. Terminal no. 10, a $24 million structure completed in 1995, was built in a modern and dramatic style, and is nicknamed the *Bahnhof*, because of its resemblance to a futuristic German railway station. Terminal no. 5, built in 1991, looks a bit like a glossy, downtown hotel. The other terminals are more industrial, like oversized Quonset huts. The port's facilities were designed to allow ships to moor parallel to the shore, partly a function of the muddy geology of the region, partly as a means of saving costs. As you head for your cruise ship, look for shrimp and fish nets drying in the sun. This port is the home base for the region's fishing industry.

The most impressive vessels at Port Canaveral are Disney Cruise Line's megaships, *Disney Magic* and *Disney Wonder.* Launched, respectively, in April and November of 1998, they're berthed within a glittering, specially built terminal (number 8) reserved exclusively for the use of Bahama-bound Disney passengers. Also sailing from this port are Cape Canaveral Cruise Line's *Dolphin IV,* Carnival Cruise Lines' megaship *Fantasy,* and Premier Cruise Line's *Big Red Boat.*

For information about the port, call the **Canaveral Port Authority** at ☎ 407/783-7831.

GETTING TO CAPE CANAVERAL & THE PORT

BY AIR   The nearest airport is the **Orlando International Airport (☎ 407/825-2001**), a 45-mile drive from Port Canaveral via Highway 528 (the Bee Line Expressway).

There is no public bus service between Orlando and the port, so many passengers arrange chartered vans or take buses organized by the cruise lines. **Cocoa Beach Shuttle (☎ 800/633-0427** or 407/784-3831) offers shuttle service between Orlando's airport and Port Canaveral; the trip costs $20 per person each way.

BY CAR   Port Canaveral and Cocoa Beach are about 35 miles southeast of Orlando and 190 miles north of Miami. They're accessible from virtually every interstate highway along the east coast. Most visitors arrive via Route 1, Interstate 95, or Highway 528 (the Bee Line Expressway from Orlando).

You can rent a car at the Orlando airport, which has branches of many car-rental companies, or in Cocoa Beach through **Budget (☎ 800/527-0700** or 407/784-0622) or **Americar (☎ 800/743-7483** or 407/868-1800).

Parking at the Port   Parking lots include the North Lots, for north terminals nos. 5 and 10, and the South Lots, for nos. 2, 3, or 4. Parking costs $7 a day.

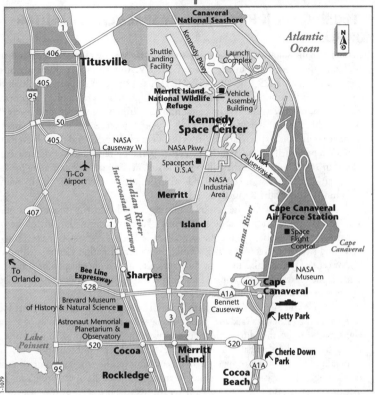

BY TRAIN **Amtrak** (☎ 800/USA-RAIL) trains make stops at Kissimmee, Sanford, and Orlando, the closest points to the port, but still about 55 to 60 miles away. You'll have to rent a car or take a taxi to the port. The Kissimmee railway station is at 316 Pleasant St. (corner of Dakin Avenue and Thurman Street). The Orlando station is at 1400 Slight Blvd., between Columbia and Miller streets. The Sanford station is at 800 Persimmon Ave., at the corner of 8th Street.

EXPLORING CAPE CANAVERAL

Most passengers spend only a night or two in Cocoa Beach, visiting the Kennedy Space Center and going to the beach, before rushing to nearby Orlando and Walt Disney World.

ESSENTIALS

VISITOR INFORMATION   Contact the **Cocoa Beach Chamber of Commerce,** 400 Fortenberry Rd., Merritt Island, FL 32952 (☎ 407/459-2200).

GETTING AROUND   You can try to flag a taxi if one happens to pass by, but it's better to call for one. However, when cruise ships arrive at the port, so do the taxis. Local operator **Cocoa Beach Cab Co.** (☎ 407/784-8294) does business under such names as **Yellow Top Taxi Service, Brevard Yellow Cab Company,** and **Banana River Cab Company.**

Buses are run by the **Space Coast Area Transit Authority (SCAT)** (☎ 407/633-1878 for information and schedules). A ticket costs $1 for adults, 50¢ for senior citizens, free for children under 6. No buses pass close to the port.

✪ TOURING THE JOHN F. KENNEDY SPACE CENTER VISITOR COMPLEX

Set amid many square miles of marshy wetlands favored by birds, reptiles, and amphibians, the **John F. Kennedy Space Center Visitor Complex,** Kennedy Space Center, Florida 32899 (☎ **407/452-2121**), has played an important role in the minds of people around the world as a symbol of America's technological prowess. Space buffs, engineers, and technological historians from around the world revere the place as the cradle of the Space Age. Even if you've never really considered yourself a science buff, you'll appreciate the sheer grandeur of the place and the achievements that are represented by the facilities here. A $79 million renovation of the site, completed in 1998, has sparked new life into the site, making it more appealing for visitors than ever. The visitor center stands with an isolated, even eerie, dignity within the municipality of the Kennedy Space Center.

The sheer scope of the site can be confusing, even baffling, without some guidance from the organization's official caretakers. Parking is free within any of the vast lots nearby. (Remember to note the location of your car!) It's best to make a stop—maps and advice are free—at a highly visible booth, Information Central, within the visitor center. It maintains the same hours (9am to 6pm daily except Christmas and some launch days) as the complex itself. Expect to spend a full day on-site to best experience the wealth of options available.

The core of the site revolves around the visitor center, site of coffeeshops, fast-food eateries, and a "**Rocket Garden,**" which displays the now-obsolete shells of at least eight space rockets that during their heydays were the hottest things in the world of Astrophysics. There are also hundreds of exhibitions and photographs detailing humankind's exploration of space, with an emphasis on the progression of visionary developments in logical sequence since the inauguration of the Space Programs. The visitor center is also home to two IMAX theaters whose screens tower a mindnumbing five stories from top to bottom. Three separate films, each about 45 minutes in length, are projected at scattered intervals throughout opening hours of the complex.

Some visitors pressed for time opt to remain entirely within the center, which does not charge admission, but which certainly succeeds at conveying NASA's curious blend of bland bureaucracy and passionate ambition. But for a more complete insight into the Space Age, take a bus tour of the complicated subdivisions that rise from the hundreds of acres of marshy flatlands nearby. Self-guided and self-timed, and conducted aboard both single-decker and double-decker buses, depending on demand, they depart at 15-minute intervals. Each bus is equipped with video screens portraying great moments of the space program's past. Tours make stops at three pivotal points within the complex, the Apollo Saturn V Center, Launch Complex 39, and the International Space Station Center.

The most comprehensive visitor package is the **Crew Pass.** Priced at $19 for adults, and $15 for children aged 4 to 11, it includes unlimited access to any of the tour buses, and entrance to any one of the ongoing IMAX movies. The tour itself, without access to any of the IMAX theaters, costs $14 for adults and $10 for children under 11. Admission to the visitor center itself is free. Individual IMAX films are $7.50 per adult, and $5.50 per child under 11. Most major credit cards are accepted throughout the complex.

You won't lack for food and drink during your exploration of the site, as there's a handful of fast-food, "theme-parkish" eateries adjacent to the visitors' center. Among the cheapest and least formal of the bunch is something called "The Launch Pad," serving family-friendly burgers and hot dogs. Better-recommended is Mila's, a fancy diner serving American-style platters, sandwiches, and salads.

Don't expect an actual space launch to be scheduled on the day of your visit, as there are only about a dozen of these every year. Call ☎ 407/449-4343 for schedule information. During launch days, some parts of the complex, including Launch Complex 39 and its Observation Gantry, are firmly closed to everyone except NASA insiders.

To get to the Kennedy Space Center from Cocoa Beach, take A1A north. About a mile after A1A takes a sharp jog to the left, you will see signs for S.R. 401 and the Kennedy Space Center. Turn right and follow signs over the NASA Causeway, which leads directly to the Space Center. It's about a half-hour drive. From Orlando, take the Bee Line Expressway (S.R. 528) east, and where the road divides, go left on S.R. 407, make a right on S.R. 405, and follow the signs. Parking is free.

ANOTHER SPACE-RELATED ATTRACTION

Six miles west of the Kennedy Space Center is the **U.S. Astronaut Hall of Fame,** State Rd. 405, 6225 Vectorspace Blvd., Titusville (☎ 407/269-6100), a satellite attraction founded by the astronauts who flew the first Mercury and Gemini missions into outer space. It contains space program memorabilia, displayed with a decidedly human and anecdotal touch. Open daily 9am to 5pm.

HITTING THE BEACH

Cocoa Beach, Merritt Island, and the surrounding landscapes are known as "the Space Coast." Most municipal entities identified as a park include a sandy beach. Here are our favorites.

Cruise ship passengers prefer **Jetty Park,** 400 E. Jetty Rd. (☎ 407/868-1108), near the port. It's more like a Florida version of Coney Island than the parks below. A massive stone, asphalt-topped jetty juts seaward as protection for the mouth of Port Canaveral. You'll see dozens of anglers there waiting for a bite. Parking costs $1 a car.

On the border between Cocoa Beach and Cape Canaveral, **Cherie Down Park,** 8492 Ridgewood Ave. (☎ 407/455-1380), is a relatively tranquil sunning and swimming area. You'll find a boardwalk, as well as showers, picnic shelters, and a public restroom. Parking is $1 per car.

Set in the heart of Cocoa Beach, **Lori Wilson Park,** 1500 N. Atlantic Ave. (☎ 407/455-1380), has children's playgrounds and a boardwalk that extends through about five acres of protected grasslands. Parking is $1 per car. Next to it is **Fischer Park** (☎ 407/868-3274), with public restrooms and a seasonal scattering of food kiosks. Parking is $2 a car.

The region's best surfing is at **Robert P. Murkshe Memorial Park,** SR A1A and 16th Street, Cocoa Beach (☎ 407/455-1380), which also has a boardwalk and public rest rooms.

SHOPPING

Cocoa Beach offers a wide array of shopping, but the most unique shopping experience is **Ron Jon Surf Shop,** 4151 N. Atlantic Ave., Cocoa Beach (☎ 407/799-8820), as you're driving down Florida A1A. The wildly original art deco building is more interesting than the merchandise, but if you're looking for a surfing souvenir, you'll find it here. The store also rents beach bikes, boogey boards, surfboards, in-line skates, and other fun stuff by the hour, day, or week.

WHERE TO STAY

Chain hotels in the area include the **Cocoa Beach Hilton,** 1550 N. Atlantic Ave. (A1A) (☎ 800/HILTONS or 407/799-0003); the **Holiday Inn Cocoa Beach Resort,** 1300 N. Atlantic Ave. (☎ 800/2BOOKUS or 407/783-2271), more upscale and better designed than the average Holiday Inn; and the **Howard Johnson Plaza Hotel/Cocoa Beach,** 2080 N. Atlantic Ave. (☎ **800/654-2000** or 407/783-9222).

Between the sea and route SR-520 and behind Ron Jon Surf Shop, ✪ **The Inn at Cocoa Beach,** 4300 Ocean Beach Blvd. (☎ **800/343-5307** or 407/799-3460), is our preferred roost. It's actually more of an upscale, personalized inn than a traditional hotel (it even calls itself an oversized bed-and-breakfast).

Closest to the port and the Kennedy Space Center is the ✪ **Radisson Resort at the Port,** 8701 Astronaut Blvd. (☎ **800/333-3333** or 407/784-0000). The bedrooms are comfortable, but not as wonderful as those at the Inn at Cocoa Beach. The hotel's only drawback is that it lies on a river; the beach is a 20-minute drive away.

Typical taxi fares from Port Canaveral to a mid-beach hotel, such as the Inn at Cocoa Beach, are $10 to $12 from the North Terminal, and $14 to $15 from the South Terminal. Call **Comfort Taxi** at ☎ **407/799-0442.**

WHERE TO DINE

In the heart of Cocoa Beach, **Bernard's Surf,** 2 S. Atlantic Ave. (☎ **407/783-2401**), has been a Florida institution since 1948. Specializing in steaks and seafood, the name Bernard's Surf should be followed by *& Turf,* as it is indeed a carnivore's paradise. The walls are adorned with pictures of astronauts who have celebrated their safe return to Earth with a filet mignon here. Try the grilled swordfish steak, or the catch of the day.

Near the port is the only five-star restaurant in town, ✪ **Flamingo's,** in the Radisson Resort at the Port, 8701 Astronaut Blvd. (☎ **407/784-0000**). Lunches are similar to those served at other restaurants, but dinners are fabulous, with a daily changing menu. The fish dishes are the best around the port, made with top-notch ingredients and deftly prepared.

Set amid the port area's densest concentration of commercial activity, **Lloyd's Canaveral Feast,** 610 Glen Cheek Dr. (☎ **407/784-8899**), is the waterfront's best-designed seafood restaurant. Outdoor tables are set on pier-like terraces over the water, and you can watch the cruise ships sail from their berths to the sea. (The best viewing times are Thursday to Monday at 5:30pm.) The luncheon buffet, served 11am to 2pm, is an amazing value. The cooking is a bit slapdash, but satisfying if you're not too demanding.

✪ **The Mango Tree,** 118 N. Atlantic Ave. (☎ **407/799-0513**), is the most beautiful and sophisticated restaurant in Cocoa Beach. Indian River crab cakes are perfectly flavored, and we especially like the sesame-seed encrusted grouper with a tropical fruit salsa, and almost any of the veal dishes. Pastas are always reliable, including the best pasta primavera on the Space Coast.

PORT CANAVERAL AFTER DARK

The Pier, 401 Meade Ave. (☎ **407/783-7549**), is the largest and busiest entertainment complex in Cocoa Beach, crowded every afternoon and evening with diners, drinkers, and sunset-watchers. Two open-air cafes, four bars, and a pair of restaurants jut 800 feet beyond the shoreline into the waves and surf. The more upscale restaurant is **Pier House,** open for dinner only, daily from 5pm to 10pm. We prefer **Marlin's Sports Bar,** where you enjoy fish platters, drinks, or sandwiches and a view of the sea that practically engulfs you. One or sometimes two bands play live 6 nights a week.

In Cocoa Beach's Heidelberg restaurant, the smoky and noisy **Heidi's Jazz Club,** 7 N. Orlando Ave. (☎ **407/783-6806**), offers jazz and classic blues. Live music is played Tuesday through Saturday, from 5 to 8pm and from 9pm to around midnight, and Monday from 5 to 8pm.

4 Tampa & the Port of Tampa

The Port of Tampa is set amid a complicated network of channels and harbors near the historic Cuban enclave of Ybor City and its deepwater Ybor Channel. The port's position on the western (Gulf) side of Florida makes it the logical departure point for ships headed for westerly ports of call, including the beaches and Mayan ruins of the Yucatan, the aquatic reefs of Central America, and the ports of Venezuela. The port's safe harbors have kept ships secure even during devastating tropical storms.

The bulk of the port's 400,000 annual passengers make their way through the modern terminal no. 2, also known as the Seaport Street Terminal, which was doubled in size in 1998. The 30-acre site also includes the constantly evolving Garrison Seaport Center, a massive complex of restaurants and shops inspired by Baltimore's Inner Harbor complex. This hub of waterfront activity and entertainment includes the Florida Aquarium and a multiscreen theater complex whose date of completion is scheduled for sometime in 1999.

Several cruise ships presently dock here, including Holland America Line's *Noordam* and Carnival Cruise Line's ***Tropicale*** and its larger mega-companion ***Sensation.***

The Port of Tampa is located at 13th and Platt streets. For information, call ☎ **813/272-0555.**

GETTING TO TAMPA & THE PORT

BY AIR   **Tampa International Airport** (☎ **813/870-8700**) lies 5 miles northwest of downtown Tampa, near the junction of Florida 60 and Memorial Highway.

The port is an easy 15-minute taxi ride away; the fare is $10 to $15. **Central Florida Limo** (☎ **813/396-3730**) also runs a minivan service, which costs $5.50 per person from the airport to Garrison Terminal and $7.50 per person to Pier 202.

BY CAR   Tampa lies 200 miles southwest of Jacksonville, 63 miles north of Sarasota, and 254 miles northwest of Miami. It's easily accessible from Interstate 275, Interstate 75, Interstate 4, U.S. 41, U.S. 92, U.S. 301, and many state roads.

The following car-rental companies have kiosks in the airport as well as offices downtown: **Avis** (☎ **800/331-1212**); **Dollar** (☎ **800/800-4000**); **National** (☎ **800/227-7368**); **Budget** (☎ **800/572-0700**); **Hertz** (☎ **800/654-3131**); **Alamo** (☎ **800/327-9633**); **Thrifty** (☎ **800/367-2277**).

Parking at the Port   The port has ample parking with good security. Parking costs $8 per day.

BY TRAIN   **Amtrak** (☎ **800/USA-RAIL**) trains arrive at the Tampa Amtrak Station, 601 Nebraska Ave. N., Tampa (☎ **800/872-7245**). Taxi fare to the port costs $5 to $7.

EXPLORING TAMPA

Tampa is best explored by car, as only the commercial district can be covered on foot. If you want to go to the beach, you'll have to head to neighboring St. Petersburg.

ESSENTIALS

VISITOR INFORMATION   Contact the Tampa/Hillsborough Convention and Visitors Association, Inc. (THCVA), 111 Madison St., Suite 1010, Tampa, FL 33602 (☎ **800/44-TAMPA** or 813/223-2752).

You can also stop by the **Tampa Bay Visitor Information Center,** 3601 E. Busch Blvd. (☎ **813/985-3601**), north of downtown in the Busch Gardens area. The office books organized tours of Tampa and the rest of Florida.

Tampa & St. Petersburg at a Glance

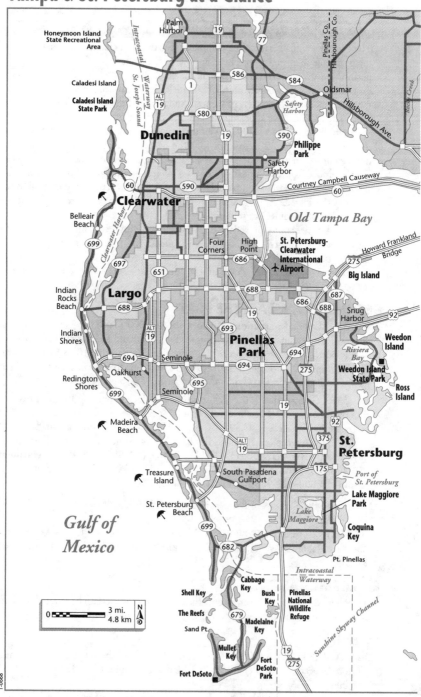

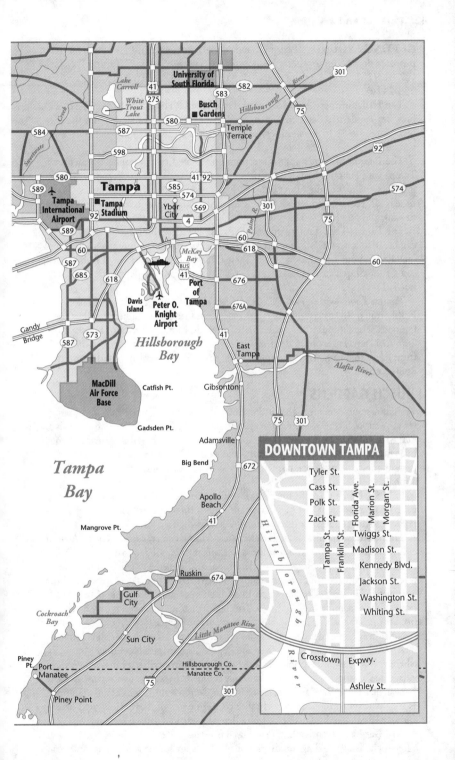

University of South Florida

Busch Gardens

Temple Terrace

Lake Carroll

White Trout Lake

Tampa

Tampa International Airport

Tampa Stadium

Ybor City

Davis Island

Peter O. Knight Airport

Port of Tampa

McKay Bay

Hillsborough Bay

MacDill Air Force Base

Catfish Pt.

Gadsden Pt.

Gibsonton

Adamsville

Big Bend

Apollo Beach

Mangrove Pt.

Tampa Bay

East Tampa

Alafia River

Ruskin

Gulf City

Sun City

Cockroach Bay

Piney Pt.

Port Manatee

Piney Point

Hillsbourough Co.
Manatee Co.

Little Manatee River

DOWNTOWN TAMPA

Tyler St.
Cass St.
Polk St.
Zack St.
Florida Ave.
Marion St.
Morgan St.
Tampa St.
Franklin St.
Twiggs St.
Madison St.
Kennedy Blvd.
Jackson St.
Washington St.
Whiting St.

Hillsborough River

Crosstown Expwy.

Ashley St.

GETTING AROUND   Taxis in Tampa do not normally cruise the streets for fares, but they do line up at public loading places. You can also call **Tampa Bay Cab** (☎ 813/251-5555), **Yellow Cab** (☎ 813/253-0121), or **United Cab** (☎ 813/253-2424).

The **Hillsborough Area Regional Transit/HARTline** (☎ 813/254-HART) provides regularly scheduled bus service between downtown Tampa and the suburbs. Fares are $1.15 for local services and $1.50 for express routes; correct change is required.

The People Mover, a motorized tram on elevated tracks, connects downtown Tampa with Harbour Island. It operates from the third level of the Fort Brooke Parking Garage, on Whiting Street between Franklin Avenue and Florida Street. Travel time is 90 seconds, and service is continuous, Monday through Saturday from 7am to 2am, and Sunday from 8am to 11pm. The fare is 25¢ each way.

The **Tampa-Ybor Trolley** interconnects the city's sites in one 15-mile loop. You can board at any of 17 stops (each clearly marked with orange-and-green signs) that include Harbour Island, downtown Tampa, the Florida Aquarium, and the Garrison Cruise Ship Terminal. Service is provided daily from 7:30am to 5:30pm. The fare is 25¢.

Tampa Town Water Taxi (☎ 813/253-3076) provides shuttle service along the Hillsborough River via a 44-passenger air-conditioned ferry, connecting downtown locations. The shuttle operates at half-hour intervals, Monday through Thursday from 2pm to 11pm, Friday from 2pm to 1am, Saturday from noon to 1am, and Sunday from noon to 11pm. Daytime round-trips cost $5 and evening round-trips (after 8pm) cost $6.

✪ BUSCH GARDENS

Yes, admission prices are high, but Busch Gardens remains Tampa Bay's most popular attraction. The 335-acre family entertainment park, at 3000 E. Busch Blvd. (☎ 813/987-5171), features thrill rides, animal habitats in natural environments, live entertainment, shops, restaurants, and games. The park's zoo, in the spirit of turn-of-the-century Africa, ranks among the best in the country, with nearly 3,400 animals.

In 1996, Busch Gardens opened Montu, the world's tallest and longest inverted roller coaster. It's part of **Egypt,** the park's ninth themed area. The area includes a replica of King Tutankhamen's tomb, plus a sand-dig area for kids.

Timbuktu is a replica of an ancient desert trading center, complete with African craftspeople at work. It also features a sandstorm ride, a boat-swing ride, a roller coaster, and an electronic games arcade. **Morocco,** a walled city with exotic architecture, has Moroccan craft demonstrations, a sultan's tent with snake charmers, and the Marrakech Theaters. The **Serengeti Plain** is an open area with more than 500 African animals roaming freely in herds. This 80-acre natural grassy veldt may be viewed from the monorail, the Trans-Veldt Railway, or the skyride.

Nairobi is home to a natural habitat for various species of gorillas and chimpanzees, a baby animal nursery, a petting zoo, reptile displays, and Nocturnal Mountain, where visitors can observe animals active at night. **Stanleyville,** a prototype African village, has a shopping bazaar and live entertainment, as well as two water rides: the Tanganyika Tidal Wave and Stanley Falls. **The Congo** features white-water raft rides, as well as Kumba, the largest steel roller coaster in the southeastern United States, and Claw Island, a display of rare white Bengal tigers in a natural setting.

Bird Gardens, the original core of Busch Gardens, offers rich foliage, lagoons, and a free-flight aviary holding hundreds of exotic birds, including golden and American bald eagles, hawks, owls, and falcons. This area also features Land of the Dragons, a new children's adventure area.

Crown Colony is the home of a team of Clydesdale horses, as well as the Anheuser-Busch hospitality center. Questor, a flight simulator adventure ride, is located here.

A 1-day ticket costs $37.97 for adults, $31.95 for children ages 3 to 9; kids 2 and under are free. The park is open daily from 9:30am to 6pm, with extended hours in summer and during holiday periods. To get here, take Interstate 275 northeast of downtown to Busch Boulevard (exit 33), and go east 2 miles to the entrance on 40th Street (McKinley Drive). Parking is $3.

MORE ATTRACTIONS

Adjacent to the Garrison Seaport Center, the ✪ **Florida Aquarium** (☎ 813/224-9583) celebrates the role of water in the development and maintenance of Florida's topography and ecosystems, with more than 4,350 specimens in all. One intriguing exhibit follows a drop of water as it bubbles through Florida limestone and wends its way to the sea. Another evokes a watery landscape as painted by Monet.

Thirteen silver minarets and distinctive Moorish architecture make the ✪ **Henry B. Plant Museum,** 401 W. Kennedy Blvd. (☎ 813/254-1891), the focal point of the Tampa skyline. Modeled after the Alhambra in Spain, this National Historic Landmark, built in 1891 as the 511-room Tampa Bay Hotel, is filled with European and Oriental art and furnishings.

The **Museum of African-American Art,** 1308 N. Marion St. (☎ 813/272-2466), features visual art by and about people of African descent. The collection covers the 19th and 20th centuries and represents more than 80 artists.

The permanent collection of the **Tampa Museum of Art,** 600 N. Ashley Dr. (☎ 813/274-8130), is especially strong in ancient Greek, Etruscan, and Roman artifacts, as well as 20th-century art. The museum grounds, fronting the Hillsborough River, contain a sculpture garden and a reflecting pool.

In St. Petersburg, the ✪ **Salvador Dalí Museum,** 1003 Third St. S. (☎ 813/823-3767), contains the largest assemblage of the artist's works outside Spain. The former marine warehouse that houses this widely divergent collection is as starkly modern as the works of art displayed within.

ORGANIZED TOURS

BY BUS   Swiss Chalet Tours, 3601 E. Busch Blvd. (☎ 813/985-3601), operates guided tours of Tampa, Ybor City, and the surrounding region. Four-hour (10am to 2pm) tours run on Monday and Thursday, and cost $35 for adults, $25 for children. Eight-hour tours on Tuesday and Friday cost $45 for adults, $35 for children. You can also book full-day tours to most Orlando theme parks, including MGM Studios, Epcot/Walt Disney World, and Sea World, as well as to the Kennedy Space Center and Cypress Gardens.

HITTING THE BEACH

You have to go to St. Petersburg, across the bay, for a north-to-south string of interconnected white sandy shores.

Most beaches have rest rooms, refreshment stands, and picnic areas. You can either park on the street at meters (usually 25¢ for each half hour) or at one of the four major parking lots, located from north to south at: Sand Key Park, beside Gulf Blvd. (also known as Route 699), just south of the Clearwater Pass Bridge; Redington Shores Beach Park, beside Gulf Boulevard at 182nd Street; Treasure Island Park, on

Gulf Boulevard just north of 108th Avenue; and St. Pete Beach Park, beside Gulf Boulevard at 46th Street.

St. Petersburg Municipal Beach lies on Treasure Island. **Clearwater Beach,** with its silky sands, is the place for beach volleyball. Water-sports rentals, lifeguards, restrooms, showers, and concessions are available. The swimming is excellent, and there's a pier for fishing. Parking is $7 a day in gated lots.

If you want to shop as well as suntan, consider **Madeira Beach,** midway between St. Petersburg and Clearwater, with a boardwalk, T-shirt emporiums, and ice-cream parlors.

Honeymoon Island isn't great for swimming, but it has its own rugged beauty and a fascinating nature trail. From here, you can catch a ferry to **Caladesi Island State Park,** a 3¹/₂-mile stretch of sand at #3 Causeway Blvd. in Dunedin (☎ 813/469-5918 for information).

You can also go south to **Fort Desoto Park,** 3500 Pinellas Bayway S. (☎ 813/866-2484), consisting of about 900 acres and 7 miles of waterfront exposed to both the Gulf of Mexico and a brackish channel. There are fishing piers, shaded picnic areas, a bird and animal sanctuary, campsites, and a partially ruined fort near the park's southwestern tip. Take Interstate 275 South to the Pinellas Bayway (exit 4) and follow the signs.

SHOPPING

In **Ybor Square,** 1901 13th St. (☎ 813/247-4497), nearly 40 shops lie within three brick buildings dating from 1886 that once housed the world's largest cigar factory. The shops sell everything, including, of course, cigars. More upscale stores are located in **Old Hyde Park Village,** Swann and Dakota avenues near Bayshore Boulevard. (☎ 813/251-3500). **The Shops on Harbour Island,** 601 S. Harbour Island Blvd. (☎ 813/202-1830), are set on an island off the coast of Tampa's commercial heart.

Malls include the **Brandon Town Center,** at the intersection of State Road 60 and Interstate 75; **Eastlake Square Mall,** 56th Street at Hillsborough Avenue; and the city's largest mall, **Tampa Bay Center,** Himes Avenue and Martin Luther King, Jr., Boulevard. You'll find substantial discounts at the **Gulf Coast Factory Shops,** 5461 Factory Shops Blvd. (corner of Interstate 75 and Highway 301, ☎ 941/723-1150).

WHERE TO STAY

The **Doubletree Guest Suites**, 11310 N. 30th St. (☎ 800/222-TREE or 813/971-7690), feels like a friendly college dormitory. Each handsomely furnished accommodation contains two separate rooms, one with a wet bar and small refrigerator.

There are two Tampa Hyatts: the **Hyatt Regency Tampa,** Two Tampa City Center (☎ 800/233-1234 or 813/225-1234), which towers over Tampa's commercial center; and the ✪ **Hyatt Regency Westshore,** 6200 Courtney Campbell Causeway (☎ 800/233-1234 or 813/874-1234), at the Tampa end of the long causeway traversing Tampa Bay. At the Westshore, some Spanish-style townhouses/villas are set about a half mile from the main hotel building.

Sheraton Grand Hotel Tampa Westshore, 4860 W. Kennedy Blvd. (☎ 800/866-7177 or 813/286-4400), is Tampa's most stylish modern hotel. The 11-story building is modeled after a butterfly.

Wyndham Harbour Island, 725 S. Harbour Island Blvd. (☎ 800/822-4200 or 813/229-5000), sits on one of Tampa Bay's most elegant residential islands.

In St. Petersburg, ✪ **The Don CeSar,** 3400 Gulf Blvd. (☎ 800/282-1116 or 813/360-1881), is the most famous landmark in town. This pink-sided Moorish/Mediterranean fantasy, listed on the National Register of Historic Places, sits on seven and a half acres of beachfront. Guest rooms are first-rate, usually with water views.

Also in St. Pete, ✪ **Stouffer Renaissance Vinoy Resort,** 501 Fifth Ave. NE at Bay Shore Drive (☎ **800/HOTELS1** or 813/894-1000), reigns as the *grande dame* of the region's hotels. Accommodations in the new wing ("The Tower") are slightly larger than those in the hotel's original core.

WHERE TO DINE

On the 14th floor of the Hyatt Regency Westshore Hotel, **Armani's,** 6200 Courtney Campbell Causeway (☎ **813/874-1234**), is a Northern Italian restaurant with flair. Dishes are all prepared with fine ingredients.

The steaks at ✪ **Bern's Steak House,** 1208 S. Howard Ave. (☎ **813/251-2421**), are close to perfect. You order according to thickness and weight. All main courses come with onion soup, salad, baked potato, garlic toast, and onion rings. Dessert is served in an upstairs warren of cubbyholes crafted from wine casks.

Le Bordeaux, 1502 S. Howard Ave. (☎ **813/254-4387**), presents competent French food at reasonable prices. The changing menu often includes bouillabaisse, pot-au-feu, salmon en croûte, veal with wild mushrooms, and filet of beef with Roquefort sauce, each impeccably cooked and presented. The Left Bank jazz club presents live jazz on Friday and Saturday nights.

In Ybor City, ✪ **Columbia Restaurant,** 2117 Seventh Ave. E., between 21st and 22nd streets (☎ **813/248-4961**), occupies a tile-sheathed building that fills an entire city block, about a mile from the cruise docks. The aura is pre-Castro Cuba. We love lunching in the big-windowed cafe, and eating dinner in the big scarlet and mahogany room with a massive crystal chandelier. The more simple your dish is, the better it's likely to be. Filet mignons, *palomillo,* roasted pork, and the black beans, yellow rice, and plantains are flavorful and well-prepared. Flamenco shows begin on the dance floor Monday through Saturday at 7:30pm.

At lunch, ✪ **Mise en Place,** 442 Kennedy Blvd. (☎ **813/254-5373**), serves an array of delicious sandwiches, as well as savory pastas, risottos, and platters. More formal dinners feature free-range chicken with smoked tomato coulis, sautéed rainbow trout with Swiss chard, and loin of venison with asparagus, tarragon mash, and red-onion balsamic marmalade.

✪ **Mojo,** 238 E. Davis Blvd. (☎ **813/259-9949**), sits on Davis Island, a residential island separated from the commercial heart of Tampa by a narrow channel. This is the most flamboyant and charming restaurant in town. Its Caribbean menu explains everything on it. At lunch, try the roast pork sandwich with lime-flavored cumin, onions, and provolone cheese on Cuban bread. Delicious dinners include *feijoada,* roasted pork with plantains, and *ropa vieja* (Cuban beef hash).

The best fish in Tampa is served at **Oystercatchers,** in the Hyatt Regency Westshore Hotel complex, 6200 Courtney Campbell Causeway (☎ **813/874-1234**). Pick the fish you want from a glass-fronted buffet or enjoy mesquite-grilled steaks, chicken rollatini, and shellfish. There's also a short list of sashimi dishes.

Selena's, 1623 Snow, Old Hyde Park (☎ **813/251-2116**), serves a mix of New Orleans Cajun and Northern Italian cuisine. The food is competently prepared, and the portions are generous. An upstairs bar/lounge hosts live jazz Thursday through Saturday.

TAMPA AFTER DARK

Nightfall now transforms Ybor City, Tampa's century-old Latin Quarter, into a hotbed of music for all tastes, ethnic food, poetry readings, and after-midnight coffee and dessert. Thousands crowd one of its main arteries, 7th Avenue, Wednesday through Saturday evenings.

The Tampa/Hillsborough Arts Council maintains **Artsline** (☎ 813/229-ARTS), a 24-hour information service about current and upcoming cultural events. The **Tampa Bay Performing Arts Center,** 1010 N. MacInnes Place (☎ 813/229-STAR, or Ticketmaster at (☎ 813/286-2100), contains four theaters and the Museum of African American Art. The restored **Tampa Theater,** 711 Franklin St. (☎ 813/274-8981), a movie palace built in 1926, is now a registered national historic site.

THE CLUB & MUSIC SCENE

The Skipper Dome/Skipper's Smokehouse, 910 Skipper Rd. (☎ 813/971-0666), is our favorite evening spot, with an all-purpose restaurant and bar (with oysters and fresh shellfish sold by the dozen and half dozen). For live music, head out back to the "Skipper Dome," a sprawling deck sheltered by a canopy of oak trees. You'll hear soca, reggae, blues, progressive New Orleans–style jazz, and more.

Set within a 1940s movie palace, **The Masquerade,** 1503 E. 7th Ave. (☎ 813/247-3319), is the first of the many nightclubs that pepper the streets of historic Ybor City. It's a raucous, high-volume emporium of dance music and electronic lights, with the main dance hall ("the theater"), a video bar, and a pub with pool tables.

5 New Orleans & the Port of New Orleans

There's power and majesty in this historic port, 110 miles upriver of the Gulf of Mexico. By some yardsticks, it's the busiest port in the nation, servicing many vessels much larger than the cruise ships that call New Orleans home. Although the bulk of business conducted here mainly involves the transport of grains, ores and mining byproducts, machinery, and building supplies, the city is poised for increased visibility as home port to a handful of cruise ships. During 1996, and again in 1997, more than 150,000 cruise passengers boarded here. Cruises from here are mainly bound for the western edge of the Caribbean, including the western "Mexican Riviera" and Cancún and Cozumel.

If you're boarding a cruise ship in New Orleans, it's virtually certain that your access will be via the Julia Street Cruise Ship Terminal on the Julia Street Wharf. Originally developed as part of the 1984 Louisiana World's Exposition, the cruise ship area was inaugurated in 1993, then doubled in size in 1996. It lies near the commercial heart of town, a 5-minute walk from the edge of the French Quarter.

Ships departing from New Orleans include Commodore Cruise Line's *Enchanted Isle* and Carnival Cruise Line's *Celebration.* Carnival's *Sensation,* while not officially using New Orleans as its home port, stops here once a week as part of its weekly cruise circuit. Other lines whose vessels make occasional stops in New Orleans en route to other sites include ACCL, Royal Caribbean, and Crystal.

The port is located at 1350 Port of New Orleans Place. For information, call the **Port of New Orleans** at (☎ 504/522-2551).

GETTING TO NEW ORLEANS & ITS PORT

BY AIR   New Orleans International Airport is 10 miles northwest of the port. A taxi to the port costs about $19 and takes about 20 minutes. **Airport Shuttle** (☎ 504/592-0555) runs vans at 10- to 12-minute intervals from outside the airport's baggage claim to the port and other points in town. It costs $11 per passenger each way, free for children under 6.

BY CAR   Highways I-10, U.S. 90, U.S. 61, and Louisiana 25 (the Lake Pontchartrain Causeway) lead directly to New Orleans.

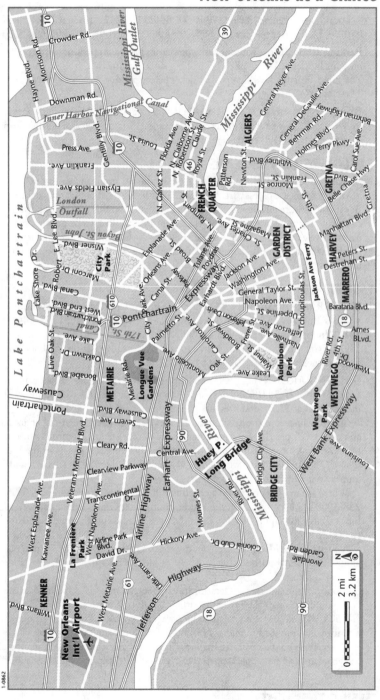

Local rental agencies include **Avis** (☎ 800/331-1212); **Budget** (☎ 800/572-07005); **Dollar Rent-a-Car** (☎ 800/800-4000); and **Hertz** (☎ 800/654-3131).

Parking at the Port   You can park your car in long-term parking at the port, but only for blocks of 1 week. Reserve parking directly with your cruise-ship operator. You must present a boarding pass or ticket before parking within the port facilities. The cost is $45 per week.

BY TRAIN   Amtrak (☎ 800/USA-RAIL) trains stop at the **Union Passenger Terminal** at 1001 Loyola Ave., in the central business district. Taxis are outside the passenger terminal's main entrance; the fare to the port is $6.

EXPLORING NEW ORLEANS

In many respects, the French Quarter *is* New Orleans, and many visitors never leave its confines. It's the oldest part of the city and still the most popular for sightseeing. But if you venture outside the French Quarter, you'll be able to feel the pulse of the city's commerce, see river activities that keep the city alive, stroll through spacious parks, drive or walk by the impressive homes of the Garden District, and get a first-hand view of the bayou/lake connection that explains why New Orleans grew up here in the first place.

ESSENTIALS

VISITOR INFORMATION   Contact the **Greater New Orleans Convention and Visitors Bureau,** 1520 Sugar Bowl Dr., New Orleans, LA 70112 (☎ 504/566-5011), for brochures, pamphlets, and information.

Once you arrive, stop at the **New Orleans Welcoming Center,** 529 St. Ann St. in the French Quarter (☎ 504/566-5031).

GETTING AROUND   Taxis are plentiful. If you're not near a taxi stand, call **United Cabs** (☎ 504/522-9771) and a cab will come within 5 to 10 minutes. The meter begins at $2.10, and rises 40¢ per mile thereafter.

Streetcar lines runs the length of St. Charles Avenue. They operate 24 hours a day and cost $1.25 per ride (you must have exact change). A transfer from streetcar to bus costs 10¢. Board at the corner of Canal and Carondelet streets in the French Quarter. A VisiTour Pass, which gives you unlimited rides on all streetcar and bus lines, sells for $4 for 1 day, $8 for 3 days.

Where the trolleys don't run, a **city bus** will. For route information call ☎ 504/248-3900 or pick up a map at the Visitor Information Center (address above). Most buses charge 80¢ (plus 30¢ for a transfer) per ride, although some express buses charge $1.25.

A **Vieux Carré Minibus** takes you to French Quarter sights. The route is posted along Canal and Bourbon streets. The minibus operates daily between 5am and 7:25pm and costs $1.

From Jackson Square (at Decatur Street), you can take a $2^{1}/_{4}$-mile horse-drawn carriage ride through the French Quarter. **The Gay Nineties Carriage Tour Co.** (☎ 504/943-8820), offers fringe-topped wagons suitable for up to 10 passengers at a time, daily from 9am to midnight. A ride costs $8 per adult and $4 per child.

A free **ferryboat** departs at frequent intervals from the foot of Canal Street, carrying cars and passengers across the river. A round-trip passage takes about 25 minutes.

SEEING THE SIGHTS

The well-designed ✪ **Aquarium of the Americas,** 1 Canal St., at the Mississippi River (☎ 504/861-2537), is a million-gallon tribute to the diversity of life within freshwater lakes and the sea. A 400,000-gallon tank holds a kaleidoscope of species from the deep waters of the nearby Gulf of Mexico.

You'll need at least 3 hours to visit the ✪ **Audubon Zoo,** 6500 Magazine St. (☎ **504/861-2537**), home to 1,500 animals in natural habitats. In a Louisiana swamp replication, alligators and other reptiles slither and hop among native birds and clusters of marsh grasses.

Despite its massive Doric columns and twin staircases, local architects nonetheless refer to **Beauregard-Keyes House,** 1113 Chartres St. (☎ **504/523-7257**), as a "Louisiana raised cottage." Built in 1826, it's one of the most impressive and socially prestigious structures in town.

Incorporating seven historic buildings connected by a brick courtyard, ✪ **The Historic New Orleans Collection,** 533 Royal St. (☎ **504/523-4662**), evokes New Orleans of 200 years ago. The oldest building in the complex escaped the tragic fire of 1794. The others hold exhibitions about Louisiana's culture and history.

Housed in a former granary four blocks from the river, the **Louisiana Children's Museum,** 420 Julia St. (☎ **504/523-1357**), divides its exhibits into activities for children over and under the age of 8. The Lab demonstrates principles of physics and math, motion, and inertia. Younger children play in a simulated supermarket and attend puppet workshops, cooking programs, and storytelling sessions.

Musee Conti Wax Museum, 917 Conti St. (☎ **504/525-2605**), is the bayou equivalent of Madame Tussaud's, featuring pivotal figures in Louisiana history and legend. Look for the replicas of the notorious politico Huey Long, jazzmeister Pete Fountain, Andrew Jackson, and Jean Lafitte.

The collections of the **New Orleans Historic Voodoo Museum,** 724 Dumaine St. (☎ **504/523-7685**), celebrate the occult and the curious mixture of African and Catholic rituals first brought to New Orleans by slaves from Hispaniola. An herb shop/apothecary is stocked with the ingredients any voodoo practitioner would need. Staff there can also put you in touch with psychics. A guided voodoo walking tour of the French Quarter departs from the museum daily at 1pm.

The collections of the **New Orleans Museum of Art (NOMA),** Lelong Avenue. (☎ **504/488-2631**), span the centuries, with one floor devoted to ethnographic and non-Western art.

The ✪ **Old Absinthe House/Tony Moran's Restaurant,** 240 Bourbon St. (☎ **504/523-3181**), is the oldest bar in America, built in 1806 by two Spanish partners. Virtually any drink is available. Upstairs is a restaurant, Tony Moran's, open only for dinner.

The **World Trade Center of New Orleans,** 2 Canal St. (☎ **504/529-1601**), one of the tallest buildings in town, has the ✪ **Viewpoint** observation platform on its 31st floor. Check out the freighters, cruise ships, tug boats, submarines, and aircraft carriers that ply the swift-flowing waters of New Orlean's harbor. A cocktail lounge spins slowly on the 33rd floor.

ORGANIZED TOURS

BY FOOT   Friends of the Cabildo (☎ 504/523-3939) lead 2-hour walking tours of Vieux Carré (the French Quarter). They leave from the Museum Store at 523 St. Ann St. every Tuesday through Sunday at 10am and 1:30pm, and Monday at 1:30pm, except holidays. Donations are expected: $10 per adult, $8 for seniors over 65 and children ages 13 to 20.

Magic Walking Tours (☎ 504/588-9693) offers theme tours associated with the city's cemeteries, its Garden District, or its voodoo traditions. Tours cost $10 per person during the day, and $14 per person at night.

You can see historic interiors on a **Hidden Treasures Tour** (☎ 504/529-4507). The **National Park Service** also conducts free 1-mile walking tours through the French Quarter. They depart from the French Quarter Folklife and Visitor Center, 916 N. Peters St. (☎ 504/589-3882).

BY BUS   A 2-hour **Gray Line** bus tour, 1300 World Trade Center of New Orleans (☎ 800/535-7786 or 504/587-0861), offers a fast overview of the city. Tours cost $18 for adults and $9.50 for children, and require advance booking.

BY BOAT   The paddlewheeler *Creole Queen* departs from the Poydras Street Wharf, adjacent to the mall Riverwalk, every day at 10:30am for a 2^1/$_2$-hour waterborne tour. Riverwalk is at the end of Canal St; the wharf is about two blocks east. There's a buffet restaurant and a cocktail lounge on board. Daytime cruises cost $14 for adults, $7 for children. Evening cruises, with live jazz, cost $39 for adults, $18 for children.

Another steam-powered stern-wheeler is the *Natchez,* departing daily from the Toulouse Street Wharf, next to the French Quarter's Jackson Street Brewery. Cruises begin at 11:30am and 2:30pm and feature live jazz and an optional Creole-style luncheon buffet. The cost is $14.75 for adults, $7.25 for children 6 to 12, free for children under 6 (food is an additional $8 for adults, $4.50 for children). Evening jazz cruises, with a buffet dinner, cost $38.75 for adults, $19.25 for children.

The riverboat *John James Audubon* departs from the Canal Street dock at Riverwalk, and travels the Mississippi as far as the Audubon Zoo and the Aquarium. The cruise costs $26.50 for adults, $15.25 for children.

The *Queen of New Orleans,* at the New Orleans Hilton Riverside (☎ 504/587-7777), is a casino paddlewheeler boat with slot machines. The 90-minute cruises run 24 hours a day, departing every 3 hours.

SHOPPING

Shopping here is, in a word, fun. Antique stores are especially well-stocked, and gift shops seem to sell more than just a cheap array of T-shirts and souvenir items.

Major shopping venues include the triple-tiered mall **Canal Place,** where Canal Street meets the Mississippi Wharves. **The Esplanade,** 1401 W. Esplanade, boasts a constantly busy food court and more than 150 retailers. **The French Market,** whose main entrance is on Decatur Street across from Jackson Square, is big on Louisiana kitsch and cookware. The **Jackson Brewery,** adjacent to Jackson Square, is a transformed suds factory filled with more than 125 retailers. **Riverwalk** is a covered mall that runs along the wharves between Poydras Street and the Convention Center.

You'll find a row of art galleries along **Julia Street,** between the Mississippi and Camp Street. A jumble of antiques and flea market–style emporiums sit along a 6-block stretch of **Magazine Street,** between Audubon Park and Canal Street. There's also **Magazine Arcade Antiques,** 3017 Magazine St. (☎ 504/895-5451).

For crafts, try the **Idea Factory,** 838 Chartres St. (☎ 504/524-5195), where woodworkers stay busy shaping and gluing letterboxes, trays, paper-towel holders, and wall brackets. You'll find new and antique silver at **New Orleans Silversmiths,** 600 Chartres St. (☎ 504/522-8333).

You can see pralines being made at **Aunt Sally's Praline Shops, Inc.,** 810 Decatur St. (☎ 504/524-5107). They'll ship anything home for you, and sell you items such as cookbooks, packaged Creole food, and Louisiana memorabilia.

French Market Gift Shop, 824 Decatur St. (☎ 504/522-6004), reigns as a tourist favorite. Whether you're setting the mood for a Christmas Eve candlelight mass or a witches' coven, you'll find everything you need to illuminate the event in soft light and soft shadows. Many of the candles are in beeswax; others are shaped into forms like pianos, country cottages, and music boxes.

Bergen Galleries, Inc., 730 Royal St. (☎ **504/523-7882**), features originals, prints, and reproductions, all with that unmistakable Creole taste that is entirely New Orleans. You're sure to find a perfect memento here, whether inspired by the Bayou country or the Bacchanalian revelry of Mardi Gras.

In New Orleans, fashion has a name: **Yvonne Lafleur/New Orleans,** 8131 Hampton St. (☎ **504/866-9666**). Yvonne Lafleur designed all of the ladies wear here. From slip dresses to formal wear to undergarments to perfume, this shop is worth a stop for even the savvy New York shopper.

Angel Wings, 710 St. Louis St. (☎ **504/524-6889**), specializes in a whimsical collection of unusual jewelry and curios. "Quirky" seems to be the buzzword here. Jewelry boxes and like items dominate the selection.

If you're looking for the originality of handmade jewelry and ornaments, stop in at **Mignon Faget, Ltd.,** Canal Place, Level One (☎ **504/524-2873**). At this unique New Orleans outlet, you can find pieces fashioned of sliver, gilded bronze, and gold.

In business since the mid-1800s, the **Bourbon French Perfume Company,** 525 St. Ann St. (☎ **504/522-4480**), still maintains its French heritage and influence. They offer nearly every major brand available, in addition to their own original creations. Here you can design and purchase a bottle of your own fragrance, diffuse a touch on your handkerchief, and stroll down the Rue St. Ann, preparing for an evening in the French Quarter.

WHERE TO STAY

Seekers of Southern charm and grace head for the **Columns Hotel,** 3811 St. Charles Ave. (☎ **800/445-9308** or 504/899-9308), a former private residence in 1883 now converted into a small hotel. One of the stateliest remaining examples of belle epoque Italiante architecture, it is listed on the National Register of Historic Places. Its columned porch is one of the city's most popular evening rendezvous points. Louis Malle selected the Columns as a site for his controversial film, *Pretty Baby.* Come here for the atmosphere, not for the rather plain rooms upstairs.

Conveniently located near both the embarkation piers for cruise ship passengers and the French Quarter, the **Doubletree Hotel,** 300 Canal St. (☎ **504/581-1300**), is at the edge of the city's business district. Rooms are comfortable and clean.

Only 11 blocks from the French Quarter, ✪ **The House on Bayou Road,** 2275 Bayou Rd. (☎ **800/882-2968** or 504/945-0992), is a rural plantation (circa 1798) just off Esplanade Avenue. This elegantly restored petite Creole plantation is set on 2 acres and offers rooms furnished with period antiques and private baths.

✪ **Lafayette Hotel,** 600 St. Charles Ave., at Lafayette Square (☎ **800/733-4754** or 504/524-4441), resembles an upscale turn-of-the-century hotel in London. From old-world architecture, French doors, and wrought-iron balconies to marble floors, polished mahogany, and English botanical prints, the ambience is consistently luxurious. Extras like thick terry robes, French-milled soaps, hair dryers, and umbrellas make the Lafayette a winner. Bedrooms have comfortable easy chairs and roomy closets.

Lafitte Guest House, 1003 Bourbon St. (☎ **800/331-7971** or 504/581-2678), is a meticulously restored elegant French manor house furnished with splendid antiques. The three-floor brick structure in a residential section of Bourbon Street was built in 1849. Its marble ceilings, wrought-iron balconies, and Victorian antiques are as alluring as each of its individually decorated bedrooms, which come in various sizes.

In the heart of the French Quarter, you can follow in the footsteps of Elizabeth Taylor and Paul Newman and head for ✪ **Maison de Ville,** 727 Toulouse St.

(☎ **800/634-1600** or 504/561-5858), located on its original 1742 site. It was here that Tennessee Williams "polished" *A Streetcar Named Desire.* Just steps from honky-tonk Bourbon Street, you find here an air of Southern gentility: Oriental rugs, Louisiana antiques, and an enchanting courtyard. Two blocks away the hotel rents its Audubon Cottages, seven suites in a series of 19th-century low buildings. Audubon actually painted his wildlife masterpieces here.

One of the best guest houses for value is **The McKendrick-Breaux House,** 1474 Magazine St. (☎ **888/570-1700** or 504/586-1700), built at the end of the Civil War by a wealthy plumber and Scottish immigrant. Located in the lower Garden District, it has been completely restored to its original charm. Each room is furnished with antiques, family collectibles, and fresh flowers.

About 7 blocks from the cruise ship terminal is the *grande dame,* of the French Quarter, the atmospheric **Monteleone Hotel,** 214 Royal St. (☎ **800/535-9595** or 504/523-2341). Decor and floor layouts are slightly different in each of the 597 rooms.

Three streets from Bourbon in the French Quarter, ✪ **P.J. Holbrook's Olde Victorian Inn,** 914 N. Rampart St. (☎ **800/725-2446** or 504/522-2446), is a beautifully restored 1840s home, with antiques and reproductions. Some rooms have balconies, and most come with fireplaces. P.J. herself exemplifies Southern hospitality.

Set within the heart of the Garden District, the ✪ **Pontchartrain Hotel,** 2031 St. Charles Ave. (☎ **800/HERITAGE** or 504/524-0581), is a full-service, if idiosyncratic, upscale establishment. It figures more prominently into local lore than any other hotel in New Orleans. Set within the heart of the Garden District, it's upscale, well-upholstered, and proud of its role as a rendezvous point for the city's bourgeois elite. Each of the bedrooms is decorated with accessories inspired by Mediterranean Europe. Suites are names after famous former occupants, including Aly Khan and Tyrone Power.

The most elegant small hotel in New Orleans, ✪ **Soniat House,** 1133 Charles St. (☎ **800/544-8808** or 504/522-0570), was selected by Condé Nast Traveler as most representative of the "essential spirit" of Louisiana. Soniat's guest rooms vary widely—they're located in everything from two Creole-style town houses to two wings of former slave quarters. Seven new suites in a renovated family town house across the street are the best New Orleans has to offer.

Only blocks from the French Quarter, ✪ **Windsor Court Hotel,** 300 Gravier St. (☎ **800/262-2662** or 504/523-6000), rents 224 beautifully furnished bedrooms, all but 50 of which are suites. From its $8 million art collection to the harpist floating celestial music over the afternoon tea drinkers, the Windsor Court provides more of an English country house experience than a Louisiana sojourn. It's the city's first and only AAA Five Diamond hotel—luxury and more luxury.

For a somewhat funky but absolutely charming gay-friendly guest house, head for **The B & W Courtyards Bed & Breakfast,** 2425 Charles St. (☎ **800/585-5731** or 504/945-9418), adjacent to the French Quarter in Faubourg Marigny. The aura here could be called "Old New Orleans meets the Caribbean." This house is actually a collection of three 1800s buildings connected by courtyards. There's a Jacuzzi in the rear.

WHERE TO DINE

Don't ask what's new at ✪ **Antoine's,** 713 St. Louis St. (☎ **504/581-4422**), established in 1840. Oysters Rockefeller, first served here in 1899, are still available. Tournedos of beef, ramekins of crawfish cardinal, and *pompano en papillote* remain perennial favorites, and rightly so. The only radical menu change occurred in the 1990s, when French menu terms were given English translations.

The legendary **Arnaud's,** 813 Bienville St. (☎ **504/523-5433**), lies within three interconnected, once-private houses from the 1700s. The five belle-epoque dining rooms here are lush with Edwardian embellishments. Shrimp Arnaud, snails *en casserole,* oysters stewed in cream, rack of lamb diablo, roasted duck *à l'orange,* and classic bananas Foster or crème brûlée are good choices here, along with other modern dishes created by chef Tommy di Giovanni. The food is better than it has been in years.

A great New Orleans bistro, **Bacco,** 310 Charles St. (☎ **504/523-6441**), stands adjacent to the De La Poste Hotel, right in the heart of the French Quarter. In an elegant setting of pink Italian marble floors and Venetian chandeliers, you can feast on wood-fired pizzas, regional seafood, and such specialties as porcini roasted duck and crabmeat and pappardelle. There's also a festive Sunday jazz brunch. You can dine in the courtyard in season.

One of New Orleans hottest new chefs is French-born Daniel Bonnot, whose culinary stage is at **Bizou,** 701 St. Charles Ave. (☎ **504/524-4114**). The place is hardly the most glamorous in New Orleans, but its cuisine, a rejuvenation of Creole and French traditional cookery, has the exuberance of a spring day. Even the vinegar potato chips you nibble on before the meal are addictive. Try the crawfish cakes with Creole mustard and baby greens in a Tabasco-infused white butter.

Broussard's, 819 Conti St. (☎ **504/581-3866**), has thrived here since 1920. It's a quieter, more dignified version of Antoine's, less heavily patronized by out-of-towners, and more authentic to the "Nawlins" ethic. Dishes include filets of Pompano Napoléon-style (with scallops and a mustard-caper sauce, served in puff pastry with a side order of shrimp) and our eternal favorite, shrimp with crabmeat Jean Lafitte.

At the corner of Washington Avenue and Coliseum Street, **Commander's Place,** 1403 Washington Ave. (☎ **504/899-8221**), still reigns as one of the city's finest dining choices, although many locals have deserted it for being "too touristy." The cuisine is haute Creole. Try anything with shrimp or crawfish, or else the Mississippi quail. Make reservations days in advance. Jazz brunches on Saturday and Sunday are a New Orleans event.

✪ **Galatoire's,** 209 Bourbon St. (☎ **504/525-2021**), feels like a bistro in turn-of-the-century Paris, still basking in its legendary reputation. Menu items include trout (*meunière* or *almondine*), *remoulade* of shrimp, oysters *en brochette,* a savory Creole-style bouillabaisse, and a good eggplant stuffed with a puree of seafood. Get here early to avoid long waits in line.

Lines often stretch halfway down the block for one of the 116 seats at **K-Paul's Louisiana Kitchen,** 416 Chartres St. (☎ **504/524-7394**), one of Louisiana's most famous restaurants. Once seated, expect company—tables on the street level are communal. Try fiery gumbos, Cajun popcorn shrimp, roasted rabbit, and the delicious spicy blackened fish (especially tuna).

Located in the Lafayette Hotel (see above), ✪ **Mike's on the Avenue,** 628 Charles St. (☎ **504/523-1709**), is a favorite with the discriminating palates of New Orleans locals. Chef Mike Fennelly has the town talking about his international and New American cuisine. What's surprising about this innovative chef is that he can take the mundane and make it truly memorable. For example, he marinates simple lamb chops in a fresh rosemary and pomegranate sauce, then covers them with a jalapeño mint glaze. The Louisiana crab cakes are also wonderful.

If you don't mind facing the world's toughest waitresses, head for **Mother's Restaurant,** 401 Poydras St. (☎ **504/523-9656**), at the corner of Tchoupitoulas. Customers have crowded to this place since 1938. Homemade biscuits and red bean omelets are featured at breakfast, giving way at lunch to po' boys—the most popular is the Ferdi special, with baked ham, roast beef, gravy, shredded cabbage and pickles, among other ingredients. For dinner you can get everything from soft shell crabs to jambalaya.

Napoléon House, 500 Chartres St. (☎ **504/524-9752**), at the corner of St. Louis Street, would have been the house of the great dictator if a wild plan had been achieved—that is, of kidnapping the Little Corporal from his island exile and bringing him to New Orleans. A landmark 1797 building, this place is a hangout for drinking and good times, but also serves food. The specialty is Italian muffuletta, with ham, Genoa salami, pastrami, Swiss cheese, and provolone. There's also a selection of po' boys and freshly made salads, including an especially good Greek salad.

At **Nola,** 534 St. Louis St. (☎ **504/522-6652**), Cajun New Orleans mingles gracefully with Hollywood. Try such intriguing dishes as slow-roasted duck with a sweet and spicy glaze, along with a buttermilk corn pudding; or else a perfectly prepared grilled fresh fish of the day. For a real Louisiana meal, opt for the grilled double cut pork chop with pecan-glazed sweet potatoes and Creole mustard.

NEW ORLEANS AFTER DARK

Life here in "The Big Easy" is conducive to all manners of nighttime entertainment, usually raucous. Visitors reel from club to club in the neighborhoods around Bourbon and St. Louis streets. There's a reason why jazz was born in this town.

THE CLUB & MUSIC SCENE

Jazz aficionados consider **Preservation Hall,** 726 St. Peter St. (☎ **514/523-8939**), the Holy of Holies. It's a world-famous monument devoted to the presentation of jazz in its most pure and elemental form. The hall itself is deliberately shabby, with very few places to sit and no air-conditioning. Nonetheless, the place is usually packed with bodies swaying, clapping, and jiving to the music of great musicians who never believed in leaving New Orleans for greener pastures.

Jazz, blues, and Dixieland pour out of the nostalgia-laden bar and concert hall, **Tipitina's,** 501 Napoleon Ave. (☎ **504/895-8477**).

Pete Fountain, the Dixieland clarinet maestro, is one of the most endearing musical celebrities of New Orleans. After running a Bourbon Street jazz club, he set up shop, with double the space, at **Pete Fountain's** in the plush third-floor interior of the New Orleans Hilton, 2 Poydras St. (☎ **504/561-0500**). If he's not on tour, Fountain usually performs several nights a week.

On a small stage in back of **Fritzel's European Bar & Cuisine,** 733 Bourbon St. (☎ **504/561-0432**), musicians will improvise, boogie, and generally shake, rattle, and roll. Very late at night, musicians from other clubs might hop on stage to jam.

One of our most recent fun nights on the town was at the **Mermaid Lounge,** 1100 Constance St. (☎ **504/524-4747**), in the Warehouse District. Here, anything goes, and music ranges from rockabilly to jazz. It's open Wednesday through Saturday, and sometimes Tuesday night, if the mood strikes. The joint keeps going at least until 2am, but if it's jumping the owners will keep it open later.

House of Blues, 225 Decatur St. (☎ **504/529-1421**), is one of the city's largest and most avant-garde live music venues. You stand and move among the several bars that pepper the club. There's also a restaurant.

Not to be confused with the Old Absinthe House/Tony Moran's Restaurant, **Old Absinthe House Bar,** 400 Bourbon St. (☎ **504/525-8108**), features antique bar fixtures and rock and blues music that attracts energetic fans from throughout Louisiana.

Follow the footsteps of Michael Jordan and U2 to the Victorian Lounge at the **Columns Hotel,** 3811 St. Charles Ave. (☎ **504/899-9308**), and try one of the staff's justly celebrated made-from-scratch Bloody Marys. A young local crowd is attracted to this bar on the fringe of the Garden District, where a jazz trio entertains on Tuesday nights.

At **Palm Court Café,** 1204 Decatur St. (☎ **504/525-0200**), you'll find an equal appreciation of good jazz and international food.

Chris Owens Club, 500 Bourbon St. (☎ **504/523-6400**), is a one-woman cabaret act. Mistress of ceremonies Ms. Owens sings, Las Vegas–style, along with whatever band happens to be accompanying her that night. Jazz legend Al Hirt performs here between two and four nights a week. On nights when Ms. Owens is indisposed, the venue becomes a dance club.

One block beyond Esplanade, on the periphery of the French Quarter, **Snug Harbor,** 626 Frenchman St. (☎ **504/949-0696**), is a jazz bistro, a classic spot to hear modern jazz in a cozy setting. Sometimes R&B combos and blues are added to the program. There's a full dinner menu as well.

Ready to rock and bowl? Check out **Mid-City Lanes Rock and Bowl,** 4133 S. Carrollton Ave. (☎ **504/482-3133**), where you can bowl and drink during the day, and continue at night, when rock bands perform. This unconventional bowling alley is tucked within a battered strip mall on Carrollton Avenue between Tulane Avenue and Ulloa Street.

Established in 1933, the quite touristy **Pat O'Brien's,** 718 St. Peter St. (☎ **504/ 525-4823**), is famous for its twin piano players, raucous high jinx, live comedians and singers, and gargantuan Hurricanes—potent rum-based libations. There's also an outdoor courtyard.

Lafitte's Blacksmith Shop, 941 Bourbon St. (☎ **504/523-0066**), is a French Quarter pub housed in an 18th-century Creole house. Tennessee Williams used to hang out here.

Vaughan's Lounge, 800 Lesseps St. (☎ **504/947-5562**), is a genuine New Orleans joint. Owner Kermit Ruffins will sometimes offer a barbecue out back. As one local patron said, "It's the best choice for live music and beans and rice." The lounge is in a residential part of the Bywater section.

If it's good ol' brass Dixieland jazz you seek, look no further than **Donna's,** 800 N. Rampart St. (☎ **504/596-6914**). This joint is often packed, especially for the more famous acts—the Marsalis family has been known to play here from time to time—so don't expect to get a seat. But don't let that stop you, either. The shows are loaded with raw energy. There's no better place to hear that authentic sound that made New Orleans famous. Cover varies, but is usually no more than a good mixed drink. When the small kitchen's open, it cooks up typical New Orleans dishes like po' boys and red beans and rice.

THE PERFORMING ARTS

The major concert halls for the presentation of opera, ballet, and symphonies include the **Mahalia Jackson Theater of the Performing Arts,** 801 N. Rampart St. (☎ **504/565-7470**), the **Contemporary Arts Center,** 900 Camp St. (☎ **504/523-1216**), and **Le Petit Théatre du Vieux Carré,** 616 St. Peter St. (☎ **504/522-2081**).

The Louisiana Philharmonic Orchestra (☎ **504/523-6530**), plays in parks and gardens throughout the city, as well as at the **Saenger Performing Arts Center,** 143 N. Rampart St. (☎ **504/525-1052**) and the **Orpheum Theater,** University Place (☎ **504/565-3680**). The **Southern Repertory Theater,** 3rd Level, Canal Place, 333 Canal St. (☎ **504/861-8163**), specializes in plays by local and southern writers. More avant-garde are the productions at the **Theatre Marigny,** 616 Frenchmen St. (☎ **504/944-2653**), just outside the borders of the French Quarter.

6 San Juan & the Port of San Juan

Navigators have recognized the strategic importance of the *Isleta de San Juan* since the days of the earliest Spanish colonization of Puerto Rico. The deepwater San Antonio Channel, which separates the southern shore of Old San Juan from the northern coast of Isla Grande, shelters the biggest megaships in the cruise industry from tropical storms, thanks to frequent dredgings and a decades-long buildup of cement wharves and piers on either side.

San Juan doesn't handle the sheer volume of Miami, but it's still the number-one cruise ship port in the Caribbean. The facilities here have recently received a $90 million upgrade, with more millions to be spent. For many cruisers, San Juan will be either their port of embarkation or a port of call. (We've covered San Juan as a port of call in chapter 3.)

Cruise ships in Puerto Rico dock on the historic south shore of Old San Juan, within the sheltered channel that was hotly contested by European powers during the island's early colonial days. As of this writing, there are eight piers, each within a short walk of the Plaza de la Marina, the Wyndham Hotel, Old San Juan's main Bus station, and most of the historic and commercial treasures of Old San Juan. Piers no. 1, 3 and 4 are the most popular and the newest or most recently remodeled. Piers no. 5, 7, and 8 are currently either out of service or being remodelled. Pier no. 6 has an odd design, parallel to the shore, and is less popular. Pier no. 2 is reserved for ferryboats that make frequent runs across the San Antonio Channel to Cataño, site of the Bacardi rum distillery, and Hato Rey, the country's financial district.

During periods of heavy volume—usually Saturday and Sunday in midwinter, when as many as 10 cruise ships might dock in San Juan on the same day—additional, less convenient piers are activated. These include the Frontier Pier, at the western edge of the Condado, near the Caribe Hilton Hotel, and the Pan American Dock, in Isla Grande, across the San Antonio Channel from Old San Juan. Passengers berthing at either of these docks need some kind of motorized transit (usually a taxi or a van provided by the cruise line as part of the shore excursion program) to get to the Old Town.

Cruise lines that sail from San Juan include Carnival, Celebrity, Norwegian Cruise Line, Princess, and Royal Caribbean International. Windjammer's sail-powered *Legacy* makes circular 1-week jaunts through Puerto Rico's offshore islands of Veiques and Culebra, as well as the British and U.S. Virgin Islands.

For information about the port, contact the Port of San Juan, P.O. 362829, San Juan, Puerto Rico 00936-2829 (☎ **787/723-2260**).

GETTING TO SAN JUAN & THE PORT

BY AIR   Visitors from overseas arrive at **Luis Muñoz Marín International Airport** (☎ **787/791-1014**), situated on the city's easternmost side. It's about 7¹/₂ miles from the port.

Taxis will be lined up outside the airport. The fixed fare is $8 to Isla Verde, $12 to Condado, and $16 to Old San Juan (including the port). The ride to the port takes about 30 minutes, depending on traffic conditions.

Renting a Car   The major car-rental companies include **Avis** (☎ **800/331-1212** or 787/791-2500); **Budget** (☎ **800/527-0700** or 787/791-3685); and **Hertz** (☎ **800/654-3131** or 787/791-0840).

Parking at the Port   Parking facilities at the port are extremely inconvenient and severely limited. If you rent a car, you must return the vehicle before you embark upon a cruise.

EXPLORING SAN JUAN

Since San Juan is a major port of call, we've covered it in chapter 3, so refer to the San Juan section there for detailed sightseeing, gambling, shopping, and restaurant information. Here we suggest where to stay and what to do after dark.

ESSENTIALS

VISITOR INFORMATION   For information before you leave home, contact one of the **Puerto Rico Tourism Company** offices: 575 Fifth Ave., New York, NY 10017 (☎ **800/223-6530** or 212/599-6262); 3575 W. Cahuenga Blvd., Suite 405, Los Angeles, CA 90068 (☎ **800/874-1230** or 213/874-5991); or 901 Ponce de León Blvd., Suite 604, Coral Gables, FL 33134 (☎ **800/815/7391** or 305/445-9112). In Canada call (☎ **800/667-0394** or 416/368-2680); or write 41-43 Colbourne St., Suite 301, Toronto, Ontario M5E 1E3.

WHERE TO STAY

At long last, cruise-ship passengers who want to stay in Old San Juan have an acceptable hotel. The **El Convento,** 100 Cristo St. (☎ **800/468-2779** or 787/723-9020), Puerto Rico's most famous (but not its best) hotel, has bounced back. The 1997 rejuvenation of this venerable structure, originally built as a Carmelite convent in the 1600's, cost about $275,000 per room. El Convento offers commodious accommodations on its third to fifth floors, often with views of the old town.

Those who prefer to be as close as possible to the cruise-ship docks should opt for **Wyndham Old San Juan Hotel & Casino,** 100 Brumbaugh St. (☎ **800/996-3426** or 787/721-5100), a nine-story waterfront property which opened in 1997. It was conceived as part of a $100 million renovation of San Juan cruise port facilities. Bedrooms are tasteful and comfortable, and Old San Juan is at your doorstep.

If you'd like your Old Town nest to be a bit funkier and more offbeat, opt for the **Gallery Inn at Galería San Juan,** Calle Norzagaray 204-206 (☎ **787/722-1808**), set on a hilltop with a sweeping view of the sea. A maze of verdant courtyards, this former 1700s home of an aristocratic Spanish family is now a whimsically bohemian hotel, with comfortable and tasteful rooms (although lacking air-conditioning). There's also an on-site artists' studio here.

In Puerto de Tierra, the **Caribe Hilton,** Calle Los Rosales (☎ **800/HILTONS** in the U.S. or Canada, or 787/721-0303), stands near the old Fort San Jerónimo, close to the walled city of San Juan. You can walk to the 16th-century fort or spend the day on a tour of Old San Juan, then come back and enjoy the beach and swimming cove.

Geared to the upscale business traveler, **Radisson Normandie,** Avenida Muñoz-Rivera at the corner of calle Los Rosales (☎ **800/333-3333** in the U.S., or 787/729-2929), is built in the shape of the famous French oceanliner, the *Normandie.* The hotel lies only 5 minutes from Old San Juan, and its beachside setting adjoins the noted Sixto Escobar Stadium. The elegant and elaborate rooms are well furnished with amenities.

In Condado, an area filled with high-rise hotels, restaurants, and nightclubs, the ✪ **Condado Plaza Hotel & Casino,** 999 Ashford Ave. (☎ **800/468-8588** in the U.S., or 787/721-1000), is one of Puerto Rico's busiest hotels. It has more style and flair than the Hilton, and is also more visible, set on a strip of beachfront at the beginning of the Condado. All rooms have private terraces. Deluxe rooms are in the Plaza Club.

Radisson Ambassador Hotel & Casino, 1369 Ashford Ave. (☎ **800/468-8512** in the U.S., or 787/721-7300), is a star-studded hotel with big-time pizzazz, but no

San Juan at a Glance

Puerto Rico

San Juan

Condado area **7**
El Morro Fortress **1**
Isla Grande Airport **6**
Isla Verde area **11**
Luís Muñoz Marín
  International
  Airport **12**
Miramar area **8**
Ocean Park **10**
Old San Juan area **4**
Piers **3**
Puerta de Tierra **5**
Santurce area **9**
Tourist Information
  Center, La Casita **2**

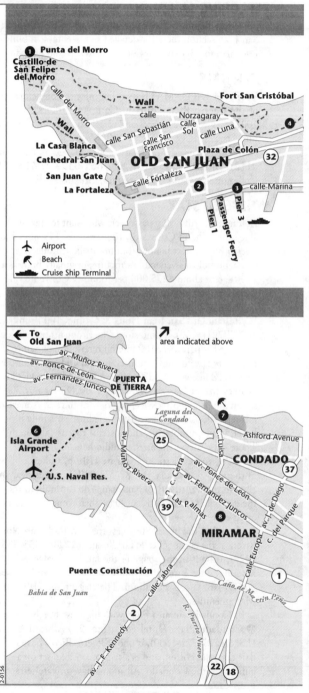

1 Punta del Morro

Castillo de
San Felipe
del Morro

calle del Morro

Wall

Fort San Cristóbal

Wall

calle

Norzagaray
calle
Sol

calle Luna

4

calle San Sebastián

La Casa Blanca

Cathedral San Juan

San Juan Gate

La Fortaleza

calle San
Francisco

OLD SAN JUAN

Plaza de Colón

32

calle Fortaleza

2

3

calle Marina

Pier 1

Pier 3

Passenger Ferry

✈ Airport
🏖 Beach
🚢 Cruise Ship Terminal

← To
Old San Juan

↗ area indicated above

av. Muñoz Rivera
av. Ponce de León
av. Fernández-Juncos

**PUERTA
DE TIERRA**

Laguna del
Condado

7

Ashford Avenue

6
Isla Grande
Airport
✈

U.S. Naval Res.

c. Luisa

25

av. Muñoz Rivera

c. Cerra

av. Ponce de León

av. Fernández-Juncos

CONDADO

av. J. de Diego

37

39

c. Las Palmas

8

MIRAMAR

calle Europa

c. del Parque

Puente Constitución

Caño de Martín Peña

1

Bahía de San Juan

2

calle Labra

R. Puerto Nuevo

av. J. F. Kennedy

22 **18**

2-0156

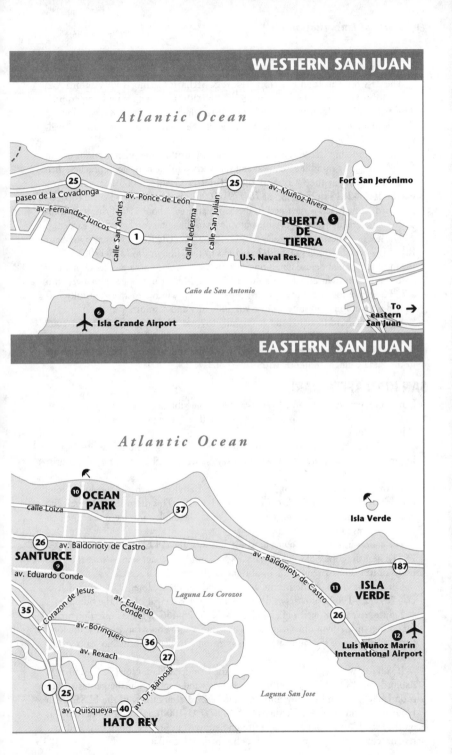

Atlantic Ocean

paseo de la Covadonga

(25)

av. Ponce de León

(25)

av. Muñoz Rivera

Fort San Jerónimo

av. Fernandez Juncos

calle San Andres

calle Ledesma

calle San Julian

(1)

PUERTA
DE
TIERRA ⑤

U.S. Naval Res.

Caño de San Antonio

To →
eastern
San Juan

✈ ⑥ Isla Grande Airport

Atlantic Ocean

⑩ OCEAN
PARK

calle Loiza

(37)

Isla Verde

(26)

av. Baldorioty de Castro

SANTURCE
⑨

av. Eduardo Conde

av. Baldorioty de Castro

(187)

⑪ ISLA
VERDE

c. Corazon de Jesus

(35)

av. Eduardo
Conde

Laguna Los Corozos

(26)

av. Borinquen

(36)

✈ ⑫
Luis Muñoz Marín
International Airport

av. Rexach

(27)

(1) (25)

av. Quisqueya (40)

av. Dr. Barbosa

HATO REY

Laguna San Jose

59

resort amenities. Accommodations are in a pair of high-rise towers, one of which is devoted to suites. Each unit has a balcony.

The 21-story **San Juan Marriott Resort & Stellaris Casino,** 1309 Ashford Ave. (☎ **800/981-8546** in the U.S., or 787/722-7000), is the tallest building around. This new entity, rebuilt after a tragic fire gutted the premises in 1989, was done in the postmodern style. One of the best beaches on the Condado lies right outside. Bedrooms are comfortable but bland.

Beach-bordering Isla Verde is closer to the airport than the other sections of San Juan. If you don't mind the isolation and want access to the fairly good beaches, then consider staying at the ✪ **El San Juan Hotel & Casino,** 6063 Isla Verde Ave. (☎ **800/468-2818** in the U.S., or 787/791-1000), the best hotel in Puerto Rico. Its 700-yard sandy beach is the finest in the San Juan area. About 150 of the accommodations are designed as comfortable bungalows in the outer reaches of the garden.

The hot hotel news in Puerto Rico is the opening of **The Ritz-Carlton,** 6961 State Rd., #187 on Isla Verde (☎ **800/241-3333** in the U.S., or 787/253-1700), one of the most spectacular deluxe hotels on the island, in a neck-to-neck race for supremacy with the El San Juan Hotel (see above). It's a trail-blazer in tropical elegance, with a 7,200 square foot pool overlooking a prime white sandy beach. Beautifully furnished guest rooms and suites encase you in luxury and comfort.

San Juan Grand Beach Hotel & Casino, 187 Isla Verde Ave. (☎ **800/443-2009** in the U.S., or 787/791-6100), is a Caribbean version of the Sands Hotel in Atlantic City. Bedrooms are comfortable, with balconies and terraces. The best rooms are in the Plaza Club, a minihotel within the hotel.

SAN JUAN AFTER DARK

San Juan nightlife comes in all varieties. From the vibrant performing-arts scene to street-level salsa or the casinos, discos, and bars, there's plenty of entertainment available almost any evening.

Qué Pasa, the official visitors' guide to Puerto Rico, lists cultural events, including music, dance, theater, film, and art exhibits. It's distributed free by the tourist office.

If you want to dance the night away, try the **Babylon,** in the El San Juan Hotel & Casino, 6063 Isla Verde Ave. (☎ **787/791-1000**). This disco attracts a rich and beautiful crowd, as well as a gaggle of onlookers. The duplex area has one of the best sound systems in the Caribbean.

For action in the Old Town, head for **Laser,** Calle del Cruz 251 ☎ 787/725-7581), near the corner of Calle Fortaleza. Once inside, you can wander over the three floors of its historic premises. Salsa and merengue are often featured.

On the Condado, **Millennium,** in the Condado Plaza Hotel, 999 Ashford Ave. (☎ **787/722-1900**), also draws disco devotees. It has a cigar bar on the side.

Egipto, Avenida Roberto H. Todd 1 (☎ **787/725-4664**), is the busiest nightclub for young, upwardly mobile singles. Many visitors come only for drinks at the long bar. Usually one of the club's two floors is devoted to Latin music. No jeans are allowed.

If you just want a drink, **Fiesta Bar,** in the Condado Plaza Hotel & Casino, 999 Ashford Ave. (☎ **787/721-1000**), attracts locals and visitors. The margaritas are appropriately salty, and the rhythms hot and Latin. **Palm Court,** in the El San Juan Hotel & Casino, 6063 Isla Verde Ave. (☎ **787/791-1000**), is the most beautiful bar on the island. After 9pm Monday through Saturday, live music, often salsa and merengue, emanates from an adjoining room, the El Chico Bar.

At **Shannon's Irish Pub,** Calle Bori 496, Rio Peidras (☎ **787/281-8466**), Ireland gets tropicalized with a Latin accent. This pub is the regular watering hole for university students. There are pool tables and a simple cafe serving inexpensive fare daily from 11:30am to 11pm.

Stylish and comfortable, **Violeta's,** calle Fortaleza 56 (☎ **787/723-6804**), occupies the ground floor of a 200-year-old beamed house two blocks from the landmark Gran Hotel Convento (see above). An open courtyard in back provides additional seating. Margaritas are the drink of choice at this bar.

The Barefoot Bar, 2 Calle Vendig on the Condado (☎ **787/724-7230**), is the most tuned-in gay bar in Puerto Rico. At least 98% of its clientele is gay and male. Across the street is its major rival, **The Beach Bar,** in the Atlantic Beach Hotel, 1 Calle Vendig (☎ **787/721-6900**) It features an outdoor terrace stretching over the sands of the beach.

Major cultural venues include **Centro de Bellas Artes,** Avenida Ponce de León 22 (☎ **787/724-4747** or 787/725-7334), with 1,883 seats in the Festival Hall, 760 in the Drama Hall, and 210 in the Experimental Theater. Standing across from the Plaza de Colón is **Teatro Tapía,** Avenida Ponce de León (☎ **787/723-2079**), built about 1832.

3 The Ports of Call

So you're about to go ashore. In this chapter, you'll find detailed coverage and insider advice about each port and island.

If you arrive at a port of call and find a harbor filled with ships, expect the shops, restaurants, beaches, or whatever, to be crowded. You may want to call a restaurant from the pier and reserve a table.

If you decide to explore an island on your own, you should always make car-rental arrangements in advance, especially during the popular winter months. Your ride will still be bumpy on most Caribbean roads, but at least you'll be at the wheel deciding where you want to go. You can always cut costs by forming a carpool with other passengers.

If you want to do something special like take a submarine ride or go horseback riding, talk with your cruise-ship director or some other knowledgeable official aboard ship before you land. Many sports activities should be reserved in advance, since a program might not be available if you just walk in and announce that's what you'd like to do. For example, St. Thomas has only one golf course, which could easily get filled if 10 ships arrive in port that day (as often happens). That's not even counting the other vacationers on the island who also want to play golf.

Or you may prefer to spend whatever time you have on land lying on the beach, soaking up the Caribbean sun. Taxi drivers meet all cruise ships and will take you to the beach you've selected. It's a good idea to arrange a pickup time with the driver to bring you back to your ship.

Finally, you may want to call home from public telephones at any port of call, because phone calls will be much cheaper than shipboard phone calls, which are extremely expensive.

Rating the Ports of Call

We've rated each port of call, and here's what each anchor means.

⚓ ⚓ ⚓ ⚓ ⚓	The Best in the Caribbean
⚓ ⚓ ⚓ ⚓	A Close Runner-Up of Wide Appeal
⚓ ⚓ ⚓	Lots to See & Do, Good Shopping
⚓ ⚓	Minor Attractions, Limited Shopping
⚓	Stay on Board

1 Antigua ⚓ ⚓ ⚓

Rolling, rustic Antigua (An-*tee*-gah) claims to have a different beach for every day of the year. This may be an exaggeration, but its numerous sugary-white, reef-protected beaches are reason enough to visit, even if just for a day. Antigua is also known for its English Harbour, home of Nelson Dockyard National Park, one of the Caribbean's major historical attractions.

English sugarcane planters settled on the island in 1623, and English Harbour was the Royal Navy's major base in the Western Hemisphere during colonial times. The dockyard is named for Admiral Horatio Nelson, who was in command here in the 1780s.

Antigua and its neighbors—Barbuda (not to be confused with Barbados) and little Redonda—today form the independent nation of Antigua and Barbuda. Despite independence, however, Antigua remains British in many of its traditions.

Sleepy, tattered St. John's, the capital, has seen better days. It's a large, neatly laid out town, 6 miles from the airport and less than a mile from Deep Water Harbour Terminal. Protected in the throat of a narrow bay, the town is full of cobblestone sidewalks, weather-beaten wooden houses, corrugated iron roofs, and louvered Caribbean verandas. The streets were built wide to let the trade winds keep them cooler. The port is the focal point of commerce, industry, and government, as well as visitor shopping.

COMING ASHORE

Only smaller ships anchor directly at English Harbour; everyone else reaches it via taxi or shore excursion from Deep Water Harbour Terminal in St. John's, the island's capital. Passengers landing here can head directly to the nearby duty-free shopping centers, Heritage Quay (pronounced *Key*) and Redcliffe Quay. You don't need a guide to walk around this sleepy town, less than a mile from the pier (see "Seeing the Sights" and "Shopping," below). Credit-card phones are located on the dock.

FAST FACTS

Currency   The **Eastern Caribbean dollar** (EC$), worth about 37¢ in U.S. currency ($1 U.S. = EC$2.70), is used on these islands; however, you'll find that nearly all prices, except those in certain tiny restaurants, are given in U.S. dollars. It's always a good idea to ask if you're not sure. Unless otherwise specified, rates quoted in this section are given in U.S. dollars.

Information   Head to the Antigua and Barbuda Department of Tourism at Long and Thames streets in St. John's (% 268/462-0480). Don't expect the staff here to tell you very much more than the basics. Open Monday to Thursday from 8am to 4:30pm and Friday from 8am to 3pm.

Language   The official language is English.

SHORE EXCURSIONS

Since we don't recommend renting a car here, it's best to take the ship's shore excursions, which are less expensive than hiring a private taxi (see "Getting Around," below). The major excursion is to Nelson's Dockyard and Clarence House at English Harbour. On the way you'll get to view some of the island's lush countryside. Most shore excursions offered by the cruise lines cost anywhere from $30 to $60, depending on the line, and last 3 hours. That will still leave you plenty of time in the day for shopping or hitting the beach.

GETTING AROUND

BUS   Buses are cheap, but we don't recommend them for the average visitor. Officially, they operate between St. John's and the villages daily from 5:30am to 6pm, but don't count on it. In St. John's, buses leave from the West Bus Station for Falmouth and English Harbour, and from the East Bus Station to other parts of the island. Most fares are $1.

CAR RENTALS   We don't recommend renting a car here, since the roads are seriously potholed and local taxi drivers remove the signs. You could get hopelessly lost. You also **drive on the left** here (a holdover from British colonial days), and there's always the temptation to have one piña colada too many. Hire a taxi to see the sights, or take a shore excursion, which is the cheaper option.

If you insist on driving, you need an Antiguan driver's license, which costs $12 (most car-rental agencies will issue them without charge). To get one, you must produce a valid driver's license from home.

Several car-rental agencies operate on Antigua, many of them precariously financed local operations with cars best described as "battered." **Avis** (☎ **800/331-1212** in the U.S.) and **Hertz** (☎ **800/654-3131** in the U.S.) both offer pickup service at the cruise dock. Advance reservations are required. If you're calling well in advance, you might try **Auto Europe** (☎ **800/223-5555**) or **Kenwel Holiday Autos** (☎ **800/ 678-0678**).

TAXIS   Taxis meet every cruise ship. The one-way fare from the airport to English Harbour is an expensive $25 and up. The taxis don't have meters; although the government fixes the rates, it's always wise to negotiate the fare before getting in. The best way to see Antigua is by private taxi, since the drivers are also guides. Most taxi tours cost $16 and up per hour.

SEEING THE SIGHTS

If you don't want to go to English Harbour, you can stay in St. John's to shop and explore. All of its minor attractions can be reached on foot from the cruise-ship dock. The people in town may impress you, if not the town itself. They're helpful, have a sense of humor, and will guide you in the right direction if you've lost your way.

ST. JOHN'S

The **market** in the southern part of St. John's is colorful and interesting, especially on Saturday morning, when vendors are busy selling their fruits and vegetables and gossiping. The partially open-air market lies at the lower end of Market Street.

The Anglican **St. John's Cathedral,** between Long Street and Newgate Street at Church Lane (☎ **268/462-4686**), has had a disastrous history. Originally built in 1683, it was replaced in 1745 by a stone structure, which was destroyed by an earthquake in 1843. The present pitch-pine interior dates from 1847. The interior was being restored in 1973 when another earthquake badly damaged the twin towers. The towers and the southern section have since been restored.

The **Museum of Antigua and Barbuda,** at Market and Church streets (☎ **268/ 462-1469**), traces the history of the nation from its geological birth to the present day. Housed in the old Court House building dating from 1750, exhibits include a wattle-and-daub house model, African-Caribbean pottery, and utilitarian objects of daily life. It's open Monday to Friday from 8:30am to 4pm, Saturday from 10am to 1pm. Admission is free.

The 3¹/₂-acre **Antigua and Barbuda Botanical Gardens,** at the corner of Nevis and Temple streets (☎ **268/462-1007**), was established in 1893 in the Green Belt

Airport ✈   Beach 🏖   Mountain ⛰

0 ▭▭▭▭ 5 km / 3 mi

N

2-0189

of the capital. As you enter, you can't miss the unfolding majesty of an 80-year-old ficus tree, contrasting sharply with the rolling lawns. The melodic sounds of tree frogs and birds emanate from the rain forest hollow, which is filled with trees draped with lianas. Ferns, tropical blossoms, herbal plants, dripping philodendrons, rare bromeliads, and a colorful carpet of flowers also await the visitor. Open daily from 9am to 6pm. Admission is by a minimum donation of $2.

AROUND THE ISLAND

✪ **Nelson's Dockyard National Park.** 11 miles southeast of St. John's. ☎ **268/460-1379.**

One of the major attractions of the eastern Caribbean, Nelson's Dockyard sits on one of the world's safest harbors. This centerpiece of the national park is the only existing example of a Georgian naval base. English ships used the harbor as a refuge from hurricanes as early as 1671, and Admiral Nelson made it his headquarters from 1784 to 1787. The dockyard played a leading role in the era of privateers, pirates, and great sea battles in the 18th century.

The restored dockyard is sometimes known as a Caribbean Williamsburg. Its colonial naval buildings stand now as they did when Nelson was here. He never lived at **Admiral House** (☎ **268/463-1379**), however, which was built in 1855. The house has been turned into a museum of nautical memorabilia. Hours are 8am to 6pm, and admission is $2.

The park itself is well worth exploring. It's filled with sandy beaches and tropical vegetation, including various species of cactus and mangroves that shelter a migrating colony of African cattle egrets. Nature trails expose the vegetation and coastal scenery. You'll also find archeological sites that date back to before the Christian era. Tours of the dockyard last 15 to 20 minutes, whereas tours along nature trails can last anywhere from 30 minutes to 5 hours. The cost is $5 per person to tour the dockyard; children under 13 are admitted free. The nature trail costs another $2.50. The dockyard and its museum are open daily from 8am to 6pm.

Dow's Hill Interpretation Center, 2½ miles east of English Harbour (☎ 268/460-1053), offers a multimedia journey through six periods of the island's history. You'll learn about the Amerindian hunters, the British military, and the struggles connected with slavery. A belvedere provides a panoramic view of the park. Admission, including the multimedia show, is $5 for adults, $2 for children under 16. The center is open daily from 9am to 5pm. It's best reached by taxi from English Harbour.

A footpath leads to **Fort Barclay,** a fine specimen of old-time military engineering at the entrance to English Harbour. The path starts just outside the dockyard gate; the fort is about half a mile away.

For an eagle's eye view of English Harbour, take a taxi up to the top of **Shirley Heights,** directly to the east of the dockyard. Still standing are Palladian arches, once part of a barracks. The **Block House** was put up as a stronghold in case of siege. The nearby Victorian cemetery contains an obelisk monument to the men of the 54th Regiment.

On a low hill overlooking Nelson's Dockyard, **Clarence House** (☎ 268/463-1026) was built by English stonemasons to accommodate Prince William Henry, who later became King William IV. The future monarch stayed here while in command of HMS *Pegasus* in 1787. The house is at present the country home of the governor of Antigua and Barbuda, and is open to visitors when His Excellency is not in residence. A caretaker will show you through (it's customary to tip). You'll see many pieces of furniture on loan from the National Trust. Princess Margaret and Lord Snowdon stayed here on their honeymoon.

Harmony Hall, in Brown's Bay Mill, near Freetown (☎ 268/460-4120), overlooks Nonsuch Bay. This partially restored plantation house and sugar mill, dating to 1843, makes an ideal lunch stopover or shopping expedition. It displays Antigua's best selection of Caribbean arts and crafts, and in November hosts the annual Caribbean Craft Fair. Lunch, served daily from noon to 4pm, features Green Island lobster, flying fish, and other specialties. Sunday is barbecue day. The entire complex is open daily from 10am to 6pm. To get there, follow the signs along the road to Freetown and Half Moon Bay. It's a 40-minute taxi ride from St. John's. You'll have to negotiate the fare, which can range from $20 to $30. The place is special and worth the effort to reach it.

SHOPPING

Most shops in St. John's are clustered on St. Mary's Street or High Street, lying within an easy walk of the cruise ship docks. There are many duty-free items for sale here, including English woolens and linens. You can also purchase Antiguan specialties, such as original pottery, local straw work, Antigua rum, hand-printed local designs on fabrics, mammy bags, floppy foldable hats, and shell curios.

If you want an island-made **bead necklace,** don't bother to go shopping; just lie on any beach and a "bead lady" will find you.

SPECIALTY SHOPS

Caribelle Batik. Redcliffe St., St. John's. ☎ 268/462-2972.

This shop is an outlet for the Romney Manor workshop on St. Kitts. The Caribelle label consists of batik and tie-dye items such as beach wraps, scarves, and a range of

⭐ A Favorite Experience: A Scenic Drive

On the way back to your cruise ship from English Harbour, ask your taxi driver to take you along **Fig Tree Drive.** Although rough and very potholed in places, this 20-some-mile circular route across the main mountain range of Antigua is the island's most scenic drive. Some of the steep hillsides are so lush they evoke a rain forest. The drive passes through tropical settings and fishing villages along the southern coast. Nearly every hamlet has a little battered church and lots of goats and children running about. There are also the ruins of several old sugar mills. However, don't expect fig trees—*fig* is the Antiguan word for bananas.

casual wear for both men and women. You'll also find silk dresses and separates in Caribbean colors from the Sensual Silk label. Accessories such as jewelry and scarves are available as well.

Island Hopper. Jardine Court, St. Mary's St., St. John's. ☎ **268/462-2972.**

This shop has a range of gifts and clothing, mainly products made in the Caribbean. The owner goes to some trouble to provide items not readily available elsewhere. The range is wide—T-shirts, spices, coffees, handcrafts, and casual wear.

The Scent Shop. Lower High St., St. John's. ☎ **268/462-0303.**

Although it doesn't aggressively advertise, this is the island's oldest perfume shop, with a loyal clientele. You'll find an array of crystal (Baccarat, Lalique, and Waterford), but the bulk of the store's income comes from exotic perfumes, some of which are not sold elsewhere on Antigua.

Shoul's Chief Store. St. Mary's St. at Market St., St. John's. ☎ **268/462-1140.**

The origins of this all-purpose department store date from the 19th century. It's one of the largest emporiums of fabric, electrical appliances, souvenir items (more than 300 kinds) and general merchandise in Antigua. Many of the customers are local elderly women, whose sewing machines were originally purchased and subsequently repaired here.

SHOPPING CENTERS

HERITAGE QUAY   Located at the cruise dock, Antigua's first shopping-and-entertainment center is a multimillion-dollar complex, featuring some 40 duty-free shops and a vendors' arcade where local artists and craftspeople display their wares. Restaurants offer a range of cuisine and views of St. John's Harbour. A food court serves visitors who prefer local specialties in an informal setting.

Island Arts (☎ 268/462-2787) was founded by Nick Maley, a makeup artist who worked on *Star Wars* and *The Empire Strikes Back*. You can purchase one of his own fine art reproductions, including the provocative *Windkissed & Sunswept*. Items for sale include everything from low-cost prints to works by artists exhibited in New York's Museum of Modern Art.

Little Switzerland (☎ 268/462-3108) is a name familiar to frequent travelers to the Caribbean. It sells Royal Doulton and Baccarat china and crystal and the best selection of Swiss-made watches. There's also a perfume shop in Heritage Quay called **La Perfumery by Little Switzerland** (☎ 268/462-2601).

Sunsneakers (☎ 268/462-4523) has one of the largest selections of swimwear in the Caribbean. It accommodates clients of all sizes, with such brand names as Gottex, Jantzen, La Perla, Speedo, and Coles of California.

REDCLIFFE QUAY   Near Heritage Quay, this historic complex is one of the best centers for shopping and dining in St. John's. Redcliffe Quay was a slave-trading quarter that filled up with grog shops and a variety of merchants after abolition. Now it has been redeveloped and contains a number of the most interesting shops in town, some in former warehouses.

A Thousand Flowers (☎ 268/462-4264) sells Indonesian batiks crafted on the island into sundresses, knock-'em-dead shirts, sarongs, and rompers, and also various accessories, such as necklaces and earrings. Many of the garments are designed in a one-size-fits-all flowing expanses of cloth, appropriate for the tropics.

Base (☎ 268/462-0920), the brainchild of English designer Steven Giles, is one of the best-known companies in the Caribbean. It carries an intriguing line of casual comfort clothing in stripes, colors, and prints, all made here at the company's world headquarters. Their cotton and Lycra beachwear is especially popular. Prices are very reasonable.

The Goldsmitty (☎ 268/462-4601) presents jewelry designs by the well-known Hans Smit. Everything is designed and made on the premises. You'll find black opal, imperial topaz, and other exotic gemstones set in exquisite, often one-of-a-kind, creations of 14- and 18-karat gold.

Jacaranda (☎ 268/462-1888) tempts you with the art of John Woodland or the place mats and prints of Jill Walker. The shop also stocks local clothing, works by local artists, herbs, and spices, as well as gels, soaps, and bath salts.

Noreen Phillips (☎ 268/462-3127) is one of the island's major fashion outlets, taking inspiration for its clothing from the colors of the sea and sunsets on Antigua. Cruise-ship passengers seek out this shop particularly, both for its casual wear and for its dressy styles. Some items are beaded with glitzy appliqué, not for everyone's taste, but a favorite at those captain's cocktail parties nonetheless.

BEACHES

Antigua is beaches, beaches, and more beaches. Some are superior, and all are public. There's a lovely one at **Pigeon Point,** in Falmouth Harbour, about a 4-minute taxi ride from Admiral's Inn. The fine beach at **Dickenson Bay,** near the Rex Halcyon Cove Hotel, is a center for water sports; for a break, you can enjoy over-the-water meals and drinks on the hotel's Warri Pier.

There are more beaches at the Curtain Bluff resort, where long **Carlisle Beach** is set against a backdrop of coconut palms. **Morris Bay** attracts snorkelers. The beach at **Long Bay** is on the somewhat remote eastern coast, but most visitors consider it worth the effort. The famous **Half Moon Bay** attracts aristocratic "blue bloods" to its mile-long stretch of sand. **Runaway Beach** is one of Antigua's most popular; its white sands make it worth fighting the crowds. **Five Islands** is actually a quartet of remote beaches with brown sands and coral reefs, located near the Hawksbill Hotel.

Warning: It's unwise to have your fun in the sun at what appears to be a deserted beach. You could be the victim of a mugging. Also, readers increasingly complain of beach vendors hustling everything from jewelry to T-shirts. The beaches are open to all, so hotels can't restrain these bothersome peddlers.

Taxis will take you from the cruise ship dock in St. John's to your choice of beach. But remember to make arrangements to be picked up at an agreed-upon time. A typical fare to Pigeon Point or Long Bay, both about 15 miles (25 minutes) from St. John's, is $20 per car. To Runaway, a distance of only 3 miles (5 minutes), the charge is $8 per car. For Five Islands, 6 miles or 10 minutes away, the fare is $12. Confirm all fares with the driver before setting out.

GOLF, SAILING, DIVING, TENNIS & WINDSURFING

GOLF   The 18-hole, par-70 **Cedar Valley Golf Club,** Friar's Hill Road (☎ 268/462-0161), is 3 miles east of St. John's, a 5-minute, $12 taxi ride from the cruise dock. The island's largest golf course, with panoramic views of Antigua's northern coast, it was designed by the late Richard Aldridge to fit the contours of the area. Greens fees are $30 for 18 holes, with club rentals going for $10.

SAILING   Antigua's famous "pirate ship," the *Jolly Roger,* at Redcliffe Quay in St. John's (☎ 268/462-2064), is one of the island's most popular attractions, lying within walking distance of the cruise ship docks. For $60 for adults and $30 for children, you're taken for a fun-filled day of sightseeing, with drinks and barbecued steak, chicken, or lobster. The *Jolly Roger* is the largest sailing ship in Antiguan waters. Lunch is combined with a snorkeling trip, and there's dancing on the poop deck. Members of the crew teach passengers how to dance calypso. The daily cruises depart at 9:30am and return at 3pm.

SCUBA DIVING   Arrange scuba diving through **Dive Antigua,** at the Rex Halcyon Cove, Dickenson Bay (☎ 268/462-3483), Antigua's oldest and most experienced dive operation. Instruction and a boat dive with all equipment costs $85 (compared to $120 on a big cruise line's boats). Dive Antigua is about a 10-minute or $6 taxi ride from the cruise ship dock.

TENNIS   The major resorts have tennis courts. The most convenient is **Rex Halcyon Cove,** at Dickenson Bay (☎ 268/462-0256), which lies a 15-minute or $12 taxi ride from the cruise ship dock. Call from the dock to reserve court time, which costs $10.

WINDSURFING   Located at the Lord Nelson Beach Hotel, on Dutchman's Bay, **Windsurfing Antigua** (☎ 268/462-9463) beckons absolute beginners, intermediates, and "shredders," or hard-core windsurfers. The outlet guarantees to have beginners enjoying the sport after a 2-hour introductory lesson, which costs $45 and includes use of equipment. The center is a $6 or 5-mile ride from the cruise ship dock.

DINING

Most cruise passengers dine either in St. John's or at nearby English Harbour or Shirley Heights. Reservations usually aren't needed for lunch, unless it's a heavy cruise ship arrival day. In that case, call from the dock before leaving.

IN ST. JOHN'S

Big Banana Holding Company. Redcliffe Quay. ☎ 268/462-2621. Reservations not required. Main courses $8–$32. AE, DC, MC, V. Mon–Sat 8:30am–midnight. PIZZA/SANDWICHES/SEAFOOD.

The best pizza on the island is served in what used to be a slave quarters. This establishment is now amid the most stylish shopping and dining area in town. With its ceiling fans and laid-back atmosphere, you almost expect Sydney Greenstreet to stop in for a drink (called "dwinks" on the menu). Frothy coconut or banana crushes are practically desserts in themselves. In addition to the zesty pizza, you can order overstuffed baked potatoes, fresh fruit salad, or conch salad.

Hemingway's. St. Mary's St. ☎ 268/462-2763. Reservations not required. Main courses EC$24–EC$60 ($8.90–$22.20). AE, MC, V. Mon–Sat 8:30am–11pm. WEST INDIAN/INTERNATIONAL.

Close to the cruise docks on the second floor of a building in the heart of St. John's, this charming and bustling cafe attracts a crowd of cruisers and land-based sightseers. It's very busy when a cruise ship docks. From its upper veranda, you can watch pedestrians in the street below and tenders unloading passengers at the landing dock. Menu items include salads, sandwiches, burgers, sautéed filets of fish, pastries, ice cream, and an array of brightly colored tropical drinks. View it more as a "refueling stop" than as a place at which to get top-notch food.

AT ENGLISH HARBOUR

✪ **Admiral's Inn.** In Nelson's Dockyard, English Harbour. ☎ **268/460-1027.** Reservations recommended. Main courses $20–$27. AE, MC, V. Daily 7:30–10am, noon–2:30pm, and 7–9:30pm. Closed Sept to mid-Oct. AMERICAN/CREOLE.

This building was designed in 1785, the year Nelson sailed into the harbor as captain of the HMS *Boreas,* and completed in 1788. Today it's one of the most atmospheric inns in Antigua, set right in the heart of Nelson's Dockyard and loaded with West Indian charm. The hostelry, constructed of weathered brick brought from England as ships' ballast, has a terrace opening onto a centuries-old garden. A tavern atmosphere prevails on the ground floor, with its brick walls, giant ship beams, island-made furniture, decorative copper, boat lanterns, old oil paintings, and wrought-iron chandeliers.

The menu changes every day. The favorite appetizer is pumpkin soup. There's usually a choice of four or five main courses, such as local red snapper, grilled steak, or lobster. The good home-style cooking pleases the inn's loyal fans. Have a drink in the bar, where you can read sailors' names carved in wood more than a century ago. The service is agreeable and the setting heavy on atmosphere.

AT SHIRLEY HEIGHTS

Shirley Heights Lookout. Shirley Heights. ☎ **268/460-1785.** Reservations recommended. Main courses EC$45–EC$65 ($16.65–$24.05). AE, MC, V. Daily 9am–10pm. AMERICAN/SEAFOOD.

This is the best alternative to the Admiral's Inn, justifiably popular with cruise passengers who come more for the view than the food, which can be overcooked. In the 1790s, the building was the lookout station for unfriendly ships heading toward English Harbour, now just a short taxi ride away. Admiral Nelson constructed it to be a powder magazine. Today, this panoramic spot is one of the most romantic on Antigua. Visitors sometimes prefer to be served on the stone battlements below the restaurant, but we'd rather dine under the angled rafters upstairs, where large, old-fashioned windows surround the room on all sides. Specialties include pumpkin soup, grilled lobster in lime butter, garlic-flavored shrimp, and good desserts, such as banana flambé and carrot cake. You can order less expensive hamburgers and sandwiches in the pub downstairs.

AT DICKENSON BAY

Coconut Grove. In the Siboney Beach Club, Dickenson Bay. ☎ **268/462-1538.** Reservations recommended. Main courses $17–$28; lunch $9–$14. AE, MC, V. Daily 5:30–10pm. INTERNATIONAL/SEAFOOD.

This restaurant is one of the best on the island, and certainly the best place outside St. John's for lunch on the beach. It's located in a coconut grove about a 10-minute or $12 taxi ride north of the docks. Sea breezes cool the simple tables, covered by a thatched roof. Each day a tangy soup is prepared fresh from local ingredients. One appetizer is a seafood delight—scallops, shrimp, crab, lobster, and local fish with a mango-and-lime dressing. Main courses include lobster and shrimp dishes, a catch of the day, a vegetarian specialty of the day, T-bone steak, and spicy Cajun chicken. The service, once not a strong feature here, has improved considerably.

2 Aruba ⚓ ⚓ ⚓

Aruba may not be a chic address like St. Barts or Anguilla, but honeymooners, sun worshippers, snorkelers, sailors, and gamblers all find it suits them just fine. Today Aruba is one of the most popular destinations in the Caribbean—so much so that the government has had to call a moratorium on hotel construction. The capital, Oranjestad, isn't a picture-postcard port, but it has glittering casinos, guaranteed sunshine, and one of the Caribbean's finest beaches.

Forget lush vegetation here. With only 17 inches of rainfall annually, Aruba is dry and sunny almost year-round, but trade winds keep the island from becoming unbearably hot. The air is clean and exhilarating, like that of Palm Springs, California. Aruba also lies outside the path of hurricanes that batter islands to the north.

Admittedly, the arid wasteland of the Aruba countryside used to have more charm than it does today. Cactus fences still surround some pastel-washed houses, and the divi-divi trees with their windblown look still stud what's left of the barren countryside. You might even come across an abandoned gold mine. But as the population has grown, the old-time quaintness is largely gone. Aruba today is overbuilt.

That said, many passengers bypass the dull guided excursion around the island, opting instead for an Atlantis submarine tour (see "A Favorite Experience," below), shopping, and, most definitely, heading for the beach. Aruba's white sugar-sand beaches, lined with palm trees and stretching for some 7 miles along the West Coast, are what put the island on the tourist maps.

As you lie on a favorite spot of beach, enjoying daytime 82°F weather, you won't be harassed by vendors peddling wares you don't want, as you would in Jamaica or Antigua. Aruba is also a safer place; chances are you won't get mugged.

COMING ASHORE

Cruise ships arrive at the Aruba Port Authority, a modern terminal with a tourist information booth and the inevitable duty-free shops. From the pier it's just a 5-minute walk to the major shopping districts of downtown Oranjestad. If you opted not to take one of the shore excursions, you can make your way around on your own, allowing some time for Aruba's famous beach in between luncheon stopovers and shopping.

FAST FACTS

Currency   The currency is the **Aruba florin (AFl)**, which is divided into 100 cents. Silver coins are in denominations of 5, 10, 25, and 50 cents and 1 and $2^1/_2$ florins. The 50-cent piece, the square "yotin," is Aruba's best-known coin. The exchange rate is 1.77 AFl to $1 U.S. (1 AFl is worth about 56¢). U.S. dollars, traveler's checks, and major credit cards are widely accepted throughout the island. Unless otherwise stated, prices quoted in this section are in U.S. dollars.

Information   For information, go to the **Aruba Tourism Authority,** 172 L. G. Smith Blvd., Oranjestad (☎ **297/8-21019**). Open Monday to Saturday from 9am to 5pm.

Language   The official language here is Dutch, but nearly everybody speaks English. The language of the street is often Papiamento, a patois. Spanish is also widely spoken.

SHORE EXCURSIONS

Skip the typical countryside tour, which usually lasts 3 hours and averages $25 per person. While it takes in the sights in both town and country, most passengers are eager to get off at the beach or the casino before it's over.

⭐ A Favorite Experience: Submerged Sightseeing

One of the island's most diverting pastimes is an underwater journey on the submarine *Atlantis* (☎ **800/253-0493** or 297/8-36090), a great opportunity for nondivers to witness firsthand the underwater life of a coral reef. Passengers submerge to about 150 feet without ever getting wet. The submarine departs from the Oranjestad harbor front every hour on the hour, Tuesday to Sunday from 10am to 2pm. Each tour includes a 25-minute transit by catamaran to Barcadera Reef, 2 miles southeast of Aruba, a site chosen for its huge variety of underwater flora and fauna. At the reef, participants transfer to the submarine for a 1-hour underwater tour and lecture. The *Atlantis* also glides over an old Danish fishing vessel sunk in 1995 to create a fascinating view for divers and submariners.

Allow 2 hours for the complete experience. The cost is $69 for adults and $32 for children 4 to 16 (no children under 4 are allowed). Advance reservations are essential. The company's offices are at Seaport Village Marina (opposite the Sonesta) in Oranjestad.

Cruise ships can book you on the Atlantis Submarine tour (see "A Favorite Experience," above). As an alternative, you might try a glass-bottom boat tour, which takes you in a 60-passenger vessel to view the extensive marine life around the island's coast. This tour costs $33 per person and lasts 2 hours. You may agree with us that the offshore seascape is more interesting than the onshore landscape.

GETTING AROUND

BUS   Aruba has an excellent bus service, with regular daily service from 6am to midnight. The round-trip fare between the beach hotels and Oranjestad is $1.75. Try to have exact change. Buses stop across the street from the cruise terminal on L. G. Smith Boulevard. They will take you to any of the hotel resorts or the beaches along the West End. For bus schedules and information, call the **Aruba Tourism Authority** at ☎ **297/8-23777.**

CAR RENTALS   Unlike most Caribbean islands, Aruba makes it easy to rent a car and explore independently. The roads connecting the major tourist attractions are excellent, and all you need is a valid U.S. or Canadian driver's license. No taxes are imposed on car rentals on Aruba, but insurance can be tricky. Even with the purchase of a collision-damage waiver (from $10 per day), a driver is still responsible for between $300 and $500 worth of damage.

Try **Budget Rent-a-Car,** 1 Kolibristraat (☎ **800/572-0700** in the U.S., or 297/8-28600); **Hertz,** 142 L. G. Smith Blvd. (☎ **800/654-3001** in the U.S., or 297/8-24545), or **Avis,** 14 Kolibristraat (☎ **800/331-1212** in the U.S., or 297/8-25496). Rates range between $35 and $90 per day. If you're calling well in advance, you might try **Auto Europe** (☎ **800/223-5555**) or **Kenwel Holiday Autos** (☎ **800/678-0678**).

MOTORCYCLES & MOPEDS   Since the roads of Aruba are good and the terrain flat, many visitors prefer to see the island by moped or motorcycle. **George's Scooter Rental,** L. G. Smith Blvd. 136, Oranjestad (☎ **297/8-25975**), rents scooters for $27 to $37 per day and motorcycles for $40 to $45 per day. **Nelson Motorcycle Rental,** Gasparito 10A, Noord (☎ **297/8-66801**), rents scooters for $30 and motorcycles from $75.

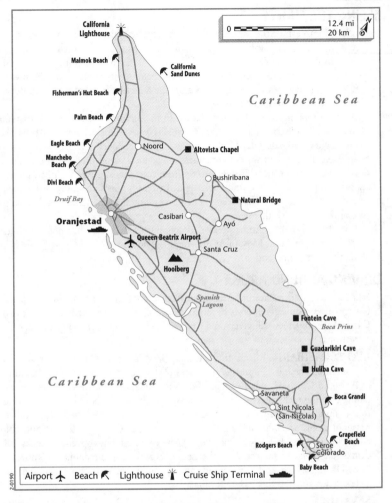

TAXIS Taxis don't have meters, but fares are fixed. Tell the driver your destination and ask the fare before getting in. The main office is on Sands Street between the bowling center and Taco Bell. A dispatch office is located at Bosabao (☎ 297/8-22116).

A ride from the cruise terminal to most of the beach resorts, including those at Palm Beach, costs about $8 to $16 per car. A maximum of four passengers is allowed. Some of the local people don't tip, although it's good to give something extra, especially if the driver has helped you with luggage.

It's next to impossible to locate a taxi on some parts of the island, so when traveling to a remote area or restaurant, ask the taxi driver to pick you up at a designated time. Some English-speaking drivers are available as guides, and most of them seem well informed about their island and eager to share with you what they know. A 1-hour tour (and you don't need much more than that) is offered at $35 per hour for a maximum of four passengers.

SEEING THE SIGHTS

Bustling **Oranjestad,** the capital and port, attracts shoppers rather than sightseers. The town has a very Caribbean flavor, with both Spanish and Dutch architecture. The main thoroughfare, Lloyd G. (L. G.) Smith Boulevard, runs from the airport along the waterfront and on to Palm Beach, changing its name along the way to J. E. Irausquin Boulevard. Most visitors cross the road heading for Caya G. F. Betico Croes, where they find the best shopping.

After a shopping trip, you might return to the harbor, where fishing boats and schooners, many from Venezuela, are moored. Nearly all newcomers to Aruba like to take a picture of **Schooner Harbor.** Colorful boats are docked along the quay, and boatpeople display their wares in open stalls. The local patois predominates. A little farther along, fresh seafood is sold directly from the boats at the fish market. On the sea side, you'll find **Wilhelmina Park,** named after Queen Wilhelmina of the Netherlands. A tropical garden has been planted here along the water, and there's a sculpture of the Queen Mother.

Aside from shopping, Aruba's major attraction is ✪ **Palm Beach,** among the finest beach in the Caribbean. Most of Aruba's high-rise hotels sit in a Las Vegas–style strip along the pure white sand.

DRIVING AROUND ARUBA

Since it's easy to drive around Aruba, consider renting a car to seek out the island's few treasures. You can cut costs by sharing the expense with another couple or two. Car-rental companies will give you a map highlighting the best routes to reach the attractions.

AYO & CASIBARI   Rocks stud the *cunucu,* which means "the countryside" in Papiamento. The most impressive are stacks of diorite boulders the size of buildings at **Ayo** and **Casibari,** northeast of Hooiberg. Ancient Amerindian drawings are painted on the rocks at Ayo. At Casibari, you can climb the boulder-strewn terrain to the top for a panoramic view of the island. Nature has carved the rocks into likenesses of prehistoric birds and animals. Casibari is open daily from 9am to 5pm. No admission is charged. There's a lodge there where you can buy souvenirs, snacks, soft drinks, and beer. In the center of the island, **Hooiberg** is affectionately known as "The Haystack." It's Aruba's most outstanding landmark. You can see Venezuela on a clear day from atop this 541-foot hill.

SAVANETA   The area called Savaneta, on the east side of Aruba, now called the Aruba Sunrise Side, has caves with Arawak artwork, the oldest trace of human habitation on the island. This region has been an industrial center since the days of phosphate mining in the late 19th century, and here you'll see the storage tanks of the Lago Oil & Transport Company Ltd., the Exxon subsidiary around which the town of **San Nicolas** developed. San Nicolas is 12 miles and a 25-minute taxi ride from Oranjestad. Tourism has become the basis of its economy. A PGA-approved golf course has sand "greens" and cactus traps. The town itself is a blend of cultures, customs, style, languages, colors, and tastes.

The one good reason to visit tacky San Nicolas is Aruba's most famous local dive, **Charlie's Bar and Restaurant** at Blvd Veen Zeppenveldstraat 56 (Main Street) (☎ 297/8-45086). Charlie's dates from 1941 and qualifies through its decor and history as one of the most authentic and raffish bars in the West Indies. It's also perhaps the most overly decorated bar, sporting an array of memorabilia and local souvenirs. Where roustabouts and roughnecks once brawled, you'll find tables filled with contented cruise-ship passengers admiring thousands of pennants, banners, and trophies dangling from the high ceiling. Two-fisted drinks are still served, just like they were when San Nicolas was one of the toughest towns in the Caribbean. You can also enjoy freshly made soup, grilled scampi, Creole-style squid, red snapper, churrasco, and sirloin steak. The chow—soup, fish, and steak—isn't bad, but most patrons come here for the good times and the brew. Hours are Monday to Saturday from noon to 9:30pm. Dishes cost from $15 to $20.

GAMBLING THE DAY AWAY

Although cruise ships have their own casinos, you can also try your luck ashore at roulette, craps, blackjack, Caribbean stud poker, baccarat, and the ubiquitous one-armed bandits. Aruba's gaming establishments are second only to San Juan in the Caribbean. Most casinos here are open both day and night, thus drawing both cruise ship passengers and land-based vacationers. They're mainly located in the big hotels on Palm Beach, an $8 to $12 taxi ride from the cruise terminal.

The casino at the **Holiday Inn Aruba Beach Resort,** L. G. Smith Blvd. 230 (☎ **297/8-67777**), wins the prize for all-around gambling action. It keeps its doors open daily from 9am to 4pm.

Closer to Oranjestad, the **Crystal Casino** at the Aruba Sonesta Resort & Casino at Seaport Village (☎ **297/8-36000**) is open 24 hours. It evokes European casinos with its luxurious furnishings, ornate moldings, marble, brass, gold-leaf, and crystal chandeliers.

Casino Masquerade, at the Radisson Aruba Caribbean Resort & Casino, J. E. Irausquin Blvd. 81 (☎ **297/8-66555**), is the newest casino in Aruba. Located in the center of the high-rise hotel area, it's open daily from 10am to 4am.

The **Casablanca Casino** occupies a large room adjacent to the lobby of the Wyndham Hotel and Resort, J. E. Irausquin Blvd. (☎ **297/8-64466**). **Casino Copacabana,** in the island's most spectacular hotel, Hyatt Regency Aruba, L. G. Smith Blvd. 85 (☎ **297/8-61234**), evokes France's Côte d'Azur. These two are open throughout the day, accommodating cruise ship passengers.

Outdrawing them all, however, is the **Royal Cabaña Casino,** at the La Cabaña All-Suite Beach Resort & Casino, J. E. Irausquin Boulevard 250 (☎ **297/8-79000**), the third largest in the Bahamian-Caribbean region. It's known for it's three-in-one venue, combining a restaurant, showcase cabaret theater, and nightclub. You might see everything from Las Vegas–style revues to female impersonators to a comedy series on the weekend. The casino, the largest on Aruba, has 33 tables and games, plus 320 slot machines.

More than just a casino, the **Alhambra,** L. G. Smith Blvd. 47 (☎ **297/8-35000**), offers a collection of boutiques, along with an inner courtyard modeled after an 18th-century Dutch village. The desert setting of Aruba seems appropriate for this Moorish-style building, with its serpentine mahogany columns, repeating arches, and sea-green domes. The casino and its satellites are open daily from 10am until very late at night.

The **Aruba Palm Beach Resort & Casino,** J. E. Irausquin Blvd. 79 (☎ **297/8-23900**), opens its slots at 9am and its other games at 1pm. **Americana Aruba Beach Resort & Casino,** J. E. Irausquin Blvd. 83 (☎ **297/8-64500**), opens daily at noon for slots, blackjack, and roulette; however, other games aren't available until 8pm, when most cruise ships have departed.

SHOPPING

An easy walk from the cruise terminal, Oranjestad's half-mile-long **Caya G. F. Betico Croes** compresses six continents into one main shopping street. While this is not technically a free port, the duty is only 3.3%, and there's no sales tax. You'll find the usual array of jewelry, liquor, Swiss watches, German and Japanese cameras, English bone china and porcelain, French perfume, British woolens, Indonesian specialties, Madeira embroidery, and Dutch, Swedish, and Danish silver and pewter. Delft blue pottery is an especially good buy, as are Edam and Gouda cheeses from Holland. Philatelists can purchase colorful and artistic issues at the post office in Oranjestad.

Shopping Centers

ALHAMBRA MOONLIGHT SHOPPING CENTER   This shopping bazaar, a blend of international shops, outdoor marketplaces, cafes, and restaurants, sells everything from fine jewelry, chocolates, and perfume to imported craft items, leather goods, clothing, and lingerie. The center is located at L. G. Smith Boulevard, next to the Alhambra Casino (☎ **297/8-35000**), and is open Monday to Saturday from 9am to 6pm.

SEAPORT VILLAGE/SEAPORT MARKET   Aruba's densest concentration of shopping options lie within these pair of nearly adjacent two-story malls, overlooking Oranjestad's harbor, at L. G. Smith Blvd. 82 (☎ **297/8-24622**). Each mall has its own casino, the Crystal Casino and the Seaport Casino, a six-screen movie theater showing recently released films from Europe and the United States, a convention center, several bars and cafes, and at least 200 purveyors of fashion, gift items, sporting goods, liquors, perfumes, and photographic supplies. Most shops within the complex are open Monday to Saturday from 9am to 6pm, and the bars and cafes usually operate on a Sunday as well. For information on the movie facilities at the Seaport Cinema, call ☎ **297/8-30318**.

One of the shops, the **Boulevard Book & Drugstore** (☎ **297/8-27358**), has everything from the latest paperback books to cosmetics, candies, gifts, toys, betterquality T-shirts and sweatshirts, sportswear, and souvenirs. You can also buy stamps, road maps, current magazines, and newspapers.

Specialty Shops

Artistic Boutique. Caya G. F. Betico Croes 25. ☎ **297/8-23142.**

If you want something made locally, the Aruban hand-embroidered linens here are the most exquisitely crafted on the entire island. The collection of Indonesian imports is equally excellent. This boutique also carries fine 14- and 18-karat gold jewelry set with precious or semiprecious stones, as well as porcelain figurines from well-known companies, Oriental antiques, handmade dhurries and rugs, Madeira fine linens, and organdy tablecloths.

Aruba Trading Company. Caya G. F. Betico Croes 14. ☎ **297/8-22602.**

Come here for Aruba's finest selection of perfumes. Brand-names are often discounted, although you'll have to search the store carefully to find the good buys. The shop also offers a complete range of such tourist items as cosmetics, souvenirs, Delft, Hummel, crystal ware, and porcelain gift items. They will deliver liquor and cigarettes to your ship.

Gandelman Jewelers. Royal Plaza. ☎ **297/8-34433.**

Gandelman offers an extensive collection of fine gold jewelry and famous-name timepieces at duty-free prices. Go here if you're in the market for a deluxe watch or a fine piece of jewelry. Prices are reasonable, and they're the real thing. This is also the place for collectors of gold bracelets. There are branch stores in the Americana Aruba Hotel, Wyndham Hotel, Royal Plaza, and Hyatt Regency Aruba.

Jewelers Warehouse. In the Seaport Village Mall. ☎ **297/8-36045.**

This popular international jewelry store is found at Sonesta's Seaport Village Mall near the center of Oranjestad. It carries a complete line of rings, earrings, and bracelets.

Les Accessories. In the Seaport Village. ☎ **297/8-37965.**

Here is where award-winning American designer Agatha Brown sells more than 70 of her exclusive designs of quality leather purses handmade in Florence, Italy. Her prices are reasonable, because she designs, imports, and retails her own bags, thus eliminating the extra cost of distributors. She also offers assorted designer sportswear collections, including hand-woven rayon shawls from Venezuela, handy as swimsuit cover-ups.

Little Switzerland Jewelers. Caya G. F. Betico Croes 47. ☎ **297/8-21192.**

Famous for its duty-free 14- and 18-karat-gold jewelry, Little Switzerland also carries a wide variety of famous-name Swiss watches. Over the years we've gotten some very good buys here on Omega and Rado watches, which are usually discounted handsomely from stateside prices. Consider this shop for fine tableware, Baccarat crystal, Lladró figurines, and Swarovski silver as well. This solid, reliable, and dependable Curaçao-based chain is anything but a fly-by-night operator peddling jewelry.

New Amsterdam Store. Caya G. F. Betico Croes 50. ☎ **297/8-21152.**

Aruba's leading department store is best for linens, with its selection of napkins, place mats, and embroidered tablecloths. It has an extensive line of other merchandise as well, from Delft blue pottery to beachwear and boutique items, along with assorted gift items, porcelain figures by Hummel, watches, French and Italian women's wear, and leather bags and shoes.

Penha. Caya G. F. Betico Croes 11-13. ☎ **297/8-24161.**

Penha offers one of the largest selections of top-name perfumes and cosmetics on the island. A household name in Aruba since 1865, it's one of the most dependable stores around, right up there with Gandelman and Little Switzerland. You'll find clothing and cosmetics by such familiar names as Pierre Cardin, Dior, Givenchy, and Cartier. Prices are usually cheaper than in the United States.

BEACHES

The western and southern shores, known as the **Turquoise Coast,** attract sun seekers to Aruba. An $8 taxi ride from the cruise terminal will get you to **Palm Beach** and **Eagle Beach,** the two best beaches on the island. The latter is closer to Oranjestad. Aruba's beaches are open to the public, so you can spread your towel anywhere along this 7-mile stretch of uninterrupted sugar-white sand, which also includes **Manchebo Beach** or **Druid Bay Beach.** But you will be charged for using the facilities at any of the hotels on this strip.

In total contrast to this leeward side, the northern, or windward, shore is rugged and wild.

GOLF, TENNIS & WATER SPORTS

GOLF Visitors can play at the **Aruba Golf Club,** Golfweg 82 (☎ 297/8-42006), near San Nicolas, on the southeastern end of the island. The 10 greens are played from different tees to simulate 18 holes. Twenty-five different sand traps add an extra challenge. Greens fees are $18 for 18 holes and $10 for 9. The course is open daily from 7:30am to 5pm, although anyone wishing to play 18 holes must begin before

1:30pm. The pro shop has golf carts and clubs for rent. There's also has an air-conditioned restaurant and changing rooms with showers.

Aruba's long-awaited **Tierra del Sol Golf Course** (☎ **297/8-67800**) opened in 1995. Designed by the Robert Trent Jones II Group, this 18-hole, par-71, 6,811-yard course is on the northwest coast, near the California Lighthouse. It was designed to combine the beauty of the island's indigenous flora, such as the swaying divi-divi tree, with lush greens. Facilities include a restaurant and lounge in the clubhouse, a swimming pool, and eight tennis courts. The course is managed by Hyatt Resorts Caribbean. Greens fees are $120 in winter, including golf cart, or $75 after 3pm. Off-season, the fees drop to $75, or $55 after 3pm. The course is open daily from 6am to 7pm.

TENNIS   Most of the island's beachfront hotels have tennis courts, often swept by trade winds, and some have top pros on hand to give instruction. We don't advise playing in Aruba's noonday sun. If you're a tennis buff, it's better to hit the courts soon after you disembark.

The best tennis is at the **Aruba Racket Club** (☎ **297/8-60215**), the island's first world-class tennis facility, with eight courts, an exhibition center court, a pro shop, a swimming pool, an aerobics center, a fitness center, and a shopping center. It's part of the Tierra del Sol complex on Aruba's northwest coast, near the California Lighthouse. The club is about a $12 taxi ride from the cruise terminal.

WATER SPORTS   Snorkelers will find the waters to be rather shallow here, but scuba divers can explore stunning marine life, with endless varieties of coral, as well as tropical fish in infinite hues. At some points visibility is up to 90 feet. Most divers head for the German freighter *Antilla,* which was scuttled in the early years of World War II off the northwestern tip of Aruba, near Palm Beach.

De Palm Tours, L. G. Smith Blvd. 142, in Oranjestad (☎ **297/8-24400**), combines boat rides with snorkeling. For $40 per person, they'll take you on a 1¹/₂-hour "fun cruise" aboard a catamaran, after which passengers stop for 3 hours at the company's private De Palm Island for snorkeling. Lunch and an open bar aboard are included in the price. If there are enough takers, the tour leaves daily at 10am and returns at 4pm, just in time to return to the cruise ship. De Palm also offers a 1-hour glass-bottom boat cruise that visits two coral reefs and the German shipwreck *Antilla.* The cruise costs $17.50 per person and operates Tuesday and Wednesday.

Red Sails Sports, Palm Beach (☎ **297/8-61603**), is the island's best water-sports center, offering an extensive variety of activities, including sailing, windsurfing, waterskiing, and scuba diving. The resort scuba-diving course is tailored for cruise-ship passengers. Certified divers pay $36 and up for one-tank excursions.

Divi Winds Center, J. E. Irausquin Blvd. 41 (☎ **297/8-23300,** ext. 623), near the Tamarind Aruba Beach Resort, is the island's windsurfing headquarters. Equipment rents for $15 per hour or $30 per half day, $50 all day. The resort is on the tranquil (Caribbean) side of the island, away from the fierce Atlantic waves. You can also arrange Sunfish lessons or rent snorkeling gear. The operation has another location at the Hyatt.

DINING

If there are many cruise ships in port, call from a pay phone in the cruise-ship terminal to make a reservation. If not, chances are you won't need them.

IN ORANJESTAD

Boonoonoonoos. Wilhelminastraat 18. ☎ **297/8-31888.** Reservations recommended for dinner in winter. Main courses $13–$32. AE, DC, MC, V. Mon–Sat 11:30am–10:30pm, Sun 5:30–10:30pm. CARIBBEAN/INTERNATIONAL.

Named after the legendary beach parties of Jamaica, this restaurant lies in an old-fashioned Aruban house on the capital's main shopping street. The decor is a confectionery blend of blues, greens, and pinks. Even if you're not visiting the rest of the Caribbean, you can go on a culinary tour by wandering through the menu. Try, for example, an appetizer known as *ajaka,* an Aruban dish seasoned with chicken and wrapped in banana leaves. Soups, such as the local callaloo and the homemade fish soup, also make good appetizers. For a main dish, the most popular is *keshi yena* (Aruban chicken casserole). You can also order Jamaican jerk ribs, based on a recipe dating back three centuries, or Bajan pepperpot, or Trinidad-style curried chicken. A small section of the menu is devoted to French cuisine, including filet mignon and Dover sole meunière. This place continues to draw mixed reactions from readers, everything from raves to attacks. Slow service is a major complaint.

✪ Chez Mathilde. Havenstraat 23. ☎ **297/8-34968.** Reservations recommended. Main courses $22–$42. AE, DC, MC, V. Mon–Sat 11:30am–2:30pm; daily 6–11pm. FRENCH.

Oranjestad's French restaurant is expensive, but most agree that it's worth the price, especially those who order the chef's bouillabaisse, made with more than a dozen different sea creatures. Other well-recommended dishes are rack of lamb chops with fine French herbs, juicy veal sirloin cooked in a raspberry liqueur and lime sauce and topped with melted Brie, and filet of red snapper prepared with a lightly peppered crust and served with lemon dressing. Not only do you get distinguished food and service, including a good wine list and a classic haute cuisine French repertoire, but you enjoy an elegant setting. The well-preserved structure housing the restaurant was built in the 1800s. Intimate dining rooms contain beautifully set tables and a restrained but romantic decor. Enjoy an aperitif beforehand. Live piano music enhances the total experience. The restaurant is near the Sonesta hotel complex, a 5-minute drive north of the airport.

Frankie's Prime Grill. In the Royal Plaza Mall, L. G. Smith Blvd. ☎ **297/8-38471.** Reservations not necessary. Main courses $9.50–$21.50. AE, DC, DISC, MC, V. Mon–Sat noon–4:30pm; daily 6–10:30pm. STEAKS/SEAFOOD.

The culinary theme here revolves around two-fisted portions of steak and seafood, some of it grilled in the *churrasco* style you might have expected on the Argentinian pampas. You can dine either inside, where it's air-conditioned, or on an outdoor terrace whose views encompass potted palms, the busy street life of downtown Oranjestad, and boats bobbing at anchor in the harbor. Menu items include selections from a well-stocked salad bar, which can also be a main course for $9.50; a wide selection of pastas, including penne with vodka sauce or a spicy *l'arrabiata* sauce; lasagna; filet mignon; and a full-fledged mixed grill. Seafood lovers should try the seafood crêpes, shrimp in garlic sauce, and various preparations of grouper and snapper.

Kowloon. Emmastraat 11. ☎ **297/8-24950.** Reservations recommended. Main courses $17–$20. Set-price rijstaffel $35 for 2 diners. AE, DISC, MC, V. Daily 11am–10pm. CHINESE/INDONESIAN.

This worthy and elegant Asian restaurant prepares great Hunan, Szechuan, Shanghai Chinese food, as well as such Indonesian staples as nasi goreng and bami goreng, made with rice or noodles and tidbits of pork, vegetables, and shrimp. Other good specialties include an elaborate *rijstaffel* (rice table), where dozens of small curried vegetables are combined into one impressive display, and a house seafood special, that combines fish, scallops, lobster, shrimp, and Szechuan-style black bean sauce. The two red-and-black dining rooms are accented with varnished hardwoods and Chinese lamps. Diners can look out over one of the main thoroughfares of the island's capital.

The Paddock. 13 L. G. Smith Blvd., Oranjestad. ☎ **297/8-32334.** Reservations not necessary. Sandwiches, snacks, and salads $3.70–$5.50. Main courses $8.50–$14.50. MC, V. Mon–
Thurs 10am–2am, Fri–Sun 10am–3am. INTERNATIONAL.

Set in the heart of Oranjestad, overlooking the harbor and within a short walk of virtually every shop in town, The Paddock is a cafe and bistro with a Dutch aesthetic
and ambience. Much of the staff is blonde, hip, and European, and no one will mind
if you opt for a drink, a cup of tea or coffee, a snack of sliced sausage and Gouda
cheese, instead of a full-fledged meal. The menu offers sandwiches of beef, crab,
salmon, shrimp, and tuna; salads; filet mignon encrusted with crushed pepper; fresh
poached or sautéed fish; and a glazed pork tenderloin. Happy hours change frequently, but when they're on, the place is as crowded and animated as anything else
in the island's capital.

The Waterfront Crabhouse. Seaport Market, L. G. Smith Blvd. ☎ **297/8-36767.** Reservations recommended. Main courses $16.95–$29.95; continental breakfast $5.95; lunch from $12.
AE, MC, V. Daily 8–11am, noon–4:30pm, and 5:30–10:30pm. SEAFOOD/STEAK.

This seafood restaurant is set at the end of a shopping mall in downtown Oranjestad,
amid painted murals, rattan furniture, and tables placed both indoors and out on a
garden terrace. Good-tasting appetizers include stuffed clams and fried squid with a
marinara sauce, and linguine with white or red clam sauce, which can also be ordered
as a main course. The chef lists "crabs, crabs, crabs" as his specialty; choices include
garlic crabs, Alaskan crab legs, and (in season) soft-shell crabs. Other main course
items are stuffed Maine lobster and some of the best steaks on the island. Blackened
Cajun shrimp is cooked over an open fire, as are a wide range of other fish dishes,
including yellowfin tuna and swordfish. Ecologists should note that all fish served are
caught with a hook-and-line, never with drift nets.

AT TIERRA DEL SOL

Ventanas del Mar. In the Clubhouse of the Tierra del Sol Golf Course, Malmokweg. ☎ **297/
8-67800.** Reservations not needed for lunch. Lunch sandwiches, salads, and platters $9–$32;
dinner main courses $21–$37. AE, MC, V. Tues–Sun 6am–10am, 11am–3pm, and 6–10:30pm.
SEAFOOD.

Until 1995, the land here was nothing more than a sunblasted, arid sand dune, dotted
with rocks and scrub. Since its transformation into an emerald oasis for golfers, the
popularity of this showcase restaurant has soared. The comfortably contemporary
decor is especially soothing considering the often blistering heat outside. Views sweep
out over the coastline and the sea. Lunches feature sandwiches and salads, in addition to steaks and grilled fish. Evening meals include Caribbean lobster, seafood pasta,
conch ceviche, grilled garlic shrimp, and sautéed grouper. One of the best dishes is
a fried whole red snapper served in a ginger soy sauce. A bar filled with golfing memorabilia remains open throughout the afternoon.

EAST OF ORANJESTAD

Brisas del Mar. Savaneta 222A. ☎ **297/8-47718.** Reservations required. Main courses $12–
$32. AE, MC, V. Tues–Sun noon–2:30pm; daily 6:30–9:30pm. SEAFOOD.

A 15-minute drive east of Oranjestad, near the police station, Brisas del Mar seems
like an outpost in Australia. Here at the water's edge, in this simple little hut with
an air-conditioned bar, locals gather to drink the day away, and to dance on weekends. Specialties include a mixed seafood platter, baby shark, and broiled lobster. You
can order meat and poultry dishes as well, including tenderloin steak and broiled
chicken. Don't expect subtlety of cuisine. This is the type of food Arubans enjoyed
back in the 1950s, and nothing much has changed since then. From the breezy

outdoor tables in back you can watch the catch of the day, perhaps wahoo, being sliced up and sold to local buyers.

3 Barbados ⬇ ⬇ ⬇ ⬇

No port of call in the southern Caribbean can compete with Barbados when it comes to diversions, attractions, and fine dining. But what really puts Barbados on world tourist maps are its seemingly endless stretches of pink-and-white sandy beaches, among the best in the entire Caribbean Basin.

Bajans, as the locals call themselves, like to think of their island as "an England in the tropics." The weather's a lot better, but this former British colony does have bandbox cottages with neat little gardens, centuries-old parish churches, and a scenic, hilly region in the northeast known as The Scotland District, where a mist rises in the morning. Narrow roads ramble through sugarcane fields trimmed with hedgerows (sugar is king here, and rum is queen). Afternoon tea remains a tradition at many places, cricket is still the national sport, and many Bajans speak with an English accent.

A young American major named George Washington came here in 1751 on his only trip outside North America—and caught smallpox. Nevertheless, the island's tropical climate turned it into the "sanitarium of the West Indies" in the 19th century, when wealthy Britons came to escape "the vapors" back home. Today, beautiful Barbados, with its mixture of coral, lush vegetation, and glorious beaches, remains healthful to the spirit.

COMING ASHORE

The cruise-ship pier, a short drive from Bridgetown, the capital, is one of the best docking facilities in the southern Caribbean. You can walk right into the modern cruise-ship terminal, which has car rentals, taxi services, sightseeing tours, and a tourist information office, plus shops and scads of vendors (see "Shopping," below). You'll also find credit-card telephones, and phone cards and stamps for sale.

If you want to go into Bridgetown instead of the beach, you can take a hot, dusty walk of at least 30 minutes, or catch a taxi. The one-way fare ranges from $4 on up.

FAST FACTS

Currency The **Barbados dollar (BD$)** is the official currency, available in $100, $20, $10, and $5 notes and $1, 25¢, and 10¢ silver coins, plus 5¢ and 1¢ copper coins. The Barbados dollar is worth 50¢ in U.S. currency. Unless otherwise specified, prices in this section are given in U.S. dollars. Most stores take traveler's checks or U.S. dollars, so don't bother to convert them if you're here only for a day.

Information The **Barbados Tourism Authority** is on Harbour Road (P.O. Box 242), Bridgetown, Barbados, W.I. (☎ 246/427-2623). Its cruise terminal office is always open when a cruise ship is in port.

Language English is spoken with an island lilt.

SHORE EXCURSIONS

It's not easy to get around Barbados quickly and conveniently, so a shore excursion is your best bet to see the major places of interest. Most cruise lines offer a 3-hour tour to Harrison's Cave in the center of the island for $33 for adults (see "Seeing the Sights," below). The second most popular tour is 1¹/₂ hours aboard the *Atlantis* submarine (see "A Favorite Experience," below).

Since most cruise lines don't really offer a comprehensive island tour, many passengers deal with one of the local tour companies. **Bajan Tours,** Glenayre, Locust

Barbados

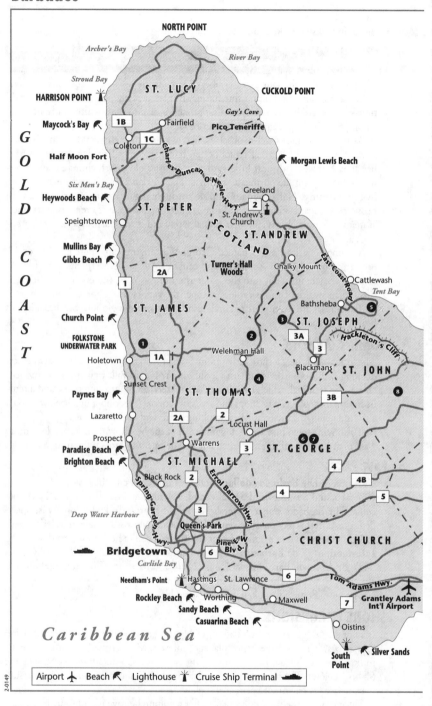

Airport ✈ Beach ☂ Lighthouse 🕯 Cruise Ship Terminal ⛴

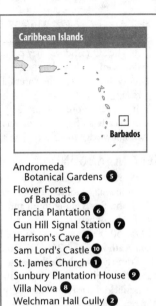

Caribbean Islands

Barbados

Andromeda
  Botanical Gardens **5**
Flower Forest
  of Barbados **3**
Francia Plantation **6**
Gun Hill Signal Station **7**
Harrison's Cave **4**
Sam Lord's Castle **10**
St. James Church **1**
Sunbury Plantation House **9**
Villa Nova **8**
Welchman Hall Gully **2**

Atlantic Ocean

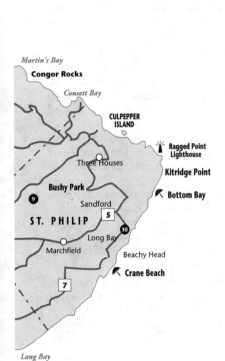

Martin's Bay
Congor Rocks

Consett Bay

**CULPEPPER
ISLAND**

**Ragged Point
Lighthouse**

Three Houses

Kitridge Point

Bushy Park

9

Bottom Bay

Sandford

ST. PHILIP

5

10

Long Bay

Marchfield

Beachy Head

7

Crane Beach

Long Bay

0 — 3 km
    1.9 mi

N

Hall, St. George (☎ **246/437-9389**), offers an island tour that leaves between 8:30am and 9am, and returns to the ship before departure. It covers all the island's highlights. On Fridays, they conduct a heritage tour, focusing mainly on the island's major plantations and museums. On Tuesdays and Wednesdays, they offer an Eco Tour, which takes in the natural beauty of the island. These tours each cost $56 per person.

If you can afford it, touring by taxi is far more relaxing than the standardized bus tour. Nearly all Bajan taxi drivers are familiar with their island and like to show off their knowledge to visitors. The standard rate is $17.50 per hour.

GETTING AROUND

BUS   Blue-and-yellow **public buses** fan out from Bridgetown every 20 minutes or so on the major routes. They're not numbered, but their destinations are marked on the front. Buses going south and east leave from Fairchild Street. Those going north and west depart from Lower Green and the Princess Alice Highway. Fares are BD$1.50 (75¢) wherever you go. Exact change is required. Call the **Barbados Tourism Authority** (☎ **246/427-2623**) for schedules and information.

Privately owned **minibuses** run shorter distances and travel more frequently. They are bright yellow, with their destinations displayed on the bottom left corner of the windshield. Board minibuses in Bridgetown at River Road, Temple Yard, and Probyn Street. These, too, cost BD$1.50 (75¢).

CAR RENTALS   We don't advise renting a car here. Roads are bad, driving is on the **left side** of the road, and the signs are totally inadequate. You could easily get lost. Furthermore, none of the major car-rental companies has affiliates on Barbados. A host of local companies rent vehicles, but they continue to draw serious complaints from readers for overcharging and for the poor condition of their vehicles. Proceed carefully if you decide to rent here.

If you don't have an International Driver's License, the rental agencies will issue a visitor's driving permit. They cost BD$10 ($5). Except in the peak of the midwinter season, cars are usually readily available without a prior reservation. No taxes apply to car rentals on Barbados.

The island's most frequently recommended car-rental firm is **National Car Rental,** Bush Hall, Main Road, St. Michael (☎ **246/426-0603**), which also has an office at the cruise terminal. This company is not affiliated in any way with the car-rental giant of the same name. Most car rentals begin at $75 per day. If you're calling well in advance, you might try **Auto Europe** (☎ **800/223-5555**) or **Kenwel Holiday Autos** (☎ **800/678-0678**).

TAXIS   As is typical of this part of the world, taxis aren't metered, but their rates are fixed by the government. Taxis are identified by the letter "Z" on their license plates. Overcharging is infrequent, and drivers have a reputation for courtesy and honesty. Standard rates for tours are about $17.50 per hour. We've given approximate fares in the listings below.

SEEING THE SIGHTS

Barbados is too diverse and spread out to see everything in a day. We've narrowed the attractions down to the most interesting few. Bridgetown is not one of them. It's hot, dry, and dirty, and the honking horns of traffic jams only add to its woes. So unless you want to go shopping, you should spend your time at calmer oases.

Welchman Hall Gully. St. Thomas (Hwy. 2 from Bridgetown). ☎ **246/438-6671.** Admission $6 adults, $3 ages 6–12 (5 and under free). Daily 9am–5pm.

This lush tropical garden owned by the Barbados National Trust contains some specimens of plants that were here when the English settlers landed in 1627. Breadfruit trees are supposed to be descended from the seedlings brought from Tahiti by Captain William Bligh of HMS *Bounty* fame. Many of the plants are labeled—clove, nutmeg, tree fern, and cocoa, among others—and occasionally you'll spot a wild monkey. The gully is 8 miles from the port and can be reached by bus from the terminal.

⊙ Harrison's Cave. Welchman Hall, St. Thomas. ☎ **246/438-6640.** Admission $8.75 adults, $4.35 children. Daily 8:45am–4pm.

The top tourist attraction of Barbados lets visitors view a beautiful, natural, underground world from aboard an electric tram and trailer. Underground, visitors see subtly lit bubbling streams, tumbling cascades, and deep pools. Stalactites hang overhead like icicles, and stalagmites rise from the floor. Visitors may disembark and get a closer look at the Rotunda Room and the Cascade Pool. A video show of the cave is shown before the tour. All cruise ship shore excursions visit here. If you'd like to go on your own, a taxi ride of about 30 minutes costs about $15.00.

Flower Forest. Richmond Plantation, St. Joseph. ☎ **246/433-8152.** Admission $7 adults, $3.50 children. Daily 9am–5pm.

This old sugar plantation sits 850 feet above sea level near the western edge of the "Scotland district," a mile from Harrison's Cave. Located in one of the most scenic parts of Barbados, it's more than just a botanical garden—people and nature have come together here to create an orchard of beauty. After viewing the grounds, visitors can purchase handcrafts at Best of Barbados. The Flower Forest is 12 miles from the cruise terminal; one-way taxi fare is about $17.50.

Francia Plantation. St. George, Barbados. ☎ **246/429-0474.** Admission $4.50. Mon–Fri 10am–4pm.

This fine home on a wooded hillside overlooking the St. George Valley is still owned and occupied by descendants of the original owner. You can explore several rooms, including the dining room with the family silver and an 18th-century James McCabe bracket clock. Antique maps and prints adorn the walls and include a West Indies map printed in 1522. The plantation lies about 20 miles from the port; one-way taxi fare is about $20.00.

Gun Hill Signal Station. Off Hwy. 4. ☎ **246/429-1358.** Admission $4.60 adults, $2.30 children under 14. Mon–Sat 9am–5pm.

One of two such stations owned and operated by the Barbados National Trust, the Gun Hill Signal Station is strategically placed on the highland of St. George and commands a panoramic view from east to west. Built in 1818, it was the finest of a chain of signal stations, and also used as an outpost by the British army. The restored military cook house now holds a snack bar and gift shop. The station is 12 miles from the port.

Heritage Park & Rum Factory. Foursquare Plantation, St. Philip. ☎ **246/423-6669.** Admission $12. Sun–Thurs 9am–5pm, Fri–Sat 9am–9pm.

After driving through cane fields, you arrive at the first rum distillery to be launched on the island since the 19th century. Inaugurated in 1996, this factory is located in a former molasses and sugar plantation dating back some 350 years. Connoisseurs praise the white rum, ESA Field, produced on-site. A one-way taxi fare costs $17.50. Nearby is a park where Barbadian handcrafts are displayed in the Art Foundry (see "Shopping," below). You'll also find an array of shops and carts selling local foods, handcrafts, and products.

Sunbury Plantation House. 6 Cross Rd., St. Philip. ☎ **246/423-6270.** Admission $6 adults, $3 children. Daily 10am–4:30pm.

This 300-year old plantation house is steeped in history. It features mahogany antiques, old prints, and a unique collection of horse-drawn carriages. This is the only great house in Barbados where all the rooms are open for viewing. The staff offers an informative tour, and later guests can patronize the Courtyard Restaurant and Bar for meals or drinks. There's also an on-site gift shop.

Synagogue. Synagogue Lane, Bridgetown. ☎ **246/432-0840.** Free admission. Mon–Fri 8am–4:30pm.

This synagogue, dating from 1833, is one of the oldest in the western hemisphere. The present building sits on the site of an even older synagogue, erected by Brazilian Jews in 1654. The synagogue was deconsecrated in the early 20th century. In 1983, an outcry went up from the island's small Jewish community when the government announced plans to raze the deteriorating building and put a courthouse on the site. Money was raised for restoration, and the building is now part of the National Trust of Barbados and serves once again as a synagogue. It's surrounded by a burial ground of early Jewish settlers. One-way taxi fare from the cruise terminal is $4.

Andromeda Botanical Gardens. Bathsheba, St. Joseph. ☎ **246/433-9261.** Admission $6 adults, $3 children. Daily 9am–5pm.

Here on a cliff overlooking the town of Bathsheba on the rugged east coast, limestone boulders make a natural eight-acre rock-garden, covered with thousands of orchids and hundreds of hibiscus and heliconia. Many varieties of ferns, bromeliads, and other species used as house plants in temperate climates grow in splendid profusion here. One section has more than 100 species of palms. A guide helps visitors identify the plants. You may also see frogs, herons, guppies, and sometimes a mongoose or monkey.

John Moore Bar. On the waterfront, Weston, St. James Parish. ☎ **246/422-2258.**

This is the most atmospheric and least pretentious bar on Barbados. A large and congenial crowd of neighborhood residents make it the nerve center of the town of Weston. Most visitors opt for a rum punch or beer, but if you're hungry, they can prepare platters of local fish, after a moderate delay, for between $6 and $8. Open daily from 9am until the last patron leaves. It's about an $8 taxi ride from the cruise terminal.

Sam Lord's Castle Resorts. Long Bay, St. Philip. ☎ **246/423-7350.** Admission $5.

The architecturally acclaimed centerpiece of this luxury resort was built in 1820 by one of Barbados' most notorious scoundrels, Samuel Hall Lord, known as the "Regency Rascal." Legend says he made his money by luring ships onto the jagged but hard-to-detect rocks of Cobbler's Reef. To build his great house near the easternmost end of the island, he brought craftspeople from England to reproduce sections of the queen's palace at Windsor. The decor includes dubiously acquired but nonetheless beautiful art by Reynolds, Raeburn, and Chippendale. The estate has 72 landscaped acres and a wide, lengthy private sandy beach edged by tall coconut trees. It's about 14 miles from Bridgetown, or a $12 taxi ride from the cruise terminal.

SHOPPING

The government's $6 million **cruise terminal** offers a variety of shopping options, including duty-free shops, local retail stores, and scads of vendors. The interior was designed to re-create an island street scene, tropical landscaping, benches, pushcarts, and storefronts that look like traditional chattel houses. The shops carry jewelry,

⭐ A Favorite Experience: Submerged Sightseeing

You no longer have to be an experienced diver to see what lives 150 feet below the surface of the sea around Barbados. Now all visitors can view the sea's wonders on sightseeing submarines. These air-conditioned submersibles seat 28 to 48 passengers and make several dives daily from 9am to 6pm. Passengers are transported aboard a ferry boat from the waterfront in downtown Bridgetown to the submarine site, about a mile from the west coast of Barbados. The ride offers a view of the west coast of the island.

The submarines have viewing ports, allowing you to see a rainbow of colors, tropical fish, plants, and even a shipwreck that lies upright and intact below the surface. You're taken aboard either *Atlantic I* or *III*. On one trip, called the Odyssey, professional divers leave the vessel and perform a 15-minute dive show for the viewing passengers; the Odyssey costs $87.50 for adults or $43.75 for children. The other trip, called the Expedition, costs $80 for adults and $40 for children. For reservations, contact **Atlantis Submarines (Barbados),** Shallow Draught, Bridgetown (☎ **246/436-8929**).

The same company also offers cruises aboard the air-conditioned *Atlantis Seatrec,* a semisubmersible boat. These trips give you a snorkeler's view of the reef through large viewing windows. You can also relax on deck as you take in the scenic coastline. The tour costs $35 for adults; children 4 to 12 are charged half fare (not suitable for those 3 or under). A second *Seatrec* tour explores wreckage sites. Divers go down with video cameras to three different wrecks on Carlisle Bay, and the video is transmitted to TV monitors aboard the vessel. The price is the same as for the first tour. For reservations, call the number above.

liquor, china, crystal, electronics, perfume, leather goods, and the arts and crafts of Barbados. You may want to go into Bridgetown or elsewhere for wider selections and certainly better prices, since retailers here pass their severely high rents along to you.

There is no duty on items made in Barbados. Some of the best duty-free buys include cameras, watches, crystal, gold jewelry, bone china, cosmetics, perfumes, and liquor (including locally produced Barbados rum and liqueurs), along with tobacco products and British-made cashmere sweaters, tweeds, and sportswear.

Among **Barbados handcrafts,** black-coral jewelry is outstanding. Local clay potters turn out a variety of products, some based on designs centuries old. You'll also find locally made vases, pots, pottery mugs, glazed plates, and ornaments. Island craftspeople also create wall hangings made from local grasses and dried flowers, straw mats, baskets, and bags with raffia embroidery. Still in its infancy, Bajan leatherwork includes handbags, belts, and sandals.

Art Foundry. Heritage Park. ☎ **246/426-0714.**

This gallery in a historic factory building is a partnership between Bajan artist Joscelyn Gardner and R.L. Seale, the rum distiller. It displays some of the finest works of art in Barbados on the ground-floor, while offering changing exhibitions upstairs. Gardner herself is both a printmaker and an artist in residence.

Articrafts. Broad St., Bridgetown. ☎ **246/427-5767.**

Here John and Rosyln Watson have assembled one of the most impressive displays of Bajan arts and crafts on the island. They make a distinctive handcrafted design. Roslyn's woven wall hangings are decorated with objects from the island, including sea fans and coral. Straw work, handbags, and bamboo items are also sold.

Best of Barbados. In the Southern Palms, St. Lawrence Gap, Christ Church. ☎ **246/420-8040.**

Part of an islandwide chain of 12 stores, Best of Barbados sells only products designed and/or made on Barbados. It's the best shop on the island for local products. An English-born painter, Jill Walker, whose prints are best-sellers, established the chain in 1975. It sells coasters, mats, T-shirts, pottery, dolls and games, and cookbooks, among other items. This tasteful shop is around the corner from the entrance to Southern Palms.

A more convenient location is in Bridgetown at Mall 34, Broad Street (☎ **246/436-1416**).

Cave Shepherd. Broad St., Bridgetown. ☎ **246/431-2121.**

The best place to shop for tax-free merchandise on Barbados is Cave Shepherd, which has branches at Sunset Crest in Holetown, Da Costas Mall, Grantley Adams International Airport, and the Bridgetown Cruise Terminal. If your time is limited and you want an overview of what's for sale on Barbados, try this outlet in Bridgetown. Cave Shepherd is the largest department store on Barbados and one of the most modern in the Caribbean. The store offers perfumes, cosmetics from the world's leading houses, fine full-lead crystal and English bone china, cameras, gold and silver jewelry, swimwear, leather goods, men's designer clothing, handcrafts, T-shirts, and souvenirs. More than 70 brands of liqueurs are sold, as well as other spirits. After shopping, relax on the top floor in the cool comfort of the Ideal Restaurant. You can also patronize the Balcony, which overlooks Broad Street and serves vegetarian dishes. It has a salad bar and beer garden as well.

Colours of De Caribbean. The Waterfront Marina, Bridgetown. ☎ **246/436-8522.**

Next to the Waterfront Café, this unique store has a very individualized collection of tropical clothing, all made in the West Indies, as well as jewelry and decorative objects. Original hand-painted and batiked clothing may hold the most interest.

Cotton Days. Lower Bay St., St. Michael. ☎ **246/427-7191.**

Boutiques abound on Barbados, but Cotton Days is the best known and most stylish. It sells a wide array of casually elegant one-of-a-kind garments, suitable for cool nights and hot climes. The collection has been called wearable art. For inspiration, the in-house designers turn to the flora and fauna of the island and the underwater world. The sales staff is skilled at selecting whimsical accessories to accompany the dresses, blouses, and shifts sold here. Magazines such as *Vogue* and *Glamour* have praised this collection.

Earthworks Pottery/The Potter's House Gallery. Edgehill Heights 2, St. Thomas Parish. ☎ **246/425-0223.**

Some serious shoppers consider this the artistic highlight of Barbados. Canadian-born Goldie Spieler erected this modern building in the 1970s deep in the island's central highlands. Trained as an art teacher and ceramic artist, Ms. Spieler and her son, David, create whimsical plates, cups, saucers, and bowls, whose blue and green colors emulate the color of the Bajan sea and sky. Fans claim that a breakfast of corn flakes in a cerulean-blue porringer on a snowy stateside morning re-creates the warmth of a Caribbean holiday. Many objects are decorated with Antillean-inspired swirls and zigzags. On the premises is the studio and a showroom that sells the output of at least half a dozen other island potters. Items can be shipped virtually anywhere.

Eurostyle, Mall 34. Broad St., Bridgetown. ☎ **246/435-8800.**

One of Bridgetown's most modern shopping complexes offers duty-free shopping in air-conditioned comfort at several outlets. You can find watches, clocks, china, jewelry, crystal, linens, sweaters, and liquor, together with souvenir items and tropical fashions.

Greenwich House Antiques. Greenwich Village, Trents Hill, St. James. ☎ **246/432-1169.**

Set within a 25-minute or $12 taxi ride from Bridgetown, in an antique planters house, this shop evokes a genteel and appealingly cluttered private home. Objects for sale seem to have come from the attic of a favorite, if slightly dotty, great-aunt. Your hostess, Mrs. Lorna Bishop, is the owner and *doyenne* of this monument to local acquisitiveness. Her grasp of local lore and gossip is profound, and she gives the impression that, at any minute, a fresh pot of tea will emerge from any of the dozens of objects that cover the tabletops and display space.

Harrison's. 1 Broad St., Bridgetown. ☎ **246/431-5500.**

In addition to this main shop, Harrison's has 14 branch stores, all selling a wide variety of duty-free merchandise, including china, crystal, jewelry, leather goods, and perfumes—all at fair prices. We've been able to find good buys here on Baccarat, Lalique, Royal Doulton, and Waterford crystal. They also sell some state-of-the-art leather products handcrafted in Colombia. Harrison's is the major competitor to Cave Shepherd on the island, but we'd give the edge to Cave Shepherd.

Little Switzerland. In the Da Costas Mall, Broad St., Bridgetown. ☎ **246/431-0029.**

At this outlet you'll find a wide selection of fragrances and cosmetics from such famous houses as Giorgio, Chanel, Guerlain, Yves St. Laurent, La Prairie, and more. Fine china and crystal from European manufacturers such as Lladró are also sold, as is an array of wares from Waterford, Lalique, Swarovski, Baccarat, and others. The shop specializes in watches and jewelry, offering a wide range of 14- and 18-karat-gold jewelry, with both precious and semiprecious stones. Watch brands include Rolex, Swatch, Omega, Raymond Weil, Tag Heuer, Ebel, and others. The store also stocks the distinctive Mont Blanc pens.

Luna Jewelers. Bay St. at Bedford Ave., Bridgetown. ☎ **246/430-0355.**

This long-standing jeweler sells an appealing but predictable collection of diamonds and precious stones, as well as watches and gift items. But what makes it unusual is its emphasis on art nouveau and art deco designs. Of special note are the pieces that elevate fossilized Bajan coral into a high art form, thanks to careful polishing, gold or silver settings, and in some cases, intricate mosaic-style inlays. The pristine whiteness of these pieces is sometimes highlighted with colored gemstones from India, Brazil, or Guatemala. The establishment lies within a 10-minute drive south of Bridgetown, about four buildings from Barbados' Parliament.

Pelican Village. Harbour Rd., Bridgetown. ☎ **246/426-4391.**

A collection of island-made crafts and souvenirs is sold here in a tiny colony of thatch-roofed shops. You can wander from one to another, and sometimes see craftspeople at work. Many of the shops here are gimmicky and repetitive, although interesting items can be found. The Pelican Village is located on Princess Alice Highway, leading down to Bridgetown's harbor.

The Shell Gallery. Carlton House, St. James. ☎ **246/422-2593.**

This is the best collection of shells in the West Indies, featuring the shell art of Maureen Edghill, the finest artist in the field. She founded this unique gallery in 1975. Shells for sale come from all over the world. Also offered are hand-painted chinaware, shell jewelry, local pottery and ceramics, and batik and papier-mâché art-work depicting shells and aquatic life.

Walker's Caribbean World. St. Lawrence Gap. ☎ **246/428-1183.**

Close to the Southern Palms, this outlet offers many locally made items, as well as handcrafts from the Caribbean Basin. Here you can buy the famous Jill Walker prints. There's also a gallery devoted to tropical prints.

BEACHES

Beaches on the island's western side—the luxury resort area called the Gold Coast—are far preferable to those on the surf-pounded Atlantic side. All Barbados beaches are open to the public, even those in front of the big resort hotels and private homes. The government requires that there be access to all beaches, via roads along the property line or through the hotel entrance.

ON THE WEST COAST   Take your pick of the West Coast beaches, which are a 15-minute, $8 taxi ride from the cruise terminal. **Payne's Bay,** with access from the Coach House or the Bamboo Beach Bar, is a good beach for water sports, especially snorkeling. There's a parking area here. This beach can get rather crowded, but the beautiful bay makes it worth it. Directly south of Payne's Bay, at Fresh Water Bay, is a trio of fine beaches: **Brighton Beach, Brandon's Beach,** and **Paradise Beach.**

  Church Point lies north of St. James Church, opening onto Heron Bay, site of the Colony Club Hotel. Although this beach can get crowded, it's one of the most scenic bays in Barbados, and the swimming is ideal. Retreat under some shade trees when you've had enough sun. You can also order drinks at the Colony Club's beach terrace.

  Snorkelers in particular seek out the glassy blue waters by **Mullins Beach.** There are some shady areas. You can park on the main road. Order food and drink at the Mullins Beach Bar.

ON THE SOUTH COAST   Depending on traffic, South Coast beaches are usually easily reached from the cruise terminal. Figure on an $8 taxi fare. **Sandy Beach,** reached from the parking lot on the Worthing main road, has tranquil waters opening onto a lagoon, a cliché of Caribbean charm. This is a family favorite, with lots of screaming and yelling, especially on weekends. Food and drink are sold here.

  Windsurfers are particularly fond of the trade winds that sweep across **Casuarina Beach,** even on the hottest summer days. Access is from Maxwell Coast Road, across the property of Casuarina Beach Hotel. This is one of the wider beaches on Barbados. The hotel has food and drink.

  Silver Sands Beach is to the east of the town of Oistins, near the very southernmost point of Barbados, directly east of South Point Lighthouse and near the Silver Rock Hotel. This white sandy beach is a favorite with many Bajans, who probably want to keep it a secret from as many tourists as possible. Windsurfing is good here, but not as good as at Casuarina Beach. You can buy drinks at Silver Rock Bar.

ON THE SOUTHEAST COAST   The southeast coast is known for its big waves, especially at **Crane Beach,** a white sandy stretch set against a backdrop of cliffs and palms. Prince Andrew owns a house overlooking this spectacular beach, and the Crane Beach Hotel towers above it from the cliffs. Crane Beach often appears in travel magazine articles about Barbados. It offers excellent body surfing, but this is ocean swimming, not the calm Caribbean, so be careful. At $17.50 from the cruise pier, the one-way taxi fare is relatively steep, so share a ride with some friends.

GOLF, RIDING, DIVING, TENNIS & WINDSURFING

GOLF   The 18-hole championship golf course of the west coast **Sandy Lane Hotel**, St. James (☎ **246/432-1311**), is open to all. Greens fees are $135 in winter and $110 in summer for 18 holes, or $100 in winter and $80 in summer for nine holes. Carts and caddies are available. Make reservations the day before you arrive in Barbados. The course is a 20- to 25-minute taxi ride from the cruise terminal. The one-way fare is $12.50.

HORSEBACK RIDING   Maintained by Swedish-born Elizabeth Roachford and her four daughters, **Caribbean International Riding Centre,** Cleland Plantation, Farley Hill, St. Andrew (☎ **246/422-7433**), offers trail rides for equestrians of all experience levels. The shortest ride is a 75-minute escorted trek through tropical forests, followed by a relaxing cool drink in the clubroom. The most scenic tour goes through the Gully Ride and continues out to a cliff with a panoramic view of almost the entire east coast of Barbados. Advance reservations are required. It's about a 20-minute or $10 taxi ride from the port. The various rides range from the 1-hour trek for $40 to a $2^1/_2$ hour ride for $82.50.

SNORKELING & SCUBA DIVING   The clear waters off Barbados have a visibility of more than 100 feet most of the year, providing great views of lobsters, moray eels, sea fans, gorgonias, night anemones, octopuses, and more than 50 varieties of fish, as well as wrecks and coral.

   The Dive Shop, Pebbles Beach, Aquatic Gap, St. Michael (☎ **246/426-9947**), offers the best scuba diving on Barbados. It charges $55 per one-tank dive or $80 for a two-tank dive, and also offers snorkeling trips and equipment rentals. Sign up for scuba at a booth next to the dock. Visitors with reasonable swimming skills who have never dived before can also take a resort course for $70. The Dive Shop provides transportation to and from the cruise terminal.

TENNIS   The deluxe **Sandy Lane** resort at St. James (☎ **246/432-1311**) emphasizes tennis more than any other establishment in Barbados, with two pros on hand, five courts, and an open-door policy to nonresidents. One court is carpeted with a material that emulates the feel of grass. The other four are hard surfaced. Court No. 1 is the most frequently used, as it's adjacent to the clubhouse, bar, and restaurant. Court rentals are $23 per hour, or $11.50 per half hour. Lessons with a pro cost $23 per hour or $11.50 per half hour. To reach Sandy Lane, take a 20- to 25-minute taxi ride from the cruise terminal. The one-way fare is $12.50.

WINDSURFING   Experts say that Barbados windsurfing is as good as any this side of Hawaii. In fact, it's a very big business between November and April, when thousands of windsurfers from all over the world come here. **Silver Sands** is rated the best spot in the Caribbean for advanced windsurfing (skill rating five to six). **Barbados Windsurfing Club,** at the Silver Sands Hotel in Christ Church (☎ **246/428-6001**), gives lessons, and rents boards for between $25 and $35 per hour or $55 to $65 per half day. To reach the center, take a taxi from the cruise terminal; it's a $10 one-way fare.

DINING
BRIDGETOWN

The Waterfront Café. The Careenage. ☎ **246/427-0093**. Reservations required. Main courses $12–$18. AE, DC, MC, V. Mon–Sat 10am–10pm. INTERNATIONAL.

   This cafe welcomes both diners and drinkers to its reverberating walls for Creole food, beer, and pastel-colored drinks. It serves international fare with a strong emphasis on

Bajan specialties. Try the peppered steak, the fish burger made with kingfish or dolphin, or the fresh catch of the day prepared Creole style. For vegetarians, the menu includes such dishes as pasta primavera, vegetable soup, and usually a featured special. The building is a turn-of-the-century warehouse originally constructed to store bananas and freeze fish. On Tuesday from 7 to 9pm, there's a Bajan buffet with live steel-pan music, costing BD$35 ($17.50).

SOUTH OF BRIDGETOWN

Brown Sugar. Aquatic Gap, St. Michael. ☎ **246/426-7684.** Reservations recommended. Main courses $14.50–$50; buffet lunch $17.50. AE, DC, DISC, MC, V. Sun–Fri noon–2:30pm; daily 6–9:30pm (last order). BAJAN.

Hidden behind lush foliage, Brown Sugar is an alfresco restaurant in a turn-of-the-century bungalow. The ceiling is latticed, with slow-turning fans, and there's an open veranda for dining by candlelight amid lots of hanging plants. The chefs prepare some of the tastiest Bajan specialties on the island. Among the soups, we suggest hot gun-go-pea soup (pigeon peas cooked in chicken broth and seasoned with fresh coconut milk, herbs, and a touch of white wine). Of the main dishes, Creole-broiled pepper chicken is popular, as are the stuffed crab backs. Conch fritters and garlic pork are especially spicy options. A selection of locally grown vegetables is also offered. For dessert, we recommend the Bajan bread pudding with rum sauce. The restaurant is known for its good-value lunches, served buffet style to local businesspeople.

ON THE SOUTH COAST

The following restaurants are about an $8 one-way taxi ride from the cruise terminal.

Josef's. St. Lawrence Gap. ☎ **246/435-6541.** Reservations recommended. Lunch main courses $10–$15; dinner main courses $24–$35. AE, DC, MC, V. Mon–Fri noon–2:30pm; daily 6:30–10pm. CARIBBEAN/CONTINENTAL.

This is one of the most durable upscale restaurants in Barbados, set within the garden of a pink-and-white Bajan house between the road and the sea. Established in the 1980s by an Austrian, and now operated by a Swede, it focuses on carefully contrived food at nighttime, with less expensive, simpler fare for lunch. Swedish specialties—a bit heavy for the tropics—include meatballs in traditional gravy, and Swedish-style steak. More tropical dishes include garlic shrimp, jerk shrimp, blackened kingfish, seafood crêpes, and curried chicken. Filet Marco Polo is made from strips of filet steak floating in a pool of red wine sauce.

Sand Dollar. In Bagshot House Hotel, St. Lawrence Coast Rd., Christ Church. ☎ **246/435-6956.** Reservations recommended. Lunch main courses $10–$20; dinner main courses $15–$32. AE, DC, MC, V. Daily 7am–10pm. INTERNATIONAL.

This hotel location has become something of a staple in the minds of many long-time island residents. It's less formal than it was in years past, with a modern outlook stemming from a complete renovation in 1996. Well-prepared menu items include a well-seasoned peppersteak, Mount Gay ribs, brochettes of jerk shrimp, a succulent chicken with a honey rum sauce, and different versions of steak and lobster. Lunches feature a roster of sandwiches and salads that aren't available at dinner. No one will object if you wear shorts, but bathing suits aren't allowed.

T.G.I. Boomers. St. Lawrence Gap, Christ Church. ☎ **246/428-8439.** Reservations not required. Main courses $11–$23; lunch specials $4–$11.50; breakfast $5.50–$7.50; Sun buffet $12.50. AE, DISC, MC, V. Daily 8am–10pm. AMERICAN/BAJAN.

Located 4 miles south of Bridgetown along Highway 7 near Rockley Beach, T.G.I. Boomers, an American/Bajan operation, offers some of the best bargain meals on the island. Patrons come here for tried-and-true dishes that never go out of favor. The restaurant has an active bar and a row of tables where food is served, usually along with frothy bright-colored drinks. The cook prepares a special catch of the day served with soup or salad, a vegetable, and rice or baked potato. You can always count on seafood, steaks, and hamburgers. For lunch, try a daily Bajan special or a jumbo sandwich. A special 16-ounce daiquiri will put a glow on your afternoon.

ON THE WEST COAST

These restaurants are an $8 to $12 taxi ride from the cruise terminal, depending on traffic.

✪ **Bagatelle Restaurant.** Hwy. 2A, St. Thomas. ☎ **246/421-6767.** Reservations recommended. Lunch $12; fixed-price dinner $45. MC, V. Mon–Sat 11am–2:30pm and 7–9:30pm. Cut inland near Paynes Bay north of Bridgetown, 3 miles from both Sunset Crest and the Sandy Lane Hotel. FRENCH/CARIBBEAN.

This restaurant is housed in one of the most historic and impressive buildings on the island, originally built in 1645 as the residence of the island's first governor (Lord Willoughby). The sylvan retreat is set with 5 acres of forest in the cool uplands, just south of the island's center, and retains the charm of its original buildings.

Bagatelle is one of the island's finest and most elegant choices, offering French cuisine with a Caribbean flair. Candles and lanterns illuminate the old archways and the ancient trees. The service is the best we found on Barbados. Try the homemade duck-liver pâté, deviled Caribbean crab backs, or smoked flying-fish mousse with horseradish mayonnaise. The beef Wellington Bagatelle style with a chasseur sauce is a favorite, as is the crisp roast duckling with an orange-and-brandy sauce. The local catch of the day, the most popular item on the menu, is prepared grilled, barbecued, or in the style of Baxters Road (spicily seasoned and sautéed in deep oil). A different list of homemade desserts is featured daily.

✪ **The Fathoms.** Paynes Bay, St. James. ☎ **246/432-2568.** Reservations recommended for dinner. Main courses $20–$29. AE, DISC, MC, V. Daily noon–3pm and 6:30–10pm (last order). INTERNATIONAL.

This pleasant, red-roofed stucco restaurant close to the surf serves meals on an outdoor terrace shaded by a mahogany tree. Its interior is decorated with terra-cotta, wood, and pottery.

The restaurant offers a fairly ambitious menu and does itself proud with appetizers like shrimp and crab étouffée, herbed conch cakes, or blackened shrimp with mango. For a main dish, try the caramelized barracuda (yes, that's right), grilled pork medallions, or the zesty and winning Dorado fish Hunan. Upstairs is a Santa Fe–style tapas bar, primarily for drinks, wines, and finger foods. A pool table and board games help you pass the time. This attractive watering hole is open daily from 5pm until the crowd finally departs.

✪ **Nico's Champagne Wine Bar & Restaurant.** Derrick's, St. James. ☎ **246/432-6386.** Reservations recommended. Lunch main courses, $8.70–$13.50; dinner main courses $11.25–$36. AE, DISC, MC, V. Mon–Sat 11:30am–10:30pm. INTERNATIONAL.

Set on the inland side of a road that bisects some of the most expensive residential real estate on Barbados, this is a great value, an informal bistro inspired by the wine bars of London. Its 19th-century building was originally constructed as the headquarters for a plantation. About a dozen kinds of wine are sold by the glass in its air-conditioned bar area. Meals are served at tables protected with a shed-style roof in the garden out back. The food is flavorful and designed to accompany the wine; menu items include deep-fried Camembert with passion-fruit sauce, chicken breasts stuffed with crab, red snapper, and some of the best lobster on Barbados. Your hosts devote a lot of care and attention to what you eat and drink.

4 British Virgin Islands: Tortola & Virgin Gorda ⚓ ⚓ ⚓

With its small bays and hidden coves, once havens for pirates, the British Virgin Islands are among the world's loveliest cruising grounds. This British colony has some 40 islands in the northeastern corner of the Caribbean, most of them tiny rocks and cays. Only Tortola, Virgin Gorda, and Jost Van Dyke are of significant size. The other tiny islets have names like Fallen Jerusalem and Ginger. Norman Island is said to have been the prototype for Robert Louis Stevenson's *Treasure Island.* Blackbeard inspired the famous ditty by marooning 15 pirates and a bottle of rum on the rocky cay known as Deadman Bay.

The islands' varied vegetation depends on rainfall, which in turn depends on both the seasons and the location on the island. In the wetter areas, palms and mangoes grow in profusion; more arid regions are studded with cactus.

Unlike most Caribbean islanders with colonial connections, the people here seem happy with their status under the Union Jack. Although they maintain a certain reserve with strangers, they're more laid-back, hospitable, and friendly than the jaded residents of nearby St. Thomas, who might see 10 cruise ships or more per day in winter.

Many of the smaller cruise lines such as Seabourn call at Tortola and the more scenic Virgin Gorda. Unlike the rigid programs at St. Thomas and other major docking ports, visits here are less structured, and each cruise line is free to pursue its own policy.

TORTOLA

Road Town, the colony's capital, sits about midway along the southern shore of 24-square-mile Tortola. Wickhams Cay, a 70-acre landfill development and marina, brought a massive yacht-chartering business to Road Town and transformed this sleepy village into a bustling center.

The island's entire southern coast is characterized by rugged mountain peaks. On the northern coast are beautiful bays with white sandy beaches, banana trees, mangoes, and clusters of palms.

COMING ASHORE

Visiting cruise ships anchor at Wickhams Cay 1 in Road Town. You'll be brought ashore by tender. The pier, built in the mid-1990s, is a pleasant 5-minute walk to Main Street. You should have no trouble finding your way around town.

FAST FACTS

Currency   The **U.S. dollar** is the legal currency, much to the surprise of arriving Britishers who find no one willing to accept their pounds.

Information   The **B.V.I. Tourist Board Office** (☎ **284/494-3134**) is at the center of Road Town near the ferry dock south of Wickhams Cay 1. Pick up a copy of the *Welcome Tourist Guide.* Open Monday to Friday from 9am to 5pm.

Language   English is spoken here.

SHORE EXCURSIONS

The shore excursions and even the organized activities here are very modest, and not as tightly structured as in major Caribbean ports such as Barbados or San Juan. The cruise ships themselves don't offer excursions, but deal through local operators. **Travel Plan Tours,** Romasco Place, Wickham's Cay, Road Town (☎ **284/494-2872**), will

The British Virgin Islands

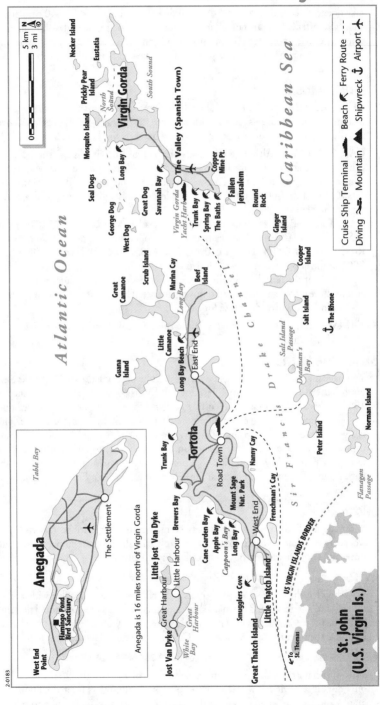

Atlantic Ocean

Caribbean Sea

N

5 km
3 mi

Necker Island
Eustatia
Prickly Pear Island
Mosquito Island

Virgin Gorda

North Sound
South Sound

Seal Dogs
Long Bay
The Valley (Spanish Town)
George Dog
West Dog
Great Dog
Savannah Bay
Copper Mine Pt.
Virgin Gorda Yacht Harbour
Trunk Bay
Spring Bay
The Baths
Fallen Jerusalem
Round Rock

Scrub Island
Great Camanoe
Marina Cay
Beef Island
Ginger Island
Long Bay

Little Camanoe
Long Bay Beach
East End
Guana Island

Cooper Island

Salt Island
The Rhone

D r a k e   C h a n n e l

Trunk Bay
Tortola
Road Town
Mount Sage Nat. Park
Nanny Cay

Salt Island Passage

Deadman's Bay

S i r   F r a n c i s

Brewers Bay
Cane Garden Bay
Apple Bay
Cappoon's Bay
Long Bay
Smugglers Cove
West End
Frenchman's Cay
Little Thatch Island

Peter Island

Norman Island

Flanagan Passage

US VIRGIN ISLANDS BORDER

Great Thatch Island

To St. Thomas

St. John (U.S. Virgin Is.)

Little Jost Van Dyke
Great Harbour
Jost Van Dyke
Little Harbour
White Bay
Great Harbour

Anegada is 16 miles north of Virgin Gorda

Table Bay

Anegada

West End Point
The Settlement
Flamingo Pond Bird Sanctuary

Cruise Ship Terminal   Beach
Diving   Mountain   Shipwreck   Airport   Ferry Route

2-0183

95

take one to three people on a 2¹/₂-hour guided tour of the island for $40 per person. They also offer 2¹/₂-hour snorkeling tours for $35 per person and glass-bottom boat tours, also 2¹/₂ hours, for $30 per person. Or you can take a 2¹/₂-hour **taxi tour.** These cost $45 for up to three people. For a taxi in Road Town, call ☎ **284/ 494-2322.**

Getting Around

BUS   Because of awkward scheduling, local buses are not a viable way to see the island in a day. Nevertheless, **Scato's Bus Service** (☎ 284/494-5873) operates all over the island, picking up passengers who hail the buses down. Fares are $1 to $3.

CAR RENTALS   Although the roads are bad and driving is **on the left,** you can rent a car and explore the island on your own. We recommend that you reserve your rental car in advance, especially in winter. A handful of local companies rent cars, but we recommend using one of the international giants, even if the cost is slightly higher.

On Tortola, **Budget** is at Wickhams Cay I, Road Town (☎ 800/527-0700 in the U.S., or 284/494-5150). **Avis** maintains offices opposite the police headquarters in Road Town (☎ **800/331-1212** in the U.S., or 809/494-3322). **Hertz** (☎ **800/654-3001** in the U.S., or 284/495-4405) has offices outside Road Town, on the island's west end near the ferry boat landing dock. All three companies require renters to be at least 25 years old and have a valid driver's license. They will issue a temporary British Virgin Islands driver's license for $10.

TAXIS   Taxis meet every arriving cruise ship. To call a taxi in Road Town, dial ☎ **284/494-2322.**

Seeing the Sights

You have mainly nature to look at on Tortola. The big attraction is ✪ **Mount Sage National Park,** which rises to 1,780 feet and covers 92 acres. It was established in 1964 to protect the remnants of Tortola's original forests not burned or cleared during its plantation era. You can still find the traces of a primeval rain forest here. This is a great place to enjoy a picnic while overlooking neighboring islets and cays. Any taxi driver can take you to the mountain. Before going, stop at the tourist office (see "Fast Facts," above) and pick up a brochure with a map and an outline of the park's trails. The two main hikes are the Rain Forest Trail and the Mahogany Forest Trail.

Shopping

Shopping on Tortola is a minor activity compared to other Caribbean ports. Most stores are on Main Street in Road Town. Only British goods are imported without duty, and they are the best buys, especially English china.

Caribbean Corner Spice House Co. Soper's Hole. ☎ **284/495-4498.**

This shop has the finest selection of spices and herbs on the island, along with a selection of local handcrafts and botanical skin-care products, most of which you'll find useful in the fierce Caribbean sun. There's also a selection of Cuban cigars, but you'll have to smoke them on the island, since U.S. Customs does not allow their importation.

Caribbean Fine Arts Ltd. Main St., Road Town. ☎ **284/494-4240.**

This store has one of the most unusual collections of art from the West Indies. Not only does it sell original watercolors and oils, but it also offers limited-edition serigraphs and sepia photographs from the dawn of the century, in addition to pottery and primitive art.

⭐ Favorite Experiences at a Bar & on a Beach

Bomba's Surfside Shack, Cappoon's Bay (☎ **284/495-4148**), is the oldest, most memorable, and most uninhibited bar on Tortola. It sits on a 20-foot-wide strip of unpromising coastline near the West End. By anyone's standards, this is the "junk palace" of the island; it's covered with Day-Glo graffiti and laced with wire and rejected odds and ends of plywood, driftwood, and abandoned rubber tires. Despite its makeshift appearance, the shack's electronic amplification system can start a great party at any time of the day. The Sunday and Wednesday night barbecue is $7 per person. Open daily from 10am to midnight (or later, depending on business).

    Cane Garden Bay, on the northwest shore, is so special you might take a taxi here in the morning and not head back to your cruise ship until departure time. With its palm-draped white sandy beach, this half-moon-shaped bay has as much South Seas charm as any place in the Caribbean. Plan to have lunch here at **Rhymer's,** Cane Garden Bay (☎ **284/495-4639**). The chef will cook some conch or whelk, or perhaps some barbecue spareribs. The beach bar and restaurant is open daily from 8am to 9pm, serving breakfast, lunch, and dinner, with main courses ranging from $12 to $20. Ice and freshwater showers are available. Rhymer's rents towels, as well as Sunfish and windsurfers.

Caribbean Handprints. Main St., Road Town. ☎ **284/494-3717.**

This store features island handprints, all hand-done by local craftspeople on Tortola. It also sells colorful fabric by the yard.

Flamboyance. Soper's Hole. ☎ **284/495-4699.**

This is the best place to shop for duty-free perfume. Fendi purses are also sold here.

Fort Wines Gourmet. Main St., Road Town. ☎ **284/494-3036.**

Picnickers should stock up on provisions here, where you can find everything from Petrossian caviar to French champagne. Sample the shop's full line of Hediard pâté terrines along with a wide selection of chocolates, including some of the best from Paris. There's also an elegant showcase of glassware, lacquered boxes, and handmade Russian filigree items plated in 24-karat gold.

J. R. O'Neal. Upper Main St., Road Town. ☎ **284/494-2292.**

Across from the Methodist church, this store has the most extensive collection of decorative pieces and home accessories on the island. You'll find terra-cotta pottery, wicker and rattan home furnishings, Mexican glassware, Dhurrie rugs, baskets, and ceramics. There's also a collection of fine crystal and China.

Little Denmark. Main St., Road Town. ☎ **284/494-2455.**

Little Denmark is your best bet for famous names in gold and silver jewelry, as well as china by Spode and Royal Copenhagen. Here you'll find many of the well-known designs from Scandinavian countries. The store also offers watches, locally made jewelry, and Cuban cigars, which you can't take back to the United States. There's even a large selection of fishing equipment.

Pusser's Company Store. Main St., Road Town. ☎ **284/494-2467.**

The long, mahogany-trimmed bar here is accented with many fine nautical artifacts and a selection of Pusser's sports and travel clothing and upmarket gift items. Pusser's Rum is a best-seller, and a Pusser's ceramic flask is a good memento of your visit.

Sunny Caribbee Herb and Spice Company. Main St., Road Town. ☎ **284/494-2178.**

This old building was the first hotel on Tortola. The shop now occupying it special-izes in Caribbean spices, seasonings, teas, condiments, and handcrafts. You can buy two world-famous specialties here: West Indian Hangover Cure and Arawak Love Potion. A Caribbean cosmetics collection, Sunsations, includes herbal bath gels, is-land perfume, and sunshine lotions. Most of the products are blended and packaged in an adjacent factory. With its aroma of spices permeating the air of the neighbor-hood, this factory is an attraction in itself. There's also a daily sampling of island products, perhaps tea, coffee, sauces, or dips. In the Sunny Caribbee Art Gallery, adjacent to the spice shop, you'll find an extensive collection of original art, prints, metal sculpture, and many other Caribbean crafts.

BEACHES

Most of the beaches are a 20-minute taxi ride from the cruise dock. Figure on about $15 one way, but discuss it with the driver before setting out. You can also ask him to pick you up at a designated time.

The finest beach is at **Cane Garden Bay** (see the "Favorite Experiences" box), which compares favorably to the famous Magens Bay Beach on the north shore of St. Thomas. It's on the northwest side of the island, across the mountains from Road Town, but it's worth the effort to get there.

Surfers like **Apple Bay,** also on the northwest side. A hotel here called Sebastians caters to the surfing crowd that visits in January and February, but the beach is ideal year-round.

Brewers Bay, site of a campground, is on the northwest shore near Cane Garden Bay. Both snorkelers and surfers come here.

Smugglers Cove is at the extreme western end of Tortola, opposite the offshore island of Great Thatch and very close to St. John in the U.S. Virgin Islands. Snorkelers also like this beach, sometimes known as Lower Belmont Bay.

Long Bay Beach is on Beef Island, east of Tortola and the site of the major air-port. To get to this mile-long stretch of white sandy beach, cross the Queen Eliza-beth Bridge, then take a left on a dirt road before the airport. From Long Bay you'll have a good view of Little Camanoe, one of the rocky offshore islands around Tortola.

Marina Cay, off Tortola's East End, is known for its good snorkeling beach. We also recommend the beach at **Cooper Island,** across Drake's Channel. Underwater Safaris (see "Riding & Diving," below) leads snorkel expeditions to both sites.

RIDING & DIVING

HORSEBACK RIDING   Shadow's Ranch, Todman's Estate (☎ 284/494-2262), offers horseback rides through Mount Sage National Park or down to the shores of Cane Garden Bay. Call for details Monday to Saturday from 9am to 4pm. The cost is $25 per person per hour. They're located about 15 miles from the cruise dock; taxi fare is $12.

SCUBA DIVING   *Skin Diver* magazine has called the wreckage of the **HMS Rhône,** which sank in 1867 near the western point of Salt Island, the world's most fantastic shipwreck dive. It teems with marine life and coral formations, and was fea-tured in the motion picture *The Deep.*

Although it's no *Rhône,* **Chikuzen** is another intriguing dive site off Tortola. It's a 270-foot steel-hulled refrigerator ship, which sank off the island's east end in 1981. The hull, still intact under about 80 feet of water, is now home to a vast array of tropical fish, including yellowtail, barracuda, black-tip sharks, octopus, and drum fish.

Baskin in the Sun, (☎ **800/233-7938** in the U.S., or 284/494-2858) a PADI five-star facility on Tortola, is a good choice for divers. It has two different locations: at the Prospect Reef Resort, near Road Town, and at Soper's Hole, on Tortola's West End. Baskin's most popular trip is the supervised "Half-Day Scuba Diving" experience for $95, catered to beginners, but there are trips for more advanced levels as well. Daily excursions are scheduled to the HMS *Rhone,* as well as "Painted Walls" (an underwater canyon formed of brightly colored coral and sponges), and the "Indians" (four pinnacle rocks sticking out of the water, which divers follow 40 feet below the surface).

Underwater Safaris (☎800/537-7032 in the U.S., or 809/494-3235) takes you to all of best sites, including the HMS *Rhône,* "Spyglass Wall," and "Alice in Wonderland." It offers a complete PADI and NAUI training facility, and is associated with The Moorings yacht charter company. Underwater Safaris' Road Town office is a 5-minute or $4 taxi ride from the docks.

DINING

Callaloo. Prospect Reef Resort, Drake's Hwy. ☎ 284/494-3311. Reservations recommended. Main courses $11–$31.50. AE, MC, V. Daily 7am–11pm. INTERNATIONAL.

One of the better hotel restaurants, Callaloo gets romantic on a balmy day when the tropical breezes are blowing. It's the kind of cliché Caribbean setting that's forever a turn-on, and the food is good, too. Begin with the conch fritters or shrimp cocktail, and don't pass on the house salad, which has a zesty papaya dressing. Main dishes include fresh lobster when available (not as good as the Maine variety, though) and also fresh fish, such as tuna, swordfish, or mahimahi. The menu is hardly imaginative, but the chefs do well with their limited repertoire. For dessert, get the orange bread pudding if featured. If not, then the Key lime pie. Downstairs is the less expensive Scuttlebutt Bar and Grill.

✪ Capriccio di Mare. Waterfront Dr., Road Town. ☎ 284/494-5369. Reservations not accepted. Main courses $6–$13.50. No credit cards. Daily 8–10:30am and 11am–9pm. ITALIAN.

Small, casual, and laid-back, this local favorite was created by the owners of the Brandywine Bay restaurant on a whim. It's the most authentic-looking Italian cafe in the Virgin Islands (U.S. or British). You might precede your meal with a mango Bellini, a variation of the famous cocktail (made with fresh peaches) served at Harry's Bar in Venice, or with an appetizer such as *tiapina,* flour tortillas with various toppings. Move on to fresh pastas with succulent sauces, well-stuffed sandwiches, or the best pizza on the island—our favorite is topped with freshly grilled eggplant. Some days, you may get specials like lobster ravioli in a rosé sauce. Their freshly made salads are consistently good—we go for the *insalata mista* with large leafy greens and slices of fresh Parmesan. In the morning, many locals stop in for a delectable Italian pastry and a cappuccino.

Pusser's Landing. Frenchman's Cay, West End. ☎ 284/495-4554. Reservations recommended. Main courses $10.95–$21.95. AE, DISC, MC, V. Daily 11am–10pm. CARIBBEAN/ ENGLISH PUB.

This second Pusser's (see below for the first) is even more desirably located in the West End, opening onto the water. Amongst this nautical setting you can enjoy fresh grilled fish, or perhaps an English-inspired dish, like shepherd's pie. Begin with a hearty bowl of homemade soup and follow it with filet mignon, West Indian roast chicken, or a filet of mahimahi. "Mud pie" is the classic dessert here, or else you can try Key lime pie, or, even better, the mango soufflé. Some dishes occasionally miss the mark, but on the whole this is a good choice. Happy hour is daily from 4 to 6pm.

Pusser's Road Town Pub. Waterfront Dr. and Main St., Road Town. ☎ **284/494-3897.** Reservations not accepted. Main courses $4.50–$21. AE, DISC, MC, V. Daily 10am–10pm. Bar until midnight. CARIBBEAN/ENGLISH PUB.

Standing on the waterfront across from the ferry dock, Pusser's serves Caribbean fare, English pub grub, and tasty pizzas. It's not as fancy or as good as the previously recommended Pusser's, but it's a lot more convenient and has faster service. The complete lunch and dinner menu includes shepherd's pie and deli-style sandwiches. *Gourmet* magazine published the recipe for its chicken-and-asparagus pie. John Courage ale is on draft, but the drink of choice is the famous Pusser's Rum, the same blend of five West Indian rums that the Royal Navy has served its men for more than 300 years.

✪ **Skyworld.** Ridge Rd., Road Town. ☎ **284/494-3567.** Reservations required. Main courses $16–$28. AE, MC, V. Daily 11am–3pm and 5:30–8:30pm. INTERNATIONAL.

Under new management, Skyworld continues to be all the rage, one of the worthiest dining excursions on the island. On one of Tortola's loftiest peaks, at a breezy 1,337 feet, it offers views of both the U.S. Virgin Islands and the British Virgin Islands. The completely renovated restaurant is now divided into two parts—an upscale section with a dress code for men (shirts with collars and long trousers) and an enclosed garden where you can dine in shorts. Both sections offer the same menu.

The fresh pumpkin soup is an island favorite, but you can also begin with seafood chowder, our favorite. The fresh fish of the day is your best bet for a main course (we prefer to skip the steak with port and peaches). Afterwards, order the finest Key lime pie on the island for dessert, unless you'd prefer the chocolate fudge ice cream pie.

VIRGIN GORDA

Instead of visiting Tortola, some small cruise ships put in at lovely Virgin Gorda, famous for its boulder-strewn beach known as the "Baths." The second-largest island in the colony, it got its name ("Fat Virgin") from Christopher Columbus, who thought the mountain framing it looked like a protruding stomach.

The island was a fairly desolate agricultural community until Laurance S. Rockefeller established Little Dix Bay Hotel here in the early 1960s, following his success with Caneel Bay on St. John a decade earlier. Other major hotels followed, but the privacy and solitude he envisioned still reign supreme on Virgin Gorda.

Virgin Gorda is one of the most irregularly shaped islands in the archipelago. The northern half is mountainous, with one peak reaching 1,370 feet. The southern half is flat, with large boulders appearing at every turn. Spanish Town, also referred to as "The Valley," lies near Virgin Gorda's southwestern corner. Although natural beauty is everywhere on this relatively unpopulated island, some of the roughest scenery is visible from either side of the narrow road that interconnects the southern edge of the island, via a narrow isthmus, to the larger land mass to the north.

COMING ASHORE

Virgin Gorda doesn't have a pier or landing facilities to suit any of the large ships. Most vessels anchor and send small craft ashore. Many others dock beside the pier in Road Town on Tortola, and then send tenders across the channel to Virgin Gorda.

SHORE EXCURSIONS

Many taxi drivers await visitors disembarking from tenders and small boats at Spanish Town. They can take you to the baths and the beach.

GETTING AROUND

The best way to see the island is to call Andy Flax at the Fischers Cove Beach Hotel (☎ 284/495-5252). He runs the **Virgin Gorda Tours Association,** which gives island tours for about $20 per person. Tours leave twice daily. They will pick you up at the dock if you give them a 24-hour notice.

BEACHES

The major reason cruise ships come to Virgin Gorda is to visit the ✪ **"Baths,"** where house-size boulders toppled over one another to form saltwater grottoes. The pools around the Baths are excellent for swimming, as is the snorkeling nearby (equipment can be rented on the beach).

Near the Baths is **Spring Bay,** one of the best of the island's beaches, with white sand, clear water, and good snorkeling. **Trunk Bay** is a wide sand beach that can be reached by boat or via a rough path from Spring Bay. **Savannah Bay** is a sandy stretch north of the yacht harbor, and **Mahoe Bay,** at the Mango Bay Resort, has a gently curving beach and vivid blue water.

Devil's Bay National Park can be reached by a trail from the Baths. The walk to the secluded coral-sand beach takes about 15 minutes through a natural setting of boulders and dry coastal vegetation.

SCUBA DIVING

Kilbrides Underwater Tours, at the Bitter End Resort at North Sound (☎ **800/ 932-4286** in the U.S., or 809/495-9638), offers the best diving in the British Virgin Islands at 15 to 20 dive sites, including the wreck of the ill-fated HMS *Rhône.* Prices range from $80 to $90 for a two-tank dive on one of the coral reefs. Equipment is supplied at no extra charge, and you can purchase a video of your dive.

DINING

Bath and Turtle Pub. Virgin Gorda Yacht Harbour, Spanish Town. ☎ **284/495-5239.** Reservations recommended. Breakfast $4.50–$8.95; lunch entrees $6.75–$9; dinner entrees $9–$20. AE, MC, V. Daily 7am–midnight. INTERNATIONAL.

At the end of the waterfront shopping plaza in Spanish Town sits the most popular pub on Virgin Gorda, packed with locals during happy hour from 4 to 6pm. Even if you don't care about food, consider joining the regulars over midmorning guava coladas or peach daiquiris. From its handful of indoor and courtyard tables, you can order fried fish fingers, nachos, very spicy chili, pizzas, Reubens or tuna melts, steak, lobster, and daily seafood specials such as conch fritters from the simple menu here.

Chez Bamboo. The Valley. ☎ **284/495-5963.** Reservations recommended. Main courses $17–$26; fixed-price menu $60–$80 per couple. MC, V. Daily 6:30–10pm. CONTINENTAL/ CARIBBEAN.

Chez Bamboo lies beside the main road, a short walk north of the yacht harbor at Spanish Town. Located on the ground floor of a clean and modern house, it is the most competent and urbanized of the privately owned restaurants on the island. The decor has been redone to look like a New York jazz club. Outside there's a shaded patio. The menu features many French-accented dishes, but also specializes in Carib-Creole dining, such as conch gumbo, New Orleans–style barbecue shrimp, and lobster with curry sauce.

Teacher Ilma's. The Valley. ☎ **284/495-5355.** Reservations not required for lunch. Full meals $18–$25. No credit cards. Daily 12:30–2pm and 7:30–9:30pm. At Spanish Town, turn left at the main road past the entrance to the Fischers Cove Hotel; the sign to Teacher Ilma's is about 2 minutes ahead to the right. WEST INDIAN.

Mrs. Ilma O'Neal, who taught youngsters in the island's public school for 43 years, began her restaurant by cooking privately for visitors and island construction workers. Main courses might be chicken, local goat meat, lobster, conch, pork, or fish (your choice of grouper, snapper, tuna, dolphin, swordfish, or triggerfish). Desserts include homemade coconut, pineapple, or guava pies. Teacher Ilma's emphasizes that her cuisine is not Creole but local in its origins and flavors.

5 Cozumel & Playa del Carmen ⇩ ⇩ ⇩

Cozumel's rich Mexican culture sets it apart from all other Caribbean ports of call. The island, 44 miles southeast of Cancún, has white sandy beaches and fabulous scuba diving, but its greatest draw is its proximity to the ancient Mayan ruins at Tulum and Chichén Itzá. Some ships also stop at nearby Playa del Carmen, 12 miles from Cozumel, on the Yucatán Peninsula. It's easier to visit the ruins from here than from Cozumel.

COZUMEL

Cozumel was the home of the Mayans for 12 centuries. Pronounced Co-soo-*mehl*, its name comes from the Mayan phrase *cuzam huzil*, or "land of the swallows." The Spanish arrived in 1518, bringing with them smallpox, which quickly devastated the native population. The island may have harbored such buccaneers as Sir Henry Morgan or Jean Lafitte, who reputedly buried gold in tunnels or catacombs dug by the Mayans. Indigenous people returned here in the mid–19th century, when they made their last-ditch stand against Spanish persecution.

As many as a million cruise passengers now visit Cozumel each year. Their presence has greatly changed San Miguel, the island's only town, which now has fast-food eateries and a Hard Rock Café. Fortunately, however, development hasn't touched much of the island's natural beauty. Here you'll see abundant wildlife, including armadillos, brightly colored tropical birds, and lizards. Offshore, the government has set aside 20 miles of coral reef as an underwater national park, including the stunning Palancar Reef, the world's second largest natural coral formation.

COMING ASHORE

Ships arriving at Muelle Fiscal on Cozumel tender passengers directly to the heart of San Miguel. From the downtown pier it's possible to walk to the shops, restaurants, and cafes. Other ships anchor off the international pier four miles from San Miguel. The beaches are close to the international pier.

You can make telephone calls from the **Calling Station**, Avenida Rafael Melgar 27 (☎ 987/2-1417), at the corner of Calle 3 in San Miguel, 3 blocks from Muelle Fiscal. The station issues prepaid phone cards, operates an international money exchange, and has a fax machine. It's open daily from 8am to 11pm.

FAST FACTS

Currency   The Mexican currency is the nuevo peso, or new peso. Its symbol is the "$" sign, but it's hardly the equivalent of the U.S. dollar. Since the peso has fluctuated wildly in recent years, we have given prices in this section in U.S. dollars. Mexican coins come in denominations of 1, 2, 5, and 10 pesos, and 20 and 50 centavos. It takes 100 centavos to equal 1 new peso. Paper currency comes in denominations of 2, 5, 10, 20, 50, and 100 new pesos. At press time, one dollar was worth 8.6 new pesos, but remember, this could be subject to dramatic change.

Currency Exchange   The following banks, all a block or less from the Muelle Fiscal pier, change currency: **Banpais,** Rafael Melgar 27A (☎ 987/2-0318), is open

The Yucatán's Upper Caribbean Coast

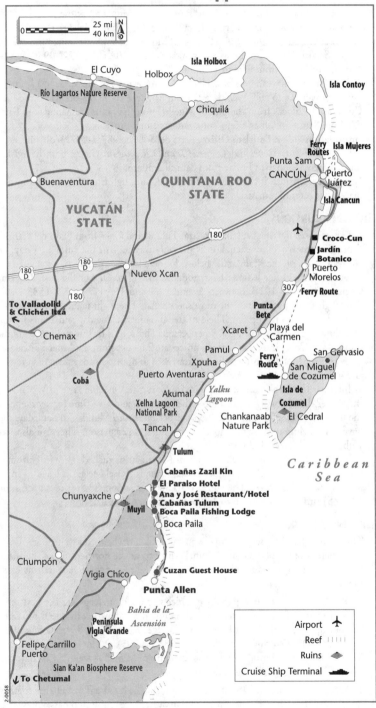

25 mi
40 km

Isla Holbox

El Cuyo
Holbox

Isla Contoy

Río Lagartos Nature Reserve

Chiquilá

Ferry Routes
Isla Mujeres

Punta Sam
CANCÚN
Puerto Juárez

Buenaventura

QUINTANA ROO STATE

Isla Cancun

YUCATÁN STATE

180

Croco-Cun
Jardín Botanico
Puerto Morelos

180 D

180 D

Nuevo Xcan

307
Ferry Route

180

Punta Bete

To Valladolid & Chichén Itzá

Xcaret
Playa del Carmen

Chemax

Pamul

San Gervasio

Xpuha

Ferry Route

San Miguel de Cozumel

Cobá

Puerto Aventuras

Yalku Lagoon

Akumal
Xelha Lagoon National Park

Isla de Cozumel

Chankanaab Nature Park
El Cedral

Tancah

Tulum

Caribbean Sea

Cabañas Zazil Kin
El Paraiso Hotel
Ana y José Restaurant/Hotel
Cabañas Tulum
Boca Paila Fishing Lodge
Boca Paila

Chunyaxche

Muyil

Chumpón

Cuzan Guest House

Vigia Chíco
Punta Allen

Bahia de la Ascensión

Peninsula Vigia Grande

Felipe Carrillo Puerto

Sian Ka'an Biosphere Reserve

To Chetumal

Airport
Reef
Ruins
Cruise Ship Terminal

2-0058

Monday to Friday from 9am to 1pm. **Bancomer,** Avenida 5A at the Plaza (☎ **987/ 2-0550**), is open Monday to Friday from 9am to 3pm. **Banco del Atlantico,** Avenida 5A Sur at Calle 1 (☎ **987/2-0142**), is open Monday to Friday from 8:30am to 6pm. **Banco Serfin,** Calle 1 Sur between Avenidas 5A and 10A (☎ **987/2-0930**), is open Monday to Friday from 9am to 1:30pm.

Foreign currency can also be exchanged at **American Express,** Calle 11 Sur 598 between Avenida 25 and Avenida 30 in San Miguel (☎ **987/2-0831**), in the Fiesta Cozumel, 15 blocks from the pier of Muelle Fiscal. Its hours are Monday to Saturday from 8am to noon and 5 to 7pm, Sunday from 4 to 5pm.

Information The **Tourism Office,** Plaza del Sol (☎ **987/2-0972**), distributes *Vacation Guide to Cozumel* and *Cozumel Island's Restaurant Guide;* both have island maps. Open Monday to Friday from 8am to 2:30pm.

Language Spanish is the tongue of the land, although English is spoken in most places that cater to tourists.

SHORE EXCURSIONS

It's easier to see the ruins at Chichén Itzá, Tulum, and Cobá from Playa del Carmen. From Cozumel, a shore excursion is the only way to visit the ruins in a day. See "Mayan Ruins on the Mainland," below, for details about the ruins.

Tour agencies offer various 1-day tours to the ruins. One of the best, **Intermar Caribe,** Calle 2 N 101B, between Avenidas 5A and 10A (☎ **987/2-1535**), offers daily flights to Chichén Itzá, the most spectacular. The flight takes 40 minutes each way and cost $115 per person. The outfitter also offers a Tuesday and Thursday tour of Tulum and Xel-Ha, costing $79 per person. This tour is by bus and ferry. Another tour goes to Coba. Intermar Caribe's offices are 2 blocks from the Muelle Fiscal pier. They're open Monday through Friday from 8am to 8pm, Saturday from 8am to 1pm and 4 to 7pm, and Sunday from 9am to 1pm.

Intermar Caribe also offers excursions on Cozumel. On Monday and Wednesday, they cover the major sights, including the museum, and save time for snorkeling at the national park. This tour costs $35 per person. From Monday to Saturday, they have a snorkeling tour by boat to Cozumel for $50 per person. They can also have scuba diving daily, with dives starting at $50.

For a 3-hour guided horseback tour of Mayan ruins tucked away in Cozumel's tropical forest, contact **Rancho Buenavista,** Avenida Rafael Melgar at Calle 11 in San Miguel (☎ **987/2-1537**). The outing costs $60 per person. The office is open Monday to Saturday from 8:30am to 1:30pm and from 4:30 to 7:30pm.

GETTING AROUND

The town of San Miguel is so small you can walk anywhere you want to go. Essentially there is only one road in Cozumel—it starts at the northern tip of the island, hugs the western shoreline, then loops around the southern tip and returns to the capital.

CAR RENTALS Four-wheel-drive vehicles or open-air Jeeps are the best rental choice because of the rough terrain and bumpy dirt side roads that lead to remote beaches and out-of-the-way Mayan ruins. **Budget Rent-a-Car,** Avenida 5A at Calle 2 N (☎ **800/527-0700** in the U.S., or 987/2-0903), 2 blocks from the pier at Muelle Fiscal, rents both. A four-door economy car rents for about $35 a day, with a Jeep Cherokee going for $45 and up.

TAXIS Taxi service (☎ **987/2-0236**) is available 24 hours a day. Cabs are relatively inexpensive, but since it's customary here to overcharge cruise ship passengers, settle

San Miguel de Cozumel

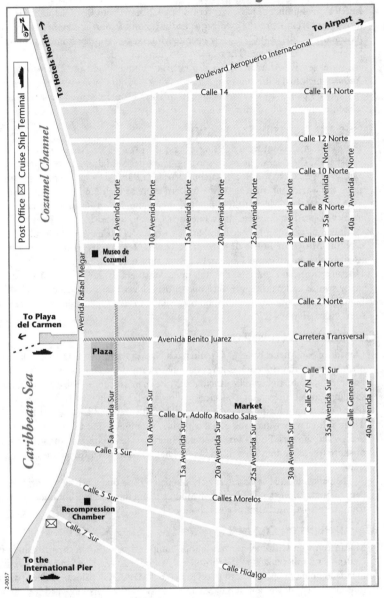

on a fare before getting in. The average fare from San Miguel to most major resorts and beaches is $7. More distant island rides cost $12 and up.

MOPEDS Mopeds are a popular means of getting about despite heavy traffic, hidden stop signs, potholed roads, and a high accident rate. The best and most convenient rentals are at **Auto Rent** (☎ 987/2-0844) in the Hotel Ceiba, a block from the pier at Muelle Fiscal. The cost is about $28 per day. Mexican law requires helmets. Hours are daily from 7am to 6:30pm.

FERRY   A number of passenger ferries link Cozumel with Playa del Carmen. The most comfortable are the two big speedboats and water-jet catamaran run by **Aviomar** (☎ **987/2-0477**). They operate Monday to Saturday from 8am to 8pm, Sunday from 9am to 1pm. The trip takes 45 minutes. Other vessels include the modern water jet **WJ México,** which also takes 45 minutes, and the **Cozmeleño and Xelha,** which make the trip in about 55 minutes. All the ferries have ticket booths at the main pier. One-way fares range from $4 to $5 per person. You'll get a ferry schedule when you buy your ticket.

SEEING THE SIGHTS IN SAN MIGUEL

The classic grid layout makes getting around the town of San Miguel easy. Directly across from the docks, the main square—Plaza del Sol (also Called *la plaza* or *el parque*)—is excellent for people watching. Avenida Rafael Melgar, the principal street along the waterfront, runs along the western shore of the island, site of the best resorts and beaches. Most of the shops and restaurants are on Rafael Melgar, though many well-stocked duty-free shops line the Malecón, the seaside promenade.

Only 3 blocks from Muelle Fiscal on Agenda Rafael Melgar between Calles 4 and 6 N, the **Museo de la Isla de Cozumel** (☎ **987/2-1434**) has two floors of exhibits displayed in what was Cozumel's first luxury hotel. Exhibits start in the pre-Hispanic times and continue through the colonial era to the present. Included are many swords and nautical artifacts; one display showcases endangered species. The highlight is a charming reproduction of a Mayan house. Open daily from 10am to 6pm. Admission is $1.75.

CHANKANAAB NATURE PARK

Outside of San Miguel is the ✪ **Chankanaab Nature Park,** where a saltwater lagoon, offshore reefs, and underwater caves have been turned into an archaeological park, botanical garden, and wildlife sanctuary. More than 10 countries have contributed seedlings and cuttings. Some 60 species of marine life occupy the lagoon, including sea turtles. Reproductions of Mayan dwellings are scattered throughout the park. There's also a wide white-sand beach with thatch umbrellas and a changing area with lockers and showers. Both scuba divers and snorkelers like examining the sunken ship offshore (there are four dive shops here). The park also has a restaurant and snack stand.

The park is located at Carretera Sur, kilometer 9 (no phone). It's open daily from 9am to 5pm. Admission is $7, free for children 9 and under. The 10-minute taxi ride from the pier at Muelle Fiscal costs about $5.

MAYAN RUINS ON COZUMEL

Mayan ruins on Cozumel are very minor compared to those on the mainland. **El Cedral** lies 2 miles inland at the turnoff at km 17.5, east of Playa San Francisco. It's the island's oldest structure, with traces of original Mayan wall paintings. The Spanish tore much of it down, and the U.S. Army nearly finished the job when it built an airfield here in World War II. Little remains now except a Mayan arch and a few small ruins covered in heavy growth. Guides at the site will show you around for a fee.

Another meager ruin is at **San Gervasio,** reached by driving west across the island to the army airbase, then turning right and continuing north four miles to San Gervasio. This was once a ceremonial center and capital of Cozumel. The Mayans dedicated the area to Ixchel, the fertility goddess. The ruins cost $3.50 to visit, plus $1 for entrance to the access road. Guides will show up to six persons what's left, including several broken columns and lintels, for $12. Open daily from 8am to 5pm.

MAYAN RUINS ON THE MAINLAND

Chichén Itzá

The largest and most fabled of the Yucatán ruins, Chichén Itzá was founded in A.D. 445 by the Mayans, then inhabited by the conquering Toltecs of Central Mexico. Two centuries later, it was mysteriously abandoned. After lying dormant for two more centuries, the site was resettled and enjoyed prosperity again until the early 13th century, when it was once more relinquished to the surrounding jungle. The area covers 7 square miles, so you can see only a fraction of it on a day trip.

The best known of the ruins is the pyramid Castillo of Kukulcán, which is actually an astronomical clock designed to mark the vernal and autumnal equinoxes and the summer and winter solstices. A total of 365 steps, one for each day of the year, ascend to the top platform. During each equinox, light striking the pyramid gives the illusion of a giant snake slithering down the steps to join its gigantic stone head mounted at the base.

The government began restoration on the site in the 1920s. Today it houses a museum, a 250-seat restaurant, and a shop. Admission is included in shore excursions; otherwise, the site and museum cost $4 Monday to Saturday, free on Sunday. Children under 12 are admitted free. Use of a video camera costs $4. It's open daily from 8am to 5pm. For more information call ☎ **985/1-0137.**

Tulum

Eighty miles south of Cancún, the walled city of Tulum is the single most visited Mayan ruin. It was the only Mayan city built on the coast and the only one inhabited when the Spanish conquistadors arrived in the 1500s. From here you can see wonderful panoramic views of the Caribbean. Tulum consists of 60 individual structures. As with Chichén Itzá, its most prominent feature is a pyramid topped with a temple to Kukulcán, the primary Mayan/Olmec god. Other important structures include the Temple of the Frescoes, the Temple of the Descending God, the House of Columns, and the House of the Cenote, which is a well. Entrance is included in shore excursions; otherwise, it's $3.50 Monday to Saturday, free on Sunday. Use of a video camera costs $4. The site is open daily from 8am to 5pm.

Cobá

A 35-minute drive northwest of Tulum puts you at Cobá, site of one of the most important city-states in the Mayan empire. Cobá flourished from A.D. 400 to 1100, its population numbering perhaps as many as 40,000. Excavation work began in 1972, but archaeologists estimate that only 5% of this dead city has yet been uncovered. The site lies on four lakes. Its 81 primitive acres provide excellent exploration opportunities for the hiker. Cobá's pyramid, Nohoch Mul, is the tallest in the Yucatán. The price of admission is included in shore excursions; otherwise, it's $2 Monday to Saturday, free on Sunday and free for children under 12. Each videocamera carries an additional $4 charge. The site is open daily from 8am to 7pm. The location is 105 miles south of Cancún.

SHOPPING

You can walk from the pier at Muelle Fiscal to the best shops, all of which are centered in San Miguel. Because of the influx of cruise ship passengers, prices are relatively high here.

To stock up on your reading while at sea, head to **Agencia Publicaciones Gracia, Avenida 5A** (☎ **987/2-0031**), Cozumel's best source for English-language books, guidebooks, newspapers, and magazines. It's a block from Muelle Fiscal.

Casablanca. Avenida Rafael Melgar 33. ☎ **987/2-1177.**

Located in front of the international port, this store has a fine selection of Mexican jewelry and loose stones, plus a well-chosen collection of Mexican crafts.

Explora. Avenida Rafael Melgar 49. ☎ **987/2-0894.**

Only 1 1/2 blocks from Muelle Fiscal, this outlet is your best bet for women's casual clothing. Its selection is the most stylish in town. It also sells attractive beachwear.

Gordon Gilchrist. Studio 1, Avenida 25 S 981 at Calle 15 S. ☎ **987/2-2659.**

This local artist produces Cozumel's finest etchings of local Mayan sites. He also displays and sells pencil drawings and limited-edition lithographs of the ruins. Open daily from 3 to 8pm or by appointment. The location is a 7-minute taxi ride from the international pier or a 3-minute taxi ride from Muelle Fiscal.

Joyería Palancar. Avenida Rafael Melgar N15. ☎ **987/2-1468.**

Established in 1978, this outlet has an amazing collection of topaz and amethyst, and also sells silver Mexican coins. It's located between Calles 2 and 4, one and a half miles from Muelle Fiscal.

La Fiesta Warehouse. Avenida Rafael Melgar 101. ☎ **987/2-2032.**

This store has a wide selection of merchandise, ranging from casual clothing (too, too many T-shirts) to a good selection of handmade Mexican crafts in wood, paper, silver, and pottery, all brought here from the mainland. It's located an easy walk from the pier at Muelle Fiscal, and as such it's likely to be packed with cruisers off the ships. Shipping is available.

Rachat & Romero. Avenida Rafael Melgar 101. ☎ **987/2-0571.**

This outlet has a wide variety of loose stones, which they will mount while you wait. Gold mountings take from 30 minutes to 1 1/2 hours.

Ultra Femme. Avenida Rafael Melgar 341. ☎ **987/2-1251.**

This is one of the most important jewelers in all of Cozumel, and the exclusive distributor of Rolex watches on the Mexican Riviera. It also sells such famous names as Ebel, Rado, and Gucci, along with Waterford and Swarovski crystal.

Unicornio. 5 Avenida Sur 2. ☎ **987/2-0171.**

Situated 2 blocks from Muelle Fiscal, this shop lures visitors with its well-chosen collection of Mexican handcrafts, which come from various provinces across the country. You'll find everything from wooden animals from Oaxaca to masks from Guerrero.

Van Cleef & Arpels. Avenida Rafael Melgar 54. ☎ **987/2-1143.**

This outlet of the fabled dealer offers the best in high-quality silver and gold jewelry. Go here only if you're seeking something toney. It also sells copper and silver figurines. Don't take seriously its claim of discounts from 5% to 15%.

Department Stores

Los Cinco Soles. Avenida Rafael Melgar N 27. ☎ **987/2-0132.**

This department store has a bit of everything, including Mexican crafts, clothing, and jewelry, all at reasonable prices. Its selection of hand-crafted items is the largest and among the best in Cozumel. Onyx, papier-mâché fruit, reproductions of Mayan art, and plenty of silver jewelry—it's all here.

Pama. Avenida Rafael Melgar S 9. ☎ **987/2-0090.**

This small department store, just a block from the port at Muelle Fiscal, offers a line of dress clothes for men, swimsuits for women, and sandals for the beach. It also carries a good assortment of perfume and designer jewelry by the likes of Cartier or Paloma Picasso. Check out its selection of leather goods, as well.

Prococo. Avenida Rafael Melgar N99. ☎ **987/2-1964.**

This is another good department store a block from the Muelle Fiscal pier. It has one of the best and widest selections of Mexican crafts in town, including Mexican religious artifacts, such as metal and wooden crosses. There's a wide array of Mexican pottery and leather goods here as well, plus everything from French perfumes to Swiss knives. It's also a good bet if you're just seeking souvenirs.

BEACHES

Cozumel's best beach of powdery white sand, **Playa San Francisco,** stretches for some 3 miles along the southwestern shoreline. It was once one of the most idyllic beaches in Mexico, but resort development is threatening to destroy its old character. You can rent equipment for various water sports here, or have lunch at one of the many *palapa* restaurants and bars on the shoreline. The beach lies a $4 taxi ride south of San Miguel's downtown pier. If you land at the international pier, you're practically at the beach already.

Many of your fellow cruisers have heard of the fine **Playa del Sol,** about a mile south of Playa del San Francisco, so it's likely to be overcrowded.

Playa Bonita is one of the least crowded beaches, but it lies on the east (windward) side of the island and is difficult to reach unless you rent a vehicle or throw yourself upon the mercy of a taxi driver. It sits in a moon-shaped cove sheltered from the Caribbean Seas by an offshore reef. Waves are only moderate here, the sand powdery and the water clear. Sometimes this beach is called Punta Chiqueros.

SCUBA DIVING & SNORKELING

Jacques Cousteau did much to extol the glory of Cozumel for scuba divers. Here he discovered black coral in profusion, plus hundreds of species of rainbow-hued tropical fish. Underwater visibility can reach 250 feet. All this gives Cozumel the best diving in the Caribbean.

Cruisers may want to confine their adventures to the finest spot, Palancar Reef. Lying about a mile offshore, this fabulous water world features gigantic elephant-ear sponges and black and red coral, as well as deep caves, canyons, and tunnels. It's a favorite of divers from all over the world.

The best scuba outfitter is **Aqua Safari,** Avenida Rafael Melgar at Calle 5, next to the Vista del Mar Hotel (☎ **987/2-0101**). Hours are daily from 8am to 2pm. One-tank dives cost $35, two-tank dives $50.

A worthwhile competitor is **Diving Adventures,** Calle 51 Sur no. 2, near the corner of Avenida Rafael Melgar (☎ **987/2-3009**). Its prices and itineraries are equivalent. Hours here are daily 8am to 2pm with a one-tank dive costing $35, a two-tank dive $50.

Snorkeling is Cozumel's biggest attraction for non-divers. Shallow reefs at Playa San Francisco or Chankanaab Bay are among the best spots. You'll see a world of sea creatures parading by, everything from parrot fish to conch. The best outfitter is **Cozumel Snorkeling Center,** Calle Primera Sur (☎ **987/2-0539**), which offers a 3-hour snorkeling tour at a cost of $30 per person, including all equipment and refreshments. They can also arrange **parasailing** at a cost of $45 for 15 minutes. Hours are Monday to Saturday from 8am to 1pm and from 4 to 8pm, Sunday from 8am to 1pm.

DINING

Because some ships anchor overnight, you may be able to have dinner as well as lunch on the island.

✪ Café del Puerto. Avenida Rafael Melgar 3. ☎ **987/2-0316.** Main courses $8–$18. AE, MC, V. Daily 5–11pm. INTERNATIONAL.

Located right in front of the in-town cruise dock, this local favorite is a good bet if your ship plans to leave late in the evening or else is anchored overnight. It's the best place for a romantic dinner and a margarita as you watch the sun go down. Piano music sets the mood. A spiral staircase leads to the main dining room and a "loft" with a view down over the diners. The international kitchen bridges the gap between Mexico and Europe. Recent high points have included a superbly prepared mustard steak flambé. The chef also produces a succulent lobster and a good prime rib. Yes, they even serve tamales. Unlike the hysteria prevailing in some San Miguel restaurants, we have found the service here professional, unobtrusive, and rather polished.

Carlos 'n' Charlie's. Avenida Rafael Melgar 11. ☎ **987/2-0191.** Reservations recommended only for groups. Main courses $10–$15. AE, MC, V. Mon–Fri 10am–1am, Sat 11am–1pm, Sun 5pm–1am. MEXICAN/INTERNATIONAL.

Just north of the ferry pier, this cornpone favorite is part of one of the most popular Mexican chains. People come here for good times and ribs. If you get past the T-shirts, auto tags, and Ping-Pong table—and if the waiter can hear your order over the rock and roll music—you can dine surprisingly well. The ribs are spicy and well flavored, almost as good as those in the Hard Rock Cozumel (see below). The stuffed shrimp with cheese wrapped in bacon is equally delectable. Fresh fish and Mexican steak are the most expensive items here. Service is often hectic, but rather professional. There's quite a party scene at night if you're still in port.

El Capi Navegante. Avenida 10A Sur 312 at Calles 3 and 5. ☎ **987/2-1730.** Reservations recommended. Main courses $9–$18. MC, V. Daily noon–11pm. SEAFOOD.

In our search for the best seafood in Cozumel, a savvy local foodie brought us here, only 5 blocks from Muelle Fiscal. The proud owner offers the freshest fish in San Miguel. We thought his kitchen was at its best with lobster flambé, although there's also a good shrimp soufflé. The chef is justifiably proud of his parilla al Capi, a grilled platter of octopus, calamari, shrimp, and whatever is good and fresh that day. Local men claim the conch ceviche—the best we've sampled here—makes them more virile. The place has a nautical decor, with a marine blue-and-white color scheme and life preservers on the walls. You can dine inside or out.

Hard Rock Cozumel. Avenida Rafael Melgar 2A. ☎ **987/2-0885.** Reservations not accepted. Main courses $10–$16. AE, MC, V. Daily 10am–midnight. AMERICAN.

Given Cozumel's growing popularity with Americans, it was bound to happen: a local branch of the Hard Rock Café chain cropped up. Its juicy burgers aren't as good as those of the stateside outlets, but they're still the best in Cozumel. The ribs here are excellent. You can also order a 14-ounce New York steak, along with a selection of well-stuffed sandwiches. Since this is Mexico, the cafe also serves grilled beef or chicken fajitas. The sassy waiters cope very well, even when the place is packed with cruise ship passengers. Naturally, there's the prerequisite rock memorabilia that has come into close bodily contact with fabled rock stars. Live music is presented daily.

La Choza. Calle Rosada Salas 198 at Avenida 10A Sur. ☎ **987/2-0958.** Main courses $8–$20. AE, MC, V. Daily 7:30am–11pm. YUCATECAN.

This restaurant, located only 2 blocks from the Muelle Fiscal pier, offers local cookery prepared by the capable hands of the Espinosa family. Their Mexican specialties are the most authentic in town. A good choice is the savory chicken in blackened pepper sauce. The red snapper is delectable in a rather sweet-tasting mustard sauce, as is the grilled lobster. Grilled beef is perfectly done. They will also grill or fry fresh fish as you like it. Of course, they have typical Mexican items such as chicken fajitas as well. For dessert, try avocado pie. You dine in a palm-covered patio with wooden tables and chairs and oilcloth coverings, and eat from handmade pottery dishes.

✪ **La Veranda.** Calle 4 Norte. ☎ 987/2-4132. Reservations required in winter. Main courses $11–$36. MC, V. Daily 5pm–1am. INTERNATIONAL/SEAFOOD.

Those remaining in port late or else overnight will find the best meal in Cozumel served here. Built in the classic Yucatan style with cutout wood trim, La Veranda is both a stylish Mexican cantina and a first-class restaurant. The mahogany bar glimmers with brass and polished glass, whereas the restaurant is more formal, with first-class tables. The portions here are large. The menu reflects the best of seasonal produce, emphasizing freshness and flavor, as exemplified by the carpaccio of salmon. The ginger chicken is zesty with flavor, but the spice isn't overpowering. Fresh fish is prepared to perfection. If you'd like a sampling of everything, opt for the Caribbean seafood platter with lobster, shrimp, octopus, and calamari. Of course, you'll also find the standard array of enchiladas, quesadillas, rice and beans, and the guacamole, but this is not where the kitchen shines. Seats are available inside or else al fresco.

Las Palmeras. Avenida Rafael Melgar. ☎ **987/2-0532.** Breakfast plates $4–$5; main courses $3–$7. AE, MC, V. Daily 7am–11pm. INTERNATIONAL/MEXICAN.

Just half a block from Muelle Fiscal, this restaurant is ideal for casual dining. Patios of red brick with ceiling fans and potted palms evoke a *Casablanca* mood. If you arrive in time, come for one of the best breakfasts in town. You can also drop in during the day for Cozumel's finest margaritas and piña coladas. For lunch or dinner, there's a selection of tempting seafood dishes or Mexican specialties. The succulent, thick grilled pork chop comes with a guacamole sauce and a salad. The filet of grouper is grilled just right (not dry) and served with freshly made french fries or rice.

Pepe's Grill. Avenida Rafael Melgar at Salas. ☎ **987/2-0213.** Reservations recommended. Main courses $10–$26. AE, MC, V. Daily 5–11:30pm. GRILL/INTERNATIONAL.

If your ship is staying late instead of leaving at 5pm, consider an early dinner at Pepe's, only 2 blocks from the international port. This romantic and bustling place by the waterfront features a variety of live music. The decor is aggressively nautical, with everything from wind vanes to fishnets. Tall windows open onto views of the *malecón* (the seaside promenade). You can also enjoy alfresco dining downstairs. Our only reservation about this restaurant is its huge popularity with the cruise ship crowd. What draws them here is the selection of succulent flame-broiled specialties, including prime rib and filet mignon. The kitchen also turns out some of the best lobster and king crab dishes on the island. Grilled mushrooms or shrimp with zesty seasonings are also delightful. *A dining tip:* The steaks, such as chateaubriand, come from the city of Chihuahua and are among the best in Mexico.

✪ **Prima Trattoria.** Avenida Adolfo Rosada 109. ☎ **987/2-4242.** Main courses $5–$19. AE, MC, V. Daily 3–11pm. ITALIAN/SEAFOOD.

When you can't face another taco, head here for an Italian food fix. This restaurant serves the best pizza on the island, and its other Italian specialties are also eminently respectable, especially the creamy lobster fettuccine Alfredo—one of the best renderings of this fattening dish we've ever had in Mexico. The bustle level is high as waiters whiz about with big pizza pies, the largest of which will feed a trio of hungry diners. The *carte* contains all kinds of pasta—those made with lobster, crab, or shrimp are the tastiest. All the bread is homemade. The preferred dining spot here is upstairs on the terrace, which is often cooled by trade winds.

Santigo's Grill. Calle Rosada Salas 299 at Avenida 15A Sur. ☎ **987/2-2137.** Reservations highly recommended if the staff will grant you one. Main courses $5–$10. MC, V. Daily 5–11pm. MEXICAN/INTERNATIONAL.

If your ship is leaving late enough for an early dinner ashore, try this restaurant, 3 blocks from Muelle Fiscal. It's so good you may find it hard to get a seat and one of its 10 tables. You can dine inside or out. Service is fast and professional, and the ambience and welcome are first rate. The shrimp with garlic is one of the best on Cozumel. Fresh lobster appears frequently on the menu, and is seldom overcooked. The seafood platter is a delight, a medley of conch, calamari, shrimp, lobster, and other fish caught in Mexican waters. The filet of sea bass is generally perfectly grilled and served with fresh vegetables and a baked potato. Seafood is king here; even the filet mignon comes stuffed with shrimp.

PLAYA DEL CARMEN

Some cruise ships spend 1 day at Cozumel, then another at Playa del Carmen. The Mayan ruins described under "Mayan Ruins on the Mainland," above, are easier to reach from Playa del Carmen, since it's on the Yucatán mainland.

The famed white sand beach here was relatively untouched by tourists not many years ago, but today the pleasure-seeking hordes have replaced the Indian families who used to gather coconuts for copra. If you can tolerate the crowds, snorkeling is excellent over the offshore reefs. Turtle-watching is another local pastime.

Avenida Juárez in Playa del Carmen is the principal business zone for the Tulum-Cancún corridor. Part of Avenida 5 running parallel to the beach has been closed to traffic, forming a good promenade. Most visitors at some point head for Rincón del Sol, which is a tree-filled courtyard built in the colonial Mexican style. This has the best collection of handcraft shops in the area, some of which offer goods of excellent quality, not the junky souvenirs peddled elsewhere.

COMING ASHORE

Some cruise ships dock at anchor, or at the pier of Cozumel, and then send passengers over to Playa del Carmen by tender. Others dock at the new Puerto Calica Cruise Pier, which lies 8 miles to the south of Playa del Carmen. Taxis meet each arriving ship, and drivers transport visitors into the center of Playa del Carmen.

SHORE EXCURSIONS: SEEING THE RUINS

Other than the beach, there is no major attraction in Playa del Carmen except Xcaret (see "An Ecological Theme Park," below). Most visitors head for the Mayan ruins the moment they reach shore. All cruise ships offer excursions to the major ones, which are booked through the travel agent **Aviomar,** Hotel Molcas Domicello, Playa del Carmen (☎ **987/3-0137**). The most popular is to the ruins of Chichén Itza on the Yucatan Peninsula. A plane tour costing $99 leaves daily; a bus tour for $74 goes only on Monday, Wednesday, and Friday. Bus tours also go to Tulum and Cobá—two important ceremonial centers—on Monday, Wednesday, and Friday, for $79 per person.

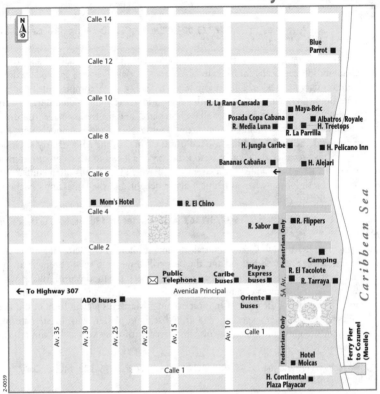

GETTING AROUND

CAR RENTALS Be sure to arm yourself with a good map if you plan to do some exploring on your own. **National,** Hotel Molcas, Avenida sur 5A (☎ **800/227-7368** in the U.S., or 987/3-0360), rents Volkswagens with no air-conditioning at $34 a day. Air-conditioned vehicle should be reserved a day ahead of time, and may cost $63 a day. Another source for rentals is **Dollar,** Hotel Diamond at Playacar (☎ **987/3-0340**), which rents Volkswagens with no air-conditioning for $50 a day and Jeep Cherokees for $72 a day. Reserve a day ahead of time.

TAXIS Taxis are readily available to take you anywhere, but you can walk to the center of town, the beach, and most of the major shops.

AN ECOLOGICAL THEME PARK

Lying 4 miles south of Playa del Carmen on the coast, **Xcaret** is a 250-acre ecological theme park in which many visitors spend their entire day. Mayan ruins are scattered about the lushly landscaped acres. Visitors can put on life jackets for an underwater river ride, which takes them through currents running throughout a series of caves. There's also a botanical garden and a dive shop. Xcaret is open Monday to Saturday from 8:30am to 8:30pm, Sunday from 8am to 5pm. General admission is a steep $39 for adults, $24 for children 5 to 12 (free for kids 4 and under). For information, call ☎ **988/3-0654.** Buses from Playa del Carmen come here frequently; a taxi costs $4 one-way.

DINING

El Chino. Calle 4 (Avenida 15). ☎ **987/3-0015**. Breakfast $2.50–$4; main courses $5–$10. Daily 8am–11pm. MEXICAN/YUCATECAN.

Visitors arriving here think this place is a chop suey joint—actually, it's a pristine restaurant known locally for its regional Yucatan specialties as well as standard dishes from throughout Mexico. The atmosphere is friendly and welcoming. Tile floors and clean, bright wooden tables, along with a side patio where you can dine al fresco, form the backdrop. The menu items are all well-prepared, and the freshly made fruit drinks are among the area's finest. Chicken breast Santo Angel is angelic enough, with prosciutto and cheese, sautéed in seasoned bread crumbs in the Milanese style. Grilled fresh fish is presented daily, often wrapped in banana leaves to which onions, tomato, and spices have been added for a Creole-like flavor. Fresh fish is often stuffed with shrimp. Fresh lobster when available is also a delight, but the fajitas and ceviche are rather standard fare.

El Tacolote. Avenida Juárez. ☎ **987/3-1363**. Main courses $6–$28. AE, MC, V. Daily 9am–3am. MEXICAN/SEAFOOD.

A popular restaurant in Cozumel installed another branch here, across from La Plaza. Both specialize in fresh seafood and the best grilled meats in town, brought to your table fresh from the broiler on a charcoal pan to keep the food warm. All the Mexican staples such as tacos or fajitas are available too. You can dine inside or out, on a terrace overlooking the ocean. On most evenings Mariachis play in front of the sidewalk tables. The chef's specialty is a grilled seafood platter, with lobster, shrimp, calamari, octopus, and fresh filet of fish, served with fresh vegetables and a baked potato or rice.

✪ **Máscaras.** Avenida Juárez. ☎ **987/3-1053**. Main courses $6–$20. MC, V. Daily 1pm–midnight. ITALIAN.

Both local residents and out-of-towners flock here for great pastas, brick-oven pizzas, and other Italian dishes. The four-cheese pizza is justifiably the most popular. The homemade pastas are equally good, especially the fettuccine in a Roquefort cream sauce. The best of the other Italian dishes is the calamari in olive oil and garlic. This place also grills some of the freshest fish in town. Several good wines are available, most of them reasonably priced, although margaritas with freshly squeezed lime juice seem to be the drink of choice. The walls are decorated with exotic masks from around the world.

6 Curaçao ⚓ ⚓ ⚓

One of the great experiences in Caribbean cruising is to sail into the harbor of Willemstad on Curaçao. A quaint "floating bridge" swings aside to welcome you into the narrow channel, set against a backdrop of rows of colorful, gabled Dutch houses. Just 35 miles north of the coast of Venezuela, this largest and most populous of the Netherlands Antilles attracts visitors with its distinctive culture, friendly people, duty-free shopping, lively casinos, water sports, and international cuisine.

Curaçao today is the most architecturally interesting island in the entire West Indies, with more European flavor than anywhere else in the Caribbean. The Dutch-colonial architecture gives Willemstad a storybook look. Hemmed in by the sea, a tiny canal, and an inlet, the streets are narrow and cross-hatched by still narrower alleyways. The three- and four-story houses are crowned by "step" gables and roofed with orange Spanish tiles. Legend says the house's pastel colors are a holdover from the

time when bright white gave headaches to one of the island's early governors. Willemstad's fairy-tale appearance may remind you of old Amsterdam, but don't let the colors deceive you. The city can be rather dirty.

Classic Dutch-style windmills stand in and around Willemstad and in some parts of the countryside, but most of this desert-like island may remind you of the American Southwest, with its amalgam of browns and russets, three-pronged cactus, spiny-leafed aloe, and divi-divi trees bent by centuries of trade winds.

Willemstad grew up on both sides of a canal. Today it's divided into the **Punda** (Old World Dutch ambience and the best shopping) and the more contemporary **Otrabanda** ("the other side"). Both sections are connected by the **Queen Emma Pontoon Bridge,** a pedestrian walkway. Powered by a diesel engine, it swings open many times every day to let ships from all over the globe pass in and out of the harbor. Vehicles must take the **Queen Juliana Bridge,** which rises 195 feet over the harbor, making it the highest bridge in the Caribbean and one of the tallest in the world.

Peter Stuyvesant, stomping on his pegleg, ruled Curaçao in 1644. Bristling with forts and thick ramparts, Willemstad served as a Dutch Gibraltar back then. The hilltop forts—many now converted into restaurants—protected the vast natural harbor and its coastal approach.

But Willemstad subsequently became a quiet, sleepy town, and remained so until Royal Dutch/Shell built one of the world's largest oil refineries here to process crude from Venezuela. Workers from some 50 countries then poured onto the island, turning it into a polyglot, cosmopolitan place with a population of more than 170,000. Politically a part of the Netherlands, Curaçao has its own governmental authority and relies on the mother country only for defense and foreign affairs.

COMING ASHORE

Cruise ships dock at the terminal just beyond the Queen Emma pontoon bridge, which leads to the duty-free shopping sector and the famous floating market. You can call home from the terminal's phone office. It's a 6- to 10-minute walk from here to the center of Willemstad, or you can take a taxi from the stand. The town itself is easy to navigate on foot. Most of it can be explored in 2 or 3 hours, leaving plenty of time for beaches or water sports. Although the ship terminal has a duty-free shop, save your serious purchases for Willemstad.

FAST FACTS

Currency Canadian and U.S. dollars are accepted for purchases, so there's no need to change money. The official currency is the **Netherlands Antillean florin (NAf)**, also called a guilder, which is divided into 100 cents. The exchange rate is 1 U.S. dollar to 1.77 NAf (or 1 NAf equals 56¢ U.S.). Shops, hotels, and restaurants usually accept most major U.S. and Canadian credit and charge cards. Unless otherwise noted, prices in this section are given in U.S. dollars.

Information For visitor information, go to the **Curaçao Tourist Board,** Pietermaai (☎ **599/9-4616000**). Open Monday to Friday from 9am to 5pm.

Language Dutch, Spanish, and English are spoken on Curaçao, along with Papiamento, a patois that combines the three major tongues with Amerindian and African dialects.

SHORE EXCURSIONS

Excursions aren't really worth the price here—you can easily see the town on your own. If you'd rather not go through the hassle of renting a car, most cruise lines will hook you up with a 3-hour countryside tour for $30 per passenger. You'll get to see the Westpunt, Mt. Christoffel, the towering cacti, and the rolling hills topped by *landhuizen* (plantation houses) built more than 3 centuries ago. You'll also stop at a beach, the Museum of Natural History, and the grotto known as Boca Tabla. Other excursions feature a submarine trip at Curaçao Seaquarium, but you can do that yourself.

In other words, you can save money and trouble by booking your own shore excursions. Up to four passengers can share the price of a tour by taxi, which costs about $30 per hour. **Taber Tours,** Dokweg (☎ **599/9-7376637**), also offers several day or night excursions to points of interest. Its tour—through Willemstad, to the Curaçao Liqueur distillery, through the residential area and the Bloempot shopping center, and to the Curaçao Museum—costs $12.50 for adults, $6.25 for children under 12, including admission to the museum.

GETTING AROUND

BUS A fleet of DAF yellow buses operates from Wilhelmina Plein, near the shopping center, to most parts of Curaçao. "C" buses are large cars that ferry small groups of tourists to different attractions or beaches. They make stops at regular bus stops and sometimes carry signs listing their destination. Be advised that drivers will often try to convince you to see all the sights of the island through a "C" bus window.

CAR RENTALS   Since all Curaçao's attractions are by paved roads, you may want to rent a car. U.S., British, and Canadian citizens can use their own licenses. Traffic moves on the right, as in the U.S. and Canada.

Avis (☎ **800/331-1212** in the U.S., or 599/9-8681163) and **Budget** (☎ **800/527-0700** in the U.S., or 599/9-8683420) offer some of the lowest rates, both with unlimited mileage. **Hertz** (☎ **800/654-3001** in the U.S., or 599/9-8880188) is slightly more expensive.

TAXIS   Since taxis don't have meters, settle on a fare before getting in. Drivers are supposed to carry an official tariff sheet, which they should produce upon request. Charges go up by 25% after 11pm. Generally, there is no need to tip. In town, the best place to get a taxi is on the Otrabanda side of the floating bridge. To summon a cab, call **Central Dispatch** (☎ **599/9-8690747**).

SEEING THE SIGHTS
WILLEMSTAD

Willemstad is the major attraction here, and you can see it on foot. After 10 years of restoration, the town's historic center and the island's natural harbor, Schottegat, have been inscribed on UNESCO's World Heritage List.

A **statue of Pedro Luis Brion** dominates the square known as Brionplein, at the Otrabanda end of the Queen Emma pontoon bridge. Born in Curaçao in 1782, Brion became the island's favorite son and best-known war hero. He was an admiral of the fleet under Simón Bolívar and fought for the independence of Venezuela and Colombia.

Fort Amsterdam, site of the Governor's Palace and the 1769 Dutch Reformed church, has the task of guarding the waterfront. The church still has a British cannonball embedded in it. The arches leading to the fort were tunneled under the official residence of the governor. A corner of the fort stands at the intersection of Breedestraat and Handelskade, the starting point for a plunge into the island's major shopping district.

A few minutes' walk from the pontoon bridge, at the north end of Handelskade, is the **Floating Market,** where scores of schooners tie up alongside the canal. Boats arrive here from Venezuela and Colombia, as well as other West Indian islands, to sell tropical fruits and vegetables, as well as handcrafts. The modern market under its vast concrete cap has not diminished the fun of watching the activity here. Either arrive early or stay late to view these marine merchants setting up or storing their wares.

Mikve Israel-Emanuel Synagogue and Jewish Cultural Historical Museum. Between the I.H. (Sha) Capriles Kade and Fort Amsterdam, at the corner of Columbusstraat and Kerkstraat. ☎ **599/9-4611067** for synagogue, ☎ **599/9-4611633** for museum. Free admission to synagogue; museum is $2. Mon–Fri 9–11:45am and 2:30–4:45pm (Sun 9am–noon if a ship is in port).

Dating from 1651, this synagogue houses the oldest Jewish congregation in the New World. The building was consecrated on the eve of Passover in 1732, thus antedating the first U.S. synagogue (in Newport, Rhode Island) by 31 years. A fine example of colonial architecture, it has a Spanish-style walled courtyard with four large portals. Sand covers the sanctuary floor, following the Portuguese Sephardic custom of representing the desert where the Israelites camped when they passed from slavery to

⭐ Favorite Experiences

Cactus, bromeliads, rare orchids, iguanas, donkeys, wild goats, and many species of birds thrive in 4,500-acre **Christoffel National Park,** about a 45-minute taxi ride from the capital near the northwestern tip of Curaçao (☎ **599/9-8640363**). The park rises from flat, arid countryside to 1,230-foot-high St. Christoffelberg, the tallest point in the Dutch Leewards. Along the way are ancient Arawak paintings and the Piedra di Monton, a rock heap piled by African slaves who cleared this former plantation. Legend says slaves could climb to the top of the rock pile, jump off, and fly back home across the Atlantic. If they had ever tasted a grain of salt, however, they would crash to their deaths.

The park has 20 miles of one-way trail-like roads. The shortest is about 5 miles long, but takes about 40 minutes to drive because of its rough terrain. One of several hiking trails goes to the top of St. Christoffelberg. It takes about 1 1/2 hours to walk to the summit (come early in the morning before it gets hot). There's also a museum in an old storehouse left over from plantation days. Guided tours of the park are available. The park is open Monday to Saturday from 8am to 4pm and on Sunday from 6am to 3pm. Admission is $9 per person.

Next door, the park has opened the **National Park Shete Boka (Seven Bays),** a turtle sanctuary. Look for the cave, with its pounding waves. Admission is $1.50 per person.

Stalagmites and stalactites are mirrored in a mystical underground lake in **Hato Caves,** F.D. Rosseveltweg (☎ **599/9-8680379**). Long ago, geological forces uplifted this limestone terrace, which was originally a coral reef. The limestone formations were created over thousands of years by water seeping through the coral. After crossing the lake, you enter two caverns known as "The Cathedral" and La Ventana, or "The Window." Displayed here are samples of ancient Indian petroglyphs. Professional local guides take visitors through the caves every hour. The caves are open daily from 10am to 4pm. Admission is $6.25 for adults, $4.75 for children 4 to 11 (free for kids 3 and under).

freedom. The *theba* (pulpit) is in the center. The highlight of the east wall is the Holy Ark, rising 17 feet. A raised *banca,* canopied in mahogany, is on the north wall.

Next door, the **Jewish Cultural Historical Museum,** Kuiperstraat 26-28 (☎ **599/9-4611633**), is housed in two buildings dating back to 1728, the rabbi's residence and the mikvah, or religious bath. The buildings were sold around 1850, but were reacquired by the Foundation for the Preservation of Historic Monuments and turned into the present museum. On display are a great many ritual, ceremonial, and cultural objects, many of which date back to the 17th and 18th centuries and are still in use for holidays and life-cycle events. There is a gift shop in the synagogue office.

WEST OF WILLEMSTAD

Curaçao Museum. Van Leeuwenhoekstraat. ☎ **599/9-4626051.** Admission $2.50 adults, $1.25 children under 14. Mon–Fri 9am–noon and 2–5pm, Sun 10am–4pm.

You can walk from the Queen Emma pontoon bridge to this tiny museum, originally a military quarantine hospital for yellow fever victims. The Royal Dutch Army constructed the building in 1853, but it was carefully restored in 1946 to 1948 as a fine example of 19th-century Dutch architecture. Furnished with paintings, objets d'art, and antique 19th-century furniture made by local cabinetmakers, the museum re-creates the atmosphere of an era gone by. Don't miss the polka-dot kitchen, and the large collection of artifacts from the Caiquetio tribes, early inhabitants described by Amerigo Vespucci as "giants 7 feet tall." There's also a modest children's science museum in the basement, with hands-on exhibits. The gardens feature specimens of the island's trees and plants. Curaçao musicians give regular performances in a reconstruction of a traditional music pavilion, also in the garden.

Curaçao Seaquarium. Off Dr. Martin Luther King Blvd. ☎ **594/9-4616666.** Admission $13.25 adults, $7.50 children under 15. Daily 8:30am–4:30pm.

The Seaquarium has more than 400 species of fish, crabs, anemones, sponges, and coral, all living in a natural environment. A rustic boardwalk connects the low-lying hexagonal buildings, which sit on a point near where the *Oranje Nassau* broke up on the rocks and sank in 1906. (The name of the site, Bapor Kibrá, means "sunken ship.") This aquarium is located a few minutes' walk along the rocky coast from the Princess Beach Resort & Casino. It also has Curaçao's only full-facility, palm-shaded beach.

A special feature here is the **"shark and animal encounter,"** in which divers, snorkelers, and experienced swimmers are able to feed, film, and photograph sharks, stingrays, lobsters, tarpons, parrot fish, and other marine life in a controlled environment. Nonswimmers can see the underwater life from a 46-foot semisubmersible observatory.

If you're here in the late afternoon, the semisubmersible *Seaworld Explorer* departs daily at 4:30pm for an hour-long journey into the deep. Passengers see submerged offshore wrecks and rainbow-hued tropical fish swimming over coral reefs. The *Explorer* has a barge top that drops about 5 feet under water, allowing views of 110 feet or so down from its wide glass windows. Reservations must be made a day in advance by calling ☎ **599/9-5604892.** Fares are $29 for adults, $19 for children 11 and under.

SHOPPING

Curaçao is a shopper's paradise, with some 200 stores lining such streets as Heerenstraat and Breedestraat in the 5-block district called the Punda. Many shops occupy the town's old Dutch houses. They also open for a few hours on Sunday and holidays if cruise ships are in port.

Look for good buys in French perfumes, Dutch Delft blue souvenirs, finely woven Italian silks, Japanese and German cameras, jewelry, silver, Swiss watches, linens, leather goods, liquor, and island-made rum and liqueurs, especially Curaçao liqueur, some of which has a distinctive blue color. The island is famous for its 5-pound "wheelers" of Gouda or Edam cheese. It also sells wooden shoes, although we're not sure what you would do with them. Some stores also offer good buys on intricate lacework imported from everywhere between Portugal and China. If you're a street shopper and want something colorful, consider a carving or flamboyant painting from Haiti or the Dominican Republic. Both are hawked by street vendors at any of the main plazas.

Bamali. Breedestraat 2. ☎ **599/9-4612258.**

The owners have designed every item of clothing in the store, and have crafted most of them. Influenced largely by Indonesian patterns, the airy garments include V-necked cotton pullovers you might wear to the grocery store here, as well as linen shifts, often in batik prints, appropriate for a glamorous cocktail party. Most garments are for women, but some are for men. Everything is made from all-natural materials, such as cotton, silk, and linen. There's also a limited array of sandals and leather bags.

Benetton. Madurostraat 4. ☎ **599/9-4614619.**

This member of a worldwide casual sportswear chain based in Italy has invaded Curaçao with all its many colors. You'll find excellent discounts on winter clothing in July and on summer clothing in December. In season items, however, are usually priced about the same as in the United States.

Bert Knubben Black Koral Art Studio. In the Princess Beach Resort & Casino, Dr. Martin Luther King Blvd. ☎ **599/9-7367888.**

Bert Knubben is a name synonymous with craftsmanship and quality. Although the Curaçao government made collection of black coral illegal, officials made an exception for Bert, a diver who has been harvesting corals from the sea and fashioning them into fine jewelry for more than 35 years. Collectors avidly seek out this type of coral, not only because of the craftsmanship of the work, but because it's becoming increasingly rare and may one day not be offered for sale at all. The black-coral jewelry here is rivaled only by Bernard I. Passman's "Black Coral and . . ." shops in George Town in the Cayman Islands and in Charlotte Amalie on St. Thomas.

Boolchand's. Heerenstraat 4B, Punda. ☎ **599/9-4612262.**

In business since 1930, Boolchand's stands for reliability in electronic equipment, which is duty-free on the island and a good buy.

Curaçao Creations. Schrijnwerkerstraat 14. ☎ **599/9-624516.**

Lying off Breedestraat on a narrow sidestreet, this outlet is a showcase for authentic Curaçao handcrafts created within the walls of a 150-year-old storefront in Otrobanda. It's within easy walking distance of the Queen Emma Bridge, the bus stop, and the cruise-ship terminal. A workshop and souvenir outlet are combined here so visitors can watch their purchases being created. This is one of the few shops on island to offer authentic, handmade Curaçao crafts; most stores sell imported items. Merchandise includes ceramics, engraved glassware, dolls, leather work, woodwork, pottery, plaques, photography, painting, jewelry, baskets, and more.

Gandelman Jewelers. Breedestraat 35, Punda. ☎ **599/9-4611854.**

This is the island's best and most reliable choice for the jewelry collector. The store has a large selection of fine jewelry, often exquisitely designed, and set with diamonds, rubies, emeralds, sapphires, and other gemstones. Of course, these items are sold all around the world; if you want something local, ask to see their selection of Curaçaoan gold pieces. They come in a vast selection of modern settings and designs, some of them worthy of awards. You'll also find timepieces by Piaget, Corum, Concord, Baume & Mercier, Tag Heuer, Gucci, Swiss Army, Fendi, Swatch, and many others. Exclusive here is the unique line of Prima Classe leather goods. Gandelman Jewelers has eight other stores in the Dutch Caribbean.

Kas di Arte Kursou. Breedestraat 126, Otrabanda. ☎ **599/9-4628896.**

This gallery and shop lies in a 19th-century mansion in Otrobanda, near the cruise-ship terminal. The shop sells unique souvenirs, such as one-of-a-kind T-shirts, all handmade by local artists. The gallery has changing exhibits of paintings and sculpture.

Little Holland. Braedestraat, Punda. ☎ **599/9-4611768.**

This is the main branch of a chain of stores with outlets in Bonaire and Aruba. Men will feel especially comfortable in this masculine-looking enclave that specializes in silk neckties, Nautica-brand shorts and shirts, and most important of all, cigars. Their sophisticated selection of stogies comes from Cuba, the Dominican Republic, and Brazil, and includes some of the most prestigious names in smoke, such as

Montecristos (five different sizes), Cohiba, and Churchills. Prices range from $3 to $27 each, and sometimes more for truly esoteric brands. Be aware that it's illegal to bring Cuban cigars into the United States. The chain maintains a second branch, where there's more focus on men's sportswear and neckties and less on cigars, at Gomez Place #6, in Punda, ☎ **599/9-4611413.**

Palais Hindu. Heerenstraat 17. ☎ **599/9-4616897.**

Palais Hindu sells a wide range of video and cassette recorders. It also stocks a lot of photographic equipment, along with cameras and watches. Go here only if you didn't find what you were looking for at Boolchand's, a better store with similar merchandise.

Penha & Sons. Heerenstraat 1. ☎ **599/9-4612266.**

Located in the oldest building in town, constructed in 1708, this traditional outlet has a history dating from 1865. It's known for its perfumes and brand-name clothes. Penha & Sons distributes such brands as Boucheron, Calvin Klein, Yves Saint Laurent, and the perfumes and cosmetics of Elizabeth Arden, Clinique, Clarins, and Estée Lauder, among others. The collection of merchandise at this prestigious store is quite varied. Their men's and women's boutiques feature travel clothes and sportswear. The firm has 10 other stores in the Caribbean.

The Yellow House (La Casa Amarilla). Breedestraat 46. ☎ **599/9-4613222.**

Housed in a yellow-and-white 19th-century building, and operating since 1887, this place sells an intriguing collection of perfume from all over the world, and is an agent of Christian Dior, Guerlain, Cartier, and Van Cleef & Arpels. It has the widest and best selection of perfume on Curaçao, though it's certainly not a "cut-rate" discount house. There's also an impressive array of cosmetics here.

BEACHES

Curaçao's beaches are not as good as Aruba's 7-mile strip of sand, but it does have some 38 of them, ranging from hotel sand-patches to secluded coves. The sea water remains an almost-constant 76°F year-round, with good underwater visibility. The **Curaçao Seaquarium** has the island's only full-facility, white sand, palm-shaded beach, but you'll have to pay the full aquarium admission to get in (see "Seeing the Sights," above). The rest of the beaches on this island are public.

A good beach on the eastern side of the island is **Santa Barbara Beach,** on land owned by a mining company between the open sea and the island's primary watersports and recreational area, known as Spanish Water. You'll also find here Table Mountain, a remarkable landmark, and an old phosphate mine. The natural beach has pure-white sand and calm water. A buoy line protects swimmers from boats. Among the amenities are rest rooms, changing rooms, a snack bar, and a terrace. You can rent water bicycles and small motorboats. Open daily from 8am to 6pm. The beach has access to the Curaçao Underwater Park.

Daaibooi is a good beach about 30 minutes from town, in the Willibrordus area on the west side of Curaçao. It's free, but there are no changing facilities.

Blauwbaai (Blue Bay) is the largest and most frequented beach on Curaçao, with enough white sand for everybody. Along with showers and changing facilities, there are plenty of shady places to retreat from the noonday sun. To reach it, take the road that goes past the Holiday Beach Hotel & Casino, heading in the direction of Juliandorp. Follow the sign that tells you to bear left for Blauwbaai and the fishing village of San Michiel.

Westpunt is known for its gigantic cliffs and the Sunday divers who jump from them into the ocean below. This public beach is located on the northwestern tip of the island. **Knip Bay,** just south of Westpunt, has beautiful turquoise waters. On weekends, live music and dancing make the beach a lively place. Changing facilities and refreshments are available. **Playa Abao,** with crystal turquoise water, is situated at the northern tip of the island.

Taxi drivers waiting at the cruise dock will take you to any of the beaches at fares to be negotiated. You can also make arrangements to be picked up at a certain time and taken back to the cruise dock.

Warning: Beware of stepping on the pines of sea urchins, sometimes found in these waters. While not fatal, their hard spines can cause several days of real discomfort. For temporary first aid, try the local remedies of vinegar or lime juice.

GOLF, SAILING, DIVING, SNORKELING, TENNIS & MORE

GOLF   The **Curaçao Golf and Squash Club,** Wilhelminalaan, in Emmastad (☎ 599/9-7373590), has the island's only course. This nine-holer is open to non-members Friday to Wednesday from 8am to 12:30pm, Thursday from 10am until sundown. Call the day before you wish to play. Greens fees are $20; you can rent clubs and carts.

SAILING   **Taber Tours,** Dokweg (☎ 599/9-7376637), offers a handful of sea-going tours, such as a snorkel/barbecue trip to Port Marie, which includes round-trip transportation to excellent reef sites and the use of snorkeling equipment. The cost is $60 per person. No children under 10 are allowed.

Travelers looking for a seagoing experience similar to the sailing days of yore should book a trip on the ***Insulinde,*** Handelskade (☎ 599/9-5601340), a 120-foot tradi-tionally rigged clipper that sails to Port Marie on the island's northwestern shore. Guests disembark onto the white sands beside a private beach house that gives wel-come protection from the sun. Trips are offered on Thursday or for cruise passen-gers by special arrangement. Included in the $55-per-person charge is a barbecue lunch and the use of snorkeling equipment. Advance reservations are necessary. The ship has a cellular phone, so the connection might be muffled.

SCUBA DIVING & SNORKELING   Scuba divers and snorkelers can see steep walls, at least two shallow wrecks, gardens of soft corals, and more than 30 species of hard corals at ☼ **Curaçao Underwater Park,** which stretches $12^{1}/_{2}$ miles along Curaçao's southern coastline, from Princess Beach Resort & Casino to East Point, the island's southeasterly tip. The park has placed 16 mooring buoys at the best dive and snorkel sites, and a snorkel trail with underwater interpretive markers just east of the Princess Beach Resort & Casino. Access from shore is also possible at Santa Barbara Beach in Jan Thiel Bay. Spearfishing, anchoring in the coral, and taking anything from the reefs except photographs are strictly prohibited.

Underwater Curaçao, in Bapor Kibrá (☎ 599/9-4618131), has a complete PADI-accredited underwater sports program and a fully stocked modern dive shop with retail and rental equipment. Dives cost $33 if you're certified. An introductory dive for novices costs $65. A snorkel trip is $20, including equipment.

TENNIS   The best tennis courts are at the hotels. Call beforehand to make sure they're available. You'll have to take a taxi to the **Curaçao Casino Resort,** Piscadera Bay, John F. Kennedy Blvd. (☎ 599/9-4625000); **Princess Beach Resort & Ca-sino,** Dr. Martin Luther King Blvd. (☎ 599/9-7367888); and **Holiday Beach Hotel & Casino,** Pater Euwensweg 31 (☎ 599/9-4625400).

WATER SPORTS   The most complete water-sports facilities are at **Seascape Dive and Watersports,** at the Curaçao Casino Resort, Piscadera Bay (☎ 599/

9-4625000). Specializing in snorkeling and scuba-diving near reefs and underwater wrecks, this company operates from a hexagonal kiosk set on stilts above the water, just offshore from the hotel's beach. Among their offerings are snorkeling excursions in an offshore underwater park for $25 per person, waterskiing for $50 per half hour, and jet-ski rentals for $50 per half hour. A Sunfish rents for $20, and an introductory PADI scuba lesson is $45. Bottom fishing (all equipment included) aboard a 38-foot Delta suitable for up to six passengers costs $180 for a half day, $300 for a full day. Open from 8am to 5pm daily.

DINING

The Cockpit. In the Hotel Holland, F. D. Rooseveltweg 524. ☎ **599/9-8688044.** Reservations required. Main courses $10–$27. AE, DC, MC, V. Daily 7am–10pm. DUTCH /INTERNATIONAL.

Located on the scrub-bordered road leading to the airport, a few minutes by taxi from the cruise dock, The Cockpit serves up international cuisine with an emphasis on Dutch and Antillean specialties. Guests enjoy such dishes as fresh fish in season (served Curaçao style), Dutch-style steak, Caribbean curried chicken, split-pea soup, and various pasta dishes such as the shrimp linguine della mama served in a lobster sauce and topped with melted cheese. Fresh vegetables and Dutch-style potatoes accompany all dishes. No one pretends that the food here is gourmet fare, but it's robust, hearty, and filled with good country flavor. Happily this place is also one of the best dining values on an island where food prices often climb to dizzying heights. Guests can enjoy their meals outside around the pool or in the dining room, where the nose of an airplane cockpit is the decorative focal point.

✪ **De Taveerne.** Landhuis Groot Vavelaar, Silena. ☎ **599/9-7370669.** Reservations recommended for street-level restaurant, not necessary for upstairs brasserie. Main courses in restaurant $19.60–$27.45; platters in brasserie $16.20. AE, DC, MC, V. Mon–Fri noon–2pm; Mon–Sat 7–11pm. FRENCH/INTERNATIONAL.

One of the most historic buildings in the district is this brick-sided manor house, originally constructed by a Venezualan revolutionary in exile in the mid-1800s. Capped with an octagonal cupola, the structure contains a formal restaurant serving French food on its street level, and a less formal brasserie serving inexpensive international food on its second floor. The third floor is devoted to an art gallery that exhibits photos, paintings, and sculpture by mostly local artists.

If you're hot, dusty, and in a hurry, your best bet might be to order a platter of food in the brasserie. Here, good choices include filet of red snapper with rice and vegetables, and a mixed grill. More formal, and more French in its orientation, is the downstairs restaurant. Menu items include lobster bisque spiked with Armagnac, carpaccio of salmon; jumbo shrimp with crabmeat stuffing; and roasted rack of lamb marinated with garlic, thyme, and rosemary, and served with a balsamic ratatouille. Furnishings within both areas evoke an antique Curaçao farmhouse, complete with polished brass, white stucco walls, dark woods, and terra-cotta tiles.

Fort Nassau. Near Point Juliana. ☎ **599/9-4613086.** Reservations recommended. Main courses $20–$28. AE, DC, MC, V. Mon–Fri noon–2pm; daily 6:30–11pm. INTERNATIONAL.

This restored restaurant and bar is set on a hilltop in the ruins of a buttressed fort dating from 1796. From the Battery Terrace, a 360° panorama of the sea, the harbor, and Willemstad unfolds. You'll even have a faraway view of the island's vast oil refinery. A signal tower on the cliff sends out beacons to approaching ships. You can visit the fashionably decorated bar just to have a drink and watch the sunset; happy hour is 6 to 7pm Monday through Friday. The decor inside remains 18th-century.

Queen Beatrix and Crown Prince Claus have dined here, and rumor has it they were more captivated by the view than by the food. Some of the more imaginative dishes on the menu perhaps should never have been thought up. However, we were impressed with the goat cheese in puff pastry and a cold terrine with layers of salmon and sole. The cream of mustard soup (yes, that's right) seems an acquired taste. Try the breast of duck with sun-dried tomatoes and basil, or even a well-prepared steak. This restaurant is a 5-minute drive from Willemstad.

☼ **Golden Star.** Socratesstraat 2 (at the corner of Dr. Hugenholtzweg and Dr. Maalweg, southeast of Willemstad). ☎ **599/9-4654795.** Reservations not required. Main courses $7.50–$25.70. AE, DC, MC, V. Daily 9am–1am. CREOLE.

The best place to go on the island for criollo, or local food, is inland from the coast road leading southeast from St. Anna Bay, 8 minutes by taxi from the cruise dock. Comparable to a roadside diner, this great-value air-conditioned restaurant is very simple, but it boasts a varied menu of very tasty Antillean dishes, such as *carco stoba* (conch stew), *bestia chiki* (goat-meat stew), *bakijauw* (salted cod), and *concomber stoba* (stewed meat and marble-size spiny cucumbers). Other specialties include *kiwa* (criollo shrimp) and *sopi carni* (meat stew). Everything is served with a side order of funchi, the cornmeal staple. The restaurant's clientele is mostly by locals, but it's not unusual for an occasional tourist to drop in. The place is almost deliberately tacky, just the way its devotees like it.

La Pergola. In the Waterfront Arches, Waterfort Straat. ☎ **599/9-4613482.** Reservations recommended. Main courses $18–$34. AE, MC, V. Mon–Sat noon–2pm; daily 6:30–10:30pm. ITALIAN.

Of the quintet of restaurants nestled into the weather-beaten core of the island's oldest fort, this is the only one focusing on the cuisine and traditions of Italy. The kitchen and one of the three dining areas are in the cellar, though the two others benefit from streaming sunlight and a view over the seafront. The decoration is enhanced by a replica of a pergola evocative of the Renaissance.

Menu items change virtually every day, and are as authentic to Italian (non-Americanized) traditions as anything else in Curaçao. Examples include gnocchi of chicken, fettuccine Giulio Cesare (with ham, cream, and mushrooms), a succulent version of grigliata mista, carpaccio della Pergola, seafood salad, and a topnotch version of exotic mushrooms, in season, garnished with Parmesan cheese and parsley. Looking for an unusual form of pasta? Ask for *maltagliata* (pasta cut at random angles and lengths) served with either Gorgonzola sauce or Genoan-style pesto. This restaurant has thrived here for more than a decade.

Pinocchio. Schottegatweg 82, Salinja. ☎ **599/9-7376784.** Reservations not required. Main courses $13–$22. AE, DC, MC, V. Mon–Sat 10am–10pm, Sun 6–10pm. INTERNATIONAL.

Set in the suburb of Salinja, a short taxi drive south of Willemstad, this plant-filled restaurant caters to couples and families. It maintains an active bar area, decorated in a tropical medley of bright colors. Simple and flavorful menu items include burgers, sandwiches, salads, steaks, fish dishes, buffalo-style chicken wings, and pita pockets filled, Lebanese style, with spiced lamb. Come here if you're on the run and want something simple, plain, and fast.

Rijstaffel Restaurant Indonesia and Holland Club Bar. Mercuriusstraat 13, Salinja. ☎ **599/9-4612999.** Reservations recommended. Main courses $10–$22; rijstaffel $22 for 16 dishes, $25 for 20 dishes, $28 for 25 dishes; all-vegetarian rijstaffel $21 for 16 dishes. AE, DC, MC, V. Mon–Sat noon–2pm; daily 6–9:30pm. INDONESIAN.

This is the best place on the island to sample the Indonesian rijstaffel, the traditional "rice table" with all the zesty side dishes. You must ask a taxi to take you to this villa in the suburbs near Salinja, near the Princess Beach Resort & Casino southeast of Willemstad. At lunchtime, the selection of dishes is more modest, but for dinner, Javanese cooks prepare the specialty of the house, a rijstaffel, consisting of 16, 20, or 25 dishes. There's even an all-vegetarian rijstaffel. Warming trays are placed on your table, and the service is buffet style. It's best to go with a party so that all of you can share in the feast. You can season your plate with peppers rated hot, very hot, and palate-melting. It's a good change of pace when you can't face another serving of steak and lobster tail.

Wine Cellar. Ooststraat/Concordiastraat (opposite the cathedral in the center of town). ☎ **599/9-4612178.** Reservations required. Main courses $18–$37. AE, DC, MC, V. Tues–Fri noon–2pm; Tues–Sun 6pm–midnight. INTERNATIONAL.

This excellent restaurant offers one of the best and most extensive wine lists on the island. The kitchen turns out a fine lobster salad and a sole meunière in a butter-and-herb sauce. You might also try, if featured, fresh red snapper or U.S. tenderloin of beef with goat cheese sauce. Game dishes are imported throughout the year from Holland and are likely to include venison roasted with mushrooms, hare, or roast goose. After years of dining here, we have found the food commendable in every way—dishes are flavorful and hearty. Be warned that there are no selections for lighter appetites. Our greatest disappointment in this restaurant always occurs when the check is presented—you'll need a small fortune to pay it.

7 Freeport/Lucaya ⚓ ⚓

There's not a lot of subtlety in bold and brassy Freeport/Lucaya on Grand Bahama Island, fourth largest of The Bahamas. It doesn't have the class of Bermuda or the chic of Paradise Island over at Nassau. But it's nonetheless a major draw among cruise-ship passengers, especially those who prefer Atlantic City to Palm Beach. Freeport/Lucaya's cosmopolitan glitz and glamour have made it the second most popular tourist destination in The Bahamas, behind Nassau. But it's a little too much for some people.

Gambling at the island's two casinos and seeing their Las Vegas–style cabaret revues are popular activities, but there are also more down-to-earth alternatives. You'll find excellent golf and tennis, along with plenty of sun, surf, and water sports. Because the island is so big and unpopulated, there are many places to get close to nature, including the Rand Memorial Nature Centre, the Garden of the Groves, and the Lucayan National Park, with its underwater caves, forest trails, and a secluded beach (see "Seeing the Sights," below). Out in the fishing village of West End, 28 miles from Freeport/Lucaya, you can enjoy Bahamian cuisine and learn about Grand Bahama's buccaneering and rum-running days.

Some Bahamians can claim descent from those pirates and privateers. A few can even trace their ancestry back to the Eleutherian Adventurers, loyalist Tories who fled the United States after the American Revolution to continue living under the British Crown. Many southern Americans also came to The Bahamas after the Civil War, bringing their slaves with them. But of the overall population of some 200,000 people, African-Bahamians are the majority, holding positions of leadership in all areas.

Once a low-lying pine forest, Freeport/Lucaya turned into one of the world's major resorts almost overnight. Freeport was developed as an industrial-free zone in 1956 to attract international financiers. Emerging 8 years later as a coastal resort area, Lucaya evolved into a blend of residential and tourist facilities. As the two communities grew, their identities became almost indistinguishable, though elements of their

Freeport/Lucaya

Freeport Harbour

Creek

Hawksbill

Harbour Rd.

Pinder's Point Rd.

Andros Dr.

Grand Bahamian Way

Aberdeen Dr.

Edenborough Pl.

Queen's Hwy.

Regency Blvd.

Shaftesbury

Ellis Lightfoot

Bahamia West

Yorkshire Rd.

Robert Maynard

Pinta Av.

Santa Maria Av.

Confederates Walk

Milton St.

Logwood Rd.

FREEPORT

Pioneers Way

Cadwallader Jones

West Sunrise Hwy.

West Atlantic Dr.

The Mall South

The Mall East

Hawksbill St.

Xanadu Beach

Northwest Providence Channel

Austin's Calypso Bar **1**
Count Basie Square **10**
Fortune Hills Golf **12**
Garden of the Groves **11**
Hydroflora Garden **6**
International Bazaar **3**
Lucayan Park Golf **8**
Princess Casino **5**
Princess Emerald Golf **4**
Princess Ruby Golf **2**
Rand Nature Centre **7**
Star Club **1**
UNEXCO **9**

2-0215

Airport ✈   Beach ⚓   Cruise Ship Dock ⛴

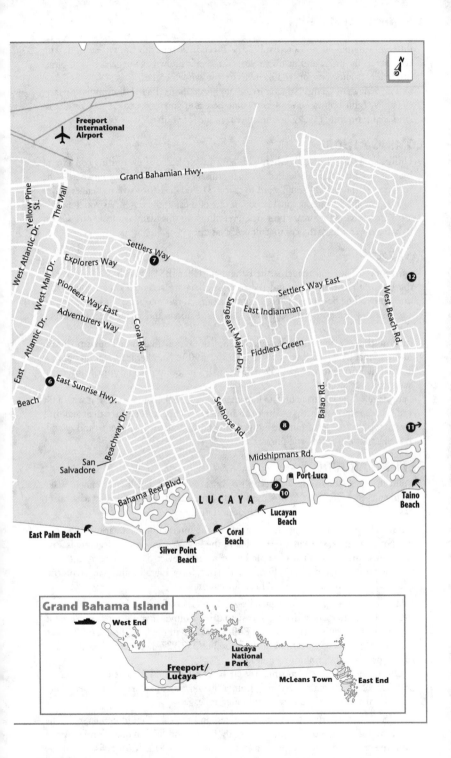

Freeport International Airport

Grand Bahamian Hwy.

West Atlantic Dr.
Yellow Pine St.
The Mall

Settlers Way
❼

Explorers Way

West Mall Dr.

Pioneers Way East

Adventurers Way

Atlantic Dr.

Coral Rd.

East
Beach

❻ East Sunrise Hwy.

Settlers Way East

East Indianman

Sargeant Major Dr.

Fiddlers Green

West Beach Rd.

❶❷

Beachway Dr.

San Salvadore

Seahorse Rd.

❽

Balao Rd.

❶❶→

Midshipmans Rd.

Bahama Reef Blvd.

■ Port Luca

LUCAYA

❾❶❿

Taino Beach

East Palm Beach

Silver Point Beach

Coral Beach

Lucayan Beach

Grand Bahama Island

⛴ West End

Lucaya National Park ■

Freeport/ Lucaya

McLeans Town

East End

different original purposes remain today. Freeport is the "downtown" section, with commerce, industry, and its own resorts. Lucaya is known as the garden city, pleasing residents and vacationers alike with its fine sandy beaches.

The reviews of Grand Bahama Island are mixed. Some highly discriminating travelers have built homes here. Others come here and vow never to set foot on the island again, finding it tacky or uninspired. Judge for yourself.

COMING ASHORE

Unlike some ports of call, where you land in the heart of everything, on Grand Bahama Island you're deposited in what cruisers call the middle of nowhere—the west end of the island. You'll want to take a $10 taxi ride (for two passengers) over to Freeport and its International Bazaar, center of most of the action. As you'll quickly learn after leaving the dreary port area, everything on this island is spread out. Grand Bahama doesn't have the compactness of Nassau.

FAST FACTS

Currency   The legal tender is the Bahamian dollar (B$1), which is on a par with the U.S. dollar. Both U.S. and Bahamian dollars are accepted on an equal basis throughout The Bahamas. There's no restriction on the amount of foreign currency a tourist can bring into the country. Most large hotels and stores accept traveler's checks.

Information   Information is available from **the Grand Bahama Tourism Board,** International Bazaar in Freeport (☎ 242/352-6909). Another information booth is located at Port Lucaya (☎ 242/373-8988). Open 9am to 5:30pm Monday to Saturday.

Language   The language of The Bahamas is English. Bahamians speak it with a lilt and with more British than American influence. They also pepper their colorful speech with words left from the indigenous Arawak tongue (like *cassava* and *guava*), as well as African words and phrases.

GETTING AROUND

You can explore the center of Freeport or Lucaya on foot, but if you want to make excursions into the West End or East End of the island, you'll either need a car or have to rely on highly erratic public transportation.

BUS   The public bus service has routes from the International Bazaar to downtown Freeport, and from the Pub on the Mall to the Lucaya area. The typical fare is 75¢. A private company, **Franco's People Express,** runs a twice-daily service from the International Bazaar and Lucaya Beach to West End, costing $8 round-trip. Unfortunately, there is no number to call for information.

CAR RENTALS   Roads are generally good on Grand Bahama Island, unlike some islands such as Barbados, making it easy to drive around. If you want to explore the island yourself, you can try **Avis** (☎ 800/331-1212 in the U.S., or 242/352-7666) or **Hertz** (☎ 800/654-3001 in the U.S., or 242/352-9277). Car rentals average $60 to $85 per day, with unlimited mileage.

One of the best local companies is **Star Rent-a-Car,** Old Airport Road (☎ 242/352-5953), which rents everything from a Suzuki Swift to a Jeep Wrangler. Rates range from $35 to $55 daily with unlimited mileage.

TAXIS   The government sets the taxi rates, and the cabs should be metered. The fare is $2 for the first quarter mile, plus 30¢ for each additional quarter mile. A trip from the cruise dock to Freeport or Lucaya costs about $10. Most taxis wait at the cruise-ship dock to pick up passengers, or you can call **Freeport Taxi Company** (☎ **242/352-6666**) or **Grand Bahama Taxi Union** (☎ **242/352-7101**), both of which are open 24 hours.

BICYCLES & MOTOR SCOOTERS   Bicycles and motor scooters are a good means of transport here. Try **Honda Cycle Shop,** Queen's Highway (☎ **242/352-7035**). A two-seat scooter requires a $100 deposit and rents from $35 per full day. Gas is provided and there's no charge for mileage. The operator must have a valid driver's license. Bicycles require a $50 deposit and cost $12 for a half day (4 hours); $20 for a full day. The rental agency also supplies helmets for drivers and passengers, which are required by law. The establishment is open daily from 9am to 6pm.

SHORE EXCURSIONS

The offerings here are weak. You can often manage better on your own. Most cruise ships tout a 25-mile round-trip sightseeing trip, during which you spend about 30 minutes at the Garden of the Groves and then are led like cattle around the International Bazaar. This latter is better explored on your own. The $2^1/_2$-hour trip cost $18 per passenger.

SEEING THE SIGHTS

Garden of the Groves. Intersection of Midshipman Rd. and Magellan Dr. ☎ **242/373-5668.** Admission $7 adults, $3.50 children 3–10 (2 and under free). Garden, Mon–Fri 9am–4pm, Sat–Sun and holidays 10am–4pm. Palmetto Café, Mon–Fri 9am–4pm, Sat 9am–noon.

The prime attraction of Grand Bahama Island is this 11-acre garden honoring Wallace Groves, the Virginia-born financier who founded Freeport/Lucaya, and his wife, Georgette. Seven miles east of the International Bazaar, this scenic preserve of waterfalls and flowering shrubs has some 10,000 trees. Tropical birds flock here, making it a lure for bird-watchers and ornithologists. There are free-form lakes, footbridges, ornamental borders, lawns, and flowers. A small nondenominational chapel, open to visitors, looks down on the garden from a hill. The **Palmetto Café** serves snacks and drinks, and there is a Bahamian straw market at the entrance gate.

Hydroflora Garden. On East Beach at Sunrise Hwy. ☎ **242/352-6052.** Admission $3 adults, $1.50 children. Guided tours $5 per person. Mon–Fri 9am–5pm, Sat 9am–4pm.

At this artificially created botanical wonder, you can see 154 specimens of plants that grow in The Bahamas. A special section is devoted to bush medicine, widely practiced by Bahamians who have been using herbs and other plants to cure everything from sunburn to insomnia since the Native Lucayans were here centuries ago.

✪ **Lucayan National Park.** Midshipman Rd. No phone. Free admission. Daily 24 hours. For information, contact Rand Nature Centre. ☎ **242/352-5438.**

Filled with mangrove, pine, and palm trees, this 40-acre park about 12 miles from Lucaya contains one of the loveliest, most secluded beaches on Grand Bahama. A wooden path winding through the trees leads to this long, wide, dune-covered stretch. As you wander through the park, you'll cross Gold Rock Creek, fed by a spring from what is said to be the world's largest underground freshwater cavern system. You can enter two of the caves that were exposed when a portion of ground collapsed. The pools there are composed of 6 feet of freshwater atop a heavier layer of saltwater. Spiral wooden steps have been built down to the pools.

The freshwater springs once lured native Lucayans, Arawak-connected tribes who lived on the island and depended on fishing for their livelihood. They would come inland to get fresh water. Lucayan bones and artifacts, such as pottery, have been found in the caves as well as on the beaches.

Rand Nature Centre. E. Settlers Way. ☎ **242/352-5438.** Admission $3. Mon–Fri 9am–4pm, Sat 9am–1pm. Guided tours at 10am and 2pm Mon–Fri.

This 100-acre pineland sanctuary, located 2 miles east of the center of Freeport, is the regional headquarters of The Bahamas National Trust, a nonprofit conservation organization. Forest nature trails highlight native flora and "bush medicine." Wild birds abound in the park, including a flock of West Indian flamingos, the national bird of The Bahamas. Other features include native-animal displays, a replica of a Lucayan Indian village, an education center, and a gift shop selling nature books and souvenirs.

GAMBLING THE DAY AWAY

Even though there are casinos aboard ships, many passengers head immediately for a land-based casino once they hit shore.

Most of the day life/nightlife in Freeport/Lucaya centers around the **Princess Casino,** the Mall at W. Sunrise Highway (☎ 242/352-7811), a glittering, giant, Moroccan-style palace. The casino is open daily from 9am to 3am.

SHOPPING
THE INTERNATIONAL BAZAAR

There's no place for shopping in The Bahamas quite like the **International Bazaar,** at East Mall Drive and East Sunrise Highway. It's one of the world's most unusual shopping marts. True, its architectural heyday peaked in the early 1960s, and some purveyors of taste cite it as a commercially viable example of Bahamian kitsch in poured concrete and plastic. But the tastelessness of these 10 acres seems perfectly suited for its role as a shopper's theme park, a sort of born-to-shop Disney World. In the nearly 100 shops, you're bound to find something that is both a discovery and a bargain. Displayed here are African handcrafts, Chinese jade, British china, Swiss watches, Irish linens, and Colombian emeralds—and that's just for starters. Continental cafes and dozens of shops loaded with merchandise await visitors. Buses marked INTERNATIONAL BAZAAR will take you right to the much-photographed Toril Gate, a Japanese symbol of welcome.

The bazaar blends architecture from 25 countries into several theme areas: the Ginza in Tokyo for Asian goods; the Left Bank of Paris, or a reasonable facsimile, with sidewalk cafes where you can enjoy a *café au lait* and perhaps a pastry under shade trees; a Continental Pavilion for leather goods, jewelry, lingerie, and gifts at shops with names such as Love Boutique; India House for exotic goods such as taxi horns and silk saris; Africa for carvings or a colorful dashiki; a Spanish section for Latin American and Iberian serapes and piñatas.

At the **Straw Market,** beside the International Bazaar, you'll find items with a special Bahamian touch—colorful baskets, hats, handbags, and place mats—all of which make good gifts and souvenirs of your trip.

Many items sold in the shops here could run about 40% less costly than in the United States, but don't count on it.

Art
Flovin Gallery. Arcade. ☎ **242/352-7564.**

This gallery sells original Bahamian and international art, frames, lithographs, posters, and Bahamian-made Christmas ornaments and decorated coral, and it also offers handmade Bahamian dolls, coral jewelry, and other gift items. Another branch is at Port Lucaya Marketplace (see below).

Favorite Freeport Experiences

In the center of the waterfront restaurant and shopping complex of Port Lucaya, **Count Basie Square** contains a vine-covered bandstand where the best live music on the island is performed nightly. And it's free. The square honors the "Count," who used to have a grand home on Grand Bahama. Steel bands, small Junkanoo groups, and even gospel singers from a local church are likely to perform here at night, their voices or music wafting across the 50-slip marina.

If you'd like to see what's left of The Bahamas "the way it was," head for **The Star Club,** Bayshore Road (☎ **242/346-6207**), in the West End. Built in the 1940s, it was the first hotel on Grand Bahama, and hosted many famous guests over the years. It's been a long time since any guests have checked in, but the place is still going strong as the only 24-hour bar on the island. Sometimes people leaving the casinos late at night and come over here to eat grouper fingers, play pool, or listen to the taped music. The "club" is still run by the family of the late Austin Henry Grant Jr., a former Bahamian senator and West End legend. You can order Bahamian chicken in the bag, burgers, fish and chips, or "fresh sexy" conch prepared as chowder, fritters, and salads. But come here for the good times, not the food. You can also drop in next door at **Austin's Calypso Bar,** a real Grand Bahama dive if there ever was one. Austin Grant, the owner, will tell you about the good ol' days.

Crystal & China
Island Galleria. Arcade. ☎ **242/352-8194.**

China by Wedgwood, Lenox, and Aynsley, and crystal by Waterford, are the major lure of this store, which has the island's most extensive collection. The store is also located in the Port Lucaya Marketplace.

Handcrafts and Gifts
Bahamian Souvenir Outlet. In the International Bazaar. ☎ **242/352-2947.**

If you're seeking just routine souvenirs of your visit to The Bahamas, along with Bahamian gift items, this outlet offers many inexpensive items. You'll find the usual array of T-shirts, key rings, mugs, and all that stuff here. The location is below the Ministry of Tourism.

Caribbean Cargo. Arcade. ☎ **242/352-2929.**

Here you'll find one of the island's best gift shops, specializing in such items as picture frames, candles, and clocks.

Jewelry
Colombian Emeralds International. South American Section. ☎ **242/352-5464.**

This is a branch of the world's foremost emerald jeweler, offering a wide array of precious gemstone jewelry and one of the island's best watch collections. Careful shoppers will find significant savings over U.S. prices. The outlet offers certified appraisals and free 90-day insurance. There are two branches at the Port Lucaya.

Jeweler's Warehouse. Spanish Section. ☎ **242/352-6425.**

This shop sells 14-karat gold, silver, and gemstone jewelry. Discounts can range to as much as 40%, but that calls for some careful shopping. Semiprecious beads and coral items are made in The Bahamas, and there is also a large selection of famous-name watches, including Fossil and Reebok that are discounted up to 60%.

Sea Treasures. Spanish Section. ☎ **242/352-2911.**

Sea Treasures sells 14- and 18-karat gold and silver jewelry inspired by the sea and handcrafted on the island. Prices go from $5 to $3,000. The staff will show you gold necklaces and bracelets, along with diamonds, topazes, pearls, and both pink and black coral.

The Leather Shop. In the International Bazaar. ☎ **242/352-5491.**

This is another good outlet, carrying a much more limited Fendi line, but also many other designers including Land and HCL. Additional leather goods include shoes and gift items. Additional locations include the Port Lucaya Marketplace (☎ **242/373-2323**), and Regent's Centre (☎ **242/352-2895**).

Unusual Centre. In the International Bazaar. ☎ **242/352-3994.**

This store is different from the competition in that it carries a wide array of items made of eel skin, as well as some goods made from exotic feathers such as peacock. There is another branch at the Port Lucaya Marketplace.

Lladró Figurines

Lladró Gallery. In the Island Galleria International Bazaar. ☎ **242/352-2660.**

Lovers of Lladró figurines welcome the chance to add to their collections by visiting the best-stocked emporium of Lladró on Grand Bahama Island. If you appreciate the elongated limbs and wistful mannerisms of characters in the 17th-century paintings of El Greco, you'll like Lladró. The gallery also stocks a less extensive collection by Swarovski, Waterford, Royal Doulton, and Wedgwood.

Miscellany

Far East Traders. In the International Bazaar. ☎ **242/352-9280.**

This outlet offers a collection of Oriental goods such as linens, hand-embroidered dresses and blouses, silk robes, lace parasols, smoking jackets, and kimonos. There's a branch location inside the Island Galleria at the Port Lucaya Marketplace.

The Old Curiosity Shop. Arcade. ☎ **242/352-8008.**

This shop specializes in antique English bric-a-brac, including original and reproduction items: Victorian dinner rings and cameos, antique engagement rings, lithographs, old and new silver and porcelain, and brass candlesticks and trivets.

Music

Intercity Music. In the International Bazaar. ☎ **242/352-8820.**

This is the best music store on the island; you get not only Bahamian music, but soca, reggae, and all the music of the islands. CDs, records, and tapes are sold. You can also purchase Bahamian posters and flags, portable radios, Walkmans, and blank audio tapes, along with accessories for camcorders. There's a branch office at the Port Lucaya Marketplace (☎ **242/373-8820**).

Perfumes & Fragrances

Les Parisiennes. French Section. ☎ **242/352-5380.**

This outlet offers a wide range of perfumes, including the latest from Paris, and it also sells Lancôme cosmetics and skin-care products. There's a branch office at the Port Lucaya Marketplace (☎ **242/373-2974**).

Parfum de Paris. French Section. ☎ **242/352-8164.**

Here you'll find practically all major French perfumes and colognes. Discounts are sometimes granted with prices up to 40% less than in the United States. There's another branch at Port Lucaya Marketplace (☎ **242/373-8404**).

The Perfume Factory Fragrance of The Bahamas, Ltd. At the rear of the International Bazaar. ☎ **242/352-9391.**

This is the top fragrance producer in The Bahamas. The shop is housed in a model of an 1800s mansion, in which visitors are invited to hear a 5-minute commentary and to see the mixing of fragrant oils. There's even a "mixology" department where you can create your own fragrance from a selection of oils. The shop's well-known products include Island Promises, Goombay, Paradise, and Pink Pearl (which has conch pearls in the bottle). The shop also sells Guanahani, a new fragrance created to commemorate the 500th anniversary of Columbus' first landfall in the New World. (Guanahani was the Indian name for the southern Bahamian island of San Salvador, traditional site of Columbus' landing.) Other perfumes and colognes include Sand, the number one Bahamian-made men's fragrance in the country.

Shoes
Gemini. In the International Bazaar. ☎ **242/352-4809.**

Although most of its inventory consists of stylish (usually Italian-made) shoes for women, this store is also well stocked with accessories, including handbags, wallets, belts, T-shirts, and a wide collection of jewelry (some of it gold-plated) inspired by the aesthetic of Coco Chanel.

Stamps & Coins
Bahamas Coin and Stamp Ltd. Arcade. ☎ **242/352-8989.**

This is not only the original but also the major coin dealer on the island. It specializes in Bahamian coin jewelry, ancient Roman coins, and relics from sunken Spanish galleons, and it also carries a vast selection of antique U.S. and English coins and paper money.

SHOPPING PORT LUCAYA MARKETPLACE

The first of its kind in The Bahamas, Port Lucaya on Seahorse Road was named after the original settlers of Grand Bahama. This is a shopping and dining complex set on 6 acres. Free entertainment, such as steel-drum bands and strolling musicians, adds to a festival atmosphere.

The complex rose on the site of a former Bahamian straw market, but the craftspeople and their straw products are back in full force after having been temporarily dislodged.

Full advantage is taken of the waterfront location. Many of the restaurants and shops overlook a 50-slip marina, home of a "fantasy" pirate ship featuring lunch and dinner/dancing cruises. A variety of charter vessels are also based at the Port Lucaya Marina, and dockage at the marina is available to visitors coming by boat to shop or dine.

A boardwalk along the water makes it easy to watch the frolicking dolphins and join in other activities at the Underwater Explorers Society (UNEXSO).

Merchandise in the shops of Port Lucaya ranges from leather to lingerie to wind chimes. Traditional and contemporary fashions are featured for men, women, and children.

Coconits by Androsia. Port Lucaya. ☎ **242/373-8387.**

This is the Port Lucaya outlet of the famous batik house of Andros Island. Its designs and colors capture the spirit of The Bahamas. Fabrics are handmade on the island of Andros, and the store sells quality, 100% cotton resort wear, including simple skirts, tops, jackets, and shorts for women, and it also offers a colorful line of children's wear.

Flovin Gallery II. Port Lucaya. ☎ **242/373-8388.**

This branch of the art gallery located in the International Bazaar sells a collection of oil paintings (both Bahamian and international), along with lithographs and posters. In its limited field, it's the best in the business. It also features a number of gift items, such as handmade Bahamian dolls, decorated corals, and Christmas ornaments.

Jeweler's Warehouse. Port Lucaya. ☎ **242/373-8400.**

This is a place for bargain hunters looking for good buys on discounted, close-out 14-karat gold and gemstone jewelry. Discounts range up to 50%. The quality of many of these items, however, remains high, and guarantees and certified appraisals are possible.

Photo Specialist. Port Lucaya. ☎ **242/373-1244.**

This is the best place on the island to purchase video and photo equipment, and it carries an extensive range of merchandise, including tapes and batteries. It has Sea & Sea 35mm underwater cameras for rent starting at $10 a day. The outlet will also repair cameras.

UNEXSO Dive Shop. Port Lucaya. ☎ **242/373-1244.**

This is the premier dive shop of The Bahamas. It sells everything related to the water—swimsuits, wetsuits, underwater cameras, shades, hats, souvenirs, state-of-the-art diver's equipment, and computers.

BEACHES

Grand Bahama has some 60 miles of white-sand beaches rimming the blue-green waters of the Atlantic. The mile-long **Xanadu Beach,** at the Xanadu Beach Resort, is the premier beach in the Freeport area. Most beaches are in the Lucaya area, site of the major resort hotels. The resort beaches, with a fairly active program of water sports, tend to be the most crowded in winter.

Other island beaches include **Taíno Beach,** lying to the east of Freeport, plus **Smith's Point** and **Fortune Beach,** the latter one of the finest on Grand Bahama. Another good beach, about a 20-minute ride east of Lucaya, is **Gold Rock Beach,** a favorite picnic spot with the locals, especially on weekends.

CRUISES, DOLPHIN ENCOUNTERS, GOLF, DIVING & MORE

CRUISES   Any tour agent can arrange for you to go from Port Lucaya Dock on the **Mermaid Kitty** (☎ 242/373-5880), supposedly the world's largest twin-diesel-engine glass-bottom boat. You'll get a panoramic view of the beautiful underwater life off the coast of Grand Bahama.

Superior Watersports in Freeport (☎ 242/373-7863) offers fun cruises on its *Bahama Mama,* a 72-foot catamaran with two semisubmersibles that dive 5 feet. Best is its Robinson Crusoe Beach Party daily from 11am to 4:30pm, costing $49 per person (including drinks). If your ship stays late, there's a sunset booze cruise daily from 5:30 to 7:30pm, costing $25.

You'll get to see porpoises up close with ✪ **The Dolphin Experience,** operated by the Underwater Explorers Society (UNEXSO), in Port Lucaya opposite Lucayan Beach Casino (☎ 800/992-3483 or 242/373-1250). UNEXSO conducts this unique dolphin/human familiarization program in which participants observe these intelligent and friendly animals close up and hear an interesting lecture by a member of the animal-care staff. This is not a swim-with-the-dolphins type of program, but all ages can step onto a shallow wading platform and interact with the animals. The dolphins are released daily to swim with scuba divers in the open ocean, however. The encounter on shore costs $36. An "Assistant Trainer" program is an all-day interactive experience in which a maximum of four people, aged 16 or older, are able to learn about dolphins and marine mammals from a behind-the-scene experience. Participants help feed the animals and swim with them for a cost of $179. For $130, dolphins also swim out from Sanctuary Bay daily to interact with scuba divers from UNEXSO in an "open ocean" program.

GOLF   This island boasts more golf links than any other in The Bahamas. The courses are within 7 miles of one another, and you usually won't have to wait to play. All courses are open to the public year-round, and you can rent clubs from any of the pro shops on the island.

Fortune Hills Golf & Country Club, Richmond Park, Lucaya (☎ 242/373-4500), was designed as an 18-hole course, but the back nine were never completed. You can replay the front nine for a total of 6,916 yards from the blue tees. Par is 72. Greens fees are $22 for 9 holes, $34 for 18. Electric carts cost $26 and $34 for 9 and 18 holes, respectively. The club is located 5 miles east of Freeport.

Lucayan Park Golf & Country Club, at Lucaya Beach (☎ 242/373-1066), is the best-kept and most manicured course on Grand Bahama. The course was recently made over and is quite beautiful. It's known for its entrance and a hanging boulder sculpture. Greens are fast, and there are a couple of par-5 holes more than 500 yards long. Total distance from the blue tees is 6,824 yards, 6,488 from the white tees. Par is 72. Greens fees are $76 for 18 holes, including a mandatory shared golf cart. We'll let you in on a secret: Even if you're not a golfer, sample the food at the club restaurant. They offer everything from lavish champagne brunches to first-rate seafood dishes.

Princess Emerald Course, The Mall South (☎ 242/352-6721), is one of two courses owned and operated by The Bahamas Princess Resort and Casino. The Emerald Course was the site of The Bahamas National Open some years back. The course has plenty of trees along the fairways, as well as an abundance of water hazards and bunkers. The toughest hole is the ninth, a par 5 with 545 yards from the blue tees to the hole. Greens fees are $51 for 9 holes or $75 for 18.

The championship **Princess Ruby Course,** on West Sunrise Highway (☎ 242/352-6721), was designed by Joe Lee in 1968 and recently hosted the Michelin Long Drive competition. Greens fees are $51 for 9 holes, $75 for 18, including electric carts. It's a total of 6,750 yards if played from the championship blue tees.

HORSEBACK RIDING   **Pinetree Stables,** N. Beachway Dr., Freeport (☎ 242/373-3600), are the best in The Bahamas, superior to rivals on New Providence Island (Nassau). Pinetree offers trail rides to the beach Tuesday to Sunday at 9am, 10am, 11am, noon, and 2pm. The cost is $35 per person for a ride lasting 1 1/2 hours. Lessons in dressage and jumping are available for $35 for 45 minutes of instruction.

SEA KAYAKING   If you'd like to explore the waters off the island's north shore, you can do so by calling **Kayak Nature Tours** (☎ 242/373-2485), which arranges trips through the mangroves where you can see wildlife as you paddle alone. The cost is $75 per person, and trips are offered daily from 8:30am to 5pm, with a Bahamian picnic lunch included. Both single and double kayaks are used on these jaunts, and children must be at least 10 years of age.

SCUBA DIVING & SNORKELING   One of the premier facilities for diving and snorkeling throughout The Bahamas and Caribbean, ☼ **Underwater Explorers Society (UNEXSO),** at Lucaya Beach (☎ 242/373-1244), has daily reef trips, shark dives, wreck dives, and night dives. This is also the only facility in the world where divers can swim alongside dolphins in the open ocean (see "The Dolphin

Experience," above). They offer a popular 3-hour learn-to-dive course every day. For $99, students learn the basics in UNEXSO's training pools. Then, the same day, they dive the beautiful shallow reef with their instructor. For experienced divers, a guided reef dive is $39, and a three-dive package is $99. A 2-hour snorkeling trip to the reef costs $35, all equipment included.

TENNIS   The Bahamas Princess Resort and Casino, The Mall at West Sunrise Highway, has the monopoly on tennis courts here. Both guests and nonguests are charged $10 per hour to use one of the three courts at the **Princess Country Club** (☎ 242/352-6721) or the three lighted surfaces at the **Princess Tower** (☎ 242/352-9661). Courts at both are open daily from 8:30am to dusk.

WATER SPORTS   Paradise Watersports, at the Xanadu Beach Resort and Marina (☎ 242/352-2887), offers a variety of activities. With snorkeling trips, you cruise to a coral reef on a 48-foot catamaran for $18 per person. Paddleboats rent for $7 for a half hour, $10 per hour. Waterskiing is priced at $15 for a 1$1/2$ mile ride. Parasailing costs $30 for a 4-minute ride. A glass-bottom-boat ride costs $20 for adults and $12 for children under 12 for a cruise lasting 1$1/2$ hours.

   Clarion Atlantik Beach Resort, on Royal Palm Way (☎ 242/373-1444), is the best center on the island for parasailing. Parasailing cost is $30 for 5 to 7 minutes.

DINING

Geneva's. Kipling Lane, the Mall at W. Sunrise Hwy. ☎ **242/352-5085.** Main courses $8.50–$16.95. No credit cards. Daily 7am–11pm. BAHAMIAN.

If you want to eat where the Grand Bahama locals dine, head for Geneva's, where the food is the way it was before the hordes of tourists invaded. The namesake is Geneva Monroe, who's aided by her sons, Francis and Robert. This restaurant sticks to the mainstay of the local diet—conch—which has fed and nourished Bahamians for centuries. In fact, Geneva's is one of the best places to sample this treat of the sea. The Monroe family will prepare it for you stewed, cracked, or fried, or in a savory conch chowder that makes an excellent starter. Grouper (there's no escaping grouper in The Bahamas) also appears, prepared in every imaginable way. To get you into the mood of things, the rum-laced Bahama Mama is the specialty drink of the bartender.

Les Fountains. E. Sunrise Hwy. ☎ **242/373-9553.** Reservations recommended. Breakfast and lunch from $6.50; dinner main courses $6.50–$17.75; all-you-can-eat buffet $8.50. MC, V. Daily 24 hours.

This affiliated restaurant of the more substantial Pepper Pot (below) offers a bit more to eat than its smaller sibling. This modern building is topped with a quintet of steeply pitched roofs designed to imitate a cluster of tropical African huts, with an English touch of exposed wood both inside and out. Don't look for five-star cuisine here—the pride of the restaurant is an all-you-can-eat buffet. If the buffet is not for you, you can order from a menu featuring chicken, steak, and lobster, or you can enjoy their jerk grill outside. Watch them prepare Bahamian fare such as ribs, chicken, or pork—jerk-style—while you sip the drink of your choice from the bar. Les Fountains is just a short 3-minute walk from the Pepper Pot.

The Pepper Pot. E. Sunrise Hwy. at Coral Rd. ☎ **242/373-7655.** Reservations not accepted. Breakfast $4–$5.25; main courses $5.50–$11.25; vegetarian plates $2.50–$6.50. No credit cards. Daily 24 hours. BAHAMIAN.

This might be the only establishment on Grand Bahama that specializes in Bahamian take-out food. You'll find it after about a 5-minute drive east of the International

Bazaar, in a tiny shopping mall. You can order take-out portions of the best carrot cake on the island, as well as a savory conch chowder, the standard fish and pork chops, chicken souse (an acquired taste), cracked conch, sandwiches and hamburgers, and an array of daily specials. The owner is Ethiopian-born Wolansa Fountain.

The Pub on the Mall. Ranfurley Circus, Sunrise Hwy. ☎ **242/352-5110.** Reservations recommended. Lunch main courses $6–$15; daily special one-course platter lunch $7.95; dinner main courses $10–$25. AE, MC, V. Prince of Wales Lounge, daily noon–2am. Islander's Roost, Mon–Sat 5:30pm–midnight. Silvano's Italian Restaurant, daily 5:30–11pm. Closed mid-Aug to mid-Sept. INTERNATIONAL.

Contained on the same floor of the same building and administered by the same management, you'll find three distinctive eating areas, each with a separate theme. This place is more interesting than its competitor, Sir Winston Churchill Pub. All three of the restaurants lie opposite the International Bazaar and attract many locals. The Prince of Wales Lounge evokes medieval Britain and serves a lunchtime menu of shepherd's pie, fish-and-chips, platters of roast beef or fish, and real English ale. The ale wins out as the best item on the menu of pub grub. The Islander's Roost has a tropical decor of bright colors such as pale yellow and marine blue with a balcony overlooking the Bazaar. The food is good—but not that good. The thrifty can order only a main platter and find it very filling and satisfying. All those fabled dishes that visitors seek when they go to London appear here on the menu, as well, including certified Angus beef, fish, fowl, and prime rib. Silvano's brings a continental touch with its copious portions of pasta and veal along with some imported beefsteaks. The homemade fettuccine wins over the cannelloni.

Ruby Swiss Restaurant. W. Sunrise Hwy. at W. Atlantic Ave. ☎ **242/352-8507.** Reservations required for dinner. Main courses $4.25–$14.75 at lunch; $13.50–$28.50 at dinner; all-you-can-eat spaghetti bar, $9.75. AE, DC, MC, V. Mon–Fri 11am–4pm; daily 6–10:30pm. INTERNATIONAL.

Airy and imaginative, this restaurant, which opened in 1986, contains two bars (one, rescued from a Victorian building, is an antique), an inviting dining room, and a less formal eating area. The restaurant, which has a Swiss owner, is popular with the increasing number of Europeans winging in to Grand Bahama Island. Although Bahamian dishes are served, most diners visit for a taste of the continent. The establishment is known for its large servings, fine service, and music at dinner. The spacious restaurant is adjacent to the Bahamas Princess Tower.

Lunch might feature such standard fare as Reuben or club sandwiches, seafood or Caesar salads, or burgers. A pâté maison, however, has the most flavor. For dinner, you can opt for the catch of the day, which is often grouper (rarely overcooked), or the zesty Creole-style shrimp. Although an odd choice for The Bahamas, the filet Stroganoff is also quite good. Finish off with a Viennese strudel, the dessert specialty.

Safari Restaurant. E. Mall Dr. ☎ **242/352-2805.** American breakfast $3.95; main dinner courses $9.95–$19.95. MC, V. Daily 7:30–11am and 5–9pm. INTERNATIONAL.

This is one of the few restaurants in the neighborhood that's as popular at breakfast as it is at dinner. The safari theme is more visible from the outside than the inside, where a simple, uncomplicated venue might remind you of the decor of an upscale coffee shop back home. Among the best values here is a two-for-one surf and turf, costing $29.95. Other items include such international and relatively straightforward staples as New York strip steaks, lamb, broiled or grilled snapper, broiled chicken, or seafood platters. Don't expect glamour, as the place is straightforward, often catering to families, and as such represents uncomplicated good value.

Scorpio's. W. Mall Dr. at Explorer's Way. ☎ **242/352-6969.** Breakfast from $3.75; lunch platters $6–$18.50; dinner main courses $8.75–$19.75. AE, MC, V. Daily 7am–1am. Bar, Mon–Wed 7am–1am, Thurs–Sun 7am–3am. BAHAMIAN.

Named after the astrological sign of its Bahamas-born owner, this restaurant offers a welcome respite from the burgers and pizza that seem to prevail in downtown Freeport. It lies at a busy traffic junction, within a cement-sided building painted both inside and out in a medley of earth-toned colors. There's a bar inside, where tropical drinks (especially rum punch) are the popular libations, and a respectable dining room where the staff wears black-and-white uniforms. Here you get the full repertoire of some Bahama Mama who knows how to rattle those pots and pans, turning out delectable lobster salads, perfectly done steaks, and steamed chicken. Naturally, the kitchen knows how to prepare conch in about every way one would want it. Peas 'n' rice, that Bahamian staple, goes with everything.

Sir Winston Churchill Pub. East Mall, next to the Straw Market and the International Bazaar. ☎ **242/352-8866.** Pizzas $8–$22.75; salads and sandwiches $3.25–$5.50; pastas $6–$13.75. AE, MC, V. Daily noon–2am. INTERNATIONAL.

In spite of its name, this has become mainly a pizzeria. In an upstairs location, it is often visited by the casino crowd when they grow bored with the slot machines. Don't expect much here in the way of cuisine, although it remains an enduring watering hole with many repeat visitors. Try one of about a dozen different pizzas, or choose from a selection of pastas, salads, and sandwiches.

THE INTERNATIONAL BAZAAR

Bavarian Beer Garden. International Bazaar. ☎ **242/352-5050.** Main courses $6–$12. No credit cards. Daily 10:30am–9pm. GERMAN/BAHAMIAN.

Its tables are reassuringly battered, and its owners may or may not have ever been to Germany, but the Teutonic aura of a Bavarian beer garden thrives here. Set beneath the Moorish-style arches of the International Bazaar, the place features at least a dozen kinds of imported beer, recorded versions of oom-pah-pah music, such German fare as knockwurst, bockwurst, and sauerkraut, and a selection of pizzas. On a hot day, all this wurst and sauerkraut may not be what you had in mind. If so, you might opt for fried chicken instead. The chef also prepares cracked conch, but you'll get better versions of that in any of the little Bahamian eateries recommended. The menu has recently been upgraded with a selection of steak, lobster, and fresh fish dishes.

Becky's Restaurant. International Bazaar. ☎ **242/352-8717.** Bahamian or American breakfasts $2.95–$9.95; lunch main courses $2.50–$14.95; dinner main courses $7.95–$22. No credit cards. Daily 7am–10pm. BAHAMIAN/AMERICAN.

This pink-and-white restaurant offers authentic Bahamian cuisine prepared in the time-tested style of the Out Islands. Go here to tank up before a day of serious shopping at the bazaar. Owned by Becky and Berkeley Smith, the place offers a welcome respite from the relentless glitter of the nearby casino.

Breakfasts are either all-American or Bahamian and are available all day. Also popular are such dishes as minced lobster, curried mutton, fish platters, baked or curried chicken, and conch salads. Stick to the Bahama Mama specialties, as the array of American dishes is lackluster. Soup is included with the purchase of steak or lobster. There's a second branch of Becky's at East Sunrise Highway (☎ 242/352-5247), which has basically the same format, hours, and prices.

Café Michel. International Bazaar. ☎ **242/352-2191.** Reservations recommended for dinner. Main courses $4.95–$27.95. AE, MC, V. Mon–Sat 11am–10:30pm. BAHAMIAN/AMERICAN.

At first you think this might be a French bistro set amid the bustle of the International Bazaar. But, alas, it turns out to be a mere coffee shop. However, it's a good place for refueling when you're shopping the bazaar. There are about 20 tables outside, placed under red umbrellas and bistro-style tablecloths. Inside are about a dozen more. Local shoppers know to come here not only for coffee, but for platters, salads, and sandwiches throughout the day. In the evening, the aura grows slightly more formal (but not much). Both American and Bahamian dishes are served, including seafood platters, steaks, and, of course, grouper. The house specialty is a Bahamian lobster platter with all the fixings.

China Temple. International Bazaar. ☎ **242/352-5610.** Main courses $9.75–$32; lunch from $6.50. AE, MC, V. Mon–Sat 10:30am–10:30pm. CHINESE.

This is a Chinese eatery—not a lot more—that also does take-out. Its food is about the same as you'd get in a similar place in New York. It has outdoor café tables, or you can retreat inside. It's recommendable because over the years it's consistently turned out to be the dining bargain of the bazaar. The menu is strictly chop suey or chow mein; this place doesn't attract the serious gourmet of the Orient. Everything's familiar and standard on the menu, including sweet-and-sour fish. The best thing about this restaurant is its prices.

PORT LUCAYA

The Brass Helmet. In the Port Lucaya Marketplace, directly above UNEXSO Dive Shop. ☎ **242/373-2032.** Reservations recommended. Main courses $7–$20; breakfast $4.95–$5.50; lunch $4.50–$8. AE, MC, V. Daily 7:30am–9pm. BAHAMIAN/INTERNATIONAL.

You may feel as if you have stepped back in time *20,000 Leagues Under the Sea* when you visit The Brass Helmet. Antique diving gear and ocean exploration are the themes here. You are greeted by an old brass diving helmet perched atop a wooden crate, along with a faux Great White shark jutting out of the wall. The food is much like what's available on rest of the island. You can get your Bahamian staples here, including cracked conch and grouper. However, there's also an array of steaks, lobster, and a variety of pastas, including a spicy Cajun pasta (obviously not indigenous to the area), seafood linguini (Alfredo or marinara), and the Caribbean seafood pasta (loaded with conch and grouper).

La Dolce Vita. Port Lucaya Marina. ☎ **242/373-8652.** Reservations required. Main courses $13–$25. AE, MC, V. Daily 11am–2:30pm and 5–11pm. Closed Sept. ITALIAN.

Next to the Pub at Port Lucaya (see below) is a small, upscale Italian restaurant with modern decor and traditional food. They serve freshly made pastas and Italian-style pizzas on a patio overlooking the marina or in the 44-seat dining room. Start with the homemade mozzarella or the arugula and baby artichoke salad, which are both quite good and much more interesting than the grilled vegetables. The main dishes from the Chef Paul Prudhomme school of cooking include veal scallopini, ravioli stuffed with lobster, linguini with clams, and angel-hair pasta with fresh tomatoes and arugula. They also offer a wide range of pizzas, made to order (as are the pastas) with whatever ingredients are in season and available. For dessert, try the tiramisu or the chocolate flan, followed by an espresso.

The Pub at Port Lucaya. Market Place, Port Lucaya Marina. ☎ **242/373-8450.** Main courses $6.95–$35. AE, MC, V. Daily 11am–midnight. INTERNATIONAL.

Your hunger pangs can be satisfied at this twin restaurant whose premises is divided between a nautical and woodsy-looking pub and a slightly more formal, big-windowed restaurant La Dolce Vita, serving mostly Italian food. Everything seems to taste better if it's preceded with a beer or a rum-based Painkiller in the pub. You can dine indoors or out, the latter offering views of the port. Menu items include cracked conch, fish strips, Caesar salads, lamb chops, and such traditional English pies as steak-and-ale or shepherd's.

8 Grand Cayman ⌇ ⌇ ⌇

Grand Cayman is one of today's "hot" ports of call, primarily because of its terrific diving and snorkeling, but also because of its laid-back civility. You can lie on the famous Seven Mile Beach and not be hustled by vendors and panhandlers, as on Jamaica and other islands. And you won't be mugged while walking the streets of George Town, the capital.

The name Cayman comes from a Spanish-Carib word, *caymanas,* or "crocodiles," although historians believe the crocodiles in reality were iguanas. The first colonists were a motley crew of shipwrecked sailors and buccaneers, including the 17th-century Welshman, Sir Henry Morgan. Later, Scottish fishermen arrived and forged a quiet, peaceful settlement. The civil manners of the locals today reflect their British heritage. To this day, Grand Cayman is a tranquil, slow-paced oasis at the western edge of the Caribbean.

Grand Cayman is a British colony 480 miles south of Miami. It's the largest of the Cayman Islands (Cayman Brac and Little Cayman are the others), though it's only 22 miles long and 8 miles across at its widest point. George Town is the colony's capital and commercial hub. With more than 500 tax-advantaged offshore banks, it's also the banking capital of the Caribbean. The town is small enough to explore easily on foot in a few hours.

COMING ASHORE

Cruise ships anchor off George Town and ferry their passengers to a pier on Harbour Drive. Located in the heart of the shopping district, the landing-point couldn't be more convenient. There's a tourist information booth at the pier, and taxis line up to meet cruise-ship passengers.

FAST FACTS

Currency   The legal tender is the **Cayman Islands dollar (CI),** which is valued at $1.25 U.S. ($1 U.S. equals 80¢ CI). Canadian, U.S., and British currencies are accepted throughout the Cayman Islands. The Cayman dollar breaks down into 100 cents. Coins come in 1¢, 5¢, 10¢, and 25¢. Bills come in denominations of $1, $5, $10, $25, $50, and $100 (note that there is no CI$20 bill). Many restaurants quote prices in Cayman Islands dollars, which can lead you to think that food is cheaper than it is. Unless otherwise noted, prices in this section are given in U.S. dollars.

Information   The **Department of Tourism** is in the Pavilion Building, Cricket Square (P.O. Box 67), George Town, Grand Cayman, B.W.I. (☎ **345/949-0623**). Open Monday to Friday from 9am to 5pm.

Language   English is the official language of the islands.

SHORE EXCURSIONS

Nearly all the shore excursions here are underwater adventures, which you can book on your own or through your cruise ship. The biggest pleaser among cruise ship passengers is a snorkeling trip to Stingray City (see the "Favorite Offshore Experiences," below), which lasts about two hours and costs $29. You can also ride in the submarine *Atlantis XI* for $72 per person (see "Seeing the Sights," below).

The Cayman Islands

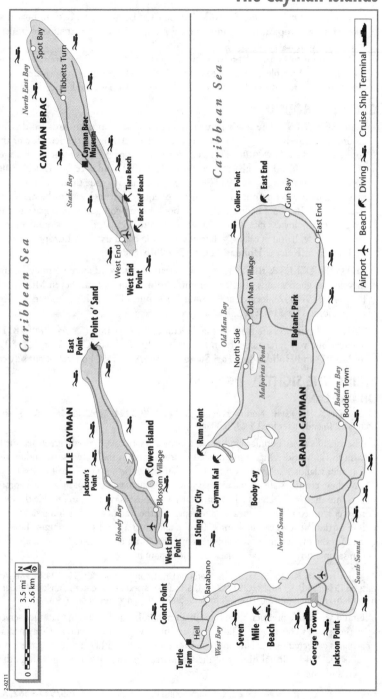

Airport ✈ Beach 🏖 Diving 🤿 Cruise Ship Terminal ⚓

CAYMAN BRAC
Spot Bay
North East Bay
Tibbetts Turn
Cayman Brac Museum
Stake Bay
Tiara Beach
Brac Reef Beach
West End
West End Point

LITTLE CAYMAN
East Point
Point o' Sand
Jackson's Point
Owen Island
Blossom Village
Bloody Bay
West End Point

Caribbean Sea

GRAND CAYMAN
Colliers Point
East End
Gun Bay
East End
Old Man Bay
Old Man Village
North Side
Malportas Pond
Botanic Park
Bodden Bay
Bodden Town
Rum Point
Cayman Kai
Sting Ray City
Booby Cay
North Sound
South Sound
Conch Point
Batabano
Hell
Turtle Farm
West Bay
Seven Mile Beach
George Town
Jackson Point

N
0 3.5 mi
   5.6 km

2-0211

Another excursion is the Seaworld Explorer Cruise on a glass-bottom boat that takes you over tropical fish, stunning coral reefs, and even the remains of sunken ships. This tour lasts about an hour and costs $29.

If you want to see the island, you can take a taxi tour for $40 per hour. Taxis can hold up to five people. A 3-hour tour would cover all the sights in a leisurely fashion. Make sure to stop in the town of "Hell" and send a postcard home.

GETTING AROUND

CAR RENTALS   The roads here are good by Caribbean standards, so driving around is relatively easy—if you can get the hang of driving on the **left side of the road**. **Cico Avis** (☎ **800/331-1212** in the U.S., or 345/949-2468), **Budget** (☎ **800/527-0700** in the U.S., or 345/949-5605), and **Ace Hertz** (☎ **800/654-3131** in the U.S., or 345/949-7861) rent cars and will issue the mandatory Cayman Islands driving permit for $5. All three require that reservations be made between 6 and 36 hours before pickup, so book before you get here. It pays to call around for the lowest rate. Count on about $35 to $55 per day, depending on the type of vehicle. If you're calling well in advance, you could try **Auto Europe** (☎ **800/223-5555**) or **Kenwel Holiday Autos** (☎ **800/678-0678**).

MOTORCYCLES & BICYCLES   The terrain is relatively flat, so motorcycles and bicycles are good means of getting around. **Soto Scooters Ltd.,** Seven Mile Beach (☎ **345/945-4652**), located at Coconut Place, offers Honda Elite scooters for $30 a day, bicycles for $15. They also have Jeeps for rent.

TAXIS   Taxis fares are fixed by the director of civil aviation (☎ **345/949-7811**). Typical one-way fares range from $11.50 to $20. **Cayman Cab Team** (☎ **809/947-4491**) and **Holiday Inn Taxi Stand** (☎ **345/945-4491**) offer 24-hour service.

SEEING THE SIGHTS
ON DRY LAND

✪ **Cayman Turtle Farm.** Northwest Point. ☎ **345/949-3894.** Admission $6 adults, $3 children 6–12 (6 and under free). Daily 8:30am–5pm.

The island's most popular land-based tourist attraction is the only green sea turtle farm in the world. Once a multitude of turtles lived in the waters surrounding the Cayman Islands (Columbus called these islands *Las Tortugas* or "The Turtles"). Today, these creatures are an endangered species (as such, you cannot bring turtle products into the United States). The turtle farm's purpose is twofold: to provide the local market with edible turtle meat and to replenish the waters with hatchlings and yearling turtles. Visitors can look into 100 circular concrete tanks that contain these sea creatures in every stage of development and size, from 6 ounces to 600 pounds. You can sample turtle dishes at a snack bar and restaurant.

Cayman Islands National Museum. Harbour Dr., George Town. ☎ **345/949-8368.** Admission CI$4 ($5 U.S.) adults, CI$2 ($2.50 U.S.) students and senior citizens, children under 6 free. Mon–Fri 9am–5pm, Sat 10am–2pm (last admission 30 minutes prior to closing).

Grand Cayman's premier museum is in a veranda-fronted building that once served as the island's courthouse. The formal exhibits include a collection of Caymanian artifacts collected by Ira Thompson from the 1930s, and others portraying the natural, social, and cultural history of the Caymans. The museum has a gift shop, theater, and cafe.

Queen Elizabeth II Botanic Park. Off Frank Sound Rd., North Side. ☎ **345/947-9462.** Admission CI$5 ($6.25 U.S.) adults, CI$2.50 ($3.15 U.S.) children (5 and under free). Daily 9am–5:30pm.

On 60 acres of rugged, wooded land, this park offers visitors a 1-hour walk through wetlands, swamp, dry thicket, and mahogany trees. Volunteers spent more than a year creating the trail, which is 0.8 miles long. Along the way, the indigenous plants are identified, including orchids and bromeliads. You're likely to spot hickatees, the freshwater turtles found only on the Caymans and in Cuba. Occasionally you'll see the rare Grand Cayman parrot, or perhaps the anole lizard, with its cobalt-blue throat pouch. Even rarer is the endangered blue iguana. There are six rest stations along the trail with more detailed information. The park has a visitor center with rotating exhibits and a canteen for food and refreshments. There's also a heritage garden with a re-creation of a traditional Cayman home, vegetable garden, and farm; a floral garden with 1¹/₂ acres of flowering plants; and a 2-acre lake with three islands, home to many native birds.

The Mastic Trail. West of Frank Sound Rd. ☎ **345/949-1996.** Tours CI$25 ($31.25 U.S.).

One of the newest attractions here is a restored 200-year-old footpath through a 2-million-year-old woodland area in the heart of the island. Named for the majestic mastic tree, the trail lies on Grand Cayman's north-central side, adjacent to the Botanic Park, and is a 45-minute drive from George Town. It showcases the reserve's natural attractions, including a native mangrove swamp, traditional agriculture, and an ancient woodland area, home to the largest variety of native plant and animal life. You can follow the trail on your own, but we recommend taking a guided tour. It's easy to get lost, rocks underfoot can be slippery and unstable, and weather can change unexpectedly for the worse.

The 3-hour guided tours, limited to eight participants, are offered Monday to Friday at 8:30am and at 3pm, and on Saturday at 8:30am. Reservations are required; call Monday to Friday from 10am to 3pm. The hike is not recommended for children under six, elderly travelers, or persons with physical disabilities. You should wear comfortable, sturdy shoes and carry water and insect repellent.

DIVING THE DEPTHS

Grand Cayman is the top of an underwater mountain, whose side—known as the Cayman Wall—plummets straight down for 500 feet before becoming a steep slope that falls away for 6,000 feet to the ocean floor. You don't have to be a scuba diver to explore this underwater wonder—the submersible ✪ *Atlantis XI*, on Goring Avenue (☎ **800/887-8591** or 345/949-7700), has three types of dives going to a depth of 100 feet.

The "Atlantis Odyssey" dive, operated both day and night, features divers communicating with submarine passengers by wireless underwater phone and moving about on underwater scooters. It costs $82 and lasts 45 minutes. The "Atlantis Expedition" dive visits the Cayman Wall; it lasts 55 minutes and costs $72. The "Atlantis Discovery" lasts 40 minutes and introduces viewers to the marine life of the Caymans. It costs $55. Children 4 to 12 are charged half price on all dives (no children under 4 allowed). *Atlantis XI* dives Monday to Saturday. Reservations are recommended 24 hours in advance.

The Atlantis company also operates two deep-diving research submersibles, each of which carries two passengers and a pilot. They go as deep as 800 feet. These trips last just over an hour and allow passengers to see the variety of sea life at different depths. If weather permits, each dive goes down to the wreck of the *Kirk Pride,* a cargo ship that sank in 1976 and lodged on a rock ledge at 780 feet. These deep dives cost $295 per person, and are available to anyone over the age of 8. Reservations should be made as early as possible, as availability is severely limited.

SHOPPING

There's duty-free shopping here for silver, china, crystal, Irish linens, British woolen goods, and such local crafts as black-coral jewelry, but we have found most prices to be similar to those in the U.S.

Don't purchase turtle products, since they cannot be brought into the United States or most other Western nations.

Artifacts Ltd. Harbour Dr., George Town (on the harborfront, across from the landing dock). ☎ **345/949-2442.**

This shop is generally recognized as the premier outlet on the island for back issues of some of the rare stamps issued by the Caymanian government. It's managed by Charles Adams, one of the country's philatelic authorities. Stamps range in price from 20¢ to $900, and inventory includes the rare War Tax Stamp issued during World War II. Other items for sale include antique Dutch and Spanish coins unearthed from underwater shipwrecks, enameled boxes, and antique prints and maps.

Black Coral and . . . . Fort St., George Town. ☎ **345/949-0123.**

Connoisseurs of unusual fine jewelry and unique objets d'art come here for the stunning black-coral creations of internationally acclaimed sculptor Bernard K. Passman, who elevated the crafting of black coral to a prized art form. In the past 2 decades, this Iowa-born artist has created many pieces of exquisite black-coral and gold jewelry and sculpture, most notably the royal wedding gift from the Cayman Islands to Prince Charles and Princess Diana—a 97-piece cutlery set of sterling silver with black-coral handles. The government also commissioned a black-coral horse and Corgi dogs for Queen Elizabeth II and Prince Philip. Signed, limited-edition pieces are excellent investments.

English Shoppe. Harbour Dr., George Town. ☎ **345/949-2457.**

Watches, black- and pink-coral jewelry, 14- and 18-karat gold jewelry, T-shirts, and souvenirs are on sale here, all with prices quoted in U.S. dollars. The shop is in front of the cruise-ship landing.

The Jewelry Centre. Fort St., George Town. ☎ **345/949-0070.**

This is one of the largest jewelry stores in the Caymans—a real jewelry department store. Its six departments specialize in loose or set diamonds, gold (sold as chains or as ornaments, including coins found in offshore shipwrecks), black coral, colored gemstones, and caymanite, the pinkish-brown striated rock found only on the Caymans. The store is located in a two-story building in the center of town.

Kennedy Gallery. W. Shore Centre, George Town. ☎ **345/949-8077.**

Opened in 1993 in a shopping center on Seven Mile Beach, this gallery specializes in watercolors by local artists (including Joanne Sibley and Lois Brezinski), as well as copies and originals of works by the establishment's founder, Robert Kennedy. The artworks cost from $15 to as much as $7,000.

Kirk Freeport Plaza. Cardinal Ave. and Panton St., George Town. ☎ **345/949-7477.**

The largest store of its kind in the Caymans, Kirk Freeport Plaza contains a treasure trove of gold jewelry, watches, china, crystal, perfumes, and cosmetics. It holds the Gucci franchise for the island and has handbags, valises, and perfumes priced 15% to 35% below suggested stateside retail prices. Also stocked are crystal and porcelain at discounts of 30% to 50%, including such names as Wedgwood, Royal Doulton, Waterford, Lladró, Baccarat, Herend, Hummel, and Daum.

⭐ **Favorite Offshore Experiences**

The waters off Grand Cayman are home to **Stingray City,** one of the world's most unusual underwater attractions. Set in the sun-flooded, 12-foot-deep waters of North Sound, about 2 miles east of the island's northwestern tip, the site was discovered in the mid-1980s, when local fishermen cleaned their catch and dumped the offal overboard. They noticed scores of stingrays (which usually eat marine crabs) feeding on the debris, a phenomenon that quickly attracted local divers and marine zoologists. Today, between 30 and 50 relatively tame stingrays hover in the waters around the site for their daily handouts from hordes of snorkelers and scuba divers.

Interestingly, most of the stingrays here are females, the males preferring to remain in deeper waters offshore. Whatever their gender, stingrays possess viciously barbed stingers capable of inflicting painful damage to anyone mistreating them. Never try to grab one by the tail. Despite the dangers, divers and snorkelers feed and pet these velvet-skinned creatures without incident.

About half a dozen entrepreneurs lead expeditions to Stingray City from points along Seven Mile Beach, traveling around Conch Point to the feeding grounds. One well-known outfit is **Treasure Island Divers** (☎ **800/822-7552** or 345/949-4456), which charges divers $45 and snorkelers $25. They go Monday, Wednesday, Friday, and Sunday at 1:30pm.

Sunflower Boutique. S. Church St., George Town. ☎ **345/949-4090.**

This is an unusual boutique. Established some quarter of a century ago in a two-story building beside the waterfront, it sells hand-painted skirts and blouses, T-shirts and shorts for men and women, jewelry fashioned from black, pink, and white coral, and an assortment of gift items and Caribbean paintings. You'll find it directly on the waterfront in the center of George Town.

BEACHES

Grand Cayman's ⭐ **Seven Mile Beach,** which begins north of George Town, an easy taxi ride from the cruise dock, has sparkling white sands with a backdrop of Australian pines. The beach is really about 5$^1/_2$ miles long, but the label of "seven mile" has stuck. It's lined with condominiums and plush resorts. The beach is known for its array of water sports and its translucent aquamarine waters. The average water temperature is a balmy 80°F.

GOLF, DIVING, SNORKELING & WATER SPORTS

GOLF   The major golf course on Grand Cayman is at the **Britannia Golf Club,** next to the Hyatt Regency on West Bay Road (☎ 345/949-8020). The course was designed by Jack Nicklaus and is unique in that it incorporates three different courses in one: a 9-hole championship layout, an 18-hole executive set-up, and an 18-hole Cayman course. The last was intended for play with the Nicklaus-designed Cayman ball, which goes about half the distance of a regulation ball. The Britannia charges $50 to $80 for greens fees in the winter season, $40 to $65 off-season, depending on which course you intend to play. Cart rentals go for $15 to $25; club rentals, $25. Nonguests of the club can reserve no more than 24 hours in advance.

SCUBA DIVING & SNORKELING   Coral reefs and other formations encircling the island are filled with marine life. It's easy to dive close to shore, so boats aren't necessary, but there are plenty of boats and scuba facilities available, as well as many dive shops renting scuba gear to certified divers.

The best dive operation is **Bob Soto's Diving Ltd.,** P.O. Box 1801, Grand Cayman, B.W.I. (☎**800/262-7686** or 809/949-2022 for reservations, or 345/949-2022), with full service dive shops at Treasure Island, the SCUBA Centre on North Church Street, and Soto's Coconut in the Coconut Place Shopping Centre. A full-day resort course for beginners costs $90. Certified divers can choose from a wide range of one-tank ($40 to $45) and two-tank ($60) boat dives daily on the west, north, and south walls, plus shore diving from the SCUBA Centre. Non-divers can take daily snorkel trips ($25), including Stingray City. The staff is helpful and highly professional.

WATER SPORTS   Universally regarded as the most up-to-date and best-equipped water-sports facility in the Cayman Islands, **Red Sail Sports** (☎ **800/255-6425** in the U.S., or 345/947-5966) has its headquarters in a gaily painted wooden house beside the beach at the Hyatt Regency Grand Cayman on West Bay Road. Their half-day deep-sea fishing excursions for up to eight people depart daily at 7am and 1pm in search of tuna, marlin, and wahoo. The cost is $600 ($800 for a full day), but the fee can be split among eight people.

Red Sail also rents 16-foot Prindle cats for about $28 an hour, and offers parasailing for $50 per ride and waterskiing for $75 per half hour. The cost can be divided among several people.

In addition, Red Sail has one of the best-designed sailing catamarans in the Caribbean, berthed in a canal a short walk from the water sports center. Some 65 feet in length, it's fast and stable. A daily 10am to 2pm sail to Stingray City, with snorkeling equipment and lunch included, costs $60 per person.

Red Sail also offers scuba diving for beginners as well as more advanced divers. A two-tank morning dive takes you to two different dive sites, at depths ranging from 50 to 100 feet. It costs $50 to $66.

DINING

Big Daddy's Restaurant and Sports Bar. W. Bay Rd. ☎ **345/949-8511.** Reservations recommended at dinner. Main courses CI$10–CI$22.50 ($12.50–$28.15). AE, MC, V. Mon–Sat 8–11am, noon–4pm, and 5–10pm, Sun 4pm–midnight. INTERNATIONAL.

This restaurant, set above a liquor store under the same management, is a bustling, informal emporium of food and drink. One area is devoted to a woodsy, nautically decorated bar area, where TV screens broadcast either CNN or sports events. Three separate dining areas, mostly isolated from the activities at the bar, serve well-prepared food. Menu items include deli sandwiches, half-pound burgers, garlic shrimp, T-bone steaks, barbecued ribs, fresh catch of the day, and pasta dishes. The food is often better than the location or ambience would suggest.

Cracked Conch by the Sea. W. Bay Rd., near Turtle Bay Farm. ☎ **345/945-5217.** Reservations recommended. Main courses CI$14.95–CI$24.95 ($18.70–$31.20). MC, V. Daily 11:30am–10pm. SEAFOOD.

Long a culinary landmark, this popular restaurant now enjoys a new location, near the famous turtle farm in West Bay. It serves some of the island's freshest seafood, including a succulent turtle steak and the inevitable conch. The menu is one of the largest on the island. There's also an array of meat dishes, including beef, jerk pork and spicy combinations of chicken. Steaks, burgers, chicken, and fish filets can be charbroiled to your specifications. The fresh fish can also be prepared as you desire it: sautéed, golden broiled, steamed in wine, or whatever. Foods are freshly prepared—nothing frozen. Each day a fresh vegetarian pasta is featured (made without oils). There's also a "crispy" salad bar.

The decor is a bit corny, including a cement floor made to look like authentic wood planking from a pirate ship. The location overlooks the Caribbean on the northwest tip of the island. There is also a dive shop here, as well as a patio bar 15 feet high overlooking the sea, and a walkway built so you can watch fish feeding at 8pm every evening.

Crow's Nest Restaurant. South Sound. ☎ **345/949-9366.** Reservations recommended. Main courses CI$11.95–CI$21.95 ($14.95–$27.45). AE, MC, V. Mon–Sat 11:30am–2pm; daily 5:30–10pm. CARIBBEAN.

With a boardwalk and a terrace jutting onto the sands, this informal restaurant has a view of both Sand Cay and a nearby lighthouse. The restaurant is on the southwesternmost tip of the island, a 4-minute drive from George Town. It's one of those places that evokes the Caribbean "the way it used to be." There's no pretense here—you get good, honest Caribbean cookery, including grilled seafood, at great prices. Many dishes are spicy, especially their signature appetizer, fiery coconut shrimp. Try one of the daily specials or perhaps the sweet, tender lobster. Other dishes might include grilled tuna steak with ackee or Jamaican chicken curry with roast coconut. For dessert, try the banana toffee pie.

✪ **Grand Old House.** Petra Plantation, S. Church St. (1 mile south of George Town, past Jackson Point). ☎ **345/949-9333.** Reservations required. Main courses CI$17.75–CI$29.75 ($22.20–$37.20). AE, MC, V. Mon–Fri 11:45am–2:30pm; daily 6–10pm. Closed Sept. AMERICAN/CARIBBEAN/PACIFIC RIM.

This mansion is a former plantation house, constructed at the turn of the century by a Boston coconut merchant. Built on bedrock near the edge of the sea, it stands amid venerable trees on 129 ironwood posts that support the main house and a bevy of gazebos. The Grand Old House is the island's premier caterer and hosts everything from lavish weddings and political functions to informal family celebrations.

The restaurant was put on the Cayman culinary map by German-born Tell Erhardt, and is often called Chef Tell's. Though this former TV celebrity chef has long gone, the Grand Old House has suffered no falloff either in food or service. The menu has been slightly updated by the new chef, India-born Kandaphil Matahi. Appetizers here remain the most delectable on island, and include home-smoked marlin and salmon or coconut beer battered shrimp. For a main course, try the sautéed fresh snapper with shallots in a Chardonnay white-butter sauce, or else the potato-encrusted tuna. Old-time favorites include turtle steak Cayman style and magret of duck breast braised in red burgundy with a thyme sauce.

Hemingway's. In the Hyatt Regency Grand Cayman, W. Bay Rd. ☎ **345/949-1234.** Reservations recommended. Main courses CI$16.50–CI$35 ($20.65–$43.75). AE, CB, DC, DISC, MC, V. Daily 11:30am–2:30pm and 6–10pm. SEAFOOD/INTERNATIONAL.

The finest seafood on the island can be found 2 miles north of George Town at Hemingway's, named after the novelist and inspired by Key West, his one-time residence. You can dine in the open air with a view of the sea. The menu is among the more imaginative on the island. Appetizers include pepperpot soup—a favorite of Papa's—and gazpacho served with a black-bean relish. The catch of the day, perhaps snapper or wahoo, is always a good choice. You can also order roast rack of lamb served on a fruit compote with caramelized-onion mashed potatoes. Want something more imaginative? Try grouper stuffed with crabmeat, or Cuban-spiced tenderloin served on white bean and fennel ragoût.

Hog Sty Bay Café and Pub. N. Church St. (near the beginning of W. Bay Rd.). ☎ **345/949-6163.** Reservations recommended in winter. Main courses CI$15–CI$20 ($18.75–$25). AE, MC, V. Daily 8am–10pm (last order). Bar open till midnight. CARIBBEAN/ENGLISH.

The Hog Sty Bay Café and Pub enjoys a loyal clientele. Set in a low-slung cottage with bright-colored verandas, this place is the creative statement of Pennsylvania-born Tom Keagy. It's divided into an amusingly decorated pub and a Caribbean-inspired dining room open to a view of the harbor. In the pub, you can order such British staples as fish and chips or cottage pie, and such drinks as a Snake Bite (equal parts of hard English cider and English lager). Also available are all the foamy tropical drinks you'd expect.

The food from the kitchen is competently prepared and satisfying, though not a lot more. Dining choices include Caesar salad topped with marinated conch, Cajun chicken, fresh catch of the day, shrimp, and pastas. There's also a seafood pastry stuffed with lobster, shrimp, and scallops. Everything is great value for the money. You can also get breakfast here—the huevos rancheros are good.

Island Taste. S. Church St. ☎ **345/949-4945.** Reservations recommended. Main courses CI$11–CI$23 ($13.75–$28.75). AE, MC, V. Mon–Sat 10:30am–4:30pm; daily 6–10pm. CARIBBEAN/MEDITERRANEAN.

This restaurant caters more to large appetites than to picky gourmets, and offers great value for the money. It sits across from the headquarters of the *Atlantis* submarine in George Town. There's an indoor and outdoor bar area and indoor tables, but the most popular seating area is on the wraparound veranda, one floor above street level. Here you'll find one of the largest "starter" selections on the island. Soups include both white conch chowder and turtle. Appetizers feature fresh oysters, Mexican ceviche, and calamari Vesuvio. At least seven pasta dishes are on the dinner menu, including linguine with small clams. You can also order T-bone steak and chicken parmigiana. However, most of the menu is devoted to seafood dishes, such as dolphin, turtle steak, and spiny lobster. The chef offers all-you-can-eat deep-fried shrimp every night for CI$15.75 ($19.70) per person.

Lobster Pot. N. Church St. ☎ **345/949-2736.** Reservations required in winter. Main courses CI$10.50–CI$25 ($13.15–$31.25). AE, MC, V. Mon–Fri 11:30am–2:30pm; daily 5:30–10pm. SEAFOOD.

One of the island's best-known restaurants, the Lobster Pot overlooks the water from its second-floor perch. It's situated at the western perimeter of George Town near what used to be Fort George. True to its name, it offers lobster prepared in different ways: Cayman style, bisque, and salad. Conch schnitzel and seafood curry are also on the menu, together with turtle steak grown commercially at Cayman Island kraals. Sometimes the seafood is a bit overcooked for our tastes, but most other dishes are right on the mark. The place is also known for its prime beef steaks. For lunch, you might try the English fish and chips or perhaps seafood jambalaya or a pasta. The Lobster Pot's pub is a pleasant place for a drink—you might find someone up for a game of darts, too.

✪ Ottmar's Restaurant and Lounge. W. Bay Rd. (side entrance of Grand Pavilion Hotel). ☎ **345/945-5879.** Reservations recommended. Main courses CI$13.95–CI$24 ($17.45–$30); Sun brunch CI$40 ($50). AE, MC, V. Daily 11:30am–3pm and 6–11pm. INTERNATIONAL.

One of the island's top restaurants, Ottmar's is outfitted in a French Empire motif with lots of paneling, rich upholstery, and plenty of space between tables. The formal bar/lounge area is decorated with deep-sea fishing trophies. This is the domain of an Austrian expatriate, Ottmar Weber, who long ago abandoned the land of his youth to roam the world, finding culinary inspiration wherever he went. The results are usually pleasing. You can try such dishes as Bavarian cucumber soup, bouillabaisse, French pepper steak, and Wiener schnitzel. Our favorite is chicken Trinidad, stuffed with grapes, nuts, and apples rolled in coconut flakes, sautéed golden brown, and served in orange-butter sauce. There's also an array of sophisticated desserts, plus a selection of vegetarian dishes. The service is professional and attentive. Lunch is served at the Waterfall Restaurant, in the same building.

The Wharf. W. Bay Rd. (about 2 miles north of George Town). ☎ **345/949-2231.** Reservations recommended. Main courses CI$18–CI$28 ($22.50–$35). AE, MC, V. Mon–Fri noon–2:30pm; daily 6–10pm. CARIBBEAN/CONTINENTAL.

The Wharf, which had been everything from a dinner theater to a nightclub, is now one of the leading restaurants on the island. This 375-seat restaurant is decorated in soft pastels. It offers dining either inside or outside on an elevated veranda or on a beachside terrace. The sound of the surf mingles with chatter from the bar and music from the strolling Paraguayan harpist and pan flute player. Many diners begin with a Wharf salad of seasonal greens; others prefer the homemade black-bean soup or the home-smoked salmon. The main dishes include everything from Cayman green-turtle steak (when available) to pepper steak Madagascar. The seafood potpourri includes lobster, shrimp, and scallops in a mild curry sauce. Veal Martinique features medallions of tender veal in a zesty citrus sauce. The kitchen makes a laudable effort to break away from typical, dull menu items, and for the most part succeeds.

Whitehall Bay. The Waterfront, N. Church St. (a short walk north of George Town's center). ☎ **345/949-8670.** Reservations recommended Sat–Sun. Main courses CI$9.50–CI$21.50 ($11.90–$26.90). AE, MC, V. Daily 11am–10pm. CARIBBEAN.

Most of this restaurant's dining tables overlook the coral reef and piers that jut out into the sea. An inner room provides additional tables, a bar, and an unusual collection of photographs depicting early Cayman Islanders. The kitchen turns out typical West Indian fare, with some charm and plenty of flavor. Menu items include salads, sandwiches, marinated conch, catch of the day, crab backs, curried chicken, steaks, turtle stew, and Cayman-style lobster.

9 Grenada ⇩ ⇩ ⇩ ⇩

St. George's, the capital of Grenada, is one of the most colorful ports in the West Indies. Nearly landlocked in the deep crater of a long-dead volcano, and flanked by old forts, it reminds many visitors of Portofino, Italy. Here you'll see some of the most charming Georgian colonial architecture in the Caribbean. The steep and narrow streets enhance the beauty of the buildings' ballast bricks, wrought-iron balconies, and red tiles on the sloping roofs. Many of the pastel warehouses here date back to the 18th century. Frangipani and flamboyant trees adding to the palette of color.

A stroll along the waterfront Carenage is certainly worth a trip, if just to have the spice vendors offer you a lifetime supply of nutmeg and mace. There are more spices per square mile on this "Spice Island" than anywhere else in the world. The air on Grenada (pronounced Gre-*nay*-dah) is fragrant with cloves, cinnamon, mace, cocoa, tonka beans, ginger, and a third of the world's supply of nutmeg. "Drop a few seeds anywhere," the locals say of their lush island, "and you have an instant garden."

Grenada is not for the serious party animal—and definitely not for anyone seeking to roll the dice in a casino. Instead, its great tropical scenery and natural bounty attract visitors who want to snorkel, sail, fish, or simply while the day away on the two-mile-long Grand Anse Beach, one of the best in the entire Caribbean. Grenada's interior, crisscrossed by nature trails, is a jungle of palms, oleander, bougainvillea, purple and red hibiscus, crimson anthurium, bananas, breadfruit, birdsong, and ferns.

The Marxists who overthrew an oppressive tyrant in 1979 were themselves booted out by United States military forces, who stormed ashore here in 1983. Its political troubles now over, this island is a worthwhile diversion.

COMING ASHORE

Ships either dock at a pier right in St. George's or anchor in the much-photographed harbor and send their passengers to the pier by tender. A tourist information center at the pier dispenses island data. Pier telephones take major credit cards, or you can buy Island Phone Cards at the tourist information desk. The Carenage (St. George's main street) is only a short walk away from the pier; a taxi into the center of town costs about $3. To get to Grand Anse, you can either take a regular taxi or a water taxi (see "Getting Around," below).

FAST FACTS

Currency   The official currency is the **Eastern Caribbean dollar (EC$),** which is worth about 37¢ U.S. Always determine which dollars—EC or U.S.—you're talking about when discussing a price.

Information   Go to the **Grenada Board of Tourism,** on the Carenage, in St. George's (☎ **473/440-2279**), for maps and general information. Open Monday to Friday from 8am to 4pm.

Language   English is commonly spoken on this island. Creole English, a mixture of African, English, and French, is spoken informally by the majority.

SHORE EXCURSIONS

Because of Grenada's lush landscape, we recommend spending at least three hours touring its interior, one of the most scenic in the West Indies. The best deal is the 3-hour Grenada Tour, costing $32 and up, depending on the cruise line. It takes you through the highlights of the interior and along the coast, including Grand Anse Beach. You get to see the most luxuriant part of Grenada's rain forest, a nutmeg-processing station, and many small hamlets along the way.

Many cruise lines will also book you on a tour that explores St. George's historical sites and forts before taking you to some of the island's natural highlights, including a private garden where some 500 species of island plants and flowers are cultivated. This 2-hour tour generally costs $16, but could be higher, depending on the cruise line.

GETTING AROUND

St. George's can easily be explored on foot, although parts of the town are steep.

BUS   Minivans, charging EC$1 to $6 (40¢ to $2.20), are the most economical means of transport. The most popular run is between St. George's and Grand Anse Beach. Most minivans depart from Market Square or from the Esplanade area of St. George's.

CAR RENTALS   Driving here is **on the left side of the road,** and finding your way around isn't easy. If you still want to rent a car, **Avis** (☎ **800/331-1212** in the U.S., or 473/440-3936) operates out of a Shell gasoline station on Lagoon Road, on the southern outskirts of St. George's. **Budget Rent-a-Car** is at Cedear's Inn, True Blue (☎ **800/527-0700** in the U.S., or 473/444-2277). Avis will pick you up at the dock if you reserve in advance. Even though U.S., British, or Canadian driver's licenses are recognized, you must obtain a local permit from the rental company. Permits cost EC$30 ($11.10).

Warning: There's such a thing as a Grenadian driving machismo. Local drivers take blind corners with abandon, resulting in an extraordinary number of accidents being reported in the lively local paper. Gird yourself with nerves of steel, don't drink and drive, and be extra alert for children and pedestrians.

Caribbean Sea

Levera Beach and National Park

Sauteurs

Victoria

Mt. St. Catherine

Gouyave (Charlottetown)

Grand Etang NationalPark

Grand Roy

Mt. Qua Qua

Grand Etang

Annandale Falls

Grenville

Mt. Sinai

Marquis

Constantine

Beaulieu

St. George's

St. David's

Grand Anse Beach

Morne Rouge

Atlantic Ocean

Woburn

Point Salines

L'Anse aux Epines

Cruise Ship Terminal
Airport ✈   Beach   Mountain ▲▲

0   5 km
     3 mi

N

2-0195

TAXIS   Fares are set by the government. Most arriving cruisers take a cab from the pier to one of the points of interest near St. George's. You can also use most taxi drivers as a guide for a day's sightseeing. The price is about $15 a hour, depending on what you want to do, but you can divide the cost among three or four passengers. Be sure to negotiate a price before setting out. You can also rent professional guides for island tours. They charge from $40 to $55, depending on how much you want to see.

WATER TAXI   An ideal way to get around the harbor and to Grand Anse Beach is by water taxi. The round-trip waterborne fare to the beach is $4. A water taxi will take you from one end of the Carenage to the other for another $2.

SEEING THE SIGHTS

In St. George's, you can visit the **Grenada National Museum,** at the corner of Young and Monckton streets (☎ **473/440-3725**), set in the foundations of an old French army barracks and prison built in 1704. This small but interesting museum houses finds from archeological digs, including ancient petroglyphs, plus a rum still, native fauna, and memorabilia depicting Grenada's history, including the island's first telegraph. There are also two bathtubs worth seeing—the wooden barrel used by the fort's prisoners and the carved marble tub used by Joséphine Bonaparte during her adolescence on Martinique. The most comprehensive exhibit illuminates the native culture of Grenada. The museum is open Monday to Friday from 9am to 4:30pm and Saturday from 10am to 1pm. Admission is $2.

The Outer Harbour is also called the **Esplanade.** It's connected to the Carenage by the Sendall Tunnel, which is cut through the promontory known as St. George's Point.

You can take a taxi up Richmond Hill to **Fort Frederick,** which the French began in 1779. The British, having retaken the island in 1783 under provision of the Treaty of Versailles, completed the fort in 1791. From its battlements you'll have a panoramic view of the harbor and the yacht marina.

Don't miss the mountains northeast of St. George's. After a 15-minute drive, you reach ✪ **Annandale Falls,** a tropical wonderland where a 50-foot-high cascade drops into a basin. The overall beauty is almost Tahitian. You can have a picnic surrounded by liana vines, elephant ears, and other tropical flora and spices. **Annandale Falls Centre** (☎ 473/440-2452) offers gift items, handcrafts, and samples of the indigenous spices of Grenada. Nearby, an improved trail leads to the falls, where you can enjoy a refreshing swim. Swimmers can use the changing cubicles at the falls at no cost. The center is open daily from 8am to 4pm.

SHOPPING

The local stores sell luxury-item imports, mainly from England, at prices that are not quite duty free. This is no grand Caribbean merchandise mart, so if you're cruising on to such islands as Aruba, St. Maarten, or St. Thomas, you may want to postpone serious purchases. On the other hand, you might locate some fine local handcrafts, gifts, or even art here.

Spice vendors will besiege you wherever you go—don't feel you have to resist them. The spices here are fresher and better than any you're likely to find in your local supermarket. Everybody comes home with a hand-woven basket of local spices. The resourceful Grenadians use every part of the nutmeg. They make the outer fruit into either a tasty liqueur or a rich jam, and ground the orange membrane around the nut into a different spice called mace.

Arawak Islands. Upper Belmont Rd., St. George's. ☎ **473/444-3577.**

This shop is a celebration of the best scents produced on an island that's legendary for spices. Look for at least nine different fragrances distilled from such island plants as frangipani, wild lilies, cinnamon, nutmeg, and cloves. You'll also find an all-natural insect repellent that some clients insist is the most effective (and safest) they're ever used; caffeine-free teas distilled from local plants; bitters that perk up any rum-based drink; and soaps scented with nutmeg. Especially interesting is the root of the khus-khus plant which, when pulverized and stuffed into potpourri bags, is used to sweeten the scents emanating from musty closets in hot climes.

Art Fabrik. Young St., St. George's. ☎ **473/440-0568.**

This shop conveys a vivid impression of the labor and detail that go into the manufacture of the boldly patterned cloth known as batik. In the showroom, you'll find for sale shirts, shifts, shorts, skirts, T-shirts, and virtually every other warm-weather garment you can think of. You can also visit the studio, to see the hot wax applications and multiple dyeing rituals that produce the psychedelic patterns of the merchandise. If you fancy yourself a seamstress or couturier, or if you're just looking for fabric to upholster some furniture, you can buy batik in long and bulky bolts, at prices that work out to around $23 a yard.

Bon Voyage. The Carenage. ☎ **473/440-4217.**

This is the island's leading purveyor of diamonds, precious stones, and gold and silver jewelry. Their selection of china and crystal includes such world-renowned names as Wedgwood, Aynsley, Blue Delft, Royal Doulton, Royal Brierley, and Coalport. Of course, if you're going on to Aruba, St. Maarten, or St. Thomas, you may want to wait and make serious purchases there. Bon Voyage also sells sunglasses, scarves, and accessories.

Creation Arts & Crafts. The Carenage. ☎ **473/440-0570.**

This is one of the few stores on Grenada selling handcrafts from off-island, which in this case includes Venezuela, St. Maarten, and Cuba. The staff here is a bit lethargic. The inventory includes Cuban cigars and cigarettes, cinnamon-scented soaps and wooden bowls, painted masks made from calabash, and sculptures of birds crafted by Grenadian artisans, plus casual wear. U.S. citizens, of course, must consume Cuban cigars and cigarettes while abroad and not attempt to bring them back into the United States.

Gift Remembered. Cross St., St. George's. ☎ **473/440-2482.**

In the center of town a block from the water, Gift Remembered sells handcrafts, straw articles, jewelry, batiks, film, beach wear, postcards, high-quality T-shirts, books, and wood carvings. It's mainly for a sort of aimless shopping, but could come in handy if you promised to bring someone a souvenir from the islands.

Imagine. Grand Anse Shopping Centre. ☎ **473/444-4028.**

This is your best bet in the Grand Anse beach area. The resort wear isn't the most fashionable we've ever seen, but the minor gift items are good. The store offers excellent value in Caribbean handcrafts, such as dolls, ceramics, and straw items, all made of natural materials.

Sea Change Bookstore. The Carenage. ☎ **473/440-3402.**

It's cramped, it's crowded, and the staff reminds you of the teachers you hated in elementary school. But this is the largest repository of recent British and American newspapers on Grenada, all piled untidily on overflowing shelves. There's also a collection of paperback books, island souvenirs, postcards, and film.

Spice Island Perfumes. The Carenage. ☎ **473/440-2006.**

This shop is a treasure trove of perfumes made from the natural extracts of local herbs and spices. If you're a collector of exotic scents, this is your store. The workshop produces and sells perfumes, potpourri, and teas. If you like, they'll spray you with scents such as island flower, spice, frangipani, jasmine, patchouli, and wild orchid. At least you'll smell differently from everybody else. The shop stands near the harbor entrance, close to the Ministry of Tourism and the public library.

Tikal. Young St., St. George's. ☎ **473/440-2310.**

This early 18th-century brick building is off The Carenage, next to the museum. You'll find here an array of tastefully chosen handcrafts from around the world, as well as the finest selection of crafts made on Grenada, including batiks, ceramics, wood carvings, paintings, straw work, and clothing. The owner, Jeanne Fisher, is designs the local crafts.

Yellow Poui Art Gallery. Cross St., St. George's. ☎ **473/440-3001.**

This shop, just a 2-minute walk from Market Square, is one of the best for souvenirs and artistic items. Here you'll find oil paintings and watercolors, sculpture, prints, photography, rare antique maps, engravings, and woodcuts, all with prices beginning at $10 and going up. There's also a comprehensive display of newly acquired works.

GRAND ANSE BEACH

One of the best beaches in the Caribbean is ✪ **Grand Anse Beach,** 2 miles of sugar-white sands. Most of Grenada's best resorts are within walking distance of Grand Anse. From the port, Grand Anse Beach is about a 10-minute, $10 taxi ride, although you can also take a water taxi from the pier for only $4 round-trip.

GOLF, SAILING, DIVING, SNORKELING & TENNIS

GOLF The **Grenada Golf Course and Country Club,** Woodlands (☎ **473/444-4128**), has a nine-hole course, with views of the Caribbean Sea and the Atlantic. Greens fees are $12. It's open Monday to Saturday from 8am to sunset and on Sunday from 8am to 1:30pm.

SAILING Two large "party boats," designed for 120 and 250 passengers, operate out of St. George's harbor. The *Rhum Runner* and *Rhum Runner II,* c/o Best of Grenada, P.O. Box 188, St. George's (☎ **473/440-4FUN**) make three trips daily, with lots of emphasis on strong liquor, steel-band musicians, and good times. Four-hour daytime tours, conducted every morning and afternoon, coincide with the arrival of cruise ships, but will carry independent travelers if space is available. Rides cost $20 per person and include snorkeling stops at reefs and beaches along the way. Evening tours are much more frequently attended by island locals and are generally louder and less restrained. They cost $7.50 per person. Regardless of when you take it, your cruise will include rum, reggae music, and lots of hoopla.

SCUBA DIVING & SNORKELING Grenada offers the diver an underwater world rich in submarine gardens, exotic fish, and coral formations. Visibility is often up to 120 feet. Off the coast is the wreck of the oceanliner *Bianca C,* which is nearly 600 feet long. Novice divers should stick to the west coast; the more experienced might search out the sights along the rougher Atlantic side.

Daddy Vic's Watersports, directly on the beach in the Grenada Renaissance, Grand Anse Beach (☎ **473/444-4371**, ext. 638), is the premier dive outfit. Night dives or two-tank dives are $45. They also offer snorkeling trips for $18 (1½ to 2 hours), windsurfer and Sunfish rentals at $16 per half hour, parasailing for $30 per 10 minutes, and waterskiing for $15 per run. They will arrange to pick you up at the pier in a courtesy bus and bring you back to the cruise ship later.

Grand Anse Aquatics, at Coyaba Beach Resort on Grand Anse Beach (☎ **473/444-4129**), gives Daddy Vic's serious competition. This Canadian-run operation is welcoming and well-equipped. They offer both scuba diving and snorkeling jaunts to reefs and shipwrecks teaming with marine life. A single dive costs $40; snorkeling trips are $20. Diving instruction is available.

Warning: Grenada doesn't have a decompression chamber. In the event of an emergency, divers must be taken to the facilities on Barbados.

TENNIS The best tennis courts are at the major resorts, which open their facilities to cruise ship passengers if they aren't occupied by hotel guests. The best kept courts are in L'Anse aux Epines at **Secret Harbour,** Mount Hartman Bay (☎ **473/444-4439**) and **Calabash,** L'Anse aux Epines (☎ **473/444-4334**); and on Grand Anse Beach at the **Grenada Renaissance,** Grand Anse Beach (☎ **473/444-4371**) and **Coyaba Beach Resort,** Grand Anse Beach (☎ **473/444-4129**).

DINING

Bird's Nest. Grand Anse (3 miles north of the airport, opposite the Grenada Renaissance). ☎ **473/444-4264.** Reservations recommended. Main courses EC$20–EC$65 ($7.40–$24.05). AE, MC, V. Mon–Sat 9am–11pm. CHINESE/CREOLE.

⭐ Favorite Experiences

Your last chance to enjoy food from old-time island recipes, many now fading from cultural memory, is at **Betty Mascoll's Morne Fendue,** at St. Patrick's (☎ 473/442-9330), 25 miles north of St. George's. This plantation house was built in 1912 of chiseled river rocks held together by a mixture of lime and molasses. Mrs. Mascoll was born that same year and has lived here ever since, continuing her long tradition of hospitality. You dine as an upper-class family did in the 1920s. Lunch is likely to include a yam-and-sweet-potato casserole or curried chicken with lots of island-grown spices. You get all of Grandmother's favorites, including fritters made of tannia (a starchy tuber) and corn coo coo (resembling spoonbread). A popular local vegetable is curried christophone, which tastes like squash. The most famous dish is Betty's legendary pepperpot stew, which includes pork and oxtail, tenderized by the juice of grated cassava. Mrs. Mascoll and her loyal, veteran staff need time to prepare, so it's imperative to call ahead. They serve a prix fixe lunch for EC$45 ($16.45) Monday to Saturday from 12:30 to 3pm.

Opened in 1994, the 450-acre **Levera National Park** has several white sandy beaches for swimming and snorkeling, although the surf is rough. Offshore are coral reefs and seagrass beds. Inland, the park contains a mangrove swamp, a lake, and a bird sanctuary—perhaps you'll see a rare tropical parrot. It's a hiker's paradise. The interpretation center (☎ 473/442-1018) is open Monday to Friday from 8am to 4pm, on Saturday from 10am to 4pm, and on Sunday from 9am to 5pm. The park, about 15 miles from the harbor, can be reached by taxi, bus, or water taxi.

For a change of pace from Caribbean fare, we suggest the Bird's Nest. This family business offers Chinese food, mainly Szechuan and Cantonese, along with seafood and Creole cuisine. You'll see the familiar shrimp egg rolls along with eight different chow meins. Sweet-and-sour fish is a favorite, along with the daily specials. Takeout service is also available. This may not be the world's greatest Chinese restaurant, and some dishes are short on flavor, but it's generally satisfying. You can order sandwiches for lunch.

Coconut's Beach Restaurant. Grand Anse Beach (about a ¹/₂ mile north of St. George's). ☎ 473/444-4644. Reservations recommended. Main courses EC$35–EC$75 ($13–$27.80); lunch platters EC$15–EC$35 ($5.60–$13). AE, DISC, MC, V. Wed–Mon noon–10pm. FRENCH/CREOLE.

Raffish and informal, this restaurant occupies a pink-and-green clapboard house directly on the sands of the beach. From the dining room you can watch the staff at work in the exposed kitchen. They'll definitely be making a callaloo soup, cooked here with local herbs and blended to a creamy smoothness. The kitchen also specializes in various kinds of lobster, including one made with spaghetti, although the lobster stir-fry with ginger chili is more imaginative. Fish choices include a catch of the day served with mango chutney, and curried conch West Indian style. Chicken and meats are also savory, especially breast of chicken cooked in local herbs and lime juice.

Warning: Many people opt to walk along the beach to reach this restaurant. Don't! Tourists have been attacked by local druggies who've robbed and threatened them. Even though it might be only a short ride, take a taxi to the door instead.

⭐ **Mamma's.** Lagoon Rd., St. George's. ☎ 473/440-1459. Reservations recommended. Fixed-price meal EC$45 ($16.65). No credit cards. Daily 8am–midnight. CREOLE.

No one else captures the authentic taste of Grenada like Mamma's. This restaurant became particularly famous during the U.S. intervention in Grenada, when U.S. servicepeople adopted the place and its owner as their own island mama.

Meals include such dishes as callaloo soup with coconut cream, shredded cold crab with lime juice, freshwater crayfish, fried conch, and rotis made of curry and yellow chickpeas. Mamma's seafoods are likely to include crab backs, octopus in a hot-and-spicy sauce, and turtle steak. Mamma is also known for her "wild meats," including armadillo, opossum, monkey, game birds, and even the endangered iguana. Gourmets flock to this restaurant to sample these delicacies, and the unusual menu has been widely written about in U.S. media. The specialty drink of the house is rum punch—the ingredients are a secret.

The Nutmeg. The Carenage, St. George's. ☎ **473/440-2539.** Main courses EC$18–EC$65 ($6.65–$24.05). AE, DISC, MC, V. Mon–Sat 8am–11pm, Sun 2–11pm. SEAFOOD/CREOLE.

The Nutmeg is located right on the harbor over the Sea Change Shop, where you can pick up paperbacks and souvenirs. Since the mid-1960s it has been a hangout for the yachting set and a favorite with expatriates and visitors. It's suitable for a snack or a full-fledged meal, and its drinks are very good, too. Try one of the Grenadian rum punches made with Angostura bitters, grated nutmeg, rum, lime juice, and syrup.

Menu choices usually include filet of fish with potato croquettes and string beans, fresh fish, and callaloo soup. The lobster Thermidor is the best in town. Lambi, that ubiquitous conch, is also done very well here. There's a small wine list with some California and German selections, and you can drop in for just a glass of beer to enjoy the sea view. Sometimes, however, you'll be asked to share a table.

Pierone. The Carenage (at the extreme northern end). ☎ **473/440-9747.** Main courses EC$25–EC$52 ($9.25–$19.25). MC, V. Mon–Sat 8am–11pm. INTERNATIONAL/WEST INDIAN/SEAFOOD.

This place was originally built as a warehouse, but when someone added a waterfront veranda to the boxy, unimaginative building, it was immediately transformed into the most desirable perch on the waterfront. It's best suited for a midday pick-me-up, with or without alcohol, partly because of the cool breezes that blow in off the port. Cocktails include U.S. bombers, mango daiquiris, and an especially potent concoction called "navy grog." Menu items include such West Indian dishes as lambi (conch) chowder, sandwiches, and the most popular dish on the menu, lobster pando, a form of ragoût. We wouldn't say it's the best food in town, but it's quite competent, and a good value.

Portofino. The Carenage, St. George's. ☎ **473/440-3986.** Reservations recommended. Pastas and pizzas EC$16–EC$40 ($5.90–$14.80); main courses EC$28–EC$35 ($10.35–$12.95). AE, MC, V. Mon–Sat 11am–11pm, Sun 6–11pm. ITALIAN/SEAFOOD.

This restaurant is spartan and simple. It's not nearly as good as Rudolf's, farther down The Carenage, but still it's not a bad choice, with fine, unpretentious food. The restaurant serves the best pizzas in the capital, Italian-style antipasti such as eggplant Parmesan, and a good bowl of minestrone. The fish and meat dishes are more ordinary, although the catch of the day, served with pasta and fresh vegetables, is usually good, as are the shrimp and lobster. The finest pasta dish is the linguine with fresh fish. There are some vegetarian choices, such as lasagna, as well.

The Red Crab. L'Anse aux Epines. ☎ **473/444-4424.** Reservations required in winter. Main courses EC$45–EC$96 ($16.65–$35.50). AE, DISC, MC, V. Mon–Sat 11am–2pm and 6–10:30pm. WEST INDIAN/INTERNATIONAL.

The Red Crab, popular with both visitors and locals alike, is only a short taxi ride from the major hotels. People come not for sublime cuisine, but for the convivial atmosphere and good times. The restaurant is especially popular with students from the medical college, although we don't know how they can afford some of the prices. The beefsteaks, especially the peppersteak, are among Grenada's finest. The seafood, however, is not as good as at other local spots. Specialties include local lobster tail; lambi (conch); locally caught fish such as snapper, dolphin, and grouper; and even garlic shrimp. Dessert might be a homemade cheesecake. Patrons can dine inside or out.

✪ **Rudolf's.** The Carenage, St. George's. ☎ **473/440-2241.** Reservations recommended. Main courses EC$25–EC$56 ($9.25–$20.70). MC, V. Mon–Sat 10am–midnight. INTERNATIONAL.

This longtime favorite restaurant, an excellent value for your money, is the most solid choice for dining in St. George's, It overlooks a deep, U-shaped harbor lined with commercial establishments. The staff is hardworking and genteel. Ceiling fans cool patrons off at midday. The ceiling is sheathed in a layer of corrugated egg cartons, which adds an unconventional, appealing touch and also muffles the noise from the sometimes very crowded bar area.

The food is well prepared, and the menu is the most extensive on the island. The steaks are the best in the capital. Conch is prepared in several different ways, as are shrimp and octopus. Flying fish and dolphin deserve the most praise. On occasion, wild game such as rabbit or duck is served, and even possum (manicou) stew. There's also a classic Wiener schnitzel—again, the best in town—in honor of the chef's origins. Rudolf's is also a good choice if you want to join the yachting machismo set in the late afternoon for some lethal rum drinks.

Spice Island Inn. Grand Anse Beach. ☎ **473/444-4258.** Reservations required for nonguests. Fixed-price dinner $40; lunch from $15. AE, DC, MC, V. Daily 7:30–9:30am, 12:30–2:30pm, and 7–9:30pm. CREOLE/SEAFOOD.

Want to dine on an uncrowded beachfront in the full outdoors, with a parapet over your head to protect you from sudden tropical showers? Some of the best hotel food on the island is found in this winning setting. At this inn, located directly north of the airport, the view is of one of the finest beaches in the Caribbean—miles of white sand sprouting an occasional grove of sea grape or almond trees. The parapet here, built of imported pine and cedar, looks like a Le Corbusier rooftop. You can eat lunch in a swimsuit. Menus change frequently, but always feature local seafood. Everything can be cooked to your specifications.

10 Guadeloupe ⚓ ⚓ ⚓

Guadeloupe's charm is not readily apparent when your ship arrives at Pointe-à-Pitre, the capital. This rather tacky port doesn't have the old-world appeal of Fort-de-France on Martinique. Modern apartments and condominiums now form a high-rise backdrop over jerry-built shacks and industrial suburbs. The narrow streets are jammed in a permanent, if colorful, traffic jam during the day. At sunset, however, the town becomes quiet again and almost deserted. The only raffish charm left is around the waterfront, where you expect to see Bogie sipping rum at a cafe table.

As in Martinique, Gallic ways combines with tropical beauty in Guadeloupe. It's a long way from Europe, but this is a part of France, since Guadeloupe, Martinique, St. Barts, and St. Martin (as well as a scattering of tiny offshore dependencies) are officially *départements de France*—the equivalent of American states. Although

Guadeloupe has much to offer, tourists generally favor Martinique, where the service and the shopping is better.

Guadeloupe actually consists of two islands separated by a narrow channel known as the Rivière Salée. Throughout both, landscape is stippled with pineapple, banana, and sugarcane. **Grande-Terre,** the eastern island, is typical of the Antilles, with rolling hills and sugar plantations. The western island, **Basse-Terre,** is rugged and mountainous, dominated by the active, 4,800-foot volcano La Soufrière. Basse-Terre's mountains are covered with tropical forests, impenetrable in many places. The island is ringed by beautiful beaches, which have attracted many tourists. The surf pounds hard against its Atlantic coast facing east, but calmer seas rule on the leeward bathing beaches.

COMING ASHORE

Cruise ships dock right in the commercial center of Pointe-à-Pitre at Centre St-Jean-Perse, a $20 million project that has transformed the port's waterfront, once a bastion of old warehouses. Named for a 20th-century poet and Nobel Laureate who was born just a few blocks away, this modern center is designed in a contemporary French Caribbean style, which blends well with the town's traditional architecture. The center, surrounded by small tropical gardens, offers an array of duty-free shops selling Guadeloupean rum and French perfume. It's located near several open-air markets and small shops.

You'll also find at Centre St-Jean-Pearse some phones and a bank, where you'll want to get some French francs (see "Fast Facts," below). Outlets labeled *Telecart en Vente Ici* sell *Telecartes,* prepaid discount phone cards that can be used in booths marked Telecom. Phone connections are difficult in Guadeloupe, especially if you don't speak French, and expensive as well (although not as pricey as on board ship).

FAST FACTS

Currency   Unlike most other parts of the Caribbean, the Yankee dollar isn't widely accepted here. Some shops will take U.S. dollars, but the official monetary unit is the **French franc (F).** The exchange rate is given in the business pages of most American newspapers. We have used 6.14 F to $1 U.S. (1 F = 16.3¢) to calculate the dollar values given in this section. Most restaurants quote prices in French francs; however, shops in and around the cruise dock generally have prices in both French francs and U.S. dollars.

Information   The major tourist office is the **Office Départmental du Tourisme,** Square de la Banque, 5, in Pointe-à-Pitre (☎ 0590/82-09-30). Open Monday to Friday 9am to 5pm.

Language   The official language is French, and Creole is the unofficial second language. English is spoken only in the major tourist centers, rarely in the countryside.

SHORE EXCURSIONS

Most cruise ships offer a 3-hour tour for $40 per person that takes in many of the scenic highlights of Grande-Terre, the island closer to the cruise terminal. Although Grande-Terre is not without its charms, Basse-Terre is much more interesting. You can also rent a car or take a taxi tour of Guadeloupe. We have described a driving tour under "Seeing the Sights," below.

GETTING AROUND

BUS   Buses link almost every hamlet to Pointe-à-Pitre, although you may need some French to use the system. From Pointe-à-Pitre, vans to Basse-Terre leave from

Guadeloupe

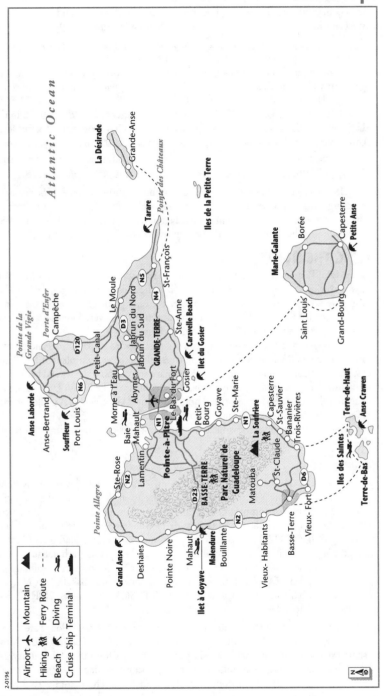

Atlantic Ocean

La Désirade

Grande-Anse

Pointe des Châteaux

Tarare

Iles de la Petite Terre

St-François

Le Moule

N5

N4

Ste-Anne

Caravelle Beach

Ilet du Gosier

Gosier

GRANDE-TERRE

Le Bas du Fort

Marie-Galante

Borée

Capesterre

Petite Anse

Saint Louis

Grand-Bourg

Jabrun du Nord

D3

Jabrun du Sud

Abymes

Morne à l'Eau

Petit-Canal

D120

Campêche

Porte d'Enfer

Pointe de la Grande Vigie

Anse Laborde

Anse-Bertrand

Souffleur

Port Louis

N6

Baie Mahault

Lamentin

Petit-Bourg

Goyave

Ste-Marie

Capesterre

St-Sauvier

Bananier

Trois-Rivières

Terre-de-Haut

Anse Crawen

Iles des Saintes

Terre-de-Bas

N1

La Soufrière

St-Claude

Matouba

BASSE-TERRE

Parc Naturel de Guadeloupe

D23

D6

Vieux-Fort

Basse-Terre

Vieux-Habitants

Bouillante

Pointe Noire

Deshaies

Ste-Rose

N2

N2

Pointe à Pitre

N1

Pointe Allegre

Grand Anse

Ilet à Goyave

Malendure

Mahaut

Airport ✈ Mountain ▲

Hiking 🚶 Ferry Route - - -

Beach 🏖 Diving 🤿

Cruise Ship Terminal

2-0196

N ⬆

159

the Gare Routière de Bergevin. Those heading to other parts of Grande-Terre depart the Gare Routière de Mortenol. Service is daily from 5:30am to 7:30pm.

CAR RENTALS   You can rent a car and drive around Basse-Terre yourself. The road all the way around the island is one of the loveliest drives in the Caribbean. Roads are in good condition and driving is on the right. If you want to be sure to get a car when you hit shore, it's best to reserve one, preferably 2 days in advance, through **Hertz** (☎ **800/654-3001** in the U.S., or 0590/21-09-35), **Avis** (☎ **800/ 331-121112** in the U.S., or 0590/21-13-54), or **Budget** (☎ **800/527-0700** in the U.S., or 0590/21-13-48). Some of your fellow readers have complained about local companies, so stick with the big three. Prices are usually 20% to 25% lower between March and early December. If you're calling well in advance, you might try **Auto Europe** (☎ **800/223-5555**) or **Kenwel Holiday Autos** (☎ **800/678-0678**).

TAXIS   You'll find taxis at the cruise dock, but no limousines or buses. The taxi drivers charge whatever they think you'll accept, although technically fares are regulated by the government. Always agree on the price before getting in. Call ☎ **0590/82-99-88** for a radio-dispatched cab. You can also sightsee by taxi. Fares are negotiable.

SEEING THE SIGHTS

Saint-John Perse once wrote about the fine time sailors had when Pointe-à-Pitre was a stopover on the famous route du Rhum. But those days are long gone, and today you may not want to linger in town, where the only point of interest is shopping. It's best to visit Pointe-à-Pitre in the morning, when the **covered market** at the corner of rue Frébault and rue Thiers is at its liveliest.

The town center is **Place de la Victoire,** a park shaded by palm trees and poincianas. Here you'll see some old sandbox trees said to have been planted by Victor Hughes, a mulatto who organized a revolutionary army of both whites and blacks and established a dictatorship just before the Napoleonic era. The British kicked Hughes out after they defeated Napoléon and briefly took over Guadeloupe. A guillotine that Hughes kept busy stood here until modern times, but it's gone now.

Below is a driving tour that touches on the best sights of Grande-Terre and Basse-Terre.

GRANDE-TERRE

LE BAS DU FORT   From town, head to the "South Riviera," which runs along the coast from Pointe-à-Pitre to Pointe des Châteaux at the eastern end of Grande-Terre. At the tourist complex of Bas du Fort, 2 miles east of Pointe-à-Pitre near Gosier, you'll come to the ✪ **Aquarium de la Guadeloupe,** Place Créole, Marina Gosier (☎ **0590/90-92-38**), one of the three most important aquariums of France and the largest and most modern in the Caribbean. The aquarium is home to tropical fish, coral, underwater plants, huge sharks, and other sea creatures. The exhibits are all clearly labeled. It's located just off the main highway near Bas-du-Fort Marina. Open daily from 9am to 7pm. Admission is 38 F ($6.35) for adults, 20 F ($3.35) for children 6 to 12, and free for kids 5 and under.

GOSIER   Some of the biggest and most important resorts of Guadeloupe are found at Gosier, with its nearly 5 miles of beach stretching east from Pointe-à-Pitre. Most shore excursions stop at **Fort Fleur-d'Epée,** which dates from the 18th century. Its dungeons and battlements are testaments to the ferocious fighting between the French and British armies seeking to control the island in 1794. The well-preserved ruins command the crown of a hill. From here you'll have good views over the bay of Pointe-à-Pitre, and on a clear day you can see the neighboring offshore islands of Marie-Galante and Iles des Saintes.

POINTE DES CHATEAUX   Seven miles east of St-François is Pointe des Châteaux, the easternmost tip of Grande-Terre, where the Atlantic meets the Caribbean. You'll hear the waves crashing all around you, and see a cliff sculpted by the sea into castle-like formations. The view from here is panoramic. At the top is a cross put there in the 19th century.

You might want to walk to Pointe des Colibris, the extreme end of Guadeloupe. From here you'll have a view of the northeastern sector of the island, and of La Désirade to the east, an island that looks like a huge vessel at anchor. Among the coved beaches found here, **Pointe Tarare** is *au naturel.*

LE MOULE   You can use the N5 as an alternative route from St-François back to Pointe-à-Pitre from Pointe des Châteaux. After 9 miles, you reach the village of Le Moule, which was founded at the end of the 17th century, long before Pointe-à-Pitre. It used to be a major shipping port for sugar, though now it's just a tiny coastal fishing village. Le Moule never regained its importance after a hurricane devastated it and many other villages in 1928. However, a holiday center is now being developed along its 10-mile crescent-shaped beach.

Musée Edgar Clerc de Préhistoire Amérindienne le Moule (Edgar Clerc Museum at Le Moule), Parc de la Rosette, Le Moule (☎ **0590/23-57-57**) is devoted exclusively to the experiences and contributions of the Arawak and Carib tribes in the Caribbean. It's one of the largest museums of its kind, containing relics gathered from throughout the Caribbean archipelago. Set 3 miles from Le Moule toward Campêche, the museum is open Tuesday to Sunday from 8:50am to 4:50pm. Admission costs 10 F ($1.65) per person.

BASSE-TERRE

You can explore Basse-Terre's northeastern, or windward, coast via the N1 from Pointe-à-Pitre. After a mile and a half, the Pont de la Gabarre crosses the Rivière Salée, the narrow strait separating Grande-Terre from Basse-Terre. For the next 4 miles the road runs straight through sugarcane fields. Turn right on the N2 toward **Baie Mahault.** Don't confuse this with the town of Mahault, which is on Basse-Terre's western coast. Leaving Baie Mahault, head northwest to Lamentin, a village settled by corsairs at the beginning of the 18th century. Here you'll see some colonial mansions scattered about.

STE-ROSE   From Lamentin, drive 6^1/$_2$ miles to Ste-Rose, where you'll find several good beaches. On your left, a small road leads to **Sofaia,** from which you'll have a panoramic view over the coast and forest preserve. The locals claim that a sulfur spring here has curative powers.

DESHAIES/GRAND ANSE   A few miles farther along the N2 is Pointe Allègre, the northernmost point of Basse-Terre. At **Clugny Beach,** you'll be at the site where the first settler landed on Guadeloupe. A couple of miles more will bring you to **Grand Anse,** one of the best beaches in Guadeloupe. It's very large, still secluded, and sheltered by many tropical trees.

Snorkeling and fishing are popular pastimes at **Deshaies.** The narrow road winds up and down and has a corniche look to it. The blue sea is underneath, and above you can see green mountains studded with colorful hamlets.

Nine miles from Deshaies, **Pointe Noire** comes into view. Its name comes from black volcanic rocks. Look for the odd polychrome cenotaph in town.

✿ PARC NATUREL DE GUADELOUPE   You reach Mahaut 4 miles from Pointe Noire. On your left begins the **route de la Traversée,** the Transcoastal Highway. We recommend going this way, to pass through the scenic wonders of **Parc Naturel de Guadeloupe.** Taking up 74,100 acres, or about one-fifth of Guadeloupe,

★ Frommer's Favorite Experiences

The country along the northeastern, or windward, coast of Basse-Terre is richer and greener than elsewhere on the island. Here near the pier in Trois Rivières are the **Roches Gravées** ("Carved Rocks"), onto which the island's original inhabitants, the Arawaks, carved petroglyphs of humans and animals. They most likely date from A.D. 300 or 400. You'll also see specimens of plants, including cocoa, pimiento, and banana, which the Arawaks cultivated long before the Europeans set foot on Guadeloupe.

this huge tract of mountains, tropical forests, and panoramic scenery is home to a variety of animals, including titi (a raccoon adopted as the island's official mascot), and such birds as the wood pigeon, turtledove, and thrush. Small exhibition huts are scattered throughout the park, providing information on the volcano and the forest, as well as coffee, sugarcane, and rum. The Parc Naturel has no gates, no opening or closing hours, and no admission fee.

From the park, the main road descends toward Versailles, a hamlet about 5 miles from Pointe-à-Pitre.

BASSE-TERRE TOWN   You can continue along winding roads to the town of Basse-Terre, Guadeloupe's seat of government. Founded in 1634, it's the oldest town on the island. The town suffered heavy destruction at the hands of British troops in 1691 and again in 1702. It was also the center of fierce fighting during the French Revolution, when explosive tensions gripped Guadeloupe. Although there's not much to see here now other than a 17th-century cathedral and Fort St-Charles, it still has its charms. The market squares are shaded by tamarind and palm trees.

★ LA SOUFRIÈRE   The big attraction of Basse-Terre is the famous sulfur-puffing **La Soufrière volcano.** The appearance of ashes, mud, billowing smoke, and earthquake-like tremors in 1975 proved that this old beast is still active. Rising to a height of some 4,800 feet, it's flanked by banana plantations and lush foliage. You can drive from Basse-Terre to the suburb of **St-Claude,** 4 miles up the mountainside at an elevation of 1,900 feet. St-Claude has an elegant reputation, with a perfect climate and tropical gardens. From here, you can drive up the narrow, winding road the Guadeloupeans say leads to hell—that is, the summit of La Soufrière. The road ends at a parking area at La Savane à Mulets, at an altitude of 3,300 feet. You can touch the ground in the parking lot and feel its heat. Hikers can climb right to the mouth of the volcano. Steam emerges from fumaroles and sulfurous fumes from the volcano's "burps."

STE-MARIE   In the town square of **Ste-Marie,** 4¹/₂ miles past Capesterre, you can stop and see the statue of Guadeloupe's first tourist: Christopher Columbus. He anchored a quarter of a mile from Ste-Marie on November 4, 1493, on his second voyage. He wrote in his journal, "We arrived, seeing ahead of us a large mountain which seemed to want to rise up to the sky, in the middle of which was a peak higher than all the rest of the mountains from which flowed a living stream." When Caribs started shooting arrows at him, however, he quickly departed.

SHOPPING

We suggest that you skip a shopping tour of Pointe-à-Pitre if you're going on to Martinique, as you'll find far more merchandise and perhaps friendlier service there.

Your best buys here will be anything French—perfumes from Chanel, silk scarves from Hermès, cosmetics from Dior, crystal from Lalique and Baccarat. We've infrequently found some of these items discounted as much as 30% below U.S. or Canadian prices, provided you pay by traveler's check. Many eager shopkeepers stay open longer than usual and even on weekends when cruise ships are in port. If you buy luxury goods, such as perfumes, with foreign currency and show your passport, you can take your purchase with you, but if you buy any alcohol, the merchant will deliver your purchase directly to the pier.

If you're adventurous, you may want to seek some native goods in little shops along the back streets of Pointe-à-Pitre. Considered collector's items are the straw hats or *salacos* made in Les Saintes islands. They look distinctly related to Chinese coolie hats and are usually well designed, often made of split bamboo. Native doudou dolls are also popular gift items.

Open-air stalls surround the **covered market** (*Marché Couvert*) at the corner of rue Frébault and rue Thiers. Here you can discover the many fruits, spices, and vegetables that are enjoyable just to view, if not to taste. In madras turbans, local Creole women make deals over their strings of fire-red pimientos. The bright fabrics they wear compete with the rich tones of the oranges, papayas, bananas, mangoes, and pineapples for sale. The sounds of African-accented French fill the air.

Distillerie Bellevue. Rue Bellevue Damoiseau. ☎ **0590/23-55-55.**

The "essence of the island" on Guadeloupe is *rhum agricole,* a pure rum fermented from sugarcane juice. Savvy locals say it's the only rum you can drink without suffering the devastation of a rum hangover the next morning. Once this liquor was available in great abundance, but now only two distilleries still process it. You can taste before purchasing here.

Phoenicia. 8 Rue Frébault. ☎ **590/83-50-36.**

This is one of the best places to buy French perfumes, at prices often lower than those charged in Paris. It also has a good selection of imported cosmetics. Other leading perfume shops include **Au Bonheur des Dames,** 49 rue Frébault (☎ **0590/82-00-30**), which is also known for its skin-care products. **L'Artisan Parfumeur,** Center St., John Perse (☎ **0590/83-80-25**), carries not only top French perfumes but also leading American brands at discounted prices. For a lark, sample one of their bottles of "tropical scents."

Rosébleu. 5 Rue Frébault. ☎ **0590/82-93-44.**

This shop has Pointe-à-Pitre's biggest stock of jewelry, perfumes, gifts, and fashion accessories. The best crystal made in France is sold here.

Soph't. Immeuble Lesseps, Centre St-John Perse. ☎ **0590/83-07-73.**

This outlet has the capital's best selection of that oh so elegant and delicate French lingerie.

Vendôme. 8-10 Rue Frébault. ☎ **0590/83-42-84.**

Here you will find imported fashions for both men and women, as well as a large selection of gifts and perfumes, including the big names. You can usually find someone who speaks English to sell you a Cardin watch.

BEACHES

There is a plenitude of natural beaches dotting the island, from the surf-brushed dark strands of western Basse-Terre to the long stretches of white sand encircling Grande-Terre.

Outstanding beaches include **Caravele Beach,** a long, reef-protected stretch of sand outside Ste-Anne, about 9 miles from Gosier, the site of many leading resorts.

Hotels welcome nonguests, but charge for changing facilities, beach chairs, and towels. On Basse-Terre, one of the best beaches is **Grande Anse,** a palm-sheltered beach north of Deshaies on the northwest coast.

Sunday is family day at the beach here. Public beaches are generally free, but some charge for parking. Unlike hotel beaches, they have few facilities. Topless sunbathing is common at hotels, less so on village beaches. Nudist beaches include **Ilet du Gosier,** off Gosier, and **Plage de Tarare,** near the eastern tip of Grande-Terre at Pointe des Châteaux, also the site of many local restaurants.

GOLF, DIVING & TENNIS

GOLF   Guadeloupe's only golf course is the well-known **Golf de St-François** (☎ 0590/88-41-87) at St-François, opposite the Hôtel Méridien about 22 miles east of Raizet Airport. The course runs alongside an 800-acre lagoon where windsurfing, waterskiing, and sailing prevail. The 6,755-yard, par-71 course designed by Robert Trent Jones, Sr. is challenging, with water traps on six holes, massive bunkers, prevailing trade winds, and a particularly fiendish 400-yard, par-4 ninth hole. The par-5 sixth is the toughest hole on the course; its 450 yards must be negotiated into the constant easterly winds. Greens fees are 250 F ($41.75) per day per person. Rental golf clubs cost 100 F ($16.70); an electric golf cart is 220 F ($36.75).

SCUBA DIVING   Scuba divers are drawn to the waters off Guadeloupe, which lack underwater currents and are relatively calm. There's also the **Cousteau Underwater Reserve,** a park with many attractive dive sites in which the underwater environment is rigidly protected. Jacques Cousteau described the waters off Guadeloupe's Pigeon Island as "one of the world's 10 best diving spots." During a typical dive, sergeant majors become visible at a depth of 30 feet, spiny sea urchins and green parrot fish at 60 feet, and magnificent stands of finger, black, brain, and star coral come into view at a depth of 80 feet. Despite damage caused by 1995 hurricanes, it's still one of the most desirable dive sites in the French-speaking world.

Centre International de la Plongée (C.I.P.), B.P. 4, Lieu-Dit Poirier, Malendure Plage, 97125 Pigeon, Bouillante, Guadeloupe, F.W.I. (☎ 0590/98-81-72), is the island's most professional dive operation, located at the edge of the Cousteau Underwater Reserve. Dive boats depart three times a day, usually at 10am, 12:30pm, and 3pm. Certified divers pay 170 F ($33.40) for a one-tank dive. What the Americans usually refer to as a "resort course" for first-time divers (the French refer to it as a *baptème*) is a one-on-one course costing 250 F ($41.75).

TENNIS   Consider an outing to the public tennis court at St-François Plage, in St-François, a durable but somewhat weathered facility which is often unused despite the fact that access is free to whomever happens to show up. For information, contact *La Mairie* (Town Hall) of St-François at ☎ 0590/88-71-37.

WINDSURFING & WATERSKIING

Head for **Sport Away (Nathalie Simon)**, Plage de St-François, St-François (☎ 0590/88-72-04). Here, a 30-minute windsurfing lesson goes for around 120 F ($20.05) per hour, and rentals, depending on the size and make of the board you rent, average 150 F ($25.05) per hour. Waterskiing costs around 230 F ($21.70) for a 15-minute ride.

DINING

Volcanic, tropically forested Guadeloupe is fabled for female Creole chefs operating simple little bistros, sometimes in their own homes.

IN GRANDE-TERRE

La Louisiane. Quartier Ste-Marthe, outside St-François. ☎ **0590/88-44-34.** Main courses 70 F–300 F ($11.70–$50.10). MC, V. Tues–Sun noon–2pm and 6–10pm. Closed 2 weeks in Sept. FRENCH/CARIBBEAN.

The oldest building in the neighborhood (about 1¹/₂ miles east of St-François), this century-old former plantation house is sheltered from the road by trees and shrub-bery. French owners Daniel and Muriel Hogon have brought some of the best cui-sine of their native regions, Provence and the Vosges. Savor the filet of swordfish with wine sauce or the shark meat with saffron sauce. What really wins us over are the scal-lops in a ginger-and-lime sauce. They are stupendously tasteful, more so than the filet of red snapper with a vermouth and basil-flavored cream sauce that you can find throughout the French West Indies. The chef proves himself again with the marmite du pêcheur, loaded with fresh lobster and whitefish, everything set off with the golden saffron flavoring. Especially captivating are the ouasous, a form of large native cray-fish prepared Creole style with tomatoes and peppers. The restaurant evokes the France of long ago, in an environment streaming with Caribbean sunlight and vegetation.

✪ **Le Bananier.** Rue Principale de Gosier, Montauban. ☎ **0590/84-34-85.** Reservations rec-ommended. Main courses 70 F–170 F ($11.70–$28.40). AE, MC, V. Tues–Sun noon–2:30pm and 7–10pm. CREOLE.

Well-established Guadeloupe-born entrepreneurs Élixe Virolan (maître-d'hôtel) and Chef Yves Clarus joined forces years ago to create a restaurant where some of the most imaginative dishes in the Creole repertoire are handled with finesse and charm. Within a 50-year-old clapboard-sided cottage, whose dining room is air-conditioned, you'll find a handful of old-fashioned staples, such as stuffed crab backs and accras (beignets) of codfish. Much more appealing, however, are such modernized dishes as filet mignon of beef served with pulverized blood sausage, port wine, and a reduction of crayfish bisque; a *clafoutis* (gratinated medley) of shellfish; a *tourtière d'oeufs aux crabes* (an omelet that combines breaded and baked crabmeat, fresh tomatoes, and a reduction of callalou leaves); and an *aiguillette de poisson façon du chef* that's composed of poached snapper, cut into strips and served with a tartly acidic *maracudja* (starfruit) and banana sauce. The menu's most appealing dessert is a flambéed banana whose alcoholic afterglow re-sults from a use of *Schrubb,* an obscure Guadeloupian liqueur made from fermented orange peels that was prized by the owners' grandparents.

Le Poisson d'Or. Rue Sadi-Carnot, 2, Port Louis. ☎ **0590/22-88-63.** Reservations required. Main courses 65 F–85 F($10.85–$14.20); fixed-price meal 85 F–150 F($14.20–$25.05). MC, V. Daily 11:30am–4pm. Drive northwest from Petit Canal along the coastal road. CREOLE.

You'll enter this green-and-white Antillean house by walking down a narrow corri-dor and emerging into a rustic dining room lined with varnished pine. Despite the simple setting, which was badly damaged during the hurricanes of 1995, the food is well prepared and satisfying. Owner-chef Esther Madel shelters a mixture of local residents and French visitors. Try the stuffed crabs, the court bouillon, the boudin of conch or fish, or octopus fricasee, and top it off with homemade coconut ice cream.

Restaurant Sucré-Salé. Blvd Le Gitimus, Pointe-à-Pitre. ☎ **0590/21-22-55.** Reservations recommended. Main courses 60 F–20 F ($10–$20.05). AE, MC, V. Mon–Sat noon–4:30pm; Tues–Sat 7–9:30pm. FRENCH.

Set in the heart of Pointe-à-Pitre, adjacent to an Air France office and near several international banks, this restaurant established in 1995 is filled at lunchtime with dealmakers and office workers from throughout the city. The decorative theme revolves around jazz, with an emphasis on portraits of such U.S. jazz greats as Billie Holliday and Miles Davis. A covered terrace overlooking the busy boulevard outside acts as an animated singles bar, with an ambience that's partially the result of the charm of Marius Pheron, the Guadeloupe-born owner whose culinary training derived from an 18-year stint in Paris. Delectable menu items include such dishes as filets of snapper served with pommes soufflés and black pepper; meal-sized salads; entrecôte steaks; sweetbreads in orange sauce (or whatever other sauce the chef feels like preparing that day); and an impressive medley of grilled fish.

✪ **Rosini.** La Porte des Caraïbes, Bas-du-Fort. ☎ **0590/90-87-81.** Reservations recommended. Main courses 45 F–175 F ($7.50–$29.25). AE, DC, MC, V. Daily noon–2:30pm and 6:30–10:30pm. NORTHERN ITALIAN.

This is the best Italian restaurant in the French West Indies, thanks to a sophisticated father-in-law/son-in-law team of Venice-born Luciano Rosini and Provence-derived Christophe Giraud. It's contained within two air-conditioned dining rooms on the ground floor of a well-heeled condominium complex across from the Novotel in Bas-du-Fort. Recorded opera music, usually as performed by Pavarotti, provides a background for succulent versions of tournedos layered with foie gras; osso bucco, Venetian-style calves liver, and freshwater prawns served *diavolo* style in a tomato, garlic, and parsley sauce with freshly made fettuccine. Ravioli comes stuffed either with veal and herbs or with lobster, according to the whims of the chef and availability of shellfish on the day of your arrival. At least five types of pizza are also available, although they're usually proposed for the small children of adults who, frankly, tend to find the restaurant's more substantial fare more appealing. Thanks to Mr. Giraud's long apprenticeship at a restaurant within Washington, D.C.'s Watergate complex, English is readily understood.

IN BASSE-TERRE

Chez Loulouse. Malendure Plage. ☎ **0590/98-70-34.** Reservations not necessary at lunch, required for dinner. Main courses 50 F–150 F ($8.35–$25.05). AE, MC, V. Daily noon–3:30pm and 7–10pm. CREOLE.

A worthy choice for an informal and colorful lunch is Chez Loulouse, a staunchly matriarchal establishment with plenty of charm. It sits beside the sands of the well-known beach, opposite Pigeon Island. Many guests like to sip rum punch on the panoramic veranda. A quieter oasis is the equally colorful dining room inside, just past the bar. Here, beneath a ceiling of palm fronds, is a wraparound series of Creole murals that seem to go well with the reggae music emanating loudly from the bar.

This is the creation of one of the most visible and charming matrons on this end of the island, Mme Loulouse Paisley-Carbon. Assisted by her children, she offers house-style Caribbean lobster, spicy versions of conch, octopus, accras, gratin of christophine (squash), and savory colombos (curries) of chicken or pork.

Chez Vaneau. Mahaut/Pointe Noire. ☎ **0590/98-01-71.** Reservations not required. Main courses 50 F–200 F ($8.35–$33.40). AE, MC, V. Daily noon–5pm; Mon–Wed and Fri–Sat 7pm–midnight. Closed Thurs and Sun night. CREOLE.

Set in an isolated pocket of forest about 18 miles north of Pointe Noire, far from any of its neighbors, Chez Vaneau offers a wide, breeze-filled veranda overlooking a gully, the sight of local neighbors playing cards beside a blaring TV set. Steaming Creole specialties come from the kitchen. Tempting specialties include oysters with a piquant sauce, crayfish bisque, ragoût of goat, fricassee of conch, brochettes of seafood, different preparations of octopus, and roast pork. In 1995 they installed a saltwater tank for the storage of lobsters, which are now featured heavily on their menu.

✪ **L'Orangerie.** Lieu-dit Desmarais, Basse Terre. ☎ **0590/81-01-01.** Reservations recommended. Main courses 98 F–125 F ($16.35–$20.90); set-price lunch 130 F ($21.70). Sun–Fri noon–2:30pm; Fri–Sat 7–10pm. MC, V. CREOLE.

This site reigns as the finest restaurant in Basse Terre, and as such, it's always filled with representatives from the city's many legal offices, government agencies, hospitals, and cultural organizations. It occupies what was originally built in 1823 as the home of a slave-owning French aristocrat (le Comte de Desmarets), and partly because of its sweeping verandas, masonry walls, and wide-plank floors, it's one of the most beautiful colonial buildings in Basse Terre. Tables fill both the Creole-inspired interior and the verandas, and are supervised, along with the wine service, by maître d'hôtel Christophe Roubenne. Food, as prepared by award-winning Frenchman Christophe Moreau, is configured as upscale and modern interpretations of old-timey Creole recipes. Examples include a *gateau* of octopus and smoked chicken, served with rondelles of leeks marinated in starfruit-enhanced vinaigrette; a moussaka of conch with a reduction of tomatoes, lentils, and smoked fish; dorado stuffed with conch and served with a gratin of christop hene and St-Émilion sauce; a filet of veal stuffed with lobster, and offered with tagliatelle and a confit of ginger-infused vegetables' and a filet of beef roasted with black Jamaican pepper and flambéed with aged rum. Views from most of the tables encompass a sprawling French-Caribbean garden loaded with tropical fruit trees.

La Touna. Malendure. ☎ **0590/98-70-10.** Reservations recommended on Sun. Main courses 55 F–250 F ($9.20–$41.75). MC, V. Tues–Sun noon–3pm; Tues–Sat 7–9:30pm. Closed mid-Sept to mid-Oct. In the village of Mahaut, turn left on Rte. 2 and drive south. SEAFOOD/CREOLE.

Built on a narrow strip of sand between the road and the sea, this restaurant specializes in seafood. Most of the tables are on a side veranda whose ceiling is covered with palm fronds. Many prefer to have a drink (the fruit-based rum drinks are among the best in the area) before a meal in the sunken bar whose encircling banquettes give the impression of a ship's cabin. The decor is French colonial and suitably blasé—you might feel like you're in a low-rent restaurant in the south of France. The smoked swordfish mousse is a smooth way to start, or go with the savory calamari Provençale. Local crabs and sea urchins are filled with a spicy stuffing. You might also try kingfish au poivre or other platters of fish and shellfish from Caribbean waters.

Restaurant Clara. Ste-Rose. ☎ **0590/28-72-99.** Reservations recommended. Main courses 45 F–120 F ($7.50–$20.05). MC, V. Thurs–Tues noon–2:30pm; Mon–Tues and Thurs–Sat 7–10pm. CREOLE.

On the waterfront near the center of town is the culinary statement of Clara Lesueur and her talented and charming semiretired mother, Justine. Clara lived for 12 years in Paris as a member of an experimental jazz dance troupe, but she returned to Guadeloupe, her home, and set up her breeze-cooled restaurant, which she rebuilt in 1990 after hurricane damage. Try for a table on the open patio, where palm trees complement the color scheme.

Clara and Justine artfully meld the French style of fine dining with authentic, spicy Creole cookery. Specialties include *ouassous* (freshwater crayfish), brochette of swordfish, *palourdes* (small clams), several different preparations of conch, sea-urchin omelets, and *crabes farcis* (red-orange crabs with a spicy filling). The "sauce chien" that's served with many of the dishes is a blend of hot peppers, garlic, lime juice, and "secret things." The house drink is made with six local fruits and ample quantities of rum. Your dessert sherbet might be guava, soursop, or passion fruit.

11 Jamaica ⇩ ⇩ ⇩

Most visitors already have opinions of English-speaking Jamaica before they arrive. They know of its boisterous culture of reggae and Rastafarianism, and of its white sandy beaches, lush growth, rivers, mountains, and clear waterfalls. The art and cuisine of the country are also famous. But Jamaica suffers from crime, drugs, muggings, and racial tension. Those who want to see "the real Jamaica," or at least the island in greater depth, had better be prepared for some hassle. Vendors on the beaches and in the markets can be particularly aggressive.

Despite a minority of thieves and annoying vendors, most of Jamaica's 2.5 million people are above all friendly, funny, opinionated, talented, and almost impossible to forget. Their sense of humor is dry and understated, subtle yet direct. Everyone pokes fun at themselves and others. National pride is specific—beating the English at cricket, or winning gold medals in the Olympics. Individuals take pride in outstandingly bright and successful family members, a new house, a successful business, and simply the ability to survive—not easy in the urban slums. Thanks to their smiles and their island's beauty, the hypnotic, haunting seduction of Jamaica remains.

This country, which lies 90 miles south of Cuba, is the third largest of the Caribbean islands, with some 4,400 square miles of predominantly green land, a mountain ridge peaking at 7,400 feet above sea level, and, on the north coast, many beautiful white-sand beaches rimmed by the clear blue sea.

Most cruise ships dock at Ocho Rios on the lush northern coast, but more and more are going instead to the city of Montego Bay ("Mo Bay"), 67 miles to the west. Both ports offer an equal but different list of attractions and some of the same shopping possibilities. Don't try to "do" both ports in one day, however, since the 4-hour round-trip ride will leave time for only superficial visits to each.

OCHO RIOS

Once a small banana and fishing port, Ocho Rios is now Jamaica's cruise ship capital. The bay is dominated on one side by a bauxite-loading terminal and on the other by a range of resort hotels with sandy beaches fringed by palm trees. Ocho Rios and neighboring Port Antonio have long drawn celebrities, such as Sir Noël Coward, who invited the world to his doorstep, and Ian Fleming, creator of James Bond. Both had homes here.

Although the Ocho Rios area has some of the Caribbean's most fabled resorts, the town itself is tacky and not a romantic place in which to stroll. Its former quaint charm has been replaced by hordes of visitors and vendors. The resorts are still good, but they are citadels on guarded grounds or behind walls. Tourism has truly ruined the town.

Ocho Rios wasn't named for eight rivers, which is its Spanish translation. In 1657 British troops repelled a Spanish expeditionary force who launched a raid from Cuba. The battle was near Dunn's River Falls, now the most important attraction here. Seeing the rapids, the Spanish called the district *las chorreras.* The British and the Jamaicans weren't too good with Spanish names back then, so *las chorreras* was corrupted into "ocho rios."

COMING ASHORE

Most cruise ships dock at the port of Ocho Rios, near Dunn's River Falls. Only a mile away is one of the most important shopping areas, Ocean Village Shopping Centre.

Vendors are particularly aggressive in Ocho Rios. Don't expect to shop in the markets without a lot of hassle and a lot of very pushy hawking of merchandise, some of which is likely to be *ganja,* locally grown marijuana (though it may be readily available, it's still illegal).

FAST FACTS

Currency   The unit of currency is the **Jamaican dollar,** designated by the same symbol as the U.S. dollar ($). For clarity, we use the symbol **J$** to denote prices in Jamaican dollars. There is no fixed rate of exchange. At press time it was J$35 to $1 U.S. (J$1 = 2.85¢ U.S.). Visitors can pay in U.S. dollars, but *be careful!* Always find out if a price is being quoted in Jamaican or U.S. dollars. In this section we've generally followed the price-quotation policy of the establishment.

Information   You'll find tourist board offices at the Ocean Village Shopping Centre in Ocho Rios (☎ 876/974-2582). Open Monday to Friday from 9am to 5pm.

Language   The official language is English, but most Jamaicans speak a richly nuanced patois. Experts say that more than 90% of the patois vocabulary is derived from English, with the remaining words largely borrowed from African languages. There are also Spanish, Arawak, French, Chinese, Portuguese, and East Indian words.

SHORE EXCURSIONS

Because of inadequate public transportation and the hassle of both renting a car and driving, we recommend shore excursions.

The most popular tour, which lasts $4^1/_2$ hours and costs $36 per passenger, visits Dunn's River Falls, where a waterfall cascades 600 feet to the beach. This is the most visited attraction in Jamaica, which means that it's hopelessly overcrowded on days when a lot of cruise ships are in port. Tourists are allowed to climb the falls. This tour also visits Shaw Park Botanical Gardens, Fern Gully, and other local attractions, with time allocated for shopping. Wear a bathing suit underneath your clothes.

On another tour, which lasts 3 hours and costs $54, you can drive through the Jamaican countryside to Brimmer Hall Plantation, a working plantation property with a Great House and tropical crops, such as bananas and pimento. On the way back, you pass the estates once occupied by Noël Coward and Ian Fleming. On yet another tour, which lasts 4 hours and costs $45, you can go to Prospect Plantation, a working Jamaican plantation.

Additional options include a 2-hour snorkeling jaunt for $29. A coral reef near the cruise pier is one of the best places in the area for snorkeling, with panoramic underwater visibility. You could also take a 1-hour cruise on a glass-bottom boat for a look at underwater Jamaica. The cost is $20 per person.

Traditionally, one of the most heavily booked tours—from either Ocho Rios or Montego Bay—is rafting on the Martha Brae River in a 30-foot, two-seat bamboo raft. This tour lasts 4 hours and costs $45. However, most people find the rafting trip disappointing, despite the lush advertising. Furthermore, two Pennsylvania men were robbed and shot on it a few years ago. We think there are more interesting ways to spend your time.

GETTING AROUND

TAXIS   Taxis are your best means of transport. Always agree on a fare before you get inside. Rates are charged per taxi, not per person. Taxis licensed by the government display red Public Passenger Vehicle (PPV) plates. All others are gypsy cabs, and you should beware of these. You can also negotiate a price for a taxi to take you around to see the sights.

Jamaica

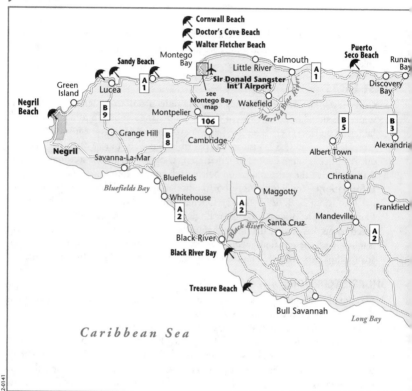

CAR RENTALS We don't recommend renting a car in Jamaica unless you absolutely want to explore that way. Roads are bad, driving is **on the left,** and Jamaicans are notorious for poor driving. Some companies require a deposit even before you come ashore. If you do rent a car, you must make arrangements through toll-free numbers in the U.S. before your ship comes in. You can call **Avis** at ☎ **800/ 331-1212, Budget Rent-a-Car** at ☎ **800/527-0700,** or **Hertz** at ☎ **800/ 654-3001.** If you're calling well in advance, you might try **Auto Europe** (☎ **800/ 223-5555**) or **Kenwel Holiday Autos** (☎ **800/678-0678**).

SEEING THE SIGHTS

South of Ocho Rios, **Fern Gully** was originally a riverbed. Today, the main A3 road winds up some 700 feet through a rain forest filled with wild ferns, hardwood trees, and lianas. For the botanist, there are hundreds of varieties of ferns, and for the less plant-minded, roadside stands sell fruits and vegetables, carved-wood souvenirs, and basketwork. The road runs for about 4 miles.

Near Lydford, southwest of Ocho Rios, are the remains of **Edinburgh Castle.** This was the lair of one of Jamaica's most infamous murderers, a Scot named Lewis Hutchinson who used to shoot passersby and toss their bodies into a deep pit. The authorities got wind of his activities, and although he tried to escape by canoe, he was captured by the navy and hanged. Rather proud of his achievements (evidence of at least 43 murders was found), he left £100 and instructions for a memorial to be built. It never was, but the 1763 castle ruins remain. To get to Lydford, take the A3 south

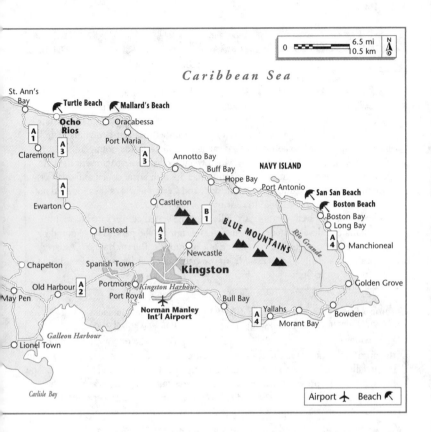

until you reach a small intersection directly north of Walkers Wood, and then follow the signpost west.

Brimmer Hall Estate. Port Maria, St. Mary's. ☎ **876/974-2244.** Tours $15. Thurs at 2pm.

If you're here on a Thursday, this 1817 estate 21 miles east of Ocho Rios is an ideal place to spend part of the day. It's often a destination of shore excursions. Brimmer Hall is a working plantation where you're driven around in a tractor-drawn jitney to see the tropical fruit trees and coffee plants. Knowledgeable guides tell you about the various processes necessary to produce the fine fruits of the island. Afterwards, you can relax beside the pool and sample a wide variety of drinks, including an interesting one called "Wow!" The Plantation Tour Eating House offers typical Jamaican dishes for lunch. There's also a souvenir shop with a good selection of ceramics, art, straw goods, woodcarvings, rums, liqueurs, and cigars.

Coyaba River Garden and Museum. Shaw Park Rd. (a mile from the center of Ocho Rios). ☎ **876/974-6235.** Admission $4.50 ages 13 and up, free for children 12 and under. Daily 8:30am–5pm.

Coyaba is a Spanish-style museum with a river and gardens filled with native flora, a cut-stone courtyard, fountains, an art gallery, and a crafts shop and bar. The complex was built on the grounds of the former Shaw Park plantation. The museum boasts a collection of artifacts from the Arawak, Spanish, and English settlements in the area. The name *coyaba* comes from the Arawak word for paradise.

⭐ **Favorite Jamaican Experiences**

There's a fantastic collection of exhibits at **Columbus Park Museum,** located in a large, open area between the main coast road and the sea along Queens Highway at Discovery Bay (☎ 876/973-2135). Here you'll see a canoe fashioned out of a solid piece of cottonwood, just as the Arawaks did it more than 5 centuries ago; and a stone cross, a monument originally placed on the Barrett family's Jamaican estate at Retreat by Edward Barrett, brother of poet Elizabeth Barrett Browning. You'll also find a tally, used to count bananas carried on men's heads from plantation to ship, as well as a planter's strongbox with a weighted lead base to prevent its theft. Other exhibits include 18th-century cannons, a Spanish water cooler and calcifier, a fish pot made from bamboo, a corn husker, and a water wheel of the type used on the sugar estates in the mid–19th century.

The museum is well worth a visit to learn of the varied cultures that have influenced Jamaica's development. Pimento trees dominate the park. A large mural by Eugene S. Hyde depicts the first landing of Columbus at Puerto Bueno (Discovery Bay) on May 4, 1494. Take a taxi from the cruise dock. Admission is free. Open daily from 9am to 5pm.

🞂 **Dunn's River Falls.** On the A3. ☎ **876/974-2857.** Admission $6 adults, $3 children 2–12, (2 and under free). Daily 9am–5pm (8am–5pm on cruise-ship arrival days).

Here you can relax on the beach or climb with a guide to the top of the 600-foot falls, the prime attraction in Ocho Rios. Swimmers can splash in the waters at the bottom of the falls or dip into the cool pools higher up between the cascades of water. The beach restaurant provides snacks and drinks. Dressing rooms are available. If you're planning to climb the falls, wear old tennis shoes to protect your feet from the sharp rocks and to prevent slipping.

Prospect Plantation. 3 miles east of Ocho Rios on the A3 (next to the Prospect Mini Golf Course). ☎ **876/994-1058.** Tours $12 adults, free for children under 12; 1-hour horseback ride $20. Tours Mon–Sat at 10:30am, 2pm, and 3:30pm; Sun at 11am, 1:30pm, and 3pm.

This working plantation is often visited on shore excursions. On your leisurely ride via covered jitney through the scenic beauty of Prospect, you'll readily see why this section of Jamaica is called "the garden parish of the island." You can view the many trees planted by such visitors as Sir Winston Churchill, Henry Kissinger, Charlie Chaplin, Pierre Trudeau, Noël Coward, and many others. You will see and learn about pimento (allspice), banana, cassava, sugarcane, coffee, cocoa, coconut, pineapple, and the famous leucaena, "Tree of Life." You can also see Jamaica's first hydroelectric plant and sample some exotic fruit and drinks.

Horseback riding is available on three scenic trails at Prospect. The rides vary from 1 to 2¼ hours. You need to reserve horses 1 hour in advance.

Firefly. Grants Pen, 20 miles east of Ocho Rios above Oracabessa. ☎ **876/997-7201.** Admission $10. Daily 8:30am–5:30pm.

Firefly was the home of Sir Noël Coward and his longtime companion, Graham Payn, who, as executor of Coward's estate, donated the house to the Jamaica National Heritage Trust. The recently restored building is as it was on the day Sir Noël died in 1973, complete with his Hawaiian-print shirts hanging in the bedroom closet. The library contains a collection of his books, and the living room is warm and comfortable, with big armchairs and two grand pianos where he composed several famous tunes. Visitors will hear Cowardian anecdotes, such as the story of how he entertained

Ocho Rios

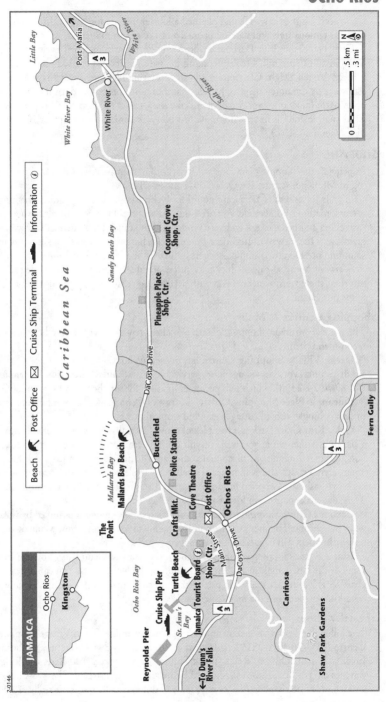

the Queen Mother here. He had planned a lobster mousse for her, but it melted; so with his famous style and flair, he opened a can of pea soup instead.

Guests housed in Blue Harbour, a villa nearer Port Maria, included Evelyn Waugh, Sir Winston Churchill, Errol Flynn and his wife Patrice Wymore, Lord Laurence Olivier, Vivien Leigh, Claudette Colbert, Katharine Hepburn, and Mary Martin. Paintings by the noted playwright, actor, author, and composer adorn the walls. An open patio looks out over the pool and the sea. Across the lawn, on his plain, flat white marble grave is inscribed simply: "Sir Noël Coward, born December 16, 1899, died March 26, 1973."

SHOPPING

In general, the shopping is better at Montego Bay than here. But if you're not going to Montego, wander the Ocho Rios crafts markets.

Literally hundreds of Jamaicans pour into Ocho Rios hoping to peddle something, often something homemade, to cruise ship passengers. Prepare yourself for aggressive selling and fierce haggling. Every vendor asks too much for an item at first, which gives them the leeway to negotiate the price. Is shopping fun in Ocho Rios? A resounding no. Do cruise ship passengers indulge in it anyway? A definite yes.

Warning: Some so-called "duty-free" prices are indeed lower than stateside prices, but then the government hits you with a 10% "General Consumption Tax" on all items purchased.

Shopping Centers & Malls

There are seven main shopping plazas. We cite a few because they are here, not to recommend them.

Ocean Village Shopping Centre has numerous boutiques, food stores, a bank, sundries purveyors, travel agencies, service facilities, and **Ocho Rios Pharmacy** (☎ **876/974-2398**), which sells perfumes, plasters for sore heels, and suntan lotion.

Pineapple Place Shopping Centre, just east of Ocho Rios, is a collection of shops in cedar-shingle–roofed cottages set amid tropical flowers.

Ocho Rios Craft Park is a complex of some 150 stalls. An eager seller will weave a hat or a basket while you wait, or you can buy from the mixture of ready-made hats, hampers, handbags, place mats, and lampshades. Other stands stock hand-embroidered goods and will make up small items while you wait. Woodcarvers work on bowls, ashtrays, wooden head-carvings, and statues chipped from lignum vitae. They also make cups from local bamboo.

Coconut Grove Shopping Plaza is a collection of low-slung shops linked by walkways and shrubs. The merchandise consists mainly of local craft items. Many of your fellow shoppers will be cruise ship passengers.

Island Plaza shopping complex is right in the heart of Ocho Rios. You can find some of the best Jamaican art here—all paintings by local artists. You can also purchase local handmade crafts (be prepared to do some haggling), carvings, ceramics, even kitchenware, and the inevitable T-shirts.

Specialty Shops

The following deserve special mention. **Swiss Stores,** in the Ocean Village Shopping Centre (☎ **876/974-2519**), sells all the big names in Swiss watches, including Juvenia, Tissot, Omega, Rolex, Patek Philippe, and Piaget. And here, the Rolex watches are real, not those fakes touted by hustlers on the streets. The Swiss outlet also sells duty-free handcrafted jewelry, some of dubious taste, but some really exquisite items as well.

One of the best bets for shopping is **Soni's Plaza,** 50 Main St., the address of all the shops recommended below. **Bollomongo** (☎ **876/974-7318**) has one of the island's widest selection of T-shirts, often in screen-printed designs. Bob Marley appears on many of them, and you can even get Bob Marley beach towels. Swimwear, such as "Sharkbite," is also sold. **Casa de Oro** (☎ 876/974-5392), specializes in duty-free watches, fine jewelry, and the classic perfumes. **Chulani's** (☎ 876/974-2421) sells a goodly assortment of quality watches and brand-name perfumes, as well as leather bags. Jewelry is set in a wide variety of 14-karat and 18-karat settings with diamonds, emeralds, rubies, and sapphires.

Gem Palace (☎ 876/974-2850) is the place to go for diamond ring solitaires, tennis bracelets, and 14-karat gold chains. **Mohan's** (☎ 876/974-9270) offers one of the best selections of 14-karat and 18-karat gold chains, rings, bracelets, and earrings in Ocho Rios. You'll also find jewelry studded with precious gems such as diamonds and rubies. **Soni's** (☎ 876/974-2303) dazzles with gold, but also cameras, French perfumes, watches, china and crystal, linen tablecloths, and even the standard Jamaican souvenirs.

Taj Gift Centre (☎ 876/974-9268) has a little bit of everything: Blue Mountain coffee, film, Jamaican cigars, and hand-embroidered linen tablecloths. For something different, look for Jamaican jewelry made from hematite, a mountain stone. **Tajmahal** (☎ 876/974-6455) beats most competitors with its name-brand watches, jewelry, and fragrances. It also has Paloma Picasso leather wear and porcelain by Lladró.

To find local handcrafts or art without the hassle of the markets, head for **Beautiful Memories,** 9 Island Plaza (☎ 876/974-2374), which has a limited but representative sampling of Jamaican art, as well as local crafts, pottery, woodwork, and hand-embroidered items.

We generally ignore hotel gift shops, but the **Jamaica Inn Gift Shop** in the Jamaica Inn, Main Street (☎ 876/974-2514), is better than most, selling everything from Blue Mountain coffee to Walkers Wood products, and even guava jelly and jerk seasoning. If you're lucky, you'll find marmalade from an old family recipe, plus Upton Pimento Dram, a unique liqueur flavored with Jamaican allspice. Local handcrafts include musical instruments for kids, brightly painted country cottages of tin, and intricate jigsaw puzzles of local scenes. The store also sells antiques, a constantly replenished collection ranging from sterling silver collectibles to 18th-century teaspoons and serving pieces. The antique maps of the West Indies are among the finest in Jamaica. We recently purchased a 1576 map of the island for a surprisingly reasonable price.

Harmony Hall

If you'd like to flee the hustle and bustle of the Ocho Rios bazaars, take a taxi to **Harmony Hall,** Tower Isle, on the A3 (☎ 876/975-4222), 4 miles east of Ocho Rios. One of Jamaica's Great Houses, Harmony Hall was built near the end of the 19th century. The restored house is now a gallery selling paintings and other works by Jamaican artists. The arts and crafts here are high-quality—not the usual junky assortment you might find at the beach. In addition, a bamboo factory makes furniture using a special trademark technique known as "plugging." You can also purchase Sharon McConnell's Starfish Oils, 100% pure essential oil blends. On the ground floor is a clothing line, "Reggae to Wear," designed and made in Jamaica from Balinese fabrics. Harmony charges no admission. The gallery is open daily from 10am to 6pm.

The Garden Café, which is also known as Alexander's after its co-owner, serves Jamaican cuisine priced at J\$550 to J\$900 ($15.70 to $25.65) for a meal. The food is full of flavor, with an authentic taste that may not be to everybody's liking. A cup of tea and a slice of homemade cake will cost about J\$100 ($2.85).

BEACHES

Most visitors to Ocho Rios head for the beach. The most overcrowded is **Mallards Beach,** shared by hotel guests and cruise ship passengers. Locals may steer you to the good and less-crowded **Turtle Beach,** southwest of Mallards.

GOLF, RIDING & TENNIS

GOLF   **Super Club's Runaway Golf Course,** at Runaway Beach near Ocho Rios on the north coast (☎ **876/973-2561**), is one of the better courses in the area, although it's nowhere near the courses at Montego Bay. Cruise ship passengers should call ahead and book playing times. The charge is $58 for 18 holes in winter. Players can rent carts and clubs.

Sandals Golf & Country Club, at Ocho Rios (☎ **876/975-0119**), is also open to the public. You can play for $50 for 9 holes or $70 for 18 holes year-round. The course lies about 700 feet above sea level. To get there from the center of Ocho Rios, travel along the main bypass for 2 miles until Mile End Road; turn right at the Texaco station there; and drive for 5 miles.

HORSEBACK RIDING   The best riding in Jamaica is in the Ocho Rios area. The island's most complete equestrian center is the **Chukka Cove Farm and Resort,** at Richmond Llandovery, St. Ann (☎ **876/972-2506**), located less than 4 miles east of Runaway Bay. A 1-hour trail ride costs $30, and a 2-hour mountain ride costs $40. The most popular ride is a 3-hour beach jaunt where, after riding over trails to the sea, you can unpack your horse and swim in the surf. Refreshments are served as part of the $55 charge. A 6-hour beach ride, complete with picnic lunch, goes for $130. Polo lessons are also available, costing $50 for 30 minutes.

TENNIS   More than any other resort here, **Ciboney Ocho Rios,** Main St., Ocho Rios (☎ **876/974-1027**), focuses on tennis. It offers three clay-surface and three hard-surface courts, all lit for nighttime play. Cruise passengers must call and make arrangements with the manager. A pro on site offers lessons for $15 an hour. Ciboney also sponsors twice-a-day clinics for both beginners and advanced players.

DINIING

✪ **Almond Tree Restaurant.** In the Hibiscus Lodge Hotel (3 blocks from the Ocho Rios Mall), 87 Main St. ☎ **876/974-2813.** Reservations recommended. Main courses $15.50–$37. AE, DC, MC, V. Daily 7am–2:30pm and 6–9:30pm. INTERNATIONAL.

The food, drink, reasonable prices, and casual cool atmosphere keep customers coming back night after night. The Almond Tree is a two-tiered patio restaurant overlooking the Caribbean with a tree growing through its roof. Lobster Almond Tree is a specialty, but lobster Thermidor is the most delectable item on the menu. We also like the bouillabaisse (made with conch and lobster), roast suckling pig, medallions of beef Anne Palmer, and fondue bourguignonne. Jamaican plantation rice is a local specialty. The wine list offers a variety of vintages, including Spanish and Jamaican. Have an aperitif in the unique "swinging bar" (with swinging chairs, that is).

Double V Jerk Centre. 109 Main St. (3 min. east of the town center). ☎ **876/974-5998.** Jerk pork or chicken J$360–J$460 ($10.25–$13.10) per pound. AE, MC, V. Mon–Sat 8:30am–1:30am. JERK/JAMAICAN.

When the moon is full and only the fiery taste of Jamaican jerk seasonings can ease your stomach growls, head here, and don't dress up. Set on Ocho Rios' main commercial boulevard, this place serves up the best jerk pork and chicken in town. Don't expect anything fancy. Just come for platters of meat that can be sold in quarter-pound or half-pound portions, depending on your appetite. Vegetables, salad, and fried breadfruit come with your main course, and you can also get a frosty Red Stripe beer. Lots of office workers and shopkeepers come here at lunch.

✪ Evita's Italian Restaurant. Eden Bower Rd. (5 min. south of Ocho Rios). ☎ **876/974-2333.** Reservations recommended. Main courses $11–$24. AE, MC, V. Daily 11am–11pm. ITALIAN.

The premier Italian restaurant in Ocho Rios, this is also one of the most fun restaurants along the entire north coast of Jamaica. It's set a few steps from the Enchanted Garden resort, in a hillside residential neighborhood with a panoramic view of the city's harbor. Its soul and artistic flair come from Eva Myers, the convivial former owner of some of the most legendary bars of Montego Bay. She established her culinary headquarters in this white, gingerbread-trimmed house in 1990. An outdoor terrace offers additional seating and enhanced views.

Even if the cuisine isn't as extraordinary as Evita claims, it's still pretty good. More than half the menu is devoted to pastas, and the selection includes almost every variety known in northern and southern Italy. If you don't want pasta, the fish dishes are excellent, especially the snapper stuffed with crabmeat and the lobster and scampi in a buttery white cream sauce. Italian (or other) wines by the bottle might accompany your menu choice.

Little Pub Restaurant. 59 Main St. ☎ **876/974-2324.** Reservations recommended. Main courses $13.50–$28.50. AE, MC, V. Daily 7am–1am. JAMAICAN/INTERNATIONAL/ITALIAN.

This indoor-outdoor pub is a bit too contrived and touristy for our tastes, but it has an undeniable appeal both for visitors and locals. Located in a redbrick courtyard with a fountain and a waterfall, the building is surrounded by souvenir shops in the center of town. No one will mind if you just enjoy a drink while seated on one of the pub's barrel chairs. But if you want a full meal, proceed to one of the linen-covered tables topped with fresh cut flowers and candles. Menu items include very familiar fare (too familiar, say some critics), such as grilled kingfish, stewed snapper, barbecued chicken, and the inevitable and overpriced lobster. The cooking is competent, but it's all very casual here. Come for the convivial atmosphere rather than for the food.

Parkway Restaurant. 60 DaCosta Dr. ☎ **876/974-2667.** Main courses $8–$20. AE, MC, V. Daily 8am–11:30pm. JAMAICAN.

Come here to eat like the Jamaicans eat. This popular spot in the commercial center of town couldn't be plainer or less pretentious, but it's always packed. Local families and businessmen know they can get some of Ocho Rios's best and least expensive local dishes here. This local watering and drinking joint is even a bit disdainful of all those resorts with their contrived international food. Hungry diners are fed Jamaican-style chicken, curried goat, sirloin steak, filet of red snapper, and to top it off, banana cream pie. Lobster and fresh fish are usually featured also. The food is straightforward, honest, and affordable.

✪ Plantation Inn Restaurant. In the Plantation Inn, Main St. ☎ **876/974-5601.** Reservations required. Main courses $20–$35; three-course fixed-price $35. AE, DC, MC, V. Daily 7:30–10am, 1–1:30pm, 4:30–5:30pm (afternoon tea), and 7–10pm. JAMAICAN/CONTINENTAL.

When you're seated at the beautifully laid tables here, you'll think you've arrived at Tara in *Gone With the Wind*. It's definitely the pampered life. The restaurant is divided into the indoor part (The Dining Room) and an outdoor section (Bougainvillea Terrace), with an annex, the Peacock Pavilion, a few steps away, where afternoon tea is served daily.

Jamaican specialties help spice up the continental cuisine in this romantic restaurant. Appetizers are always spicy and tangy, our favorite being "Fire & Spice," which is a chicken and beef kebab with a ginger-pimiento sauce. For the main course, we always ask the chef to prepare a whole roast fish from the catch of the day, served boneless and seasoned with island herbs and spices. The fish is always perfectly cooked and presented with fresh country vegetables. Since this place attracts a lot of meat eaters, the chefs always prepare the classics, such as lamb chops Provençale. Opt for the creamy and tasty banana cream pie for dessert, if it's featured.

Ruins Restaurant, Gift Shop, and Boutique. Turtle River, DaCosta Dr. ☎ **876/974-2442.** Reservations recommended. Main courses $13–$37. AE, DC, MC, V. Mon–Sat noon–2:30pm; daily 6–9:30pm. CHINESE/INTERNATIONAL/JAMAICAN.

Here you dine in the center of town at the foot of waterfalls, which are so inviting that they're a tourist attraction in their own right. In 1831 a British entrepreneur constructed a sugar mill on the site, using the powerful stream to drive his water wheels. Today, all that remains is a jumble of ruins. After you cross a covered bridge, perhaps stopping off for a drink at the bar in the outbuilding first, you find yourself in a fairyland where the only sounds come from the tree frogs, the falling water from about a dozen cascades, and the discreet clink of silver and china. Tables are set on a wooden deck leading all the way up to the pool at the foot of the falls, where moss lines the stones at the base. At some point you may want to climb a flight of stairs to the top of the cascade, where bobbing lanterns and the illuminated waters below afford one of the most delightful experiences on the island.

The only problem is that the setting is more dramatic than the cuisine. It's more "Chinese-American" than authentic regional Chinese—witness the several kinds of chow mein or chop suey and the sweet-and-sour pork. Lobster in a stir-fry is the house specialty. Dishes such as chicken Kiev try to justify the restaurant's "international" label, but this chicken wouldn't be allowed out of the Russian Tea Room's kitchen in New York. Your best bet is to stick with the vegetarian dishes, which aren't bad.

MONTEGO BAY

Montego Bay is sometimes less of a hassle than the port at Ocho Rios. Its beaches are better, its shopping is better, and its restaurants are better. Some of the best golf courses in the Caribbean are also found here, superior even to those on Puerto Rico and the Bahamas. Like Ocho Rios, Montego Bay has its crime, traffic, and annoyance, but there is much more to see and do here.

There is little of interest in the town of Montego Bay itself except shopping. The good stuff lies in the environs, which you'll have to reach by taxi or shore excursion. In fact, getting around from place to place will be one of the major difficulties here, as it is in Barbados. Whatever you want to visit seems to be in yet another direction.

COMING ASHORE

Montego Bay has a modern cruise dock with lots of conveniences, including duty-free stores, telephones, tourist information, and plenty of taxis to meet all ships. This rather dull cruise port isn't at a center of town, however, so you'll have to take a $5 taxi ride to get to the main tourist board in the heart of "Mo Bay."

INFORMATION

You'll find a tourist board office at Cornwall Beach, St. James (☎ **876/952-4425**). It's open Monday to Friday from 9am to 5pm.

SHORE EXCURSIONS

Most cruise ships offer such weak shore excursions here that they may not be worth your time or money. One of the most highly touted is the rafting on the Martha Brae River (see "Shore Excursions" under Ocho Rios, above). You can also book independent tours yourself.

The **Croydon Plantation,** Catadupa, St. James (☎ **876/979-8267**), is a 25-mile ride from Montego Bay. It can be visited on a half-day tour from Montego Bay on Tuesday, Wednesday, and Friday. Included in the $55 price are round-trip transportation from the dock, a tour of the plantation, a tasting of varieties of pineapple and other tropical fruits in season, and a barbecued chicken lunch.

Another tour of Croydon is the **Hilton High Day Tour,** (☎ **876/952-3343**). Your day starts with a continental breakfast served at the old plantation house. Afterwards, you can roam around the 100 acres of the plantation and visit St. Leonards village or the nearby German village of Seaford. Calypso music is played throughout the day, and a Jamaican lunch of roast suckling pig with rum punch, chicken or fish, and 12 Jamaican vegetables is served at 1pm. The charge for the day is $50 per person for the plantation tour, breakfast, lunch, and round-trip transportation on a scenic drive through historic plantation areas. Tour days are Tuesday, Wednesday, Friday, and Sunday. The company's office is on Beach View Plaza.

GETTING AROUND

MOTOR BIKES **Montego Honda/Bike Rentals,** 21 Gloucester Ave. (☎ **876/952-4984**), rents Hondas for $30 to $35 a day (24 hours), plus a $300 deposit. Bikes cost $35 a day, plus a $200 deposit. Deposits are refundable if the vehicles are returned in good shape. It's open daily from 7:30am to 5pm. You'll need your valid home driver's license.

TAXIS If you don't book a shore excursion, a taxi is the best—perhaps the only—means of getting around. Renting a car here is a lot of hassle. For more information about taxis, see "Getting Around" under Ocho Rios, above. The same conditions apply to Montego Bay.

SEEING THE SIGHTS

All of the following attractions can be reached by taxi from the cruise dock.

Barnett Estates and Bellfield Great House. Barnett Estates. ☎ **876/952-2382.** Admission $10. Daily 9:30am–5pm.

Once a totally private estate sprawled across 50,000 acres, this Great House has hosted everybody from President Kennedy to Churchill and even Queen Elizabeth II over the years. Now anybody who pays the entrance fee can come in and take a look. The domain of the Kerr-Jarret family during 300 years of high society, this was once the seat of a massive sugar plantation. At its center is the 18th-century Bellfield Great House (not as ornate as Rose Hall, see below). Restored in 1994, it is a grand example of Georgian architecture. Guides in costumes offer narrated tours of the property. After the tour, drop in to the old Sugar Mill Bar for a tall rum punch.

Greenwood Great House. On the A1 (14 miles east of Montego Bay and 7 miles west of Falmouth). ☎ **876/953-1077.** Admission $10 adults, $5 children under 12. Daily 9am–6pm.

Greenwood is even more interesting than Rose Hall (see below). This Georgian-style building was the residence from 1780 to 1800 of Richard Barrett, a relative of Elizabeth Barrett Browning. On display is the original library of the Barrett family, with rare books dating from 1697, along with oil paintings of the family, china made by

Montego Bay

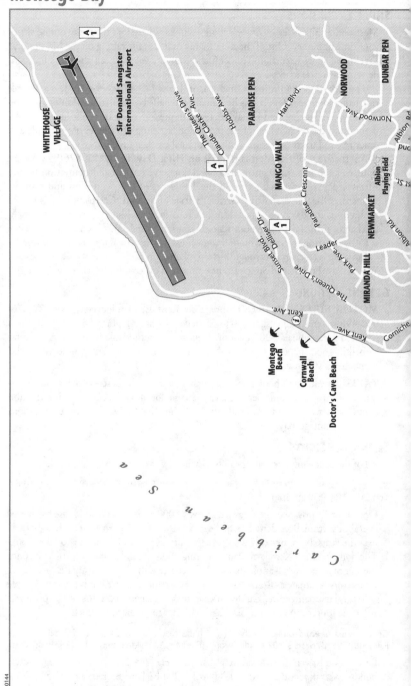

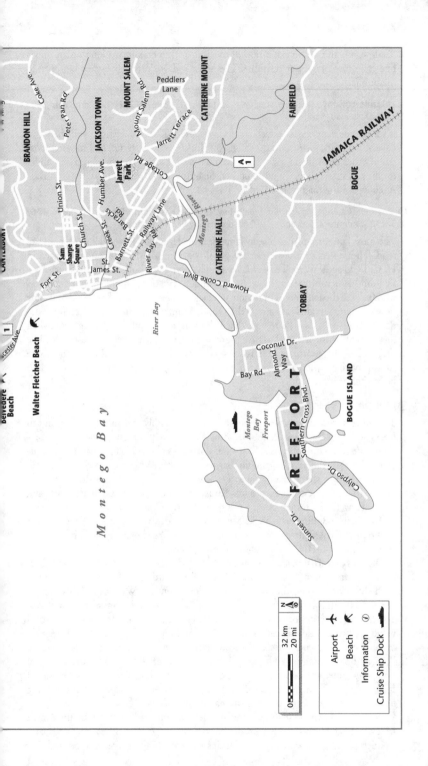

Wedgwood, and a rare exhibition of musical instruments in working order, plus a fine collection of antique furniture. The house today is privately owned but open to the public.

Rocklands Wildlife Station. Anchovy, St. James. ☎ **876/952-2009.** Admission J$300 ($8.55). Daily 2:30–5pm.

It's a unique experience to feed small doves and finches millet from your hand, to have a Jamaican doctor bird perch on your finger to drink syrup, and to watch dozens of other birds flying in for their evening meal. Don't take children 5 and under to this sanctuary, as they tend to bother the birds. Rocklands is about a mile outside Anchovy on the road from Montego Bay.

✪ **Rose Hall Great House.** Rose Hall Hwy. (9 miles east from Montego Bay). ☎ **876/953-2323.** Admission $15 adults, $10 children. Daily 9am–5:15pm.

The most famous Great House in Jamaica is the legendary Rose Hall, on the coastal road. The subject of at least a dozen gothic novels, Rose Hall was immortalized in H. G. DeLisser's *White Witch of Rosehall*. The house was built about 2 centuries ago by John Palmer. However, it was Annie Palmer, wife of the builder's grandnephew, who became the focal point of fiction and fact. "Infamous Annie," was said to dabble in witchcraft. Servants called her "the Obeah woman" (*Obeah* is Jamaican for "voodoo"). Annie was also said to have taken slaves as lovers, and then killing them when they started boring her, and to have murdered several of her coterie of husbands while they slept—she eventually suffered the same fate herself. Long in ruins, the house (now privately owned by U.S.-based philanthropists) has been restored. Annie's Pub lies on the ground floor.

SHOPPING

The same warnings about shopping in Ocho Rios apply to Mo Bay. Still, you can find good duty-free items here, including Swiss watches, Irish crystal, French perfumes, English china, Danish silverware, Portuguese linens, Italian handbags, Scottish cashmeres, Indian silks, and liquors and liqueurs. Appleton's overproof, special, and punch rums are excellent values. Tìa Maria (coffee-flavored) and Rumona (rum-flavored) are the best liqueurs. Khus Khus is the local perfume. Jamaican arts and crafts are available throughout the resorts and at the Crafts Market.

The main shopping areas are at **Montego Freeport,** within easy walking distance of the pier; **City Centre** (where most of the duty-free shops are, aside from at the large hotels); and **Holiday Village Shopping Centre.**

Old Fort Craft Park, a shopping complex with 180 vendors licensed by the Jamaica Tourist Board, fronts Howard Cooke Boulevard up from Gloucester Avenue in the heart of Montego Bay, on the site of Fort Montego. With a varied assortment of handcrafts, this is browsing country for both souvenirs and more serious purchases. You'll see a selection of wall hangings, hand-woven straw items, and hand-carved wood sculptures, and you can even get your hair braided. Vendors can be extremely aggressive, so be prepared for some major hassles, as well as some serious negotiation. Persistent bargaining on your part will lead to substantial discounts. Fort Montego, now long gone, was constructed by the British in the mid–18th century as part of their defense of "fortress Jamaica." But it never saw much action, except for firing its cannons every year to salute the monarch's birthday.

You can find the best selection of handmade Jamaican souvenirs at the **Crafts Market,** near Harbour Street in downtown Montego Bay. Straw hats and bags, wooden platters, straw baskets, musical instruments, beads, carved objects, and toys are all available here. That "jipijapa" hat will come in handy if you're going to be out in the island sun.

One of the newest and most intriguing places for shopping is a mall, **Half Moon Plaza,** set on the coastal road about 8 miles east of the commercial center of Montego Bay. This upscale mini-mall caters to the shopping and gastronomic needs of residents of one of the region's most elegant hotels, the Half Moon Club. Also on the premises are a bank and about 25 shops, each arranged around a central courtyard and purveying a wide choice of carefully selected merchandise.

Ambiente Art Gallery. 9 Fort St. ☎ **876/952-7919.**

A 100-year-old clapboard cottage set close to the road houses this gallery. The Austrian-born owner, Maria Hitchins, is the doyenne of the Montego Bay art scene. She has personally encouraged and developed scores of local fine artworks and prints by local artists.

Blue Mountain Gems Workshop. At the Holiday Village Shopping Centre. ☎ **876/953-2338.**

You can take a tour of the workshops to see the process from raw stone to the finished product available for purchase later. Wooden jewelry, local carvings, and one-of-a-kind ceramic figurines are also sold.

Caribatik Island Fabrics. Rock Wharf on the Luminous Lagoon, Falmouth (2 miles east of Falmouth on the north coast road). ☎ **876/954-3314.**

You'll recognize this place easily by the huge sign painted across the building's side. This is the private living and work domain of Keith Chandler, who established the shop with his late wife, Muriel, in 1970. Chic boutiques in the States view the batiks Muriel created as stylish and sensual. You'll find a full range of fabrics, scarves, garments, and wall hangings, some patterned after such themes as Jamaica's "doctor bird." Muriel's Gallery continues to sell her original batik paintings. Either Keith or a member of the staff will be glad to describe the intricate process of batiking. Closed in September.

Golden Nugget. 8 St. James Shopping Centre, Gloucester Ave. ☎ **876/952-7707.**

Golden Nugget has an impressive collection of watches for both women and men, and a fine assortment of jewelry, especially gold chains. The shop also carries leading brand-name cameras and a wide assortment of French perfumes. It's set in the manicured confines of one of Montego Bay's most modern shopping compounds.

Jolie Madame Fashions. 30 City Centre Bldg. ☎ **876/952-3126.**

This shop's racks of clothing for women and girls might contain evening dresses, casual clothes, and beach attire. Many garments range from $25 to $200. Norma McLeod, the establishment's overseer, designer, coordinator, and founder, is always on hand to arrange custom-made garments.

Klass Kraft Leather Sandals. 44 Fort St. ☎ **876/952-5782.**

Located next door to Things Jamaican, this store offers sandals and leather accessories made on location by a team of Jamaican craftspeople. All sandals cost less than $35.

Nevlle Budhai Paintings. Budhai's Art Gallery, Reading Main Rd., Reading. ☎ **876/979-2568.**

This is the art center of a distinguished artist, Nevlle Budhai, the president and cofounder of the Western Jamaica Society of Fine Arts. He has a distinct style and

> ## ⭐ More Favorite Jamaican Experiences
>
> It's a unique experience to have a Jamaican doctor bird perch on your finger to drink syrup, or to feed small doves and finches from your hand, or simply to watch dozens of birds flying in for the evening at **Rocklands Wildlife Station,** Anchovy, St. James (☎ 876/952-2009). Lisa Salmon, known as the "Bird Lady of Anchovy," established this sanctuary. It's perfect for nature lovers and bird watchers, but don't take children 5 and under, as they tend to worry the birds. Smoking and playing transistor radios are forbidden. Rocklands is about a mile outside Anchovy on the road from Montego Bay. It's open daily from 2:30 to 5pm, and charges an admission of J$300 ($8.55).
>
> You may want to skip all the public beaches and head instead for the **Rose Hall Beach Club** (☎ 876/953-2323), lying on the main road 11 miles east of Montego Bay. It sits on half a mile of secure, secluded, white sandy beach, by crystal-clear water. The club offers a full restaurant, two beach bars, a covered pavilion, an open-air dance area, showers, restrooms, and changing facilities, plus beach volleyball courts, various beach games, and a full water sports activities program. There's also live entertainment. Admission fees are $8 for adults, $5 for children. The club is open daily from 10am to 6pm.

captures the special flavor of the island and its people. The artist may sometimes be seen sketching or painting in Montego Bay or along the highways of rural Jamaica. His studio is 5 miles west of Montego Bay on the way to Negril.

Things Jamaican. 44 Fort St. ☎ **876/952-5605.**

This is a showcase for the talents of the artisans of Jamaica. Here you'll find a wealth of products, including rums and liqueurs, along with jerk seasoning. Look for Busha Browne's fine Jamaican sauces, especially spicy chutneys or planter's spicy piquant sauce. These recipes are prepared and bottled by the Busha Browne Company in Jamaica just as they were 100 years ago. Many items for sale are carved from wood, including sculpture, salad bowls, and trays. You'll also find large hand-woven Jamaican baskets.

Look for reproductions of the Port Royal collection. Near Kingston, the Jamaican capital, Port Royal was buried by an earthquake and tidal wave in 1692. After resting underwater for 275 years, beautiful pewter items were recovered and are living again in reproductions. They include Rat-tail spoons (spoons with the heads of the monarchs William and Mary), Splay-Footed Lion Rampant spoons, and spoons with Pied-de-Biche handles. The items were reproduced faithfully, right down to the pit marks and scratches. To complement the pewter assortment, Things Jamaican created the Port Royal Bristol-Delft Ceramic Collection, based on original pieces of ceramics found in the underwater digs.

BEACHES

Cornwall Beach (☎ 876/952-3463) is a long stretch of white sand beach with dressing cabanas. Daily admission is $2 for adults, $1 for children. A bar and cafeteria offer refreshment. Hours are 9am to 5pm daily.

Doctor's Cave Beach, on Gloucester Avenue across from the Doctor's Cave Beach Hotel (☎ 876/952-2566), helped launch Mo Bay as a resort in the 1940s. Admission to the beach is $2 for adults, half price for children up to 12. Dressing rooms, chairs, umbrellas, and rafts are available from 8:30am to 5pm daily.

One of the premier beaches of Jamaica, **Walter Fletcher Beach** in the heart of Mo Bay (☎ 876/952-5783) is noted for its tranquil waters, which make it a particular favorite for families with children. Changing rooms are available; lifeguards are on duty. There's also a restaurant for lunch. The beach is open daily from 9am to 5pm, with an admission charge of $1 for adults, half price for children.

DIVING, GOLF, RAFTING, RIDING, SAILING & TENNIS

SCUBA DIVING **Seaworld Resorts Ltd.,** Cariblue Hotel, Rose Hall Main Rd. (☎ 876/953-2180), operates scuba diving as well as deep-sea fishing jaunts, plus many other water sports, including sailing and windsurfing. Its scuba dives go to off-shore coral reefs that are among the most spectacular in the Caribbean. There are three PADI-certified dive guides, one dive boat, and all the necessary equipment for either inexperienced or certified divers. Most day dives begin at $35.

GOLF **Wyndham Rose Hall Golf & Beach Resort,** Rose Hall (☎ 876/953-2650), has a noted course with an unusual and challenging seaside and mountain layout. Its eighth hole skirts the water, then doglegs onto a promontory thrusting 200 yards into the sea. The back nine are even more scenic and interesting, rising up steep slopes and falling into deep ravines on Mount Zion. The 10th fairway abuts the family burial grounds of the Barretts of Wimpole Street, and the 14th passes the vacation home of singer Johnny Cash. The 300-foot-high 13th tee offers a rare panoramic view of the sea and the roof of the hotel, and the 15th green is next to a 40-foot waterfall, once featured in a James Bond movie. A fully stocked pro shop, a clubhouse, and a professional staff are among the amenities. Cruise passengers pay $60 for 18 holes and $40 for 9 holes. Mandatory cart rental costs $33 for 18 holes, and the use of a caddy (also mandatory) is another $12 for 18 holes.

The excellent, regal course at the **Tryall** (☎ 876/956-5660), 12 miles from Montego Bay, has often been the site of major golf tournaments, including the Jamaica Classic Annual and the Johnnie Walker Tournament. For 18 holes, players pay $75 from mid-April to mid-December and $150 in winter.

Half Moon, at Rose Hall (☎ 876/953-2560), features a championship course—designed by Robert Trent Jones, Sr.—which opened in 1961. The course players has manicured and diversely shaped greens. For 18 holes pay $110 year-round. Carts cost $30 for 18 holes, and caddies (mandatory) cost $15.

Ironshore Golf & Country Club, Ironshore, St. James, Montego Bay (☎ 876/953-2800), a well-known, par-72, 18-hole golf course is privately owned, but open to the public. Greens fees for 18 holes are $57.50.

RAFTING **Mountain Valley Rafting,** 31 Gloucester Ave. (☎ 876/956-0020), offers excursions on the Great River. They depart from the Lethe Plantation, about 10 miles south of Montego Bay. One-hour trips operate daily from 8:30am to 4:30pm; the cost is $36 for up to two people. Bamboo rafts are designed for two, with a raised dais to sit on. In some cases, a small child can accompany two adults on the same raft, although caution should be exercised. Ask about pickup by taxi at the end of the run. For $45 per person, a half-day experience includes transportation to and from the pier, an hour's rafting, lunch, a garden tour of the Lethe property, and a taste of Jamaican liqueur.

HORSEBACK RIDING The best program for equestrians is offered by the helpful staff at the **Rocky Point Riding Stables,** at the Half Moon Club, Rose Hall, Montego Bay (☎ 876/953-2286). The stables, built in the colonial Caribbean style in 1992, are the most beautiful in Jamaica. They hold about 30 horses. A 90-minute beach or mountain ride costs $50; a 2¹/₂-hour combination ride (including treks through hillsides, forest trails, and beaches, and ending with a saltwater swim) goes for $70.

SAILING   Day cruises are offered aboard the *Calico,* a 55-foot gaff-rigged wooden ketch that sails from Margaritaville on the Montego Bay waterfront. An additional vessel, *Calico B,* carries another 40 passengers per ride. They will transport you to and from the cruise pier for either journey. Departing daily at 10am and returning at 1pm, the day voyage provides sailing, sunning, and snorkeling (with equipment included), plus a Jamaican buffet lunch served on the beach, all to the sound of reggae and other music. The cost is $50 per person. For information and reservations, call Capt. Bryan Langford, North Coast Cruises Ltd. (☎ 876/952-5860). A 3-day notice is recommended.

TENNIS   Half Moon Golf, Tennis, and Beach Club, outside Montego Bay (☎ 876/953-2211), has the finest tennis courts in the area, even outclassing Tryall (see below). Its 13 state-of-the-art courts attract players from around the world. Lessons cost $25 per half hour, $45 per hour. The pro shop, which accepts reservations for court times, is open daily from 7am to 8pm. If you're not a guest of the hotel, you must purchase a day pass ($50 per person) at the front desk. It will allow you access to the resort's tennis courts, gym, sauna, Jacuzzi, pools, and beach facilities.

Tryall Golf, Tennis, and Beach Club, St. James (☎ 876/956-5660), offers nine hard-surface courts near its Great House. Nonguests pay $25 per hour. All players are charged an extra $12 per hour for nighttime illumination. Four pros on-site provide lessons, costing $17 to $25 per half hour, or $25 to $40 per hour, depending on the rank of the pro.

Wyndham Rose Hall Golf & Beach Resort, Rose Hall (☎ 876/953-2650), outside Montego Bay, is also an outstanding tennis resort, though it's not the equal of Half Moon or Tryall. Wyndham offers six hard-surface courts. To play, you must get permission from the manager. The resident pro charges $50 per hour for lessons, or $30 for 30 minutes.

DINING

Calabash Restaurant. In the Winged Victory Hotel, 5 Queen's Dr. ☎ **876/952-3892.** Reservations recommended. Main courses $12–$22. AE, MC, V. Daily noon–2:30pm and 6–10pm. INTERNATIONAL/JAMAICAN.

Over the years the kitchen here has been consistently good, and savvy locals keep returning. Perched on a hillside road in Montego Bay, 500 feet above the distant sea, this restaurant is often favored by celebrities. It was originally built as a private villa by a doctor in the 1920s. More than 25 years ago owner Roma Chin Sue established the courtyard and elegantly simple eagle's-nest patio as a well-managed restaurant. The seafood, Jamaican classics, and international favorites here include curried goat, lobster dishes, the house specialty of mixed seafood en coquille (served with a cheese-and-brandy sauce), and a year-round version of a Jamaican Christmas cake. Flavors are blended beautifully.

Georgian House. 2 Orange St. ☎ **876/952-0632.** Reservations recommended. Main courses $16–$33; lunch $6.50–$13. AE, DC, MC, V. Mon–Fri noon–3pm; daily 6–11pm. INTERNATIONAL/JAMAICAN.

The landmark Georgian House, which includes a restaurant and an art gallery, brings grand cuisine and an elegant setting to the heart of town. An English gentleman constructed the 18th-century buildings for his mistress, or so it is said. You can select either the upstairs room, which is more formal, or the garden terrace, with its fountains, statues, lanterns, and cut-stone exterior.

You might begin with a traditional Jamaican appetizer such as ackee and bacon. Baked spiny lobster is another specialty, but ask that it not be overcooked. Continental dishes, such as tournedos Rossini, are also prepared with flair. The lunch menu is primarily Jamaican, but dinner offerings are broader in scope, with a variety of fresh seafood pastas and vegetarian choices. There's a fine wine list, too.

✪ **The Native Restaurant.** Gloucester Ave. ☎ **876/979-2769.** Reservations recommended. Main courses $10–$35. AE, MC, V. Daily 7:30am–10pm. JAMAICAN.

This restaurant continues to win converts as a self-styled "sis & bro" act, turning out dishes that Jamaican foodies love. Visitors have also discovered it. You might start with a tropical drink while selecting one of the international wines to go with your meal. You know you're getting island flavor when faced with such appetizers as jerk reggae chicken, ackee and saltfish (an acquired taste), or perhaps smoked marlin. Consider following these with our favorite dish here, steamed fish. The cook will also serve you jerk or fried chicken, each filled with flavor. Lobster with garlic butter, although more costly, actually pales next to the curried shrimp. A more recent specialty is Boonoonoonoos, billed as "A Taste of Jamaica," a big platter with a little bit of everything, meats and several kinds of fish and vegetables. Although fresh desserts are prepared daily, you may choose instead just to have a Jamaican Blue Mountain coffee, which rounds the meal off nicely.

✪ **Norma at the Wharfhouse.** Reading Rd. ☎ **876/979-2745.** Reservations recommended. Main courses $26–$32. AE, MC, V. Thurs–Sun noon–3:30pm; Tues–Sun 6:30–10pm. 15 min. west of the town center along Rte. A1. NOUVELLE JAMAICAN.

Set in a coral-stone warehouse, with 2-foot-thick walls bound together with molasses and lime, this is the finest restaurant in Montego Bay. It's a favorite of many of Jamaica's visiting celebrities. Originally built in 1780, the building was restored by Millicent Rogers, heiress of the Standard Oil fortune, and now serves as the northshore domain of Norma Shirley, one of Jamaica's foremost restaurateurs. You can request a table either on the large pier built on stilts over the coral reef (where a view of Montego Bay glitters in the distance) or in an elegantly formal, early–19th-century dining room illuminated only with flickering candles. Before or after dinner, you can get drinks either in the restaurant or in an informal bar, much favored by locals, called the Wharf Rat (in a separate building).

Service in the restaurant is impeccable, and the food is praised throughout the island. Specialties include grilled deviled crab backs, smoked marlin with papaya sauce, chicken breast with callaloo, nuggets of lobster in a mild curry sauce, and chateaubriand larded with pâté in a peppercorn sauce. Many of the main dishes are served with a garlic sauce. Dessert might be a rum-and-raisin cheesecake or a piña-colada mousse. Each of these dishes is individually prepared and filled with flavor. This is the type of food you hope to find in Jamaica, but so rarely do.

Pier 1. Howard Cooke Blvd. ☎ **876/952-2452.** Reservations not required. Main courses $15–$28. AE, MC, V. Daily 11am–11pm (later on Sat–Sun if business warrants it). SEAFOOD.

Pier 1, one of the major dining and entertainment hubs of Mo Bay, is set in an appealing waterfront location, on a landfill in the bay. The place remains a local favorite. Fisherfolk bring fresh lobster, which the chef prepares in a number of ways, including Creole style or curried. You might begin with one of the typically Jamaican soups, such as conch chowder or red pea (which is actually red bean). At lunch the hamburgers are the juiciest in town, and the steak sandwich with mushrooms is excellent as well. The chef also prepares such famous island dishes as jerk pork and chicken, and Jamaican red snapper. (The jerk dishes, however, are better at the Pork Pit, listed below.) Finish your meal with a slice of moist rum cake. Service is very laid-back.

✪ **Pork Pit.** 27 Gloucester Ave., near Walter Fletcher Beach. ☎ **876/952-1046.** Reservations not required. One pound of jerk pork $10. No credit cards. Daily 11am–11:30pm. JAMAICAN.

Pork Pit, an open-air gazebo right in the heart of Montego Bay, is the best place to go for the famous Jamaican jerk pork and jerk chicken. Many beachgoers come over here for a big lunch. Picnic tables encircle the building, and everything is open-air and informal. Half a pound of jerk meat, served with a baked yam or baked potato and a bottle of Red Stripe beer, is usually sufficient for a meal. The menu also includes steamed roast fish. Prices are very reasonable.

Richmond Hill Inn. 45 Union St. ☎ **876/952-3859.** Reservations recommended. All main courses (including soup, salad, garlic bread, and dessert) $35. AE, MC, V. Daily 7:30am–9:30pm. Take a taxi (a 4-minute ride uphill, east of the town's main square). INTERNATIONAL/ CONTINENTAL.

This plantation-style house was originally built in 1806 by owners of the Dewar's whisky distillery, who happened to be distantly related to Annie Palmer, the "White Witch of Rose Hall" (see "Seeing the Sights," above). Today it's run by an Austrian family team, who prepare well-flavored food for an appreciative clientele. Dinners include a shrimp-and-lobster cocktail, an excellent house salad, breaded breast of chicken, surf and turf, Wiener schnitzel, filet mignon, several different versions of dolphin, and a choice of dessert cakes. Many of the dishes are of a relatively standard international style, but others, especially the lobster, are worth the trek up the hill.

Sugar Mill Restaurant. At the Half Moon Club, Half Moon Golf Course, Rose Hall, along Rte. A1. ☎ **876/953-2314.** Reservations required. Main courses $18.50–$39.50. AE, MC, V. Daily noon–2:30pm and 7–10pm. INTERNATIONAL/CARIBBEAN.

You need to drive through the rolling landscape to get to this restaurant, near the stone ruin of a water wheel for a sugar plantation. Guests dine on an open terrace with a view of a pond, the water wheel, and plenty of greenery. You can also dine inside.

Although he came from Switzerland, it was in the Caribbean that chef Hans Schenk blossomed as a culinary artist. He has entertained everyone from the British royal family to Farouk, the former king of Egypt. Smoked north-coast marlin is a specialty. The chef makes the most elegant Jamaican bouillabaisse on the island and zesty jerk versions of pork, fish, or chicken. He also prepares the day's catch with considerable flair. Ask the waiter what's cooking in the curry pot. Chances are, it will be a Jamaican specialty such as goat, full of flavor and served with island chutney. Top your meal with a cup of unbeatable Blue Mountain coffee. Lunch is a simpler affair, perhaps an ackee burger with bacon, preceded by Mama's pumpkin soup and followed by a homemade rum-and-raisin ice cream.

Town House. 16 Church St. ☎ **876/952-2660.** Reservations recommended. Main courses $15–$30. AE, DC, MC, V. Mon–Sat 11:30am–3:30pm; daily 6–10:30pm. JAMAICAN/ INTERNATIONAL.

Housed in a redbrick building dating from 1765, the Town House is a tranquil luncheon choice. It offers sandwiches and salads, or more elaborate fare if your appetite demands it. At night it's floodlit, with outdoor dining on a veranda overlooking an 18th-century parish church. You can also dine in what used to be the cellars, where old ship lanterns provide a warm light. Soups, increasingly ignored in many restaurants, are a specialty here. The pepper pot or pumpkin is a delectable opening to a meal. The chef offers a wide selection of main courses, including the local favorite, red snapper en papillote (wrapped in parchment paper). We're also fond of the large rack of barbecued spareribs, with the owners' special Tennessee sauce. The pasta and steak dishes are good as well, especially the homemade fettuccine with whole shrimp and the perfectly aged New York strip steak. This restaurant often attracts the rich and famous.

12 Key West ⚓ ⚓ ⚓ ⚓ ⚓

Key West can't compete with the exotica of Martinique and Barbados, or with the shopping bargains of St. Thomas and St. Maarten. But no other Caribbean-area port of call offers such a sweeping choice of fine dining, easy-to-reach attractions, music, street entertainment, and roguish bars as this heavy-drinking, fun-loving town at the very end of the Florida Keys.

Key West has been growing in cruise-line popularity, much to the disdain of many local residents, who think the ships are making their town even more of a "carnival" than it already is. In the kind of civic action they say can only happen here, the locals have barred cruise ships from Mallory Dock after 5:30pm. No hulk of ocean-going metal is going to interfere with their long-standing, drink-in-hand ritual of watching the sun set over the Gulf of Mexico. Ships staying later must move to the Truman Annex, only a few blocks away, but well out of the sunset sight line.

The extraordinary 19th-century houses in Old Town are reason enough to visit Key West. It's the largest historical district on the National Register of Places. Nowhere else in the Caribbean offers such a vast assortment of clapboard-sided Bahamian architecture—all in the Victorian style and trimmed in gingerbread. But with a few exceptions, such as Harry S Truman's Little White House and Ernest Hemingway's writing abode, few of these structures are open to the public. And the Truman and Hemingway homes, as well as other attractions here, are likely to be crowded on cruise-ship days.

It's difficult to digest Key West without surrendering yourself for some time to its laid-back attitude and *joie de vivre*. But since you only have a day, flee the busy cruise docks and touristy Duval Street for a walk through hidden and more secluded byways, such as Olivia or William Street. Then you'll understand why Hemingway, Tennessee Williams, and so many other writers came to live in Key West.

Or you might want to spend your day in more active pursuits—playing golf or going diving or snorkeling. Be warned that Key West's beaches are severely limited and rather poor, so if you're a true beach buff, you may prefer a cruise to eastern Mexico, the U.S. Virgin Islands, Aruba, Barbados, or another island with better sand and surf.

COMING ASHORE

No port of call in the Caribbean is as convenient for cruise ship arrivals as Key West. Ships dock at Mallory Square, Old Town's most important plaza, or at nearby Truman Annex, a 5-minute stroll away. Both are on the Gulf of Mexico side of the island. Except for esoteric pockets, virtually everything is at your doorstep, including the two main arteries, Duval Street and Whitehead Street, each filled with shops, bars, restaurants, and the town's most important attractions.

FAST FACTS

Currency   Obviously, U.S. dollars are used here. You can change other major currencies at First State Bank, 1201 Simonton St. (☎ **305/296-8535**), open Monday through Friday from 9am to 3pm. On Friday they also reopen 4 to 6pm. There's a 2% to 4% exchange fee.

Information   **The Greater Key West Chamber of Commerce,** 402 Wall St. (☎ **305/294-5988**), lies near the cruise ship docks. This helpful agency answers questions about local activities, distributes free maps, and assists in arranging tours and fishing trips. Ask for *Pelican Path,* a free walking guide that documents the history and architecture of Old Town, and *Solares Hill's Walking and Biking Guide to Old Key West,* which contains eight walking tours.

SHORE EXCURSIONS

In Key West, it's a waste of time and money to take a shore excursion. You can get around on your own, seeing what you want to see and doing what you choose.

GETTING AROUND

The island is only 4 miles long and 2 miles wide, so getting around is easy. Hundreds of people who live here own bicycles instead of cars. The most popular sights, including the Hemingway House and the Harry S Truman Little White House, are within walking distance of the cruise docks, so you're hardly dependent on public transportation unless you wish to go to the beaches on the Atlantic side of the island.

The **East Martello Museum and Gallery,** (☎ **305/296-3913**) a National Historic Site housed in a Civil War fort, is out by the airport, an $18 round-trip taxi ride. Other than a handful of intriguing nautical exhibits and the great view you'll get of the Atlantic Ocean here, it isn't worth the time or money if you're on a limited schedule. It's open daily from 9:30am to 5pm, and it costs $6 for adults and $2 for children.

BICYCLES   Key West is a paradise for bikers, especially the historic Old Town. Except for the main thoroughfares, most streets are generally free of traffic. *Solares Hill's Walking and Biking Guide to Old Key West* is distributed free by the Greater Key West Chamber of Commerce (see "Fast Facts," above). The guide contains eight tours, including one of the Key West Cemetery.

One of the largest and best places to rent a bicycle or motorbike is **Keys Moped and Scooter Rental,** 523 Truman Ave., about a block off Duval Street (☎ **305/294-0399**). Cruise ship passengers might opt for a 3-hour motor scooter rental for $12, or all day for $14. One-speed, big-wheeled "beach-cruiser" bicycles with soft seats and big baskets for toting beachwear rent for $4 for 8 hours. The outlet is open daily throughout the year from 9am to 6pm.

BUS   The cheapest way to see the island is by bus, which costs only 75¢ for adults, 35¢ for senior citizens and children 6 years and older (kids 5 and under ride free). You don't get the narration provided by the trolley tours described below, but you can ride around the island in about an hour. For information, call **The City of Key West and Transit Authority** (☎ **305/292-8165**).

CAR RENTALS   Walking or cycling is better than renting a car here. But if you do rent, try **Hertz,** 3491 S. Roosevelt Blvd. (☎ **800/654-3131** or 305/294-1039), **Tropical Rent-a-Car,** 1300 Duval St. (☎ **305/294-8136**), or **Enterprise Rent-a-Car,** 3031 N. Roosevelt Blvd. (☎ **800/325-8007** or 305/292-0222). If you're visiting in winter, make reservations at least a week in advance.

TAXIS   Island taxis operate around the clock, but are small and not suited for sightseeing tours. They will, however, take you to the beach and arrange for you to be picked up at a certain time. You can call one of four different services: **Florida Keys Taxi** (☎ **305/294-2227**), **Maxi-Taxi Sun Cab System** (☎ **305/294-2222**), **Pink Cabs** (☎ **305/296-6666**), or **Island Transportation Services** (☎ **305/296-1800**). Prices are uniform; the meter starts at $1.40, and adds 35¢ per quarter mile.

TROLLEY CAR TOURS   These tours are the best way to see Key West in a short time. In fact, the **Conch Tour Train** is Key West's most famous tourist attraction. It's a narrated 90-minute tour, going up and down all the most interesting streets and

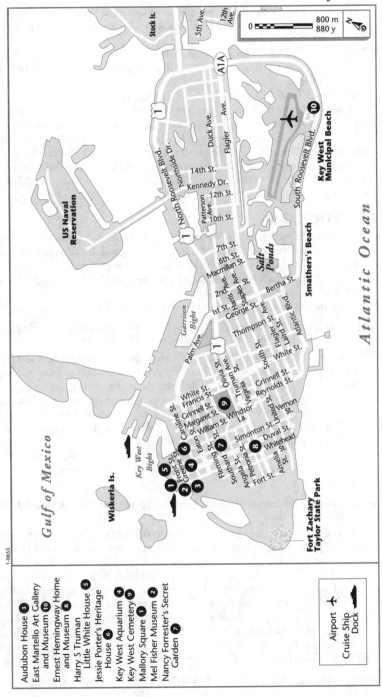

Key West

0	800 m
	880 y

Stock Is.

5th Ave.
12th Ave.

A1A

1

Duck Ave.

Flagler Ave.

US Naval Reservation

North Roosevelt Blvd.
Northside Dr.

14th St.
Kennedy Dr.
12th St.
Patterson Ave.
10th St.

1

7th St.
6th St.
Macmillan St.
2nd Ave.
Harris Ave.
George St.
Staples Ave.

Salt Ponds

Bertha St.

Garrison Bight

Thompson St.

Palm Ave.

1

White St.
Francis St.
Olivia St.
Truman Ave.
Flagler St.
Laird St.
Atlantic Blvd.

South St.

Smathers's Beach

South Roosevelt Blvd.

Key West Municipal Beach

🔟

Gulf of Mexico

Atlantic Ocean

Wiskeria Is.

Key West Bight

White St.
Caroline St.
Grinnell St.
Margaret St.
William St.
Eaton St.
Fleming St.
Southard St.
Angela St.
Petronia St.
Fort St.
Amelia St.

Front St.
Greene St.

Windsor La.
Simonton St.
Duval St.
Whitehead St.
United St.

Virginia St.
Reynolds St.
Grinnell St.
Vernon St.

①
②
③
④
⑥
⑨
⑦
⑧

Fort Zachary Taylor State Park

1-0653

Audubon House ③
East Martello Art Gallery and Museum ⑩
Ernest Hemingway Home and Museum ⑧
Harry S Truman Little White House ⑤
Jessie Porter's Heritage House ⑥
Key West Aquarium ④
Key West Cemetery ⑨
Mallory Square ①
Mel Fisher Museum ②
Nancy Forrester's Secret Garden ⑦

✈ Airport
⚓ Cruise Ship Dock

commenting on 60 local sites, giving you lots of lore about the town. The depot is located at Mallory Square near the cruise ship docks. Trains depart every 30 minutes. The trip is nonstop, unlike tours on the Old Town Trolley (see below), which allow you to get on and off. Departures are daily from 9am to 4:30pm and cost $15 for adults, $7 for children ages 4 to 12 (3 and under free). Call ☎ **305/294-5161** for more information.

Old Town Trolley is less popular than the Conch Tour Train, but appeals to visitors who want more flexibility. It lets you get off and explore a particular attraction, then reboard another of its trains later. Professional guides spin tall tales about Key West as you ride. The trolleys operate 7 days a week from 9am to 4:30pm, with departures every 30 minutes at convenient spots throughout town. You can board the trolley near the cruise docks (look for signposts). Call ☎ **305/296-6688** for more information. Tours cost $16 for adults, $7 for children ages 4 to 12, free for children under 4.

SEEING THE SIGHTS

If the lines aren't too long, you'll want to visit the Harry S Truman Little White House and the Hemingway House. But don't feel obligated. If you want to see and capture the real-life mood and charm of Key West in a short time, you'll need to leave the most-visited attractions to your fellow passengers and head for the ones we've indicated with stars below.

These sites all lie within an easy walk of the cruise ship docks.

Audubon House. 205 Whitehead St. at Greene St. ☎ **305/294-2116.** Admission $7.50 adults, $5 students, $3.50 children 6–12 (5 and under free). Daily 9:30am–4:45pm.

This house is dedicated to the 1832 Key West sojourn of the famous naturalist and ornithologist John James Audubon. Audubon didn't live in this three-story building dating from the mid-1840s, but it's filled with the largest collection of his engravings in Florida. Many of the master artist's original works are here, some from his famous "Birds of America" and double "Elephant" folios produced between 1826 and 1838. Though Audubon didn't live here, Capt. John Geiger, once one of the wealthiest men in Florida, did. The main reason to visit this house is not necessarily to learn about Audubon, but to see how wealthy sailors lived in Key West in the 19th century. The lush tropical gardens surrounding the house are worth the price of admission.

Harry S Truman Little White House. 111 Front St. ☎ **305/294-9911.** Admission $7.50 adults, $3.75 children 12 and under. Daily 9am–5pm.

This small house, the president's vacation home, offers a rare glimpse of a president at play. It's part of the 103-acre Truman Annex near the cruise ship docks. During his first visit in November 1946, Truman became enamored of Key West, and he returned every few months until he left the presidency in 1953. Here he wore those florid "From Here to Eternity" sports shirts mocked by news cameramen of the day. First Lady Bess fled when local politicos like flamboyant Monroe County Sheriff John Spottswood showed up for bourbon and poker games. Truman took swims, long walks, and held press conferences in Key West. File this statistic under presidential trivia: It cost only $35,000 for Miami interior designer Haygood Lassiter to restore the Little White House for Bess and Harry. The house takes less than an hour to tour.

Hemingway House. 907 Whitehead St. ☎ **305/294-1575.** Admission $6.50 adults, $4 children ages 6–12 (5 and under free). Daily 9am–5pm (last tour at 4:30pm).

The long lines may discourage a visit here, especially when both cruise ships and tour buses from Miami arrive at the same time. Still, many sightseers endure the wait to see where "Papa" lived with his second wife, Pauline. He first occupied the Spanish-colonial-style house in 1931 and owned it until his death in 1961. Today it's furnished much as the Nobel Prize winner left it. The chandeliers, for example, came from Spain, Africa, and Cuba.

Standing up at a raised typewriter in a studio annex, Hemingway wrote such classics here as *For Whom the Bell Tolls, The Green Hills of Africa, A Farewell to Arms,* and *The Snows of Kilimanjaro*. The Hemingways installed Key West's first swimming pool here at a cost of $20,000—"Papa" was furious at his wife for "taking the last penny I've got" to pay for it. He had some 50 polydactyl (many-toed) cats, whose descendants—including Marilyn Monroe, Ava Gardner, and Greta Garbo—still live on the grounds. Ginger Rogers can usually be found snoozing away on the cool tile floor of the bathroom at the top of the stairs.

⭐ **Jessie Porter's Heritage House & Robert Frost Cottage.** 410 Caroline St. ☎ **305/296-3575.** Admission $6, free for children 11 and under. Mon–Sat 10am–5pm, Sun 11am–4pm.

Time was, if Jessie Porter Newton called you over for a shrimp dinner on her back porch, you thought you'd been summoned to paradise. A woman of immense charm, "Miss Jessie" was the *grande dame* of Key West. This Steel Magnolia virtually launched the old-island restoration movement. She loved to invite the celebrities of her day to visit—everyone from Tennessee Williams ("I get so angry at Tenn for the way he depicts Southern womanhood") to "my girlhood friend" Gloria Swanson ("when she lived in Key West she was just an army brat"). On occasion, family friend Robert Frost stayed in a cottage out back, which can be visited. Although Miss Jessie might one day send down a bolt of lightning to stop the invasion, the world—cruise passengers, mainland tourists, etc.—now crosses her once hallowed ground, rubbernecking its way through her antique-filled rooms, inspecting her mementos and the exotic treasures collected by six generations of the Porter family.

Key West Aquarium. 1 Whitehead St., at Mallory Market (on the waterfront at Mallory Square). ☎ **305/296-2051.** Admission $8 adults, $4 children (2 and under free). Daily 10am–6pm. Daily tours at 11am, 1, 3, and 4:30pm.

This aquarium, in operation since 1932, was the first tourist attraction built in the Florida Keys. A variety of colorful tropical fish and sea turtles live here in a 50,000-gallon tank. The aquarium's special feature is a "touch tank," where you can feel such creatures as a horseshoe crab, sea squirt, sea urchin, starfish, and, of course, conch, the town's mascot and symbol. Try to time your visit for one of the tours, as the guides are not only knowledgeable in explaining the habits and habitats of these creatures, but entertaining as well. You'll have the chance to pet a shark, too, if that's your idea of a good time.

⭐ **Key West Cemetery.** Main entrance at Margaret St. and Passover Lane. ☎ **305/296-2175.** Free admission. Daily sunrise to sunset. Guided tours ($10) Tues–Wed at 9am and 11am. From Mallory Square proceed south on Whitehead to Angela St., then east 4 blocks.

A visit to a spooky graveyard might not be your idea of a good time while cruising the Caribbean, but in Key West the cemetery—21 prime acres in the heart of the historic district—is the island's foremost offbeat attraction. Stone-encased caskets rest on top of the earth, because graves dug into the ground would hit the water table. The cemetery is filled with remembrances, including a memorial and resting place for those who died when the U.S. battleship *Maine* was sunk in Havana Harbor in 1898, touching off the Spanish-American War. There's also a touch of humor here: one gravestone proclaims, "I Told You I Was Sick." A grieving widow left this message etched on stone on her husband's plot: "At Least I Know Where He Is Sleeping Tonight."

○ **Mel Fisher Maritime Heritage Society Museum.** 200 Greene St. ☎ **305/294-2633.**
Admission $6.50 adults, $3 children 6–12 (5 and under free). Daily 9:30am–5pm.

Treasure hunter Mel Fisher wears heavy gold necklaces that he likes to say are worth a "king's ransom." He isn't exaggerating. After long, arduous, and risky dives, Fisher and his associates plucked more than $400 million in gold and silver from the ship-wrecked Spanish galleons *Santa Margarita* and *Nuestra Señora de Atocha,* which were lost on hurricane-tossed seas some 350 years ago. A 77.76-karat natural emerald crystal was appraised at Tiffany's at a quarter of a million dollars. Now this array of extraordinary long-lost Spanish jewelry, doubloons, and silver and gold bullion are displayed at this museum, a true treasure trove near the cruise ship docks.

○ **Nancy Forrester's Secret Garden.** 1 Free School Lane, off Simonton between Southard and Fleming sts. ☎ **305/294-0015.** Admission $6 adults, $2 children 6–12 (5 and under free). Nov–Mar, daily 10am–5pm. Apr–Oct, call for appointment.

Perhaps inspired by Margaret O'Brien's 1940s film, *The Secret Garden,* this garden in the heart of Key West is the most lavish and verdant in town. In 1969, Pennsylvania-born Nancy Forrester, rescued a cluster of towering sapodillas from chain saws and bulldozers and cleared away carloads of litter and broken glass. She then planted some 130 to 150 species of palms, palmettos, climbing vines, and ground covers, creating a blanket of lush, tropical greenery. The location is near the highest point of Key West, Solares Hill. Botanists cite this as the only frost-free garden in the United States devoted exclusively to exotic tropical plants. Before coming here from your cruise ship (a 30-minute walk from the docks), stop at a deli to get supplies for a picnic, which you can enjoy at tables in the garden.

FLIGHTSEEING

For a bird's eye view of the Florida Keys and surrounding waters, take a ride with **Island Aeroplane Tours,** 3469 S. Roosevelt Blvd., Key West Airport (☎ **305/294-8687**). Up to two passengers in an open cockpit biplane can choose from seven different tours, ranging from $55 to $300 for two. One tour takes in the south shore, beaches, and resorts, but the best tour blankets a vast area of the Florida Keys, flying over all of Key West (especially the Old Town) and uninhabited islands such as Mud Key. Flights range from 20 minutes to 1 hour and 15 minutes. It's a $9 one-way taxi fare to reach the airport from the cruise ship docks.

Seaplanes of Key West, (☎ **305/294-0709**), follows a different route, offering a half-day tour of remote Dry Tortugas (70 miles west of Key West) in a five-passenger single-engine plane. During the 40-minute flight, you'll fly low over shallow waters where you can view colorful sea life and sunken vessels. Landing at Fort Jefferson National Park, you can visit a remote and interesting national fort, where Dr. Samuel Mudd was imprisoned for treating John Wilkes Booth after Booth assassinated President Lincoln in 1865. You can then go swimming or snorkeling over the island's rainbow-hued coral reefs. This is an unusual trip generally overlooked by cruise ship passengers yet fitting well between cruise ship departures and arrivals. Half-day tours cost $159 per person.

SHOPPING

Shopping by cruise ship passengers has become a local joke in Key West. "Just how many T-shirts can you buy?" asked one local merchant, trying to peddle his jewelry.

Within a 12-block radius of Old Town, you'll find mostly tawdry and outrageously overpriced merchandise. The most touristy shops, some hustling T-shirts at $125 to $150 each, are clustered at the cruise ship docks.

But Key West also has many merchants who have assembled interesting and unusual merchandise. Their stores lie much farther along Duval Street, the main drag leading to the Atlantic, and on hidden back streets. Arm yourself with a good map, and seek them out. You can reach all the stores recommended below from the cruise ship docks in a 15-to-20-minute stroll. Store hours are generally daily from 10am to 6pm, but most shops are always open if a cruise ship is in port.

Key West isn't filled with bargains, but in most stores you can generally negotiate the price downward, especially on big-ticket items.

Bird in Hand. 203 Simonton St. ☎ **305/296-6324.**

This is the number-one gift store in Key West, with collectibles ranging from the sophisticated to the corny scattered over two rambling floors. Its wares are not remotely related to Key West, the tropics, or your cruise experience, but business is nevertheless brisk. Especially appealing are the Indonesian statues and the Swarovski crystal from Austria. They will ship anything.

✪ **Cavanaugh's.** 520 Front St. ☎ **305/296-3343.**

A treasure trove of merchandise from all over the world, Cavanaugh's is likely to have anything, especially the most unusual furnishings and exotic artwork in the Keys. A shopping trip here is like wandering through the souks in the dusty back alleys of the Arab world. The merchandise isn't cheap, since you pay a high price to subsidize someone else's buying spree in the East.

Emeralds International. 718 Duval St. ☎ **305/294-2060.**

The owner of the store, Marcial de Gomar, developed "emerald fever" while working as the teenage interpreter for a geologist exploring the mines of Colombia. The green stones, which have been prized by everyone from the ancient Egyptians to the Incas, are often opaque; unlike diamonds, they're prized more for their seductive color than their glitter. Prices in this small but select boutique range from $50 to $150,000. Many cruise ship passengers shop here more modestly for "conch pearls."

✪ **Fast Buck Freddie's.** 500 Duval St., at Fleming St. ☎ **305/294-2007.**

Old-timers looking for the Kress Five & Dime that stood for years on this spot are in for a shock—no store in all the Florida Keys is as fun and hip as this one. But the emporium appeals to all people—or at least all those who appreciate style and whimsy. It's a small, eclectic department store with fashions, table settings, costumes, chic sportswear, beachwear, linens, and toys. Sometimes the stock depends on what's happening in Key West at the time—during October's Fantasy Fest, for example, they stockpile costumes ghoulish, glittery, and gauche.

✪ **Fletcher's.** 1024 Duval St. ☎ **305/294-2032.**

No other store in town celebrates the bedrock that forms the foundation of Key West as brilliantly as Fletcher's, whose inventory is based on high style and a sense of respect for the millenniums. As any salesperson will tell you, the Keys are a relatively youthful conglomeration of coral, formed 300,000 years ago from the exoskeletons of sea creatures that thrived in the warm, shallow waters south of the Florida peninsula. For anywhere between $50 and $5,000, you can buy a slice of Keys limestone, artfully crafted into lamps, tables, bookends, or the kind of soaring columns that would look good embedded on an outdoor terrace or in a tropical greenhouse. The best pieces have fossilized seashells and ancient crustacea visibly embedded in the rock. Other objects and artifacts here (chandeliers, mirrors, furniture, wrought iron) from South America, Mexico, and Asia are suitably rare, eclectic, and stylish, but prices are high.

✪ **Gingerbread Square Gallery.** 1207 Duval St. ☎ **305/296-8900.**

This is the most prestigious art gallery in town, with paintings celebrating the whimsy of Key West itself. The owner, former Green Beret Sal Salinero, displays many of his own decorative award-winning paintings, but space is devoted to other artists as well. Best known is John Kiraly, whose canvases manage to infuse Key West with Capri, Jamaica, and the lost kingdom of Atlantis. The gallery is "re-hung" every 2 weeks, and always features an assortment of ceramics, crystal, and paintings ranging from $25 to $35,000.

Haitian Art Company. 600 Frances St. ☎ **305/296-8932.**

Established in 1978 in an unpretentious clapboard-sided cottage at the corner of Southard Street, this art gallery claims to inventory the largest collection of Haitian paintings in the United States. More than 300 artists are represented here, their work graphically illustrating a changing and troubled nation. Prices range from $15 to $5,000. St-Louis Blaise, Gourgue, and Jean-Baptiste Jean are among the Haitian artists represented.

H. T. Chittum & Co. 725 Duval St. ☎ **305/292-9002.**

On first glance this clothing and sporting goods emporium looks like an L.L. Bean rip-off, but a second look confirms it has its own distinctive style. The clothing is actually less folksy and more sophisticated than L.L. Bean, with everything you'd need to wear to go canoeing, hiking, or rock climbing. Some items are also suitable for casual street wear.

✪ **Key West Aloe, Inc.** 524 Front St. or 540 Greene St. ☎ **800/445-2563** in the U.S., or 305/295-0775.

No other establishment in Florida bases its profits as firmly upon the healing qualities of a single plant. The aloe plant is a hardy desert shrub whose spear-shaped leaves contain fluids that Native Americans knew were beneficial for the healing of the skin. Established in the early 1970s, this organization imports massive quantities of dried and pulverized aloe from plantations in West Texas. The powder is then rehydrated and mixed with perfumes and additives to create one of the most instantly recognizable lines of skin and sun-care products in Florida. The shop's inventory includes shaving cream, after-shave lotion, sunburn ointments, and fragrances for men and women based on such tropical essences as hibiscus, frangipani, and white ginger. One scent was specifically formulated to suggest the smell of the ocean and is marketed as the perfect cruise cologne. The largest selection of products is available at the company's Front Street branch near the cruise ship dock.

Key West Hand Print Fashions and Fabrics. 201 Simonton St. ☎ **800/866-0333** in the U.S., or 305/294-9535.

This company's juicy compendium of scandals, near-bankruptcies, deceptions, and resurrections has titillated Key Westers for years. It was launched in 1961 by a group of gay men. Long ago, designer Lily Pulitzer popularized its silk-screened fabrics, which were all the rage for 2 decades. Today, the shop is still committed to bold, tropical prints despite current fashion trends. They display handprinted scarves with coordinated handbags, and rack after rack of busily patterned sundresses and cocktail dresses that will make you look jaunty on the deck of an oceanliner.

Key West Island Bookstore. 513 Fleming St. ☎ **305/294-2904.**

This has been called a bookstore for writers. The store is well stocked in books on Key West and has Florida's largest collection of works by and about Hemingway. In the rear is a rare-book section where you may want to browse, if not buy.

⭐ Favorite Key West Experiences

WHERE THE WRITERS LIVED   Key West has been home to many writers besides Hemingway. **Tennessee Williams,** who wrote some of his most performed plays here, lived in a red-shuttered cottage at 1413 Duncan St. Many major stars arrived on his doorstep in the 1950s and 1960s, hoping for a casting recommendation. The house—now privately owned—was Williams' principal residence from the late 1940s until his death in 1983. He built a writing studio and added a swimming pool with a mosaic based on one of his most famous plays, *The Rose Tattoo.*

Phil Caputo, Pulitzer Prize–winning author of *Rumor of War* (a journalistic account of the Vietnam conflict) and other bestsellers, lived at 621 Caroline St. in the 1970s. The Classic Revival house represents one of the most beautiful examples of architecture created by ship carpenters in the 19th century. They worked with Dade County pine, which resists termites. You can view the house from the outside.

A SUNSET RITUAL   If your ship leaves late enough, you can take in a unique local celebration: viewing the sunset from Mallory Dock. Sunset-watching is good fun all over the world, but in Key West it's been turned into a carnival-like, almost pagan celebration—a "blazing festival of joy," some call it. People from all over the world begin to crowd Mallory Square even before the sun starts to fall, bringing the place alive with entertainment—everything from a string band to a unicyclist wriggling free of a straitjacket. A juggler might delight the crowd with a machete and a flaming stick. You're likely to see everything here, including the Cookie Lady hustling her brownies. Hers are safe and good to eat, but on occasion other peddlers have pushed illegal hashish brownies made from Alice B. Toklas' special recipe. The main entertainment, however, is that massive fireball falling out of view, which is always greeted with hysterical applause.

Michael. 400C Duval St. ☎ **305/294-2488.**

Coins from sunken wrecks such as the *Atocha* are widely available for sale in Key West. Other antique coins for sale here were discovered at sites in the Middle East. Before buying, check the settings—all are not created equal. Settings at Michael are "numismatically correct"—that is, they don't damage or alter the shape of the coin. Settings range from the strong and simple to the elaborate and ornate, with prices going from $60 to $22,000. Skip the branches of this store near the cruise docks and head instead for this main store, which has far superior stock.

✪ **Pandemonium.** 825 Duval St. ☎ **305/294-0351.**

This shop reigns unchallenged as the most avant-garde art gallery in Key West. It defines its work as Oriental Art Deco/Tropical Art Deco. The fastest-moving objects are one-of-a-kind ceramics created by China-born, London-educated Valerie Hoh and her colleague, Dan Gore. Even if you hadn't necessarily planned to install a tile mural or frieze in your bathroom, kitchen, or bar, take a second look at these tongue-in-cheek homages to the tropics *à la Key West.* Also available are couture-quality, one-of-a-kind silk and linen cruising garments for him or for her.

Tikal Trading Co. 129 Duval St. ☎ **305/296-4463.**

This outlet designs and manufactures its own line of women's clothing. They have original floral prints in a 40/60 blend and hand-woven linen clothing without prints. The two lines are made as mother/daughter wear—in other words, you can buy two outfits with similar designs and matching accessories.

Waterfront Market. 201 William St. ☎ **305/294-8418.**

This is a deli, bakery, seafood market, gourmet shop, and the best place for hot sauces, beer, and wine. Come here if you want supplies for a picnic lunch. The best of their array of freshly made salads is the curried chicken salad. Sandwiches can be prepared as you want them and while you wait from a wide variety of breads, Boar's Head meats, cheeses, and vegetables.

✪ **Whitehead Street Pottery.** 1011 Whitehead St. ☎ **305/294-5067.**

This pottery shop is tucked into an unpretentious residential neighborhood in a former Cuban *bodega* (grocery store), built before 1890. About a decade ago, potters Charles Pearson and Timothy Roeder converted what had been a termite-infested shack into a seamless showroom whose clean lines might remind you of a meditation chamber in Japan. Pottery includes traditional, fully rounded objects, often fired with copper oxides, as well as slab-built pots reminiscent of T'ang and Sung Dynasty pieces from China. Many of their works have been praised for their strong emphasis on architectural line and form and *raku* glazes.

BEACHES

Beaches are not the compelling reason to visit this land of mangrove-edged marshes and rocky outcroppings. Most beaches are manmade, often with imported Bahamian or mainland Florida sand. Those we mention below are free and open to the public daily from 7am to 11pm. There are few facilities, except locals hawking beach umbrellas, food, and drinks.

    Fort Zachary Taylor State Beach is the best and the closest to the cruise ship docks, a 12-minute walk away. This 51-acre manmade beach is adjacent to the ruins of Fort Taylor, once known as Fort Forgotten because it was buried under tons of sand. The beach is fine for sunbathing and picnicking and is suitable for snorkeling, but rocks make it difficult to swim. To get there, go through the gates leading into Truman Annex. Watering holes near one end of the beach include the raffish Green Parrot Bar and a booze-and-burger joint, *Gato Gordo* (Fat Cat).

    If you want to escape your fellow cruise ship passengers, consider **Higgs Memorial Beach,** a 25-minute walk from the harbor near the end of White Street, one of the main east-west arteries. You'll find lots of sand and picnic tables sheltered from the sun. Named in honor of one of Florida's most colorful former senators, **Smathers Beach** is the longest (about 1½ miles), most isolated, and least accessorized beach in town. Unfortunately it's a $9 one-way taxi ride from the cruise docks. The beach borders South Roosevelt Boulevard. Regrettably, there's no shade here.

    In the 1950s, **Southernmost Beach** drew Tennessee Williams and a gay coterie, but today it's likely to fill up with visitors staying in the lackluster motels nearby. Except for a nearby restaurant, facilities are nonexistent. The beach lies at the foot of Duval Street on the Atlantic side, across the island from the cruise ship docks. It takes about 20 minutes to walk there along Duval Street from the docks. The beach boasts some white sand, but is not good for swimming. Nevertheless, it's one of the island's most frequented.

FISHING, GOLF, DIVING, KAYAKING, SAILING & BOATING

FISHING As Hemingway, an avid fisherman, would attest, the waters off the Florida Keys are some of the world's finest fishing grounds. You can follow in his wake aboard the 40-foot *Linda D III* and *Linda D IV* (☎ **800/299-9798** in the U.S., or 305/296-9798), which offer the best deep-sea fishing here. Arrangements should be made a week or so before you are due in port. Four-hour jaunts, with all equipment included, cost $375 to $450 for the entire boat or $100 for a chair.

GOLF   The Florida Keys contain a smattering of golf courses, some better than others. The only golf course that's easily accessible lies 6 miles from the cruise docks, near the southern tip of neighboring Stock Island. Redesigned in 1982 by architect Rees Jones, the **Key West Resort Golf Course,** 6450 E. Junior College Rd. (☎ 305/294-5232), features a challenging terrain of coral rock, sandtraps, mangrove swamp, and pines. The course is a 10- to 15-minute, $15 taxi ride from the dock each way. Greens fees are $80, including use of a motorized cart, for 18 holes. A full set of golf clubs rents for $30. The pursers of many cruise ships do a brisk business booking tee-off times at least a day in advance. In some cases, the cruise line itself will provide transportation from the docks directly to the golf course.

SCUBA DIVING   The resort's largest dive outfitter is **Captain's Corner,** 0 Duval St., opposite the Pier House Hotel a block from the dock (☎ 305/296-8865). In fact, this is the most versatile dive outfit in the Florida Keys. The five-star PADI operation has 11 instructors, a 60-foot dive boat (used by Timothy "James Bond" Dalton during the filming of *License to Kill*), and a well-trained staff. Most cruise-ship passengers opt for a two-tank dive departing every morning at 9:30am and returning at 1:15pm. The $60-per-person cost includes use of equipment and two 1-hour dives at two different locations above the teeming reef. To reach the departure point, make a left along the docks, then walk for about a block to the northern tip of Duval Street.

KAYAKING   For years, ecologically conscious visitors to the Keys have focused on skin-diving above the coral reefs of the Keys' Atlantic coast, ignoring the marine treasures thriving in the murkier, and much shallower, waters of the Gulf of Mexico. In the early 1990s, an enterprising group of nature lovers changed that focus and established ✪ **Florida Keys Back Country Adventures,** 6810 Front St., Stock Island (☎ 305/296-0362). The only way to transit the shallow waters of the middle and lower keys is via kayak. Most cruise ship passengers opt for the half-day tours, which depart daily at 9am from Cudjoe Marina and last 3¹/₂ hours. These shallow waters, from 12 to 36 inches deep, are home to endless fish, stingrays, spiny lobsters, and crustaceans. You'll also see abundant bird life, especially hawks, bald eagles, and ospreys. Kayak tours are an ecologically sensitive way to avoid the "party cruise" mode of sun and booze—and many visitors emerge with a renewed sense of respect for the fragile ecosystems comprising the Florida Keys. There's no time for snorkeling during the half-day tour, although you can always dip into the cool waters wherever you came across a clean, sandy bottom.

The main drawback is the time and expense of getting to the boats. The company will, however, send a minivan for up to six passengers, and charge $20 round-trip for everyone if notified in advance. Otherwise it's a $12 ride by taxi. The half-day tour costs $35 per person.

SAILING & BOATING   Two of the largest and most crowded of the craft available for tours are **Fury Catamarans,** a pair of double-hulled vessels with metal stairs descending directly into the sea (☎ 305/294-8899). They depart from the Hilton Resort Marina, at the western end of Greene Street. A half-day tour devoted to reef snorkeling, priced at $38, offers a first-hand view of underwater marine life. Morning tours last from 9:30am to 12:30pm; afternoon sessions are from 1 to 4pm.

You'll have a different type of experience aboard the ***Reef Chief,*** a 65-foot, two-masted wooden schooner built in the 1970s and modeled on the forms made popular in the Chesapeake Bay during the 19th century (☎ 305/292-1345). The 3¹/₂-hour snorkeling jaunts are closely synchronized with the arrival and departures of cruise ships, departing daily at 9am, 10:30am, or 2:30pm. Morning tours cost $35 per participant; afternoon tours cost $40. The craft moors at the Safe Harbor Marina on

Stock Island, a 15-minute, $12 one-way taxi ride from the docks. *Reef Chief's* dark green hull always drops anchor for around 90 minutes above reefs teeming with aquatic life. The shoals you'll visit will be less crowded than those visited by ships berthed at points closer to the cruise docks.

The ***Pride of Key West*** (☎ **305/296-6293**) is a 65-foot catamaran power boat. Its cruises depart at noon and 2pm, last 2 hours, and cost $20 for adults or $10 for children 5 to 12 (ages 4 and under sail free). The boat is wheelchair accessible. Departures are from the foot of Duval Street, 2 blocks from Mallory Square, close to the cruise ship docks. Two TV monitors show videos during the cruise. Viewing wells are found on either end of the boat.

A radically different type of seagoing experience—one more concerned with life below the waves than the view from above—is available here on the only ship of its kind plying U.S. waters. The **MV *Discovery*** (☎ **305/293-0099**) is a 78-foot motor craft with 20 large viewing windows (angled at 45 degrees) set below the water line. Passengers can view reef life from the safety and comfort of below deck. The 2-hour tour costs $18 for adults, $12 for children under 12, and departs from Land's End Village & Marina at the western end of Margaret Street, a 6-block walk from the cruise ship docks. Morning tours depart daily at 9:30am in the off-season, daily at 10:30am December through April.

DINING

All the restaurants listed below are within an easy 5- to 15-minute walk of the docks. Many passengers prefer to have their lunch at one of Key West's legendary bars (see "Pub Crawling," below). Several "raw bars" near the dock area offer seafood, including oysters and clams, although the king here is conch—served grilled, ground in burgers, made into a chowder, fried in batter as fritters, or served raw in a conch salad.

Even if you don't have lunch, at least sample the local favorites, a slice of Key lime pie with a Cuban coffee. The pie's unique flavor is achieved from the juice and minced rind of the local, piquant Key lime.

✪ **Bagatelle.** 115 Duval St., at Front St. ☎ **305/296-6609.** Main courses $17–24; lunches from $8. AE, DC, DISC, MC, V. Daily 11:30am–3pm and 5:30–10:30pm. CARIBBEAN/INTERNATIONAL.

Cruise ship passengers on a return visit to Key West often ask for "The Rose Tattoo," a historic old restaurant named for the Tennessee Williams film partially shot on the island. The restaurant is now the Bagatelle, one of Key West's finest. It's housed in what once was a cigar-factory foreman's home built in the 1890s. In the 1970s owners added a curving veranda—a great place to dine in fine weather. Bagatelle is one of the few so-called special restaurants open at lunch—look for daily specials or stick to the chef's better dishes, such as conch ceviche (thinly sliced raw conch marinated in lime juice and herbs). Keys pasta is served with fresh local seafood, and Jamaican chicken (sautéed in curry with banana, rum, papaya, and coconut) is a spicy local favorite, though too sweet for some tastes. Most offerings here are imaginative, particularly in the use of island spices. The waiters are often more hip than the clients.

✪ **Blue Heaven.** 729 Thomas St. ☎ **305/296-8666.** Main courses $9–$18; lunches $4.75–$11; breakfast from $4. DISC, MC, V. Tues–Sun 8am–3pm and 6–10:30pm. INTERNATIONAL.

The long lines often forming outside tell the story: This dive serves some of the best food in town. The building housing this restaurant once served as a bordello and later, in the 1930s, as the site of Friday night boxing matches. At times, Hemingway, himself a boxer, would oversee the fights. Today the neighborhood is one of the roughest in Key West. Jimmy Buffett shows up on occasion, and he wrote a song about the place, "Blue Heaven Rendezvous."

The chefs get the freshest produce they can find and enhance their dishes with herbs and delicately dosed spices. Their carrot and curry soup and their zesty barbecue shrimp make for good openings. Some of their finest food is fresh local fish, most often grouper or red snapper. Their hot and spicy jerk chicken is as fine as that served in Jamaica. You can also order vegetarian dishes. Save room for the worthy dessert special, Banana Heaven, with Betty's banana bread and flambéed bananas in spicy rum served with homemade vanilla bean ice cream. It's almost a meal unto itself.

✪ **Camille's.** 703½ Duval St., between Angela and Petronia sts. ☎ **305/296-4811.** Breakfast from $3.50; lunch platters/sandwiches $5.95–$12.95. AE, MC, V. Sun–Mon 8am–3pm, Tues–Sat 8am–10pm. AMERICAN.

This unpretentious, hip cafe, decorated with pictures of movie stars, serves the best breakfast in town, as well as best lunch value. Pancakes "made from scratch" are delectable, as are the waffles and French toast. The three-egg omelets are without competition on Duval Street; some of them feature broccoli and smoked Gouda. In the afternoon, sample one of the homemade soups, a perfectly prepared chicken salad, or perhaps a sandwich made from the catch of the day served on fresh bread. The Key lime pie appears beneath a cloud of meringue sprinkled with perfectly shaped drops of caramel. It's the island's best.

El Siboney. 900 Catherine St. ☎ **305/296-4184.** Main courses $5.95–$13.95. No credit cards. Mon–Sat 11am–9:30pm. Closed 2 weeks in June and July. CUBAN.

Key West is famous for its Cuban restaurants, which flourished here long before anybody ever heard of Fidel Castro. A $6 taxi ride will bring you back to their golden days of the 1950s. At El Siboney, no one's ever heard of nouvelle Cuban cuisine. Instead, all the time-tested favorites appear on the menu, especially the delectable *ropa vieja* or shredded beef. Roast pork is pungently flavored with garlic and tart sour oranges grown in the Keys' limestone soil. The cook makes the best shrimp *enchilado* in town, or you can happily settle for the *paella Valenciana* (minimum of two). Black beans, of course, accompany everything, and you can wash it all down with homemade *sangría*. This is an aggressively ugly establishment, with plastic-covered tables and a flaming red decor, but that's part of its allure.

Flamingo Crossing. 1105 Duval St., at Virginia St. ☎ **305/296-6124.** Ice cream and sorbets $2.25–$3.75. Daily 11am–midnight. ICE CREAM.

This corner parlor serves the best ice cream in the Florida Keys, each luscious scoop made with natural ingredients, often pure fruit and cream. Cuban coffee, soursop, rum raisin, even frothy guanabana, mango, and papaya are just some of the flavors. After ordering, select a table outside this little cottage and feast on the additive-free delight. They also offer milkshakes and frozen yogurt. The operation was set up by Eleanor and Dan McConnell, who came to Key West from Chicago in 1987. Dan operates Mosquito Coast next door, which specializes in nature tours and ocean kayaking.

Half Shell Raw Bar. Land's End Marina, foot of Margaret St. ☎ **305/294-7496.** Main courses $10.50–$24.95; sandwiches $6.95–$8.95. Mon–Sat 11am–11pm, Sun noon–10:30pm. SEAFOOD.

This is Key West's original raw bar, offering fresh fish, oysters, and shrimp direct from its own fish market. In season, the best offerings are succulent stone crab claws and tasty Florida lobster. The Raw Bar also features Gulf oysters, top-neck clams, and beer-steamed shrimp. It was deservedly voted "best raw bar" in the Keys by *The*

Miami Herald. For appetizers, the chefs make a tasty conch chowder and a perfectly smoked fish. Their "cracked" conch dinner is the island's finest. If you'd like a delectable platter of "everything from the sea," try the seafood combo. One of the best items is the famous Gulf shrimp, which is grilled just right. The setting is nautical and macho. Don't come here for glitz and glamour and don't bother to dress up. You'll be seated at varnished picnic tables and benches.

Harbour View Restaurant. The Pier House, 1 Duval St. ☎ **305/296-4600.** Main courses $14.95–$22.95; lunches $7.50–$9.25. AE, DC, MC, V. Daily 7:30am–10pm. INTERNATIONAL.

This restaurant at the foot of Duval Street near the cruise ship docks is housed in Key West's premier hotel, where the overpaid big-time movie stars stay. It's a good choice on a hot day for light meals, including a Pier burger grilled as you like it. There's always a selection of sandwiches, filled with good things and served on bread fresh from the oven. Try their conch chowder, which uses fresh cream instead of tomatoes. The fish and chips here is better than in London. The best one-dish meal? Try their Reuben on Cuban bread topped with purple cabbage kraut.

Hard Rock Café. 313 Duval St., at the corner of Caroline St. ☎ **305/293-0230.** Reservations recommended. Main courses $5.99–$15.99. AE, MC, V. Daily 11am–2am. AMERICAN.

Set 3 short blocks from the cruise ship dock, this is the only Hard Rock Café in the world that occupies an antique house. Unlike other members of its chain (and partly because of local building codes), it doesn't have a vintage car suspended from its ceiling, and its setting is distinctly tropical. But it does feature the largest collection of 1960s rock 'n' roll memorabilia of any Hard Rock in the world. Enjoy a potent version of the bartender's special, a Hard Rock Hurricane, on one of several porches before settling down to eat. Menu items include conch chowder, burgers, meal-sized salads (including an Oriental salad loaded with grilled chicken, snow peas, and mandarin oranges), sandwiches and steaks.

La-Te-Da (aka La Terrazza di Martí). 1125 Duval St. ☎ **305/296-6706.** Reservations recommended. Breakfast, brunch, and lunch dishes $4–$10; main courses $8–$10. AE, DC, DISC, MC, V. Mon–Sat 8am–11pm, Sun 11am–11pm. INTERNATIONAL.

Le-Te-Da is still the queen of camp restaurants in Key West, although in its old age it's far more respectable than it was in the 70s, when you might have seen a nude man stroll by and jump into the pool. Today a more subdued gay clientele still shows up, along with the mayor, celebrities in town, and Mr. and Mrs. Smith from Kansas.

The belle epoque white-trimmed house was once the headquarters of José Martí, the exiled 19th-century Cuban writer and revolutionary. Guests dine in or out of doors, or else find a seat at the mahogany bar, officially called Godfrey's now. The food is better than it's been in years, quite good really. Try the spicy seafood bisque, or the Caesar salad with sliced grilled chicken. For a lunch sandwich, opt for the sautéed filet of hog snapper. It sounds dreadful, but it's really first rate, especially when accompanied by the bartender's famous Bloody Mary.

Latitudes. Sunset Key. ☎ **305/292-5300.** Reservations required and made through the concierge at Key West Hilton Resort & Marina, 245 Front St. Lunch salads and sandwiches $7.95–$12.95; main courses $18.95–$30. AE, DC, DISC, MC, V. Daily 7am–10pm. INTERNATIONAL.

Here's a little secret dining selection on its own little island, allowing you to escape from the hordes roaming Duval. The restaurant opened in the fall of 1997 and became an instant success. It's really just a horseshoe-shaped bar with about a dozen tables off the sandy beach, and more on a surrounding stone terrace. Plastic and canvas sides protect you in inclement weather. The island itself lies 500 yards offshore and is reached by regular launch service from the Hilton.

Begin with one of the alcoholic fruit drinks (more fresh fruit than alcohol). The food is adequately prepared and often quite tasty, although not the major reason to come here. The setting is so appealing that almost anything tastes delightful. Try the chef's favorite sandwich: filet of beef with avocado. Or else you can opt for a peppery crabcake po' boy. The potato salad accompanying the sandwiches is often made with sweet potatoes. Finish off with one of the freshly made tortes.

Louie's Backyard. 700 Waddell Ave. ☎ **305/294-1061.** Reservations required. Main courses $25–$31; lunch main dishes $9.50–$15.95; Sunday brunch dishes $4.95–$14.95. AE, CB, DC, MC, V. Daily 11:30am–3pm and 6–10:30pm. MODERN CARIBBEAN/SEAFOOD.

Louie's Backyard, once the most elegant and best restaurant in Key West, ain't what it used to be back in its golden era when it was billed as "an inexpensive place for people with money." It's no longer inexpensive, and the food has gone downhill, too. But you might want to come here anyway for lunch, because the seaside setting is the most romantic in Key West. Even if you visit only at the end of the afternoon before your ship departs, you can sit at the dockside bar and enjoy a drink at sunset.

The chef specializes in seafood—mostly served fusion style with Asian spices. Citrus and other tropical fruits are worked into many dishes. Try the seared lamb roulade with goat cheese, or the seared tuna atop strands of green wakame. A recent sample of the filet of fresh grouper splashed with blood-orange sauce and served on a bed of trendy purple potatoes showed an improvement over the cuisine the year before. Instead of the ubiquitous Key lime pie, order the Key lime cheesecake for dessert instead.

✪ Pepe's Café & Steak House. 806 Caroline St., between William & Margaret sts. ☎ **305/294-7192.** Main courses $12.50–$19.80. DISC, MC, V. Daily 6:30am–10:30pm. SEAFOOD/STEAK.

This is the oldest eating house in the Florida Keys, established in 1909. It moved to its present location on the old commercial waterfront of Caroline Street in 1962. Key West mayors can be found having breakfast here, catching up on the latest gossip with shrimpers, police officers, and local construction crews. Diners eat under slow-moving paddle fans at tables or at dark pine booths with high backs. A towering rubber tree shades a garden outside. Cruise ship passengers enjoy the "in between" menu served daily from noon to 4:30pm. You get to choose from zesty homemade chili, perfectly baked oysters, fish sandwiches, and Pepe's deservedly famous steak sandwiches, as well as other dishes. The freshly squeezed screwdriver is the best in town. If you arrive before noon, go for the shrimp and mushroom omelet—there's nothing finer.

Planet Hollywood Key West. 108 Duval St., at the corner of Front St. ☎ **305/295-0003.** Reservations recommended. Main courses $9–$18. AE, DC, MC, V. Daily 11am–11pm. INTERNATIONAL.

This vast restaurant and bar boasts a seating capacity of 140, a mezzanine bar area with a Hollywood Hills diorama, and a trio of outside terraces, plus the main dining room—all with an extensive memorabilia collection. A merchandise shop offers a full line of Planet Hollywood clothing and accessories. This clone of so many other Planets opened in the summer of 1997, hosted by Sylvester Stallone and Jim Belushi. Danny Glover also showed up, along with the likes of Kevin (Hercules) Sorbo.

Does anyone ever really care about the food here? It's child-friendly, perfect for unsophisticated palates. Pizzas, burgers, fajitas, and the like round out the menu, similar to the Hard Rock Café's. The apple strudel comes from the secret recipe of Arnold Schwarzenegger's mother.

Siam House. 829 Simonton St., parallel to Duval St. ☎ **305/292-0302.** Main courses $9.95–17.95. AE, DC, DISC, MC, V. Daily 11:30am–2:30pm and 5–11pm. THAI.

Your taste buds will thank you if you skip most Asian eateries in Key West, but the Thai specialties here are worth the detour. It's just a 12-minute walk from the cruise docks. The only criticism we've heard is that the fiery-hot, spicy dishes have been "cooled" for the American palate. But the results are still first class. Begin with a spicy appetizer, perhaps a Thai beef salad flavored with lemon dressing, and follow with one of the chef's specialties. There's none better than crispy fish, a whole red snapper fast-fried and served with a sauce flavored with tamarind, garlic, and red peppers. Other good choices are the crispy roast duck drained of fat, or frog's legs "Pad Ped" made extra hot with a black pepper seasoning.

Turtle Kraals Wildlife Bar & Grill. Land's End Village, foot of Margaret St. ☎ **305/294-2640.** Main courses $8.95–$25. MC, V. Daily 11am–11pm. SEAFOOD/SOUTHWEST.

Established in 1980, this bustling restaurant and bar opens right on the harbor. We prefer the food here to the better-known Half Shell Raw Bar nearby. The island's shrimp fleet used to pull in here following the discovery in 1950 of "pink gold," a new species of Gulf Coast shrimp that ran from Conpeche to the Dry Tortugas. The Thompson Fish House and later the Singleton Packing Company were headquartered here also, near the turtle kraals where these giant animals were kept alive in salt-water prior to being turned into soup. You can't order green turtle steak today, but try tender Florida lobster, spicy conch chowder, or perfectly cooked fresh fish (often dolphin with pineapple salsa or baked stuffed grouper with mango crabmeat stuffing). Experience has taught us to bypass the many Southwestern specialties such as nachos, tostadas, and stuffed jalapeños in favor of the fish.

PUB CRAWLING

Most places recommended below offer fast food to go with their drinks. The food isn't the best on the island, but usually arrives shortly after you order it, which suits most rushed cruise ship passengers just fine.

Captain Tony's Saloon. 428 Green St. ☎ **305/294-1838.** Mon–Sat 10am–2am (sometimes 4am), Sun noon–2am.

Heavily patronized by cruise ship passengers, this is the oldest active bar in Florida, and has it ever grown tacky. The 1851 building was the original Sloppy Joe's, a rough and tumble fisherman's saloon (Sloppy Joe's is now on Duval Street, see below). Hemingway drank here from 1933 to 1937, and Jimmy Buffett got his start here before opening his own bar and going on to musical glory. The name refers to Capt. Tony Tarracino, a former Key West mayor and rugged man of the sea who owned the place until 1988. Memorabilia of this self-styled "legend" abounds, including T-shirts adorned with his picture. Now in his 80s, this "captain, hustler, rumrunner, and bootlegger" still drops in occasionally. But Bob Dylan, the Key West literati, and the gay crowd have now gone elsewhere, abandoning the bar to others who've decorated it with macho paraphernalia like women's bras and G-string underwear. The house special is a lethal Pirates' Punch.

Havana Docks Bar & Sunset Deck. The Pier House, 1 Duval St. ☎ **305/296-4600.** Daily 4–9pm.

This longtime favorite rivals Sunset Pier Bar & Grill as the best place from which to observe Key West's legendary sunsets. Live local island music toasts the setting sun. You might pop in here for a farewell drink before your ship departs. It's the type of convivial open-air bar that many people think exists all over the Caribbean, but is really only found in Key West.

It was in this general area, once filled with ramshackle warehouses and sleazy sailor joints, that playwright William Inge went wandering one night, eventually discovering a strip club that ignited his imagination. The result was his play *Bus Stop*, later a film starring Marilyn Monroe in one of her most memorable roles.

Hog's Breath Saloon. 400 Front St. ☎ **305/296-HOGG.** Salads/sandwiches/platters $4.95–11.95. AE, DC, MC, V. Bar daily 11:30am–2am; food daily 11:30am–11pm. AMERICAN.

This watering hole near the cruise docks has been a Key West tradition since 1976. Drinking is a sport here, especially among the fishermen who come in after a day chasing the big one. This open-air place is very laid-back. Live entertainment is offered from 1pm to 2am. You can still get raw oysters here, in spite of the health risk, but in season, you may prefer the steamed, sweet stone crab claws instead. Sandwiches are served throughout the day, including a quarter pound all-beef hot dog first made famous on New York's Coney Island. Local favorites include a fish plate (usually a 9-ounce piece of dolphin), followed by the only dessert offered, Key lime pie.

Jimmy Buffett's Margaritaville. 500 Duval St. ☎ **305/292-1435.** Main courses $9.95–14.95; sandwiches $5.25–$5.75. AE, MC, V. Daily 11am–2am. AMERICAN.

The third most popular bar with cruise ship passengers, after Captain Tony's and Sloppy Joe's, is Jimmy Buffett's Margaritaville. Buffett, who in the words of one critic "made a fortune rewriting the same song 3 dozen times," is the hometown boy done good. His cafe, naturally, is decorated with pictures of himself. And, yes, it sells T-shirts and Margaritaville memorabilia in a shop off the dining room. Actually Buffett's "Cheeseburger in Paradise" isn't bad. His margaritas are without competition, but then they'd have to be at his place, wouldn't they?

✪ **Schooner Wharf.** 202 William St., Key West Bight. ☎ **305/292-9520.** Food items $1.95–$14.95. MC, V. Mon–Sat 8am–4am, Sun noon–4am. AMERICAN.

For a real local hangout within an easy walk of the cruise ship docks, head to this dive, rarely discovered by tourists. It bills itself as the last funky area of Old Key West. The waterfront bar looks out on charter boats and classic old yachts in the slips. It's the most robust and hard-drinking bar in Key West, drawing primarily a young crowd, many of whom cater to the tourist industry or work on the town's fleet of fishing boats. Come here for margaritas, screwdrivers, or whatever else you want to drink. If you're hungry, one of the staff will throw "something" on the grill. There's often live entertainment.

Sloppy Joe's. 201 Duval St. ☎ **305/294-5717.** Sandwiches/salads $6–$10. MC, V. Mon–Sat 9am–4am, Sun noon–4am. AMERICAN.

This is the most touristy bar in Key West, visited by virtually all cruise ship passengers, even those who don't normally go to bars. It aggressively plays up its association with Hemingway, although the bar stood on Greene Street back then (see Captain Tony's). In 1962, someone discovered the original manuscript of *To Have and Have Not* and notes on *A Farewell to Arms* in the back room. It's said that Papa liked to gamble with the locals in the back room. This former speakeasy was founded by charterboat captain and Hemingway crony Joe Russell (the original "Sloppy"). Today, marine flags decorate the ceiling, and its ambiance and decor evoke a Havana bar from the 1930s. Although most patrons come here just to drink, you can order from a selection of platters and sandwiches, everything from a Sloppy Joe's sandwich to a Key West fish sandwich. You can even buy Hemingway T-shirts. The place is often packed, noisy, and raucous. Live entertainment packs them in from noon to 2am.

Sunset Pier Bar & Grill. 0 Duval St. (behind the Ocean Key House). ☎ **305/295-7040.** Main courses $4.75–$25; salads/sandwiches $4.75–$7.50. AE, DC, DISC, MC, V. Mon–Thurs 11am–10pm, Fri–Sat 11am–11pm, Sun noon–10pm. INTERNATIONAL.

When the crowds at Mallory Square get you down, retreat to this bar and restaurant that overlooks the docks. You can still see everything, but you don't have to put up with the hassle. Tropical drinks, including a Sunset Pier margarita, are the bartender's specialties. A jumbo Hebrew National hot dog, charbroiled and served on a toasted bun, satisfies as sometimes nothing else can. You can also order a number of salads, including a veggie pasta, while listening to the live music. Much beer is consumed here with spicy conch fritters.

13 Martinique ⚓ ⚓

When you arrive at the port section of Fort-de-France, the capital of Martinique, you would never guess that you've arrived at one of the most beautiful islands in the Caribbean. You face either a long, hot, dull walk into town or a hassle with an overcharging taxi driver—either way, a jolt back to reality after the well-ordered life aboard ship. But afterwards, you can proceed to take in the charms of this raffish town and this ever-fascinating, sensual island. And don't overlook the food. The Creole cuisine here is among the most distinctive in the West Indies, rivaled only by Guadeloupe.

Martinique appeals to a diverse crowd. Many vacationers, especially those from France, are drawn to the miles of white sandy beaches along an irregular coastline. Shoppers love to explore Martinique's boutiques, looking perhaps for a Hermès scarf, or a bottle of Chanel perfume, or even some Baccarat crystal. Bird-watchers and nature lovers will find a number of hummingbirds, as well mountain whistlers, blackbirds, and multicolored butterflies. The early Carib peoples, who gave Columbus a hostile reception, called Martinique "the island of flowers," and indeed it has remained so. The vegetation is lush with hibiscus, poinsettia, bougainvillea, coconut palm, breadfruit, and mango trees. Almost any fruit sprouts out of the rich, volcanic soil—pineapples, avocados, bananas, papayas, and custard apples.

Martinique is mountainous, especially in the rain-forested northern region, where the volcano Mount Pelée rises to a height of 4,656 feet. In one of the most famous eruptions of all time, Mount Pelée blew its stack in 1902, calcifying 30,000 people in the city of St-Pierre, then known as the Paris of the West Indies. Only a convict named Siparis survived, saved by the thick walls of his cell (he later toured as a side-show attraction with the Barnum & Bailey Circus).

Like Guadeloupe, Martinique is not a colony, as many visitors wrongly assume, but a *département* of France, meaning that these *citoyens* are full-fledged citizens of *la belle France*. Martinique has been France's anchor in the Caribbean since it relinquished rights to Canada in exchange for the French West Indies in 1763. Napoléon's Empress Joséphine was born here that same year. In her youth, Madama de Maintenon, mistress of Louis XIV, lived here in the small fishing village of Le Précheur.

COMING ASHORE

The **Maritime Terminal** is in a dreary commercial district of Fort-de-France, about a mile east of the center. Many passengers make the usually hot and humid walk to downtown. Taxi drivers have a monopoly on transportation here and will charge $10 to make the trip (or more if they think they can get away with it). If you walk, keep to the left after leaving the dock. This will take you to Place de la Savane, the heart of Fort-de-France.

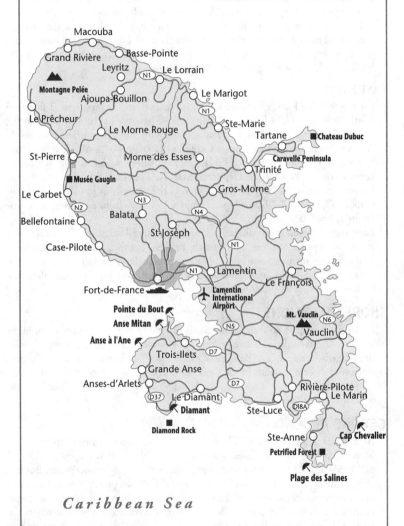

Atlantic Ocean

Macouba

Basse-Pointe

Grand Rivière

Leyritz

Le Lorrain

N1

▲▲ Montagne Pelée

Ajoupa-Bouillon

Le Marigot

Le Prêcheur

N1

Le Morne Rouge

Ste-Marie

Tartane

■ Chateau Dubuc

St-Pierre

Morne des Esses

Caravelle Peninsula

■ Musée Gaugin

Trinité

Le Carbet

Gros-Morne

N2

Bellefontaine

Balata

N3

N4

Case-Pilote

St-Joseph

N1

Fort-de-France

N1

Lamentin

Le François

Lamentin
International
Airport

Pointe du Bout ↖

Mt. Vauclin

Anse Mitan ↖

N5

▲▲

N6

Anse à l'Ane ↖

Vauclin

Trois-Ilets

D7

Grande Anse

D7

Anses-d'Arlets

Rivière-Pilote

D37

Le Diamant

Le Marin

↖ Diamant

Ste-Luce

D18A

■

Cap Chevalier ↖

Diamond Rock

Ste-Anne

Petrified Forest ■

↖

Plage des Salines

Caribbean Sea

| Airport ✈ | Beach ↖ | Mountain ▲▲ | Cruise Ship Terminal 🚢 |

2-0197

At the pier you'll find a less-than-helpful tourist information office, a telephone, and a duty-free shop that is best skipped. Save purchases for the town center unless you're getting right back on the ship.

Placing long distance calls in Martinique is just as difficult and frustrating as it is in Guadeloupe. Avoid calling home unless there's an emergency. If you must call, it's less expensive to use a *Telecarte*. These prepaid cards are sold at outlets labeled *Telecarte en Vente Ici*. The tourist office at the port will help you find them.

In some cases your cruise line may anchor in the Baie des Flamands. If so, passengers will be transported by tender to the waterfront of Fort-de-France, thus putting you right into the heart of the city. The tourist office lies across the street from the landing dock in a building with an Air France logo.

FAST FACTS

Currency   The French franc (F) is the legal tender here. At press time, 1 franc was worth 16.3¢ U.S. (6.14 F = $1 U.S.), the rate we have used to convert prices in this section. Exchange your money at banks, which give much better rates than hotels. A money-exchange service, **Change Caraibes** (☎ 0596/60-28-40), is at rue Ernest Deproge 4. It's open Monday to Friday from 7:30am to noon and 2:30 to 4pm.

Information   The **Office Départemental du Tourisme** (tourist office) is on boulevard Alfassa in Fort-de-France, across the waterfront boulevard from the harbor (☎ 0596/63-79-60). Open Monday to Friday from 8am to 5pm and on Saturday from 8am to noon.

Language   Almost everyone speaks French, the official language. The local Creole patois uses words borrowed from French, English, Spanish, and African languages. In the wake of increased tourism, English is occasionally spoken in the major hotels, restaurants, and tourist organizations—but don't count on driving around the countryside and asking for directions in English.

SHORE EXCURSIONS

If you don't want to go through the hassle of renting a car or the expense of hiring a private taxi, consider a shore excursion. The classic tour—and sometimes the only one offered—is called "The Pompeii of Martinique" (see below). It's one of the most intriguing shore excursions in the Caribbean. You're taken through the lush countryside to St-Pierre, where Mount Pelée killed 30,000 people in 1902. The 2^1/$_2$-hour tour costs $40; the 4-hour version is $50.

GETTING AROUND

BUS AND TAXI COLLECTIF   There are two types of buses operating on Martinique. Regular buses, called *grand busses,* hold about 40 passengers and cost 5 F to 8 F (85¢ to $1.35) to go anywhere within the city limits of Fort-de-France. But *taxis collectifs* are used to travel beyond the city limits. These are privately owned minivans that traverse the island and bear the sign TC. Traveling in one of these is for the adventurous tourist—they are crowded and uncomfortable. A simple one-way fare is 30 F ($5) from Fort-de-France to Ste-Anne. *Taxis collectifs* depart from the heart of Fort-de-France, at the parking lot of Pointe Simon. There's no phone number.

CAR RENTALS   The scattered nature of Martinique's geography makes renting a car especially tempting. There are several local car-rental agencies, but clients have complained of mechanical difficulties and billing irregularities. We recommend renting from **Avis,** rue Ernest-Deproge, 4 (☎ **800/331-1212** in the U.S., or 0596/51-17-70); **Budget,** rue Félix-Eboué, 12 (☎ **800/527-0700** in the U.S., or 0596/63-69-00); or **Hertz,** rue Ernest-Deproge, 24, at Lamentin Airport (☎ **800/**

654-3001 or 0596/60-64-64). If you're calling well in advance, you might try **Auto Europe** (☎ **800/223-5555**) or **Kenwel Holiday Autos** (☎ **800/678-0678**).

You'll need a valid home driver's license to rent a car for up to 20 days. After that, an International Driver's License is required.

Most car-rental rates are about $60 a day, including unlimited mileage. Prices are usually lower if you reserve a car from North America at least two business days before your arrival. You'll also be hit with a 9.5% value-added tax (VAT). Collision-damage waivers (CDWs) are an excellent idea in a country where the populace drives somewhat recklessly.

TAXIS   Travel by taxi is popular but expensive. Most of the cabs aren't metered, so you'll have to agree on the price of the ride before getting in. Night fares, in effect from 8pm to 6am, come with a 40% surcharge. For a radio taxi, call ☎ **0596/ 63-63-62.** If you want to rent a taxi for the day, it's better to have a party of at least three or four people to keep costs down. Based on the size of the car, expect to pay 700 F ($116.90) to 850 F ($141.95) and up for a 5-hour tour, depending on the itinerary you negotiate with the driver.

FERRY   The least expensive way to go between quai d'Esnambuc in Fort-de-France and Pointe du Bout, the main tourist zone, is by ferry (*vedette*). These usually run every day from 6am to midnight. The one-way fare is 32 F ($5.35) per passenger. Schedules are printed in the free visitor's guide *Choubouloute,* which is distributed by the tourist office. However, if the weather is bad and/or the seas are rough, all ferryboat services may be canceled.

A smaller ferryboat runs between Fort-de-France and Anse Mitan and Anse-à-l'Ane, across the bay, home to many two- and three-star hotels and several modest and unassuming Creole restaurants. The boat departs daily at 30-minute intervals between 6am and 6:30pm from quai d'Esnambuc in Fort-de-France. The trip takes about 15 minutes. The fare is 15 F ($2.50) per passenger each way.

BICYCLES & MOTOR SCOOTERS   Motor scooters and, to a lesser extent, bicycles, can be rented from **Funny,** rue Ernest-Deproge, 80, in Fort-de-France (☎ **0596/63-33-05**). The new 18-speed VTT (*velo tout terrain,* or all-terrain bike) is gradually making inroads from mainland France into the rugged countryside of Martinique. For tour information and possible rentals, contact **Jacques-Henry Vartel,** VT Tilt, Anse Mitan (☎ **0596/66-01-01**).

SEEING THE SIGHTS
FORT-DE-FRANCE

Once past Fort-de-France's disappointing port, you'll find the town to be a mélange of New Orleans and Menton (French Riviera). Iron grillwork balconies overflowing with flora are commonplace here. Narrow streets climb up to houses on the steep hills. Almost a third of the island's year-round population of 360,000 lives in the capital, so it's not a small town.

That said, Fort-de-France isn't that great. But if you would like to explore it further, the tourist office will direct you to a guided walking tour costing $15 for 1 1/2 hours.

At the center of the town lies **La Savane,** a broad garden with many palms and mangoes and bordered by shops and cafes. In the middle of this grand square stands a statue of Joséphine, "Napoléon's little Creole," carved in white marble by Vital Debray. The graceful statue looks toward Trois-Ilets, where she was born.

St. Louis Roman Catholic Cathedral, on rue Victor-Schoelcher, was built in 1875. The religious centerpiece of the island, it's an extraordinary iron building, which someone once likened to a Catholic railway station. A number of the island's former governors are buried beneath the choir loft.

A statue in front of the Palais de Justice portrays the island's second main historical figure, Victor Schoelcher (you'll see his name a lot in Martinique). He worked to free the slaves more than a century ago. The **Bibliothèque Schoelcher,** rue de la Liberté, 21 (☎ **0596/70-26-67**), also honors this popular hero. This elaborate structure was first displayed at the Paris Exposition in 1889. The Romanesque portal in red and blue, the Egyptian lotus-petal columns, and even the turquoise tiles were taken apart and reassembled piece by piece here. It's open Monday from 1 to 5:30pm, Tuesday through Thursday from 8:30am to 5:30pm, Friday from 8:30am to 5pm, and Saturday from 8:30am to noon.

Guarding the port is **Fort St-Louis,** built in the Vauban style on a rocky promontory. In addition, **Fort Tartenson** and **Fort Desaix** stand on hills overlooking the port as well.

Musée Départemental de la Martinique, rue de la Liberté, 9 (☎ **0596/71-57-05**), is the one place on Martinique that preserves its pre-Columbian past, with relics left from the early settlers, the Arawaks and the Caribs. The museum faces La Savane and is open Monday to Friday from 8:30am to 5pm, and on Saturday from 9am to noon. Admission is 15 F ($2.50) for adults, 10 F ($1.65) for students, and 5 F (85¢) for children.

Sacré-Coeur de Balata Cathedral, overlooking Fort-de-France at Balata, is a copy of the basilica looking down from Montmartreon Paris—and this one is just as incongruous, maybe more so. To get there, take the route de la Trace (Route N3). Balata is 6 miles north of Fort-de-France.

A few minutes' taxi ride away on Route N3, the **Jardin de Balata** or **Balata Garden** (☎ **0596/64-48-73**) is a tropical botanical park created by Jean-Phillippe Thoze on land near his grandmother's house. He has restored the house, furnishing it with antiques and engravings depicting life in other days, and with bouquets and baskets of fruit renewed daily. The garden contains a profusion of flowers, shrubs, and trees. Balata is open daily from 9am to 5pm. Admission is 35 F ($5.85) for adults, 15 F ($2.50) for children 7 to 12, and free for children under 6.

AROUND THE ISLAND
The Pompeii of Martinique

The major goal of all shore excursions, St-Pierre was the cultural and economic capital of Martinique—until May 7, 1902. That very morning, locals read in their daily newspaper that "Montagne Pelée does not present any more risk to the population than Vesuvius does to the Neapolitans." Then at 8am, the southwest side of Pelée exploded in fire and lava. At 8:02am, all but one of St-Pierre's 30,000 inhabitants were dead.

St-Pierre never recovered its past splendor. Ruins of the church, the theater, and some other buildings can be seen along the coast.

One of the best ways to get an overview of St-Pierre is to ride a rubber-wheeled "train," the **CV Paris Express** (☎ **0596/78-31-41**), which departs from the Musée Volcanologique (see below). Tours cost 50 F ($8.35) for adults, and 25 F ($4.20) for children, and run Monday through Friday from 10:30am to 1pm and 2:30 to 7pm. In theory, tours depart about once an hour, but actually they only leave when there are enough people to justify a trip.

Musée Volcanologique, rue Victor-Hugo, St-Pierre (☎ **0596/78-10-32**), was created by American volcanologist Franck Alvard Perret, who turned the museum over to the city in 1933. In pictures and relics excavated from the debris, you can trace the story of what happened to St-Pierre. Dug from the lava is a clock that stopped at the exact moment the volcano erupted. The museum is open daily from 9am to 5pm. Admission is 15 F ($2.50), free for children 7 and under.

LE CARBET

An idyllic excursion north of Fort-de-France is to Le Carbet, where Columbus landed in 1502 and the first French settlers arrived in 1635. The painter Paul Gauguin lived here for 4 months in 1887 before going on to do his most famous work on Tahiti. The landscape looks pretty much as it did when Gauguin depicted the beach in his *Bord de Mer*. **Centre d'Art Musée Paul-Gauguin,** Anse Turin (☎ **0596/78-22-66**), housed in a five-room building near the beach, commemorates the French artist's stay with books, prints, letters, and other memorabilia. There are also paintings by René Corail, sculpture by Hector Charpentier, and examples of the artwork of Zaffanella. Of special interest are faïence mosaics made of pieces of colored volcanic rock excavated from nearby archaeological digs. They were formed when the fires of Montagne Pelée devastated St-Pierre in 1902. There are also changing exhibits of works by local artists. The museum is open daily from 9am to 5:30pm. Admission is 15 F ($2.50) for adults and students, 5 F (85¢) for children under 8.

POINTE DU BOUT

Pointe du Bout is a narrow peninsula across the bay from Fort-de-France. It's the most lavish resort area of Martinique, with at least four of the island's largest hotels, an impressive marina, about a dozen tennis courts, swimming pools, and facilities for horseback riding and all kinds of water sports. There's also a golf course designed by Robert Trent Jones Sr., a handful of restaurants, a gambling casino, and boutiques. Except for the hillside that contains the Hôtel Bakoua, most of the district is flat and verdant, with gardens and rigidly monitored parking zones. You can get here by ferry (see "Getting Around," above).

PLANTATION DE LEYRITZ

If you're driving yourself around or taking a taxi tour, you will find no better goal than **Hotel Plantation de Leyritz** near Basse-Pointe (☎ **0596/78-53-92**), one of the best restored plantations on Martinique and a good place for lunch. It occupies the site of a plantation established around 1700 by Bordeaux-born Michel de Leyritz. Sprawled over flat, partially wooded terrain a half-hour's drive from the nearest beach (Anse à Zerot, in Sainte-Marie), it was the site of the "swimming pool summit meeting" in 1974 between Presidents Gerald Ford and Valéry Giscard d'Estaing. Part of the acreage still functions as a working banana plantation. The resort includes 16 acres of tropical gardens. At the core is a stone-sided 18th-century Great House.

The dining room is in a rum distillery, which takes advantage of the fresh spring water running down from the hillside. Your authentic (and expensive) Creole lunch—90 F ($15.05) to 150 F ($25.05) and up—might consist of chicken covered in coconut-milk sauce, along with ouassous (freshwater crayfish in a herb sauce), sautéed breadfruit, and sautéed bananas. Lunch is served daily from 12:30 to 3pm.

SHOPPING

Your best buys on Martinique are French luxury imports, such as perfumes, fashions, Vuitton luggage, Lalique crystal, or Limoges dinnerware. Sometimes prices are as much as 30% to 40% below those in the United States, but don't count on it. Some luxury goods—including jewelry—are subject to a value-added tax as high as 14%.

If you pay in dollars, store owners supposedly will give you a 20% discount; however, their exchange rates are almost invariably far less favorable than those offered by the local banks, so your real savings will only be 5% to 11%. Actually, you're better off shopping in the smaller stores, where prices are 8% to 12% less on comparable items, and paying in francs.

The main shopping street in Fort-de-France is **rue Victor-Hugo.** The other two leading shopping streets are **rue Schoelcher** and **rue St-Louis.**

Facing the tourist office and alongside **quai d'Esnambuc** is an open market where you can purchase local handcrafts and souvenirs, many of them tacky. Far more interesting is the display of vegetables and fruit—quite a show—at the open-air stalls along **rue Isambert.** Gourmet chefs will find all sorts of spices in the open-air markets, and such goodies as tinned pâté or canned quail in the local *supermarchés.*

Shops on every street sell bolts of the ubiquitous, colorful, and inexpensive local fabric—madras. So-called haute couture and resort wear are sold in many boutiques dotting downtown Fort-de-France.

Cadet-Daniel. Rue Antoine-Siger, 72. ☎ **0596/71-41-48.**

This shop, which opened in 1840, competes with Roger Albert (see below) to offer the best buys in French china and crystal. The crystal from the major designers might be priced more attractively at Roger Albert one month, or Cadet-Daniel the next. So before buying, do some comparison shopping. Cadet-Daniel sells Christofle silver, Limoges china, and crystal from Daum, Baccarat, Lalique, and Sèvres. Like some nearby stores, it also offers island-made 18-karat-gold baubles, including the beaded *collier chou,* or "darling's necklace," long a required ornament for a Creole costume.

Centre des Métieres d'Art. Rue Ernest-Deproge, adjacent to the tourist office. ☎ **0596/70-25-01.**

This is the best and most visible arts and crafts store in Martinique, set within a low-slung building fronting the waterfront. You'll find both valuable and worthless local handmade artifacts for sale, including bamboo, ceramics, painted fabrics, and patchwork quilts suitable for hanging. There's also a collection of original tapestries.

Galeries Lafayette. Rue Victor-Schoelcher, 10, near the cathedral. ☎ **0596/71-38-66.**

This is a small-scale, rather pale branch of the most famous department store in Paris. It specializes in fashion for men, women, and children, but also offers leather goods, jewelry, watches, and all the predictably famous names in French perfume and fashion. The store offers 20% off for purchases made with U.S. dollars, traveler's checks, or a credit card.

La Belle Matadore. Immeuble Vermeil-Marina (midway between the La Pagerié Hôtel and the Méridien Hotel), Pointe du Bout. ☎ **0596/66-04-88.**

The owner of this shop, Martinique-born Marie-Josée Ravenel, has carefully researched the history and traditions of the island's jewelry. Virtually all the merchandise sold here derives from models developed during slave days by the *matadores* (prostitutes), midwives, and slaves. Designs are vivid and bold, and for the most part crafted on the island from 18-karat gold. Especially popular are the necklaces, brooches, and pendants popularized during the 18th and 19th centuries. The store carries baubles that range in price from 60 F ($10) for a pendant shaped like the island of Martinique to 12,000 F ($2,004) for a gold necklace.

La Case à Rhum. In the Galerie Marchande, rue de la Liberté, 5. ☎ **0596/73-73-20.**

Martinique rum is considered by aficionados to be the world's finest. Hemingway, in *A Moveable Feast,* lauded it as the perfect antidote to a rainy day. This shop is the best place for browsing, offering all the brands of Martinique rum, as well as several others famous for their age and taste. Bottles range in price from 42 F ($7) for

---

⭐ Favorite Experiences

Marie-Josèphe-Rose Tascher de la Pagerié was born in the charming little village of **Trois-Ilets** in 1763. As Joséphine, she was to become the wife of Napoléon I and empress of France from 1804 to 1809. She'd been previously married to Alexandre de Beauharnais, who had actually wanted to wed either of her two more attractive sisters. Six years older than Napoléon, she pretended that she'd lost her birth certificate so he wouldn't find out her true age. Although many historians call her ruthless and selfish (she certainly was unfaithful), she is still revered by some on Martinique as uncommonly gracious. Others, however, blame Napoléon's "re-invention" of slavery on her influence.

To reach her birthplace in Trois-Ilets (pronounced Twaz-ee-lay), take a taxi from the pier through lush countryside 20 miles south of Fort-de-France. In la Pagerié, a small museum, Musée de la Pagerie (☎ **0596/68-33-06**), displaying mementos relating to Joséphine, sits in the former estate kitchen (the plantation house was destroyed in a hurricane). You'll see a passionate love letter from Napoléon, along with her childhood bed. Here in this room Joséphine gossiped with her slaves and played the guitar. Still remaining are the partially restored ruins of the Pagerié sugar mill and the church where she was christened (the latter is in the village itself). A botanical garden, the **Parc des Floralies,** is adjacent to the golf course Golf de l'Impératrice Joséphine (see below).

---

ordinary rum to 5,400 F ($901.80) for a connoisseur's delight—a bottle of rum distilled by the Bally Company in 1924 in the nearby hamlet of Carbet. They offer samples in small cups to prospective buyers. We suggest a taste of Vieux Acajou, a dark, mellow Old Mahogany, or a blood-red liqueur-like rum bottled by Bally.

La Galleria. Route de Lamentin.

Set midway between Fort-de-France and the Lamentin airport, this is, by anyone's estimate, the most upscale and elegant shopping complex on Martinique. On the premises are more than 60 different vendors, from both France and the Caribbean. There's also a handful of cafes and restaurants, as well as an outlet or two selling the pastries and sweets for which Martinique is known.

Nouvelles Galeries. Rue Lamartine, 87. ☎ **0596/63-04-60.**

This is another of the capital's large department stores, stocked with a downscale, not-very-glamorous assortment of products for the home and kitchen. It's also known for its toys, luggage, beauty accessories, china, crystal, and silver, as well as many workaday items. Come here to look for occasional bargains. The emphasis is French with Caribbean overtures.

Paradise Island. Rue Ernest-Deproges, 22. ☎ **0596/63-93-63.**

This shop maintains the most stylish and upscale collection of T-shirts in Martinique, each displayed as a kind of couture-conscious art form. Carefully folded shelves ring the all-white showroom. Whatever you like will probably be available in about a dozen different colors, and priced at between 49 F ($8.20) and 69F ($11.50) per garment. Many display a slogan—sometimes in gold lettering—concerning Martinique and its charms.

Roger Albert. Rue Victor-Hugo, 7-9. ☎ **0596/71-71-71.**

This is by far the largest emporium of luxury goods on Martinique. Roger Albert has five branches scattered throughout the island, although this one near the waterfront is the busiest. You'll find both fun and expensive wristwatches, perfumes, sportswear by La Coste and Tacchini, Lladró and Limoges porcelain, and crystal by Swarovski and other manufacturers such as Daum and Lalique. For anyone with a non-French passport, there are reductions of 20%; seasonal discounts and promotions often take off another 20%.

BEACHES

The beaches south of Fort-de-France are white and sandy, whereas the those to the north are mostly of gray sand. Outstanding in the south is the 1 1/2-mile **Plage des Salines,** near Ste-Anne, with palm trees and a long stretch of white sand, and the 2 1/2-mile **Diamant,** with the landmark Diamond Rock offshore. Swimming on the Atlantic coast is for experts only, except at **Cap Chevalier** and **Presqu'ile de la Caravelle Nature Preserve.**

The clean white-sand beaches of **Pointe du Bout,** site of Martinique's major hotels, were created by developers. The sandy beaches to the south at **Anse Mitan** have always been there welcoming visitors, however, including many snorkelers.

Nudist beaches are not officially sanctioned, but topless sunbathing is widely practiced at the big hotels, often around their swimming pools. Public beaches rarely have changing cabins or showers. Resorts charge nonguests for the use of changing and beach facilities, and request a deposit for towel rentals.

GOLF, HIKING, RIDING, DIVING, SNORKELING & TENNIS

GOLF   The famous golf course designer Robert Trent Jones, Sr. visited Martinique and left behind the 18-hole **Golf de l'Impératrice-Joséphine** at Trois-Ilets (☎ 0596/68-32-81), a 5-minute, 1-mile taxi ride from the leading resort area of Pointe du Bout and about 18 miles from Fort-de-France. The only golf course on Martinique, it unfolds its greens from the birthplace of Empress Joséphine, across rolling hills with scenic vistas down to the sea. Amenities include a pro shop, a bar, a restaurant, and three tennis courts. Greens fees are 270 F ($45.10) per person for 18 holes.

HIKING   Personnel of the **Parc Naturel Régional de la Martinique** organize inexpensive guided excursions for small groups of tourists year-round. Contact them at the Excollège Agricole de Tivoli, B.P. 437, 97200 Fort-de-France (☎ 0596/64-42-59). This should be done 2 or 3 days before your cruise ship arrives in Martinique.

Presqu'ile de la Caravelle Nature Preserve, a well-protected peninsula jutting into the Atlantic Ocean, has safe beaches and well-marked trails through tropical wetlands, and to the ruins of historic Château Debuc.

At certain times of the year, the park organizes serious hiking excursions up Montagne Pelée, into the Gorges de la Falaise, or through the thick coastal rain forest between Grand Rivière and Le Prêcheur.

HORSEBACK RIDING   The premier riding facility on Martinique, established in 1974, is **Ranch Jack,** Morne Habitué, Trois-Ilets (☎ 0596/68-37-69). It offers morning horseback rides for both experienced and novice riders, at 350 F ($58.45) per person for a ride of 3 1/2 to 4 hours. The daily promenades pass through the beaches and fields of Martinique, and the leaders offer a running commentary of the history, fauna, and botany of the island. Cold drinks are included in the price. Call Ranch Jack for transportation arrangements to and from the cruise dock. This is an ideal way to discover both botanical and geographical Martinique. Between 4 and 15 participants are required.

SCUBA DIVING & SNORKELING   Scuba divers come here to explore the Diamond Rock caves and walls and the ships sunk at St-Pierre in the 1902 volcanic eruption. Snorkeling equipment is also available at dive centers.

Across the bay from Fort-de-France, in the Hotel Méridien, **Espace Plongée** (☎ **0596/66-00-00**) is a major scuba center and the best in Pointe du Bout. They welcome anyone who shows up. Dive trips leave from the Méridien Hotel's pier. Prices include equipment rental, transportation, guide, and drinks on board. Dives are conducted twice daily, from 9am to noon and 2:30 to 6pm, and cost 250 F ($41.75) per person. Full-day charters can be arranged. Cruise ship passengers should opt for the morning dives, as afternoon dives may not allow enough time to get back to the ship. The dive shop on the Méridien's beach stocks everything from weight belts and tanks to partial wetsuits and underwater cameras.

TENNIS   The large resorts at Pointe du Bout have courts; non-guests pay 50 F ($8.35 per hour). The best are at the **Hotel Méridien** (☎ **0596/66-00-00**), which has tennis pros on hand to instruct for a fee. Another good choice is to play at one of three courts on the grounds of **Golf de l'Impératrice-Joséphone** at Trois-Ilets (☎ **0596/68-32-81**), a 5-minute taxi ride from the major hotels at Pointe du Bout. The setting here is one of the most beautiful on Martinique.

WINDSURFING   Windsurfing is the most popular sport in the French West Indies. Equipment and lessons are available at all resort water-sports facilities, especially the **Hotel Méridien**, Pointe du Bout (☎ **0596/66-00-00**), where 30-minute lessons cost 100 F ($16.50). Board rentals are only 120 F ($20.05) per hour.

DINING
IN FORT-DE-FRANCE

✪ **À La Bonne Viande.** 11 rue Lamartine. ☎ **0596/63-56-93**. Reservations recommended. Main courses 120 F–185 F ($20.05–$30.90). AE, MC, V. Mon–Sat noon–3pm and 7pm–midnight. STEAK.

If you ask a local for an atmospheric, charming restaurant in the center of town, you'll be directed here. This is the premier steakhouse on Martinique, with a warm and woodsy decor and a location close to La Savane in the heart of town. It's maintained by restaurateur Alphonse Sintive, who trained as a master butcher before World War II on the French mainland. He can regale you with stories of his experiences in the French Foreign Legion in Indochina and Algeria. He brings the juicy steaks and chops from France by regular air shipments. Hearty eaters will appreciate the large portions. Specialties include tournedos Rossini with foie gras, filet steak with pepper sauce; T-bones with béarnaise, and even succulent versions of Japanese-style Kobe steak that's been massaged by a butcher before it's cooked. One of the most generous and likable hosts on the island, Monsieur Sintive usually offers a free after-dinner drink to anyone who mentions this guidebook.

La Fontane. Km 4, Rte. de Balata (2¹/₂ miles north of Fort-de-France on Hwy. N3). ☎ **0596/64-28-70**. Reservations recommended. Fixed-price lunch 100 F ($16.70); main courses 100 F–300 F ($16.70–$50.10). MC, V. Tues–Sat noon–3pm and 7–10pm. FRENCH/CARIBBEAN.

This restaurant in the verdant suburb of La Fontane, easily reached by taxi from the docks, occupies a completely renovated century-old historic villa. The setting is dotted with dowdy antiques, fresh flowers, and Oriental rugs. In the far distance you can see a chain of volcanic hills, Les Pitons de Carbet. Menu items include crayfish au gratin, fresh fish filets with coconut, lobster Thermidor, Caribbean bouillabaisse *à la*

Fontane, seawolf stuffed with shrimp, cassolette of lamb, and a flavorful salad known locally as a *bambou de la Fontane* (fresh fish, crayfish, melon, tomato, and corn). The wine list is among the island's best.

La Mouina. Rte. de Redoute, 127. ☎ **0596/79-34-57.** Reservations recommended only at dinner Sat–Sun. Main courses 85 F–205 F ($14.20–$34.25). MC, V. Mon–Fri noon–2:30pm; Mon–Sat 7:30–9:30pm. FRENCH/CREOLE.

La Mouina, a Creole word for a meeting house, is a venerable restaurant established some 20 years ago by members of the French-Swiss-Hungarian Karschesz family. Sitting next to the police station in the suburb of Redoute, about 1½ miles north of Fort-de-France, this 65-year-old white colonial house is the domain of some of the island's most experienced chefs. You might begin with *crabes farcis* (stuffed crabs) or *escargots de Bourgogne,* then follow with tournedos Rossini, *rognon de veau entier grillé* (whole grilled veal kidneys), or duckling in orange sauce. The owners are particularly proud of their red snapper baked in parchment.

✪ **La Plantation.** In Martinique Cottages (near the airport), Pays Mélé Jeanne-d'Arc, Lamentin. ☎ **0596/50-16-08.** Reservations required. Main courses 75 F–195 F ($12.55–$32.55). AE, DC, MC, V. Mon–Fri noon–2pm; Mon–Sat 7:30–9:30pm. FRENCH.

La Plantation, a 20-minute taxi ride south of Fort-de-France, is one of the finest restaurants on the island. It's housed in a small French Antillean hotel designed about 25 years ago to resemble a 19th-century private home. An imaginative cuisine is the aim of the chef, Gilles Jiacomo, a native of Lyon. The foie gras may have come from France, but the herbs flavoring it are Antillean. Foie gras appears again in a salade folle with lobster. We found a traditional version of rack of lamb was perfectly cooked. A hardworking brother-and-sister team, Jean-Marc and Peggy Arnaud, run the restaurant.

Le Planteur. 1 rue de la Liberté (on the southern edge of La Savane). ☎ **0596/63-17-45.** Reservations recommended. Main courses 85 F–140 F ($14.20–$23.40); set menus 120 F ($20.05) and 150 F ($25.05). AE, MC, V. Mon–Fri noon–2:30pm; Mon–Sat 7–10:30pm. FRENCH/CREOLE.

This restaurant, established in 1997 in the heart of town, has a growing number of local fans, especially among the island's business community. Its hardworking, somewhat distracted staff run around hysterically trying to be all things to all clients. Menu items are fresh, flavorful, and usually received with approval. They include a hot *velouté* (soup) concocted from shrimp and *giraumons,* a green-skinned tropical fruit with a succulent yellow core; a cassolette of minced conch; filet of *daurade* with coconut; snapper *Belle Doudou,* served with a tomatoe, onion, and chive sauce; and a *blanquette* (white, slow-simmered stew) of shellfish, available only when the local catch can provide the ingredients. The restaurant is livened up by several somewhat idealized painted depictions of colonial Martinique, as well as flowered napery on the small rectangular tables.

AT POINTE DU BOUT

Au Poisson d'Or. L'Anse Mitan (near the entrance to the resort community of Pointe du Bout). ☎ **0596/66-01-80.** Reservations recommended. Main courses 85 F–240 F ($14.20–$40.10); set menu 110 F–200 F ($18.35–$33.40). AE, MC, V. Tues–Sun noon–2:30pm and 7–10pm. Closed July. CREOLE.

There's no view of the sea here, and the traffic runs close to the edge of the veranda and terrace, but the reasonable prices and the complete change of pace make this restaurant a good choice. The rustic dining room offers grilled fish, grilled conch, grilled seafood, scallops sautéed in white wine, poached local fish, and, for dessert, flan.

These dishes are common in Martinique, of course, but they're prepared here with a certain flair and served with style. Visitors are warmly welcomed.

Pignon sur Mer. Anse-à-l'Ane (a 12-minute drive from Pointe du Bout). ☎ **0596/68-38-37.** Reservations not necessary. Main courses 55 F–170 F ($9.20–$28.40). AE, MC, V. Tues–Sun 12:15–4pm; Tues–Sat 7–9:30pm. CREOLE.

Simple and unpretentious, this small-scale Creole restaurant contains about 15 tables, inside a rustically dilapidated building beside the sea. Menu items are island-inspired, and might include *delices du Pignon,* a platter of shellfish, or whatever grilled fish or shellfish was hauled in that day. *Lambi* (conch), shrimp, and crayfish are almost always available. Brochettes of chicken are filling and flavorful.

✪ La Villa Créole. Anse Mitan. ☎ **0596/66-05-53.** Reservations recommended. Set menus 200 F–650 F ($33.40–$108.55); main courses 85 F–150 F ($14.20–$25.05). AE, MC, V. Tues–Sat noon–2pm; Tues–Sun 7–10:30pm. CREOLE.

This restaurant, which lies within a 3 or 4-minute drive from the hotels of Pointe du Bout, has thrived since the late 1970s, offering a colorful, small-scale respite from the island's high-rise resorts. Set within a simple but well-maintained Creole house, with no particular views other than the small garden that surrounds it, the restaurant serves reasonably priced set-price menus that offer a selection of such staples as *accras de morue* (beignets of codfish); *boudin creole* (blood sausage); and *un féroce* (a local form of pâté concocted from fresh avocados, pulverized codfish, and manioc flour). Especially flavorful is the *filet de vivaneau* (red snapper) prepared either with tomato sauce or grilled "facon Villa Créole."

THE NORTH COAST: TWO "MAMA" CHEFS

Like Guadeloupe, Martinique is famous for its female Creole chefs. If you opted for a taxi tour or a rented car, you can seek out two of the best of these Martinique "mamas" on the north coast.

Chez Mally Edjam. Rte. de la Côte Atlantique (36 miles from Fort-de-France), Basse-Pointe. ☎ **0596/78-51-18.** Reservations required. Main courses 70 F–180 F ($11.70–$30.05); fixed-price menu 70 F ($11.70). AE, MC, V. Daily noon–3pm. Closed mid-July to mid-Aug. FRENCH/CREOLE.

This local legend operates from a modest house beside the main road in the center of town. Many visitors prefer to taxi all the way from the cruise docks to dine here, instead of at the Leyritz Plantation. You sit either at one of a handful of tables on the side porch, or in the somewhat more formal dining room.

Grandmotherly Mally Edjam (assisted to an ever-increasing degree by her younger, France-born friend, Martine Hugé) is usually busy in the kitchen turning out her Creole delicacies. Both women know how to prepare all the dishes for which the island is known: stuffed land crab with a hot seasoning, small pieces of conch in a tart shell, and a classic *colombo de porc* (the Creole version of pork curry). Equally delectable are the lobster vinaigrette, the papaya soufflé (which must be ordered in advance), and the highly original confitures, which are tiny portions of fresh island fruits, such as pineapple and guava, preserved in a vanilla syrup.

Yva Chez Vava. Boulevard de Gaulle (west of Basse-Pointe). ☎ **0596/55-72-72.** Reservations recommended. Main courses 60 F–150 F ($10–$25.05); set menu 80 F ($13.35). AE, DC, MC, V. Daily noon–6pm. FRENCH/CREOLE.

Located in a low-slung building painted the orange color of a papaya fruit, Yva Chez Vava is a combination private home and restaurant, representing the hard labor of three generations of Creole women. It was established in 1979 by a well-remembered, long-departed matron, Vava, whose daughter, Yva, is now assisted by her own daughter, Rosy. Local family recipes are the mainstay of this modest bistro, infused with a simple country-inn style. À la carte menu items include Creole soup, lobster, and various colombos or curries. Local delicacies have changed little since the days of Joséphine and her sugar fortune, and include *z'habitants* (crayfish), *vivaneau* (red snapper), *tazard* (kingfish), and *accras de morue* (cod fritters).

14 Nassau ⇩ ⇩ ⇩ ⇩

One million visitors a year have cast their vote for Nassau, capital of The Bahamas, and its adjoining Cable Beach and Paradise Island. Many of them come on 3- to 4-day cruises leaving from Miami, Fort Lauderdale, and Port Canaveral. There's good reason for their preference—the historic city of Nassau, on the north side of New Providence Island, offers the charm of an indolent tropical antique, yet boasts up-to-date tourist facilities. It also has The Bahamas's best shopping, best entertainment, and best beaches.

Nassau, Cable Beach, and Paradise Island (linked by high-rise bridge to the city) have luxury resorts set on powdery-soft beaches and an array of water sports, golf, tennis, and plenty of duty-free shopping. The stores outdraw the museums here.

Despite its close proximity to Miami, Nassau hasn't lost its British colonial charm. Stately old homes and public buildings coexist with modern high-rises and new government edifices. Plentiful tropical plant life lines the streets, on which horse-drawn surreys take visitors for leisurely town tours (the most romantic way to see Nassau). Police officers in immaculate white starched jackets and colorful pith helmets still direct traffic on the principal streets.

You'll have lots of company enjoying this charm, for Nassau is one of the busiest cruise ship ports in the world. In recent years, the government has spent millions of dollars on its facilities, so that now 11 cruise ships can pull into dock at one time. When they do, you'll have to stake out your space on the beach and elbow your way into the shops and attractions.

COMING ASHORE

Cruise ships dock near Rawson Square, the very center of the city and its main shopping area. The Straw Market, at Market Plaza, is nearby, as is the main shopping artery of Bay Street. The Nassau International Bazaar is at the intersection of Woodes Rogers Walk and Charlotte Street.

FAST FACTS

Currency   The legal tender is the **Bahamian dollar (B$1),** which is on a par with the U.S. dollar. Both U.S. and Bahamian dollars are accepted on an equal basis throughout The Bahamas. There is no restriction on the amount of foreign currency tourists can bring into the country. Most large hotels and stores accept traveler's checks.

Information   You can get help from the Information Desk at the **Ministry of Tourism's** office, Bay Street (☎ **242/356-7591**). Open Monday to Friday from 9am to 5pm. A smaller information booth can be found at Rawson Square near the dock.

Language   The language of The Bahamas is English, spoken with a lilt and more of a British Isles influence than American.

SHORE EXCURSIONS

Shore excursions in Nassau are relatively minor and aren't really necessary, as you can easily get around on your own. The most heavily booked tour visits the heart of Nassau and Ardastra Gardens (see "Seeing the Sights," below). You're taken along

Bay Street, the main shopping district, and later treated to the famous marching flamingo review in the gardens. Other stops include the Queen's Staircase and Fort Charlotte. This jaunt lasts 2¹/₂ hours and costs $22 per person. Another 2-hour tour visits Fort Fincastle for the view, the Queen's Staircase, and some of the most beautiful homes of Nassau. It also takes passengers across the bridge to view the highlights of Paradise Island, including the Cloisters and its side gardens. This tour costs $18.

Free **Goombay Guided Walking Tours** (☎ 242/326-9772), arranged by the Ministry of Tourism, leave from the Tourist Information Booth on Rawson Square. Make an advance reservation, as schedules may vary. Usually the tours leave the booth at 10am and again at 2pm, except on Thursday and Sunday afternoon. These tours last for about 45 minutes and include descriptions of some of the city's most venerable buildings, with commentaries on the history, customs, and traditions of Nassau.

Many cruise passengers opt for a visit to Crystal Cay (see "Seeing the Sights," below), the country's most popular attraction, but you can go there on your own. The 3-hour tour costs $34 and includes a scenic boat ride to the marine park.

Majestic Tours Ltd., Hillside Manor (☎ 242/322-2606), will book 3-hour cruises on two of the biggest catamarans in the Atlantic, offering views of the water, sun, sand, and outlying reefs. This is the biggest and most professionally run of the tour boats. Its major drawback—at least to some passengers—is that there are too many other passengers aboard. *Yellow Bird* carries up to 250 passengers, and *Tropic Bird* up to 170. They depart from Prince George's Dock; ask for the departure point when you make your reservation. The cruises include a 1-hour stop on a relatively isolated portion of Paradise Island's Cabbage Beach. The cost is $15 per adult, with children under 12 paying $7.50, and snorkeling equipment is $10 extra. Departures are Tuesday, Wednesday, Friday, and Saturday at 1:15pm.

GETTING AROUND

Unless you rent a horse and carriage, the only way to see Old Nassau is on foot. All the major attractions and the principal stores are close enough to walk to. You can even walk to Cable Beach or Paradise Island, although many prefer taking a taxi or bus.

JITNEYS   The least expensive means of transport is by jitney, medium-size buses that leave from the downtown Nassau area to outposts on New Providence. The fare is 75¢; exact change is required. They operate daily from 6:30am to 7pm. Buses to the Cable Beach area leave from Navy Lion Road Depot. Buses to the eastern area depart from the Frederick Street North Depot, and buses to the malls leave from Marlborough Street East. Some hotels on Paradise Island and Cable Beach run their own free jitney service.

CAR RENTALS   **Avis** (☎ 800/331-1212 in the U.S., or 242/326-6380), **Budget** (☎ 800/527-0070 in the U.S., or 242/377-7405), and **Hertz** (☎ 800/654-3131 in the U.S., or 242/377-8684) maintain branches across the street from the main terminal at Nassau International Airport. Avis also has branches at the cruise ship docks, and in downtown Nassau on Marlborough Street. The companies' rates are approximately the same, but insurance regulations differ.

The best local companies include **Teglo Rent-a-Car,** Mount Pleasant Village (☎ 242/362-4361), and **McCartney Rent-a-Car,** 7th Terrace, Centreville (☎ 242/328-0486), which rents only compact cars.

There's no tax on car rentals in Nassau. Drivers must present a valid driver's license, plus a credit card or a cash deposit. Remember to **drive on the left,** British style.

Nassau

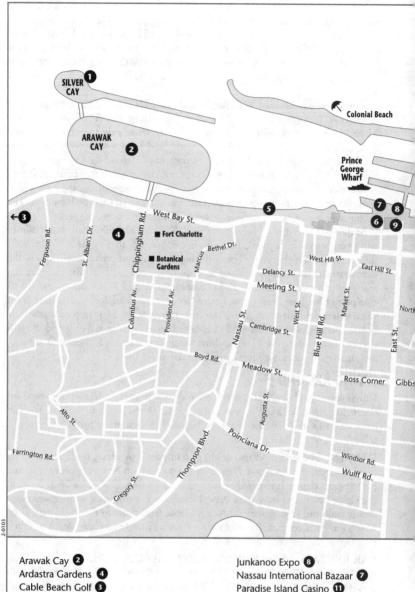

Arawak Cay ❷
Ardastra Gardens ❹
Cable Beach Golf ❸
The Cloister ⑫
Crystal Cay ❶
Crystal Palace Casino ❺
Fort Fincastle ❿
Hairbraider's Centre ❾

Junkanoo Expo ❽
Nassau International Bazaar ❼
Paradise Island Casino ⑪
Paradise Island Golf ⑬
Potter's Cay ⑭
Rawson Square ❻
The Retreat ⑮
Straw Market ❾

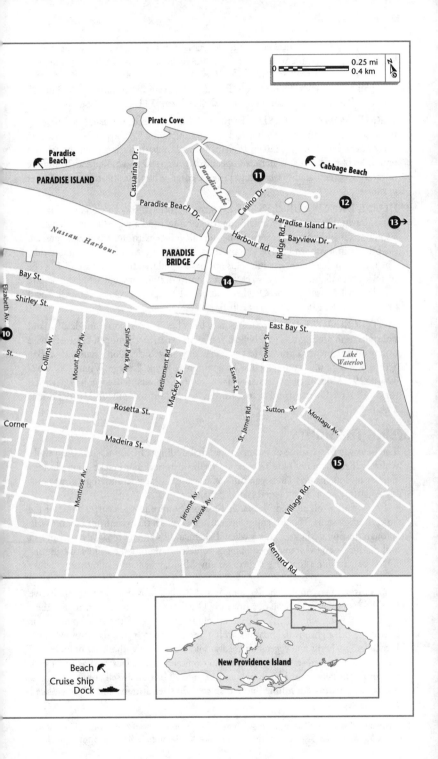

Pirate Cove

Paradise Beach

Cabbage Beach

PARADISE ISLAND

Casuarina Dr.

Paradise Lake

11

Casino Dr.

12

Paradise Beach Dr.

Paradise Island Dr.

Ridge Rd.

Bayview Dr.

13→

Nassau Harbour

Harbour Rd.

PARADISE
BRIDGE

14

Bay St.

Shirley St.

10

Elizabeth Av.

St.

*Lake
Waterloo*

East Bay St.

Fowler St.

Collins Av.

Mount Royal Av.

Shirley Park Av.

Retirement Rd.

Mackey St.

Essex St.

St. James Rd.

Sutton St.

Montagu Av.

Rosetta St.

Corner

Madeira St.

15

Montrose Av.

Jerome Av.

Arawak Av.

Village Rd.

Bernard Rd.

0.25 mi
0.4 km

N

Beach
Cruise Ship
Dock

New Providence Island

TAXIS　Taxis are practical, at least for longer island trips. Fares on New Providence are set by the government, and taxis are required to have working meters. The official fare is $2 at flag fall and 30¢ for each quarter of a mile for the first two passengers, plus $2 for each extra passenger. Five-passenger cabs can be hired for $23 to $25 per hour. The radio-taxi call number is ☎ **242/323-5111.**

FERRIES & WATER TAXIS　Ferries run from the end of Casuarina Drive on Paradise Island across the harbor to Rawson Square for $2 per person round-trip. They operate daily from 9:30am to 4:15pm, with departures every half hour from both sides of the harbor. Water taxis operate daily from 9am to 5:30pm at 20-minute intervals between Paradise Island and Prince George Wharf. Round-trip fare is $2 per person.

HORSE-DRAWN SURREYS　The elegant, traditional way to see Nassau is in a horse-drawn surrey—the kind with the fringe on top and a wilted hibiscus stuck in a straw hat shielding the horse from the sun. Negotiate with the driver and agree on the price before you get in. The average charge is $5 per person for a 25-minute ride. The maximum load is three adults plus one or two children under the age of 12. The surreys are available 7 days a week from 9am to 4:30pm, except when horses are rested from 1 to 3pm May to October, and from 1 to 2pm November to April. You'll find the surreys at Rawson Square, off Bay Street.

MOTOR SCOOTERS　Motor scooters have become a favorite mode of island transportation among tourists. Unless you're an experienced moped rider, it's wise to stay on quiet roads until you feel at ease with your vehicle. Don't start out on Bay Street. For a rental, contact **Ursa Investment,** Prince George Wharf (☎ **242/ 326-8329**). Mopeds cost $20 per hour or $30 for 2 hours, $40 for a half day, $50 for a full day. Open Monday to Saturday from 8am to 6pm. A $10 deposit is required.

SEEING THE SIGHTS

The best way to see some of the major public buildings of Nassau is to take a walk, which will give you not only an overview of the historical monuments, but a feel for the city and its history. Later you can concentrate on specific outlying sights, notably Ardastra Gardens and Coral Island Bahamas.

Begin your stroll around Nassau at **Rawson Square** in the center, home of the Straw Market stalls. We also enjoy the native market on the waterfront, a short walk through the Straw Market. This is where Bahamian fishermen unload a variety of fish and produce—crates of mangoes, oranges, tomatoes, and limes, plus lots of crimson-lipped conch. For a look, it's best to go any Monday to Saturday morning before noon.

✪ **Potter's Cay,** under the Paradise Island Bridge, provides a chance to observe local life as nowhere else. Sloops from the Out Islands pull in here, bringing their fresh catch along with plenty of conch. You are likely to see the chef buying your lunchtime fish right off the boat (assuming he's not using frozen fish from Miami). Freshly grown herbs and vegetables are also sold here, along with plenty of limes (the Bahamians' preferred seasoning for fish) and tropical fruits, such as *paw-paw* (papaya), pineapple (usually from Eleuthera), and bananas. Little stalls sell conch in several forms: raw, marinated in lime juice, as spicy deep-fried fritters, and in conch salad and conch soup.

✪ **Ardastra Gardens.** Chippingham Rd. (near Fort Charlotte, about a mile west of downtown Nassau). ☎ **242/323-5806.** Admission $10 adults, $5 children. Daily 9am–5pm. Bus: 10.

A flock of pink flamingos parading in formation is the main attraction at this lush, 5-acre tropical garden. The Caribbean flamingo, national bird of The Bahamas, had almost disappeared in the early 1940s but was brought back to significant numbers through efforts of the National Trust. These Marching Flamingos have been trained to obey the drillmaster's oral orders with long-legged precision and discipline. They perform daily at 11am, 2pm, and 4pm.

Other exotic wildlife to be seen here are very tame boa constrictors, kinkajous (honey bears) from Central and South America, green-winged macaws, peafowl, blue-and-gold macaws, capuchin monkeys, iguanas, ring-tailed lemurs, red-ruff lemurs, margays, brown-headed tamarins, and a crocodile. There are also numerous water-fowl in Swan Lake, including black swans from Australia and several species of wild ducks.

You can get a good look at the flora of the gardens by walking along the sign-posted paths, as many of the more interesting and exotic trees bear identification plaques. Guided tours of the gardens and the aviary are given Monday to Saturday at 10:15am and 3:15pm.

Atlantis **Submarine.** Clifton Pier, Lyford Cay. ☎ **242/356-2548.**

If you'd like a fish-eye view of New Providence, take a tour in this air-conditioned submarine. They offer about seven to eight trips per day, starting at 7:30am. The whole cast of "Waterworld" in The Bahamas parades before your eyes on this trip, lasting 2¹/₂ hours. The cost is $74 for adults, half fare for children. The 7:30am special is only $59 per adult, half price for children. When you make your reservation, you can also arrange to have the company van appear at the cruise dock to take you the 18 miles to Lyford Cay and the submarine.

The Cloister. In front of the Ocean Club, Ocean Club Dr., Paradise Island. ☎ **242/363-3000.** Free admission. Open anytime.

A 14th-century cloister built in France by Augustinian monks was reassembled here stone by stone. Huntington Hartford, the A&P stores heir, purchased the cloister from the estate of William Randolph Hearst at San Simeon in California. Regretta-bly, the dismantled parts arrived unlabeled and unnumbered on Paradise Island. The deconstructed cloister baffled the experts until artist and sculptor Jean Castre-Manne set about to reassemble it. It took him 2 years, and what you see today presumably bears some similarity to the original. The gardens, extending over the rise to Nassau Harbour, are filled with tropical flowers and classic statuary.

✪ **Crystal Cay.** On Silver Cay just off W. Bay St., between downtown Nassau and Cable Beach. ☎ **242/328-1036.** Admission $16 adults, $11 children 5–12 (5 and under free). Daily 9am–6pm. Bus: 10.

This marine park has a network of aquariums, landscaped park areas, lounges, a gift shop, and a restaurant, but its outstanding feature is the Underwater Observation Tower. You descend a spiral staircase to a depth of 20 feet below the surface of the water, where you view coral reefs and abundant sea life in their natural habitat. The tower rises 100 feet above the water to two viewing decks, which have a bar where you can enjoy a panoramic view of Nassau, Cable Beach, and Paradise Island.

In the Reef Tank, visitors have a 360-degree view of the world's largest manmade living reef, maintained by an "open system" that provides more than 48,000 gallons of unfiltered sea water every hour into Coral Island's tank and ponds. Graceful stin-grays, endangered sea turtles, and Caribbean sharks swim in Shark Tank, which has both an overhead viewing deck and a "below-water" viewing area. Visitors can spend hours in the Marine Gardens Aquarium, a complex of 24 individual saltwater aquariums that tell the story of life on the reef. The brilliant sea horses and baby sea turtles are striking highlights. Feeding time at the marine exhibits is a favorite of visitors and park employees alike.

Nature trails with lush tropical foliage, waterfalls, exotic trees, and wildlife further enhance this setting. A cluster of small seaside shops offers souvenirs, seashells, and island-inspired jewelry. Near the shops, the Wishing Well is believed to have been the island's only source of freshwater for the early Indians and marauding pirates. There's even a Pearl Bar where oysters containing pearls can be selected and purchased right on the spot.

You can get here via a scenic 10-minute ferry ride from the Prince George Dock. There are panoramic views of the harbor along the way.

Fort Fincastle. Elizabeth Ave. ☎ **242/322-2442.** Admission 50¢ adults and children. Mon–Sat 9am–4pm. Bus: 10, 17.

This fort, which can be reached by climbing the Queen's Staircase, was constructed in 1793 by Lord Dunmore, the royal governor. From here you can take an elevator ride to the top and walk on an observation floor (a 126-foot-high water tower and lighthouse) for a view of the harbor. The tower is the highest point on New Providence.

Although the ruins of the fort can hardly compete with the view, you can walk around on your own or take a guided tour. You don't have to ask for a guide, for very assertive young men wait to show you around. Frankly, there isn't that much to see except some old cannons. The so-called bow of this fort is patterned like a paddle-wheel steamer, the kind used on the Mississippi. The fort was built to defend Nassau against a possible invasion, but no shot was ever fired here.

✪ **Junkanoo Expo.** Prince George Wharf. ☎ **242/356-2731.** Admission $1 adults, 50¢ children. Mon–Sat 9am–5pm, Sun 3–5pm.

It's quite likely you'll miss the Junkanoo parade beginning at 2am on Boxing Day, December 26, but you can relive the Bahamian Junkanoo carnival at this expo in the old Customs Warehouse. All the glitter and glory of Mardi Gras comes alive in this museum, with its fantasy costumes used for the holiday bacchanal.

✪ **The Retreat.** Village Rd. ☎ **242/393-1317.** Admission $2. Mon–Fri 9am–5pm. Tours Tues–Thurs noon.

A true oasis in Nassau, these 11 acres of unspoiled gardens are even more intriguing than the Botanical Gardens. They are home to about 200 species of exotic palm trees, as well as the headquarters for The Bahamas National Trust. Half-hour tours of the acres are given Tuesday to Thursday at noon.

GAMBLING THE DAY AWAY

Many cruise ship passengers spend almost their entire time ashore at one of the casinos on Cable Beach or Paradise Island.

All gambling roads eventually lead to the extravagant ✪ **Paradise Island Casino,** in the Atlantis, Casino Drive (☎ **242/363-3000**). For sheer gloss, glitter, and show-biz extravagance, this mammoth 30,000-square-foot casino, with adjacent attractions, is the place to go. It's the only casino on Paradise Island, and is superior to the Crystal Palace Casino. No visit to The Bahamas would be complete without a promenade through the Bird Cage Walk, an assortment of restaurants, bars, and cabaret facilities. Doric columns, a battery of lights, and a mirrored ceiling vie with the British colonial decor in the enormous gaming room. Some 1,000 whirring and clanging slot machines operate 24 hours a day.

From mid-morning until early the following morning, the 38 tables for blackjack, 8 for craps, 3 for baccarat, and 1 for big six, along with the 9 roulette wheels, are all seriously busy with the exchange of large sums of money.

The dazzling **Crystal Palace Casino,** West Bay Street, Cable Beach (☎ **242/ 327-6200**)—the only one on New Providence Island—is run by Nassau Marriott Resort. Although some savvy gamblers claim you get better odds in Las Vegas, this casino nevertheless stacks up well against all the major casinos of the Caribbean. Decorated in hues of purple, pink, and mauve, the 35,000-square-foot casino is also filled with flashing lights. The gaming room features 750 slot machines in true Las Vegas–style, along with 51 blackjack tables, 7 craps tables, 9 roulette wheels, a baccarat table, and 1 big six. An oval-shaped casino bar extends onto the gambling floor, and a Casino Lounge, with its bar and bandstand, offers live entertainment. Open Sunday to Thursday from 10am to 4am, Friday and Saturday 24 hours.

SHOPPING

In 1992, The Bahamas abolished import duties on 11 categories of luxury goods, including china, crystal, fine linens, jewelry, leather goods, photographic equipment, watches, fragrances, and other merchandise. Antiques are exempt from import duty worldwide. Even though prices are duty-free, you can still end up spending more on an item in The Bahamas than you would back home. If you're contemplating buying a good Swiss watch or some expensive perfume, it's best to look in your hometown discount outlets before making serious purchases here. While the advertised 30% to 50% reductions off stateside prices might be true in some cases, they're not in most.

The principal shopping area is a stretch of Bay Street, the main drag, and its side streets. There are also shops in the hotel arcades. In lieu of street numbers along Bay Street, look for signs advertising the various stores.

THE MARKETS

We have listed specialty shops below, but a few places are good for one-stop browsing. The **Nassau International Bazaar** is comprised of some 30 shops selling goods from around the globe. This new arcade is pleasant for strolling and browsing. The bazaar runs from Bay Street down to the waterfront near the Prince George Wharf. The alleyways here have been cobbled and storefronts are garreted, evoking the villages of old Europe.

Prince George Plaza, Bay Street (☎ **242/322-5854**), can be crowded with cruise ship passengers. Many fine shops here sell Gucci and other quality merchandise. You can also patronize an open-air rooftop restaurant overlooking the street.

The **Straw Market** in Straw Market Plaza on Bay Street seems to be on every shopper's itinerary. Even those who don't want to buy anything come here to look around. You can watch the Bahamian craftspeople weave and pleat straw hats, handbags, dolls, place mats, and other items, including straw shopping bags. You can buy items ready-made—often in Taiwan—or order special articles, perhaps bearing your initials. Try bargaining to get the stated prices reduced.

ANTIQUES

Marlborough Antiques. Corner of Queen and Marlborough sts. ☎ **242/328-0502.**

This store carries the type of antiques you'd expect to find in London: antique books, antique maps and engravings, English silver (both sterling and plate), and the kinds of unusual table settings (fish knives, etc.) that might have been better appreciated by older, more formal generations. Among the most appealing objects for nostalgia buffs are the store's many antique photographs of Old Bahamas, any of which might be treasured by an island historian. Also displayed are works by Bahamian artists Brent Malone and Maxwell Taylor.

ART

Charlotte's Gallery. Charlotte St. ☎ **242/322-6310.**

This nonprofit organization sells only Bahamian-produced art. Some of it isn't to everybody's taste, but much of the collection is interesting. Though there are some large-size original oil paintings, many pieces are small, ideal for the souvenir collector.

The Green Lizard. W. Bay St. ☎ **242/356-3439.**

This store specializes in Haitian art, but also offers some Bahamian handcrafts. Its handmade wood chimes are collector's items. The place also carries one of The Bahamas' most celebrated creations: the hammock.

Kennedy Gallery. Parliament St. ☎ **242/325-7662.**

Although many locals come here for custom framing, the gallery also sells original art work by well-known Bahamian artists, along with pottery and sculpture.

CIGARS

Pipe of Peace. Bay St., between Charlotte and Parliament sts. ☎ **242/325-2022.**

Pipe of Peace is called the "world's most complete tobacconist." You can buy both Cuban and Jamaican cigars here; however, the Cuban cigars can't be brought back to the United States. For the smoker, the collection is amazing. The shop also sells such name-brand watches as Casio, Guess, and Anne Klein. Even if you don't smoke, you might slip in here looking for some souvenirs or perhaps some locally made handcrafts. They even sell chocolates and pecans.

COINS & STAMPS

Bahamas Post Office Philatelic Bureau. In the General Post Office, at the top of Parliament St. on E. Hill St. ☎ **242/322-3344.**

Here you'll find beautiful Bahamian stamps, slated to become collector's items. One of the most sought-after stamps uses seashells as a motif.

Coin of the Realm. Charlotte St., just off Bay St. ☎ **242/322-4497.**

This family-run shop lies in a lovely building, more than 2 centuries old, hewn out of solid limestone. It offers not only fine jewelry, but also mint and used Bahamian and British postage stamps, as well as rare and not-so-rare Bahamian silver and gold coins. You'll also find old and modern paper currency of The Bahamas. Bahama pennies, the ones minted in 1806 and 1807, are now rare and expensive items.

CRYSTAL & CHINA

Treasure Traders. Bay St. ☎ **242/322-8521.**

This offers the biggest selection of gifts made of crystal and china in The Bahamas. All the big names in china are here, including Rosenthal and Royal Copenhagen. The crystal selection includes Waterford, Lalique, and Orrefors. The store offers not only a multitude of traditional designs but also modern sculpted glass.

FASHION

Barry's Limited. Bay and George sts. ☎ **242/322-3118.**

One of Nassau's more formal and elegant clothing stores, this shop sells garments made from lamb's wool, English cashmere, and the kinds of upscale garments you might wear to a meeting of local bankers. Elegant sportswear (including Korean-made Guayabera shirts) as well as suits are also sold here. Most of the clothes are for men, but women often stop in for a look at the fancy handmade Irish linen handkerchiefs and the stylish cuff links, studs, and other accessories.

The Bay. Bay St. ☎ **242/356-3918.**

This Manhattan-style boutique carries a wide selection of designer clothing for both genders, but we didn't find any great bargains. The selection is elegant in a casual way. If you pick and choose carefully, you'll probably come up with something you can't find back home.

Bonneville Bones. Bay St. ☎ **242/328-0804.**

The name alone will intrigue, but it hardly describes what's inside. This is the best men's store we've found in Nassau. You can get everything here, from the usual T-shirts and designer jeans to elegantly casual clothing, including suits. A lightweight Perry Ellis suit will look especially good at the casino later.

Cole's of Nassau. Parliament St. ☎ **242/322-8393.**

This boutique offers the most extensive selection of designer fashions in Nassau. Women can find everything from swimwear to formal gowns, sportswear, and hosiery. Cole's also sells sterling gift items, silver designer and costume jewelry, hats, shoes, bags, scarves, and belts.

Fendi. Charlotte St. at Bay St. ☎ **242/322-6300.**

This is Nassau's only outlet for well-crafted Italian-inspired accessories (handbags, luggage, shoes, watches, cologne, wallets, and portfolios) endorsed by the famous leather-goods company. Its choice of gift items might solve some of your present-giving quandaries.

The Girls from Brazil. Bay St. ☎ **242/323-5966.**

This is the best outlet for swimwear in Nassau. The walls alone are intriguing, featuring wooden cutouts of well-endowed Brazilian women in bikinis. Prices are reasonable when compared to similar outlets in the Caribbean and Florida. The store on the upper floor sells a collection of casual clothing for children and women, plus craft and gift items from Central America. There's another branch on the lower floor of an outlet at Charlotte and Bay streets.

Mademoiselle, Ltd. Bay St. at Frederick St. ☎ **242/322-5130.**

This store specializes in the kinds of resort wear appropriate at either a tennis club or a cocktail party. It features locally made batik garments by Androsia. Swimwear, sarongs, jeans, and halter tops are also on offer here, as well as all the wonderfully scented soaps, lotions, and paraphernalia (through their on-site "Body Shop" boutique) you need for herbal massages and beauty treatments.

Gifts & Souvenirs

Planet Hollywood. Bay St. at East St. ☎ **242/325-7827.**

No one wanted to deny Nassau easy access to a Hollywood hipster's sense of American popular culture, so in 1995, Hollywood's grit-and-glitter *kulturmeisters* (Sly, Arnold, and Bruce and Demi, plus two less visible partners) opened a branch here in the heart of town. But despite official linkage with other members of the chain, this one doesn't sell liquor, or even food. Instead, look only for a nonalcoholic juice bar (selling such conventional juices as apple, cranberry, and grapefruit juice, as well as nonalcoholic daiquiris) and a daunting collection of pop-Hollywood souvenirs.

The inventory is broad-based and endlessly perky, featuring American trinkets (such as T-shirts, polo shirts, stuffed animals, jackets, keychains, bathing suits, and memorabilia inspired by the Age of Sputnik), many of them destined for eventual disposal in garage sales the world over.

HANDCRAFTS

Bahamas Plait Market. Wulff Rd. ☎ 242/394-6180.

This outlet right in the heart of Nassau is another good choice for 100% Bahamian-made products. It's far superior to the Straw Market, where some of the items are imported from Asia. You'll find a fine collection of place mats, jewelry boxes, hats, and bags. This process of turning palm fronds into plait takes 4 weeks, which explains the relatively high prices.

Island Tings. Bay St. between East St. and Elizabeth Ave. ☎ 242/326-1024.

Everything inside this shop pays homage to the skill of Bahamians. Expect a mini-library of books on the archipelago's culture and cuisine, as well as sculptures crafted from driftwood and conch shells, utilitarian jewelry, straw goods, natural sea sponges, wall hangings, and Junkanoo masks made both from all-natural traditional materials as well as from new-fangled fiberglass. The collection also includes aloe-based skin lotions and perfumes distilled from local plants and flowers.

The Plait Lady. The Regarno Bldg., Victoria and Bay sts. ☎ 242/356-5584.

Bahamians are proud of their handmade straw items, woven from fronds of the pond-top or silver-top palms, which are harvested only during a new moon. If you look carefully at some of the items sold at the famous Straw Market, you'll often see the label "Made in Taiwan" (unless the vendor has removed the tag already). However, if you're looking for the real thing—100% Bahamian—head to this outlet near The Sugar Reef Restaurant. The handmade straw wares here are the finest in Nassau. Conch-shell mats, trays, and baskets, and many other handcrafts are also sold. Especially intriguing are the coiled baskets from Red Bays on Andros. Sometimes these are woven with fabric from the famed Androsia Batik.

Seagrape. W. Bay St. ☎ 242/327-1308.

The main focus of this shop is Bahamian arts and crafts, some of which are made by persons with disabilities. You'll also find gift items, costume jewelry, and casual wear, including Androsia batik made on the island of Andros. There's a second branch in the Radisson Mall (☎ 242/327-5113), also on West Bay Street.

JEWELRY

John Bull. Corner of Bay and East sts. ☎ 242/322-4253.

This is the best name in the jewelry business. You'll find here classic selections from Tiffany & Co.; cultured pearls from Mikimoto; the creations of David Yurman, Stephen Lagos, Carrera y Carrera, and Sea Life by Kanbana; and Greek and Roman coin jewelry, as well as Spanish gold and silver pieces. The store also features a wide selection of watches, cameras, perfumes (including Estée Lauder, Chanel, and Calvin Klein, offered at 25% or more off stateside prices), cosmetics, leather goods, and accessories. It's one of the best places in The Bahamas to buy a Gucci or a Cartier watch, and has been the authorized agent for Rolex in The Bahamas for 30 years. The store itself has been doing business since 1929.

Little Switzerland. Bay St. ☎ 242/322-1493.

You'll never have to worry that you're getting ripped off here. Little Switzerland features a wide variety of jewelry, watches (including Ebel, Rado, Omega, and

Tag-Heuer), china, perfume (Oscar de la Renta, Dior, and Chloe), crystal, and leather in top brands. With various branches in The Bahamas and throughout the Caribbean, this store has long stood for quality. It also sells figurines from Royal Doulton and Lladró, as well as crystal by Lalique and Baccarat and, of course, Waterford.

LEATHER

Gucci. Saffrey Sq., Bay St., corner of Bank Lane. ☎ **242/325-0561.**

This shop, opposite Rawson Square, is the best for leather goods in Nassau. It offers a wide selection of designer handbags, wallets, watches, perfume, luggage, briefcases, gift items, scarves, ties, umbrellas, shoes, sandals, and designer casual wear and evening wear for men and women, all by Gucci of Italy.

Leather Masters. Parliament St. ☎ **242/322-7597.**

This well-known retail outlet carries an internationally known collection of leather bags, luggage, and accessories by Ted Lapidus, Lanvin, and Lancel of Paris; Etienne Aigner of Germany; and "i Santi" of Italy. Leather Masters also carries luggage by Piel and Marroquinera of Colombia, leather wallets by Bosca, and pens, cigarette lighters, and watches by Colibri. You'll also find silk scarves and neckties, as well as cigar accessories.

LINENS

The Linen Shop. Ironmongery Bldg., Bay St., near Charlotte St. ☎ **242/322-4266.**

This is the best outlet for linens in Nassau. It sells beautifully embroidered bed linens, Irish handkerchiefs, hand-embroidered women's blouses, and tablecloths. Look also for the most exquisite children's clothing and christening gowns in town.

MAPS

Balmain Antiques. Mason's Bldg., Bay St., (on the second floor, 3 doors east of Charlotte St.). ☎ **242/323-7421.**

This shop offers a the best collection in Nassau of 19th-century etchings, engravings, and maps, many of them antique and all reasonably priced. Some items go back 400 years. The assortment is wide and varied. It's usually best to discuss your interests with Mr. Ramsey, the owner, so he can direct you to the proper drawers. His specialties include The Bahamas, America at the time of the Civil War, and black history. He also has a collection of military historical items.

MUSIC

Cody's Music and Video Center. E. Bay St., corner of Armstrong St. ☎ **242/325-8834.**

The finest record store in The Bahamas, Cody's specializes in the contemporary music of The Bahamas and the Caribbean. The father of owner Cody Carter was mentor to many of the country's first Goombay and Junkanoo artists. The store also sells videos, compact discs, and tapes.

PERFUMES & COSMETICS

The Beauty Spot. Bay and Frederick sts. ☎ **242/322-5930.**

The largest cosmetic shop in The Bahamas, this duty-free outlet sells Lancôme, Chanel, YSL, Elizabeth Arden, Estée Lauder, Clinique, Prescriptives, and Biotherm, among others. It also operates facial salons.

Lightbourn's. Bay and George sts. ☎ **242/322-2095.**

A pharmacy 100 years ago, Lightbourn's is today a family-owned and operated business that carries a wide selection of duty-free fragrances and cosmetics. It's known for its service and the quality of its goods.

Special Bahamian Moments

You'll get all the conch you can possibly eat on **Arawak Cay,** a small manmade island across West Bay Street. The Bahamian government created the cay to store large tanks of freshwater, of which New Providence Island often runs out. You don't go here to see the water tanks, however, but to join the locals in sampling their favorite food. The conch is cracked before your eyes (not everybody's favorite attraction), and you're given some hot sauce to spice it up. The locals wash it down with their favorite drink, coconut milk laced with gin (an acquired taste, to say the least). This ritual is a very local tradition, and you'll feel like a real Bahamian if you participate.

You'll be aggressively solicited to have your hair braided in the local style at the **Hairbraider's Centre,** Prince George Dock. The government sponsors this open-air pavilion where all sorts of braiding experts gather. By the time you get back to the ship, you'll definitely have a new look.

The Perfume Bar. Bay St. ☎ **242/322-3785.**

Nassau has several good perfume outlets, notably John Bull and Little Switzerland, but this little gem has exclusive rights to market Boucheron and Sublime in The Bahamas. It also stocks the Clarins line (but not exclusively).

The Perfume Shop. Corner of Bay and Frederick sts. ☎ **242/322-2375.**

In the heart of Nassau, within walking distance of the cruise ships, The Perfume Shop offers duty-free savings on world-famous perfumes. Women can treat themselves to a flacon of Eternity, Giorgio, Poison, Lalique, Shalimar, or Chanel. For men, the selection includes Drakkar Noir, Polo, and Obsession.

SCOTTISH PRODUCTS
The Scottish Shop. Charlotte St. ☎ **242/322-4720.**

This specialist features products from Scotland, including stoneware, bone china, and especially crystal made in factories outside Edinburgh. It also offers the finest selection of Scottish woolens in the islands, along with kilts and fabrics.

SHOES
Alexis. Corner of Rosetta and Montgomery sts. ☎ **242/328-7464.**

Need a pair of leather pumps for an impromptu, spur-of-the-moment rendezvous with the prime minister and his wife? This outlet has one of the best selections of quality shoes, including women's footwear by Evan Picone, Timothy Hitsman, and Bandolino.

STEEL DRUMS
Pyfroms. Bay St. ☎ **242/322-2603.**

If you've fallen under the Junkanoo spell and want to take home some steel drums, you've come to the right place. Admittedly, they're not for everybody, but they'll be useful if island fever overtakes you after you return home.

BEACHES
The allure of New Providence Island for sun lovers is **Cable Beach,** one of the best-equipped in the Caribbean, with all sorts of water sports as well as easy access to

shops, casinos, bars, and restaurants. The area was named for the telegraph cable laid in 1892 from Jupiter, Florida, to The Bahamas. Cable Beach runs for some 4 miles and is incredibly varied. Keep searching until you find a spot that suits you. Waters can be rough and reefy, then turn calm and clear. The beach is about 2 miles from the port and can be reached by taxi or bus no. 10.

Cable Beach is far superior to the meager one in town, the **Western Esplanade,** which sweeps westward from the British Colonial hotel. But Western Esplanade is closer and more convenient for those arriving in a cruise ship. It has restrooms, changing facilities, and a snack bar.

Even Cable Beach buffs like **Paradise Beach** on Paradise Island. It's convenient to Nassau—all visitors have to do is walk or drive across the bridge or take a boat from the Prince George Wharf (see "Getting Around," above). Admission to the beach is $3 for adults, $1 for children, including use of a shower and locker. An extra $10 deposit is required for towels.

Paradise Island has a number of smaller beaches, including **Pirate's Cove Beach** and **Cabbage Beach,** both on the north shore. Bordered by casuarinas, palms, and seagrapes, Cabbage Beach's broad sands stretch for at least 2 miles. It's likely to be crowded with guests of the island's megaresorts. Escapists find something approaching solitude on the northwestern end, accessible only by boat or foot.

GOLF, RIDING, SAILING, TENNIS, DIVING & MORE

GOLF **South Ocean Golf Course,** Southwest Bay Road (☎ 242/362-4391), is the best course on New Providence Island and one of the best in The Bahamas. It's located 30 minutes from Nassau on the southwest edge of the island. This 18-hole, 6,706-yard, par-72 beauty has some first-rate holes with a backdrop of trees, shrubs, ravines, and undulating hills. The lofty elevation offers some panoramic water views, including an area of the Atlantic called "Tongue of the Ocean." Golf architect Joe Lee factored in four challenging water holes and made very effective use of the rolling terrain. Greens fees are $45, plus $35 for a golf cart. It's best to phone ahead in case there's a tournament scheduled.

Cable Beach Golf Course, Cable Beach, West Bay Road (☎ 242/327-6000), is a spectacular 18-hole, 7,040-yard, par-72 championship golf course, though not as challenging as South Ocean, above. Under the management of Radisson Cable Beach Hotel, this course is often used by guests of the other nearby hotels. Greens fees are $55 for all players. You can rent carts for $60.

Paradise Island Golf Club, Paradise Island Drive (☎ 242/363-3925), is a superb 18-hole championship course at the east end of Paradise Island. The 14th hole of the 6,771-yard, par-72 course has the world's largest sand trap: the entire left side over the hole is white sand beach. From May through November, greens fees are $100 for 18 holes; in winter, the rate is $135, including cart. There is a fully stocked pro shop.

HORSEBACK RIDING On the southwest shore, 2 miles from the Nassau Airport, **Happy Trails Stables,** Coral Harbour (☎ 242/362-1820), offers a 1-hour, 20-minute horseback trail ride for $60 per person, including free round-trip transportation from your hotel. The weight limit for riders is 200 pounds. Children must be 8 or older. Reservations are required, especially during the holiday season.

SAILING A number of operators offer cruises from the harbors around New Providence Island. **Flying Cloud,** at the Paradise Island West Dock (☎ 242/393-1957), features trips on a 57-foot catamaran capable of carrying up to 50 people. That's too large a crowd to be intimate, but you'll have fewer shipmates than on Majestic Tours' catamarans (see below). A half-day charter costs $35 per person, including snorkeling equipment and transportation to and from the boat. Tours depart daily, but times vary.

Majestic Tours Ltd., at Prince George's Dock (☎ 242/322-2606), has 3-hour cruises on two of the biggest catamarans in the Atlantic. These are the most professionally run of the local cruise boats. *Yellow Bird* is suitable for up to 250 passengers, and *Tropic Bird* carries up to 170. The cruises include a 1-hour stop on a relatively isolated portion of Paradise Island's Cabbage Beach. The cost is $15 per adult; children under 12 pay $7.50 on either cruise. Departures are Tuesday, Wednesday, Friday, and Saturday at 1:15pm.

Nassau Cruises Ltd., at the Paradise Island Bridge (☎ 242/363-3577), maintains a trio of three-deck motorized yachts, *Calypso I, Calypso IV,* and *The Islander.* These are the most luxurious of the cruises, and their trips to uninhabited Blue Lagoon Island are reason enough to take them. The yachts depart from a point just west of the toll booth at the Paradise Island Bridge. Daytime trips leave every day for the secluded beaches of Blue Lagoon Island, a 4-mile sail east of Paradise Island. The day sails leave at 10am and 11:30am and come back from the island at 1:30pm, 3pm, and 4:30pm. The Day Pass is $20 for adults and $10 for children, and pays for the boat ride only. The all-inclusive day pass is $50 for adults and $25 for children (3 to 12), and covers transportation, the boat ride, lunch, two daiquiris for adults, and all non-motorized water sports.

SCUBA DIVING & SNORKELING   Dive operators here cater to snorkelers as well as scuba enthusiasts. **Bahama Divers,** East Bay Street (☎ 242/393-5644), offers a half day of snorkeling at offshore reefs for $25 per person, and a half-day scuba trip with preliminary pool instruction for beginners for $65. Half-day excursions for certified divers to deeper outlying reefs, dropoffs, and blue holes cost $60. Participants receive free transportation to the boats. Children must be 8 or older to go snorkeling. Reservations are required, especially during the winter season.

Stuart Cove's Dive South Ocean. Southwest Bay Street, South Ocean. (☎ 800/879-9832 in the U.S., or 242/362-4171) is about 10 minutes from top dive sites, including the coral reefs, wrecks, and underwater airplane structure used in filming James Bond thrillers. The Porpoise Pen Reefs and steep sea walls are also on the diving agenda. An introductory scuba program costs $85, with morning two-tank dives priced at $70. All prices for boat dives include tanks, weights, and belts. An open-water certification course starts at $660. Bring along two friends and the price drops to $360 per person. Escorted boat snorkeling trips cost $30. A special feature is a series of shark-dive experiences priced from $115. In one outing, Caribbean reef sharks swim among the guests. In another dive, called "Shark Arena," a dive master feeds the sharks off a long pole.

Sea & Ski Ocean Sports, at the Radisson Grand Resort on Paradise Island (☎ 242/363-3370), offers scuba diving and snorkeling. A one-tank dive, all equipment included, costs $35; a two-tank dive goes for $60. Snorkeling reef trips depart daily at 10am and 2pm, and cost $25, with all equipment included.

One way to stay underwater without holding your breath or getting certified first is with **Hartley's Undersea Walk,** East Bay Street (☎ 242/393-8234), which takes you on a 3¹/₂-hour cruise on the yacht *Pied Piper.* At one point you don a breathing helmet and spend about 20 minutes walking along the ocean bottom through a "garden" of tropical fish, sponges, and other undersea life. Entire families can make this walk, which costs $45 per person in groups of five. You don't even have to be able to swim. Trips are operated Tuesday to Saturday at 9:30am and 1:30pm. Arrive 20 minutes before departure times.

TENNIS   Cruise passengers can pay to play at some resorts' courts. The **Radisson Cable Beach Hotel** at Cable Beach, West Bay Street (☎ 242/327-6000), has 18 courts. Nonguests pay $10 per person. Other hotels offering tennis courts include **Nassau Beach Hotel,** West Bay Street, Cable Beach (☎ 242/327-7711), with six Flexipave lighted courts, and **British Colonial Beach Resort,** 1 Bay St., Nassau (☎ 242/322-3301), with three hard-surface lighted courts.

Hotels with courts on Paradise Island include **Atlantis,** Casino Drive, (☎ 242/363-3000), with nine courts; **Pirate's Cove Beach,** Casuarina Drive, (☎ 242/326-2101), with three courts; and the **Radisson Grand Resort,** Casino Drive, (☎ 242/363-2011), with four lighted Har-Tru courts and lessons available.

Another major venue for tennis is the **Ocean Club,** Ocean Club Drive on Paradise Island (☎ 242/363-3000), which has nine Har-Tru courts. Although beginners and intermediate players are welcome, the courts are often filled with first-class competitors. Two major tennis championships a year are played here, drawing from among the world's professionals.

WATER SPORTS   Your best bet is **Sea Sports,** at the Nassau Marriott Resort & Crystal Palace Casino on West Bay Street (☎ 242/327-6200), the oldest and the best water-sports company in The Bahamas. It offers a full water-sports program. You can rent Hobie cats, Sunfish, windsurfers, or even a kayak. Prices range from $5 for 30 minutes in a kayak up to $40 for an hour's use of a Hobie Cat. Parasailing costs $40 for 5 to 6 minutes. Waterskiing goes for $70 for 1 hour. A snorkel trip, including gear, costs $25. You can also arrange many other activities here, such as scuba diving or deep-sea fishing.

Sea & Ski Ocean Sports, at the Radisson Grand Resort on Casino Drive (☎ 242/363-3370), is the best all-around center for water sports on Paradise Island. It offers scuba diving and snorkeling trips, parasailing for $40, and windsurfing for $20 an hour. Sailors can rent a Sunfish for $20 per hour or a Hobie Cat for $35 per hour.

DINING
IN NASSAU

Bahamian Kitchen. Trinity Place, off Market St. (next to Trinity Church). ☎ 242/325-0702. Reservations not accepted. Main courses $9.95–$24; lunches $6–$12. AE, DC, MC, V. Mon–Sat 11:30am–10pm. Bus: 10, 17. BAHAMIAN.

This honest, decent, and upright restaurant is one of the best places for good, down-home Bahamian food at modest prices. Specialties include lobster Bahamian style, fried red snapper, conch salad, stewed fish, curried chicken, okra soup, and pea soup and dumplings. Most dishes are served with peas and rice. You can also order such old-fashioned Bahamian fare as stewed fish and corned beef and grits, all served with johnnycake. This is the type of food the Bahamians have loved and survived on for decades. There's a take-out service if you're planning a picnic.

Café Kokomo. 18 Parliament St. ☎ 242/322-2836. Lunch main courses $6.50–$14; dinner main courses $9–$15. AE, MC, V. Mon–Sat 11am–4pm and 5–10pm. Bus: 10. BAHAMIAN/AMERICAN.

This downtown restaurant lies within the palm-studded tropical garden of Nassau's oldest continually operating hotel, the Parliament. Casually dressed diners come here for well-prepared Bahamian seafood in a verdant setting. Appetizers include conch salad and chowder. Try the food the regulars grew up on, either cracked conch or grilled or blackened grouper, the house specialty. Desserts include Key lime pie or mud pie. There's a also large tropical drink menu featuring the best frozen fruit daiquiris in Nassau. Ever had a soursop daiquiri?

Caribe Café Restaurant and Terrace. In the British Colonial Beach Resort, 1 Bay St. ☎ **242/ 322-3301.** Reservations recommended. Breakfast $3.50–$10; lunch $6–$9. Daily 7:30–11am, 11:30am–2:30pm. Bus: 10, 17. STEAKS/SEAFOOD.

Cruise ship passengers flock here for convenience, low prices, and familiar fare. Renovated in 1995, this down-home eatery was once the dank Blackbeard's Forge, recalling the days when Nassau was a haven for buccaneers. But the place has been considerably lightened up, both in its decor and in its food. Because it's near the cruise-ship docks, it's likely to be overrun on the days when a heavy armada is in port. You may want to retreat elsewhere if all the tables are full, since service tends to get worse then. Otherwise, at lunch you can get the food your kids have been crying for, including beef burgers or freshly made salads. This place also makes an excellent breakfast.

Europe. In the Ocean Spray Hotel, W. Bay St. ☎ **242/322-8032.** Lunch main courses $8– $14; set lunch $12; dinner main courses $8–$24. AE, MC, V. Mon–Fri 8am–midnight, Sat 4:30pm–midnight. Bus: 10. GERMAN/CONTINENTAL.

Attached to an inexpensive hotel, Europe offers the best German specialties in Nassau. Admittedly, it's a little heavy for the tropics, but the dishes are properly rendered and politely served. Admirers are drawn to Europe's low prices and to its change-of-pace fare—this is where you go when you think you can't stare another grouper or conch in the face.

The robust flavors have traveled across the ocean rather well. When the waiter suggests hearty soups to begin, he means it—perhaps lima bean and sausage. Naturally, you can get bratwurst and quite good sauerbraten. If you don't opt for the Wiener schnitzel, you might order the perfectly done pepper steak cognac. The chef will also prepare two kinds of fondue: bourguignonne and cheese. Everyone's favorite dessert is the meltingly moist German chocolate cake. All right, we said it was heavy. Diet tomorrow.

Gaylord's. Dowdeswell St. at Bay St. ☎ **242/356-3004.** Reservations not necessary. Main courses $11.50–$25; set-price lunches $13.95–$16.95; set-price dinners $21.95–$41.95. AE, MC, V. Mon–Fri noon–3pm; daily 6–10:30pm. NORTHERN INDIAN.

The Indian owners of this restaurant arrived in The Bahamas via Kenya and then England, and are wryly amused at their success "in bringing India to The Bahamas." A member of a respected worldwide franchise, it's the only Indian restaurant in the country, and as such, is now a culinary staple of Nassau. Within a beige-painted room lined with Indian art and artifacts, you'll hear recorded Indian music and dine on a wide range of Punjabi, tandoori, and curried dishes. Recently, such concessions to local culture as curried or tandoori-style conch have cropped up on the menu. If you don't know what to order, consider any of the curries, or perhaps a Tandoori mixed platter which, if you accompany it with a side dish or two, might comprise a meal for two persons. Any of the *korma* dishes, which combine lamb, chicken, beef, or vegetables in a creamy curry sauce, are also very successful. Take-out meals are available.

✪ **Graycliff.** W. Hill St. (opposite Government House). ☎ **242/322-2796.** Reservations required. Lunch main courses $17.75–$22.75; dinner main courses $32.75–$42.75. AE, DC, MC, V. Mon–Fri noon–3pm; daily 7–10pm. Bus: 10, 17. CONTINENTAL.

Graycliff, part of a deluxe hotel, is the only restaurant in The Bahamas that deserves a five-star rating. It's the domain of connoisseur and bon vivant Enrico Garzaroli. The chefs use local Bahamian products and delicacies whenever available and fashion them into a spicy and hearty cuisine. Neither provincial nor unduly French, they apply their original standards and measures to interesting and innovative dishes. They take plump, juicy pheasant and cook it with pineapple grown on Eleuthera in an award-winning combination. Lobster is another specialty, covered on one side with white butter and on the other with a sauce prepared from the lobster's head. The Grand Marnier soufflé is worth the trip across town. The wine list is the finest in the country, and the collection of Cuban cigars—almost 90 types—is said to be the most varied in the world. The balcony bar is an ideal spot for a drink.

Green Shutters Restaurant. 48 Parliament St. (2 blocks south of Rawson Sq.). ☎ **242/325-5702.** Lunch main courses $6.95–$21.50; dinner main courses $10.50–$27; fixed-price lunch $6.95. AE, MC, V. Mon–Sat 11:30am–4pm and 6–11pm. Bar open Mon–Sat 11am–midnight. Bus: 10, 17. ENGLISH/BAHAMIAN.

This place, a favorite with British expatriates, is an English pub transplanted to the tropics. It offers three imported English beers along with pub grub favorites such as steak-and-kidney pie, bangers and mash, shepherd's pie, and fish-and-chips. These dishes taste like what mother used to make (provided your mother's from the English Midlands). Bahamian specialties, including the inevitable grouper and conch chowder, are also available and are often an improvement over the pub grub. Sandwiches at lunch are particularly good and well stuffed. Courage beer is on tap, but the bartender can also make you a frozen daiquiri.

This place is macho and sporty, with a giant TV screen and secondary monitors airing live sporting events throughout the year.

House of Wong. Marlborough St. ☎ 242/326-0045. Reservations recommended. Main courses $8.50–$30; lunch from $6.95. AE, MC, V. Daily 11am–11pm. ASIAN.

Located in the heart of downtown Nassau, House of Wong is the latest incarnation of the famed Mai Tai Chinese-Polynesian Restaurant, which used to stand near Fort Montagu. You get a lot of good food and polite service here for the price. Peter Wong and his family brought all their recipes for Polynesian, Szechuan, and Cantonese dishes, and even some Hawaiian ones, to their new kitchen. It's still the leading Asian restaurant in Nassau, although the kitchen staff may be stretching itself a bit far with all these culinary influences. Before your meal, try one of the exotic drinks: a Volcanic Flame (served with flaming rum), a Lover's Paradise, or perhaps a Fog Cutter.

In the Polynesian mood? You might choose deviled Bahamian lobster, Mandarin orange duck, or sizzling steak. Szechuan dishes include hot shredded spiced beef, kung pao chicken ding, and lemon chicken. Among the Cantonese selections are chicken almond ding, moo goo gai pan, and sweet-and-sour chicken or pork. The restaurant also has take-out service.

☼ Pink Flamingo Trading Company. Bay St., 2 buildings east of Charlotte St. ☎ **242/322-7891.** Coffee or tea from $1.50; pastries from $2.50. AE, MC, V. Mon–Thurs 9am–5:30pm, Fri–Sat 9am–6pm. TEA/COFFEE/CIGARS.

This is the island's premier cigar, tea, and coffee bar. You can rifle through their racks of T-shirts and souvenirs on the street level, and then have a pick-me-up in the upstairs cafe. The only food options are bagels and pastries, steaming cups of tea and coffee, and wine or beer. Clients, at management's urging, are more seriously preoccupied with cigars, smoked by both deeply committed connoisseurs and gasping-for-breath neophytes. The cigars all come from the Dominican Republic and Cuba, and range from an unpretentious $3.95 stogie to a $50 Monte Cristo "Grade A," usually shared among friends at the same table.

Poop Deck. Nassau Yacht Haven Marina, E. Bay St. ☎ 242/393-8175. Main courses $12.95–$39; lunch $9.95–$39. AE, MC, V. Daily noon–5pm and 5:30–10:30pm. Bus: 10, 17. BAHAMIAN.

If you like your dining with a view, there's no better place than here on the second-floor, open-air terrace, overlooking the harbor and Paradise Island. At lunch, you can order such standard fare as conch chowder (perfectly seasoned) or else some juicy beef burgers. The waiters are friendly, the crowd convivial, and the festivities continue into the evening with lots of drinking and good cheer. For traditional Bahamian food, try the native grouper fingers served with peas and rice, or more spicy dishes like Rosie's special chicken or Bahama Mama's grouper. Two of the best seafood selections are the fresh lobster and the stuffed deviled crab. The creamy homemade lasagna with crisp garlic bread is another fine choice.

Shoal Restaurant and Lounge. Nassau St. ☎ **242/323-4400.** Main courses $9–$25. AE, DISC, MC, V. Daily 7:30am–1am. BAHAMIAN.

Far removed from the well-trodden tourist path, this restaurant is a steadfast local favorite. We rank it near the top for authentic flavor. After all, where can you get a good bowl of okra soup these days? Naturally, conch chowder is the favorite opener. Many diners follow it with more conch—"cracked" this time. But you can also order more unusual dishes such as Bahamian-style mutton seasoned with local spices and herbs. The seafood platter is more international in appeal. The restaurant is at its most active on Saturday morning, when half of Nassau seems to show up for the chef's specialty, boiled fish and johnnycake—it may not sound great, but this dish to a Bahamian is like pot liquor and turnip greens with cornbread to a Southerner.

Sugar Reef Harbourside Bar & Grill. Bay St. ☎ **242/356-3065.** Reservations recommended. Main courses $14.95–$26.95. AE, MC, V. Daily 11am–10:30pm. CARIBBEAN.

Sometimes you like to dine with a view. In Nassau, one of the best options is this restaurant, which has dining both inside and out. Its view of the harbor and Paradise Island is excellent. Fortunately, the food is worthy, too. The owner likes to show off the cookery, especially the use of sauces, many of which are made with tropical fruits, such as papaya, guava, and banana. The grilled chicken breast in mango sauce is a delight. Dishes are lighthearted in texture and taste. The chef always shops for fresh seafood—your best choice is usually the catch of the day. You can also order cracked conch, zesty crab cakes, and on most nights Bahamian lobster (ask that it not be overcooked to be on the safe side).

AT CABLE BEACH

Café Johnny Canoe. In the Nassau Beach Hotel, W. Bay St. ☎ **242/327-3373.** Breakfast $5–$7; main courses $7–$22. AE, DC, MC, V. Daily 7:30am–12:30am. Bus: 10 or 38. INTERNATIONAL.

Even its setting on the less desirable side of the Nassau Beach Hotel (the one facing West Bay Street) doesn't seem to detract from this popular place. Here you can order a wide range of the kind of dishes that everybody (especially families) seems to like, such as burgers, all kinds of steaks, seafood, and chicken dishes. The best items on the menu are blackened grouper and barbecued fish.

The yellow interior is accented with framed antique photographs of Old Nassau. College students often mob the outdoor terrace (site of volleyball games and other competitions), especially during spring break. There's often live music and karaoke, too.

Dickie Mo's. Cable Beach Hwy. (2 blocks west of the Radisson Hotel), Cable Beach. ☎ **242/327-7854.** Reservations recommended. Main courses $12.50–$39.95. AE, MC, V. Daily noon–midnight. SEAFOOD.

This well-maintained newcomer has competed successfully with better-financed establishments located within the nearby megahotels. Its fine cooking keeps customers coming back. The decor is unashamedly nautical, complete with fishnets, wide-plank flooring you might have found aboard a clipper ship, and memorabilia of the sailing days of yore. You'll find such dishes as barbecued chicken and ribs; grilled salmon or mahimahi in garlic-flavored butter sauce; yellowfin tuna with onion and sweet peppers sauce; and shark filet.

Tequila Pepe's. In the Radisson Cable Beach Hotel, W. Bay St. ☎ **242/327-6000.** Main courses $15–$24. Thurs–Tues 11:30am–2:30pm and 6–11pm. Bus: 10, 38. MEXICAN.

Although stateside visitors are used to such dining, a Mexican restaurant is an oddity in The Bahamas. Waitresses here tote shot glasses on their hips—they believe in keeping that tequila pouring. The buffet-style food is all familiar fare to Tex-Mex fans. Appetizers include black-bean soup and tortilla chips with queso or salsa. For a main course, you get what you'd expect: fajitas, tacos, burritos, tamales, and chimichangas. But is it any good? We've found that after enough margaritas, you, like Rhett, won't really give a damn. On Sunday, there's a live band and salsa contest.

ON PARADISE ISLAND

Café Casino. In the Paradise Island Casino, Casino Dr. ☎ **242/363-3000.** Main courses $8.50–$18. AE, DC, MC, V. Daily 11am–4am. AMERICAN.

If you want a snack or a break from the gaming tables, head over to this coffee shop at the far end of the casino. It offers pizza and well-stuffed sandwiches—such as corned beef, pastrami, and Reubens—as well as many kinds of salad. You can also order full meals, including New York sirloin or broiled, blackened, or fried grouper, but your best bet is to stick to the sandwiches. Go here only for the convenience and when you get bored of winning all that money.

The Cave. In the Atlantis, Casino Dr. ☎ **242/363-3000.** Lunch platters $5.50–$12. AE, DC, MC, V. Daily 8am–6pm. BURGERS/SALADS/SANDWICHES.

This burger and salad joint is located near the beach of the most lavish hotel and casino complex on Paradise island. It caters to the bathing suit and flip-flops crowd. To reach the place, you pass beneath a simulated rock-sided tunnel illuminated with flaming torches. It seems like a pirate rendezvous. The selection of ice creams is suitable for mid-afternoon cool-offs.

Club Paradise. In the Paradise Hotel, Casuarina Dr. ☎ **242/363-3000.** Main courses $19–$32. AE, DC, MC, V. Daily 8–11am, noon–4:30pm, and 6–9:45pm. STEAKS/SEAFOOD.

This is a good choice for those who want a casual ambience combined with ocean views, good value, and tasty, although relatively plain, food. The restaurant is in a thatch-roofed pavilion directly on the beach. You can order everything from Bahamian fried chicken and veal T-bone to seafood paella and cracked conch. The food is standard, not outstanding, essentially the kind of cuisine you'd find in a good tavern.

Columbus Tavern. Paradise Island Dr. ☎ **242/363-2534.** Reservations required for dinner. Main courses $19–$35. AE, MC, V. Daily 7am–11:30pm. CONTINENTAL/BAHAMIAN.

Far removed from the glitz and glamour of the casinos, this tavern seems relatively unknown. But it deserves to be sought out, as it serves good food at affordable (not cheap) prices. You can sit either inside or out (the better option), with views overlooking the harbor. The bar is worth a visit in itself, with its long list of tropical drinks. Appetizers include the ubiquitous conch chowder, as well as the more elegant cheese-stuffed mushrooms and foie gras. Even though imported frozen, both the chateaubriand and rack of lamb are flawless. You can also order a decent veal cutlet and a quite good filet of grouper with a tantalizing lobster sauce.

Seagrapes Restaurant. In the Atlantis, Casino Dr. ☎ **242/363-3000.** Breakfast buffet $15.95, lunch buffet $16.95, weekend brunch $22.95, dinner buffet $26.95. AE, DC, MC, V. Daily 7–11am, noon–3pm, and 5:30–10pm. INTERNATIONAL.

Buffet lunches and dinners are the specialties here. This is one of the mass-market restaurants of the Atlantis, catering mainly to those, especially families, who want an alternative to the more expensive options on Paradise Island. You can order tropical food from around the world, including Cuban, Caribbean, and Cajun dishes. The emphasis is on quantity rather than quality. The restaurant, which can seat 200 to 300 diners at a time, overlooks the lagoon and has a marketplace feel, with little stalls and different stations making up the buffet offerings.

The Water's Edge. In the Atlantis, Casino Dr. ☎ **242/363-3000.** Reservations recommended. Main courses $19.50–$35. AE, DC, MC, V. Daily, 7:30am–noon and 6:30–10pm. EURO/MEDITERRANEAN.

This is one of the most upscale of the many dining spots within the resort. Outside the dining room's windows, three 15-foot waterfalls splash into an artificial lagoon. Huge chandeliers illuminate the interior. Inside the open kitchen, a battalion of chefs create such dishes as paella Valencia and grilled salmon with French beans, potatoes, olives, and artichokes. The oak-smoked and spit-roasted duckling with figs and braised cabbage won our hearts. The pizzas here are standard fare, but some of the pastas have a bit of zest, including the penne à l'arrabbiata with a spicy tomato sauce. Depending on the day, some of these dishes are better than others. Mainly, the problem here is that the food has a hard time competing with the ambience.

15 St. Barts ⚓ ⚓ ⚓ ⚓

St. Barts is sophistication in the tropics—chic, rich, and so very Parisian, yet with a touch of Normandy and even Sweden in its personality. Forget such things as historical sights or ambitious water sports here. Come instead for white sandy beaches, fine French cuisine, and relaxation in ultimate comfort. Only small cruise ships can visit this little French pocket of posh.

New friends call the island "St. Barts," while old-time visitors prefer "St. Barths." Either way, it's short for St. Barthélemy—named by Columbus in 1493 and pronounced San Bar-te-le-MEE. The island's only town and capital is Gustavia, named after a Swedish king. It's a little dollhouse-sized port in a sheltered harbor.

For a long time, St. Barts was a paradise for a few millionaires, such as David Rockefeller, who has a hideaway on the northwest shore, and Edmond de Rothschild, who occupies some fabulous real estate at the "other end" of the island. The Biddles of Philadelphia are in the middle. These days, St. Barts is developing a broader base of tourism, but it continues to be a celebrity favorite. In February, its guest list reads like a roster from "Lifestyles of the Rich and Famous." You might run into Tom Cruise, John F. Kennedy, Jr., Harrison Ford, or Mikhail Baryshnikov.

The population is small, about 3,500 living on only 8 square miles of island. For the most part, St. Bartians are descendants of Breton and Norman fishermen. Many are of French and Swedish ancestry, the latter evident in their fair skin, blond hair, and blue eyes.

Occasionally you'll see St. Bartians dressed in the provincial costumes of Normandy, and when you hear them speak Norman French, you'll think you're back in the old country. In the little village Corossol, more than anywhere else on the island, people follow traditions brought from 17th-century France. You might see elderly women wearing starched white bonnets, at least on special occasions. This headgear was called *quichenotte*, a corruption of "kiss-me-not," and protected women

Airport ✈ Beach 🏖 Mountain ▲▲ Ferry Route - - - - Cruise Ship Terminal ⚓

from the close attentions of English or Swedish men on the island. Look for the bonneted women at local celebrations, particularly on August 25, St. Louis's Day. Many are camera-shy, but some offer their homemade baskets and hats for sale to tourists.

COMING ASHORE

Cruise ships anchor right off Gustavia; tenders then ferry passengers to the heart of town. There are usually shaded refreshment stands on shore. A short walk will get you into Gustavia's restaurant and shopping district.

FAST FACTS

Currency The official monetary unit is the **French franc (F),** but most stores and restaurants prefer U.S. dollars. At press time the exchange rate was 6.14 F to $1 U.S. (1 F = 16.3¢). We've used this rate to convert currency throughout this section.
Information Go to the **Office du Tourisme** in the Town Hall, quai du Général-de-Gaulle, in Gustavia (☎ **0590/27-87-27**). Open Monday to Friday 9am to 5pm.
Language St. Barts is technically part of France, so the official language is French. However, nearly everyone speaks English.

SHORE EXCURSIONS

Many passengers prefer to spend their time ashore walking around and exploring Gustavia, which should take no more than 2 hours. Most cruise ships offer a standard minibus tour of the island, which takes only 1¼ hours and costs $25. The duration is so short because there are almost no attractions, other than the island's natural beauty and beaches.

The minibus goes through the port, and then past the village of St-Jean to an overlook in Salinos, where you can take in the view. On the windward side of the island, you'll notice the different architecture required to withstand the heavy breezes. Next you'll head to Grand Cul-de-Sac for a view of the lagoon, and then have a brief stop at La Savone. You'll be brought back to the ship via Corossol, a tiny fishing village where the locals make straw from lantana palms.

GETTING AROUND

TAXIS   Taxis meet all cruise ships and aren't very expensive, since no destination is all that far. Dial ☎ **0590/27-66-31** for taxi service. The fare is 25 F ($4.20) for rides up to 5 minutes; each additional 3 minutes is another 20 F ($3.35).

CAR RENTALS   Never have we seen as many open-sided Mini-Mokes and Suzuki Samurais for rent as on St. Barts. Painted in vivid colors, they're fast, fun, and very windy. You'll enjoy driving one, as long as you're handy with a stick shift and don't care about your coiffure.

Budget (☎ **800/527-0700** in the U.S., or 0590/27-66-30) offers the best terms for its midwinter rentals, as well as some of the best prices. For the lowest rate, reserve at least 3 business days before your arrival.

Hertz (☎ **800/654-3001** in the U.S.) operates on St. Barts through a local dealership, Henry's Car Rental. With branches in St-Jean (☎ **0590/27-71-14**), it offers open-sided Samurais and more substantial Suzuki Sidekicks.

At **Avis** (☎ **800/331-1212** in the U.S., or 0590/27-71-43), whose local name is St. Barts Centre-Auto, you'll need a reservation a full month in advance during high season, plus leave a $100 deposit. These requirements may make it too much of a hassle for a cruise ship passenger. **Auto Europe** (☎ **800/223-5555**) also requires advance reservations.

MOTORBIKES & MOTOR SCOOTERS   Denis Dafau operates **Rent Some Fun,** rue Gambetta, in Gustavia (☎ **0590/27-70-59**). They provide helmets. Bikers must pay a $200 deposit as well as daily rental fee of $24 to $30. You'll need a driver's license.

SHOPPING

You don't pay any duty on St. Barts, so it's a good place to buy liquor and French perfumes at some of the lowest prices in the Caribbean. In fact, perfume and champagne are cheaper here than in metropolitan France. You'll also find good buys in sportswear, crystal, porcelain, watches, and other luxuries. The only trouble is that selections here are limited.

If you're in the market for island crafts, try to find those convertible-brim, fine straw hats St. Bartians like to wear. *Vogue* once featured them in its fashion pages. There are also some interesting block-printed cotton resort clothes on the island.

La Boutique Couleur des Îles. Rue du Général-de-Gaulle, 8. ☎ **0590/27-51-66.**

Tucked off a courtyard that's adjacent to one of the main streets of Gustavia, this shop sells shirts and blouses with hand-embroidered references to the flora and fauna of St. Barts. Suitable for both men or women at a "casually elegant" onboard cocktail party, they sell for between $30 and $50 each. Also available are what might be the worlds' most elegant beach towels, embroidered in gold letters with yachty-looking references to St. Barts.

Le Comptoir du Cigare. Rue du Général-de-Gaulle, 6. ☎ **0590/27-50-62.**

Very few shops in the Caribbean are as elegant and upscale as this one, and of those, this might be the only one designed exclusively for the tastes of gentlemen. It was established in 1994 by Patrick Gerthofer, as a branch of his cigar and cognac emporium based in Bordeaux, France. Elegantly sheathed in exotic hardwood, and enhanced by a glass-sided, walk-in humidor for the storage of thousands of cigars, this shop caters to the December-to-April crowd of super-upscale villa and yacht owners who flock to St. Barts. Cigars hail from Cuba and the Dominican Republic; connoisseur-quality rums come from Martinique, Cuba, and Haiti. Remember that Cuban cigars cannot be brought into the United States, so you must smoke them abroad. There's also a worthy collection of silver ornaments suitable for the desk of a CEO; artisan-quality Panama hats from Ecuador; and the most beautiful collection of cigar boxes and humidors in the Caribbean.

Diamond Genesis/Kornérupine. Rue du Général-de-Gaulle, 12/Les Suites du Roi-Oskar-II. ☎ **0590/27-66-94.**

Established in 1984 by a third-generation descendent of a French jeweler, this well-recommended gold, gemstone, and diamond shop is strongly influenced by French and European tastes. Although the price of objects here can go as high as $60,000, a particularly appealing best-seller is an 18-karat-gold representation of St. Barts, which sells for around $20. This is one of the few shops on the island where jewelry is handcrafted on the premises—in this case, from an atelier that's visible from the establishment's showroom. You can also peruse the selection of watches by Corum and Jaeger Lecoultre (both of which are available only through this store), and Brietling and Tag Heuer.

Laurent Eiffel. Rue du Général de Gaulle. ☎ **0590/27-54-02.**

Nothing sold in this elegant store is original; everything is either "inspired by" or crafted "in imitation of" designer models that usually cost 10 times as much. Look for belts, bags, and accessories modeled after Versace, Prada, Hermès, Gucci, and Chanel, and sold at lower prices. One of the few objects specifically advertised as a direct copy of a designer model is the "Kelly" purse, made famous by Grace Kelly around the time of her marriage to Prince Rainier. Originally crafted by Hermès, its copyright expired, in accordance with French law, after 30 years, and the design is now more or less in the public domain.

Little Switzerland. Rue de la France. ☎ **0590/27-64-66.**

This is the largest purveyor of luxury goods on St. Barts, a glittering tribute to the good life of conspicuous consumption. The entire second floor is devoted to perfumes and crystal, the street level to jewelry and a densely packed inventory of all kinds of watches. Prices are usually 15% to 20% less than on the North American mainland. Always ask about special sales.

La Maison de Free Mousse. Carré d'Or, quai de la République. ☎ **0590/27-63-39.**

This is the most unusual gift shop on St. Barts, with an intensely idiosyncratic roster of wood carvings and handcrafts from throughout Europe, especially Italy, and other countries such as Nepal, Thailand, Brazil, Mexico, Indonesia, and The Philippines. Your hostess is Italian-born Tina Palla, who selects her merchandise intuitively, focusing on whatever she thinks might look exotic or mysterious within a well-conceived private home. Anything you buy can be shipped. The shop's bizarre name comes from a nearby shop selling health and beauty aids, including hair gels (*la mousse*).

⭐ Favorite Experiences

The most popular gathering place in Gustavia is **Le Select,** rue de la France (☎ **0590/27-86-87**), apparently named after its more famous granddaddy in the Montparnasse section of Paris. It's utterly simple. A game of dominoes might be under way as you walk in. Tables are placed outside on the gravel in an open-air cafe garden near the port. The outdoor grill promises a "cheeseburger in Paradise." Jimmy Buffett might show up here—or perhaps Mick Jagger. The place is open Monday to Saturday from 10am to 11pm. The locals like it a lot, and outsiders are welcomed, but not necessarily embraced until they get to know you a bit. If you want to spread a rumor and have it travel fast across the island, start it here.

We are fond of St. Barts' secluded beaches. **Gouverneur** on the south is gorgeous and offers some waves, but wear lots of sunscreen—there's no shade. Get there by driving or taking a taxi through Gustavia and up to Lurin. Turn at the Sante Fe Restaurant (see "Dining," below), and head down a narrow road. To get to the beach **Saline,** to the east of Gouverneur, drive up the road from the commercial center in St-Jean. A short walk over the sand dune and you're there. Like Gouverneur, it offers some waves but no shade.

Marigot, also on the north shore, is narrow but good for swimming and snorkeling. **Colombier** is difficult to get to, but well worth the effort, for swimmers and snorklers. You'll have to take a boat or a rugged goat path from Petite Anse past Flamands, a 30-minute walk. You can pack a lunch and eat in the shade.

Polo Ralph Lauren. Carré d'Or, quai de la République. ☎ **0590/27-90-06.**

Predictably upscale, this branch of the worldwide arbiter of good taste does a thriving business close to the northern edge of Gustavia's harbor front. You'll find Ralph Lauren home products, sportswear for men and women, and a more elegant line of clothing (women only) for evening and gala wear.

St. Barts Style. Rue Lafayette, near the corner of rue du Port. ☎ **0590/27-76-17.**

This multicultural shop is closely tuned to France's idea of what hip Californians might wear for an off-the-record weekend on the French Riviera. It's owned by Dominique Gauthier, and staffed by a crew who mixes doses of Parisian *froideur* with *Franglais* and American slang. You'll find racks of beachwear by Jams World and Vicidomine in citrus colors of lemon, lime, grapefruit, and orange, as well as psychedelic-looking T-shirts from about a dozen different manufacturers. There's also an array of garments whose rumpled "I just had time to throw this together look" has proved enormously popular as an après nudist cover-up at certain beaches.

Sud, Etc. Galerie du Commerce, St.-Jean. ☎ **0590/27-98-75.**

Set within a cluster of stores adjacent to the island's airport, this shop is known for its stylishly off-handed clothing, both day and evening wear. Most of the inventory is for women, although there's a roster of bathing shorts and Bermuda shorts for men as well. If you're a high-fashion model, or just trying to look like one, chances are that this boutique will have something whimsical, light-textured, and *insouciant* for you.

Versace. Carré d'Or, quai de la République. ☎ **0590/27-99-30.**

Chic and relentlessly upscale, this stylish boutique perpetuates the memory of the late designer, and also pays homage to the semitropical climate of St. Barts. Don't even think of gaining access to Versace Enterprises' winter collections, as the inventory focuses almost exclusively on an "endless summer" motif.

BEACHES

There are 14 white-sand beaches on St. Barts. You're likely to be alone on the four we mentioned in the "Favorite Experiences" box, but few beaches here are ever crowded, even during winter. All are public and free, and easily accessible by taxi from the cruise pier. You can also make arrangements to be picked up at a scheduled time. Nudism is officially prohibited, but topless sunbathing is nevertheless quite common.

The most famous beach is **St-Jean,** which is actually two beaches divided by the Eden Rock promontory. It offers water sports, beach restaurants, and a few hotels, as well as some shady areas. **Flamands,** to the west, is a very wide beach with a few small hotels and some lantana palms.

If you want a beach with hotels, restaurants, and water sports, the **Grand Cul-de-Sac** area on the northeast shore fits the bill. There's a narrow beach here protected by a reef.

TENNIS & WATER SPORTS

TENNIS   Nonguests can play at the **Hôtel Manapany Cottages,** Anse des Cayes (☎ **0590/27-66-55**), for 80 F ($13.35) per hour.

WATER SPORTS   **Marine Service,** quai du Yacht-Club in Gustavia (☎ **0590/27-70-34**), is the most complete water-sports facility on the island. It operates from a one-story building set directly on the water at the edge of a marina, across the harbor from the more congested part of Gustavia. The outfit is familiar with at least 15 unusual dive sites scattered at various points offshore. The most interesting of these include The Grouper, a remote reef west of St. Barts, close to the uninhabited cay known as Ile Forchue. Almost as important are the reefs near Roche Rouge, off the opposite (i.e., eastern) edge of St. Barts. The island has only one relatively safe wreck dive, to the rusting hulk of *Kayali,* a trawler that sank offshore in 1994. It's recommended only for experienced divers. A *baptème* (baptism, or resort course) that includes two open-water dives for persons who are strong swimmers but inexperienced divers, costs 650 F ($108.55). A "scuba review" for certified divers who are out of practice, goes for 350 F ($58.45). A one-tank dive for certified divers begins at 300 F ($50.10).

Marine Service can also arrange waterskiing, offered daily from 9am to 1pm and again from 4:40pm to sundown. Because of the shape of the coastline, skiers must remain at least 80 yards from shore on the windward side of the island and 110 yards off the leeward side. The cost is about 210 F ($35.05) per half hour.

WINDSURFING   Windsurfing is one of the most popular sports here. Try **St. Barth Wind School** near the Tom Beach Hotel on Plage de St-Jean (☎ **0590/27-71-22**). It's open daily from 9am to 5pm. Windsurfing generally costs 100 F to 120 F ($16.70 to $20.05) per hour. Professional instructors are on hand.

DINING
IN GUSTAVIA

L'Escale. Rue Jeanne-d'Arc, La Pointe. ☎ **0590/27-81-06.** Reservations required in season. Main courses 100 F–180 F ($16.70–$30.05). AE, MC, V. Daily noon–2pm and 6:30pm–midnight. Closed Sept 1–Oct 20. ITALIAN/FRENCH.

Some villa owners cite L'Escale, a hip, sometimes raucous, and always irreverent hangout for the raffish and wealthy, as their favorite restaurant on the island. It's set in a simple, industrial-looking building on the relatively unglamorous south side of Gustavia's harbor, adjacent to dozens of moored yachts. You can either dine lightly and inexpensively here or spend a lot of money. Typical fare might include one of about a half-dozen pizzas or meal-sized salads, as well as pasta such as lasagna (a perennial favorite here), penne a l'arrabiata, or any of several gnocchis. You can also get Newfoundland lobster, carpaccio of raw marinated fish and beef, Mileanese-style veal, and a range of grilled meats and fish.

L'Iguane. Carré d'Or, quai de la République. ☎ **0590/27-88-46.** Reservations recommended for dinner. Continental breakfast 35 F ($5.85); sushi 14.50 F–17.50 F ($2.40–$2.90) per piece; main courses 150 F–175 F ($25.05–$29.25). AE, MC, V. Mid-Nov to May, cafe daily 8–11am; restaurant daily 11am–11pm; off-season, cafe Mon–Sat 8–11am; restaurant Mon–Sat 11am–3pm, daily 7–11pm. Closed Sept–Oct. JAPANESE/INTERNATIONAL.

This restaurant and cafe offers an international menu that includes sushi, American breakfasts, and California-style sandwiches and salads. The walls are ocher and blue, and the lighting fixtures are filtered to flatter even the most weather-beaten skin. The clients all seem to be watching their waistlines. The ambiance grows more Asian as the day progresses. Sushi, processed and served according to time-honored Japanese techniques, and imported twice a week from suppliers in Miami, is the main allure here, with special emphasis on tuna, snapper, salmon, and eel.

Wall House Restaurant. La Pointe (adjacent to the public library and municipal museum), Gustavia. ☎ **0590/27-71-83.** Reservations recommended for dinner. Lunch platters 50 F–80 F ($8.35–$13.35); dinner main courses 120 F–155 F ($20.05–$25.90); dinner set menus 195 F–280 F ($32.55–$46.75). AE, MC, V. Sun–Fri 11:45am–3pm; daily 6:45–10pm. FRENCH/INTERNATIONAL.

This restaurant, on the less congested peninsula of Gustavia's busy harbor, boasts one of the best views in town. Its name derives from a nearby ruin ("The Wall"), originally constructed during the island's Swedish occupation, and in recent years carefully incorporated by the island's government into newer buildings. Lunches here are unpretentious, sunlit affairs, featuring such lighthearted fare as burgers, simple grills, salads, and sandwiches. Dinners are more elaborate and ritualized. A set-price "lobster menu," priced at 280 F ($46.75), includes lobster ravioli, and a delicious version of parmentier of lobster in a crispy thyme crust. The à la carte menu features foie gras of duckling, shellfish salads, a gratin of scallops with vanilla, and noisettes of lamb with a *brunoise* of baby vegetables and turnip chips.

AT MORNE LURIN

Santa Fe Restaurant. Morne Lurin. ☎ **0590/27-61-04.** Reservations not required. Burgers 25 F–50 F ($4.20–$8.35); meal platters 60 F–100 F ($10–$16.70). No credit cards. Mon–Tues and Thurs–Sat noon–2pm; Thurs–Tues 5–10pm. Closed lunch Apr–Oct. AMERICAN.

Set inland from the sea, atop one of the highest elevations on the island, this burger house and sports bar has carved out a formidable niche for itself among the island's English-speaking clientele. It features wide-screen TVs that present American shows like the Super Bowl to as many as 450 viewers. You can take in the view of the surrounding landscapes for free, but most clients order one of the good hamburger, steak, shrimp, or barbecued-chicken dishes. This place made its reputation on its burgers, cheeseburgers, and fries, which some diners compare to the best in the States.

GRANDE SALINE

Le Tamarin. Plage de Saline. ☎ **0590/27-72-12.** Reservations required for dinner. Main courses 120 F–170 F ($20.05–$28.40). AE, DC, MC, V. Daily 12:30–3pm; Fri–Sun 7–9:30pm. Closed June–Oct. FRENCH/CREOLE.

One of the island's genuinely offbeat places is Le Tamarin, a deliberately informal bistro that caters near the Plage de Saline. It's isolated amid rocky hills and forests east of Gustavia, within a low-slung cottage. Inside, a teak-and-bamboo motif prevails. Lunch is the more popular and animated meal here, and most customers dine in T-shirts and bathing suits. If you have to wait, you can order an aperitif in one of the hammocks stretched under a tamarind tree (hence the name of the restaurant). Menu items are mostly light, summery meals that go well with the streaming sunlight and tropical heat. Examples include gazpacho, a *pavé* of cajun-style tuna with Creole sauce and baby vegetables; a carpaccio of fish, and chicken roasted with lemon and ginger. There's also a broad-based wine list, and a dessert specialty (chocolate cake) that appeals to chocoholics. Service can be slow, but if you're in a rush you shouldn't be here. This restaurant is made for a lazy afternoon on the beach.

GRAND CUL-DE-SAC

Club Lafayette. Grand Cul-de-Sac (east of Marigot). ☎ **0590/27-62-51.** Reservations recommended. Main courses 195 F–350 F ($32.55–$58.45). AE, MC, V. Daily noon–4pm. Closed May–Oct. FRENCH/CREOLE.

Come here for a wine-soaked meal in the sun amid beach-loving clients. Lunching here, at a cove on the eastern end of the island, is like taking a meal at your own private beach club—and a very expensive beach club at that. After a dip in the ocean or pool, you can order a planteur in the shade of a sea grape, and later proceed to lunch itself. You might begin with a *tarte fine aux tomates, mozzarelle, et herbes de Provence* that's lighter and more flavorful than most pizzas. Be warned that the congenial owners and chefs, Toulouse-born Nadine and Georges Labau, would be horrified to hear it compared to a pizza. There's also warm foie gras served with apples; grilled chicken breast with mushroom sauce; an *émincé* of lobster with basil-flavored pasta, and one of the best meal-sized lobster salads on the island. In other words, this is no hamburger fast-food beach joint. Afterward, have a refreshing citrus-flavored sherbet.

West Indies Café. In El Sereno Beach Hotel, Grand Cul-de-Sac (4 miles east of Gustavia). ☎ **0590/27-64-80.** Reservations recommended. Main courses 100 F–210 F ($16.70–$35.05). AE, MC, V. Daily noon–2:30pm and 7:30–8:30pm (last dinner order). Closed Sept–Oct 25. FRENCH/INTERNATIONAL.

One of the most endearing restaurants on the island incorporates aspects of a Parisian cabaret with simple but well-prepared meals served on a breeze-filled tropical terrace. At lunchtime, you'll be shaded from the sun by a wooden roof like a giant parasol. The design allows for a 360-degree view that overlooks a lagoon and a swimming pool. Menu items are midmarket in price, but are actually more carefully conceived and prepared than you might have expected. Examples include fish tartare, eggplant mousse, grilled lobster, and grilled tuna and snapper.

VITET

Hostellerie des Trois Forces. Vitet. ☎ **0590/27-61-25.** Reservations required. Main courses 120 F–170 F ($20.05–$28.40); fixed-price menu 230 F ($38.40). AE, MC, V. Mon–Sat noon–3pm and 6–10:30pm. FRENCH/CREOLE/VEGETARIAN.

Isolated from the bulk of St. Barts' tourism, this restaurant is located midway up the island's highest mountain (Morne Vitet). It has a resident astrologer and French provincial decor. In 1995 its food won an award from France's prestigious Confrérie de la Marmite d'Or. Although the same menu is available throughout the day and evening, dinners are more formal than lunches, and might include fish pâté, beef shish kebab with curry sauce, grilled fresh lobster, veal kidneys flambé with cognac, a cassolette of snails, and such desserts as crêpes Suzette flambé. Count on a leisurely meal here and a well-informed host who has spent years studying astrology.

16 St. Croix ⟱ ⚓ ⚓

St. Croix competes with St. Thomas, its smaller sibling in the U.S. Virgin Islands, for the Yankee cruise ship dollar. Although it gets nowhere near the number of visitors as St. Thomas, St. Croix is bigger, a lot more tranquil, and less congested. It has fewer shopping options, but the same good deals and generous duty-free allowances for U.S. shoppers. The major attraction here, however, is Buck Island National Park, a national offshore treasure. Some call it the single greatest attraction in the Caribbean.

In 1493, Columbus anchored off Salt River Point, on the island's north shore, but hostile Caribs drove him away. Eventually the island fell into Spanish, English, and French hands. The Danes bought it from the French in 1733 and owned it until the United States took over during World War I. The Danish influence still permeates the island and its architecture.

Large cruise ships moor at Frederiksted on the island's western end, where the Danes built a fort. Today, however, most of the action is in Christiansted, on a coral-bound bay about midway along the north shore. In the process of being handsomely restored, Christiansted is more historic, and has more sights and better restaurants and shopping. It's filled with Danish buildings erected by prosperous merchants during the island's sugar heyday in the 18th century. These red-roofed structures are often washed in pink, ochre, or yellow. Arcades over the sidewalks make ideal shaded colonnades for shoppers. The entire harbor front area is a national historic site.

St. Croix has some of the best beaches in the Virgin Islands. The east end of the island is rocky and arid. The west end is more lush, with a rain forest of mango, mahogany, tree ferns, and dangling lianas. In between are rolling hills and upland pastures dotted with former grinding mills. African tulips and other flowers add splashes of color to the landscape.

Most local-born residents are descended from African slaves brought to work the sugar plantations (the Danes abolished slavery here in 1848). Today, they live in a territory of the United States, carry U.S. passports, vote in presidential elections, and send a non-voting delegate to the U.S. House of Representatives.

COMING ASHORE

Only cruise ships with fewer than 200 passengers can land directly at the dock at Christiansted. Others moor at a 1,500-foot pier at Frederiksted, a sleepy town that only springs to life when the ships arrive. Both piers have information centers and telephones.

We suggest you spend as little time as possible in Frederiksted and head immediately for Christiansted, some 17 miles away. It's easy to explore either Frederiksted or Christiansted on foot (the only way, really), although you may want to consider one of the shore excursions outlined below to see more of the island, especially its underwater treasures.

FAST FACTS

Currency   The U.S. dollar is official currency.

Information   The **U.S. Virgin Islands Division of Tourism** has offices in Christiansted at Queen Cross Street (☎ **340/773-0495**), and at the Customs House

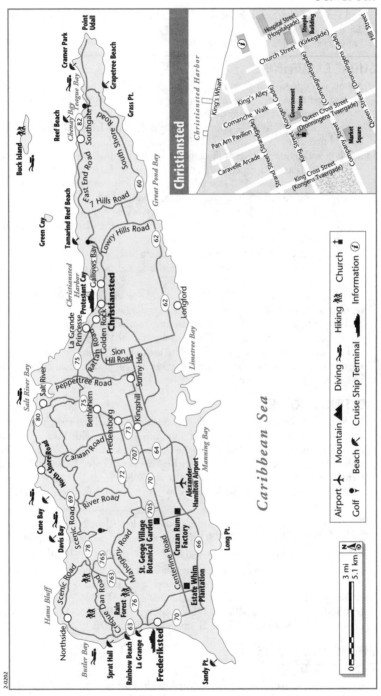

St. Croix

Christiansted

Hospital Street (Hospitalgade)
Steeple Building
Church Street (Kirkegade)
Hill Street
Christiansted Harbor
King's Wharf
King's Alley
Comanche Walk
Pan Am Pavillion
Caravelle Arcade
King Street (Kongens Gade)
Strand Street (Strandgade)
Government House
Queen Cross Street (Dronningens Tvaergade)
Company Street (Compagniets Gade)
Queen Street (Dronningens Gade)
Queen Cross Street
Market Square
King Cross Street (Kongens Tvaergade)
Company Street

Point Udall
Cramer Park
Grapetree Beach
Chenay Bay
Teague Bay
Southgate
82
Reef Beach
Grass Pt.
South Shore Road
Buck Island
East End Road
60
Great Pond Bay
Green Cay
1 Hills Road
Tamarind Reef Beach
Lowry Hills Road
62
Gallows Bay
Christiansted Harbor
Protestant Cay
La Grande Princesse
Christiansted
Longford
Golden Rock
62
Raftan Road
75
Sion Hill Road
Sunny Isle
Limetree Bay
Salt River
Peppertree Road
Salt River Bay
80
75
Bethlehem
Kingshill
Fredensborg
73
707
64
Canaan Road
Manning Bay
North Shore Road
72
70
Alexander Hamilton Airport
69
Scenic Road
River Road
Cane Bay
Davis Bay
705
Long Pt.
78
St. George Village Botanical Garden
Cruzan Rum Factory
Northside
765
763
Mahogany Road
Centerline Road
66
Rain Forest
76
Estate Whim Plantation
Hams Bluff
Creque Dan Road
63
70
Butler Bay
Sprat Hall
Rainbow Beach
La Grange
Frederiksted
Sandy Pt.

Caribbean Sea

Airport ✈ Mountain ▲ Diving ≥ Church ✝
Golf ⛳ Beach ⚲ Cruise Ship Terminal Information ⓘ
Hiking 🥾

N
3 mi
5.1 km
0

2-0202

247

Building, Strand Street in Frederiksted (☎ **340/772-0357**). Open Monday to Friday from 9am to 5pm.

Language   English is spoken here.

SHORE EXCURSIONS

Although it's possible to get around St. Croix on your own, you'll find here some of the best and most varied shore excursions in the Caribbean. For convenience alone, you might consider taking one of them.

The premier tour is the 4-hour, $60 tour of ✪ **Buck Island National Park,** a tropical underwater wonderland of blue water and colorful coral reefs. Transportation is provided from the pier at Frederiksted to Christiansted, where a boat takes you over to Buck Island. An experienced guide provides snorkel lessons.

An alternative 3-hour, $50 tour takes visitors on a sail-and-snorkel trip in a six-passenger boat. Another 3-hour tour includes 2 hours of hiking through a 225-acre preserve. Walks start at the Ghut Bird Sanctuary, where you can observe 30 different species, then continue up to Estate Mount Washington Plantation. You should be in good shape to take this tour, which costs $20.

A reef party cruise, lasting 3 hours and costing $32, takes cruisers on a double-decker glass-bottom boat over several sunken wrecks and reefs. The cruise leaves from the pier at Frederiksted.

Golf at Carambola, one of the Caribbean's most famous courses, is yet another destination. If booked as part of an excursion, golfing here costs $93.

If you're more interested in land sightseeing, consider the 3^1/$_2$-hour, $28 tour of the major island sights, including Christiansted and the Whim Great House.

Taxi tours are also a great way to explore the island. For one or two passengers, the cost is about $30 for 2 hours or $40 for 3 hours. All prices should be negotiated and agreed upon in advance.

GETTING AROUND

BUS   Air-conditioned buses run daily between Christiansted and Frederiksted about every 40 minutes between 5:30am and 9pm. Buses begin at Tide Village and head east of Christiansted along Route 75 to the Golden Rock Shopping Center, and then to Route 70, with stopovers at the Sunny Isle Shopping Center, La Reine Shopping Center, St. George Village Botanical Garden, and Whim Plantation Museum, before reaching Frederiksted. Fares are $1 or 55¢ for senior citizens. For more information, call ☎ **340/778-0898.**

TAXIS   Taxis are unmetered, so agree on the rate before you get in. The **St. Croix Taxicab Association** (☎ **340/778-1088**) offers door-to-door service. Expect to pay $20 to go from the cruise pier at Frederiksted to Christiansted, across the island.

CAR RENTALS   Driving can be dangerous here. The island has a higher-than-usual accident rate, and you drive on the **left side of the road.**

Budget (☎ **800/527-0700** in the U.S., or 340/778-9636), **Hertz** (☎ **800/654-3001** in the U.S., or 340/778-1402), and **Avis** (☎ **800/331-1212** in the U.S., or 340/778-9355) all maintain rental offices here. Rates vary.

SEEING THE SIGHTS
FREDERIKSTED

If you decide to hang around Frederiksted, begin your tour at russet-colored **Fort Frederick,** next to the cruise ship pier (☎ **340/772-2021**). Some historians claim that this was the first fort to sound a foreign salute to the U.S. flag, in 1776. The structure, at the northern end of Frederiksted, has been restored to its 1840 look. You can explore the courtyard and stables, and examine an exhibit area in what was once the Garrison Room. Admission is free. Open Monday to Saturday from 8am to 5pm.

CHRISTIANSTED

Begin your visit to Christiansted at the **visitors' bureau** (☎ 340/773-0495), a yellow building with a cedar-capped roof near the harbor front. It was built as the Old Scalehouse in 1856 to replace a similar, older structure that burned down. In its heyday, all taxable goods leaving and entering the harbor were weighed here. The scales could once accurately weigh barrels of sugar and molasses of up to 1,600 pounds each.

Another major attraction is the **Steeple Building** (☎ 340/773-1460) or Church of Lord God of Sabaoth, which was completed in 1753 as St. Croix's first Lutheran church. It, too, stands near the harbor front; get there via Hospital Street. The building was deconsecrated in 1831, and has served at various times as a bakery, a hospital, and a school. Admission is $2, which also includes admission to Fort Christiansvaern (see below). Open daily 8am to 5pm.

Overlooking the harbor, **Fort Christiansvaern** (☎ 340/773-1460) is the best preserved colonial fortification in the Virgin Islands. The National Park Service maintains the fort as a historic monument. Its original star-shaped design was at the vanguard of the most advanced military planning of its era. Open Monday to Thursday 8am to 5pm, Friday and Saturday 9am to 5pm. Admission is included in the ticket to the Steeple Building (see above).

AROUND THE ISLAND

Cruzan Rum Factory. W. Airport Rd., Rte. 64. ☎ **340/692-2280.** Admission $4. Tours Mon–Fri 9–11:30am and 1–4:15pm.

This factory distills the famous Virgin Islands rum, which residents consider to be the finest in the world. Guided tours depart from the visitors' pavilion; call for reservations and information.

Estate Whim Plantation Museum. Centerline Rd. (about 2 miles east of Frederiksted) ☎ **340/772-0598.** Admission $5 adults, $1 children. June–Oct Tues–Sat 10am–3pm, Nov–May Mon–Sat 10am–4pm.

This museum, restored by the St. Croix Landmarks Society, is unique among the many old sugar plantations dotting the island. It's composed of only three rooms. Some say the house resembles a luxurious European château. Its 3-foot-thick walls are made of stone, coral, and molasses,

Milling Road, a division of Baker Furniture Company, used the Whim Plantation's collection for one of its most successful lines of reproductions, the "Whim Museum–West Indies Collection." A showroom in the museum sells some of these reproductions, including pineapple-motif four-poster beds, cane-bottomed planters' chairs with built-in leg rests, and Caribbean adaptations of Empire-era chairs with cane-bottomed seats.

Also on the museum's premises is a woodworking shop, the estate's original kitchen, a museum store, a servant's quarters, and tools from the 18th century. The ruins include remains of the plantation's sugar-processing plant, complete with a restored windmill.

SHOPPING

Americans get a break here, since they can bring home $1,200 worth of merchandise from the U.S. Virgin Islands without paying duty, as opposed to a paltry $400 from most other Caribbean ports. And liquor here is duty-free.

In recent years, shopping in Frederiksted has improved. An urban mall is currently under construction here, mainly to appeal to cruise ship passengers arriving at Frederiksted Pier. The site occupies a 50-foot strip of land from Strand Street to King Street, the town's main thoroughfare. When it opens, it will be bustling with merchants, vendors, and restaurants.

In Christiansted, the emphasis is on hole-in-the-wall boutiques selling one-of-a-kind merchandise, especially handmade items.

A major redevelopment of the waterfront at Christiansted, following the hurricanes of 1995, was **King's Alley Complex** (☎ 340/778-8135), a pink-sided compound filled with the densest concentration of shopping options on St. Croix.

Caribbean Clothing Co. 41 Queen Cross St. ☎ **340/773-5012.**

This outlet sells hip sports clothing by top name U.S. designers in all the latest styles. It carries Calvin Klein, Guess, Polo, and Dockers, among others. Evening clothes for women are available as well. They also sell a small stock of shoes for both men and women, along with a good selection of jewelry, belts, scarves, and purses.

Colombian Emeralds. 43 Queen Cross St. ☎ **340/773-1928.**

Rubies and diamonds dazzle here, along with stunning emeralds, called "the rarest gemstones in the world." The staff will also show you their large range of 14-karat-gold jewelry, as well as the best buys in watches, including Seiko quartz. Colombian Emeralds sells the real thing.

Crucian Gold. 59 King's Wharf. ☎ **340/773-5241.**

Here you encounter the unique gold creations of island-born Brian Bishop. He designs all the gold jewelry himself. The shop also sells less expensive versions of his work in sterling silver. The most popular item is the Crucian bracelet, which contains a "True Lovers' Knot" in its design. You'll also find hand-tied knots (bound in gold wire), rings, pendants, and earrings.

Elegant Illusions Copy Jewelry. 55 King St. ☎ **340/773-2727.**

This branch of a hugely successful California chain sells convincing fake jewelry. The look-alikes range in price from $9 to $1,000, and include credible copies of the baroque and antique jewelry your great-grandmother might have worn.

If you want the real thing, you can go next door to **King Alley Jewelry** (☎ 340/773-4746), owned by the same company. King Alley specializes in fine designer jewelry, including Tiffany and Cartier.

Estate Mount Washington Antiques. 2 Estate Mount Washington. ☎ **340/772-1026.**

This place is a remarkable discovery: the best treasure trove of colonial West Indian furniture and "flotsam" in the Virgin Islands. Try to arrive on Sunday when owners Tony and Nancy Ayer are on site to provide professional guidance and commentary. After browsing through there, you can walk around the grounds of an 18th-century sugar plantation, now under restoration.

Folk Art Traders. 1B Queen Cross St. ☎ **340/773-1900.**

Since 1985, the operators of this store have traveled throughout the Caribbean ("in the bush") to acquire a unique collection of local art and folk-art treasures, such as carnival masks, pottery, ceramics, original paintings, and hand-wrought jewelry. The wide-ranging assortment includes batiks from Barbados and high-quality iron sculpture from Haiti. There's nothing else like it in the Virgin Islands.

From the Gecko. 1233 Queen Cross St. ☎ **340/778-9433.**

Hip and eclectic are the buzz words for this clothier/gift shop. You can find anything from handpainted USVI cottons and silks to the old West Indian staple, batiks. We found the Indonesian collection among the most imaginative in the Virgin Islands—everything from ornate candle holders to banana leaf knapsacks.

Gone Tropical. 5 Company St. ☎ **340/773-4696.**

About 60% of the merchandise in this unique shop is made in Indonesia (usually Bali). New, semiantique, or antique sofas, beds, chests, tables, mirrors, and decorative carvings are all priced the same as or better than similar new pieces at more conventional furniture stores. The store also sells worthy art objects (which can be shipped wherever you want) ranging in price from $5 to $5,000, as well as jewelry, batiks, candles, and baskets.

Harborside Market & Spirits. 59 King's Wharf. ☎ **340/773-8899.**

This outlet sells one of the island's best selections of duty-free liquors, wine, and beer. The location is one of the most convenient in town.

Larimar. The Boardwalk/King's Walk. ☎ **340/692-9000.**

Everything in this shop is produced by the largest manufacturer of larimar gold settings in the world. Discovered in the 1970s, larimar is a pale-blue pectolyte prized for its sky-blue color. It's found only in one place in the world, a mountain on the southwestern edge of the Dominican Republic. Objects range in price from $25 to $1,000. Other shops also sell larimar, but this emporium has the widest selection.

Little Switzerland. 1108 King St. ☎ **340/773-1976.**

This store has branches throughout the Caribbean. It's the island's best source for crystal, figurines, watches, china, perfume, flatware, leather, and fine jewelry. For luxuries like a Rolex watch, Paloma Picasso leather goods, or heirloom crystal by Lalique, Swarovski, and Baccarat, this is the place. At least a few items are said to sell for up to 30% less than on the U.S. mainland, but don't take anyone's word for that unless you've checked prices carefully.

Many Hands. In the Pan Am Pavilion, Strand St. ☎ **340/773-1990.**

Many Hands sells Virgin Islands handcrafts exclusively. You'll find West Indian spices and teas, shellwork, stained glass, hand-painted china, pottery, and handmade jewelry. Their collection of local paintings is intriguing, as is their year-round "Christmas tree."

The Royal Poinciana. 1111 Strand St. ☎ **340/773-9892.**

This store, which looks like an antique apothecary, is actually the most interesting gift shop on St. Croix. You'll find such Caribbean-inspired items as hot sauces ("fire water"), seasoning blends for gumbos, island herbal teas, Antillean coffees, and a scented array of soaps, toiletries, lotions, and shampoos. There's also a selection of museum-reproduction greeting cards and calendars, as well as fun and educational gifts for children.

Skirt Tails. In the Pam Am Pavilion. ☎ **340/773-1991.**

This little boutique is one of the most colorful and popular on the island. It specializes in hand-painted batiks for both men and women. The women's silks are bright and easy to care for.

Sonya Ltd. 1 Company St. ☎ **340/778-8605.**

There's a cult of local residents who wouldn't leave home without one of Sonya Hough's bracelets. She's most famous for her sterling silver or gold (from 14- to 24-

⭐ **Favorite Experiences**

The only known site where Columbus landed in what is now U.S. territory was at Salt River, on the island's northern shore. To mark the 500th anniversary of his arrival, President George Bush signed a bill creating the 912-acre **Salt River Bay National Historical Park and Ecological Preserve.** The landmass includes the site of the original Carib village explored by Columbus and his men, along with the only ceremonial ball court ever discovered in the Lesser Antilles.

At the Carib settlement, the men of Columbus liberated several Taíno women and children held as slaves. On the way back to their vessels, the Spaniards faced a canoe filled with hostile Caribs, armed with poison arrows. One Spanish soldier was killed, and perhaps six Caribs were either slain or captured. This is the first documented case of hostility between invading Europeans and the Native Americans. Sailing away, Columbus named this part of St. Croix "Cape of the Arrows."

The park today is in a natural state. It contains the largest mangrove forest in the Virgin Islands, sheltering many endangered animals and plants, plus an underwater canyon attracting scuba divers from around the world. The St. Croix Environmental Association, 3 Arawak Building, Gallows Bay, conducts tours of the area. Call them at ☎ **340/773-1989** for details.

Just north of Centerline Road, 4 miles east of Frederiksted at Estate St. George, lies the **St. George Village Botanical Garden of St. Croix** (☎ **340/692-2874**), a veritable Eden of tropical trees, shrubs, vines, and flowers. Built around the ruins of a 19th-century sugarcane workers' village, the garden is a feast for the eye and the camera—from the entrance drive bordered by royal palms and bougainvillea to the towering kapok and tamarind trees. Restoration of the ruins is a continuing project, but two sets of workers' cottages provide space for a gift shop, rest rooms, a kitchen, and an office. These have been joined together with a Great Hall, which the St. Croix community uses for various functions.

Other completed projects include the superintendent's house, the blacksmith's shop, and other smaller buildings used for a library, a plant nursery, workshops, and storehouses. Self-guided walking tour maps are available at the entrance to the Great Hall. Admission is $5 for adults, $1 for children 12 and under. From November to May hours are daily from 9am to 5pm; from June to October, Tuesday to Saturday from 9am to 4pm.

---

karat) version of the C-clasp bracelet. Locals use them to communicate discreet messages: If the cup of the C is turned toward your heart, it means you're emotionally committed. If the cup is turned outward, you're available. Prices range from $20 to $2,500. She also sells rings, earrings, and necklaces.

Trader Bob's Dockside Book Store. 5030 Anchor Way, Gallows Bay. ☎ **340/773-6001.**

This is one of the better bookstores in St. Croix, but that's not saying much. Of course, you might come across some intriguing West Indian titles. You'll also find a collection of toys for various age groups, ranging from puzzles to dolls.

Urban Threadz/Urban Kidz. 52C Company St. ☎ **340/773-2883.**

This is the most comprehensive clothing store in Christiansted's historic core, with a two-story, big-city scale and a different appeal from the other nearby T-shirt shops. Island residents prefer to shop here, because of the hip, urban styles. Garments for men are on the street level, women's garments are upstairs. The inventory includes everything from Bermuda shorts to lightweight summer blazers and men's suits. They carry Calvin Klein, Nautica, and Oakley, among others.

Violette Boutique. In the Caravelle Arcade, 38 Strand St. ☎ **800/544-5912** or 340/773-2148.

A small department store, Violette stocks many exclusive fragrances and hard-to-find toiletry items. It also has the latest from Estée Lauder, Fendi, Christian Dior, and Gucci. A selection of gifts for children is also carried. Many famous brand names found here aren't available elsewhere on the island, though they can definitely be found elsewhere in the Caribbean.

The White House. King's Alley Walk. ☎**340/773-9222.**

This White House is not about politics, but fashion, and it definitely lives up to its name. Everything is white or off-white. The style of clothing for women ranges from dressy to casual and breezy. "Sometimes you might want something in black," a staff member said, "and that's just fine. But when only white will do, we're waiting for you."

BEACHES

Beaches are the biggest attraction on St. Croix. The drawback is that getting to them from Christiansted or Frederiksted isn't always easy. Taxis will take you, but they can be expensive. In Christiansted, take a ferry to the **Hotel on the Cay,** a palm-shaded island in the harbor.

Most convenient for passengers arriving at Frederiksted is **Sandy Point,** the largest beach in all the U.S. Virgin Islands. Its waters are shallow and calm, perfect for swimming.

Cramer Park, at the northeastern end of the island, is a special public park operated by the Department of Agriculture. Lined with sea-grape trees, the beach has a picnic area, a restaurant, and a bar.

We highly recommend **Cane Bay** and **Davis Bay.** They're both the type of beaches you'd expect to find on a Caribbean island—palms, white sand, and good swimming and snorkeling. Cane Bay attracts snorkelers and divers, with its rolling waves, coral gardens, and dropoff wall. It's near Route 80 on the north shore. Davis Beach draws bodysurfers. There are no changing facilities here. It's off the South Shore Road (Route 60), in the vicinity of the Carambola Beach Resort.

Windsurfers like **Reef Beach,** which opens onto Teague Bay along Route 82, East End Road, a half-hour ride from Christiansted. You can order food at Duggan's Reef. On Route 63, a short ride north of Frederiksted, **Rainbow Beach** invites with its white sand and ideal snorkeling conditions. **La Grange** is another good beach in the vicinity, also on Route 63, about 5 minutes north of Frederiksted. You can rent lounge chairs here, and there's a bar nearby.

At the **Cormorant Beach Club,** about 5 miles west of Christiansted, palm trees shade some 1,200 feet of white sands. A living reef lies just off the shore, making snorkeling ideal. **Grapetree Beach** offers a similar amount of clean white sand on the eastern tip of the island. Follow the South Shore Road (Route 60) to reach it. Water sports are popular here.

GOLF, RIDING, DIVING, SNORKELING, TENNIS & MORE

GOLF   St. Croix has the best golfing in the U.S. Virgins. In fact, guests staying on St. John and St. Thomas often fly over for a day's round on the island's two 18-hole and one 9-hole golf courses.

The ✪ **Carambola Golf Course,** on the northeast side of St. Croix (☎ **340/ 778-5638**), was designed by Robert Trent Jones, Sr., who called it "the loveliest course I ever designed." The course, formerly the site of "Shell's Wonderful World of Golf," has been likened to a botanical garden. Golfing authorities consider its collection of par-3 holes to be the best in the tropics. Carambola's course record of 65 was set by Jim Levine in 1993. The greens fees of $80 per person in winter ($48 in summer) allow you to play as many holes as you like. Cart rental is included in the greens fees.

The **Buccaneer** (☎ **340/773-2100,** ext. 738), 2 miles east of Christiansted, is a challenging 5,810-yard, 18-hole course with panoramic vistas. Player can knock the ball over rolling hills right to the edge of the Caribbean. Greens fees are $35 for 9 holes or $50 for 18 holes, with a cart rental going for $14.

A final course is the **Reef,** at Teague Bay on the east end of the island (☎ **340/ 773-8844**), a 3,100-yard, nine-hole course, charging greens fees of $10 to $14. Carts rent for $5 to $8. The longest hole is a 579-yard par 5.

HORSEBACK RIDING   Paul and Jill's Equestrian Stables, Sprat Hall Plantation, Route 58 (☎ **340/772-2880**), is the only equestrian stable in the Virgin Islands. The owners are Paul Wojcie and his wife, Jill Hurd, a daughter of the establishment's original founders. The stables, set on the sprawling grounds of the island's oldest plantation, are known throughout the Caribbean for the quality of the horses and the scenic trail rides through the forests. You'll pass ruins of abandoned 18th-century plantations and sugar mills and climb the hills of St. Croix's western end. Tour guides give running commentaries on island fauna and history, and riding techniques. Beginners and experienced riders alike are welcome.

A 2-hour trail ride costs $50 per person. Tours usually depart daily in winter at 10am and 4pm and off-season at 5pm, with slight variations according to demand. The afternoon tours are often too late for returning cruise ship passengers. Make reservations at least a day in advance.

SCUBA DIVING & SNORKELING   **Diver's love St. Croix's sponge life, beautiful black-coral trees, and steep dropoffs near the shoreline. This island is home to the largest living reef in the Caribbean. Its fabled north shore wall begins in 25 to 30 feet of water and drops—sometimes almost straight down—to 13,200 feet. There are 22 moored diving sites. Favorites among them include the historic **Salt River Canyon, the coral gardens of **Scotch Banks,** and **Eagle Ray,** filled with cruising rays. **Pavilions** is yet another good dive site, with a pristine virgin coral reef.

The best site of all, however, is ✪ **Buck Island,** an underwater wonderland with a visibility of more than 100 feet and an underwater nature trail. All the minor and major agencies offer scuba and snorkeling tours to Buck Island.

Dive St. Croix, 59 King's Wharf (☎ **800/523-DIVE** in the U.S., or 340/ 773-2628; fax 340/773-7400), operates the 38-foot dive boat *Reliance.* The staff offers complete instruction, from beginners courses through full certification. A resort course is $75; a two-tank dive is $70. Scuba trips to Buck Island are $65.

V.I. Divers Ltd., in the Pan Am Pavilion on Christiansted's waterfront (☎ **800/ 544-5911** in the U.S., or 340/773-6045), is the oldest and one of the best dive operations on the island. *Rodales Scuba Diving* magazine rated its staff as among the top 10 worldwide. This full-service PADI five-star facility offers daily two-tank boat dives, as well as guided snorkeling trips to Green Cay. A two-tank boat or beach dive is $75. A guided snorkeling tour to Green Cay costs $35; another snorkeling tour costs $25.

TENNIS   **Some authorities rate the tennis at the **Buccaneer (☎ **340/773-2100,** ext. 736) as the best in the West Indies. This hotel offers a choice of eight courts, all open to the public. Nonguests pay $8 per person per hour. You must call to reserve a court. There's a pro shop, and a tennis pro available for lessons.

WINDSURFING   The best place for this increasingly popular sport is the **St. Croix Water Sports Center** (☎ **340/773-7060**), located on a small offshore island in Christiansted Harbor. It's part of the Hotel on the Cay. The hours are daily from 9am to 5pm in winter and daily from 10am to 5pm in off-season. Windsurfing rentals are $25 per hour. You can also get lessons. The center also offers Sea Doos, which seat two and cost $50 per half hour, as well as parasailing for $50 per person, and snorkeling equipment for $15 per day.

DINING

IN CHRISTIANSTED

Annabelle's Tea Room. 51-ABC Company St. ☎ **340/773-3990.** Reservations recommended. Sandwiches, salads, and platters $6.50–$12. No credit cards. Mon–Sat 9am–3pm. INTERNATIONAL.

This restaurant occupies a quiet courtyard filled with tropical plants and surrounded by clapboard-sided buildings evoking New Orleans. Don't expect grand cuisine here—what you get is a shady place to rest your feet, a warm welcome from Anna Deering or a member of her staff, a sense of Cruzan history, and a simple but refreshing assortment of sandwiches, salads, soups, and platters. Try the dolphin (the fish, not the mammal) in herb-flavored butter sauce, Cubano or "Lazy Virgin" sandwiches ("all vegetables and cheese, with no meat"), or the conch Creole.

Antoine's. 58A King St. (on King's Wharf). ☎ **340/773-0263.** Reservations required in winter. Main courses $15–$18. AE, MC, V. Daily 7:30am–2:30pm and 6:30–9:30pm. CARIBBEAN/INTERNATIONAL.

This restaurant, on the second floor overlooking Christiansted's harbor and marina, is a local institution. But in spite of its fame, the dinners are only mediocre. Many visitors come just for the bar, which dispenses more than 35 different kinds of frozen drinks, and the island's largest selection of beer. There's a covered terrace, a satellite bar in back (the Aqua Lounge), and a cubbyhole Italian restaurant (Pico Bello) serving lunch and dinner daily. Regardless of where you dine, a range of pastas and veal dishes is available, as well as such specialties as goulash, knockwurst salad, roulade of beef, and Wiener schnitzel. Local dishes like fish chowder and lobster are also on hand. Antoine's is better for breakfast, when you can try one of the "creative" alpine omelets.

Harvey's. 11B Company St. ☎ **340/773-3433.** Main courses $8–$12. No credit cards. Mon–Wed 11:30am–6pm, Thurs–Sat 11:30am–9pm. CARIBBEAN/CONTINENTAL.

The setting might be a back room in Truman Capote's "House of Flowers," which is no great compliment. But try to ignore the plastic and the flowery tablecloths that give this place its 1950s aura, and grab one of the dozen tables. If you do, you'll enjoy the thoroughly zesty cooking of island matriarch Sarah Harvey, who takes joy in preparing her basic but tasty food. There's plenty of it, too. Begin with one of her homemade soups, such as callaloo or chicken. She'll even serve you conch in butter sauce as an appetizer. Main dishes are the type of food she was raised on: barbecue chicken, barbecue spareribs (barbecue is big here), boiled filet of snapper, and even lobster when they can get it. Fungi comes with virtually everything. For dessert, try one of her delectable tarts made from guava, pineapple, or coconut.

✪ **Indies.** 55–56 Company St. ☎ **340/692-9440.** Reservations recommended. Main courses $13.50–$21.50. AE, DISC, MC, V. Mon–Fri 11:30am–2:30pm; daily 5:30–9:30pm. CARIBBEAN/INTERNATIONAL.

Catherine Plav-Drigger is one of the best chefs in the Caribbean, and at her restaurant you're likely to get your finest meal on St. Croix. Indies is a welcoming retreat. You dine adjacent to a carriage and cookhouse from the 1850s in a sheltered courtyard protected from the noise of the street outside. Catherine's fresh, mostly tropical ingredients are first-rate.

The menu changes depending on what's fresh. The swordfish with fresh artichokes, shiitake mushrooms, and thyme has a savory flavor, as does the baked wahoo with lobster curry and fresh chutney and coconut. For a soup, try either the excellent island lobster and shrimp bisque or the spicy black-bean soup. Appetizers might be anything—perhaps a superb lobster vegetable strudel or steamed mussels in white wine. All the desserts are homemade.

✪ **Paradise Café.** Queen Cross St. at 53B Company St. (across from Government House). ☎ **340/773-2985.** Reservations not required. Main courses $13–$16; sandwiches $4–$8; breakfast from $3. No credit cards. Mon–Sat 7:30am–10pm. DELI/AMERICAN.

Locals frequent this neighborhood enclave in a setting of brick walls and beamed ceilings, originally part of an 18th-century guest house. It serves New York deli–style sandwiches throughout the day—everything from a Reuben to a tuna melt. Of course, burgers are always featured. After 5pm, you can order from a limited—but good value—list of main dishes, including a grilled fresh fish dinner and a beef stir-fry. All mains come with a tossed salad and garlic bread. Fresh local lobster is occasionally available also. Many in-the-know residents arrive for breakfast, to feast on such delights as banana pancakes or sausage, pepper, and onion omelets with french fries.

St. Croix Chop House & Brew Pub. King's Alley Walk. ☎ **340/713-9820.** Reservations recommended for upstairs dining room, not for meals in the Brew Pub. Platters in Brew Pub $8–$11.50; main courses in upstairs restaurant $18–$23. AE, V. Lunch (available in Brew Pub only) Mon–Sat 11am–3pm and 6–10:30pm. AMERICAN.

Boasting one of the best harbor views in Christiansted, this restaurant is the extension of the Virgin Island's only brewery (The Virgin Island Ale Company), which was established in 1997. Its beers include a pale ale (Frigate), a red beer (Blackbeard's), and a dark stout (Jump-Up)—all of which have already earned a formidable local reputation. Most of the serious beer-drinking occurs on the building's street level (The Brew Pub). Many of the clients come here just to drink, and stay until the pub closes at around 1am. But if you're hungry, a burgers and sandwiches are served at street level for lunch and dinner. In the evening, the upstairs dining room offers a two-fisted menu that includes garlic-stuffed filet steak, New York–style pepper steak, brown ale chicken, and such fish as wahoo and marlin. All sauces and breads are concocted with some kind of brew, which adds a welcome heartiness to the cuisine.

Tutto Bene. 2 Company St. ☎ **340/773-5229.** Reservations accepted only for parties of 5 or more. Main courses $12.95–$21.95; lunch $5.95–$10.95. AE, V. Mon–Fri 11:30am–2:30pm; daily 6–10pm. ITALIAN.

In the heart of town, Tutto Bene has more the allure of a bistro-cantina than of a full-fledged restaurant. The Connecticut-born owner, Tony Cerruto, believes in simple, hearty, and uncomplicated *paysano* dishes, the kind mammas fed their sons in the old country. You'll dine on wooden tables covered with painted tablecloths, amid warm colors and often lots of hubbub. Menu items are written on a pair of oversize mirrors against one wall. A full range of delectable pastas is offered daily. At lunch you can enjoy bistro-style veggie frittatas, a chicken pesto sandwich, or spinach lasagna. Great care goes into the seafood dishes. Fish might be served parmigiana, or you can order seafood Genovese with mussels, clams, and shrimp with a white wine/

pesto sauce over linguine. There's also a large mahogany bar in back that does a brisk business of its own.

IN FREDERIKSTED

Le St. Tropez. Limetree Court, 67 King St. ☎ **340/772-3000.** Reservations recommended. Main courses $14.50–$24.50. AE, DISC, MC, V. Mon–Fri 11:30am–2:30pm and 6–10pm, Sat 6–10:30pm. FRENCH/MEDITERRANEAN.

This bistro is the most popular in Frederiksted. Since it's small, it's always better to call ahead for a table. If you're visiting for the day, make this bright little cafe your luncheon stopover, and enjoy crêpes, quiches, soups, or salads in the sunlit courtyard. At night the atmosphere glows with candlelight, and assumes more *joie de vivre*. Try the Mediterranean cuisine, beginning with mushrooms aïoli, escargots (snails) Provençale, or one of the freshly made soups. Main dishes are likely to include medallions of beef with mushrooms, the fish of the day, or a magret of duck. Ingredients are always fresh. Look for the daily specials, such coq au vin (chicken cooked in wine).

Pier 69. 69 King St. ☎ **340/772-0069.** Reservations not accepted. Sandwiches and platters $4.25–$17. AE, DC, DISC, MC, V. Mon–Thurs 10am–midnight, Fri–Sun 10am–4pm. AMERICAN/CARIBBEAN.

Although you can get a worthy platter of food here, this place is far more interesting for its resemblance to a funky bar in New York's Greenwich Village than for its cuisine. New York–born Unise Tranberg is the earth-mother/matriarch of the place, which looks like a warm and somewhat battered combination of a 1950s living room and a nautical bar. Counterculture fans from Christiansted make this their preferred hangout, often opting for a mango colada or a lime lambada. If you're stepping off a ship and want something to eat, you can order from the predictable array of salads, sandwiches, and platters.

AROUND THE ISLAND

Duggan's Reef. East End Rd., Teague Bay. ☎ **340/773-9800.** Reservations required for dinner in winter. Main courses $14.50–$29; pastas $10–$24. AE, MC, V. Daily noon–3pm and 6–9:30pm. Bar, daily 11am–11:30pm. Closed for lunch in summer. CONTINENTAL/CARIBBEAN.

Set only 10 feet from the still waters of Reef Beach, and open to the sea breezes, Duggan's Reef is an ideal perch for watching the windsurfers and Hobie cats gliding through the nearby waters. This restaurant, owned for more than a decade by Boston-born Frank Duggan, is the most popular on St. Croix—it seems that all visitors dine here at least once during their stay. At lunch, a simple array of salads, crêpes, and sandwiches is offered. Appetizers include fried calamari and conch chowder. House specialties include Duggan's Caribbean lobster pasta and Irish whiskey lobster. The local seafood, prepared as you wish, is fresh and depends on the day's catch; in other words, it's fresh fish or no fish. Try it Cajun style or island style (with tomato, pepper, and onion sauce). Main dishes include New York strip steak and veal piccata. The cuisine remains consistently reliable.

Sprat Hall Beach Restaurant. Rte. 63 (1 mile north of Frederiksted). ☎ **340/772-5855.** Reservations not required. Lunch $7–$15. No credit cards. Daily 9am–4pm (hot food 11:30am–2:30pm). CARIBBEAN.

This informal restaurant is on the western coast of St. Croix, near Sprat Hall Plantation. It's the best place on the island to combine lunch and a swim. The place has been in business since 1948, feeding both locals and visitors. Try the conch chowder, pumpkin fritters, tannia soup, and the fried fish of the day. These local dishes have an authentic island flavor, perhaps more than anywhere else on St. Croix. They also do salads and burgers. The owners are Cruzan-born Joyce Merwin Hurd and her husband, Jim. They charge $2 for use of the showers and changing rooms.

17 St. Kitts ⚓ ⚓ ⚓

Massive beach-oriented tourism may soon overtake St. Kitts, but this small island has yet to make a name for itself in the ports-of-call sweepstakes. For now, St. Kitts is a delightful, relatively uncrowded stop with beaches, shops, restaurants, and a capital that looks like a Hollywood set for an 18th-century West Indies port.

St. Kitts is far more active and lively than Nevis, its companion island 2 1/2 miles across a strait, but it's still fairly sleepy. The major source of income remains sugar, not tourists. Cane fields climb right up the slopes of a volcanic mountain range reaching nearly 4,000 feet, and you'll see ruins of old mills and plantation houses as you drive around the island. Any farmer will sell you a huge stalk of cane. To get the sweet juice, strip off the hard exterior and chew on the tasty reeds. It's best with ice and a little rum.

The original Carib inhabitants called St. Kitts Liamuiga, or "fertile isle." The interior virgin rain forests are alive with hummingbirds and green vervet monkeys, brought here as pets by early French settlers and turned loose when the British took over in 1783. The local people, some 35,000 of them, are proud of their British heritage and traditions, but there's a lingering French influence as well.

The capital and chief port, **Basseterre,** still sports its 18th-century waterfront, white colonial houses with toothpick balconies, and the Circus—the town square (it's actually round). The green Victorian Berkeley Memorial Clock standing in the center of the Circus is one of the most photographed landmarks on the island. Another landmark, Independence Square, once a thriving slave market, is surrounded by Georgian-style homes.

Just like in the old days, country people still come to the marketplace with baskets brimming with just-picked mangoes, guavas, soursop, mammy apples, and wild strawberries and cherries.

COMING ASHORE

In April of 1997, the government of St. Kitts and Nevis began investing massive sums in the construction of a pier stretching from the center of Basseterre into deep waters offshore. It now welcomes at regular intervals such ships as Holland America's *Veendam* and *Statendam*, Costa Cruise Line's *Costa Victoria*, and NCL's *Seaward*. Its name is Port Zante, because of its visual similarities to a port with the same name in Greece. The new development has virtually replaced the older, drab-looking industrial piers that used to receive cruise ships. For information about Port Zante, contact Jason, the harbormaster, at ☎ **869/466-5021.**

FAST FACTS

Currency   The local currency is the **Eastern Caribbean dollar (EC$).** The exchange rate is about EC$2.70 for $1 U.S. Many shops and restaurants quote prices in U.S. dollars. Always determine which currency locals are talking about. We have used U.S. dollar prices in this section.

Information   You can get local tourist information at the **St. Kitts/Nevis Department of Tourism,** Pelican Mall, Bay Road, in Basseterre (☎ 869/465-4040). Open Monday to Friday from 9am to 5pm.

Language   English is the language of the island.

St. Kitts

SHORE EXCURSIONS

The premier excursion is the Brimstone Hill Tour, which lasts $2^{1}/_{2}$ hours and costs $28. This inspiring 17th-century citadel (see "Seeing the Sights," below) is some 800 feet above sea level, and offers a panoramic view of the coastline and the island. You can explore its museum.

On the Beach Horseback Ride, cruise ship passengers ride well-trained horses along the Atlantic coastline, where trade winds ensure a cool trip. The tour lasts an hour and costs $38. Another active tour is the Catamaran Adventure, a leisurely 45-minute sail along the southern coast of the island. The boat stops in a sheltered cove for snorkeling. The trip lasts $3^{1}/_{2}$ hours and costs $50.

GETTING AROUND

CAR RENTALS The only U.S.-based car-rental firm represented on St. Kitts is **Avis,** South Independence Square (☎ 800/331-1212 in the U.S., or 869/465-6507). They charge $45 to $50 per day. Tax is an additional 5%. The company offers free delivery service to the cruise dock. You also might get a good deal at **Delisle Walwyn & Co.,** Liverpool Row, Basseterre (☎ 869/465-8449), a local company offering cars and Jeeps at daily rates ranging from $40 to $55.

Reflecting British tradition, **driving is on the left.** You'll need a local driver's license, which can be obtained for EC$53 ($19.60) at the Traffic Department, on Cayon Street in Basseterre. The staff at your car-rental agency will usually drive you to the Traffic Department to get one.

TAXIS   This is the best means of getting around. You don't even have to look for a taxi—it will find you at the cruise dock. The taxis aren't metered, so before heading out you must agree on the price. Be sure to ask if the rates quoted are in U.S. dollars or the Eastern Caribbean dollars. Most drivers are versed in the lore of the island and will take you on a 3-hour tour for about $60. On the tour, you can also arrange lunch at one of the local inns. We'd suggest either **Golden Lemon** at **Dieppe Bay** or **Rawlins Plantation,** Mount Pleasant (see "Dining" below).

SEEING THE SIGHTS

The ✪ **Brimstone Hill Fortress** (☎ **869/465-6211**), 9 miles west of Basseterre, is the major stop on any tour of St. Kitts. This historic monument, among the largest and best preserved in the Caribbean, is a complex of bastions, barracks, and other structures ingeniously adapted to the top and upper slopes of a steep, 800-foot hill.

The structure dates from 1690, when the British fortified the hill to help recapture Fort Charles below from the French. In 1782, an invading force of 8,000 French troops bombarded the fortress for a month before its small British garrison, supplemented by local militia, surrendered. When the British took the island back the next year, they proceeded to enlarge the fort into "The Gibraltar of the West Indies."

Today the fortress is the centerpiece of a national park featuring nature trails and a diverse range of plant and animal life, including green vervet monkeys. It's also a photographer's paradise, with views of mountains, fields, and the Caribbean Sea. On a clear day you can see six neighboring islands.

Visitors will enjoy the self-directed tours among the many ruined or restored structures, including the barrack rooms at Fort George. The gift shop sells prints of rare maps and paintings of the Caribbean. Admission is $5 for adults, $2.50 for children. The park is open daily from 9:30am to 5:30pm.

SHOPPING

The best buys here are in local handcrafts, including baskets, coconut shells, and leather items made from goatskin. You can also find some decent values in clothing and fabrics, especially Sea Island cottons. Prices on some luxury goods can range from 25% to 30% below those on the North American mainland.

For one-stop shopping, head to **Pelican Shopping Mall,** which has some two dozen shops as well as banking services, a restaurant, and a philatelic bureau, where collectors can buy St. Kitts stamps and everyone else can mail letters. Little Switzerland and some major Caribbean retail outlets have branches here. Also check out the unusual merchandise in the shops on **Liverpool Row.** The shops along Fort Street are also worth browsing. Stores in St. Kitts are generally open Monday to Saturday from 9am to 5pm, but most are also open whenever a cruise ship docks.

Ashburry's. The Circus/Liverpool Row, Basseterre. ☎ **869/465-8175.**

This well-respected emporium is the local branch of a chain based on St. Maarten. It sells discounted luxury goods, including fragrances, fine porcelain, crystal by Baccarat, handbags by Fendi, watches, and jewelry. Discounts range from 25% to 30% below what you might pay in North America, although the selection is similar to dozens of equivalent stores throughout the Caribbean.

Cameron Gallery. 10 N. Independence Sq., Basseterre. ☎ **869/465-1617.**

Britisher Rosey Cameron-Smith displays her watercolors and limited-edition prints of scenes from St. Kitts and Nevis at this gallery. In her work, she makes an effort to capture the essence of West Indian life. Rosey is well-known on the island for her

Favorite Experiences

Mount Liamuiga, in the northwest of the island, was dubbed "Mount Misery" long ago. This dormant volcano sputtered its last gasp around 1692. Today, it's a major goal for hikers. A round-trip to the usually cloud-covered peak takes about 4 hours—2¹/₂ hours going up, 1¹/₂ coming down. Hikers usually make the ascent from Belmont Estate near St. Paul on the north end of St. Kitts. The trail winds through a rain forest and travels along deep ravines up to the rim of the crater at a cool 2,625 feet. Many hikers climb—or crawl—down a steep, slippery trail to a tiny lake in the caldera, some 400 feet below the rim.

You can reach the rim without a guide, but it's absolutely necessary to have one to go into the crater. **Greg's Safaris** (☎ **869/465-4121**) offers guided hikes to the crater for $60 per person (a minimum of four hikers required), including breakfast and a picnic at the crater's rim. The same outfit also offers half-day rain forest explorations, also with a picnic, for $35 per person.

Anyone with a taste for rum will enjoy a trip to the **Sugar Factory,** where raw cane is processed into bulk sugar from February through July. The factory also produces a very light liqueur, CSR, which the locals use in a grapefruit drink they call "Ting." You can also visit the **Carib Beer Plant,** an English lager brewery. If sales are any indication, Carib Beer is the best in the West Indies. You get to sample a cold bottle at the end of the plant tour. Reservations aren't required, but check with the tourist information office in Basseterre first to find out if the brewery is open (see "Fast Facts," above).

paintings of Kittitian Carnival clowns. She also produces greeting cards, postcards, and calendars, and she displays the works of some 10 to 15 other artists.

Island Hopper. The Circus, Basseterre. ☎ **869/465-1640.**

Located in the Circus, below the popular Ballahoo Restaurant, Island Hopper is one of St. Kitts's most patronized shops. It has the biggest inventory, both West Indian and international, of any store on the island. Look for the all-silk, loose-fitting shift-style dresses from China, the array of batiks made on St. Kitts, and also outfits from formal wear to casual sportswear.

Kate Design. Mount Pleasant. ☎ **869/465-7740.**

Set in an impeccably restored West Indian house, on a hillside below the Rawlins Plantation, this is the finest art gallery on St. Kitts. Virtually all the paintings on display are by English-born Kate Spencer, whose work is well-known throughout North America and Europe. Her still lifes, portraits, and island scenes range in price from $200 to $3,000 and have received critical acclaim from several different sources. Also for sale are a series of Ms. Spencer's silk-screened scarves, each crafted from extra-heavy stonewashed silk.

Lemonaid. At the Golden Lemon Hotel, Dieppe Bay. ☎ **869/465-7260.**

This bazaar-style shop at the Golden Lemon specializes in local antiques, crafts, artwork, jewelry, and silverware, and also carries a full line of elegant fragrances, plus spa products and skin-care lotions. Island clothes include those from John Warden's Island collection. The shop also sells Kisha batik fashions from Bali.

The Linen and Gold Shop. In the Pelican Mall, Bay Rd., Basseterre. ☎ **869/465-9766.**

There's a limited selection of gold and silver jewelry sold here, usually in bold modern designs, but the real appeal of this shop is the tablecloths and napery, such as doilies and napkins. They were all laboriously handcrafted in China from cotton and linen. The workmanship is as intricate as anything you'll find in the Caribbean.

Little Switzerland. In the Pelican Shopping Mall, Basseterre. ☎ **869/465-9859.**

This is the most elaborate emporium of luxury goods on St. Kitts, with a medley of jewels, wristwatches, porcelain, and crystal specifically selected for North American tastes. Lots of business is conducted when cruise ships pull up to the nearby wharves. Prices are set at about 25% to 30% less than in North America, but the true bargains appear during the promotional sales, when specific items are discounted as much as 40%. These sales continue almost without a break throughout the year. Most items can be wrapped and shipped for an additional charge.

The Palms. In the Palms Arcade, Basseterre. ☎ **869/465-2599.**

The Palms specializes in island "things." You'll find handcrafts; larimar, sea opal, pottery, and amber jewelry; West Indies spices, teas, and perfumes; tropical clothes by Canadian designer John Warden; and Bali batiks by Kisha.

Romney Manor. Old Road, 10 miles west of Basseterre. ☎ **869/465-6253.**

This is the most unusual factory in St. Kitts. It was built around 1625 as a manor house for sugar baron Lord Romney, during the era when St. Kitts was the premier stronghold of British military might in the Caribbean. For years, it has been the headquarters and manufacturing center for a local clothier, Caribelle batiks, whose tropical cotton wear sold widely to cruise ship passengers and holiday-makers from at least three outlets in the eastern Caribbean.

In 1995, hurricanes and a tragic fire completely gutted the historic building. Currently, the manor is being rebuilt, and about half of it has been completed. A temporary structure now serves as the retail outlet. Consider a stopover here to admire the 5 acres of lavish gardens, where 30 varieties of hibiscus, rare orchids, huge ferns, and a 250-year-old saman tree still draw horticultural enthusiasts. Entrance to the gardens is free.

Rosemary Lane Antiques. 7 Rosemary Lane. ☎ **869/465-5450.**

This little nugget is housed in an early 19th-century Caribbean building painted purple and white to stand out. The owner, Robert Cramer, has a choice collection of Kittitian, Caribbean, and international antiques, including furniture, paintings, silver, china and glass. He'll ship them to anywhere in the world.

A Slice of the Lemon. Fort St., Basseterre. ☎ **869/465-2889.**

This store has the largest selection of perfumes on St. Kitts, but frankly, we're not sure that they're sold at the lowest prices available. One room of the lemony-yellow shop functions as an outlet for Portmeirion English bone china.

BEACHES

The narrow peninsula in the southeast contains the island's salt ponds and also boasts the best white-sand beaches. You'll find the best swimming at **Conaree Beach,** 3 miles from Basseterre; **Frigate Bay,** with its talcum-powder fine sand; the twin beaches of **Banana Bay** and **Cockleshell Bay,** at the southeast corner of the island; and **Friar's Bay,** a peninsula beach opening onto both the Atlantic and the Caribbean. All beaches, even those that border hotels, are open to the public. However, you must usually pay a fee to use a hotel's beach facilities.

GOLF, TENNIS & WATER SPORTS

GOLF   The **Royal St. Kitts Golf Course,** Frigate Bay (☎ **869/465-8339**), is an 18-hole, par-72 championship course featuring seven beautiful ponds. It's bounded on the south by the Caribbean Sea and on the north by the Atlantic Ocean. Greens fees are $35 for 18 holes; cart rentals are $40 for 18 holes. It's open daily from 7am to 7pm. A bar and restaurant on site opens daily at 10am.

TENNIS   To play tennis you have to call one of the hotels for a court. The best are at **Bird Rock Beach Hotel,** 2 miles southwest of Basseterre (☎ **869/465-8914**), and at **Golden Lemon,** Dieppe Bay, which is the finest place on island for lunch if you're touring (see "Dining," below).

WATER SPORTS   At **Pro-Divers,** at Turtle Beach (☎ **869/465-3223**), you can swim, sail, float, paddle, or head out for scuba diving and snorkeling expeditions. A two-tank dive costs $50 with your own equipment, or $60 without.

One of the best diving spots is **Nagshead,** at the south tip of St. Kitts. This is an excellent shallow-water dive for certified divers starting at 10 feet and extending to 70 feet. You'll see a variety of tropical fish, eaglerays, and lobster here. Another good site is **Booby Shoals,** between Cow 'n' Calf Rocks and Booby Island. Booby Shoals has abundant sea life, including nurse sharks, lobster, and stingrays. Dives here are up to 30 feet in depth, and are good for both certified and beginning divers.

DINING

The Anchorage. Frigate Bay. ☎ **869/465-8235.** Main courses $13.50–$23. AE, MC, V. Mon–Thurs 11am–11pm, Fri–Sat 11am–midnight. WEST INDIAN/CONTINENTAL.

This isolated beachfront restaurant on the rolling acres of Frigate Bay isn't exactly famous for appearing in guidebooks, but it comes in handy. There's not much here in the way of decor: Its tables are under a plain roof on a plain concrete floor. But if you're looking for that unspoiled, casual beach restaurant, you've come to the right place. Try a rum-based drink, while you peruse the menu. At lunch you can order hamburgers or a dozen kinds of sandwiches along with fresh fish. The chef often features lobster, either broiled or Thermidor, and can prepare the fresh catch of the day as you like it. You can also get such old standbys as spareribs.

Ballahoo Restaurant. The Circus, Fort St., Basseterre. ☎ **869/465-4197.** Reservations recommended. Main courses EC$25–EC$60 ($9.25–$22.20). AE, MC, V. Daily 8am–10pm. CARIBBEAN.

The Ballahoo is about a block from the sea, on the second story of a traditional stone building overlooking the Circus Clock. Its open-air dining area is one of the coolest places in town on a hot afternoon, thanks to the sea breezes. Try the Blue Parrot fish filet. The chef also makes some of the best chili and baby back ribs in town. Seafood platters, such as chili shrimp or fresh lobster, are served with a coconut salad and rice. For more elegant fare, there's Italian-style chicken breast topped with pesto tomatoes and cheese and served with a pasta and salad. The service is casual. Because of its central location, this restaurant draws the cruise ship crowd.

✪ **The Golden Lemon.** Dieppe Bay (on the northern coast beyond St. Paul's). ☎ **869/ 465-7260.** Reservations usually required but walk-ins accepted if space available. Fixed-price dinner $25–$50; lunch main courses $3.50–$20; Sun brunch $24. AE, MC, V. Daily noon–3pm and 6:30–10:30pm. CONTINENTAL/CREOLE.

If you're touring St. Kitts, the best luncheon stop is at the Golden Lemon, a 17th-century house converted into a fine hotel. The food is very good, and the service is polite. You can eat either in an elegant, candlelit dining room, in the garden, or on the gallery. The cuisine features Creole, continental, and American dishes, all with locally grown produce. Many of the recipes were created by the hotel's sophisticated owner, Arthur Leaman, one-time decorating editor of *House & Garden*. The menu changes daily, but is likely to include baked Cornish hen with ginger, fresh fish of the day, and Creole sirloin steak with a spicy rum sauce. Vegetarian dishes are also available. Dress is casually chic.

Ocean Terrace Inn. Fortlands. ☎ 869/465-2754. Reservations recommended. Main courses $15–$22; fixed-price 3-course lunch $15; fixed-price 4-course dinner $35. AE, DC, DISC, MC, V. Daily 7:30–9:30am, noon–2pm and 7:30–10:30pm. Drive or take a taxi west on Basseterre Bay Rd. to Fortlands. CARIBBEAN/INTERNATIONAL.

You'll find some of Basseterre's finest cuisine here, along with one of the best views of the harbor. A meal might include tasty fish cakes, accompanied by breaded carrot slices, creamed spinach, a stuffed potato, johnnycake, a cornmeal dumpling, and a green banana in a lime-butter sauce, topped off by a tropical fruit pie and coffee. You can also get French or English dishes along with some flambé specialties, including Arawak chicken, chateaubriand, steak Diane, and veal Fantasia. The kitchen is best when preparing the real down-home island dishes, instead of the blander international specialties. Some form of entertainment is often presented. Dining is on an open-air veranda.

Pisces Restaurant & Bar. Cayon St. (behind the Glimbara Guest House), Basseterre. ☎ **869/465-5032.** Reservations recommended for dinner. Main courses EC$20–EC$55 ($7.40–$20.35). No credit cards. Daily 7am–midnight. CARIBBEAN.

Pisces has been a local favorite since it opened in 1993. It's owned and operated by Nerita Godfrey, or "Rita," as she's affectionately known. She specializes in seafood, such as lobster, shrimp, and whelk. Each day she prepares some local dish, perhaps bullfoot soup with dinner rolls or a "cookup" (saltfish, pigtail, pig snout, chicken, and red peas), traditionally served on Wednesday. Her barbecued spareribs and conch stew are justly praised. On Saturday locals visit to sample her "goatwater," a savory goat stew. Lamb chops, pork chops, shrimp fried rice, and her special chicken are good choices for those who don't want to go too local. Throughout the day you can order a cheap breakfast, sandwiches, and burgers (cheese, fish, and a veggie).

Rawlins Plantation. Mount Pleasant (outside St. Paul's, on the island's northwest coast). ☎ **869/465-6221,** Reservations required. Lunch buffet $28; fixed-price dinner $45. AE, MC, V. Daily noon–2:30pm; Mon–Sat 7–9pm. INTERNATIONAL/CARIBBEAN.

This hotel near Dieppe Bay serves the island's tastiest lunch buffet. This cuisine here has been called a mix of Kittitian, serious Cordon Bleu, and love and inspiration. Originally, this was the site of an old musovado sugar factory. Today, the dining area is a cool courtyard where guests eat amid flowers and tropical birds. A delectable West Indian buffet is served daily. Begin with the breadfruit salsa, before going on to the choices of the day, perhaps flying fish fritters, shrimp ceviche, or bobote (a combination of ground beef, spices, curry, eggplant, and homemade chutney). Finish with such sinful desserts as guava and lime parfait and most definitely the chocolate terrine with passion-fruit sauce. A four-course fixed-price dinner is served in the evening.

✪ The Royal Palm. In Ottley's Plantation Inn, north of Basseterre, on the east coast. ☎ **869/465-7234.** Reservations required. Fixed-price 4-course dinner from $50; lunch main courses $8.95–$17.95; Sun champagne brunch $25. AE, MC, V. Mon–Sat noon–3pm; Sun brunch noon–2pm; daily dinner seating 7:30–8:30pm. CARIBBEAN/FUSION.

The Royal Palm is an island favorite, serving the most creative cuisine on St. Kitts. It also has a colorful setting: You can gaze through the ancient stone arches to the ocean on one side and Mount Liamuiga and the inn's Great House on the other.

The restaurant is set beside the pool. The menu changes daily. You might start with Brazilian gingered chicken soup or chili-flavored shrimp corn cakes, each equally tempting. The quesadillas with local lobster, if featured, are worth crossing the island to sample. The dinner menu is international and elaborate. Appetizers include a white Cheddar and green chili bisque. The main courses are usually impeccably prepared, especially the French roast of lamb or the breast of chicken Molyneux with almonds, country ham, mozzarella, and mushroom stuffing.

Turtle Beach Bar & Grill. Near the Ocean Terrace Inn, on the Southeastern Peninsula. ☎ **869/469-9086.** Reservations recommended. Main courses $8.50–$18.50. AE, MC, V. Daily noon–5pm; Sat 7:30–10pm. Follow the Kennedy Simmonds Hwy. over Basseterre's Southeastern Peninsula; then follow the signs. SEAFOOD.

This airy, sun-flooded restaurant is set on the sands above Turtle Beach. Many clients spend time before their meal swimming or snorkeling beside the offshore reef; others simply relax beneath the verandas or shade trees (hammocks are available), perhaps with a drink in hand. Scuba diving, ocean kayaking, windsurfing, sailing, and volleyball are available. Menu specialties are familiar, but often scrumptious. Typical dishes might be stuffed broiled lobster, conch fritters, barbecued swordfish steak, prawn salads, and barbecued honey-mustard spareribs.

18 St. Lucia ⚓ ⚓ ⚓ ⚓

Nobel Prize–winning poet Derek Walcott, a native of St. Lucia, prefers not to tout the charms of his home island. "I don't want everyone to go there and overrun the place," he told the media not long ago. His wish has gone unfulfilled, however, for St. Lucia (pronounced *Loo*-sha) has become one of the most popular cruise ship stopovers in the southern Caribbean.

And with good reason. St. Lucia offers beautiful white sandy beaches on its northwest coast, an unspoiled interior of green-mantled mountains, and two dramatic Piton peaks, giving it more of a South Pacific look. You'll find on this island gentle valleys, banana plantations, a bubbling volcano, giant tree ferns, wild orchids, fishing villages, and a mixed French and British heritage.

Castries, the capital, grew up around an extinct volcanic crater that forms a large, sheltered harbor surrounded by hills. Because of devastating fires, the town today has a look of newness. Glass-and-concrete buildings has replaced the French colonial or Victorian appearance typical of many West Indian capitals.

The 140,000 or so St. Lucians are a mix of Indian, African, French, and British blood. The old-fashioned Saturday-morning market on Jeremy Street in Castries is our favorite "people-watching" site on the island. Country women dress up in traditional cotton headdresses to sell their luscious fruits and vegetables. The number of knotted points on a woman's headdress reveals her marital status (ask a local to explain it to you). Meanwhile, weather-beaten men sit close by playing *warrie,* a fast game with pebbles on a carved board.

COMING ASHORE

Most cruise ships arrive at the fairly new pier at Pointe Seraphine, a short taxi ride from the center of Castries. Unlike piers on other islands, this one contains St. Lucia's best shopping. You'll find a money exchange, a small visitor information bureau, and a cable and wireless office. Phone cards are sold for use at specially labeled phones.

If Pointe Seraphine is too crowded, your ship might dock at the Elizabeth II pier. This facility is not geared to cruisers the way Point Seraphine is, but it's only a short walk to the center of Castries.

Some smaller vessels, such as Seabourn's, anchor off Soufrière and carry you ashore by tender.

FAST FACTS

Currency   The official monetary unit is the **Eastern Caribbean dollar (EC$),** worth about 37¢ in U.S. currency. Most of the prices quoted in this section are in U.S. dollars, which are accepted by nearly all hotels, restaurants, and shops.

Information   The **St. Lucia Tourist Board** is at Point Seraphine in Castries (☎ **758/452-4094**). Open Monday to Friday from 9am to 5pm.

Language   English is the official language.

SHORE EXCURSIONS

Because of the difficult terrain, shore excursions are the best means of seeing this beautiful island in a day or less.

A trip from Castries to the Piton peaks takes you across St. Lucia, with visits to the La Soufrière volcano, the Diamond Baths, and a sulfur springs (see "Seeing the Sights," below). Lunch is included in the $45 cost. This trip takes about 8 hours, so it will occupy your full day. Small ships anchoring off La Soufrière offer a 2-hour tour of the surroundings for $30 per person. You'll see the same sights mentioned above, but you'll get there a lot faster than the passengers who arrived at Castries.

GETTING AROUND

BUS   Minibuses (with names like "Lucian Love") and jitneys connect Castries to main towns such as Soufrière and Vieux Fort. These vehicles are generally over-crowded and often filled with produce on the way to market, so they should be your last resort. Buses for Cap Estate, in the northern part of the island, leave from Jeremy Street in Castries, near the market. Buses going to Vieux Fort and Soufrière depart from Bridge Street, in front of the department store.

CAR RENTALS   **Budget** (☎ **800/527-0700** in the U.S., or 758/452-0233), **Avis** (☎ **800/331-1212** in the U.S., or 758/452-2046), and **Hertz** (☎ **800/654-3001** in the U.S., or 758/452-0679) maintain offices on St. Lucia. Rates begin at $50 per day. If you're calling in advance, you might try **Auto Europe** (☎ **800/223-5555**). Remember to drive **on the left side of the road,** and be very careful on the narrow, hilly, switchback roads outside the capital. You'll need a St. Lucia driver's license, which can be purchased easily for $12 at the car-rental kiosks.

TAXIS   Taxis are ubiquitous on the island, and most drivers are eager to please. Many have been trained in special programs to serve as guides. Their cars are unmetered, but tariffs for all standard trips are fixed by the government. Make sure you determine if the driver is quoting a rate in U.S. or EC dollars.

SEEING THE SIGHTS
CASTRIES

The principal streets of Castries are William Peter Boulevard and Bridge Street. A Roman Catholic cathedral stands on Columbus Square, which has a few restored buildings. **Government House** is a late Victorian structure.

Beyond Government House lies **Morne Fortune,** which means "Hill of Good Luck." Actually, no one's had much luck here, certainly not the French and British that battled for **Fort Charlotte.** The fort changed nationalities many times. You can visit the 18th-century barracks complete with a military cemetery, a small museum, the Old Powder Magazine, and the "Four Apostles Battery" (the apostles being a quartet of grim muzzle-loading cannons). The view of the harbor of Castries is

St. Lucia

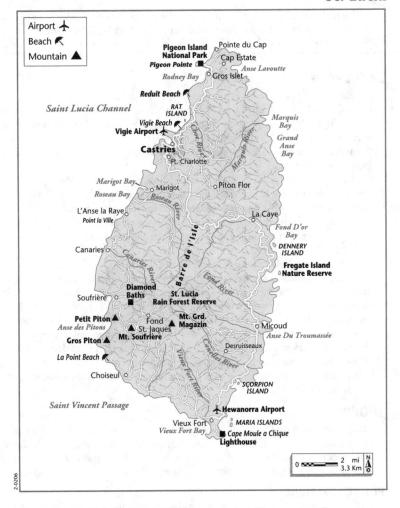

Airport ✈
Beach ⏃
Mountain ▲

Pointe du Cap
**Pigeon Island
National Park**
Cap Estate
Pigeon Pointe ■
Anse Lavoutte
Rodney Bay
Gros Islet

Reduit Beach ⏃

Saint Lucia Channel
RAT
ISLAND
*Marquis
Bay*

Vigie Beach ⏃
Vigie Airport ✈
Choc River
*Grand
Anse
Bay*

Castries
Ft. Charlotte
Marquis River

Marigot Bay
Marigot
Piton Flor
Roseau Bay
Roseau River

L'Anse la Raye
Point la Ville
La Caye

*Fond D'or
Bay*

Canaries
Canaries River
Barre de l'Isle
Fond River
*DENNERY
ISLAND*

**Fregate Island
Nature Reserve**

**Diamond
Baths** ■
**St. Lucia
Rain Forest Reserve**

Soufrière

Petit Piton ▲
Fond
**Mt. Grd.
Magazin**
Micoud
Anse des Pitons
▲ St. Jaques
Anse Du Troumassée

Gros Piton ▲
Mt. Soufrière
Canelles River
Desruisseaux

La Point Beach ⏃
Vieux Fort River

Choiseul

*SCORPION
ISLAND*

Saint Vincent Passage

✈ **Hewanorra Airport**

Vieux Fort ○
Vieux Fort Bay
MARIA ISLANDS
■ **Cape Moule a Chique
Lighthouse**

0 ⬛⬛⬛ 2 mi
3.3 Km
N

2-0206

panoramic. You can also see north to Pigeon Island or south to the Pitons. To reach Morne Fortune, head east on Bridge Street.

PIGEON ISLAND NATIONAL LANDMARK

St. Lucia's first national park was originally an island. It's now joined to the northwest shore of the mainland by a causeway. Forty-four-acre Pigeon Island got its name from the red-neck pigeon, or ramier, which once made this island home. It's ideal for picnics, and nature walks. Its Interpretation Centre is equipped with artifacts and a multimedia display of local history, ranging from the Amerindian occupation of A.D. 1000 to the Battle of Saints, when Admiral Rodney's fleet set out from Pigeon Island and defeated Admiral De Grasse in 1782.

On Pigeon Island's west coast are two white-sand beaches. There's also a restaurant, Jambe de Bois ("Leg of Wood"), named after a peg-legged pirate who once used the island as a hideout. The Captain's Cellar Olde English Pub, under the interpretive center, evokes an 18th-century English bar

The park is open daily from 9am to 5pm. Admission is EC$10 ($3.70). For more information, call the St. Lucia National Trust (☎ 758/452-5005). The best way to get here is to take a taxi here and arrange to be picked up in time to return to the ship.

LA SOUFRIÈRE

This little fishing port, St. Lucia's second largest settlement, is dominated by the dramatic ✪ **Pitons,** two pointed peaks called Petit Piton and Gros Piton, which rise to 2,460 and 2,619 feet, respectively. Formed by lava and once actively volcanic, these mountains are now clothed in green vegetation. Their sheer rise from the sea makes them such visible landmarks that they've become the very symbol of St. Lucia. Waves crash around their bases.

Near the town of Soufrière lies the famous "drive-in" volcano, ✪ **Mont Soufrière,** a rocky lunar landscape of bubbling mud and craters seething with fuming sulfur. You literally ride into an old crater and walk between the sulfur springs and pools of hissing steam. The fumes are said to have medicinal properties. A local guide is usually waiting nearby; for a fee, he'll give you a tour. If you do hire a guide, agree—then doubly agree—on what the fee will be.

Nearby are the ✪ **Diamond Mineral Baths** (☎ 758/452-4759), surrounded by a tropical arboretum. They were constructed in 1784 by order of Louis XVI, whose doctors told him that these waters were similar in mineral content to the waters at Aix-les-Bains. Their purpose was to recuperate French soldiers fighting in the West Indies. Later destroyed, they were rebuilt after World War II. The water's average temperature is 106°F. You'll also find here another fine attraction, a waterfall that changes colors (from yellow to black to green to gray) several times a day. For EC$7 ($2.60), you can bathe and benefit from the recuperative effects yourself.

It's extremely difficult to get to these attractions on your own from Castries, so opt for a shore excursion.

SHOPPING

Many stores sell duty-free goods; they will also deliver tobacco products and liquor to the cruise dock. You'll find some good, but not remarkable, buys in bone china, jewelry, perfume, watches, liquor, and crystal. Souvenir items include bags and mats, local pottery, and straw hats—again, nothing remarkable.

POINTE SERAPHINE

Built for cruise ship passengers, **Pointe Seraphine** has the best collection of shops on the island. You must present your cruise pass when making purchases from the merchants here. Liquor and tobacco will be delivered to the ship. All shops in the red-roofed, Spanish-style complex are open in winter, Monday to Friday from 8am to 5pm, Saturday from 8am to 2pm; off-season, Monday to Friday from 9am to 4pm, Saturday from 9am to 4pm. They also open on Sunday if cruise ships are in port.

Benetton. Pointe Seraphine. ☎ **758/452-7685.**

All the sportswear here was made in either Italy or Spain, and any of these pieces would be appropriate for a cruise wardrobe. In addition to T-shirts, tennis shirts, and shorts, there's an assortment of women's pantsuits, men's business suits, and children's wear. Prices are about 20% lower than stateside.

Colombian Emeralds. Pointe Seraphine. ☎ **758/453-7721.**

Colombian Emeralds's major competitor in this mall is Little Switzerland. Of the two, Little Switzerland's stock of porcelain, crystal, perfume, and luggage is larger, but Colombian's selection of watches and gemstones is more diverse. There are two adjoining buildings here, one of which sells only gold chains (14- and 18-karat) and wristwatches; the other features a sophisticated array of precious and semiprecious stones that would tempt a Turkish vizier. Chains range from $85 to $1,100, and wristwatches from $90 to $14,000. Gemstones, set in twinkling and tempting settings, are often reasonable in price. Of special value are the wristwatches, which sometimes sell for up to 40% less in North America.

Images. Pointe Seraphine. ☎ **758/452-6883.**

Images operates two shops within Castries' wharf-side shopping mall. The more interesting of them sells the most exhaustive collection of enameled Indian jewelry on St. Lucia. Laboriously handcrafted with lots of exotic swirls, the ornaments (necklaces, bracelets, and earrings) range in price from $10 to $60. Also worthwhile are Indian-made evening bags lavishly adorned with sequins (a bargain at $24 each), and bags by Ted Lapidus. A few steps away, the establishment's second store specializes in perfumes that cost around 20% less than in North America. Most fragrances are from France and the States, although some are locally made.

The Land Shop. Pointe Seraphine. ☎ **758/452-7488.**

This store specializes in elegant handbags, garment bags, and briefcases. Some come with English-made labels affixed; others are made by relatively obscure manufacturers in Colombia whose quality is nonetheless very high. Prices are at least 25% less than in North America, and your purchases are, like everything else in the complex, tax-free. Also available is a selection of shoes; the inventory for women is more varied and interesting than the choices for men. Bags and briefcases range from $79 to $550.

Little Switzerland. Pointe Seraphine. ☎ **758/451-6799.**

Its inventory includes a broad-based but predictable array of luxury goods, including porcelain, crystal, watches, and jewelry. Prices are usually around 25% less than on the North American mainland, but wise shoppers take advantage of special promotions (with savings of up to 40%).

Oasis. Pointe Seraphine. ☎ **758/452-1185.**

This shop sells well-known brand name resort clothing and beach wear. Look for Revo sunglasses, Reef and Naot footwear, Kipling bags, Gottex swimwear, and Gear casual clothing. There's also a wide range of quality T-shirts for adults and children.

Peer. Pointe Seraphine. ☎ **758/453-0815.**

One of the 75 worldwide franchised Peer stores, this outlet offers high-quality, creative, colorful prints and embroidery designs on T-shirts, shorts, camp shirts, and more. There's a wide range for children, as well as bags, caps, women's wear, and bright tropical prints. It's a good place to visit for a wearable souvenir or gift.

ELSEWHERE ON THE ISLAND

Gablewoods Mall, on Gros Islet Highway, 2 miles north of Castries, contains three restaurants and one of the densest concentrations of stores on St. Lucia. The best clothing and sundry shop here is **Top Banana** (☎ 758/451-6389). Inventory includes beachwear, scuba and snorkeling equipment, gifts, inflatable rafts, and casual resort wear. **Made in St. Lucia** (☎ 758/453-2788) sells only gifts and souvenirs made by local craftspersons. Most of the inventory is small enough to be carried off-island in a suitcase. It includes woodcarvings, clay cooking pots, sandals, a medley of spices and cooking sauces, a wide assortment of T-shirts, paintings, and such jewelry items as necklaces and "love beads" made from seeds and dried berries.

> ### ★ Favorite Experiences
>
> **Bananas** are St. Lucia's leading export, so as you're being hauled around the island by taxi drivers, ask them to take you to one of the huge plantations. We suggest a look at one of the three biggest: the Cul-de-Sac, just north of Marigot Bay; La Caya, in Dennery on the east coast; and the Roseau Estate, south of Marigot Bay.

Another worthwhile outlet at this mall is **Sea Island Cotton Shop** (☎ 758/452-3674), catering almost exclusively to visitors. This is one of the center's largest shops, offering an array of quality T-shirts, hand-painted souvenirs, Caribbean spices, beach and swimwear, and elegantly casual clothing.

Shops in St. Lucia are generally open Monday through Saturday from 9am to 5pm, but most are also open whenever a cruise ship docks.

Bagshaws. La Toc. ☎ **758/451-9249.**

Just outside Castries, this is the leading shop for hand-printing of silk-screen designs. An American, Sydney Bagshaw, founded the operation in the mid-1960s, and today it's operated by his daughter-in-law, Alice Bagshaw. The company has devoted its considerable skills to turning out a high-quality line of fabric as colorful as the Caribbean. The birds (look for the St. Lucia parrot), butterflies, and flowers of St. Lucia are all incorporated into original designs. Highlights include an extensive household line in vibrant prints on linen, as well as clothing and beachwear for both men and women, and the best T-shirt collection on the island. At La Toc Studios, you can view the printing process Monday through Friday. The company has another retail outlet in the Pointe Seraphine duty-free shopping mall (☎ **758/452-7570**).

Caribelle Batik. Howelton House, Old Victoria Rd., The Morne. ☎ **758/452-3785.**

In this workshop, just a 5-minute taxi ride from Castries, you can watch St. Lucian artists creating intricate patterns and colors through the ancient art of batik. You can also purchase batik in cotton, rayon, and silk, made up in casual and beach clothing, and in wall hangings and other gift items. The Dyehouse Bar and Terrace serves drinks in the renovated Victorian-era building.

Eudovic Art Studio. Goodlands, Morne Fortune. ☎ **758/452-2747.**

Vincent Joseph Eudovic, a native of St. Lucia, is a master artist and wood carver whose sculptures have gained increasing fame. He usually carves from local tree roots, such as teak, mahogany, and red cedar. Some of his sculptures are from Laurier Cannelle trees, which have disappeared from the island, although their roots often remain in a well-preserved state. He also teaches his art. His pupils' work is on display in the main studio. However, ask to be taken to his private studio, where you'll see his own remarkable creations. The shop is open daily 7:30am to 4:30pm. Take a taxi from the cruise pier. While here, you can pop into the bar for a drink.

Choiseul Art & Craft Center. La Fargue, Choiseul. ☎ **758/459-3226.**

The coastal village of Choiseul, southwest of Castries, picked up its name under St. Lucia's French-speaking regime, and has ever since been the home of the descendants of Carib Indians whose bloodlines mingled long ago with African slaves. The village's artistic centerpiece is a government-funded retail outlet and training school that perpetuates the tradition of handmade Amerindian pottery and basketware. Some of the best basketweaving on the island is done here, using techniques practiced only in St. Lucia, St. Vincent, and Dominica. Look for place mats, handbags, woodcarvings (including bas-reliefs crafted from screw pine), and pottery. Artfully contrived bassinets, priced at EC\$250 (\$92.50) each, might make a worthwhile present for parents-to-be.

Noah's Arkade. Jeremie St. ☎ **758/452-2523.**

Many of the Caribbean handcrafts and gifts here are routine tourist items, yet you'll often find something interesting if you browse around. They sell local straw place mats, baskets, and rugs, wall hangings, maracas, shell necklaces, locally made bowls, dolls dressed in banana leaves, and warri boards. A branch is found at Pointe Seraphine duty-free shopping mall.

BEACHES

If you don't take a shore excursion, you may want to spend your time on one of St. Lucia's famous beaches. We prefer the calmer shores along the western coast, since the rough surf on the windward Atlantic side makes swimming potentially dangerous.

Leading beaches include **Pigeon Island,** off the northern shore, with white sand and picnic facilities. **Vigie Beach,** north of Castries Harbour, is one of the most popular on St. Lucia. It has fine sands, often light beige in color. **Reduit Beach,** with its fine brown sands, lies between Choc Bay and Pigeon Point. For a novelty, you might try the black volcanic sand at Soufrière. The beach there is called **La Toc.**

Just north of Soufrière is that beach connoisseur's delight, **Anse Chastanet** (☎ **758/459-7000**), with its white sands set at the foothills of lush, green mountains. While here, you might want to patronize the facilities of the Anse Chastanet Hotel.

All beaches are open to the public, even those along hotel properties. But you must pay to use a hotel's beach equipment.

GOLF, RIDING, DIVING, TENNIS & WATER SPORTS

GOLF St. Lucia has a nine-hole golf course at the **Cap Estate Golf Club,** at the northern end of the island (☎ **758/450-8523**). Greens fees are \$35 for 18 holes, \$25 for nine. There are no caddies. Hours are daily from 8am to sunset. Another nine-hole course is located at the all-inclusive **St. Lucia Sandals** resort (☎ **758/452-3081**). It does, however, give preference to its guests.

HORSEBACK RIDING You can rent a horse at **Cas-En-Bas and Cap Estate Stables,** north of Castries. To make arrangements, call René Trim at ☎ **758/450-8273.** The cost is \$35 for a 1-hour ride, \$45 for 2 hours. Ask about a picnic trip to the Atlantic side of the island, with a barbecue lunch and drink included for \$55. Departures are at 8:30am, 10am, 2pm, and 4pm. Nonriders can also join the excursion; they are transported to the site in a van and pay half price.

SCUBA DIVING In Soufrière, **Scuba St. Lucia,** in the Anse Chastanet Hotel (☎ **758/459-7000**), at the southern end of Anse Chastanet's quarter-mile secluded beach, is a five-star PADI dive center. It offers great diving and comprehensive facilities. Some of the most spectacular coral reefs of St. Lucia—many only 10 to 20 feet below the surface—provide shelter for sea creatures just a short distance offshore. A 2- to 3-hour introductory lesson in shallow water and a tour of the reef costs \$75. Single dives cost \$30. Hours are from 8am to 5:45pm daily.

Rosemond Trench Divers, Ltd., at the Marigot Beach Club, Marigot Bay (☎ **758/451-4761**), is on the waters of the most famous bay in St. Lucia. This establishment will take both novices and experienced divers to shallow reefs or to some of the most challenging trenches in the Caribbean. A resort course, including a practice dive in sheltered waters and one dive above a reef, costs \$75. A one-tank dive for certified divers costs \$50, including equipment.

TENNIS One of the best tennis facilities in the Lesser Antilles is the **St. Lucia Racquet Club,** adjacent to Club St. Lucia in Smugglers Village (☎ **758/450-0551**). Its seven courts are maintained in state-of-the-art condition. There's also a good pro shop on site. Call ahead to reserve a court.

WATER SPORTS The best center for all water sports except diving is **St. Lucian Waterspsorts,** on Reduit Beach at the Rex St. Lucian Hotel (☎ **758/452-8351**). You can rent windsurfers here for $10 to $20 an hour; lessons cost $38 per person for a 3-hour course. Snorkeling is free for guests of the hotel; nonresidents pay $5, including equipment. Waterskiing costs $15 for a 15-minute ride.

DINING
IN CASTRIES

Green Parrot. Red Tape Lane, Morne Fortune (about 1¹/₂ miles east of the town center). ☎ **758/452-3399.** Reservations recommended. Fixed-price dinner EC$95–EC$115 ($35.15–$42.55); lunch main courses EC$35–EC$80 ($12.95–$29.60). AE, MC, V. Daily 7am–midnight. EUROPEAN/WEST INDIAN.

Green Parrot, overlooking Castries Harbour, remains the local hot spot for visitors, expats, and locals. This elegant place is the home of its chef, Harry, who had many years of training in prestigious restaurants and hotels in London, including Claridges. Guests take their time and make an evening of it; many enjoy a before-dinner drink in the Victorian-style salon. You might try a Grass Parrot (made from coconut cream, crème de menthe, bananas, white rum, and sugar).

There's an emphasis on St. Lucian specialties and home-grown produce. Try the christophine au gratin (a Caribbean squash with cheese) or the Creole soup made with callaloo and pumpkin. There are also five kinds of curry with chutney, as well as a selection of omelets and sandwiches at lunchtime. Steak Pussy Galore is a specialty.

Jimmie's. Vigie Cove Marina. ☎ **758/452-5142.** Reservations not accepted. Main courses EC$37.50–EC$65 ($13.90–$24.05). AE, MC, V. Mon–Sat 9am–10:30pm. Closed mid-July to Aug. CREOLE.

Near Vigie Field, with a view of Castries Harbour and the Morne, Jimmie's is known for its fresh-fish menu and tasty Creole cookery. Jimmie is a native St. Lucian, and after training in England, he returned to his homeland to open this spot, popular with visitors and locals alike. St. Lucia divides into two camps: those who prefer the Green Parrot and those who prefer Jimmie's. Both are equally fun. The bar here is a prime rendezvous point, and guests like the open-air terrace dining. The dishes are delicious. Order the fish, prepared in any number of ways; Jimmie's special is a Caribbean seafood risotto seasoned with fresh herbs. Conch is made according to Jimmie's secret recipe, which he claims is a known aphrodisiac. Lobster is classic, but for something truly delectable try octopus Helen, cooked from an old St. Lucian recipe. Nearly a dozen banana desserts are also featured (St. Lucians call bananas "figs").

San Antoine. Morne Fortune. ☎ **758/452-4660.** Reservations recommended. Main courses EC$40–EC$100 ($14.80–$37). AE, MC, V. Mon–Fri 11:30am–2:30pm; daily 6:30–10:30pm. CONTINENTAL/WEST INDIAN.

Constructed in the 19th century as a Great House, this restaurant lies up the Morne hill. It offers vistas over the capital and the water. Sometime in the 1920s, Aubrey Davidson-Houston, the British portrait painter whose subjects included W. Somerset Maugham, turned it into the first hotel on St. Lucia. However, in 1970 it was destroyed by fire. When it was restored in 1984, whatever could be retained, including the original stonework, was cleaned and repaired.

You might begin with the classic callaloo soup, then follow with fettuccine Alfredo, or perhaps fresh fish en papillote (baked in parchment). Lobster Thermidor might also be featured. Frankly, many visitors have found the view and ambience far more stunning than the cuisine, but if you order grilled fish and fresh vegetables, you should have a most satisfying meal.

AT MARIGOT BAY

Café Paradis. At the Marigot Beach Club (take a ferry across Marigot Bay). ☎ 758/451-4974. Reservations recommended. Main courses EC$26–EC$50 ($9.60–$18.50); barbecue EC$45 ($16.65). AE, MC, V. Daily 8am–10:30pm. FRENCH/INTERNATIONAL.

This is a culinary showplace, the proud domain of a French-trained chef who was eager to escape to the Caribbean. The restaurant derives some of its income from its award-winning rum punches. A view of the water beckons from the restaurant's veranda. Lunch items include rotis (Caribbean burritos), brochettes, burgers, salads, and grilled fish platters—nothing imaginative here. Daily specials enhance the menu at dinner. Rack of lamb and lobster, prepared in different ways, are upscale staples. The linguine with king prawns and scallops is delectable. The best deal here is the barbecue—for one price you get a soup or salad, a choice of baby back ribs, chicken, or steak, plus dessert. The barbecue starts at 6:30pm, which unfortunately is too late for most cruise passengers.

To reach the place, you'll have to take a ferryboat across Marigot Bay. Attached by a cable to either end of Marigot Bay, the ferry makes the short run from its origin at the Moorings Marigot Bay Resort about every 10 minutes throughout the day and evening. Show a staff member the return half of your ferryboat ticket and you'll receive a $1 discount off your food or bar tab.

Hurricane Hole. In the Moorings, Marigot Bay. ☎ **758/451-4357.** Reservations recommended. Main courses EC$19–EC$28 ($7.05–$10.35). AE, MC, V. Daily 7:30–10am, noon–2:30pm, and 6:30–10pm. INTERNATIONAL/ST. LUCIAN.

This is the cozy restaurant of the Marigot Bay Resort, which charters yachts to clients from around the hemisphere. The congenial bar does a brisk business; try the Marigot Hurricane (rum, banana, grenadine, and apricot brandy). Ceiling fans spin languidly as you peruse the menu, which is geared to surf-and-turf fans, although many dishes have genuine island flavor. Okra gives added zest to the callaloo soup with crab, and we're equally fond of the pumpkin soup blended with herbs and cream. A stuffed crab back is an alluring appetizer. For a main course, try the fresh fish of the day, which can be served in any number of ways, although we prefer au natural with herbs, fresh butter, lemon, and garlic. Meats and poultry range from a spicy Indian curried chicken to smoked pork chops grilled to perfection.

IN THE SOUFRIÈRE AREA

Chez Camilla Guest House & Restaurant. 7 Bridge St. (1 block inland from the waterfront). ☎ **758/459-5379.** Main courses $10–$20. AE, MC, V. Mon–Sat 8am–11pm. WEST INDIAN.

Chez Camilla is the only really good place to eat in the village of Soufrière itself. This clean and decent Caribbean-style restaurant, one floor above sea level, offers simple, unpretentious food. It's operated by a local matriarch, Camilla Alcindor, who will welcome you for coffee, a soda, or Perrier, or for full-fledged dinners that include Caribbean fish Creole, lobster Thermidor, and prime loin of beef with garlic sauce. The food is straightforward but with good flavor. Opt for the fish and shellfish instead of the beef, although the chicken curry is a savory choice as well. Lunches are considerably less elaborate and include an array of sandwiches, cold salads, omelets, and burgers. Our favorite tables are the pair on the balcony overlooking the energetic activities in the street below. The inside tables can get a bit steamy, as there's no air-conditioning.

☻ **Dasheene Restaurant & Bar.** In the Ladera Resort, between Gros and Petit Piton. ☎ **758/459-7323.** Reservations recommended. Main courses EC$55–EC$85 ($20.35–$31.45). AE, MC, V. Daily 8–10am, 11:30am–2:30pm, and 6:30–9pm. CARIBBEAN/CALIFORNIAN.

One of the most widely heralded restaurants in St. Lucia, and definitely the one with the most dramatic setting, this hideaway features Caribbean/Creole cuisine with the innovative cookery of California as an added inspiration. The result is perhaps the most refined and certainly the most creative cuisine in St. Lucia. Begin with a garden salad made with locally grown greens or else christophene and coconut soup. We're especially fond of the chilled Creole seafood soup, which is reminiscent of gazpacho. As for main dishes, the chef has a special flair for seafood pasta or marinated sirloin steak, and chicken appears stuffed with bread crumbs, sweet peppers, and onions. But the best bet is the catch of the day, likely to be kingfish or red snapper, grilled to perfection.

The Still. Less than a mile east of Soufrière. ☎ **758/459-7224.** Reservations not required. Main courses $10–$32. AE, V. Daily 8am–5pm. CREOLE.

There are far better restaurants on St. Lucia, but if it's lunchtime and you're near Diamond Falls, you don't have a lot of choices. The first thing you'll see as you drive up the hill from the harbor is a very old rum distillery set on a platform of thick timbers, the home of this restaurant. The site is a working cocoa and citrus plantation that has been in the same St. Lucian family for four generations. The front blossoms with avocado and breadfruit trees, and a mahogany forest is a few steps away. The bar near the front veranda is furnished with tables cut from cross sections of mahogany tree trunks. A more formal and spacious dining room is nearby. St. Lucian specialties are served here, depending on what's fresh at the market that day.

IN RODNEY BAY

☻ **The Lime.** Rodney Bay, north of Reduit Beach. ☎ **758/452-0761.** Reservations recommended. Main courses EC$35–EC$70 ($12.95–$25.90). MC, V. Wed–Mon 11am–2pm and 6:30–11pm. Closed mid-June to July 7. AMERICAN/CREOLE.

The Lime stands north of Reduit Beach in an area known as restaurant row. Some of these places here are rather expensive, but the Lime continues to keep its prices low, its food good and plentiful, and its service among the finest on the island. This open-air restaurant is very West Indian in atmosphere. Both locals and visitors come here for "limin'," or hanging out. Try the "lime special" drink. Specialties include stuffed crab backs and fish steak Creole, and it also serves shrimp, steaks, lamb and pork chops, and roti (Caribbean burritos). The steaks are done over a charcoal grill. Nothing is fancy, nothing is innovative, and nothing is nouvelle—just like the savvy local foodies like it.

The Mortar & Pestle. In the Harmony Marina Suites, Rodney Bay Lagoon. ☎ **758/452-8711.** Reservations recommended. Main courses EC$45–EC$85 ($16.65–$31.45). MC, V. Daily 7am–3pm and 7–11pm. CARIBBEAN/INTERNATIONAL.

This restaurant offers indoor-outdoor dining with a view of the boats moored at the nearby marina. It serves select recipes from the various islands of the southern Caribbean, with their rich medley of African, British, French, Spanish, Portuguese, Dutch, Indian, Chinese, and even Amerindian influences. To start, try the rich and creamy conch chowder, followed by crab farci (a delicious stuffed crab in the shell). Trinidad rule Jol (salt codfish with tomatoes, onions, peppers, and lime juice, with pepper sauce), an unusual dish and an acquired taste for some, is also available. For something truly regional, try the Barbados souse, with marinated pieces of lean cooked pork, or the frogs' legs from Dominica. All the good stuff is here, including Jamaican ackee and saltfish or Guyana Casareep pepperpot, an Amerindian specialty with beef, pork, and salt meats simmered slowly in Casareep syrup, cloves, star anise, cinnamon, and chili. Music by a steel band or some other local group sometimes accompanies the meals.

19 St. Maarten & St. Martin ⚓ ⚓ ⚓

Legend has it that a gin-drinking Dutchman and a wine-guzzling Frenchman walked around this island one day in 1648 to claim territory for their countries. The Frenchman covered the most ground, but the canny Dutchman got the more valuable real estate.

Whether the story is true or not, this island is today the smallest territory in the world shared by two sovereign states. The Dutch side is known as St. Maarten; the French side, St. Martin. Once you've cleared Customs on either side, the only way you'll know you're crossing from Holland into France is by the "Bienvenue Française" signs marking the boundary. Coexistence between the two nations is very peaceful. Muggings and robberies of tourists, however, have been on the rise.

Most cruise ships land at Philipsburg, capital of the Dutch side, though smaller ships can maneuver into the harbor of Marigot on the French side.

Don't come to either side to escape the crowds. Thousands of tourists arrive every week, many of them tour groups and conventioneers. The 100% duty-free shopping has turned the island into a virtual mall, and Philipsburg is bustling with cruise ship passengers.

Although the boom was severely slowed by the hurricanes of 1995, the island quickly rebuilt. The island's 36 white-sand beaches remain unspoiled, though somewhat rearranged by Mother Nature, and the clear turquoise waters are as enticing as ever.

ST. MAARTEN

Founded in 1763 by Comdr. John Phillips, a Scot in Dutch employ, **Philipsburg** curves along the shores of Great Bay. The main thoroughfare is busy Front Street, which stretches for about a mile and is lined with stores selling international merchandise. More shops lie along the little lanes, known as *steegijes,* that connect Front Street with Back Street, another shoppers' mart.

COMING ASHORE

Most vessels land at Philipsburg, docking about a mile southwest of town at A.C. Wathey Pier at Point Blanche. Some passengers walk the distance, but taxis do await all cruise ships. There are almost no facilities at A.C. Wathey Pier except for a few phones. Passengers can use an AT&T credit card or call collect here cheaper than they can aboard ship. Some ships anchor in the mouth of the harbor, then take passengers by tender to Little Pier in the heart of town.

FAST FACTS

Currency   The legal tender in Dutch St. Maarten is the **Netherlands Antilles guilder (NAf).** The official rate of exchange is 1.80 NAf for each $1 U.S. Dollars, however, are also accepted here. Prices in this section are usually given in U.S. currency.

Information   Go to the **Tourist Information Bureau,** in the Imperial Building at 23 Walter Nisbeth Rd. (☎ **599/5-22337**). Open Monday to Friday from 8am to noon and 1 to 5pm.

Language   Although the official language is Dutch, most people also speak English.

St. Maarten & St. Martin

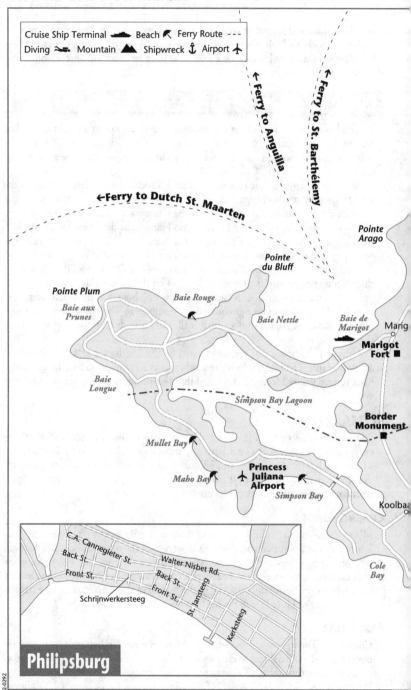

Cruise Ship Terminal 〜 Beach ⚓ Ferry Route - - -
Diving 〜 Mountain ▲ Shipwreck ⚓ Airport ✈

← Ferry to Anguilla

← Ferry to St. Barthélemy

←Ferry to Dutch St. Maarten

Pointe Arago

Pointe du Bluff

Pointe Plum

Baie aux Prunes

Baie Rouge

Baie Nettle

Baie de Marigot

Marig

Marigot Fort ■

Baie Longue

Simpson Bay Lagoon

Border Monument ■

Mullet Bay

Maho Bay

Princess Juliana Airport

Simpson Bay

Koolba

Cole Bay

C.A. Cannegieter St.

Walter Nisbet Rd.

Back St.

Front St.

Back St.

Front St.

St. Jansteeg

Kerksteeg

Schrijnwerkersteeg

Philipsburg

2-0292

Anse
Marcel

Bell Point

Red Rock

Grandes
Cayes

La Tintamarre→

Baie de
Grand Case

Grand Case

Cul-de-Sac

Aérodrome
de l'Espérance

ILET PINEL

Orient Beach

Baie Orientale

GRANDE-TERRE

Colombier

Paradise Peak

CAYE VERTE

Orléans

Baie de l'Embouchure

ST. MARTIN

Mt. Flagstaff

ST. MAARTEN

Beneden
Prinsen

Boven
Prinsen

Oyster
Pond

Dawn Beach

Dutch
Cul de Sac

Great
Salt
Pond

Genève
Bay

Philipsburg

AREA OF INSET

Little Bay

Great Bay

Caribbean Sea

0   1 km
     .6 mi

N

Point
Blanche

SHORE EXCURSIONS

There aren't many attractions here except the beaches, so you won't miss much if you skip the 3-hour sightseeing tour, which costs $20, covers both sides of the island, and usually includes a stopover in Marigot for sightseeing and shopping.

Most cruise ships also offer sports-oriented tours. These include a 3-hour, $28 snorkeling excursion to Pinel Island at Cul-de-Sac on the French side, and a 2-hour, $22 sun-and-sea cruise, which offers offshore views of the beach resorts on both the French and Dutch sides. You can also take a sea and island tour, which lasts 3¹/₂ hours and combines the best of both. It costs $40 per person.

GETTING AROUND

BUS   The privately owned and operated minibuses are a reasonable way to get around, if you don't mind some inconveniences and possible overcrowding. They run daily from 7am to midnight and serve most major locations on St. Maarten. Fares range from $1.15 to $2. The most popular run is from Philipsburg to Marigot on the French side.

CAR RENTALS   Rental cars are a practical way to see both the Dutch and the French sides of the island. **Budget** (☎ **800/527-0700** in the U.S., or 599/5-54030), **Hertz** (☎ **800/654-3131** in the U.S., or 599/5-54314), and **Avis** (☎ **800/ 331-1212** in the U.S. or 599/5-52847) all have agencies here. If you're calling in advance, you might try **Auto Europe** (☎ **800/223-5555**). Rates begin at $45 per day with unlimited mileage for a subcompact car. Drive on the **right-hand side of the road** on both sides of the island.

TAXIS   Taxis are unmetered, but Dutch St. Maarten law requires drivers to list fares to major destinations on the island. There are minimum fares for two passengers, and each additional passenger pays another $2. Call a cab at ☎ **599/5-54317.**

GAMBLING THE DAY AWAY

In the absence of natural wonders or man-made attractions, the biggest on-shore lure for cruise ship passengers are the casinos on the Dutch side.

Most of the casinos are in the big hotels. **Casino Royale,** at the Maho Beach Hotel on Maho Bay (☎ **599/5-52115**), which opened in 1975, has 6 roulette wheels, 3 craps tables, 16 blackjack tables, and 3 Caribbean stud-poker tables. It also offers baccarat, minibaccarat, and more than 250 slot machines. It's open daily from 1pm to 4am. There's no admission, and a snack buffet is complimentary.

Another popular casino is at the **Pelican Resort and Casino** on Simpson Bay (☎ **599/5-42503**), built to a Swiss design incorporating a panoramic view of the water. This Las Vegas–style casino has 2 craps tables, 3 roulette tables, 9 blackjack tables, 2 stud-poker tables, and 120 slot machines. It's open daily from 1pm to 3am.

The Roman-themed **Coliseum Casino,** on Front Street in Philipsburg (☎ **599/ 5-32102**), tries hard to attract gaming enthusiasts, especially "high rollers," and has the highest table limits ($1,000 maximum) on St. Maarten. Upon the management's approval, the Coliseum also offers credit lines for clients with a good credit rating at any U.S. casino. This casino features about 225 slot machines, 4 blackjack tables, 3 poker tables, and 2 roulette wheels. The Coliseum is open daily from 11am to 3am.

SHOPPING

The main shopping area is in the center of Philipsburg. Most stores are on the two leading streets, Front Street (*Voorstraat* in Dutch), which is closer to the bay, and Back Street (*Achterstraat*), which runs parallel to Front.

In general, the price marked on the merchandise in the major retail outlets is what you're supposed to pay. At small, very personally run shops, however, some polite bargaining might be in order.

Antillean Liquors. Queen Juliana Airport. ☎ **599/5-54267.**

This duty-free shop attracts the last-minute shopper. It has a complete assortment of liquor and liqueurs, as well as cigarettes and cigars. In general prices are lower here than in other stores on the island, and the selection is larger. Many bottles are priced anywhere from 30% to 50% lower than in the States. The only local product sold is an island liqueur called Guavaberry, which is made from rum (see the Guavaberry Company, below).

Caribbean Camera Centre. 79 Front St. ☎ **599/5-25259.**

This outlet has a wide range of merchandise, but it's always wise to know the prices charged back home. Cameras here may be among the lowest priced on St. Maarten; however, we've found better deals on St. Thomas.

Colombian Emeralds International. Old St. ☎ **599/5-23933.**

If you're seriously shopping for emeralds, this is the place. Here you'll find stones ranging in style from collector to investment quality. Unmounted, duty-free emeralds from Colombia, as well as emerald, gold, diamond, ruby, and sapphire jewelry, will tempt you. Prices here are approximately the same as in other outlets of this famous chain throughout the Caribbean. There are some huckster fly-by-night vendors around the island pawning fakes off on unsuspecting tourists; Colombian Emeralds offers the genuine item.

Guavaberry Company. 10 Front St. ☎ **599/5-22965.**

This place sells the rare "island folk liqueur" of St. Maarten, which for centuries was made in private homes but is now available to everyone. Sold in square bottles, the liqueur is aged and has a fruity, woody, almost bittersweet flavor. It's made from rum that's given a unique flavor by rare, local berries usually grown in the hills in the center of the island. You can blend it with coconut for a unique guavaberry colada or pour a splash into a glass of icy champagne. Don't confuse guavaberries with guavas—they're very different. Stop in at their shop and free-tasting house.

H. Stern Jewelers. 56 Front St. ☎ **599/5-23328.**

This is the Philipsburg branch of a worldwide firm that engages in mining, designing, manufacturing, exporting, and retailing jewelry in all price ranges. If you're looking for quality jewelry, sometimes at 25% off stateside prices, H. Stern is the place. Over the years we've made some good buys here in elegant watches. Unlike all those shady vendors in St. Maarten and elsewhere, Stern gives guarantees that you might say are written in gold.

Little Europe. 80 Front St. ☎ **599/5-24371.**

This upscale purveyor of all the "finer things" in life is a favorite of cruise ship passengers because its prices are inexpensive compared to North American boutiques. Its inventory includes porcelain figurines by Hummel, watches by Concorde, Piaget, Corum, and Movado, and jewelry.

Little Switzerland. 42 Front St. ☎ **599/5-23530.**

These fine-quality European imports are sold at attractive prices, often 25% or more lower than stateside. You'll find elegant famous-name watches, china, crystal, and jewelry, plus perfume and accessories. Little Switzerland has the best overall selection of these items of any shop in the Dutch side.

Old Street Shopping Center. With entrances on Front St. and Back St. ☎ **599/5-24712.**

The Old Street Shopping Center, built in a West Indian-Dutch style, lies 170 yards east of the courthouse. Its lion's-head fountain is the most photographed spot on St. Maarten. The center features more than two dozen shops and boutiques, including branches of such famous stores as Colombian Emeralds. Dining facilities include the Philipsburg Grill and Ribs Co. and Pizza Hut. The stores are open Monday to Saturday from 9:30am to 6pm, but the Philipsburg Grill and Ribs Co. is open on Sunday if a cruise ship docks.

New Amsterdam Store. 54 Front St. ☎ **559/5-22787.**

A tradition in the islands since 1925, this is a general store with a little bit of everything—from fine linen to fashion, footwear to swimwear, even porcelain. If your time is limited, you might want to visit this place first because it's so comprehensive. Prices are competitive with other stores in town.

Shipwreck Shop. Front St. ☎ **599/5-22962.**

Here you'll find West Indian hammocks, beach towels, sea salt, cane sugar, spices, baskets, jewelry, T-shirts, postcards, books, and much more. The shop also sells a variety of Caribbean handcrafts, including native art and woodcarvings. If you're looking for gifts or handcrafts in general, this might be your best bet, especially if funds are low.

Yellow House (Casa Amarilla). Wilhelminastraat. ☎ **599/5-23438.**

This shop is a branch of a century-old establishment on Curaçao. All kinds of perfumes and luxury items are sold here, including Christian Door cosmetics. Although primarily known for its cosmetics and perfumes, the store also carries a number of discounted luxury gift items as well.

BEACHES

St. Maarten has 36 beautiful white-sand beaches, so it's comparatively easy to find one for yourself. But if it's too secluded, be careful: There have been reports of robberies on some remote beaches. Don't carry valuables to the beach.

You can often use the changing facilities at some of the bigger resorts for a small fee. Nudists should head for the French side (see the "Favorite Beach Experiences" box), although the Dutch side is getting more liberal about such things.

On the west side of the island, **Mullet Bay Beach** is shaded by palm trees, but can get crowded on weekends. You can arrange water-sports equipment rentals through the Mullet Bay Resort.

Great Bay Beach is best if you'd like to stay near Front Street in Philipsburg. This mile-long beach is sandy, but since it borders the busy capital it may not be as clean as some of the more remote beaches. Immediately to the west, at the foot of Fort Amsterdam, **Little Bay Beach** looks like a Caribbean postcard, but it, too, can be overrun with visitors.

Stretching the length of Simpson Bay Village, white sand **Simpson Bay Beach,** is shaped like a half moon. It lies west of Philipsburg, just east of the airport. You can rent water-sports equipment here.

West of the airport, **Maho Bay Beach,** at the Maho Beach Hotel and Casino, is ideal in many ways, if you don't mind the planes passing overhead. Palms provide shade, and food and drink can be purchased at the hotel.

The sands are pearly white at **Oyster Pond Beach,** near the Oyster Pond Hotel northeast of Philipsburg. Bodysurfers like the rolling waves here. Nearby, **Dawn Beach** is noted for its underwater tropical beauty, with reefs lying offshore.

Beyond the sprawling (and severely hurricane-damaged) Mullet Beach Resort on the Dutch side, **Cupecoy Bay Beach** lies just north of the Dutch-French border on the western side of the island. It's a string of three white sandy beaches set against a backdrop of caves and sandstone cliffs that provide morning shade. The beach doesn't have facilities, but is nonetheless popular. One section of the beach is "clothing optional." The 1995 storms unearthed some rocky parts that sunbathers find uncomfortable.

GOLF, RIDING, SAILING, DIVING, SNORKELING & TENNIS

GOLF   The **Mullet Bay Resort** (☎ 599/5-52801, ext. 1850) has an 18-hole course designed by Joseph Lee. It's one of the most challenging in the Caribbean. Mullet Pond and Simpson Bay lagoon provide both beauty and hazards. Greens fees are $108 for 18 holes.

HORSEBACK RIDING   At **Crazy Acres,** Dr. J.H. Dela Fuente Street, Cole Bay (☎ 599/5-42793), riding expeditions invariably end on an isolated beach where horses and riders can enjoy a cool post-ride romp in the water. Two experienced escorts accompany a maximum of eight people on the 2^1/$_2$-hour outings, which begin at 9:30am and 2:30pm Monday to Saturday and cost $55 per person. Riders of all experience levels are welcome. Wear a bathing suit under your riding clothes. Reservations should be made at least 2 days in advance.

SAILING   A popular pastime here is to sign up for a day of picnicking, sailing, snorkeling, and sightseeing aboard one of several sleek sailboats. The boats usually pack large wicker hampers full of victuals and stretch tarpaulins over sections of the deck to protect sun-shy sailors. *Random Wind* operates in conjunction with **Fun in the Sun,** Great Bay Marina (☎ 599/5-70210) on the Dutch side. This 47-foot traditional clipper circumnavigates the island, carrying 15 passengers for $70 apiece.

SCUBA DIVING & SNORKELING   Crystal-clear bays and countless coves make for good snorkeling as well as scuba diving. Underwater visibility runs from 75 to 125 feet. The biggest attraction for scuba divers is the 1801 British man-of-war HMS *Proselyte,* which came to a watery grave on a reef a mile off the coast.

You'll find the best water sports—and the best values—at **Pelican Watersports,** Pelican Resort & Casino, Simpson Bay (☎ 599/5-42604). Its PADI-instructed program features the most knowledgeable guides on the island, each one familiar with St. Maarten dive sites. Divers are taken out in custom-built 28- and 35-foot boats. Many say that this is the best reef diving in the Caribbean. A single tank dive costs $45, a double tank dive $90. Snorkeling trips can also be arranged.

TENNIS   In St. Maarten, you'll have to call a hotel and see if courts are free. Try **Maho Beach Hotel and Casino,** Maho Bay (☎ 599/5-52115), and **Oyster Pond Beach Hotel,** Oyster Pond (☎ 599/5-36040), which both accept nonguests.

DINING

Antoine's. 119 Front St., Philipsburg. ☎ **599/5-22964.** Reservations recommended, especially in winter. Main courses $17.75–$36. AE, MC, V. Daily 11:30am–10pm. FRENCH/CREOLE/ITALIAN.

Antoine's offers *la belle cuisine* in an atmospheric building by the sea. Its sophistication and style are backed up by first-class service and an impressive wine list. The Gallic specialties with Creole overtones are among the best on the island, ranking favorably with any of the better restaurants in the French zone. The cuisine is mainly old continental favorites. For an appetizer, you could order gazpacho or vichyssoise, but we prefer the chef's savory kettle of fish soup, or the good homemade pâté. Main courses are almost equally divided between meat and fish dishes. If available, opt for the baked red snapper filet, which is delicately flavored with white wine, lemon, shallots, and a butter sauce. Although the veal and beef dishes are shipped in frozen, they're thawed out and fashioned into rather delectable choices, especially the veal scaloppini with a smooth, perfectly balanced mustard-and-cream sauce. Enjoy an aperitif in the bar while you peruse the menu.

✪ **Cheri's Café.** 45 Cinnamon Grove, Shopping Centre, Maho Beach. ☎ **599/5-53361.** Reservations not accepted. Main courses $5.75–$16.75. No credit cards. Daily 11am–midnight. AMERICAN.

The island hot spot, Cheri's was the *Caribbean Travel and Life* readers' pick for best bar in the West Indies. Known for its inexpensive food and live bands, it has been an island institution ever since it opened in 1988. This open-air cafe serves some 400 meals a night.

The place is really only a roof without walls, and it's not on a beach. But everybody comes here, from movie stars to rock bands, from high rollers at the casino to beach bums. You can get really fresh grilled fish, 16-ounce steaks, and juicy burgers. Some come for the inexpensive food, others for the potent drinks. The bartender's special is a frozen "Straw Hat" made with vodka, coconut, tequila, both pineapple and orange juice, and strawberry liqueur. Maybe even one more ingredient, we suspect, although nobody's talking.

Chesterfields. Great Bay Marina, Philipsburg. ☎ **599/5-23484.** Reservations recommended. Lunch main courses $6.95–$13.95; dinner main courses $14.95–$18.95. No credit cards. Daily 7:30am–10:30pm. AMERICAN/CARIBBEAN.

Just a few steps from Great Bay Marina, east of Philipsburg's center, this restaurant occupies a breezy veranda that's popular among yachties. Breakfasts are hearty and wholesome, with main courses ranging from $3.50 to around $6. The seafood omelets are especially tasty. The bar dispenses bottled beer and mixed drinks from midmorning until long after sundown, and also does a brisk lunch business, serving platters of fish, grilled steaks and other meats, sandwiches, and salads. Dinners are more elaborate, and include yellowfin tuna or mahimahi, which can either be grilled and served with garlic butter, or pan-fried with a Creole sauce. Roasted duck is accompanied by banana-pineapple sauce, and has been a longtime favorite here.

✪ **Crocodile Express Café.** Casino Balcony, at the Pelican Resort & Casino, Simpson Bay. ☎ **599/5-42503,** ext. 1127. MC, V. Daily 7:30am–11pm. DELI/GRILL/AMERICAN.

Start the day looking out at Simpson Bay while feasting on extra thick French toast made with homemade bread, or eggs any style. Otherwise, maybe lunch, or snacks in the afternoon? Hearty deli fare includes well-stuffed sandwiches. You might also try the grilled local fish or tasty kebabs. A specialty is grilled chicken breast West Indian style, marinated in tropical fruit juices and served with grilled onions. For dessert there are home-baked pies and other choices. Drinks include fresh mango or frozen passion fruit.

✪ **Da Livio Ristorante.** 159 Front St. (at the bottom of Front St.), Philipsburg. ☎ **599/5-23363.** Reservations recommended for dinner. Lunch main courses $16–$25; dinner main courses $18–$30. AE, MC, V. Mon–Fri noon–2pm; Mon–Sat 6:30–10pm. ITALIAN.

This is the finest Italian dining in St. Maarten. The food here is consistently excellent, and the service is graciousness itself (something rarely found on the island). The place is as Italian as they come, even if all the staff isn't. Bergamasco Livio himself hails from near Venice, and he purchases most of his ingredients from the finest suppliers in his home country.

The restaurant sets a romantic mood in the evening with its panoramic view of the Great Bay and background music. Da Livio obviously adores Pavarotti. The kitchen offers daily specials with an emphasis on fresh pastas, fresh local fish, and such favorites as lobster and prime meats. Our favorite dish is homemade manicotti della casa, filled with ricotta, spinach, and a zesty tomato sauce. For a main course, we also suggest the Fra Diavolo with linguine or else the tender and juicy veal chop with sage-flavored butter. Tony Bennett and even Eddie Murphy have sung the praises of these dishes. This is obviously a kitchen staff who cares, even going so far as to grow tomatoes in their own garden.

Don Carlos Restaurant. Airport Rd. (5 min. east of the airport), Simpson Bay. ☎ **599/5-53112.** Reservations not required. Main courses $10.50–$28.50. AE, DC, DISC, MC, V. Daily 7:30am–10pm. MEXICAN/CARIBBEAN/INTERNATIONAL.

From the hacienda-style dining room in this down-home restaurant, you can watch arriving and departing planes through the floor-to-ceiling windows. This place serves breakfast, lunch, and dinner, providing consistently decent fare at reasonable prices. Have a drink in the Pancho Villa Bar before your meal. Quantity, instead of quality, is the rule here, but diners seem to view this as a "fun" choice.

The Greenhouse. Bobby's Marina (off Front St.), Philipsburg. ☎ **599/5-22941.** Reservations not required. Main courses $12.25–$18.70. AE, MC, V. Daily 11am–1am. AMERICAN.

Open to a view of the harbor, the Greenhouse is a breezy, open-air restaurant, filled with plants. Lunches include the catch of the day, a wide selection of burgers, and conch chowder. The menu might also feature chunks of lobster in wine sauce or a whole red snapper. By no means does this place serve the best food on the island, but it's plentiful and a good value. Some patrons use it merely as a drinking venue.

Indiana Beach. Simpson Bay (on the road to the Pelican Resort & Casino). ☎ **599/5-42797.** Reservations recommended. Main courses $19.75–$21.50; breakfast buffet from $4.95. AE, MC, V. Daily 8am–11pm. Closed Sept. CONTINENTAL.

A good choice for an alfresco meal, this place is at its most romantic during candlelit dinners, but is also a viable choice for cruise ship passengers during the day. Seating selections range from intimate sheltered booths to outdoor tables set within sight and sound of the sea. The lobster pasta is sublime; otherwise, the main dishes are all too familiar, though well prepared, including the filet mignon. The fresh fish and other seafood specialties are also good bets.

Lynette's. Simpson Bay Blvd. (near the airport). ☎ **599/5-52865.** Reservations recommended. Main courses $13.75–$32. AE, MC, V. Winter daily 11:30am–10:30pm; off-season daily 6–10:30pm. WEST INDIAN.

This is the most noteworthy West Indian restaurant on St. Maarten. It's completely unpretentious, and rich in local flavors and understated charm. St. Maarten-born Lynette Felix, along with Clayton Felix, are the creative forces here, serving flavorful ethnic food. The setting is a concrete-sided, wood-trimmed building beside the highway, with a color scheme of pink, maroon, cream, and brown. The menu reads like a lexicon of tried-and-true Caribbean staples, including colombos (ragoûts) of goat and chicken, stuffed crab backs, curried seafood, and filet of snapper with green plantains and Creole sauce or garlic butter. An ideal lunch might be a brimming bowlful of pumpkin (squash) soup followed by one of the main-course salads. Try the one made from herbed lobster. The dishes here have true island flavor.

ST. MARTIN

The St. Martin side of the island is decidedly French. The tricolor flies over Marigot's *gendarmerie;* towns have names like Colombier and Orléans; the streets are called "rue de la Liberté" and "rue de la République." Its advocates say St. Martin is decidedly more sophisticated, prosperous, stylish, and cosmopolitan than its neighboring *départements d'outre-mer,* Guadeloupe and Martinique.

Marigot, the principal town in Saint Martin, has none of Philipsburg's frenzied pace and cruise ship crowds. In fact, Marigot looks like a French village transplanted to the Caribbean.

COMING ASHORE

Medium-sized vessels can dock at the pier at Port-Royale, at the bottom of the Boulevard de France in the heart of Marigot. When you disembark, you'll see a rather lavish marina, the headquarters of the island's tourist office, and arcades of shops nearby. In the event that a cruise ship is already at the pier, which can only accommodate one at a time, the second ship will have to anchor and send tenders ashore.

FAST FACTS

Currency   French St. Martin uses the **French franc (F),** although U.S. dollars seem to be preferred here. The exchange rate is 6.14 F to $1 U.S. (1 F = 16.3¢), which we have used to convert prices in this section. Canadians should convert their money into U.S. dollars and not into francs.

Information   The **Office du Tourisme** is at the Port de Marigot (☎ **0590/87-57-21**). Open Monday to Friday from 9am to 5pm.

Language   Although the official language is French, most people also speak English.

SHORE EXCURSIONS

See the "Shore Excursions" section in St. Maarten, above. You may be able to take a 3-hour, $28 snorkeling excursion to Pinel Island at Cul-de-Sac. Sun-and-sea cruises usually last 2 hours, cost $22, and offer views offshore of the beach resorts on both the French and Dutch sides.

GETTING AROUND

BUS   Local drivers operate a diverse armada of privately owned minivans and minibuses. There's a departure every hour from Marigot to the Dutch side. Because it's sometimes difficult for a newcomer to identify the buses, it's best to ask a local.

CAR RENTALS   Rental cars are a practical way to see the island. **Budget** (☎ **800/527-0700** in the U.S., or 0590/87-38-22), **Hertz** (☎ **800/654-3001** in the U.S., or 0590/87-73-01), and **Avis** (☎ **800/331-1212** in the U.S., or 0590/87-50-60) all have agencies here. Rates begin at $35 per day with unlimited mileage. Drive on **the right-hand side** of the road.

TAXIS   Taxis are the most common means of transport. A **Taxi Service & Information Center** operates at the port of Marigot (☎ **0590/87-56-54**). It also books 2-hour sightseeing trips around the island. Always agree on the rate before getting into an unmetered cab.

SHOPPING

Many day-trippers come over to Marigot just to look at the collection of French boutiques and shopping arcades. Whether you're seeking jewelry, perfume, or St-Tropez bikinis, you'll find it in one of the boutiques along rue de la République and rue de la Liberté. Because it's a duty-free port, the shopping here is some of the best in the Caribbean here. There's a wide selection of European merchandise, much of it geared to the luxury trade. Crystal, perfumes, jewelry, and fashions are sometimes 25% to 50% less expensive than in the United States and Canada. You'll also find fine liqueurs, cognacs, and cigars.

Prices are often quoted in U.S. dollars, and salespeople frequently speak English. U.S. dollars, credit and charge cards, and traveler's checks are usually accepted. Shops are generally open Monday through Saturday from 9am to noon and from 2 to 6pm. Some of the larger shops are also open on Sunday and holidays if cruise ships are in port.

At harbor side in Marigot, there's a frisky **morning market** with vendors selling spices, fruit, shells, and local handcrafts. Mornings are even more alive at **Port La Royale,** the bustling center of everything. Schooners unload produce from the neighboring islands, boats board guests for picnics on deserted beaches, and a brigantine sets out on a sightseeing sail. The owners of a dozen different little dining spots get ready for the lunch crowd. The largest shopping arcade on the French side is here, with many boutiques that often come and go rapidly.

Galerie Périgourdine, another cluster of boutiques, faces the post office. Here you might pick up some designer wear for both men and women, including items from the collection of Ted Lapidus.

Act III. 3 rue du Général-de-Gaulle. ☎ **0590/29-28-43.**

Since it open in 1994, this shop has often been cited as the most glamorous women's store in St. Martin. It prides itself on a higher percentage of evening gowns and chic cocktail dresses than any of its competitors, and limits its roster of bathing suits to a simple, short-lived springtime collection. If you've been invited to a reception aboard a private yacht, get your outfit here. Designers include Alaïa, Thierry Mugler, Gianni Versace, Christian Lacroix, Cerruti, Gaultier, and others. The staff is accommodating and bilingual, and usually serves with tact and charm.

Gingerbread & Mahogany Gallery. 4-14 Marina Royale (in a narrow alleyway at the marina). ☎ **0590/87-73-21.**

Owner Simone Seitre scours Haiti four times a year to secure the best works of a cross-section of Haitian artists, both the "old masters" and the talented amateurs. One of the most knowledgeable purveyors of Haitian art in the Caribbean, Seitre has promoted Haitian art at exhibits around the world. Even if you're not in the market for an expensive piece of art, you'll find dozens of charming and inexpensive handcrafts. The little gallery is a bit hard to find, but it's worth the search.

Havane. Port La Royale. ☎ **0590/87-70-39.**

Havane offers exclusive collections of French clothing, in both casual and high-fashion designs for men. This is the leading choice for French designer fashions on the island. Sometimes you get discounts, depending on how willing they are to move the merchandise.

Lipstick. Port La Royale, rue Kennedy. ☎ **0590/87-73-24.**

This is the leading purveyor of women's cosmetics and skin-care products on French St. Martin. A beauty parlor one floor above street level is devoted to the intelligent and tasteful use of the store's impressive inventory. You'll find virtually every conceivable cosmetic or beauty aid made by such manufacturers as Chanel, Lancôme, Guerlain, Yves St. Laurent, Door, and an emerging brand from Japan known as Shiseido. Hair removals, massages, manicures, pedicures, facials, and hair styling are available on the premises. The company maintains another outlet a few storefronts away (Lipstick, rue de la République, ☎ **0590/87-53-92**) that sells the cosmetics but lacks a beauty parlor.

⭐ Favorite Beach Experiences

Orient Beach is one of the Caribbean's most famous clothing-optional beaches. A taxi will take you to the **Club Orient Naturist Hotel** (☎ **0590/87-33-85**), where you can join in the stripped-down fun. When your eyes tire of body-watching, you can also rent sports equipment.

Uninhabited **Pinel Island,** a little sandy islet off the northeast coast of St. Martin, only has about 500 yards of beach, but it's choice. The island is located off the coast of Cul-de-Sac in St. Martin. You can picnic here, but there are no facilities. Snorkelers can take in the beauty of coral reefs inhabited by tropical fish that you can hand feed. To reach the islet, rent a small boat called a putt putt on the beach at Cul-de-Sac. It's a memorable way to spend 3 or 4 hours in the sun.

Little Switzerland. Rue de la Liberté. ☎ **0590/87-50-03.**

As you travel through the islands, especially on a cruise, you'll see branches of this store everywhere. You'll find the widest array of duty-free luxury items in French St. Martin here, including French perfume and French leather goods. There's even another outlet on the Dutch side, but the merchandise is different here, with more French products.

Maneks. No. 24 rue de la République. ☎ **0590/87-54-91.**

This place has a little bit of everything: video cameras, electronics, household appliances, liquors, beach accessories, gifts, souvenirs, Kodak film, watches, T-shirts, sunglasses, and pearls from Majorca. You can even get Cuban cigars, but these will have to be smoked abroad, as they can't be brought back into the United States.

Oro de Sol Jewelers. Rue de la République. ☎ **0590/87-56-51.**

This is the St. Martin branch of a small but choice chain of jewelers whose other outlets lie within upscale neighborhoods of Anguilla and St. Barts. Its inventory includes high-fashion jewelry studded with precious stones, and gold watches by Cartier, Chopard, Ebel, Patek Philippe, and Bulgari. Within the neighboring, affiliated shops, you'll find lots of other upscale items, including perfumes, porcelain, crystal, flatware, and leather handbags.

Roland Richardson. Blvd. de France (on the waterfront). ☎ **0590/87-32-24.**

Local artist Roland Richardson welcomes visitors to his beautiful small gallery. A native of St. Martin, Mr. Richardson is recognized today as one of the Caribbean's premier artists. He works in oil, watercolor, pastel, charcoal, and etching. Often referred to as a "modern-day Gauguin," he is a gifted Impressionist painter known for his landscape, portraiture, and colorful still life paintings. His work has been exhibited in more than 70 one-man and group exhibitions in museums, major trade centers, and fine art galleries around the world, and is included in many fine private and public collections. Gallery hours are Monday through Friday, 10am to 6pm, Saturday, 9am to 2pm; the gallery is closed on Sunday. Special appointments are available.

La Romana. 12 rue de la République. ☎ **0590/87-88-16.**

Specializing in a roster of chic women's clothing, this store sells garments that are a bit less pretentious and, at their best, more fun and lighthearted than those of the most visible competitor, Act III. The motif is Italian rather than French, with brand names that include La Perla swimwear and, to a much greater extent, day and evening wear. Other trademarks include Anna Club, Ritmo de la Perloa, handbags by

Moschino, and perfumes. A small collection of menswear is also available, but overall, the focus here is on garments for women.

BEACHES

Top rating on the French side goes to **Baie Longue,** a long, beautiful beach that's rarely overcrowded. Chic and very expensive La Samanna, a deluxe hotel, opens onto this beachfront, which is one of the few on the island that grew rather than diminished in size during the 1995 hurricanes. Unfortunately, the storms created unexpected holes offshore, which makes swimming here more hazardous than before. The beach lies to the north of Cupecoy Beach, by the Lowlands road. Don't leave any valuables in your car, as many break-ins have been reported along this stretch of highway.

If you continue north, you reach the approach to **Baie Rouge,** another long and popular stretch of sand and jagged coral. Snorkelers are drawn to the rock formations at both ends of this beach, many of which were exposed through erosion caused by the 1995 storms. There are no changing facilities, but that doesn't matter for some, who get their suntan *au naturel.*

On the north side of the island, to the west of Espérance airport, **Grand-Case Beach** is small but select. Despite the many tons of storm debris left in 1995 by the hurricanes, the sands are once again white and clean.

DIVING, SNORKELING, TENNIS & WINDSURFING

SCUBA DIVING   Scuba diving is excellent around French St. Martin, with reef, wreck, cave, and drift dives ranging from 20 to 70 feet. Dive sites include Ilet Pinel for shallow diving; Green Key, a barrier reef; Flat Island for sheltered coves and geologic faults; and Tintamarre, known for its shipwreck. The island's premier dive operation is **Marine Time,** whose offices are in the same building as L'Aventure, Chemin du Port, 97150 Marigot (☎ **0590/87-20-28**). Operated by England-born Philip Baumann and his Mauritius-born colleague, Corine Mazurier, this outfit offers morning and afternoon dives in deep and shallow water, to wrecks and over reefs. The price is $45 per dive. A resort course for first-time divers costs $75.

SNORKELING   The island's tiny coves and calm offshore waters make it a snorkeler's heaven. The waters off the northeastern shore are protected as a regional underwater nature reserve, **Reserve Sous-Marine Régionale.** This area includes Flat Island (also known as Tintamarre), Pinel Islet, Green Key, and Petite Clef. The use of harpoons and spears is strictly forbidden. Snorkeling can be enjoyed individually or on sailing trips. You can rent equipment at almost any hotel on the beach.

TENNIS   Tennis buffs can play at most hotels. **Le Méridien L'Habitation,** Anse Marcel (☎ **0590/87-67-00**), has six courts. There are three courts at the exclusive **La Samanna,** Baie Longue (☎ **0590/87-64-00**).

WATERSKIING & PARASAILING   Most of St. Martin's large beachfront hotels maintain facilities for waterskiing and parasailing, often from makeshift kiosks that operate from the sands of the hotel's beaches. Waterskiing costs around $40 per 20-minute ride. Two independent operators that function from side-by-side positions on Orient Bay, close to the cluster of hotels near the Esmeralda Hotel, are **Kon Tiki Watersports** (☎ **0590/87-46-89**), and **Bikini Beach Watersports** (☎ **0590/ 87-43-25**). High-velocity, highly maneuverable water scooters—also known as jet skis—rent for between $35 and $45 per half-hour session. Parasailing, where you'll hang from a parachute while being towed behind a motorboat, costs $45 for a vertiginous 10-minute experience.

WINDSURFING   Because of prevailing winds and calmer, more protected waters, most windsurfers gravitate to the island's easternmost edge, most notably Coconut Grove Beach, Orient Beach, and to a lesser extent, Dawn Beach. The best of the several outfits that specialize in windsurfing is **Tropical Wave,** Coconut Grove, Le Galion Beach, Baie de l'Embouchure (☎ **0590/87-37-25**), set midway between Orient Beach and Oyster Pond, amid a sunblasted, scrub-covered, isolated landscape. The combination of wind and calm waters here is considered almost ideal. Mistral boards rent for $20 an hour, with instruction priced at $30 an hour.

DINING

In Baie Longue

✪ **La Samanna.** Baie Longue. ☎ **0590/87-51-22.** Reservations required for dinner, not for lunch. Main courses 200 F–425 F ($33.40–$71). AE, MC, V. Daily 12:30–2:30pm and 7–10:30pm. Closed Sept–Oct. FRENCH.

Judges of the food here have declared it among the best in the Caribbean, equal to that of the finest world-class restaurants in Paris. The high prices reflect the establishment's reputation. Innovatively prepared and impeccably presented, dishes are likely to include lobster risotto, a hot and cold array of California foie gras, and Norwegian salmon with a sauce of red flame seedless grapes. Many dishes are a modernized version of the cuisine of Provence, priced at levels higher than you'd find even in that expensive region of France. The Dover sole and the oysters are flown in fresh from France, and the steaks are imported from New York.

The alfresco dining terrace overlooks the sea. Dinner is served by candlelight. Each table is set with Rosenthal china, lit by lamps from the Orient Express, and, at lunch, adorned with local flowers. Lunches are slightly less expensive than dinners; try the theatrically prepared steak tartare. La Samanna's underground, air-conditioned wine cellar houses more than 25,000 bottles from elite vineyards around the world.

In & Around Marigot

La Brasserie de Marigot. Rue du Général-de-Gaulle, 11. ☎ **0590/87-94-43.** Reservations not required. Main courses 45 F–88 F ($7.50–$14.70). AE, MC, V. Mon–Sat 7am–9pm, Sun 9am–4pm. FRENCH/CARIBBEAN.

This is where the real French eat, a great choice for good food at good prices. The brasserie, located in the center of town, is air-conditioned, with sidewalk tables overlooking the pedestrian traffic outside. Opened in a former bank, it has a marble-and-brass decor, a sort of retro 1950s style with green leather banquettes. Meals include all those good dishes the French enjoyed at blue-collar bistros "between the wars," such as pot-au-feu, duck breast with peaches, filet of beef with mushroom sauce, blanquette de veau, and even chicken on a spit and steak tartare. Naturally, you can order interesting terrines here. Wine is sold by the glass, carafe, or bottle. The kitchen also prepares a handful of Caribbean dishes such as red snapper in vanilla or passion-fruit sauce. It also features the most glamorous "take-out" service on St. Martin.

La Maison sur le Port. Blvd. de France. ☎ **0590/87-56-38.** Reservations recommended. Main courses $14–$19 at lunch, $15–$38 at dinner; fixed-price dinner $21.75. AE, DISC, MC, V. Mon–Sat noon–2:30pm; daily 6–10:30pm. FRENCH.

The staff welcomes people to enjoy their French cuisine in a refined atmosphere and elegant surroundings, in a covered terrace with a view of three waterfalls in the garden. Overall, this is a grand, Parisian, and upscale choice. The tables are dressed with snowy tablecloths and Limoges china. At lunch, you can choose from a number of salads as well as fish and meat courses. Dinner choices include fresh fish, such as snapper, salmon, or swordfish with coconut sauce; and filet of lamb, veal, or steak, each with a light sauce. Duck with mango has always been a specialty, as has bouillabaisse or giant shrimp in garlic butter. The cookery is grounded firmly in France, but there are Caribbean twists and flavors, which come as delightful surprises. You can order from a wine list with an extensive selection of imported French products at moderate prices. Many guests come here at sundown to enjoy the harbor view.

✪ **La Vie en Rose.** Blvd. de France at rue de la République. ☎ **0590/87-54-42.** Reservations recommended, especially in winter, as far in advance as possible. Lunch main courses $7–$26; dinner main courses $25–$33. AE, MC, V. Daily 11:30am–2:30pm and 6:30–9:45pm. Closed Sun off-season. FRENCH.

The dining room in this balconied second-floor restaurant evokes the nostalgia of the 1920s, with ceiling fans and a romantic atmosphere. If you don't like the parlor, you can sit at one of the tables on a little veranda overlooking the harbor, but you need to request this when you make a reservation. Even though the menu is classic French, it still has Caribbean flavors. Lunches are relatively simple affairs, with an emphasis on fresh, meal-sized salads, simple grills that include steaks and fresh fish, and sandwiches. Dinners are more elaborate, and might begin with a seafood tartare with medallions of lobster, or fried foie gras with pears marinated in red wine. Main courses include grilled filet of red snapper with fresh basil sauce; fresh medallions of lobster floating on a bed of Caribbean lime sauce; boneless breast of duck with raspberry sauce and fried bananas; and an unusual version of roasted rack of lamb with a gratin of goat cheese and sliced potatoes.

Le Mini Club. Rue de la Liberté. ☎ **0590/87-50-69.** Reservations required. Main courses 95 F–165 F ($15.85–$27.55); Wed and Sat dinner buffet 210 F ($35.05). AE, MC, V. Daily noon–3pm and 6–11pm. FRENCH/CREOLE.

After you climb a flight of wooden stairs, you'll find yourself on a wooden deck suspended above the sands of the beach, like a tree house built among coconut palms. This popular establishment is filled with Haitian murals and grass carpeting. It's not the best, and certainly not the most innovative restaurant on the island, but it prepares every dish exceedingly well and uses quality ingredients. The specialties include lobster soufflé (made for two or four people), an array of fish and vegetable terrines, red snapper with Creole sauce, sweetbreads in puff pastry, and many kinds of salad. Dessert might be bananas flambéed with cognac. Lavish buffets are held every Wednesday and Saturday night, with unlimited wine included. The restaurant is along the seafront at Marigot.

In & Around Grand Case

Il Nettuno. 70 Blvd. de Grand-Case (on the main street of Grand-Case, close to the pier) ☎ **0590/87-77-38.** Reservations recommended. Main courses $17–$22; lunch platters $12–$14. AE, MC, V. Daily noon–2:30pm and 6–10:30pm. Closed June and Sept. ITALIAN/SEAFOOD.

This cozy trattoria, in a clapboard-sided house, is not the most refined place on the island, but it's interesting and has a devoted local following. Its interior is painted in shades of pink and white and draped with fish nets, Chianti bottles, and memorabilia of the Washington Redskins (its French-Italian owner lived in the U.S. capital for a time, and considers the Redskins his "home team"). Agnolotti stuffed with ricotta and porcini mushrooms is a worthwhile pasta, as is the chef's penne with salmon or the ravioli stuffed with spinach and ricotta. Main courses include saltimbocca (veal with ham) and fresh fish, such as mahimahi, tuna, and swordfish; there's also a choice of traditional Italian veal and chicken dishes. Fish choices can be blackened, grilled, or fried, and are served with a choice of sauces, including one made of saffron. The bar here is popular.

La Marine. 158 Blvd. de Grand-Case. (on the seaward side of the main road through Grand-Case) ☎ **0590/87-02-31.** Reservations recommended. Main courses 120 F–195 F ($20.05–$32.55). AE, MC, V. Mon–Sat 6–10:30pm (and noon–2:30pm mid-Dec to mid-Mar). Closed Sept to mid-Oct. FRENCH.

This is one of the most appealing restaurants in town. It's set within an antique, much-enlarged Creole house, with a color scheme of blue and white. Gilles Briand, the capable French-trained chef here, crafts sophisticated variations on grand classical French cuisine. Everything is made fresh, from ingredients imported at frequent intervals from the French or U.S. mainland. Worthy beginnings include lobster-stuffed ravioli with Antillean herbs; a galette of crabmeat with a confit of red peppers; and a *croustillant* of snails with vinaigrette made from equal portions of cider vinegar and balsamic vinegar. There's also a roulade of halibut with Japanese algae, stuffed with a mixture of crabmeat and smoked salmon and drizzled with a curry sauce. An example of a dish that seems to come directly from provincial 19th-century France is a *confit* of rabbit cooked in goosefat, served with cabbage stuffed with smoked lard, and accompanied by a chive-flavored cream sauce.

Rainbow. Grand Case (on the seaward side of Grand Case's main road). ☎ **0590/87-55-80.** Reservations recommended. Main courses 115 F–200 F ($19.20–$33.40). MC, V. Dec–Mar only, Mon–Sat noon–2pm; Oct 16–Aug Mon–Sat 6:30–10:30pm. Closed Sept–Oct 15. CARIBBEAN/ CONTINENTAL.

The staff and owners here are a bit blasé; you might get the idea that they'd rather be sailing than preparing your meal. But, don't be turned off by their attitude. You'll be pleasantly surprised by a delectable platter of tuna, snapper, mahimahi, or lobster, if you can stand the wait. The blue-and-white dining room is in a 70-year-old Creole house. For lunch, there are burgers and salads, along with some of the main courses served at night. Dinner choices include a fricassee of shrimp with scallops and Caribbean chutney; a sauté of Atlantic salmon with lobster-studded mashed potatoes; or a very French version of *magret* of duckling.

In Oyster Pond
Captain Oliver Restaurant. In Captain Oliver's Hotel Resort (at the Dutch border). ☎ **0590/ 87-30-00.** Reservations recommended. Main courses $11.50–$25. AE, DC, MC, V. Daily noon–10:30pm. FRENCH/CREOLE.

Partially built on piers above the bay, Captain Oliver is reached from either Marigot or Philipsburg along a twisting and much-potholed road. Once here, in a wood-sheathed setting overlooking some very expensive yachts, you'll find West Indian conch, "fish soup of the captain," a fisher's platter, tuna steak grilled with caper sauce, and fresh grilled lobster. This place has been known to island gourmets since it opened in 1983.

20 St. Thomas & St. John ⚓ ⚓ ⚓ ⚓

One of the busiest ports in the Caribbean, St. Thomas often hosts more than 10 cruise ships a day during the peak winter season. Charlotte Amalie, its somewhat seedy capital, has become the Caribbean's major shopping center.

Vacationers discovered St. Thomas right after World War II, and they've been flocking here in increasing numbers ever since. Tourism and U.S. government programs have raised the standard of living here to one of the highest in the Caribbean. The island is now the most developed of the U.S. Virgins. Condominium apartments have grown up over the debris of bulldozed shacks.

In stark contrast to this busy scene, more than half of nearby St. John, the smallest of the U.S. Virgin Islands, is pristinely preserved in the gorgeous Virgin Islands

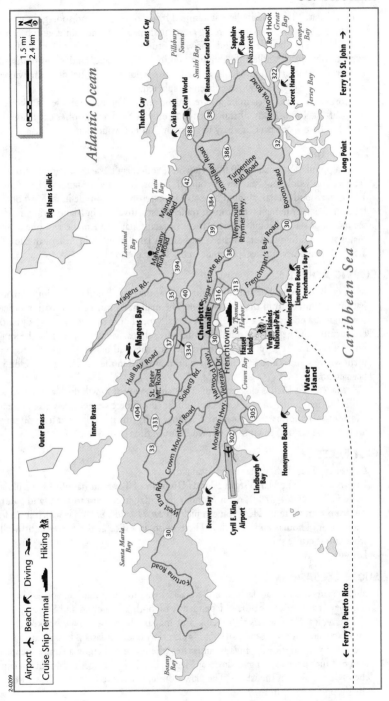

National Park. The wildlife here is admired by ornithologists and zoologists around the world. A rocky coastline, forming crescent-shaped bays and white-sand beaches, rings the whole island. Panoramic views and ruins of 18th-century Danish plantations dot St. John's miles of serpentine hiking trails. Island guides can point out mysterious geometric petroglyphs incised into boulders and cliffs; of unknown age and origin, the figures have never been deciphered.

Most cruise ships dock in Charlotte Amalie on St. Thomas, but a few anchor directly off St. John. Many of those that stop only at St. Thomas offer excursions to St. John. If yours doesn't, it's easy to get to St. John on your own.

ST. THOMAS

With a population of some 50,000, tiny St. Thomas isn't exactly a tranquil tropical retreat. You won't any beaches to yourself. Shops, bars, and restaurants (including a lot of fast-food joints), abound here, as well as resorts and simple inns. Most of the locals make their living by the tourist trade. Most native Virgin Islanders are the descendants of slaves brought from Africa. In fact, Charlotte Amalie was one of the major slave-trading centers in the Caribbean. A large number of American expatriates and temporary sun-seekers reside in St. Thomas also.

COMING ASHORE

Most cruise ships anchor at Havensight Mall, at the eastern end of Charlotte Amalie harbor, 1 1/2 miles from the town center. The mall has a tourist information office, restaurants, a bookstore, a bank, a U.S. postal van, phones that accept long-distance credit cards, and a generous number of duty-free shops. Many people make the long, hot walk to the center of Charlotte Amalie, but the road passes a housing development where some cruise passengers have been mugged in the past. Take a taxi for $3 per person.

If Havensight Mall is clogged with cruise ships, your ship will dock at the Crown Point Marina, to the west of Charlotte Amalie. From here we definitely recommend a taxi into Charlotte Amalie instead of a long, dusty, dreary walk of at least 30 minutes. A taxi ride into town from Crown Point Marina costs $4.

FAST FACTS

Currency   The U.S. dollar is the local currency.

Information   The **U.S. Virgin Islands Division of Tourism** has offices at Tolbod Gade (☎ **340/774-8784**), open Monday to Friday from 8am to 5pm, and Saturday from 8am to noon. Here you can pick up *St. Thomas This Week,* which includes maps of St. Thomas and St. John. There's also an office at the Havensight Mall, where most cruise ships dock.

Language   It's English.

SHORE EXCURSIONS

Shore excursions here are lackluster. Because it's easy to get around on your own, you may want to spend your time independently on both St. Thomas and St. John.

The typical St. Thomas sightseeing tour may be the most heavily booked cruise ship excursion in the Caribbean, but it's also the dullest. It lasts 2 hours, costs $24, and takes you up into the hills to an estate, where you can enjoy a complimentary rum or fruit punch as you gaze down at Magens Beach. It also goes to Mountain Top, the highest point on the island. The view from up there is a lot more pleasant than the shopping down in town.

Shore excursions often feature water adventures, which are much better and more interesting than the sightseeing jaunt.

One tour offers snorkeling at Coki Beach. It lasts 3 hours and costs $25, instruction and equipment included. Often you can spot a wide variety of wildlife. This is a good tour for snorkeling neophytes. Sometimes cruise lines offer a 3-hour sailing and snorkeling tour for $47. These tours include snorkeling lessons and a romantic sail. The boat might be a single hull sailing yacht or a modern catamaran. Certified divers can generally hook up with a scuba diving jaunt, lasting 3 hours and costing $40.

GETTING AROUND

BUS   Comfortable and often air-conditioned, government-run **Vitran buses** serve Charlotte Amalie and the countryside as far away as Red Hook, a jumping-off point for St. John. They run daily between 5am and 10:40pm. You rarely have to wait more than 30 minutes during the day. A one-way ride costs 75¢ within Charlotte Amalie, $1 to outer neighborhoods, and $3 for rides as far as Red Hook. For routes, stops, and schedules, call ☎ 340/774-5678.

Less structured and more erratic are **"taxi vans,"** a miniflotilla of privately owned vans or minibuses operated by a frequently changing cast of local entrepreneurs. They make unscheduled stops along major traffic arteries and charge the same fares as the Vitran buses. They may or may not have their final destinations written on a cardboard sign displayed on the windshield. They tend to be less comfortable than Vitran buses. If in doubt, stick to Vitran.

CAR RENTALS   St. Thomas has many car-rental firms, and competition is stiff. The big companies tend to be easier to deal with than local firms. Before you go, compare the rates of **Avis** (☎ 800/331-1212), **Budget** (☎ 800/527-0700), and **Hertz** (☎ 800/654-3001). A 1-day car rental generally ranges from $55 to $75, with unlimited mileage. There is no tax on car rentals in the Virgin Islands.

Be careful when driving here. Although this is a U.S. territory, Virgin Islanders drive **on the left side of the road.** St. Thomas has a high accident rate. Roads are narrow, and the steep, hilly terrain often shelters blind curves and entrance ramps. Also, some drivers here take the wheel after too many drinks.

TAXIS   Taxis are the chief means of transport here. They're unmetered, so agree with the driver on a fare before you get in. The official fare for sightseeing is $30 for two passengers for 2 hours; each additional passenger pays another $12. For 24-hour radio-dispatch service, call ☎ 340/774-7457. Many taxis transport 8 to 12 passengers in vans to multiple destinations, for a lower price.

SEEING THE SIGHTS

The color and charm of a slightly seedy Caribbean waterfront come vividly to life in **Charlotte Amalie.** In days of yore, seafarers from all over the globe flocked to this old-world Danish town. Confederate sailors used the port during the Civil War.

The old warehouses once used for storing pirates' loot still stand and, for the most part, house today's shops. In fact, the main streets (called "Gades" here in honor of their Danish heritage) are now a virtual shopping mall and are usually packed with visitors. Sandwiched among these shops are a few historic buildings, most of which can be covered on foot in about 2 hours. Before starting your tour, stop off in the so-called **Grand Hotel,** near Emancipation Park. No longer a hotel, it contains shops and a visitor center.

Dating from 1672, **Fort Christian** rises from the harbor to dominate the center of town. Named after the Danish king Christian V, the structure has been everything from a governor's residence to a jail. Many pirates were hanged in its courtyard. Some of the cells have been turned into the rather minor **Virgin Islands Museum,** displaying Native American artifacts of only the most passing interest. Admission is free. The fort is open Monday to Friday from 8am to 5pm.

Seven Arches Museum, Government Hill (☎ **340/774-9295**), is a 2-century-old Danish house completely restored to its original condition and furnished with antiques. You can walk through the yellow ballast arches and visit the great room with its view of the busy harbor. You can also view the original separate stone Danish kitchen above the cistern. The $5 admission includes a cold tropical drink served in a walled garden filled with flowers. It's open Tuesday to Saturday from 10am to 3pm.

The Paradise Point Tramway (☎ **340/774-9809**), opened in 1994, affords visitors a dramatic view of Charlotte Amalie harbor at a peak height of 697 feet, although you'll pay dearly for the privilege. The tramways, similar to those used at ski resorts, transport customers from the Havensight area to Paradise Point, where riders disembark to visit shops and a popular restaurant and bar. The four cars, each with a 10-person capacity, take about 15 minutes for the trip. Admission is $10 per person round-trip, children half-price. Open daily 9am–5pm.

✪ **Coral World Marine Park & Underwater Observatory.** 6450 Coki Point (off Rte. 38, 20 min. from downtown Charlotte Amalie). ☎ **340/775-1555.** Admission $17 adults, $10 children under 12. Daily 9am–5:30pm.

This aquarium is the number one attraction in St. Thomas. The 3¹/₂-acre complex features a three-story underwater observation tower 100 feet offshore. Through windows you'll see sponges, fish, coral, and other underwater life in their natural state. In the Marine Gardens Aquarium, saltwater tanks display everything from sea horses to sea urchins. An 80,000-gallon reef tank features exotic Caribbean marine life. Another tank is devoted to sea predators, including circling sharks and giant moray eels, among other creatures. The entrance is hidden behind a waterfall.

The latest addition to the park is a semisubmarine that lets you enjoy the panoramic view and the underwater feeling of a submarine without truly submerging. Coral World's guests can also take advantage of adjacent Coki Beach for snorkel rental, scuba lessons, or simply swimming and relaxing. Lockers and showers are available.

Also included in the marine park are a cafe, duty-free shops, and a tropical nature trail. Activities include daily fish and shark feedings and exotic bird shows.

SHOPPING

St. Thomas is famous for its shopping. As with St. Croix, American shoppers can bring home $1,200 worth of merchandise without paying duty. You'll sometimes find well-known brand names at savings of up to 40% off stateside prices—but you'll often have to plow through a lot of junk to find the bargains. Look around before leaving home so you'll recognize the good deals here.

Many cruise ship passengers shop at the **Havensight Mall,** where they disembark, but the major shopping goes on along the harbor of Charlotte Amalie. **Main Street** (or Dronningens Gade, its old Danish name) is the main shopping area. Just north of Main Street is merchandise-loaded **Back Street,** or Vimmelskaft. Many shops are also spread along the **Waterfront Highway** (also called Kyst Vejen). Running between these major streets is a series of side streets, walkways, and alleys—all filled with shops. Among these are Tolbod Gade, Raadets Gade, Royal Dane Mall, Palm Passage, Storervaer Gade, and Strand Gade.

All the major stores in St. Thomas are located by number on an excellent map in *St. Thomas This Week,* distributed free to all arriving cruise passengers. Nearly all stores here are closed on Sundays and major holidays unless a cruise ship is in port. Friday is the busiest cruise ship day.

Charlotte Amalie

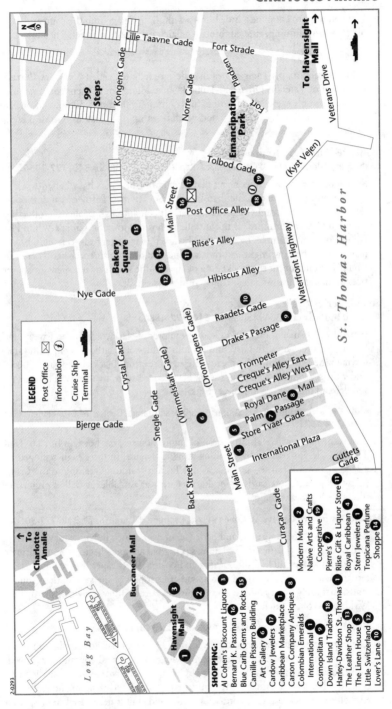

SHOPPING:
Al Cohen's Discount Liquors **3**
Bernard K. Passman **16**
Blue Carib Gems and Rocks **15**
Camille Pissarro Building
Art Gallery **6**
Cardow Jewelers **17**
Caribbean Marketplace **1**
Carson Company Antiques **8**
Colombian Emeralds
International **1**
Cosmopolitan **9**
Down Island Traders **18**
Harley-Davidson St. Thomas **1**
The Leather Shop **13**
The Linen House **5**
Little Switzerland **12**
Lover's Lane **10**
Modern Music **2**
Native Arts and Crafts
Cooperative **1**
Pierre's **7**
Riise Gift & Liquor Store **11**
Royal Caribbean **4**
Stern Jewelers **1**
Tropicana Perfume
Shoppe **14**

If you want to combine a little history with shopping, go into the courtyard of the old **Pissarro Building,** entered through an archway off Main Street. The impressionist painter lived here as a child, and the old apartments have been turned into a warren of interesting shops.

Street vendors ply their trades in a designated area called **Vendors Plaza,** at the corner of Veterans Drive and Tolbod Gade. Hundreds of them converge under oversize parasols there Monday to Saturday from 7:30am to 5:30pm, and on Sunday if a cruise ship is expected. Food vendors set up on sidewalks outside Vendors Plaza.

Antique Furniture Reproductions

Mahogany Island Style. Al Cohen's Plaza, Raphune Hill, Rte. 38. ☎ **340/777-3060.**

St. Thomas locals sometimes regret that neighboring St. Croix has a better-developed sense of historic plantation life than bustling St. Thomas. Partly as a means of correcting that, Jane Coombs created this store. It contains high-quality reproductions, crafted by Baker Furniture, of the antique furniture within St. Croix's Whim Plantation Museum. Examples include lavishly carved four-poster beds (certain to become heirlooms in their own right), and wicker-and-mahogany planters chairs. There's also a built-in humidor for the stockpiling of cigars—the store's owner spent an apprenticeship in Cuba learning the nuances of the cigar trade.

Art Galleries & Fine Crafts

Bernard K. Passman. 38A Main St. ☎ **340/777-4580.**

Bernard K. Passman is the world's leading sculptor of black coral art and jewelry. He's famous for his "Can Can Girl" and his four statues of Charlie Chaplin. On Grand Cayman, he learned to fashion exquisite treasures from black coral found 200 feet under the sea. Some of Passman's work has been treasured by royalty. There are also simpler and more affordable pieces for sale.

Camille Pissarro Building Art Gallery. Caribbean Cultural Centre, 14 Dronningens Gade. ☎ **340/774-4621.**

This is the house where Pissarro, dean of Impressionism, was born on July 10, 1830. The art gallery is reached by climbing a flight of stairs. In three high-ceilinged and airy rooms, you'll can see all the available Pissarro paintings relating to the islands. Many prints and note cards of local artists are also available, as well as original batiks, alive in vibrant colors.

Mango Tango Art Gallery. Al Cohen's Plaza, Raphune Hill, Rte. 38. ☎ **340/777-3060.**

Associated with Mahogany Island Style (see above), which lies next door, this is one of the largest art galleries in St. Thomas. Original artworks begin at $200, rising to a maximum of around $7,000. Prints and posters are cheaper. Represented are internationally recognized artists who spend at least part of the year in the Virgin Islands, including Don Dahlke, Max Johnson, Anne Miller, David Millard, Dana Wylder, and Shari Erickson.

Native Arts and Crafts Cooperative. Tarbor 1. ☎ **340/777-1153.**

The largest arts and crafts emporium in the U.S. Virgin Islands combines the output of 90 different artisans into one sprawling shop. It's all contained within the former headquarters of the U.S. District Court, a 19th-century brick building adjacent to Charlotte Amalie's tourist information office. Most items here are small enough to be packed into a suitcase or trunk, and almost never need to be specially shipped. Examples include spice racks, paper towel racks, lamps crafted from conch shells, salad utensils and bowls, crocheted goods, and straw goods.

Bags

Coki. Compass Point Marina. ☎ **340/775-6560.**

Coki of St. Thomas has a factory at Compass Point Marina amidst a little restaurant row. You might want to combine a gastronomic tour with a shopping expedition. From the factory's expansive cutting board come some of the most popular varieties of shoulder tote bags in the Virgin Islands. These include beach bags, zip-top bags, and drawstring bags. All Coki bags are 100% cotton, stitched with polyester sailmaker's thread.

Bric-a-Brac

Carson Company Antiques. Royal Dane Mall, off Main St. ☎ **340/774-6175.**

Its clutter and eclecticism might appeal to you, especially if you appreciate small spaces loaded with merchandise, tasteless and otherwise, from virtually everywhere. Much of it is calculated to appeal to the tastes of cruise ship passengers. Bakelite jewelry is cheap and cheerful, and the African artifacts are often especially interesting.

Clothes & Memorabilia

Harley-Davidson St. Thomas. In the Havensight Mall, Bldg. 5. ☎ **340/776-7162.**

It comes as no surprise that the macho memorabilia associated with Harley-Davidson's motorcycles has been elevated to new levels of either hipness or kitsch, depending on your point of view. If you're interested in actually buying a motorcycle, you'll find models beginning at around $8,000 and going much higher. More feasible, however, especially in terms of transporting your purchase off-island, are any of the roster of sunglasses, pins, watches, "fanny packs," T-shirts, and leather belts, vests, and jackets designed by Harley for him and/or her. Cheerful and chipper, with a wholesomeness far removed from the image of Hell's Angels bikers roaring down the highways of California, this place is ready, willing, and eager to help transform even the most staid of tourists into Road Warriors.

Electronics

Royal Caribbean. 33 Main St. ☎ **340/776-4110.**

This is the largest camera and electronics store in the Caribbean, selling Nikon, Minolta, Pentax, Canon, and Panasonic products. It's also good source for watches, such as Seiko, Movado, Corum, Fendi, and Zodiac. They even have a complete collection of Philippe Charriol watches, jewelry, and leather bags, and a wide selection of Mikimoto pearls, 14- and 18-karat jewelry, and Lladró figurines.

There's an additional branch at Havensight Mall (☎ **340/776-8890**).

Fashion

Cosmopolitan. Drakes Passage and the waterfront. ☎ **340/776-2040.**

Since 1973, this store has drawn a lot of repeat business. Its shoe salon features shoes and handbags by Bally of Switzerland. In swimwear, it offers one of the best selections of Gottex for women and Gottex, Hom, Lahco, and Fila for men. A menswear section offers Paul & Shark from Italy and Burma Bibas sports shirts. The shop also features ties by Gianni Versace and Pancaldi of Italy (priced at least 30% less than on the U.S. mainland), and Nautica sportswear for men, discounted at 10%.

Fragrances

Tropicana Perfume Shoppe. 2 Main St. ☎ **800/233-7948** or 340/774-0010.

This store at the beginning of Main Street is billed as the largest perfumery in the world. It offers all the famous names in perfumes, skin care, and cosmetics, including Lancôme and La Prairie, among others. Men will find Europe's best colognes and aftershave lotions here.

Gifts & Liquors

Al Cohen's Discount Liquors. Long Bay Rd. ☎ **340/774-3690.**

In a big warehouse at Havensight, across from the docks where cruise ship passengers disembark, you can make purchases from one of the island's biggest storehouses of liquor and wine. The wine department is especially impressive. The quarters have been recently expanded and remodeled, and there are now more brands and items on sale than ever before. You can also purchase fragrances, T-shirts, and souvenirs.

A. H. Riise Gift & Liquor Stores. 37 Main St. at A. H. Riise Gift & Liquor Mall (perfume and liquor branch stores at the Havensight Mall). ☎ **800/524-2037** or 304/776-2303.

St. Thomas's oldest outlet for luxury items, such as jewelry, crystal, china, and perfumes, is still the largest. It also offers the widest sampling of liquors and liqueurs. Everything is displayed in a 19th-century Danish warehouse, extending from Main Street to the waterfront. The store sells fine jewelry and watches from Europe's leading craftspeople, including Vacheron Constantin, Bulgari, Omega, and Gucci, as well as a wide selection of Greek gold, platinum, and precious gemstone jewelry.

Imported cigars are stored in a climate-controlled walk-in humidor. Delivery to cruise ships and the airport is free. A. H. Riise also offers a vast selection of fragrances for both men and women, along with the world's best-known names in cosmetics and treatment products. Waterford, Lalique, Baccarat, and Rosenthal, among others, are featured in the china and crystal department. Specialty shops in the complex sell Caribbean gifts, books, clothing, food, art prints, note cards, and designer sunglasses.

Caribbean Marketplace. Havensight Mall (Bldg. III). ☎ **340/776-5400.**

The best selections of island handcrafts are found here, in addition to some distinctively Caribbean food items, including Sunny Caribbee products, a vast array of condiments ranging from spicy peppercorns to nutmeg mustard. There's also a wide selection of Sunny Caribbee's botanical products. Other items include Trinidadian steel-pan drums, wooden Jamaican jigsaw puzzles, Indonesian batiks, and bikinis from the Cayman Islands. Do not expect very attentive service.

Down Island Traders. Veterans Dr. ☎ **340/776-4641.**

The aroma of spices will lead you to these markets, which have Charlotte Amalie's most attractive array of spices, teas, seasoning, candies, jellies, jams, and condiments, most of which are packaged from natural Caribbean products. The owner also carries a line of local cookbooks, as well as silk-screened T-shirts and bags, Haitian metal sculpture, handmade jewelry, Caribbean folk art, and children's gifts. Be sure to ask for their collection of tropical coconut-mango bath and body products and the Calypso Spa Sun Care line.

Little Switzerland. 5 Main St. ☎ **800/524-2010** or 340/776-2010.

A branch of this shop seems to appear on every island in the Caribbean. Its collection of watches, including Omega and Rolex, is second to none. Its china, especially the Rosenthal collection, is outstanding, as are its crystal and jewelry, including gorgeous South Seas pearls. The store also maintains the official outlets for Hummel, Lladró, and Swarovski figurines. There are several other branches of this store on the island (at the Havensight Mall, for example), but the main store has the best selection.

Jewelry

Blue Carib Gems and Rocks. 2 Back St. (behind Little Switzerland). ☎ **340/774-8525.**

The owners of this shop have scoured the Caribbean for gemstones to bring to their workshop. Here the raw stones are cut, polished, and then fashioned into jewelry by the lost-wax process. On one side of the premises you can see the craftspeople at work, and on the other, view their finished products. All handcrafted jewelry comes with a lifetime guarantee. Since the items are locally made, they are duty-free and not included in the $1,200 customs exemption.

Cardow Jewelers. 39 Main St. ☎ **340/776-1140.**

Often called the Tiffany's of the Caribbean, Cardow Jewelers boasts perhaps the largest selection of fine jewelry in the world. This fabulous shop, where more than 20,000 rings are displayed, offers savings because of its worldwide direct buying, large turnover, and duty-free prices. Unusual and traditional designs are offered in diamonds, emeralds, rubies, sapphires, Brazilian stones, and pearls. Cardow has a whole wall of Italian gold chains, and also features antique-coin jewelry. The Treasure Cove, a discount area within the store, has cases of fine gold jewelry all priced under $200.

Colombian Emeralds International. Havensight Mall. ☎ **340/774-2442.**

Colombian Emeralds stores are renowned throughout the Caribbean for offering the finest collection of Colombian emeralds, both set and unset. Here you buy direct from the source, which can mean significant savings. In addition to jewelry, the shop stocks fine watches. There's another outlet on Main Street.

H. Stern Jewelers. Havensight Mall. ☎ **800/524-2024** or 340/776-1223.

This international jeweler is one of the most respected in the world, with some 175 outlets. In a world of fake jewelry, it's good to know that there's still a name you can count on. Stern is Cardow's (see above) leading competitor on the island. You'll find colorful gem and jewel creations here. There are two other branches on Main Street, and another at Marriott Frenchman's Reef. Stern gives worldwide guaranteed service, including a 1-year exchange privilege.

Pierre's. 24 Palm Passage. ☎ **800/300-0634** or 340/776-5130.

Connoisseurs of colored gemstones consider this store one of the most impressive repositories of rare and sought-after collector's items in the Caribbean. It's the 12-year-old branch of a store based in Naples, Florida. Here you'll find glittering and mystical-looking gemstones you might never have heard of before. Look for alexandrites (garnets in three shades of green), spinels (pink and red), sphenes (yellow-green sparklers from Madagascar), and tsavorites (a difficult-to-pronounce green stone from Tanzania). The creative forces behind all this are Jennifer and Gerald Rathkolb, who spent year studying gemology and doing goldsmithing work in Austria and South Africa. Virtually everything for sale here is tax-free.

Leather
The Leather Shop. 1 Main St. ☎ **340/776-0290.**

Here you'll find the best selection from Italian designers such as Desmo, Longchamp, Furla, and Il Bisonte. There are many styles of handbags, belts, wallets, briefcases, and attaché cases, plus reasonably priced bags from around the world.

Linens
The Linen House. A. H. Riise Mall. ☎ **340/774-1668.**

The Linen House is the best store for linens in the Caribbean. You'll find a wide selection of place mats, decorative tablecloths, and hand-embroidered goods, many of them handmade in China.

Merchandise for Lovers
Lover's Lane. Raadets Gade 33 (beside Veteran's Dr., on the second floor), Charlotte Amalie. ☎ **340/777-9616.**

Though this store expends a lot of effort cloaking its merchandise in an aura of "sex within the confines of marriage" respectability, much of the inventory here is as earthy and in some cases, raunchy, as anything you'll find on St. Thomas. That doesn't prevent a visit here from being amusing, if you're in the mood for it. Set within an ever-so-tasteful decor of muted grays and mirrors, this shop sells provocative lingerie; edible panties; inflatable men and women; massage aids of every conceivable type; the largest inventory of electric or battery-operated vibrators in the Virgin Islands; and all the lace, leather, or latex you'll need to make your dreams come true.

Music
Modern Music. Across from Havensight Mall and cruise ship docks. ☎ 340/774-3100.

Modern Music features nearly every genre of music, from rock to jazz to classical, and definitely Caribbean. It was opened nearly 10 years ago by New Jersey cold-weather refugee Chris Hansen. You'll find new releases from Caribbean stars such as Jamaica's Byron Lee and Virgin Island's The Violators, as well as the usual stuff from the U.S. They also have two other stores: at Nisky Center (☎ 340/777-7877) and at Four Winds Mall (☎ 340/775-3310).

BEACHES

Instead of looking at the minor attractions or going shopping, many cruise ship passengers prefer to spend their time ashore on a beach. St. Thomas has some good ones, and you can reach them all relatively quickly in a taxi (arrange for the driver to return and pick you up at a designated time). If you're going to St. John, you may want to do your beaching there (see "Beaches," under St. John, below).

All the beaches in the U.S. Virgin Islands are public, but some still charge a fee. Mind your belongings at the beach, as St. Thomas has pickpockets and thieves who target visitors.

THE NORTH SIDE   Magen Bay lies across the mountains 3 miles north of the capital. Once hailed as one of the world's 10 most beautiful beaches, its reputation has faded. Though still beautiful, it isn't as well-maintained as it should be and is often overcrowded, especially when many cruise ships are in port. It's less than a mile long and lies between two mountains. Admission is $1 for adults and 25¢ for children under 12. Changing facilities are available, and you can rent snorkeling gear and lounge chairs. If you're driving, take Route 35 north all the way from Charlotte Amalie. There's no public transportation here. The gates are open daily from 6am to 6pm (you'll need insect repellent after 4pm).

Located in the northeast near Coral World, **Coki Beach** is good, but it, too, becomes overcrowded when cruise ships are in port. Snorkelers come here often, as do pickpockets—protect your valuables. Lockers can be rented at Coral World, next door. An East End bus runs to Smith Bay and lets you off at the gate to Coral World and Coki.

Also on the north side is **Renaissance Grand Beach Resort,** one of the island's most beautiful beaches. It opens onto Smith Bay, right off Route 38, near Coral World. Many water sports are available here.

THE SOUTH SIDE   On the south side, **Morningstar** lies about 2 miles east of Charlotte Amalie at Marriott's Frenchman's Reef Beach Resort. You can wear your most daring swimwear here, and you can also rent sailboats, snorkeling equipment, and lounge chairs. The beach can be easily reached via a cliff-front elevator at the Marriott.

Limetree Beach, at the Bolongo Bay Beach Club, has been called a classic. It lures those who love a serene spread of sand. You can feed hibiscus blossoms to iguanas

✪ Favorite Experiences

West of Charlotte Amalie, **Frenchtown** was settled by a French-speaking citizenry uprooted when the Swedes invaded and took over in St. Barts. They were known for wearing *cha-chas,* or straw hats. Many of the people who live here today are the direct descendants of those long-ago residents. This colorful fishing village contains several interesting restaurants and taverns. To get there, take Veteran's Drive (Route 30) west and turn left at the sign to the Admirals Inn.

The lush **Estate St. Peter Greathouse Botanical Gardens,** at the corner of St. Peter Mountain Road (Route 40) and Barrett Hill Road (☎ **340/774-4999**), decorates 11 acres on the volcanic peaks of the island's northern rim. It's the creation of Howard Lawson DeWolfe, a Mayflower descendant who, with his wife, Sylvie, bought the estate in 1987 and set about transforming it into a tropical paradise. It's filled with self-guided nature walks that will acquaint you with some 200 varieties of plants and trees, including an umbrella plant from Madagascar. There's also a rain forest, an orchid jungle, a monkey habitat, waterfalls, and reflecting ponds. From a panoramic deck you can see some 20 of the Virgin Islands. The house itself is worth a visit, its interior filled with local art. The complex is open daily from 9am to 5pm. Admission is $8 for adults, $4 for children.

For a Jules Verne–type thrill, the ✪ *Atlantis* **submarine** takes you on a 1-hour voyage to depths of 150 feet, unfolding a world of exotic marine life for you and 45 other passengers. Divers swim with the fish and bring them close to the windows for photos. You take a surface boat from the West Indies Dock outside Charlotte Amalie to the submarine moored near Buck Island (different from the more famous Buck Island at St. Croix, 40 miles to the south). The fare is $72 for adults, $36 for teens, and $27 for children 4 to 12. Kids under 4 are not permitted. Hours and days vary depending on the arrival of cruise ships. Reservations are imperative. Go to the Havensight Shopping Mall, Building 6, or call ☎ **340/776-5650.**

and rent snorkeling gear and lounge chairs. There's no public transportation, it's easy to get here by taxi from Charlotte Amalie.

One of the most popular, **Brewer's Beach** lies in the southwest near the University of the Virgin Islands. It can be reached by the public bus marked "Fortuna" heading west from Charlotte Amalie. **Lindberg Beach,** near the airport, also lies on the Fortuna bus route heading west from Charlotte Amalie.

THE EAST END   Small and special, **Secret Harbour** sits near a collection of condos whose owners you'll meet on the beach. With its white sand and coconut palms, it's a cliché of Caribbean charm. No public transportation stops here, but it's an easy taxi ride east of Charlotte Amalie heading toward Red Hook.

✪ **Sapphire Beach** is one of the finest on St. Thomas, set against the backdrop of the fine Doubletree Sapphire Beach Resort & Marina complex, where you can lunch or order drinks. Windsurfers like this beach a lot. You can also rent snorkeling gear and lounge chairs here. A large reef lies close to the shore, and there are great views of offshore cays and St. John. To get to this beach, you can take the East End bus from Charlotte Amalie, going via Red Hook. Ask to be let off at the entrance to Sapphire Bay; it's not too far to walk from there to the water.

GOLF, SAILING, DIVING, SNORKELING, TENNIS & WINDSURFING

GOLF   Designed by Tom and George Fazio, **Mahogany Run** on the north shore, Mahogany Run Road (☎ **800/253-7103** or 340/777-6006), is one of the most beautiful courses in the West Indies. This 18-hole, par-70 course rises and drops like a roller coaster on its journey to the sea. Cliffs and crashing sea waves are the ultimate hazards at the 13th and 14th holes. Greens fees are $85 for 18 holes. A cart is mandatory and costs $15. The golf course is an $8 taxi ride from the cruise dock.

SAILING   You can avoid the crowds by sailing aboard *Fantasy* (☎ 340/775-5652), which departs from the American Yacht Harbor at Red Hook at 9:30am daily. It sails to St. John and nearby islands, carrying a maximum of six passengers, for swimming, snorkeling, beach combing, or trolling. Snorkel gear with expert instruction is provided, as is a champagne lunch. An underwater camera is also available. The cost of a full-day trip is $95 per person. A half-day sail, morning or afternoon, lasts 3 hours and costs $60.

SCUBA DIVING & SNORKELING   With 30 spectacular reefs just off St. Thomas, the waters off the U.S. Virgin Islands are rated as one of the "most beautiful areas in the world" by *Skin Diver* magazine.

Dive In!, in the Doubletree Sapphire Beach Resort & Marina, Smith Bay Road, Route 36 (☎ 800/524-2090), offers some of the finest diving services in the U.S. Virgin Islands, including professional instruction, daily beach and boat dives, custom dive packages, underwater photography and videotapes, and snorkeling trips. An introductory course costs $60, a one-tank dive $55, and a two-tank dive $70.

TENNIS   The best tennis on the island is at the **Wyndham Sugar Bay Beach Club,** 6500 Estate Smith Bay (☎ 340/777-7100), which has the Virgin Island's first stadium tennis court, seating 220, plus six additional Laykold courts. There's also a pro shop.

Another good resort for tennis is the **Bolongo Bay Beach Club,** Bolongo Bay (☎ 340/775-1800), which has two well-maintained tennis courts.

At **Marriott Frenchman's Reef Tennis Courts,** Flamboyant Point (☎ 340/776-8500,** ext. 444), four courts are available. Nonresidents are charged $10 a half hour per court.

WINDSURFING   This increasingly popular sport is practiced at the major resort beaches and at some public beaches, including Brewers Bay, Morningstar Beach, and Limetree Beach. **Renaissance Grand Beach Resort,** Smith Bay Road, Route 38 (☎ 340/775-1510), is the major hotel offering windsurfing. Nonresidents pay $30 per hour.

DINING

In Charlotte Amalie

Beni Iguana's Sushi Bar. In the Grand Hotel Court, Veteran's Dr. ☎ 340/777-8744. Reservations recommended. Sushi $4.50–$6 per portion (2 pieces); salads $7.95–$12.45; main courses $6–$15.95; combo plates for 4–5 diners $25–$35 each. AE, MC, V. Daily 11:30am–10pm. JAPANESE.

This is the only Japanese restaurant on St. Thomas, a good change of pace from the Caribbean, steak, and seafood restaurants nearby. Along with a handful of shops, it occupies a sheltered courtyard across from Emancipation Square Park. Select a table outside, or pass through wide Danish colonial doors into a red- and black-lacquered interior. Most meals begin with a selection of sushi (freshwater eel, tuna, yellowtail, or amberjack), which the chefs dub "edible art." This is often followed by a salad or a roll of seafood wrapped in rice. A perennial favorite is the "13" roll, stuffed with spicy crabmeat, salmon, lettuce, cucumbers, and scallions. Todd Reinhard, an American carefully trained in the art of Japanese cuisine, is your host.

Greenhouse. Veterans Dr. ☎ 340/774-7998. Main courses $6–$21; breakfast $2.50–$6.95. AE, DISC, MC, V. Daily 8am–2am. AMERICAN/CARIBBEAN.

Fronted by big sunny windows, this waterfront restaurant attracts cruise ship passengers who have shopped and need a place to drop. The food is not the island's best, but it's perfectly satisfying if you're not too demanding. A breakfast menu of eggs, sausages, and bacon segues into the daily specialties, including much American fare and some Jamaican-inspired dishes. You could order a pretty good freshly grilled mahimahi with Florida Key lime ginger butter and Jamaican jerk seasoning, or one of the delectable specialties such as barbecued pork ribs, again with Jamaican jerk spices. Happy hour is daily from 4:30 to 7pm. This is one of the safest places to be in Charlotte Amalie after dark.

Hard Rock Café. 5144 International Plaza (on the second floor of a pink-sided mall), the Waterfront, Queen's Quarter. ☎ **340/777-5555.** Reservations not accepted. Main dishes $7.95–$16.95. AE, MC, V. Mon–Sat 10am–9pm, Sun 10am–3pm. AMERICAN.

This hot spot overlooking Charlotte Amalie's harbor is a member of the international Hard Rock chain. Entire walls are devoted to the memorabilia of such artists as John Lennon, Eric Clapton, and Bob Marley. The place serves barbecued meats, salads, sandwiches, burgers, fresh fish, and steaks. Its burgers are the best in town, but people mainly come for the good times.

✪ **Hervé Restaurant & Wine Bar.** Government Hill (next to Hotel 1829). ☎ **340/777-9703.** Reservations requested. Main courses $17.75–$24.75; lunch $5.50–$16.75. AE, MC, V. Mon–Sat 11:30am–3pm and 6–10pm. AMERICAN/CARIBBEAN/FRENCH.

Hervé has quickly become the hot new restaurant in St. Thomas, surpassing all competition in town. A panoramic view of Charlotte Amalie and a historic setting are minor benefits—it's the cuisine here that matters. Hervé P. Chassin, a veteran of such stellar properties as the Hotel du Cap d'Antibes on the French Riviera, is a restaurateur with a vast, classical background. Here in his own unpretentious setting, he offers high-quality food at reasonable prices.

Study the menu in a room decorated with classic black-and-white photographs of St. Thomas at the turn of the century. There are two dining areas: a large open-air terrace and a more intimate wine room. Contemporary American dishes are served with the best of classic France, along with Caribbean touches. Start with the pistachio-encrusted brie, shrimp in a stuffed crab shell, or conch fritters with mango chutney. From here, you can let your taste buds march boldly forward to such temptations as red snapper poached with white wine, or a delectable black-sesame-crusted tuna with a ginger/raspberry sauce. Well-prepared nightly specials of game, fish, and pasta are also featured. Desserts here are equally divine—you'll rarely taste a creamier crème caramel or a lighter, fluffier cheesecake.

✪ **Virgilio's.** 18 Dronningens Gade (entrance on a narrow alleyway running between Main and Back sts.). ☎ **340/776-4920.** Reservations recommended. Main dishes $16.95–$39.95. AE, MC, V. Mon–Sat 11:30am–10:30pm. NORTHERN ITALIAN.

Virgilio's is the best northern Italian restaurant in the Virgin Islands. Heavy ceiling beams and brick vaulting shelter its neo-Baroque interior, with stained-glass windows and crystal chandeliers. A well-trained staff attends to the tables. Try the delicious house special: *cinco peche,* clams, mussels, scallops, oysters, and crayfish simmered in a saffron broth. The lobster ravioli here is the best there is, and the rack of lamb has a distinctive flair, filled with a porcini mushroom stuffing and glazed with a roasted garlic aïoli. You can even order an individual pesto pizza. Fresh fish and cold marinated duck are also featured.

Virgilio's Wine Cellar & Bistro. 16 Dronningsgade. ☎ **340/774-8086.** Reservations not necessary. Main courses $18.95–$38.95. AE, MC, V. Mon–Sat 11:30am–10:30pm; wine bar 11:30am–1am. ITALIAN.

Set within an 80-year-old building, this restaurant was conceived as a clone of its neighbor, Virgilio's, and is under the same management. The cellar contains the closest thing in St. Thomas to the kind of sophisticated wine bar you might have expected in London. It offers about 1,000 vintages, selling for between $3.75 and $6.50 a glass. You can visit just for a drink, or stop to consume an entire meal in the street-level dining room. Begin with any of about 17 kinds of pasta. Main courses include well-flavored chicken cacciatore, osso buco, and three different preparations of veal chops (breaded and baked, grilled, or stuffed with prosciutto, mozzarella, and porcini mushrooms). There's also lobster, prepared virtually any way you want. Technically, both the Wine Cellar and Virgilio's main restaurant maintain separate kitchens, but in fact, there's a lot of communication between the two, and some sharing of ideas.

In Frenchtown

Alexander's. Rue de St. Barthélemy (west of town). ☎ **340/776-4211.** Reservations recommended. Main courses $13–$21.50. AE, MC, V. Mon–Sat 11:30am–10pm. AUSTRIAN/GERMAN.

Alexander's will accommodate you in air-conditioned comfort at one of its 12 tables with picture windows overlooking the harbor. The Teutonic dishes are the best on the island. There's a heavy emphasis on seafood—the menu even includes conch schnitzel on occasion. Other dishes are a mouthwatering Wiener schnitzel and homemade pâté. For dessert, try the homemade strudel, either apple or cheese. Lunch consists of a variety of sandwiches, salads, and smaller versions of main courses offered at dinner. At both lunch and dinner, the menu offers 10 to 13 different pasta dishes. Alexander's also has a Bar and Grill, open daily from 11am to midnight; and Epernay, a wine bar open Monday through Friday from 4 to 11pm and Saturday from 4 to 11:30pm (closed Sunday).

✪ **Craig & Sally's.** 22 Honduras, Frenchtown. ☎ **340/777-9949.** Reservations recommended. Main courses $14–$29. AE, MC, V. Wed–Fri 11:30am–3pm; Wed–Sun 5:30–10pm. INTERNATIONAL.

Craig and Sally Darash, a husband-wife team who escaped from the snowbelt, operate this airy, open-sided, Caribbean cafe. Sally prepares all the eclectic food. Craig is the greeter and coordinator. He says that the food is not "for the faint of heart, but for the adventurous soul." His affection for fine wines has led him to create the most extensive and sophisticated wine list on St. Thomas. Views of the sky and sea complement a cuisine that ranges from pasta to seafood, with influences from Europe and Asia. Roast pork with clams, filet mignon with macadamia-nut sauce, and grilled swordfish with a sauce of fresh herbs and tomatoes are some items from a menu that changes every day. The lobster-stuffed twice-baked potatoes are examples of creative cuisine at its most inspired.

On the North Coast

Eunice's Terrace. 66-67 Smith Bay, Rte. 38 (just east of the Coral World turnoff). ☎ **340/775-3975.** Reservations not accepted. Main courses $9.95–$29.95. AE, MC, V. Mon–Sat 11am–10pm, Sun 5–10pm. Take the Red Hook bus. WEST INDIAN/AMERICAN.

This is one of the island's best-known West Indian restaurants. It's devoid of a romantic atmosphere but oozes with lots of local color. Locals and tourists alike crowd into its confines for savory platters of island food served in generous portions. Eunice Best and her restaurant made news around the world on January 5, 1997, when Bill and Hillary Clinton showed up unexpectedly for lunch. Surrounded by secret service men, they shared a conch appetizer, then Mrs. Clinton went for the vegetable plate, and the president for the catch of the day, a fish called "Old Wife," which Clinton declared he loved. A popular concoction called a Queen Mary (tropical fruits laced with dark rum) is a favorite starter. Dinner specialties include conch fritters, broiled or fried fish (especially dolphin), sweet-potato pie, and a number of dishes usually served with fungi, rice, or plantain. A bottle of hot yellow sauce enhances the flavors. On the lunch menu are fish burgers, sandwiches, and such daily specials as Virgin Islands doved pork or mutton. (Doving, pronounced *DOUGH-ving*, involves baking sliced meat while basting it with a combination of its own juices, tomato paste, Kitchen Bouquet, and island herbs.) Key lime pie is a favorite dessert.

On Sapphire Beach

Seagrape. In the Doubletree Sapphire Beach Resort & Marina, Rte. 6, Smith Bay Rd. ☎ **340/775-6100.** Reservations recommended. Main courses $12.95–$27.95; Sun brunch $9.50–$15.95. AE, DC, MC, V. Mon–Sat 7:30–10:30am, 11am–3pm, and 6–10pm, Sun 11am–3pm (brunch) and 6–10pm. CONTINENTAL/AMERICAN.

Seagrape is counted among the finest dining rooms along the east coast of St. Thomas. The restaurant's attractions are the sounds of the waves from of one of the most famous beaches in the Virgin Islands, a well-trained staff, and fine-quality food. The lunch menu includes the grilled catch of the day and freshly made salads. A children's menu is also available. The dinner menu offers traditional items like teriyaki chicken breast, veal marsala, and New York strip steak. Everything is prepared with style and flair. The rib eye comes with mashed potatoes laced with garlic for added flavor. The chicken breast is made more delightful with a mushroom salsa. The well-attended Sunday brunches include such favorites as Grand Marnier French toast and Belgian waffles with fresh fruit.

Near the Sub Base

L'Escargot. 12 Sub Base. ☎ **340/774-6565.** Reservations recommended. Main courses $15–$22. AE, MC, V. Tues–Sat 11:45am–2:30pm and 6–10pm. FRENCH/INTERNATIONAL.

This place has been in and out of fashion for so long it's an island legend for sheer endurance. But it also serves a first-rate cuisine. Its setting is a low-slung semioutdoor terrace with close-up views of Crown Bay Marina. Menu items include the standard repertoire of French dishes, including rack of lamb with rosemary sauce, lobster Thermidor, onion soup, fresh mushroom salad, and chocolate mousse. You can also order dishes with more flair and imagination, including scampi in pesto sauce with linguine and grilled swordfish in a spicy mango sauce.

Victor's New Hide Out. 103 Sub Base, off Rte. 30. ☎ **340/776-9379.** Reservations recommended. Main courses $10.95–$29.95. AE, MC, V. Mon–Sat 11am–3:30pm; daily 4–10pm. SEAFOOD/CARIBBEAN.

Victor's is operated by Victor Sydney, who comes from Montserrat. You never know who's going to show up here—maybe Bill Cosby, perhaps José Feliciano. Victor's has some of the best local dishes on the island, but first you have to find it—this hilltop perch is truly a place to hide out. If you're driving, call for directions; otherwise, take a taxi. Its dishes have much sophisticated flair and zest, as opposed to the more down-home cookery found at Eunice's Terrace (see above), but this place is also an excellent value for your money. The large, airy restaurant serves fresh lobster prepared Montserrat style (that is, in a creamy sauce) or grilled in the shell. You might also ask for a plate of juicy barbecued ribs. For dessert, try the coconut, custard, or apple pie.

ST. JOHN

St. John lies about 3 miles east of St. Thomas across Pillsbury Sound. The island, the smallest and least populated of the U.S. Virgins, is about 7 miles long and 3 miles wide, with a total land area of some 20 square miles. When held under Danish control, it was slated for big development, but a slave rebellion and a decline of the sugarcane plantations ended that idea. Since 1956, more than half its landmass, as well as its shoreline waters, have been set aside as the Virgin Islands National Park.

Since St. John is easy to reach from St. Thomas, many cruise ship passengers spend their entire day here.

COMING ASHORE

Cruise ships cannot dock at either of the piers in St. John. Instead, they moor off the coast of Cruz Bay, sending in tenders to the National Park Service Dock, the larger of the two piers. Most cruise ships docking at St. Thomas offer shore excursions to St. John's pristine acres and beaches.

If your ship docks on St. Thomas and you don't take a shore excursion to St. John, you can get here from Charlotte Amalie by ferry. Ferries leave the Charlotte Amalie waterfront for St. John's Cruz Bay at 1-to-2-hour intervals, from 9am until the last departure around 5:30pm. The last boat leaves Cruz Bay for Charlotte Amalie at 3:45pm. The ride takes about 45 minutes and costs $7 each way. Call ☎ 340/776-6282 for more information.

Another ferry leaves from the Red Hook pier on St. Thomas' eastern tip more or less every half hour, starting at 6:30am. It's a 30-minute drive from Charlotte Amalie's port to the pier at Red Hook; the ferry trip to Cruz Bay on St. John takes another 20 minutes each way. The one-way fare is $3 for adults, $1 for children under 11. Schedules can change without notice, so call in advance (☎ 340/776-6282). You can take a Vitran bus from a point near Market Square directly to Red Hook for $1 per person each way, or negotiate a price with a taxi driver.

SHORE EXCURSIONS

The best way to see St. John is to take a 2-hour taxi tour. Taxi tours cost from $30 for one or two passengers, or $12 per person for three or more riders. Almost any taxi at Cruz Bay will take you on these tours, or you can call ☎ 340/693-7530. Some shipping lines will also hook you up on an organized tour of the national park, allowing time for swimming, snorkeling, or sunbathing. Most 4^1/$_2$-hour tours of St. John cost $36.

GETTING AROUND

TAXIS   The most popular way to get around is by surrey-style taxi. Typical fares from Cruz Bay are $3 to Trunk Bay, $3.50 to Cinnamon Bay, or $7 to Mahoe Bay. For more information, call ☎ 340/693-7530.

CAR & JEEP RENTALS   The extensive Virgin Islands National Park has kept the island's roads undeveloped and uncluttered, with some of the most panoramic vistas anywhere. Renting a vehicle is the best way to see these views, especially if you like to linger at particularly beautiful spots. Open-sided Jeep-like vehicles are the most fun of the limited rentals here. There's sometimes a shortage of cars during the busy midwinter season, so try to reserve early. Remember to **drive on the left.**

The two largest car-rental agencies are located on St. John: **Avis** (☎ 800/331-1212 or 340/776-6374), charges between $78 and $82 per day, and **Hertz** (☎ 800/654-3001 or 340/693-7580), $63 to $80 per day.

Gasoline is seldom included in the price of a rental, and your car is likely to come with just enough fuel to get you to one of the island's two gas stations. Because of the distance between stations, it's never a good idea to drive around St. John with less than half a tank of gas.

BIKING   Bicycles are available for rent, at $25 per day, from the Cinnamon Bay Watersports Center on **Cinnamon Bay Beach** (☎ 340/776-6330). St. John's steep

St. John

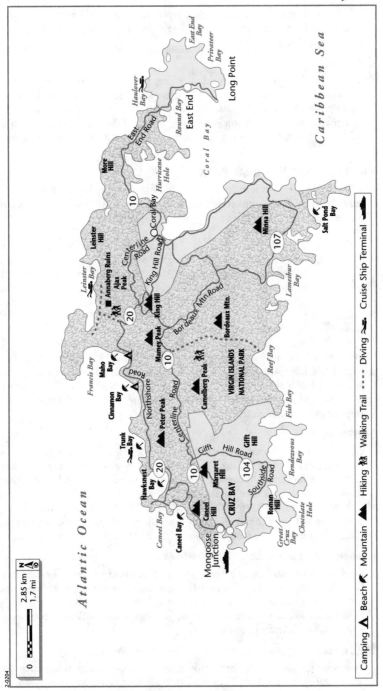

Camping ▲ Beach ⚓ Mountain ▲ Hiking 🥾 Walking Trail - - - - Diving ≋ Cruise Ship Terminal ⬛

hills and off-road trails can challenge the best of riders, but cyclists in search of more moderate rides can visit the ruins at Annaberg or the beaches at Maho, Francis, Leinster, or Watermelon Bay.

CRUZ BAY

Most cruise ship passengers dart through Cruz Bay, a sleepy little West Indian village with interesting bars, restaurants, boutiques, and pastel-painted houses. **Elaine Ione Sprauve Museum** (☎ 340/776-6359) isn't big, but it does contain some local artifacts, and will teach you some of the history of the island. It's located at the public library and can be visited Monday to Friday from 9am to 5pm. Admission is free.

VIRGIN ISLANDS NATIONAL PARK

Two-thirds of St. John is national park land. If you want to explore the **Virgin Islands National Park,** stop off first at the visitor center (☎ 340/776-6201), right on the dock at St. Cruz. Here you'll see some exhibits and learn more about what you can see and do in the park.

Established in 1956, the park totals 12,624 acres, including submerged land and water adjacent to St. John. You can explore the park on the more than 20 miles of biking trails, or rent your own car, Jeep, or Mini-Moke. Make sure you drive on the left. If you want to hike, stop at the office of the park ranger, adjacent to the pier, to watch an 18-minute video about the park. Also pick up maps and instructions before setting out on any of the clearly marked hiking trails. You can take a taxi for about $5 to the starting point of whatever trail you select.

Within the park, try to see the **Annaberg Ruins,** Leinster Bay Road, where the Danes founded a thriving plantation and sugar mill in 1718. You'll find tidal pools, forest lands, hilltops, wild scenery, and the ruins of several Danish plantations. It's located off North Shore Road east of Trunk Bay on the north shore. On certain days of the week (dates vary) guided walks of the area are given by park rangers. Check with the park's visitor center.

SHOPPING

Compared to St. Thomas, there's not a lot of shopping on St. John. Nevertheless, the boutiques and shops at Cruz Bay are unique, interesting, and quite special. Most of them are clustered at **Mongoose Junction,** in a woodsy area beside the roadway, about a 5-minute walk from the ferry dock.

As you wait at Cruz Bay for the ferry back to St. Thomas, you can browse through **Wharfside Village,** a complex of courtyards, alleys, and shady patios with a mishmash of boutiques, restaurants, fast-food joints, and bars.

Bamboula. Mongoose Junction. ☎ **340/693-8699.**

Bamboula has an unusual and very appealing collection of gifts from the Caribbean, Haiti, India, Indonesia, and Central Africa. Its exoticism is unexpected and very pleasant. The store also sells clothing for both men and women under its own label—hand-batiked soft cottons and rayons made for comfort in a hot climate. You can also buy many locally crafted items here.

The Canvas Factory. Mongoose Junction. ☎ **340/776-6196.**

This outlet produces its own handmade, rugged, and colorful canvas bags in its "factory" at Mongoose Junction. Their products range from sailing hats to soft-sided luggage to cotton hats.

The Clothing Studio. Mongoose Junction. ☎ **340/776-6585.**

The Caribbean's oldest hand-painted clothing studio has been in operation since 1978. You can watch talented artists create original designs on fine tropical clothing, including swimwear and daytime and evening clothing, mainly for babies and women, with a few items for men.

Coconut Coast Studios. Frank Bay. ☎ **340/776-6944.**

A 5-minute stroll from the heart of Cruz Bay (follow along the waterfront bypassing Gallows Point) will lead you to the studios of Elaine Estern and Lucinda Schutt. One of the best watercolorists on the island, Elaine is especially known for her Caribbean landscapes. She's the official artist for Westin Resorts, St. John. Lucinda is the artist for Caneel Bay. Note cards begin at $8, with unmatted prints costing $15 to $275.

Donald Schnell Studio. Mongoose Junction. ☎ **800/253-7107** or 340/776-6420.

In this working studio and gallery, Mr. Schnell and his assistants have created one of the finest collections of handmade pottery, sculpture, and blown glass in the Caribbean. The staff can be seen working daily and are especially noted for their rough-textured coral work. Water fountains are another specialty item, as are house signs. The coral-pottery dinnerware is also unique and popular. The studio will mail works all over the world and discuss with you any particular design you have in mind.

Fabric Mill. Mongoose Junction. ☎ **340/776-6194.**

This shop features silk-screened and batik fabrics from around the world. Vibrant rugs and bed, bath, and table linens might add the perfect touch to your home, if you like a Caribbean flair. Whimsical soft sculpture, sarongs, and handbags are also made in this studio shop.

Pusser's of the West Indies. Wharfside Village, Cruz Bay. ☎ **340/693-8489.**

This store offers a large collection of classically designed, old-world travel and adventure clothing, along with unusual accessories. It's a unique shop. Look for clothing for women, men, and children, along with T-shirts emblazoned with the Pusser's emblem.

R and I Patton Goldsmithing. Mongoose Junction. ☎ **340/776-6548.**

Established in 1973, this is one of the oldest tourist businesses here. Three-quarters of its merchandise is made on St. John. It has a large selection of island-designed jewelry in sterling silver, gold, and precious stones. Also featured are the works of goldsmiths from outstanding American studios, plus Spanish coins.

BEACHES

For a true beach-lover, missing the great white sweep of **Trunk Bay** would be like touring Europe and skipping Paris. Trouble is, the word is out. This gorgeous beach is likely to be overcrowded, and there are pickpockets lurking about. The beach has lifeguards and offers rentals, such as snorkeling gear. The underwater trail near the shore attracts beginning snorkelers in particular. Both taxis and "safari buses" to Trunk Bay meet the ferry as it docks at Cruz Bay.

Caneel Bay, the stamping ground of the rich and famous, has seven perfect beaches on its 170 acres—but only one open to the public. That's **Hawksnest Beach,** a little gem of white sand beloved by St. Johnians. The beach is a bit narrow and windy, but beautiful, as filmmakers long ago discovered. Close to the road you'll find barbecue grills. Safari buses and taxis from Cruz Bay will take you along North Shore Road.

The campgrounds of **Cinnamon Bay** and **Maho Bay** have their own beaches, where forest rangers sometimes have to remind visitors to put their swimsuits back on. Snorkelers find good reefs here. Changing rooms and showers are available.

Salt Pond Bay is known to locals but often missed by visitors. The bay here is tranquil, but there are no facilities. The Ram Head Trail begins here and winds for a mile to a panoramic belvedere overlooking the bay.

HIKING, DIVING, TENNIS & WATER SPORTS

HIKING   Hiking the network of trails is the big thing here. The visitor center at Cruz Bay gives away free trail maps of the park. However, we suggest a tour by Jeep first, just to get your bearings. It's best to set out with someone experienced in the mysteries of the island. Both **Maho Bay** (☎ 340/776-6226) and **Cinnamon Bay** (☎ 340/776-6330) conduct nature walks.

DIVING & SNORKELING   Divers can ask about scuba packages at **Low Key Watersports,** Wharfside Village (☎ 800/835-7718 or 340/693-8999). All wreck dives are two-tank/two-location dives. A one-tank dive costs $55 per person. Snorkel tours are also available at $25 to $35 per person. Parasailing costs $50. The center uses its own custom-built dive boats and also specializes in water sports gear, including masks, fins, snorkels, and "dive skins." It can arrange day-sailing charters, kayaking tours, and deep-sea sport fishing.

Cruz Bay Watersports, P.O. Box 252, Palm Plaza, St. John, U.S.V.I. 00831 (☎ 800/835-7730 or 340/776-6234), is a PADI and NAUI five-star diving center on St. John. Two-tank reef dives with all the dive gear go for $70 to $78. Beginner scuba lessons start at $68. Snorkel tours are available daily, as well as trips to the British Virgin Islands (bring your passport), which cost $80, including food and beverages.

TENNIS   There are public courts near the fire station at Cruz Bay, available on a first-come, first-serve basis (no phone). Otherwise, nonguests who make reservations are allowed to use the six state-of-the-art courts at **Westin Resort St. John,** Great Cruz Bay (☎ 340/693-8000).

WATER SPORTS   The most complete line of water sports available on St. John is offered at the **Cinnamon Bay Watersports Center** on Cinnamon Bay Beach (☎ 340/776-6330). For the adventurous, there's windsurfing, kayaking, and sailing.

The windsurfing here is some of the best anywhere, for both the beginner and the expert. High-quality equipment is available for all levels, even for kids. Boards rent for $12 an hour; a 2-hour introductory lesson costs $40.

Want to paddle to a secluded beach, explore a nearby island with an old Danish ruin, or be able to jump overboard anytime you like for snorkeling or splashing? Then try a sit-on-top kayak; one- and two-person kayaks are available for rent for $10 to $17 per hour.

You can also sail away in a 12- or 14-foot Hobie monohull sailboat, which can be rented for $20 to $30 per hour.

DINING

The Fish Trap. In the Raintree Inn, Cruz Bay. ☎ 340/693-9994. Reservations not accepted except for parties of 6 or more. Main courses $7.95– $22.95. AE, DISC, MC, V. Sat–Sun 10:30am– 2:30pm; Tues–Sun 3–9:30pm. SEAFOOD.

The Fish Trap, in the midst of coconut palms and banana trees, attracts both locals and vacationers. It's known for its wide selection of fresh fish, but also caters to the vegetarian and burger crowd. Most diners begin with conch fritters or fish chowder. For a main course, we recently enjoyed an herb-crusted snapper with a Dijon tarragon cream sauce. Blackened swordfish with roasted red pepper aïoli is another crowd-pleasing choice, as is the ginger-seared snapper. Obviously, this is not just another fish-and-chips joint.

Mongoose Restaurant and Deli. Mongoose Junction. ☎ **340/693-8677.** Reservations recommended during winter. Main dishes $12–$26. AE, MC, V. Daily 8am–10pm. CARIBBEAN.

You've had similar food elsewhere, and probably better versions of it, but the setting, locale, long hours, and reasonable prices make this a winning choice. Visitors have compared the soaring interior design here to a large Japanese birdcage, because of the strong vertical lines and the 25-foot ceiling. Set among trees and built above a stream, it also looks like something you might find in Northern California. Some guests perch at the open-centered bar for a drink and sandwich, while others sit on an adjacent deck where a canopy of trees filters the sunlight. The bar offers more than 20 varieties of frothy island libations.

Lunches include soups, well-stuffed sandwiches, salad platters, burgers, and pastas. Dinner is more formal, with such specialties as grilled steaks, fresh catch of the day, and surf and turf. The fresh fish is served in different ways, including grilled and blackened. The Sunday brunch is mobbed with St. Johnians, who love the eggs Benedict.

✪ **Paradiso.** Mongoose Junction. ☎ **340/693-8899.** Reservations recommended. Main courses $16.95–$26.95. AE, MC, V. Daily 11am–3pm and 5:30–9:30pm. Bar, daily 5–10pm. ITALIAN/AMERICAN.

One of the most talked-about restaurants on St. John, and the only one that's air-conditioned, is located in the island's best shopping center, Mongoose Junction. The decor features lots of brass, glowing hardwoods, and nautical antiques. Paradiso has the most beautiful bar on the island, crafted from mahogany, purpleheart, and angelique.

The Italian food here is the best on the island. To get started, opt for the Caesar salad, or the platter of smoked seafood is a winning selection. Afterwards, try the seafood puttanesca, mussels and shrimp with tomatoes, capers, and garlic in a marinara sauce with linguini. The chicken Picante Willie—a spicy, creamy picante sauce over crispy chicken with linguini and ratatouille—was featured in *Bon Apétit*. The house drink is Paradiso Punch, the bartender's version of plantation punch.

Pusser's. Wharfside Village (near the ferry dock), Cruz Bay. ☎ **340/693-8489.** Reservations recommended. Main courses $9.95–$24.95. AE, DISC, MC, V. Daily 11am–3pm and 6–10pm. INTERNATIONAL/CARIBBEAN.

A double-decker, air-conditioned store and pub overlooking Cruz Bay, Pusser's is part of a chain unique to the Caribbean. It serves Pusser's Rum, a blend of five West Indian rums that the Royal Navy has served to its men for 3 centuries. There's a choice of three bars: the Beach Bar, where you can enjoy food while still in your bathing suit, the Oyster Bar (the main dining area), and the Crow's Nest. The same food is served at each bar. You might try the jerk tuna filet, the jerk chicken with a tomato basil sauce over penne, or the spaghetti with lobster cooked in rum, wine, lemon juice, and garlic. Caribbean lobster is an eternal favorite, or else you might be seized with island fever and order the chicken Tropical, which features coconut-encrusted, pan-seared chicken served up with a rum and banana sauce. You can also enjoy traditional

English fare, including steak and ale. Finish your meal with Pusser's famous mud pie. The food is satisfying and competent, and not a lot more, but after all that Pusser rum, who can judge?

✪ Shipwreck Landing. 34 Freeman's Ground, Rte. 107, Coral Bay (8 miles east of Cruz Bay on the road to Salt Pond Beach). ☎ **340/693-5640.** Reservations requested. Main courses $9.75–$15.25; lunch from $6. AE, MC, V. Daily 11am–10pm. Bar, daily 11am–11pm. SEAFOOD/ CONTINENTAL.

Here you dine amid palms and tropical plants on a veranda overlooking the sea. The intimate bar specializes in tropical frozen drinks. For lunch there's a lot more than sandwiches, salads, and burgers—try a pan-seared blackened snapper in Cajun spices, or conch fritters to get you going. At night, the chef offers a pasta of the day along with such specialties as a tantalizing Caribbean blackened shrimp. A lot of the fare is routine, including New York strip steak and fish and chips, but the grilled mahimahi in lime butter is worth the trip.

21 San Juan ⚓ ⚓ ⚓ ⚓

The capital of Puerto Rico, San Juan is an urban sprawl. The look of this old city ranges from decaying ruins that recall the Spanish empire to modern beachfront hotels that evoke Miami Beach.

Around 1521 the Spanish began to settle in what is now Old San Juan. At the outset, the city was called Puerto Rico ("Rich Port"), and the whole island was known as San Juan. Today, the Port of San Juan is the busiest ocean terminal in the West Indies. It's estimated that half the trade in the Caribbean passes through here. There are about 710 cruise ship arrivals every year, bringing nearly 851,000 passengers. See chapter 2 for more information on San Juan as a port of embarkation.

The harbor where both commercial cargo and cruise ships arrive lies outside San Juan Bay, a body of water about 3 miles long and 1 mile wide—and almost completely landlocked. The long bay protects vessels from any rough seas in the Atlantic Ocean. The dock area, now restored, is an attractive place for strolling, with its plazas, fountains, promenades, and beaches. A spacious walkway connects the piers to the cobblestone streets of Old San Juan. You can head for this district to shop or take a waiting taxi and head for the beaches of Condado.

COMING ASHORE

Cruise ships in Puerto Rico dock on the historic south shore of Old San Juan, within the sheltered channel that was hotly contested by European powers during the island's early colonial days. As of this writing, there are eight piers, each within a short walk of the Plaza de la Marina, the Wyndham Hotel, Old San Juan's main bus station, and most of the historic and commercial treasures of Old San Juan. Piers nos. 1, 3 and 4 are the most popular and the newest or most recently remodeled. Piers nos. 5, 7, and 8 are currently either out of service or being remodelled. Pier no. 6 has an odd design, parallel to the shore, and is less popular. Pier no. 2 is reserved for ferryboats that make frequent runs across the San Antonio Channel to Cataño, site of the Bacardi rum distillery, and Hato Rey, the country's financial district.

During periods of heavy volume—usually Saturday and Sunday in midwinter, when as many as 10 cruise ships might dock in San Juan on the same day—additional, less convenient piers are activated. These include the Frontier Pier, at the western edge of the Condado, near the Caribe Hilton Hotel, and the Pan American Dock, in Isla Grande, across the San Antonio Channel from Old San Juan. Passengers berthing at either of these docks need some kind of motorized transit (usually

Old San Juan

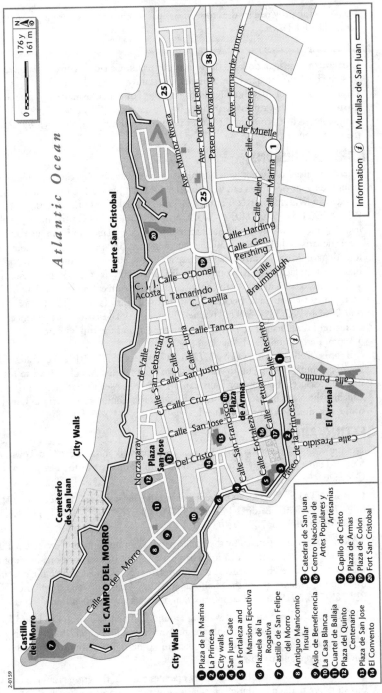

Information (i)   Murallas de San Juan

- ① Plaza de la Marina
- ② La Princesa
- ③ City walls
- ④ San Juan Gate
- ⑤ La Fortaleza and Mansion Ejecutiva
- ⑥ Plazuela de la Rogativa
- ⑦ Castillo de San Felipe del Morro
- ⑧ Antiguo Manicomio Insular
- ⑨ Asilo de Beneficencia
- ⑩ La Casa Blanca
- ⑪ Cuartel de Ballaja
- ⑫ Plaza del Quinto Centenario
- ⑬ Plaza de San Jose
- ⑭ El Convento
- ⑮ Catedral de San Juan
- ⑯ Centro Nacional de Artes Populares y Artesanias
- ⑰ Capillo de Cristo
- ⑱ Plaza de Armas
- ⑲ Plaza de Colon
- ⑳ Fort San Cristobal

2-0159

a taxi or a van provided by the cruise line as part of the shore excursion program) to get to the Old Town.

FAST FACTS

Currency   The U.S. dollar is the coin of the realm. Canadian currency is accepted by some big hotels in San Juan, although reluctantly.

Information   For advice and maps, contact the **Tourist Information Center at La Casita,** Paseo de la Princesa near Pier 1 in Old San Juan (☎ 787/721-2400).

Language   Most people in the tourist industry speak English, although Spanish is the native tongue.

SHORE EXCURSIONS

There's no need to bother with organized shore excursions. It's easy enough to get around on your own. You can walk through Old San Juan in less than a day.

Castillo Watersports & Tours, 2413 calle Laurel, Punta La Marias, Santurce (☎ **787/791-6195** or 787/726-5752), offers bus tours. One of the most popular half-day tours travels along the northeastern part of the island to El Yunque rain forest. It departs daily between 8:30 and 9am and costs $30 per person. A 4-hour city tour departs Monday through Saturday at 1 or 1:30pm, and includes a stop at Bacardi's rum factory (and a complimentary rum drink). It costs $30 per person.

For a day sea excursion to the best islands, beaches, reefs, and snorkeling in the area, contact **Capt. Jack Becker,** Villa Marina Yacht Harbor, Fajardo (☎ **787/ 860-0861** or 787/385-3509 cell phone). Captain Jack takes two to six passengers at a time on his sailboat. The cost is $50 per person, and the trip lasts from 10am to 3:30pm. Reservations can be made at any hour.

Tropix Wellness Tours (☎ **787/268-2173** or fax 787/268-1722) operates a series of ecotours, opening up to visitors Puerto Rico's varied and often hard-to-reach natural treasures. Four major tours explore either the sea turtles' nesting sites in Culebra, the phosphorescent bay in Vieques, the Río Camuy cave system in Camuy, or the dry, desert-like forest in Guánica.

GETTING AROUND

Driving is a hassle in congested San Juan. You can walk most of the Old Town on foot or take a free trolley. You can also take buses or taxis to the beaches in the Condado.

CAR RENTALS   The major car-rental companies include **Avis** (☎ **800/331-1212** or 787/791-2500), **Budget** (☎ **800/527-0700** or 787/791-3685), and **Hertz** (☎**800/654-3001** or 787/791-0840).

TAXIS   Taxis are operated by the Public Service Commission, and are metered in San Juan—or should be. The initial charge is $1, plus 10¢ for each one-tenth of a mile and 50¢ for every suitcase. A minimum fare is $3. Various taxi companies are listed in the *Yellow Pages* of the phone book under "Taxis," or you can call the PSC (☎ 787/756-1919) to request information or report any irregularities.

TROLLEY   When you tire of walking around Old San Juan, you can board one of its free trolleys. Departure points are the Marina and La Puntilla, but you can get on any place along the route. Relax and enjoy the sights as the trolleys rumble through the old and narrow streets.

BUS   The Metropolitan Bus Authority operates buses in the greater San Juan area. Bus stops are marked by upright metal signs or yellow posts, reading PARADA. Bus terminals in San Juan are in the dock area and at Plaza de Colón. A typical fare is 25¢ to 50¢. For route and schedule information, call ☎ 787/250-6064.

SEEING THE SIGHTS

Metropolitan San Juan includes the old walled city on San Juan Island; the city center, which contains the Capitol building, on San Juan Island; Santurce, on a larger peninsula, reached by causeway bridges from San Juan Island (the lagoon front section here is called Miramar); Condado, the narrow peninsula that stretches from San Juan Island to Santurce; Hato Rey, the business center; Río Piedras, site of the University of Puerto Rico; and Bayamón, an industrial and residential quarter. See the map on page 58 in chapter 2.

The Condado strip of beachfront hotels, restaurants, casinos, and nightclubs is separated from Miramar by a lagoon. Isla Verde, another resort area, is near the airport, which is separated from the rest of San Juan by an isthmus.

A WALKING TOUR OF OLD SAN JUAN

The streets are narrow and teeming with traffic, but a walk through Old San Juan (in Spanish, *El Viejo San Juan*) is a stroll through 5 centuries of history. Within this 7-square-block landmark area in the city's westernmost part are many of Puerto Rico's chief historic attractions.

Begin your walk near the post office, amid the taxis, buses, and urban congestion of **Plaza de la Marina,** a sloping, many-angled plaza situated at the eastern edge of one of San Juan's showcase promenades—*el paseo de la Princesa.*

Walk westward along paseo de la Princesa, past heroic statues and manicured trees, until you reach **La Princesa,** the gray-and-white building on your right, which for centuries served as one of the most feared prisons in the Caribbean. Today it houses a museum and the offices of the Puerto Rico Tourism Company.

Continue walking westward to the base of the heroic fountain near the edge of the sea. Turn to your right and follow the seaside promenade as it parallels the edge of the **City Walls,** once part of one of the most impregnable fortresses in the New World and even today an engineering marvel. At the top of the walls you'll see balconied buildings that have served for centuries as hospitals and residences of the island's governors.

Continue walking between the sea and the base of the city walls until the walkway goes through the walls at the **San Juan Gate,** at calle San Juan and Recinto del Oeste. This is actually more of a tunnel than a gate. Now that you're inside the once-dreaded fortification, turn immediately right and walk uphill along calle Recinto del Oeste. The wrought-iron gates at the street's end lead to **La Fortaleza and Mansion Ejecutiva,** the centuries-old residence of the Puerto Rican governor, located on calle La Fortaleza.

Now retrace your steps along calle Recinto del Oeste, walking first downhill and then uphill for about a block until you reach a street called las Monjas. Fork left until you see a panoramic view and a contemporary statue marking the center of **Plazuela de la Rogativa,** the small plaza of the religious procession.

Continue your promenade westward, passing between a pair of urn-capped gateposts. You'll be walking parallel to the city walls. The boulevard will fork (bear to the right); continue climbing the steeply inclined cobble-covered ramp to its top. Walk westward across the field toward the neoclassical gateway of a fortress believed impregnable for centuries, the **Castillo de San Felipe del Morro** ("El Morro"), whose treasury and strategic position were the envy of both Europe and the Caribbean. Here, Spanish Puerto Rico struggled to defend itself against the navies of Great Britain, France, and Holland, as well as the hundreds of pirate ships that wreaked havoc throughout the colonial Caribbean. The fortress walls were designed as part of a network of defenses that made San Juan *La Ciudad Murada* (the Walled City).

After your visit, with El Morro behind you, retrace your steps through the sunlit, treeless field to the point you stood at when you first sighted the fortress. Walk down the calle del Morro past the **Antiguo Manicomio Insular,** originally built in 1854 as an insane asylum. It now houses the Puerto Rican Academy of Fine Arts. Farther on, the stately neoclassical building (painted buff with fern-green trim) on your right is the **Asilo de Beneficencia** ("Home for the Poor"), which dates from the 1840s.

Continue walking uphill to the small, formal, sloping plaza at the street's top. On the right-hand side, within a trio of buildings, is **La Casa Blanca,** built by the son-in-law of Juan Ponce de León to be the great explorer's island home (he never actually lived here, though). Today, this "White House" accommodates a small museum and has beautiful gardens.

Exit by the compound's front entrance and walk downhill, retracing your steps for a half block, and then head toward the massive and monumental tangerine-colored building on your right, the **Cuartel de Ballajá.** The military barracks of Ballajá evokes the most austere and massive monasteries of Old Spain. On the building's second floor is the **Museum of the Americas.**

After your visit, exit through the barracks's surprisingly narrow back (eastern) door, where you'll immediately spot one of the most dramatic modern plazas in Puerto Rico, the **Plaza del Quinto Centenario,** a terraced tribute to the European colonization of the New World, and one of the most elaborate and symbolic formal piazzas in Puerto Rico.

Now, walk a short block to the southeast to reach the ancient borders of the **Plaza de San José,** dominated by a heroic statue of Juan Ponce de León, cast from English cannon captured during a naval battle in 1797. Around the square's periphery are three important sites: the **Museo de Pablo Casals,** where exhibits honor the life and work of the Spanish-born cellist who adopted Puerto Rico as his final home; **Casa de los Contrafuertes** (House of the Buttresses); and **Iglesia de San José,** where the conquistador's coat-of-arms hangs above the altar. Established by the Dominicans in 1523, this church is one of the oldest places of Christian worship in the New World.

Exiting from the plaza's southwestern corner, walk downhill along one of the capital's oldest and best-known streets, Calle del Cristo. Two blocks later, at the corner of las Monjas, is **El Convento,** originally a convent in the 17th century, but now for many decades one of the few hotels within the old city. Recently restored, it is today better than ever. Across the street from El Convento lies the island's most famous church and spiritual centerpiece, the **Catedral de San Juan.**

Now walk 2 more blocks southward along Calle del Cristo, through one of the most attractive shopping districts in the Caribbean. After passing calle La Fortaleza, look on your left for the **Centro Nacional de Artes Populares y Artesanias,** a popular arts and crafts center run by the Institute of Puerto Rican Culture.

Continue to the southern-most tip of Calle del Cristo (just a few steps away) to the wrought-iron gates that surround a chapel no bigger than a newspaper kiosk, the **Capilla de Cristo.** Its silver altar is dedicated to the "Christ of Miracles."

Retrace your steps about a block along the Calle del Cristo, walking north. Turn right along calle La Fortaleza. One block later, go left onto calle de San José, which leads to the site of the capital's most symmetrical and beautiful square, **Plaza de Armas,** a broad and open plaza designed along Iberian lines during the 19th century. Two important buildings flanking this square are the neoclassic **Intendencia** (which houses certain offices of the U.S. State Department) and **San Juan's City Hall** (Alcaldía).

You can either end your tour here, or forge ahead to two important sites on the east side of Old San Juan. To continue, leave the square eastward along the Calle San

Francisco. Eventually you'll come to **Plaza de Colón,** with its stone column topped with a statue of Christopher Columbus. On the south side of the square is the Tapía Theater, which has been restored to its original 19th-century elegance.

Then continue along Calle San Francisco to its intersection with Calle de Valle, and follow the signs to **Fort San Cristóbal,** built as part of the string of fortifications protecting of one Spain's most valuable colonies. Today, like its twin, El Morro, it is maintained by the National Park Service and can be visited throughout the day.

GAMBLING THE DAY AWAY

Casinos are one of the island's biggest draws. Most are open daily from noon to 4pm and again from 8pm to 4am.

The casino generating all the excitement today is the 18,500-square-foot **Casino at The Ritz-Carlton,** 6961 State Rd., #187, Isla Verde (☎ **787/253-1700**), the largest facility of its kind in Puerto Rico. It combines the elegant decor of a bygone era (the 1940s), with tropical fabrics and patterns. This is one of the plushest and most exclusive entertainment complexes in the Caribbean. You expect to see Joan Crawford arrive beautifully gowned and on the arm of Clark Gable. It features traditional games such as blackjack, roulette, baccarat, craps, and slot machines.

You can also try your luck at the **Caribe Hilton,** Calle Los Rosales (☎ **787/ 721-0303**), the **Wyndham Old San Juan Hotel & Casino,** 100 Brumbaugh St. (☎ **787/721-5100**); **El San Juan Hotel and Casino,** 6063 Isla Verde Ave., Carolina (☎ **787/791-1000**); and the **Condado Plaza Hotel & Casino,** 999 Ashford Ave. (☎ **787/721-1000**).

More gambling is found at the **Radisson Ambassador Plaza Hotel & Casino,** 1369 Ashford Ave. (☎ **787/721-7300**), the **Diamond Palace Hotel & Casino,** 55 Condado Ave. (☎ **787/721-0810**), the Stellaris Casino at the **San Juan Marriott Resort,** 1309 Ashford Ave. (☎ **787/722-7000**), and the **Crowne Plaza Hotel and Casino,** Route 187, Isla Verde (☎ **787/253-2929**), which is one of the newest in the area.

The **San Juan Grand Beach Hotel & Casino,** 187 Isla Verde Avenue in Isla Verde (☎ **800/443-2009** in the U.S., or 787/791-6100), is a 10,000-square-foot gaming facility and an elegant rendezvous. One of its Murano chandeliers is longer than a bowling alley. The casino offers 207 slot machines, 16 blackjack tables, 3 dice tables, 4 roulette wheels, and a minibaccarat table.

BEACHES

Beaches on Puerto Rico are open to the public, although you will be charged for use of *balneario* facilities, such as lockers and showers, as well as parking if you drive. Public beaches shut down on Mondays; if Monday is a holiday, the beaches are open for the holiday but close the next day, Tuesday. Beach hours are from 9am to 5pm in winter, to 6pm in the off-season.

Bordering some of the Caribbean's finest resort hotels, the **Condado** and **Isla Verde** beaches are the most popular in town. Both are good for snorkeling, and have rental equipment for water sports. **Condado Beach** is the single most famous beach strip in the Caribbean, despite the fact it's not the best beach and can be crowded in winter. Its long bands of white sand border some of the Caribbean's finest resort hotels. Locals prefer to head east of El Condado to the beaches of **Isla Verde,** which are less rocky and better sheltered from the waves. You can reach the beaches of **Ocean Park** and **Park Barboa,** on San Juan's north shore, by bus.

Luquillo Beach, lying about 30 miles east of San Juan, is edged by a vast coconut grove. This crescent-shaped beach is not only the best in Puerto Rico, but one of the finest in the entire Caribbean. Coral reefs protect the crystal-clear lagoon from the fierce Atlantic. There are changing rooms, lockers, showers, and picnic facilities. However, the beach isn't as well-maintained as it used to be.

Dorado Beach, Cerromar Beach, and **Palmas del Mar** are the chief centers for those seeking the golf, tennis, and beach life. Sometimes they're overcrowded, especially on Saturday and Sunday, but at other times they're practically deserted. If you find a secluded beach, be careful. You'll have no way to protect yourself or your valuables.

BOATING, FISHING, GOLF, DIVING, SNORKELING & MORE

BOATING & SAILING The **San Juan Bay Marina, Avenida Fernández Juncos** (☎ 787/721-8062), rents sailboats and powerboats. The 10-minute taxi ride here from the cruise docks should cost about $6.

DEEP-SEA FISHING It's top-notch! You can catch allison tuna, white and blue marlin, sailfish, wahoo, dolphin, mackerel, and tarpon.

It's said in deep-sea fishing circles that **Capt. Mike Benitez,** who has chartered out of San Juan for more than 40 years, sets the standard by which to judge other captains. Benitez Fishing Charters can be contacted directly at P.O. Box 5141, Puerto de Tierra, San Juan, PR 00906 (☎ **787/723-2292** until 9pm). The captain offers a 45-foot air-conditioned deluxe Hateras, the *Sea Born.* Fishing tours for parties of up to six cost $450 for a half-day excursion, and $750 for a full day, with beverages and all equipment included.

In the waters just off Palmas del Mar, the resort complex on the southeast coast of Puerto Rico, **Capt. Bill Burleson,** P.O. Box 8270, Humacao, PR 00792 (☎ **787/850-7442**), operates charters on his fully customized 46-foot sport-fisherman, *Karolette.* Burleson prefers to take fishing groups to Grappler Banks, 18 nautical miles away. It costs $500 for a maximum of 6 people for 4 hours, $675 for 6 hours, and $900 for 9 hours. He also offers snorkeling expeditions to Vieques Island and other locations at $85 per person for up to 5 hours.

GOLF Puerto Rico may be a golfer's dream, but you'll need a rented car to reach the major courses, which lie 45 minutes to 1 1/2 hours from San Juan.

The **Hyatt Resorts Puerto Rico at Dorado** (☎ **787/796-1234**), with 72 holes of golf, offers the greatest concentration of golf in the Caribbean, including the 18-hole Robert Trent Jones, Sr. courses at the Hyatt Regency Cerromar and the Hyatt Dorado Beach, and the par-72 east course at Dorado Beach, with the famous par-5, 5,540-yard 14th hole. Greens fees are $85 to $120 for non-residents.

The **Golf Club,** at Palmas del Mar in Humacao (☎ **787/852-6000,** ext. 54), is 45 miles east of San Juan. The par-72, 6,803-yard course was designed by Gary Player. Greens fees range from $90 to $130.

Rio Mar Golf Course, at Palmer (☎ **787/888-8815**), is a 45-minute drive from San Juan along Route 187, on the northeast coast. The greens fees are $140 per person at this 6,145-yard course. After 2pm, fees are reduced to $90.

SCUBA DIVING, SNORKELING, & WINDSURFING The continental shelf, which surrounds Puerto Rico on three sides, is responsible for an abundance of coral reefs, caves, sea walls, and trenches for scuba diving and snorkeling.

Migrating whales and manatees visit the open-water reefs off the central coast near Humacao, 45 miles east of San Juan. The Great Trench, off the island's south coast, is ideal for experienced sport divers. Mona Island, off the west coast, offers unspoiled reefs at depths averaging 80 feet; seals are one of its attractions.

Many of Puerto Rico's dive operators and resorts offer packages that include daily or twice-daily dives, scuba equipment, instruction, and excursions to the island's popular attractions.

In San Juan, the best option for underwater diving is **Caribe Aquatic Adventures,** P.O. Box 9024278, San Juan Station, San Juan, PR 00902 (☎ **787/724-1882**). Its dive shop is located in the rear lobby of the Radisson Normandie Hotel. The company offers diving certification from both PADI and NAUI. A resort course for first-time divers costs $97. Also offered are local daily dives in San Juan or windsurfing, and a choice of full-day diving expeditions to various reefs off the east coast of Puerto Rico. Bay cruises start at $29.95 per person, with a maximum boat capacity of 35 people on a 60-foot motor yacht. If time is limited, the outfitter will take you to sites in San Juan. But since the best sites for scuba diving are out on the island's coasts, the serious scuba diver will have to commit to a full-day tour. Caribe Aquaticalso offers windsurfer rentals for $25 per hour, and lessons for $45.

The best place for windsurfing and snorkeling on the island's north shore is along the well-maintained beachfront of the Hyatt Dorado Beach Hotel, near the 10th hole of the hotel's famous east golf course. Here, **Penfield Island Adventures** (☎ **787/ 796-1234,** ext. 3768, or 787/796-2188) offers 90-minute windsurfing lessons for $60 each; board rentals cost $50 per half day. Boards designed specifically for beginners and children are available. The school benefits from the north shore's strong, steady winds and an experienced crew of instructors. A kayaking/snorkeling trip, departing daily at 9:15am and 11:45am, and lasting 1¹/₂ hours, costs $45. Two-tank boat dives go for $119 per person. Waverunners, a fast, light boat, often compared to "a snowmobile that skims along the surface of the water" cost $55 per half hour for a single rider, and $70 for two riders. A Sunfish rents for $50 an hour. The owner and namesake of this establishment, incidentally, is a well-known professional athlete, and winner of a world-class windsurfing competition in Australia in 1981.

SURFING   Puerto Rico's northwest beaches attract surfers from around the world. October through February are the best surfing months. The most popular areas are from Isabela around Punta Borinquén to Rincón, with beaches such as Wilderness, Surfers, Crashboat, Los Turbos in Vega Jajja, Pine Grove in Isla Verde, and La Pared in Luquillo. Surfboards are available at many water-sports shops. You'll need to drive to these beaches.

TENNIS   There are approximately 100 tennis courts in Puerto Rico. Many are located at hotels and resorts, but others can be found in public parks throughout the island.

In San Juan, the **Caribe Hilton** and the **Condado Plaza** have tennis courts. Also in the area is a public court at the old navy base, Isla Grande, in Miramar. Enter from avenida Fernández Juncos at bus stop 11.

SHOPPING

U.S. citizens don't pay duty on items bought in Puerto Rico and brought back to the United States. You can find great bargains in San Juan; prices are often lower than those in St. Thomas.

The streets of the **Old Town,** such as Calle San Francisco and Calle del Cristo, are the major venues for shopping. Most stores in Old San Juan are closed on Sunday.

Native handcrafts can be good buys, including *santos* (hand-carved wooden religious figures), needlework, straw work, ceramics, hammocks, *guayabera* shirts for men, papier-mâché fruit and vegetables, and paintings and sculptures by Puerto Rican artists.

The biggest and most up-to-date shopping plaza in the Caribbean Basin is **Plaza Las Americas,** which lies in the financial district of Hato Rey, right off the Las Americas Expressway. The complex, with its fountains and advanced architecture, has more than 200 shops, most of them upmarket. Open Monday through Thursday and on Saturday from 9:30am to 6pm, Friday from 9:30am to 9:30pm.

ANTIQUES

El Alcazar. Calle San José 103. ☎ **787/723-1229.**

Established in 1986 by retired officers of the U.S. Army and the U.S. State Department, this is the largest emporium of antique furniture, silver, and art objects in the Caribbean. The best way to sift through the massive inventory is to begin at the address listed above, on Calle San José between Calle Luna and Calle Sol, and ask the owners, Sharon and Robert Bartos, to guide you to the other three buildings, all stuffed with important art and antiques. Each lies within a half-block of the organization's headquarters, and each is within a historic building of architectural importance.

Some of the objects, such as the 1930s-era dining-room sets, derive from Puerto Rico; the majority of the objects, however, come from estates and galleries throughout Europe. *Hint:* If you're looking for antique silver, crystal, delicate porcelain, glittering chandeliers, Russian icons, and objects of religious devotion such as santos, stick to the organization's headquarters.

José E. Alegria & Associates. Calle del Cristo 152-154. ☎ **787/721-8091.**

For generations, this shop reigned as the most stylish and prestigious repository of 19th-century art and antiques in San Juan, with an inventory of stately furniture that often evoked the grandest days of the Spanish colonial empire. In the mid-1990s, however, it diversified its premises, retaining part of its floor space for the antique trade, and transforming another part ("La Arcada") into an old-fashioned arcade lined with gift shops and boutiques. You'll still find art and antiques here, although there's not as much as before. The remaining space is devoted to modern inventories of leather goods, Mexican artifacts, and gift items, including Caribbean herbs and spices.

ART

Galería Botello. Calle del Cristo 208. ☎ **787/723-2879.**

A contemporary Latin American art gallery, Galería Botello is a living tribute to the late Angel Botello, one of Puerto Rico's most outstanding artists. Born in a small village in Galicia, Spain, he fled to the Caribbean after the Spanish Civil War, and spent 12 years in Haiti. His unique paintings and bronze sculptures evoke his colorful background. This galería, which he restored himself, is his former home. Today it displays his paintings and sculptures, and also offers a large collection of Puerto Rican antique santos. The gallery also showcases many outstanding local artists.

Galería Palomas. Calle del Cristo 207. ☎ **787/725-2660.**

This and the also recommended Galería Botello are the two leading art galleries of Puerto Rico. Works are priced from $75 to $35,000, include some of the leading painters of the Latin American world, and are rotated every 2 to 3 weeks. The setting is a 17th-century colonial house. Of special note are works by such local artists as Homer, Moya, and Alicea.

Haitian Souvenirs. Calle San Francisco 206. ☎ **787/723-0959.**

This is our favorite of the three stores in San Juan specializing in Haitian art and artifacts. Its walls are covered with primitive Haitian landscapes, portraits, crowd scenes, and whimsical visions of jungles where lions, tigers, parrots, and herons take on quasi-human personalities and forms. Most paintings cost from $35 to $350, although they can usually be bargained down a bit. Look for the brightly painted wall-hangings crafted from sheets of metal (priced at around $120 each). Also look for cheaper satirical metal wall-hangings, brightly painted, representing the *tap-taps* (battered public minivans and buses) of Port-au-Prince. These sell for around $45 each, and make amusing and whimsical souvenirs of a trip to the Caribbean.

BEACH WEAR

W. H. Smith. In the Condado Plaza Hotel, 999 Ashford Ave. ☎ **787/721-1000**, ext. 2094.

This outlet sells mostly women's clothing, everything from bathing suits and beach attire to jogging suits. For men, there are shorts, bathing suits, and jogging suits. There's also a good selection of books and maps.

BUTTERFLIES (MOUNTED)

Butterfly People. Calle Fortaleza 152. ☎ **787/723-2432.**

Butterfly People is a gallery and cafe in a handsomely restored building in Old San Juan. Butterflies are sold here in artfully arranged boxes. Prices range from $20 for a single mounting to thousands of dollars for wall-sized murals. This dimensional artwork is sold in limited editions and can be shipped worldwide. Most of these butterflies come from farms around the world, particularly Indonesia, Malaysia, and New Guinea. The butterflies are well-preserved and will last forever. Tucked away, within the same premises is **Malula Antiques,** which specializes in tribal art from the Moroccan sub-Sahara and Syria. This shop contains a sometimes startling collection of primitive and timeless crafts and accessories.

FASHION

Lindissima Shop. Calle Fortaleza 300. ☎ **787/721-0550.**

This outlet offers women's contemporary sportswear and dresses for both daytime and evening. If you lack an outfit for a formal evening aboard ship, look for it here. Garments generally range from $59 to $700.

London Fog. Calle del Cristo 156. ☎ **787/722-4334.**

The last thing you need in steamy San Juan is a winter overcoat or parka, but the prices at this factory outlet are so low that a purchase is often well worth it. Prices are usually 30% to 35% less than on the U.S. mainland. Men's, women's and children's garments are displayed on two floors of a colonial house.

Nono Maldonado. 1051 Ashford Ave. ☎ **787/721-0456.**

Named after its owner, a Puerto Rico–born designer who worked for many years as the fashion editor for *Esquire* magazine, this shop is one of the most fashionable and upscale in the Caribbean. It sells both men's and women's clothing, including everything from socks to dinner jackets, as well as ready-to-wear versions of Maldonado's twice-a-year collections. Both ready-to-wear and couture are available.

Polo Ralph Lauren Factory Store. Calle del Cristo 201. ☎ **787/722-2136.**

It's as stylish and carefully orchestrated as anything you'd expect from one of North America's leading clothiers. Even better, its prices are often 35% to 40% less than on the U.S. mainland. You can find even greater discounts on irregular or slightly damaged garments. The store occupies two floors of a pair of colonial buildings, with one upstairs room devoted to home furnishings. Men's sizes larger than a 42 waist are almost never in stock.

GIFTS & HANDCRAFTS
Anaiboa. Calle San Francisco 100. ☎ **787/724-8017.**

This shop occupies a cubbyhole off a pedestrians-only stretch adjacent to Calle del Cristo. Its owners, a married team of artists (Edgard Rodriguez and Marianne Ramirez), sell one-of-a-kind items, including ceramic boxes, hat racks, mirrors, serving trays, and small-scale furniture accented with whimsical drawings of faces, plants, and animals. Many objects cost as little as $15. Recently, the owners have been offering stained glass and mosaics.

Bared & Sons. Calle Fortaleza 65 (at the corner of Calle San Justo). ☎ **787/724-4811.**

Now in its fourth decade, this is the main outlet of a chain of at least 20 upper-bracket jewelry stores on Puerto Rico. You'll find a worthy inventory of gemstones, gold, diamonds, and wristwatches on the street level, all popular with cruise ship passengers. But the real value of this store lies one floor up, where a monumental collection of porcelain and crystal is displayed in claustrophobic proximity. It's a great source for hard-to-get and discontinued patterns (priced at around 20% less than at equivalent outlets in the States) from Christofle, Royal Doulton, Wedgwood, Limoges, Royal Copenhagen, Lalique, Lladro, Herend, Baccarat, and Daum.

El Artesano. Calle Fortaleza 314. ☎ **787/721-6483.**

If your budget doesn't allow for an excursion to the Andes, head for this shop. You'll find Mexican and Peruvian icons of the Virgin Mary; charming depictions of fish and Latin American birds in terra-cotta and brass; all kinds of woven goods; painted cupboards, chests, and boxes; and mirrors and Latin dolls.

Galería Bóveda. Calle del Cristo 209. ☎ **787/725-0263.**

This long, narrow space is crammed with exotic jewelry, clothing, greeting cards, some 100 handmade lamps, antiques, Mexican punched tin and glass, and art nouveau reproductions, among other items.

Olé. Calle Fortaleza 105. ☎ **787/724-2445.**

Browsing this store is a learning experience. Practically everything comes from Puerto Rico or Latin America. If you want a straw hat from Ecuador, hand-beaten Chilean silver, Christmas ornaments, or Puerto Rican santos, this is the place.

Puerto Rican Arts & Crafts. Calle Fortaleza 204. ☎ **787/725-5596.**

Set in a 200-year-old colonial building, this unique store is one of the premier outlets on the island for authentic handcrafts. Of particular interest are papier-mâché carnival masks from the town of Ponce; their grotesque and colorful features were designed to chase away evil spirits. Most of the sterling-silver jewelry sold here incorporates Taíno designs inspired by ancient petroglyphs. There's also an art gallery in back, with silk-screened serigraphs by local artists.

This well-respected store specializes in traditional santos, which are carved and sometimes polychromed representations of the Catholic saints and the infant Jesus. Santos here were laboriously carved by artisans in private studios around the island, and cost from $44 to $225 each. They're easy to pack in a suitcase, since the largest one measures only 12 inches from halo to toe. This store also has a gourmet Puerto Rican food section with items like coffee, rum, and hot sauces for sale.

JEWELRY
200 Fortaleza. Calle Fortaleza 200 (at the corner of Calle La Cruz). ☎ **787/723-1989.**

Known as a leading cost-conscious jewelry outlet in Old San Juan, this shop offers 18-karat gold, emerald, ruby, diamond, and pearl jewelry, along with platinum bridal jewelry. You can also get 14-karat Italian gold chains and bracelets (measured, fitted, and sold by weight), as well as watches.

Barrachina's. Calle Fortaleza 104 (between Calle del Cristo and Calle San José). ☎ **787/ 725-7912.**

The birthplace, in 1963, of the piña colada, Barrachina's is a favorite of cruise ship passengers. It offers one of the largest selections of jewelry, perfume, cigars, and gifts in San Juan. There's even a patio for drinks, where you can order (what else?) a piña colada. A Bacardi rum outlet here sells bottles cheaper than in the States. You'll also find a costume-jewelry department, a gift shop, and a section for authentic silver jewelry, plus a restaurant.

The Gold Ounce. Plaza los Muchachos, Calle Fortaleza 201. ☎ **787/724-3102.**

This is the direct-factory outlet for the oldest jewelry factory on Puerto Rico, the Kury Company. Most of the output is shipped stateside. Many of the designs are repeated endlessly, but don't overlook this place for 14-karat-gold ornaments. Prices are about 20% less than on the North American mainland. In addition, the outlet has opened an art store called Arts and More, featuring regional works, plus a cigar store called The Cigar Shop.

Joyería Riviera. Calle La Cruz 205 (Adjacent to Plaza de Armas). ☎ **787/725-4000.**

This emporium of 18-karat gold and diamonds is the island's leading jeweler and has an impeccable reputation. Its owner, Julio Abislaiman, collects his stock from such diamond centers as Antwerp, Tel Aviv, and New York. The store is also the major distributor of Rolex watches on Puerto Rico. Prices are high, but, according to the owner, you can get "whatever you want" here.

Vergina Gallery. Calle del Cristo 202. ☎ **787/721-0592.**

The most exotic jewelry emporium in San Juan, this is the only outlet in the Caribbean showcasing the neo-Byzantine and ancient Greek designs of Zolotos, one of Greece's most spectacular jewelers. Most of the pieces are made of hammered 18- and 22-karat gold, inset with colorful glittering gemstones. There's also an inventory of streamlined platinum jewelry from Germany, and worthy reproductions of medieval Greek and Russian icons, priced from $10 to $3,000.

Yas Mar. Calle Fortaleza 205. ☎ **787/724-1377.**

This shop sells convincing, glittering fake diamonds, as well as real diamond chips, emeralds, sapphires, and rubies.

LACE

This traditional Puerto Rican craft has undergone a major revival, just as it seemed about to disappear forever. Originating in Spain, *mundillos* (tatted fabrics) are the product of a type of bobbin lacemaking that exists today only in Puerto Rico and Spain.

The first lace made in Puerto Rico was called *torchon* ("beggar's lace"). Early examples were of indifferent quality, but artisans today have transformed the practice into a delicate art form, eagerly sought by collectors. Lace bands called *entrados* have two straight borders, whereas the other traditional style, *puntilla*, has both a straight and a scalloped border. The best place to see the craft of the *mundillos* is the **Folk Arts Center** at the Dominican Convent, 98 Calle Norzagaray (☎ 787/721-6866) in Old San Juan. This center has information on craftspeople who make and sell mundillos. There are no major stores in San Juan, however, that specialize in this collector's item.

The island's headquarters for lace-making is in the hamlet of Moca, near Aquadilla. Here the best artisans are **Nelly Vera** (☎ 787/877-0387) and **Jolanda Romero** (☎ 787/877-2971). You can call for an appointment to visit them. If you don't speak Spanish, ask the staff on your ship to call and make arrangements for a personal shopping visit. They don't want their addresses published because they don't want customers showing up without calling first. If you happen to be in Puerto Rico in the end of April, you might attend the **Puerto Rican Weaving Festival,** held in the town of Isabela.

LEATHER

Leather & Pearls. Calle Tanca 252 (at the corner of Calle Tetuán). ☎ **787/724-8185.**

This shop sells Majorca pearls and fine leather garments (bags, shoes, suitcases, briefcases, and accessories) from manufacturers such as Gucci and Fendi. Also look for leather goods from the same Iberian company that sells Lladró porcelain. A relative newcomer to the field of leather goods, this store has impressed consumers with their quality and pizzazz.

LINENS

The Linen House. Calle Fortaleza 250. ☎ **787/721-4219.**

This unpretentious store has the island's best selection of napery, bed linens, and lace. Some of the more delicate pieces are expensive, but most are moderate in price. You'll find embroidered shower curtains selling for around $35 each, and lace doilies, bun warmers, place mats, and tablecloths that seamstresses took weeks to complete. Some astonishingly lovely items are available for as little as $30. The aluminum/pewter serving dishes have strikingly beautiful Spanish-colonial designs. Prices here are sometimes 40% lower than on the North American mainland.

DINING
IN OLD SAN JUAN

Al Dente. Calle Recinto Sur 309. ☎ **787/723-7303.** Reservations recommended. Main courses $10–$17. AE, MC, V. Mon–Fri noon–2pm and 5:30–10pm, Sat noon–10:30pm. Bus: A7, T1, or 2. SICILIAN.

In the heart of Old San Juan, this unpretentious restaurant evokes a trattoria from Palermo. Nearly all dishes are genuinely satisfying and reasonably priced. Both the dress code and the ambiance are relaxed and casual. Brochettes of fresh tuna laced with pepper and Mediterranean herbs is an excellent choice. You might also sample the scallops on a bed of spinach sautéed in cream, or gnocchi with pesto, fettuccine maestro, ravioli (cheese or shrimp versions), or well-seasoned calamari. The chef also makes his own desserts, including cheesecake, tiramisu, and chocolate tortes.

✪ **Amadeus.** Calle San Sebastián 106 (across from the Iglesia de San José). ☎ **787/722-8635.** Reservations recommended. Main courses $7–$22. AE, MC, V. Tues–Sun noon–2am (kitchen closes at 12:30am). Bus: M2, M3, or T1. CARIBBEAN.

Housed in a brick-and-stone 18th-century building, Amadeus offers Caribbean cuisine with a nouvelle twist. The appetizers alone are worth the trip here, especially the Amadeus dumpling with guava sauce and arrowroot fritters. You can enjoy dishes *de la tierra* (from the land) or *del mar* (from the sea), including a fresh catch of the day. One zesty specialty is pork scaloppini with sweet and sour sauce. More recent and rather delectable additions to the menu include chicken breast with escargots and mushrooms, linguini with shrimp in an Alfredo sauce, and an array of freshly made sandwiches and salads available at lunch. The chef will even prepare a smoked salmon and caviar pizza.

Butterfly People Café. Calle Fortaleza 152. ☎ **787/723-2432.** Reservations not required. Main courses $4.50–$10. AE, DC, MC, V. Mon–Sat 10am–6pm. Bus: A7, T1, or 2. CONTINENTAL/AMERICAN.

This restaurant is on the second floor of a restored mansion in Old San Juan, next to the world's largest gallery devoted to butterflies. The cafe overlooks a courtyard and has 15 tables inside. The cuisine is tropical and light European fare made with fresh ingredients. You might begin with gazpacho or vichyssoise, follow with quiche or one of the daily specials, and finish with chocolate mousse or the tantalizing raspberry chiffon pie with fresh raspberry sauce. A full bar offers tropical specialties such as piña coladas, fresh-squeezed Puerto Rican orange juice, and Fantasias (frappes of seven fresh fruits). Wherever you look, framed butterflies will delight or horrify you.

✪ **Chef Marisoll.** Calle del Cristo 202. ☎ **787/725-7454.** Reservations required. Main courses $24–$30. AE, MC, V. Tues–Sat noon–2:30pm; Tues–Sun 7–10:30pm. CONTEMPORARY.

Marisoll Hernández is one of the top chefs in Puerto Rico. Trained in Hilton properties, including one in London, she broke away to become an independent restaurateur in the Old Town of San Juan. Her eight-table restaurant, set in a Spanish colonial building, with a courtyard patio for dining, is warm and intimate. Instead of settling for a sandwich at lunch, try one of her imaginative dishes. Two of the soups should be featured in *Gourmet* magazine, including a cream of exotic wild mushrooms with an essence of black truffles, and a butternut-squash soup with crisp ginger. Caesar salads are garnished with duck or lobster. There's usually a catch of the day, such as dorado with a medley of sauces—whatever strikes the chef's fancy. A truly elegant and beautifully flavored tenderloin with foie gras is another specialty, as is the risotto with shrimp, lobster, and scallops in a saffron sauce. Service is low key, a bit distracted, and slightly formal.

El Patio de Sam. Calle San Sebastián 102 (across from the Iglesia de San José). ☎ **787/ 723-1149.** Reservations not required. Main courses $17.50–$22; sandwiches, burgers, salads $7.50–$12. AE, DC, DISC, MC, V. Sun–Thurs 11am–midnight, Fri–Sat 11am–1:30am. Bus: A7, T1, or 2. AMERICAN/PUERTO RICAN.

This is a popular gathering spot for American expatriates, newspeople, and shopkeepers. It's known for having the best burgers in San Juan. Even though everything is indoors, you'll swear you're dining alfresco: each table is placed near a cluster of potted plants, and canvas panels and awnings cover the skylight. For a satisfying lunch, try the black-bean soup, followed by the burger platter, and top it off with a Key lime tart. Visitors have complained about the nonburger items on the menu. Nevertheless, meals satisfy most clients, and Sam's Patio remains the Old Town's most popular restaurant.

Hard Rock Café. Calle Recinto Sur 253. ☎ **787/724-7625.** Reservations not required. Main courses $6.99–$16.99. AE, MC, V. Daily 11:30am–midnight. Bar, daily 11am–2am. Bus: A7, T1, or 2. AMERICAN.

Serving a "classic" American cuisine against a backdrop of loud rock music, the Hard Rock is here to stay, packing in the crowds for drinks, burgers, and T-shirts. Check out the artifacts from the rock 'n' roll hall of fame, including a wig worn by Elton John, John Lennon's jacket, and Phil Collins's drumsticks. Throughout the day well-stuffed sandwiches and juicy burgers are served. For dinner, you can fill up on fajitas, barbecued chicken, pork ribs, or even the catch of the day. The chili will set you ablaze.

La Bombonera. Calle San Francisco 259. ☎ **787/722-0658.** Reservations recommended. Main courses $6.45–$17.75; American breakfast $5. AE, DISC, MC, V. Daily 7:30am–8pm. Bus: M2, M3, or T1. PUERTO RICAN.

This favorite offers exceptional food at affordable prices. It was established in 1902, and ever since has been offering homemade pastries and endless cups of coffee amid traditional colonial decor. For decades a rendezvous for the island's literati and Old San Juan families, La Bombonera has now been discovered by foreign visitors. Its atmosphere evokes turn-of-the-century Castile transplanted to the New World. The food is authentically Puerto Rican, homemade, and inexpensive. The sandwiches are the biggest in town. The regional dishes include rice with squid, roast leg of pork, and seafood asopao. For dessert, there's apple, pineapple, or prune pie, as well as many types of flan. Service is polite, if a bit rushed. The place fills up quickly at lunchtime.

La Mallorquina. Calle San Justo 207. ☎ **787/722-3261.** Reservations not accepted at lunch, recommended at dinner. Dinner courses $13.95–$23.95. AE, MC, V. Mon–Sat 11:30am–10pm. Bus: A7, T1, or 2. PUERTO RICAN.

The food here seems little changed over the decades; visit for tradition and exceptional value rather than innovation. San Juan's oldest restaurant was founded in 1848. It's in a three-story, glassed-in courtyard with arches and antique wall clocks. Even if you've already eaten, you might want to stop by for a drink at the old-fashioned wooden bar. The chef specializes in the most typical Puerto Rican rice dish: asopao. You can have it with either chicken, shrimp, or lobster and shrimp. *Arroz con pollo* (rice with chicken) is almost as popular. Begin with garlic soup or gazpacho. Other good main dishes are grilled pork chop with fried plantain, beef tenderloin Puerto Rican style, and assorted seafood stewed in wine. Paella is an enduring favorite. Lunch is busy; dinners are sometimes quiet.

✪ Parrot Club. 363 Calle Fortaleza. ☎ **787/725-7370.** Reservations not accepted. Lunch main courses $8.50–$13; brunch main courses $13.50–$17; dinner main courses $12–$21. MC, V. Tues–Sat 11:30am–3pm, Sun noon–4pm; Tues–Wed 6–11pm, Thurs–Sat 6pm–midnight, Sun 6:30–10pm. Closed 2 weeks in July. MODERN PUERTO RICAN.

The hot, hot restaurant of Old San Juan is this bistro and bar. Its Nuevo Latino cuisine blends traditional Puerto Rican cookery with Spanish, Taíno, and African influences, heightened by rich, contemporary touches. The Parrot Club is located in a neighborhood known as SOFO (South of Fortaleza Street), within a stately-looking building from 1902 that was originally a factory for hair tonic. Today, you'll find a cheerful dining room where Gloria Vanderbilt, San Juan's mayor, and the governor of Puerto Rico can sometimes be spotted, and a verdantly landscaped courtyard where tables for at least 200 diners are scattered amid potted ferns, palms, and orchids. Live music, either Brazilian, salsa, or Latino jazz, is the norm every night of the week, as well as during the popular Sunday brunches. Menu items are updated interpretations of old-fashioned Puerto Rican specialties.

Index

Page numbers in italics refer to maps.

FROMMER'S® COMPLETE TRAVEL GUIDES

(Comprehensive guides with selections in all price ranges—from deluxe to budget)

Alaska
Amsterdam
Arizona
Atlanta
Australia
Austria
Bahamas
Barcelona, Madrid & Seville
Belgium, Holland & Luxembourg
Bermuda
Boston
Budapest & the Best of Hungary
California
Canada
Cancún, Cozumel & the Yucatán
Cape Cod, Nantucket & Martha's Vineyard
Caribbean
Caribbean Cruises & Ports of Call
Caribbean Ports of Call
Carolinas & Georgia
Chicago
China
Colorado
Costa Rica
Denver, Boulder & Colorado Springs
England
Europe
Florida

France
Germany
Greece
Hawaii
Hong Kong
Honolulu, Waikiki & Oahu
Ireland
Israel
Italy
Jamaica & Barbados
Japan
Las Vegas
London
Los Angeles
Maryland & Delaware
Maui
Mexico
Miami & the Keys
Montana & Wyoming
Montréal & Québec City
Munich & the Bavarian Alps
Nashville & Memphis
Nepal
New England
New Mexico
New Orleans
New York City
Nova Scotia, New Brunswick & Prince Edward Island
Oregon
Paris
Philadelphia & the Amish Country

Portugal
Prague & the Best of the Czech Republic
Provence & the Riviera
Puerto Rico
Rome
San Antonio & Austin
San Diego
San Francisco
Santa Fe, Taos & Albuquerque
Scandinavia
Scotland
Seattle & Portland
Singapore & Malaysia
South Pacific
Spain
Switzerland
Thailand
Tokyo
Toronto
Tuscany & Umbria
USA
Utah
Vancouver & Victoria
Vermont, New Hampshire & Maine
Vienna & the Danube Valley
Virgin Islands
Virginia
Walt Disney World & Orlando
Washington, D.C.
Washington State

FROMMER'S® DOLLAR-A-DAY GUIDES

(The ultimate guides to comfortable low-cost travel)

Australia from $50 a Day
California from $60 a Day
Caribbean from $60 a Day
England from $60 a Day
Europe from $50 a Day
Florida from $60 a Day
Greece from $50 a Day
Hawaii from $60 a Day
Ireland from $50 a Day

Israel from $45 a Day
Italy from $50 a Day
London from $70 a Day
New York from $75 a Day
New Zealand from $50 a Day
Paris from $70 a Day
San Francisco from $60 a Day
Washington, D.C., from $60 a Day

FROMMER'S® MEMORABLE WALKS

Chicago
London

New York
Paris

San Francisco

FROMMER'S® PORTABLE GUIDES

Acapulco, Ixtapa/	Dublin	Puerto Vallarta, Manzanillo
Zihuatenejo	Las Vegas	& Guadalajara
Bahamas	London	San Francisco
California Wine	Maine Coast	Sydney
Country	New Orleans	Tampa Bay & St. Petersburg
Charleston & Savannah	New York City	Venice
Chicago	Paris	Washington, D.C.

FROMMER'S® NATIONAL PARK GUIDES

Grand Canyon	Yosemite & Sequoia/
National Parks of the American West	Kings Canyon
Yellowstone & Grand Teton	Zion & Bryce Canyon

THE COMPLETE IDIOT'S TRAVEL GUIDES
(The ultimate user-friendly trip planners)

Cruise Vacations	Las Vegas	New York City
Planning Your Trip to Europe	Mexico's Beach Resorts	San Francisco
Hawaii	New Orleans	Walt Disney World

SPECIAL-INTEREST TITLES

The Civil War Trust's Official Guide to	Outside Magazine's Adventure Guide
the Civil War Discovery Trail	to the Pacific Northwest
Frommer's Caribbean Hideaways	Outside Magazine's Guide to Family Vacations
Israel Past & Present	Places Rated Almanac
New York City with Kids	Retirement Places Rated
New York Times Weekends	Washington, D.C., with Kids
Outside Magazine's Adventure Guide	Wonderful Weekends from Boston
to New England	Wonderful Weekends from New York City
Outside Magazine's Adventure Guide	Wonderful Weekends from San Francisco
to Northern California	Wonderful Weekends from Los Angeles

THE UNOFFICIAL GUIDES®
(Get the unbiased truth from these candid, value-conscious guides)

Atlanta	Florida with Kids	Miami & the Keys	Skiing in the West
Branson, Missouri	The Great Smoky	Mini-Mickey	Walt Disney World
Chicago	& Blue Ridge	New Orleans	Walt Disney World
Cruises	Mountains	New York City	Companion
Disneyland	Las Vegas	San Francisco	Washington, D.C.

FROMMER'S® IRREVERENT GUIDES
(Wickedly honest guides for sophisticated travelers)

Amsterdam	London	New Orleans	San Francisco
Boston	Manhattan	Paris	Walt Disney World
Chicago			Washington, D.C.

FROMMER'S® DRIVING TOURS

America	Florida	Ireland	Scotland
Britain	France	Italy	Spain
California	Germany	New England	Western Europe

www.frommers.com

rthur Frommer's OUTSPOKEN ENCYCLOPEDIA OF TRAVEL

You've Read our Books, Now Visit our Website...

With more than 6,000 pages of the
most up-to-date travel bargains
and information from the
name you trust the most,
Arthur Frommer's
Outspoken Encyclopedia of
Travel brings you all the
information you need to plan
your next trip.

Register to Win free tickets, accommodations and more!

Arthur Frommer's Daily Newsletter

Bookmark the daily newsletter to read about the
hottest travel news and bargains in the industry or
subscribe and receive it daily on your own desktop.

Hot Spot of the Month

Check out the Hot Spot each month to get the
best information and hottest deals for your favorite
vacation destinations.

200 Foreign & Domestic Destinations

Choose from more than 200 destinations and get
the latest information on accommodations, airfare,
restaurants, and more.

Frommer's Travel Guides

Shop our online bookstore and choose from more
than 200 current Frommer's travel guides. Secure
transactions guaranteed!

Bookmark www.frommers.com for the most up-to-date travel bargains and information—updated daily!

MACMILLAN
DIGITAL PUBLISHING USA
A VIACOM COMPANY

Regal Cruises™

TWO CATEGORY UPGRADE

Call Your Local Travel Agent
or for information call Regal Cruises at
1-800-270-SAIL

Regal Cruises™

Reminiscent of the Golden Age of Cruising

Regal Cruises™

Terms & Conditions:

Subject to availability. This upgrade offer cannot be combined with any other promotional offer. Two category upgrade valid for Category 10 through Category 3. Not valid for group bookings. Upgrade based on brochure rate only. Travel must be completed by April 30, 1999.

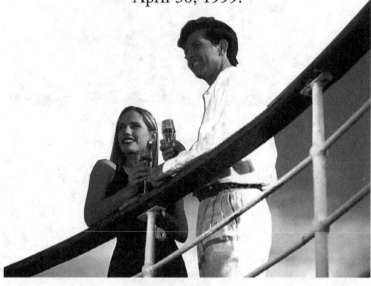

Reminiscent of the Golden Age of Cruising

Holland America Line

A TRADITION OF EXCELLENCE®

Free Upgrade

Purchase an outside
ocean view cabin on a
Holland America Line
cruise and receive a

Free, one category upgrade!

Valid for sailings through December 15, 1999.
Please see reverse side for more information.

Important Information

1. Valid on new bookings made with this original coupon. Photocopies not accepted. Upgrade must be requested at time of initial booking.

2. Offer valid on all Holland America cruises and Alaska cruisetours through December 15, 1999, excluding Grand Voyages.

3. Upgrades into the following categories are not permitted: Westerdam, categories S, A & B; Noordam and Nieuw Amsterdam, categories A & B; Veendam, Rotterdam, Volendam, Ryndam, Statendam and Maasdam, categories PS, S, A & B.

4. Upgrade is based on availability and may not be available on all sailings.

5. Upgrade is not combinable with any other special offer.

Travel Agent: Please submit this certificate with deposit.

Name
_____

Ship   Sailing Date
_____

Booking #
_____

Agency Contact Name
_____

Agency Address
_____

City   State/Province   Zip/Postal Code
_____

Phone   Fax